Buddy Holly

ALSO BY ELLIS AMBURN

Pearl: The Obsessions and Passions of Janis Joplin
Dark Star: The Roy Orbison Story

Buddy Holly

a biography

ELLIS AMBURN

ST. MARTIN'S PRESS ❦ NEW YORK

Photo credits: Frontispiece. Buddy Holly, 1959, AP/Wide World. Part One, page 2. Buddy Holly, *Westerner*. Part Two, page 111. Buddy Holly, AP/Wide World. Part Three, page 280-81. Edwin L. Musser photo.

Library in Congress Cataloging-in-Publication Data

Amburn, Ellis,
    Buddy Holly, : a biography / Ellis Amburn.
       p.   cm.
     ISBN 0-312-13446-0
     1. Holly, Buddy, 1936–1959. 2. Rock musicians—United States—Biography I. Title.
  ML 420.H595A8 1995
    782.42166'092—dc20
  [B]   95-19980
                                        CIP
                                      MN

First Edition: October 1995

10 9 8 7 6 5 4 3 2 1

To Cy Egan

Kindest and wisest of mentors

Contents

Part One

Beginnings

Prologue: Young Man in a Hurry

Lubbock, Texas, Palm Sunday, 1992—The Tabernacle Baptist Church, where Buddy Holly was baptized in adolescence and eulogized at age twenty-two, is one of those severe "modern" structures built in the 1950s—shedlike, functional, and without religious ornamentation of any kind, not even a steeple. It could easily pass for a Holiday Inn. The Holley family—Buddy dropped the "e" on his first Decca contract—has come to pray in force today. In the pulpit, the short, red-faced preacher angrily harangues the congregation, denouncing "pip-squeak modernists" and insisting on a literal interpretation of every word in the Bible. In a pew on the right side of the church, a couple of teenagers are making out. The boy, in a punk buzzcut and Bugle Boy denims, pretends to follow the sermon as his girl surreptitiously runs her hand up the inside of his thigh. Bristling with life and energy, they seem to mitigate the words of the fusty, out-of-touch minister. Nothing has changed since the days when Buddy Holly sat squirming in these pews in the 1950s. The struggle between piety and the lure of hot sex is still very much alive.

After the service, Buddy's brother, Larry, now sixty-four, rises from his pew. He is a tall, lanky cowpoke with Buddy's intense brown eyes and wiry physique. He is cautious at first but warms up when I tell him, truthfully, that he looks about forty. We meet the following day at Holley Tiles, a tile-installation company, which he owns and operates. "Forget about that movie completely," he says, dismissing *The Buddy Holly Story*, the 1978 film in which Gary Busey portrayed Buddy. "Put it completely out of your mind. That movie was completely erroneous. We were very disappointed in it. . . . I would advise people not to even see it. I don't look at it anymore." For the next few hours he tries to be honest about Buddy. "He wasn't no saint by any means," Larry begins. "He certainly wasn't a goody-goody. He was a saint in the fact that he was a saved Christian. He accepted Christ as his savior when he was younger."

From my talk with Larry, a picture of Buddy emerges that is radically different from the books, movies, and stage shows that have formed our impression of him. The true portrait is etched out by Larry and in my interviews with Buddy's widow Maria Elena, Crickets Sonny Curtis and

Niki Sullivan, and other musicians with whom he worked. Classmates, teachers, former juvenile delinquents and churchgoers, DJs, record people, groupies, and ordinary folk who saw Buddy play at teen hops in the fifties tell me during my trips across the country he was far different from the likable "dork" he appeared to be.

He was exactly the opposite. On the most basic, physical level, he was hardly the awkward geek that his amateurish, poorly lit promotional photos suggest. Duane Eddy, the twangy guitar rocker who appeared with him in 1958, once described Buddy as a "well-built" six-footer who had "wavy hair" and was "very good looking." And Buddy's innocent public image, carried like a sacred torch for over three decades now, is far from the whole story. He was an impetuous, reckless youth in a perpetual rush, and couldn't wait to grow up and earn money. His adolescence was dotted with incidents of what was then called juvenile delinquency. He got into fights. He hung out with—and was protected by—a fearless young man who carried a chain and beat up anyone who bothered Buddy. His first sexual foray was not with a proverbial gum-chewing sweetheart who seduced him in the back of a pickup truck. The circumstances were far more Rabelaisian. There are even reports, though they are still disputed by some Holly experts, that he fathered an illegitimate offspring with a Lubbock teenager who liked to dance in juke joints.

As he moved further and further from the stifling strictures of his fundamentalist boyhood on the South Plains, he discovered—at the same time as did beat writer Jack Kerouac—the pleasures of New York. He became sexually adventurous, a moral outlaw in his time, not above mixing things up racially and bisexually. He romped in a little-known orgy with Little Richard—a no-no in the uptight, segregationist fifties. It was only a hint of things to come.

Buddy fit Norman Mailer's description of "the white Negro," which Mailer defined in his famous 1957 *Dissent* essay as a hipster poised on the boundaries of repression and freedom. While not avowedly political, fifties rock was revolutionary. It urged people to do whatever they wanted to do, even if it meant breaking the rules. The original rockers of the fifties and their relatively small following were on the cutting edge of their time, trailblazers not only of rock 'n' roll but of the political and social revolutions of the sixties. Like so many of his generation, Buddy was transformed by rock 'n' roll from a warbling C&W bluegrass country boy into an early Freedom Rider who went into a hostile South with a busload of black R&B stars. His relationship with black musicians became a powerful symbol of the fusion of R&B and rockabilly—the spark that ignited rock 'n' roll as we know it today.

Discovering Buddy Holly at last as a flesh-and-blood human being, with all his flaws, does not make him any less attractive. Through all the drama of a short but eventful life, he remains one of the more appealing public figures of mid-century America. He was capable of heroically transcending his ingrained Texas prejudices, yet he remained loyal to family and friends. He was a tireless discoverer and supporter of then-new singers, like Waylon Jennings. As a friend he could be generous to a fault, yet crafty as a fox. In the music business, he was a gullible youth who was cheated out of a fortune. As a visionary, he established the basic rock-band lineup (two guitars, bass, and drums), expanded the parameters of rock to include string-drenched ballads, pioneered independent record deals, and started his own studio and publishing company. He was attracted to all sorts of women. He bedded his manager's wife, whom some people considered a lesbian. He kept one of the Crickets waiting out on the street in New York while he "got it on" with a girl songwriter. He proposed to his wife, according to my 1993 interview with her, on their first date. The same spontaneity that made his life so tumultuous also infused his music with bursts of unbridled energy and invention, leading to a string of hit records and one of the seminal careers in rock.

As DJ Alan Freed said, Buddy was always in a hurry and wanted to be the first person to get anywhere. On the night of his death, his plane flew headlong into a snowstorm and crashed a few minutes later. Killed were Buddy, twenty-two, Ritchie Valens, seventeen, and the Big Bopper, twenty-eight. Popular culture has been fixated on that plane crash ever since. For those first introduced to rock in the fifties, Buddy's death was a chilling experience. The death of a teenage legend was more shocking then than now, in the wake of the premature deaths of Jim Morrison, Jimi Hendrix, Janis Joplin, John Lennon, and Kurt Cobain, among many others. To millions, it will always feel as if Buddy was the first of their age group to die. Indeed, the crash of his Bonanza Beechcraft in Clear Lake, Iowa, on February 3, 1959, shocked a very naive generation into an awareness that it was not immortal. The event took on mythic proportions. It was a tragedy that came to personify the loss of innocence, just as Buddy's music and fast-torqued falsetto captured that indescribable blend of joy, sweetness, and excitement that defined the end of the 1950s.

The early morning crash also marked the end of something else: the first extraordinary phase of rock 'n' roll, the period from 1955 to 1959 during which the basic innovations were introduced by Buddy, Elvis Presley, Little Richard, Chuck Berry, Jerry Lee Lewis, and Carl Perkins. Death or misadventure claimed the founding fathers of rock, who were never to repeat the successes of those years. The Army drafted Elvis in his heyday, while religious fervor temporarily derailed Little Richard. The others fell rapidly too. Scandal damaged Jerry Lee's reputation. The law unmercifully hounded Berry. A near-fatal car smashup sidetracked Perkins, and Buddy was forever silenced in a snowy cornfield.

Thirteen years later, the poignant phrase "the day the music died" came to be associated with Buddy's death in "American Pie," Don McLean's haunting melody that summarized the history of rock in eight and a half minutes. "American Pie" mourned the passing of pure, danceable fifties rock 'n' roll and its plunge in the following decade into drugs, satanism, and witchcraft. But in an even deeper sense, early rock was stymied not only by the stark disaster at Clear Lake, but by forces that had been trying to destroy it from the beginning. Terrified by its message of freedom, the establishment marshaled formidable forces—the church, the police, and the press—to discourage the young musicians and their audiences. Even the music industry seemed to turn against rock 'n' roll, attempting to bury it in the payola scandal that ended the decade.

Buddy's life is a story of exploitation, betrayal, and distortion—by his manager, by insensitive record business entrepreneurs, by tour packagers who sent him into the frozen North Woods in harrowing travel conditions, and by a film biography after his death that trivialized the complex realities of the artist's life. His fatal Mason City-to-Fargo flight has a frightening parallel in the present-day controversy over commuter planes, which are not regulated as strictly as commercial airlines. If I seem heartlessly graphic in my description of the catastrophic crushing wounds sustained by Buddy, Ritchie, the Bopper, and pilot Roger Peterson in the crash of their small aircraft, it is to draw attention to the fact that safety reforms are still overdue.

While Elvis Presley was worshiped as a sex idol, people reserved a special love for Buddy Holly. He mirrored the ordinary teenager and symbolized both the guilelessness of the era and its repression and conformity. In his square suits and Slim Jim ties, he looked like an honor student who made A's in algebra, but when he went onstage and blasted off with "Oh Boy," the anchors of the past no longer held. His music marked a tumultuous end of the sedate Eisenhower years. From Buddy the burgeoning youth culture received rock's message of freedom, which presaged the dawn of a decade of seismic change and liberation. Buddy was above all a product of the time—the decade of the Cold War, the H-bomb, and tragic antiheroes such as Marlon Brando, James Dean, and Marilyn Monroe. He embodied as much as they did the central conflict of the fifties—conformity with establishment values versus individuality and rebellion. While he wore leather and rode a motorcycle, he was a devout fundamentalist Christian, hounded by a puritanical conscience that condemned rock as evil. Perhaps it was this innate contradiction that made him so great.

The songs Buddy wrote and sang are among the most original and ecstatic rock would ever know. They helped shape the new musical genre of rock 'n' roll. He became the model for countless singer-songwriters, from John Lennon and Paul McCartney to Bob Dylan and Elton John. As Keith Richards pointed out, it was Buddy who first demonstrated that the most exciting rock comes from bands performing their own material. With songs like "That'll Be the Day" and "Peggy Sue," Buddy influenced the music and lifestyles of generations to come. He put the hiccup in Bob Dylan's singing style and the falsetto in the Beatles' hits and made horn-rim glasses and Edwardian elegance hip. His use of echo chambers, over-dubbing, syllable-shattering scats, and high-flying trills gave rock 'n' roll many of its trademark sounds.

In Lubbock I heard people say that God killed Buddy Holly to prevent the spread of rock 'n' roll. Their beliefs, of course, are formed by the hand of fundamentalism, for his music died only to be resurrected and played back to us a few years later by the Beatles, whose popularity spread the Buddy Holly sound to every corner of the globe. That some of the persons close to Buddy could make statements such as "Sometimes the Lord snuffs people out when He sees He's not going to get any more good out of them. I have felt like that might have been the case with Buddy," indicates the kind of conflict Buddy overcame in order to help establish rock 'n' roll as the most dominant musical form of the last half of the twentieth century. It explains, too, the suffering that underlies his darker-hued ballads, such as "Learning the Game," written only days before his death. Gigantic as his achievement was, we barely glimpsed the dawn of his talent.

This book completes my trilogy, begun in 1990 with *Dark Star: The Roy Orbison Story* and continued in *Pearl: The Obsessions and Passions of Janis Joplin*, on the Texas roots of rock 'n' roll. Holly, Orbison, and Joplin all grew up in Texas in the fifties—a scene every bit as steamy and sexual as Larry McMurtry portrayed in *The Last Picture Show*. Roy's hometown, Wink, was a wild and woolly oil camp. Port Arthur, where Janis lived, was a sailor's port known for its rollicking whorehouses. Lubbock, the "Buckle of the Bible Belt," where Buddy was born in 1936, has a Pentagon-sized church in the middle of town, testimony that religion is the overpowering fact of life here. But despite its pious façade, Lubbock's population of 230,000 seems more hot and bothered than virtually anything I encountered in either Port Arthur or Wink. While their fundamentalist religion makes the good burghers of Lubbock at first appear to be straitlaced, beneath the veneer they're as untamed and dangerous as the Lubbock weather. It's easy to see why rock 'n' roll as we know it started here. Perhaps repression breeds such things.

Tornadoes were zigzagging across the South Plains as I explored the city in the spring of 1992. Most of the downtown area had been leveled by a tornado on May 11, 1970, and when Lubbock was rebuilt, a statue of Buddy was erected in front of the new Civic Center. Bill Griggs, the amiable founder of the Buddy Holly Memorial Society, takes me on a tour of the inner city, now a bleak and desolate slum. We pause before 1911 Sixth Street, where Buddy was born in one of the worst years of the Great Depression. It's now a vacant lot, full of rattlesnakes, the house having been condemned by the city in 1977 and hauled out beyond the city limits. No one seems to know where it is.

Three blocks down is the garage apartment where Jerry Allison, Buddy's drummer, and Peggy Sue Gerron lived after they got married. Nearby, at University and Second, is the roller rink where the Crickets played; the art deco brick structure still stands but today houses Bell Dairy, an ice-cream warehouse. Across the railroad tracks is Tommy's Burgers, where one of Lubbock's three Hi-D-Ho Drive-ins once stood. The Hi-D-Ho was a favorite hangout of Buddy's. One night in 1957, just after the release of "That'll Be the Day," Buddy and the Crickets climbed on top of the drive-in and serenaded dozens of kids in parked cars. The only Hi-D-Ho that survives today is located in a shabby strip mall at 6419 University Avenue. Buddy's niece, Sherry Holley, greets me warmly and slaps a Hidy Burger on the grill for me. She serves it in a tight pocket of wax paper that keeps it piping hot. The incredibly fresh, soft bun is packed with a thin, pancake-sized patty of succulent ground beef, minced onions, pickles, lettuce, tomatoes, and mayonnaise—a classic Texas hamburger, one of the finest I've ever eaten.

"Uncle Buddy used to hold me and serenade me when I was little," Sherry says. "He sang me my first lullabye." Sherry's a pretty woman in her thirties and she has those bright brown Holley eyes. She also has a melodic country singer's voice, as I learn when I listen to her album *Don't Say Hello; Say Hi-D-Ho*. She shows me a picture of Buddy and her sitting around a campfire in Colorado in 1955. He's nothing like the familiar nerd in the Crickets' publicity still—grinning and toying with his bow tie, looking like a cross between Archie, Henry Aldridge, and Dagwood Bumstead. In the campfire photo, he's a handsome, broad-shouldered teenager whose face, in the orange glow of the fire, is luminous and serene.

In probing deeper into's Buddy's intimate life than previous writers have attempted, I have uncovered personal details that are the key to the man and his music. I have tried to portray Buddy as he truly was: bright, quick, visionary, torn by internal polarities—at once willful and submissive, impatient and long-suffering, independent yet always clinging to stronger personalities. Like Jack Kerouac he was a young man in a hurry. He was plagued by a fire in the belly, which he tried to quench, but only succeeded in tamping down with the fast times and high spirits of the rock 'n' roll life.

Buddy was a complex human being with a river of talent coursing through his veins. That is what comes home to me as I stand at his grave in the Lubbock cemetery, which is located between an automobile junk-yard and a grain elevator, under a vast blue Texas sky. Musical notes and a guitar decorate his granite gravestone. Nearby stands a stone angel with cupped hands that are full of buzzing bees, a ready-made tableau of both the tranquillity and the manic impetuousness that made up Buddy's character. It was his frenetic, hard-rocking songs as well as the late ballads that are so tough, mournful, and wise that transformed the agonies and joys of his brief days into lasting art.

Chapter One

The Cradle Will Rock

We all sorta spoiled him, because he was so much younger than the rest of us," says Larry Holley. When Buddy was born in 1936, Larry was already ten years old and the other Holley children, Travis and Patricia, were nine and seven, respectively. Sex was a forbidden subject in Baptist families, so Larry didn't even suspect his parents, Ella, thirty-four and L.O., thirty-five, were expecting a baby until a friend told him. Hurt and bewildered by his parents' silence, Larry was so confused that he began to cry. The Holleys were a poor, decent family of hard-shell Baptists; Buddy would be the first of them to graduate from high school. His father, L. O. Holley, was a laborer who sometimes earned as little as $12 a week, going from job to job, toiling as a cook, carpenter, construction worker, car salesman, and clerk in a men's clothing store.

Buddy was born September 7, Labor Day, in the family's white-frame house at 1911 Sixth Street in Lubbock. The day had dawned cloudy and overcast, but by the time Buddy arrived a gentle, southerly wind was blowing across the South Plains. Born at the end of an age when the bedroom still served as the delivery room, Charles Hardin Holley was named after both grandparents. Mostly of English and Welsh descent, Buddy also had Indian blood from a grandfather who was one-fourth Cherokee. The Cherokees, originally from North Carolina and Georgia, had been forced to resettle in Oklahoma after a brutal march along what came to be known as "The Trail of Tears." Among their illustrious sons was the great humorist Will Rogers, who made America laugh during the Depression. Rogers died in the crash of a small airplane just a year before Buddy was born. He came from Claremore, Oklahoma, about four hundred miles from Lubbock. Of his Cherokee heritage he once quipped, "My ancestors didn't come over in the *Mayflower*, they met the boat."

Lawrence Odell Holley, Buddy's father, came from a farm near Honey Grove, a town in Fannin County near the Oklahoma border in northeast Texas. In his youth L.O. moved two hundred miles westward across the state to Vernon, a town situated on the Old Chisholm Trail, where he found work as a short-order cook. He met Ella Pauline Drake and they were married in 1924. Ella's parents had decided to move to Lubbock, 150 miles west of Vernon, where the construction of Texas Tech had opened up new jobs. There was also the promise of work in the sprawling cotton fields of West Texas. In 1925 L.O. and Ella Holley moved to Lubbock, settling in a rented house and moving to a different place almost every year. Larry was born in 1925, Travis in 1927, and Patricia in 1929.

The family was still poor when Buddy arrived. The Great Depression, described by John Steinbeck in his 1939 novel *The Grapes of Wrath*, lingered much longer in the Southwest—well into the 1940s—than in the rest of the nation. When Buddy was still very small, his mother said his given name of Charles Hardin Holley was "too long for such a small boy." So she nicknamed him Buddy. He grew into a smiling towheaded charmer, the pet of the family. The Holley home was intensely musical, one that resounded with country-and-western songs and Protestant hymns. As soon as Buddy was old enough to carry a tune, his mother taught him "Have You Ever Gone Sailing on the River of Memories." In 1941, when he was five, he won a $5 contest singing the song at County Line, a rural school, accompanying himself on the violin.

Later the same year, on December 7, World War II began, robbing him of both his brothers, Larry and Travis, who joined the Marines and went off to the Pacific to fight the Japanese. Buddy entered the first grade in 1943 at Roscoe Wilson Elementary and quickly found he didn't like to study—nor did he need to. When he brought home his first report card, it was full of A's. "He was the first of the Holley children to excel scholastically," says Larry.

Even so, he preferred the outdoors, which are nowhere grander or more alluring than the wide-open spaces of West Texas. He spent the summer of 1944 horseback riding, hunting, and fishing on his Uncle Jud's farm with his cousin from New Mexico, Sam Modrall, whose mother was Ella Holley's twin sister. Nights he sat in front of the radio with his parents tensely listening to war news. Travis was with the Marine Corps' 4th Division when it stormed ashore on Iwo Jima on February 18, 1945. "Right after Iwo Jima we were in Hawaii," Travis later told writer William J. Bush. There a shipmate with a $15 Harmony guitar got Travis hooked on the instrument. Throughout the war, soldiers from Texas had been spreading C&W all over the globe. Everywhere from Piccadilly Circus to Pearl Harbor people were singing "You Are My Sunshine" and "San Antonio Rose," wartime megahits that launched the crossover phenomenon that would vitalize the pop scene for decades to come. When the war ended later in 1945, Travis brought his guitar home and taught Buddy how to play.

Later Buddy got his own guitar, an acoustic Epiphone, and "made a clean sound," says Larry, who had managed to make it home from the war safely. "I would have swore it was another instrument entirely—the way he pressed down on it," adds Larry. Soon Buddy progressed to banjo and mandolin, applying a driving attack on any instrument he took up. His singing was equally spirited. One day the family heard him belting "Love Sick Blues," a difficult tune full of vocal somersaults. Though his voice hadn't changed yet, he managed every trick and turn of the 1949 No. 1 hit that heralded to Buddy the arrival of C&W's greatest star, Hank Williams, Sr., who became Buddy's musical model. Williams and Holly, by age only separated by thirteen years, by sound a great deal more, had in common a passion for breaking and twisting words into almost as many fragments as Handel, making them spin and loop to the delight of the listener. Before his thirtieth year, Hank Williams, Sr., would die, of alcoholism, on New Year's Day 1953.

Buddy's idol in every other respect was his brother Larry, whom Buddy seemed to cling to, perhaps because his mother and father were growing old and showed little understanding of the particularly treacherous adolescent years Buddy was entering. Larry let Buddy tag along, although Larry was far more interested in chasing girls and soon found and married the woman of his dreams, Maxine. When they went on a camping trip to the Red River, Buddy not only came along but insisted on sleeping between them when coyote howls alarmed him at night.

In the years just before adolescence, from ten to twelve, Buddy was the star of his class—a cute, lovable show-off. Lois Keeton, the playground director, adored his "infectious laugh. He just bubbled all over," she remembers. "He was a good-lookin' little fellow at ten, just as cute as he could be, but very small." He was also clever, quick, and sly. Lois, who always wore huge dark sunglasses in the glaring Texas sun, taught him to play Canasta. After he won every game for a month, she inquired, "How is it you manage to beat me every time?"

"Because I can see your hand in your big black sunglasses," he replied.

Still financially strapped, the Holleys experienced little of the prosperity that others enjoyed in the years following the Depression. To make ends meet, they moved outside the Lubbock city limits in 1946, to the less expensive Loftland Addition. Ineligible to attend city schools, Buddy transferred to suburban Roosevelt Elementary and had to ride the bus twenty miles daily. When he was twelve he could tell from the way girls flirted with him that he was the most popular kid in class. At one point, he peroxided his hair, and looked a little like Marlon Brando in The Young Lions. At an age awkward for most kids, he turned out to be at the peak of his physical attractiveness. So much so that in 1948, his classmates voted him and a girl named Barbara Denning "King and Queen of the Sixth Grade." On the school bus, everyone gathered around when he played his Epiphone guitar and sang Bill Monroe's "Gotta Travel On." One day classmate Wayne Maines brought his guitar and they performed duets on the bus, singing C&W hits such as "Pistol Packin' Mama" and "Born to Lose." Wayne was more advanced in his guitar playing but Buddy quickly soaked up everything he knew and left his classmate far behind.

Buddy's guitar playing progressed with such remarkable speed that his family was astonished at his proficiency and individual style, and by the fact that he'd memorized the words to all the traditional Texas cowboy songs, such as "Home on the Range" and "Bury Me Not on the Lone Prairie." Like Williams, he was deeply influenced by the spiritual sound of the old country church. He loved Mahalia Jackson's "Move On Up a Little Higher." The Baptist gospel singer with the deep, emotion-drenched voice, astonishing control, and awesome inflections was Buddy's introduction to the glories of black music. Adapting both Jackson's and Hank Williams's bizarre vocal feats, Buddy learned to mimic Williams's yodel-like falsetto and the elaborate jazz spins Mahalia had picked up while marching in New Orleans funeral parades as a child. He blended in his own vocal tricks, which included hiccuping or stuttering in the middle of a word or stretching it until he shattered it to pieces. The word "Well," for example, became the multisyllabic "Weh-eh-eh-eh-el."

In 1949, when Buddy was thirteen, the Holley family moved back to Lubbock, renting a house at 3315 Thirty-sixth Street. The move provided him with an introduction into a faster, more socially aggressive world. He entered J. T. Hutchinson Junior High School and met Bob Montgomery, Don Guess, and Jerry Allison, precocious musicians who played important roles in his life for years to come. A multitalented youth just a year Buddy's junior, Don Guess could play stand-up bass and steel guitar and was beginning to write songs. From Lampasas, Texas, dark-haired Bob Montgomery could play guitar and sing C&W and rhythm and blues.

R&B, the precursor of rock 'n' roll, was the creation of black musicians and was known as "race records" or—in Texas in the late forties—"nigger music." Buddy Holley was racially prejudiced in his youth but overcame it, his brother Larry revealed in a 1992 interview. This family secret, heretofore unknown, emerged as Larry recounted Buddy's falling out with a famous bluegrass singing star in 1958. The star had "a bigoted attitude, like Buddy used to be," Larry said. It was in Buddy's adolescence, as he listened to R&B on Gatemouth Page's radio program on KWKH from Shreveport, Louisiana, that he began to question his racial intolerance. How could he be better than anyone who left him so far behind musically, in the dust of simplistic hillbilly and bluegrass? Blacks were cool. Their music was dirtier than sin, with titles like "It's Not the Meat, It's the

Motion," "Sixty Minute Man," and "Big Long Slidin' Thing." Unlike the segregated whites at Tabernacle Baptist, blacks knew the score. He wanted to be like them. So he shed those bigoted Texas ways.

Bluegrass has been called C&W in overdrive, and Buddy and Bob cooked up a sensational act around it—a combustible mix of R&B and bluegrass that sometimes shocked the staid Protestants of the prairie. Buddy's mother later told Bill Griggs that Buddy and Bob were "big hams . . . [W]here there are two, there is more enthusiasm and push." By 1949 they were making home recordings such as a cover of Hank Snow's "My Two Timin' Woman," using equipment that a friend who worked in a local electronics store temporarily "borrowed."

In 1950 when they were in the eighth grade, Buddy and Bob scandalized half of Lubbock by singing a notorious C&W novelty song, "Too Old to Cut the Mustard," at a PTA open-house program. Jerry Allison, a transfer student from Plainview, Texas, who was a grade below Buddy, heard them sing the suggestive Jumping Bill Carlisle tune and was "really impressed," he later recalled, by Buddy's gutsy singing and guitar playing. Jerry had been playing drums since the fifth grade. One day he asked Buddy to come home with him after school and played Fats Domino's record "Goin' to the River." When Buddy heard rock 'n' roll, he saw his future; it was as if the heavens had opened. But it was more than just the music. From that moment on, Buddy identified closely with blacks. At first Buddy just wanted to be uninhibited, black from the waist down—hip, cool, sexy, and rhythmic. Later this would become the essence of his whole being and culminate in the most important relationship of his life—an interracial marriage. Fortunately, Buddy's moral development out of prejudice started early, freeing him for personal and artistic growth. Ultimately, all Americans are defined by the attitude they take toward race; until that is right, nothing can be right.

Though he was coming of age in a segregated town before the beginning of the civil rights movement, Buddy identified with blacks so much that when he acquired his first cat, he named it after Booker T. Washington, the founder of Alabama's Tuskegee Institute and the first published black author. The small black kitten began life as "Booker T" but eventually became known simply as "Booker."

When Buddy's first sexual urges hit during his junior high school years, he was thrown into confusion. Tabernacle Baptist had taught him that sexual desire without marriage was evil. His parents, typically reticent Baptists, were no help. "I was ten years older than Buddy, and he looked to me for a lot of his fathering," Larry says. "He had his ornery side and his good side." When asked in a 1992 interview how Buddy learned the facts of life, Larry responds, "I just talked to him a little bit about it. I was more wild myself than I should have been at that time."

Buddy broke out of his Baptist shell in his teens when he began to disobey his parents and stay out late, hanging out with his gang in front of the Tech Café, smoking, and drinking. Friends from that period say they "stole, cussed, and chased little ol' girls." Around the time his drinking began, Buddy sprouted an ulcer. Since he and his friends were underage, they depended on the older boys in the group to acquire the beer, and they'd split a quart between five or six people. A quart of bootleg cost about three dollars.

Buddy smoked Winstons. A photograph taken of him at the time shows a pack of Salems clearly visible through the transparent material of his shirt pocket, but he only smoked menthols when he had a cold. Occasionally he bummed unfiltered Camels from his boyhood friend Tinker Carlen, but "choked to death on them," Tinker remembers. The older boys had cars and often drove to Mexico in groups looking for a good time. They returned from Acuña or Ojinaga complaining of "crotch crickets"—crabs—and the clap. "I went down and got fucked for *dos pesos*," one of them remembers in 1992. "She got the pesos and I got the dose."

Buddy's first sexual encounter was a "gang bang." For many young men growing up in West Texas in the fifties, this was a common rite of passage to sexual maturity. For Buddy Holley, it was a significant turning point, marking his transformation from God-fearing Baptist boy into prototypical fifties teen rebel. Tinker Carlen described the gang bang in a 1992 interview in Lubbock. He and Buddy were with several other boys one night when they spotted a girl standing in front of Tom Halsey's Pharmacy on the corner of Broadway and Avenue K. "She just had on a little halter top and a pair of Levi britches," Tinker recalls.

In the fifties, at least in West Texas, such girls were not prostitutes. They were just rebellious, and they sometimes came from the families of the clergy, high school teachers, doctors, or other prominent local citizens. When they became pregnant, as they frequently did, they had to drop out of school and were often sent into permanent exile by their parents, to live with relatives in distant cities such as Galveston or Houston.

"We drove by in a car and there was six boys of us in there," Tinker remembers. "We was out lookin', because Buddy hadn't been to bed with anybody and wondered what it was like. . . . Back then they called it gang bangin'. There was very few little ol' gals who'd put out and the ones that did, you could really bang 'em.

"One guy was on the rough side. He'd been used to all this wild and reckless stuff. Back then we didn't call it 'gettin' laid'; we said, 'We're going to get him bred.' We stopped at the Hi-D-Ho to get a Coke or something. Over here by Fourth Street, there's this little underpass and all of us old boys got out and in underneath a little bridge there."

The more experienced boys took the girl one by one. Tinker remembers that Buddy was uncircumcized and "had to skin it back to pee." When the other boys had finished and it was Buddy's turn, he said, "How do I do it?" Tinker says. Evidently Buddy figured it out by the time he joined the girl in the car. "He quickly became so passionate he started kissing the girl," Tinker recalls, "and one of the boys stuck his head in the window and poked Buddy in the ass with a cotton stalk. 'Hey,' he said, 'are you a pervert or something? You've got your mouth where my dick was.' The guy had had the girl give him a blow job."

After making the rounds of the easier girls around Lubbock, Buddy's attendance at Tabernacle Baptist Church dropped off noticeably. Some of the guys he was running with were shoplifting. One night Buddy was in a crowd that ended up at someone's "grandmother's house," Tinker remembers. "It was about four maybe in the morning when we got there. She got up and cooked us a nice breakfast. A real down-to-earth grandma. She took care of her little grandson. He was about ten years old [and was] so delighted to see us. Wonderful little kid. They made pallets on the floor for us. We were laying down there and that little kid was showing us all his toys. He made the mistake of showing us ten dollars that he'd saved up. Next morning it was gone."

Buddy and some of the local boys would shoplift when they stopped for gas at service stations, loading up on food while the attendant was outside pumping gas. Larry Holley noticed that musical instruments started disappearing from the house when Buddy realized they could be hocked for pocket money. When a banjo worth $10 couldn't be found, Larry "wondered if Buddy had hocked it," but decades later, after Buddy Holly became a legend, it turned up in a storage room in the home of Buddy's parents. "We sold it in the auction for a tremendous price," Larry reveals. "Buddy'd hocked every other instrument around the house. I had a mandolin that was the keenest thing you'd ever seen, one of them gourd-shaped [ones, with] different-colored wood, and I could play it. Buddy couldn't. The mandolin disappeared. I had a Steiner fiddle, a really pretty one. I could play it, but Buddy couldn't play it. It disappeared, and I know where. He'd hock them every time he needed some money. Mother and Daddy were poor and couldn't help him any."

In our 1992 interview, Larry reflects, "Baptists seem like a wilder bunch of people. They realize that they're not good and can't be good enough to get to heaven on their own merits." Looming before Buddy and his brothers was Baptism, which Baptist youths customarily undergo as the path to salvation. It involves a physical dunking in water in front of the whole congregation. Larry was the first to face it and says he was initially reluctant. "When I was a little boy of fourteen," he recalls, "we was havin' a revival. I mean we had a good preacher. It was in my heart and my mind that I needed to take Christ as my savior sometime, but not right now. Mother got us in the room over there—me and Travis and Pat. Buddy was too little to know. Mom said, 'I want to read something to you in the Bible—the plan of salvation God has for us.'

" 'Mother, I don't want to hear it,' I said. 'I'm readin' a book, *Silver Chief*.'

" 'Well, you don't have to if you don't want to, but I'm goin' to read to Travis and Pat.'

"I got in there and covered up my ears with pillows and I tried to read that book and I went over and over the same lines. Directly I got up and went in and listened and I could see that I was a sinner. I went to church and confessed that I'd done this and was baptized into the church. . . . It's showin' the world that you've died the old life and took Christ as your savior."

Even as Buddy outgrew his church's narrow-minded dogma and ran wild, he never lost his spirituality. This was confirmed by Bill Griggs during the 1992 interview in Lubbock, when he displayed some of Buddy's keepsakes from this period, which Buddy's parents had given to him over the years. They included spiritual literature and copies of hymns that Buddy had carefully saved. Buddy studiously underlined his copy of the Gospel of John, his favorite book of the Bible. That he highlighted the lines "*These are written that ye might believe that Jesus is the Christ the Son of God and that believing ye might have life through his name*" indicates that Buddy's faith was strong and that he felt it would bring him everything he needed.

Another key teaching of St. John that Buddy heeded was "*He that is without sin among you, let him first cast a stone.*" Despite the white-supremacist, homophobic society he grew up in, he cleansed himself of racial prejudice and macho snobberies and began to embrace people who were different from him, notably blacks, Hispanics, and gays.

Along with the Gospel of John, he always kept a copy of the hymn "What a Friend We Have in Jesus" handy. Like Hank Williams, he loved hymns and was fascinated by "What a Friend," in which the composers Joseph Scriven and Charles C. Converse describe a way to turn over worries and achieve inner peace. According to Scriven and Converse, all anxieties and guilts can be unburdened regularly on God, who is better equipped to dispose of them than human beings. Peace of mind comes from devoting a portion of each day to meditation or prayer, according to the wise old hymn. Buddy discovered that when he turned his trials, temptations, troubles, sorrows, weaknesses, and pain over to his higher power, as prescribed in the song, even if he had to do so over and over, they went away. The hymn gave him a powerful weapon for dealing with a life that would be anything but easy. As Scriven and Converse put it, "Take it to the Lord in prayer, in His arms He'll take and shield thee, thou wilt find a solace there."

Not long after his sexual initiation, Buddy told Tinker Carlen, "I think I'm going to get baptized. I've been putting it off since I was twelve." The fact that he considered it carefully and discussed it with a friend shows Buddy knew exactly what he was doing. Despite his differences with Tabernacle Baptist, he felt good enough spiritually to want to declare in public that he believed in and trusted his higher power. And that was *all* he intended by his baptism—he wasn't about to give up the newly discovered pleasures of sex. "I'm ashamed of a lot of the stuff we do, but it's not going to stop me," Buddy said. "I like girls and like to git out and be noticed."

"Hell, we may be wilder than a peach-orchard boar, but we know there's a God and a hereafter," said his friend.

"Yeah, looks like ever' time you screw up, God is there to put His arms around you and say, 'Let's get goin' again,' " Buddy said.

Buddy was baptized by Ben D. Johnson at the old Tabernacle Baptist Church that was located at Fifteenth and N Streets before moving in 1955 to its present location at 1911 Thirty-fourth Street. A schoolmate of Buddy's, Ken Johnson (no relation to pastor Ben D. Johnson), was baptized around the same time. The baptistry, Ken remembered, was behind the pulpit and the choir, in full view of the congregation. Buddy's favorite Biblical author was St. John, who wrote of baptism, "I saw the Spirit descending from heaven like a dove, and it abode upon him. Behold the Lamb of God, which taketh away the sins of the world."

According to Ken, who later became a minister, baptism means that "you are dead to sin, buried in the watery grave, and raised to walk in newness of life. That is a walk that portrays the Christian teaching of the New Testament." Like Hank Williams, whose "I Saw the Light" is one of his finest recordings, the influence of the Lord and Jesus, as well as the sound of gospel, would influence Buddy's music.

In the months and years after his baptism, Buddy often rose from his pew during the "Invitation" at the close of the church service, as the congregation sang, "Just as I am, O Lamb of God, I come! I come!" He would go down to the altar and face the congregation, often with his family. "Their lives in serving the Lord in the church this way was always very open and conspicuous," explains Ken. "Many times in revival meetings or just a regular church service on Sunday morning the Holleys would become burdened about doing more for the Lord and would openly or publicly dedicate themselves to do more for the Lord."

The unity and dynamism the family displayed at church was not always reflected in their home life. In 1951, when Buddy was fifteen and in his final year at Hutchinson Junior High, he came home from school and told his mother that he needed glasses. His mother's response, by her own description, was scatterbrained. "He didn't talk a lot, he was a quiet boy, and I didn't pay him any mind," she said. A few days later he again asked for glasses, and his mother again did nothing. All of her other children had demanded glasses, but when she'd taken them to the optometrist, "they didn't need them very bad," she explained. "I thought that this would turn out the same way." The third time Buddy mentioned his vision problem, he at last got her attention.

"Why do you think you need glasses?" she asked.

"Because the school nurse examined my eyes and told me so," Buddy said.

An optometrist's examination revealed that Buddy's vision was 20/800 in both eyes. After the test the optometrist turned to Mrs. Holley and said, "This boy needs glasses pretty bad. He should have had them several years ago."

Buddy loved his mother, but sometimes she could be obtuse. His father left his parenting to Mrs. Holley and then complained that Buddy was "tied to his mother" by "his umbilical cords," L. O. Holley later said in John Goldrosen and John Beecher's book *Remembering Buddy*. Not equal to the job of handling the difficult, headstrong boy Buddy was, his mother left the job to her older son Larry. Buddy turned to Larry for guidance "on many things, some private," Larry revealed in his autobiographical booklet "The Buddy I Knew!" "Buddy seemed to think that I hung the moon because I was an older brother and had been around a little."

It never seemed to have occurred to L.O. that if Buddy was a "mama's boy" it was due to the absence of a strong father figure. The situation would have far-reaching consequences for Buddy, who would make the mistake of relying on stronger personalities who were not always trustworthy.

Chapter Two

KDAV's "Sunday Party"

Around 1951, L. O. Holley was in charge of a construction crew putting up a house in Lubbock. One of the young men working for him as a carpenter's helper, Jack Neal, was also a gifted musician. Born in Fort Worth, Texas, Neal had moved with his family to Tahoka on the South Plains in 1940 and then to Lubbock in 1942. He could play banjo, guitar, steel guitar, and piano, and his favorite singers were Hank Williams, Lefty Frizzell, Webb Pierce, and Ray Price. One day at work, during lunch break, Jack took his guitar from his car and joined the rest of the construction workers on the porch of the house they were building. He started to play and sing. L. O. Holley walked over to him and stood listening intently.

"My son plays the guitar," L.O. said as they started back to work. "It sounds like you oughta get together."

Neal met Buddy that evening and was immediately intrigued with his guitar playing. "We liked the toe-tapping type," Neal later told Bill Griggs. "We had that feeling in our blood." The pair sang some C&W and a couple of gospel songs and discovered that they sounded good as a duo. It was a period of musical growth that marked the beginning of Buddy's dream to become a professional musician.

Neal was also a lot of fun. Two years older than Buddy, he liked the rugged outdoors and knew his way around the South Plains, showing Buddy a side of life that was the birthright of every plainsman but remained foreign to many of the city folk of Lubbock, Dallas, Fort Worth, Houston, Amarillo, and San Antonio, Texas's major urban areas. Neal took Buddy to Tahoka, 110 miles south of Lubbock, where Jack still had relatives. They rode horses across the prairie and shot rabbits with their .22s. Sometimes they went fishing and duck-hunting. "We wore out the road going back and forth to Tahoka," Neal said. A member of the Texas Wild Varmint Association, Neal's father encouraged the young men to go after bigger game, and soon they were bagging coyotes, foxes, and bobcats. On their way to shoot ducks one day, Buddy poked his rifle out the car window.

"Look at that coyote," he said, taking aim.

Betraying a streak of cruelty, Buddy grazed the animal and "was tickled to death," according to Neal, when the injured, disoriented creature started running around in circles. Fortunately, it managed to escape with its life, but only because Buddy "was too far away to hurt him," Neal added. In some respects Buddy was a typical West Texan, especially when it came to guns.

Buddy and Neal practiced their music as hard as they played. Both were passionate, compulsive aficionados of the guitar. Buddy's style was "unique," Neal told Griggs. In an interview with Philip Norman, Neal explained: "I played rhythm. Buddy played lead. . . . We'd go out to these black cafés on the other side of the tracks and just sit and listen. They mostly served barbecue, which we liked as well. He'd say, 'Jack, I don't want to be rich. I don't even want to be in the limelight. But I want people to remember the name Buddy Holley.' " Buddy and Jack developed into such an entertaining C&W act that when Lubbock's movie theaters announced a new policy of live entertainment for Saturday morning kiddie shows, they went onstage and had the children calling for encores. After that, they became a regular attraction. Proud of his ability to hold the attention of restless, fidgety tykes, Buddy, now pushing sixteen, began to think seriously of a singing career.

During the blisteringly hot Texas summer of 1952, just before Buddy entered high school, the temperature regularly hit a hundred degrees in Lubbock. Overseas, the Korean War was raging. In Chicago, Ike won the Republican presidential nomination, and President Truman saluted the Democratic nominee, Adlai Stevenson. Millions of people were singing "High Noon" that summer and reading *The Power of Positive Thinking*. On September 7 Buddy turned sixteen and reported for his first day at Tom S. Lubbock High School, named after one of Texas's Civil War heros. In a theme he wrote for his English class he expressed pride at being a Lubbock High Westerner. Standing in assembly with his classmates, he sang the school song, which exhorted the students to conquer the Texas plains, waving the Westerner banner of black and gold.

"He was still just a little fellow, very short," says Lois Keeton, who'd been his playground director during grade school recesses and was now his homeroom teacher at Lubbock High. "Buddy Holley was rather hyper—bubbly and vivacious," she remembers. "He didn't want to study. He bounced around in his seat, refusing to open a book. I worked with him gently, and after the first few days, he settled down."

On Wednesdays the homeroom students were expected to elect committees and set up programs as a way of learning organization and responsibility. Listless and lazy, Buddy's class was so lacking in initiative that "Wednesdays came around too often for those kids to have a program ready," Lois recalls. At Christmas they were allowed to have refreshments in addition to staging a program, but again no one made the necessary arrangements.

"Well, it's not too late—why don't *you* go get us some refreshments yourself?" Buddy cheekily suggested to Miss Keeton. His charm was such that Miss Keeton trudged over to a grocery store across the street and loaded up on candy and cookies while the class, no doubt under Buddy's direction, hastily improvised a Christmas program. "He was pretty bold to say that to me," she says, laughing, recalling the incident over forty years later. "He was a bit of a smart aleck, but he was sweet. He wasn't ugly or belligerent or I would have taken care of *that*."

The winter of Buddy's sophomore year, 1952–53, was frigid and violent throughout Texas and New Mexico. The snow, tornadoes, and freezing rain were as punishing as the summer had been the previous year. South of Lubbock, a nine-foot-high tumbleweed rolled through downtown Midland. In the pastures around Clovis, New Mexico, ninety miles northwest of Lubbock, livestock stoically leaned into 70-mile-per-hour winds. Thermometers in the Panhandle read 10 degrees. On February 20, 1953, Westerner Round-up Day at Lubbock High, the capricious Texas weather was up to its usual tricks—64 degrees in the morning, dropping to 21 degrees at noon. All the homerooms held an election to pick Westerner Round-up Day Favorite Boy and Girl. The winners were to be announced at the main event that evening in the school auditorium. Buddy and a girl named Joyce Howard won in Miss Keeton's homeroom, showing Buddy's popularity had remained intact during the tricky transition from junior to senior high.

By the spring semester he wrote in a school paper that he wanted to become a professional C&W singer, but he was realistic enough to know that the chances of that were slim. Niki Sullivan, later one of the Crickets but already a distant admirer of Buddy's in high school, saw him perform during lunch hour, singing Hank Thompson's C&W hit "Wild Side of Life" and Lloyd Price's R&B classic "Lawdy, Miss Clawdy."

Not all the attention Buddy attracted was favorable. It was the first time his brother Larry had seen him wearing tight pants, and it struck Larry as absurd. Tight pants couldn't be bought in Lubbock stores in the early fifties, a time when men concealed their bodies in loose-fitting gabardine slacks and tuniclike sport shirts. Buddy had prevailed upon his mother to take in the legs of his jeans, all the way from the crotch to the cuff, making them snug and form-fitting. Another Buddy Holley fashion innovation in Lubbock was the common T-shirt. At a time when T-shirts were regarded as underwear or something for laborers to wear, Buddy wore them with his jeans. He soon discovered that innovative style is often unrecognized or ridiculed, whether in music, fashion, or other forms of art. Newness triggers a strong response, which is generally negative, from those who are fearful of losing power or being left behind. Buddy's detractors were mostly mediocre C&W pickers who envied his talent, but they had a shattering effect on his self-esteem. From a bubbly, irrepressible personality, he turned into a defensive loner when husky peers derided his slender build. He began to withdraw from the crowd, turning inward. "Buddy sidled along the hallway, clutching his books," says Arlene Burleson, a member of the class of '55 who was dating a football player. "Buddy looked like he was afraid someone would speak to him."

Despite his standoffishness, Buddy's smart-aleck persona quickly reasserted itself anytime he felt secure, especially when he was with other musicians, a girl who liked him, or one of his tougher buddies, such as the dude who carried a chain. Toward the end of the 1953 spring semester, he carved his name on his homeroom desk. "He sat in the fourth seat down, over by the window," Miss Keeton remembers. "I didn't see him do it because he crunched down behind the guy in front of him. When school let out that summer he was just beginning to get his growing pains. Then he began to grow and he grew very tall in just a year's time, from a little fellow as a sophomore to a tall boy. Growing that fast in just a little while is hard on a person, hard on the nervous system."

It was hard on Buddy's scholastic record, too. In the last week of the semester, he was expelled from Plane Geometry and was derelict in his Biology assignments. Expecting to flunk out, he borrowed his father's truck and gave a new meaning to the phrase hell on wheels. In a single day he totaled both the windshield and the hood. A few days later, on his way to a job interview at a drafting firm, he crashed into a Chrysler and destroyed the front of the Holleys' car. He got the job and started drawing blueprints for Panhandle Steel. Around this time he considered electrical engineering as a profession. During his last two years of school he dreamed of becoming a recording artist, but he was enough of a realist to know that the chances against this happening were overwhelming. He knew he had to have something to fall back on.

Working every angle to break into local radio, he boldly invaded station KSEL one day and informed a startled employee that he wanted to see Ben Hall, the DJ who was taking the one-to-three-P.M. shift. Impressed with Buddy's moxie, Hall, a singer-songwriter, invited Buddy to perform with him at a local sports arena where occasional musical programs were held. For their first gig together Buddy arrived carrying an electric guitar and wearing a large white cowboy hat. Weldon Myrick, an outstanding young steel guitarist who'd played with Jim Reeves and Ferlin Husky by the time he was sixteen, performed with Buddy and Jack Neal that night. The gig went so well that, afterwards, Hall frequently used Buddy as a backup instrumentalist. In 1953, Hall and the entire staff of KSEL bolted and moved to KDAV, establishing America's first all-C&W

radio station. Buddy had his heart set on appearing on KDAV's popular "Sunday Party," hosted by station owner Dave Pinkston, whose professional name was "Pappy" Dave Stone. Pinkston once explained that his surname was too hard for callers to the station to pronounce, so he dropped the first syllable of his surname and changed "ston" to Stone.

Buddy and Jack Neal were still doing Saturday morning kiddie shows, which were regularly scouted by KDAV assistant manager Hi Pockets Duncan. In the latter part of September 1953, Hi Pockets auditioned them. They sang a duet at KDAV's studio at 6602 Quirt Avenue. Hi Pockets described their music as C&W "with a little upbeat" or rockabilly, as it would shortly be known.

"You have a beat of your own," Hi Pockets told Buddy. "You're destined to be a star." He offered to host Buddy's radio debut. "The Buddy and Jack Show" went on the air November 8, 1953, opening with Hank Williams's "Your Cheatin' Heart." The newly discovered pair received fan mail almost immediately. Their fans wrote out the titles of songs they wanted to hear them sing on the air.

Grateful to Hi Pockets for discovering him, Buddy carefully handtooled a western belt and presented it to his benefactor. Larry described the belt as "a beautiful professional job." Unfortunately, it was too small for the paunchy Hi Pockets, who nevertheless kept it and treasured it for many years.

William Joseph "Hi Pockets" Duncan, Buddy's champion and staunchest supporter, was a big, bright-eyed, good-natured DJ with a toothy grin like actor James Whitmore's. Injured in World War II, he walked with a cane for years before completely recovering from his wounds. Originally from Amarillo, Texas, he launched his nickname by opening a fifteen-minute hillbilly radio show with the impromptu announcement, "This is Hi Pocket Hank's Hillbilly Hop presented by Henry Clay's Food Store." He also formed a band, Hi Pockets Duncan and His Texas Hot Shots, and played local events like Lubbock's 1953 Labor Day dance at the VFW Hall.

Now a hit at KDAV, Buddy and Jack felt free to hang out there, teaching themselves everything there was to know about broadcasting and recording equipment and listening to the station's extensive record collection. Hi Pockets and Ben Hall always greeted them warmly and made them feel at home. Dave Stone, another ardent advocate of Buddy's, recorded the duo on acetate on November 10, 1953. Buddy played lead guitar and Jack sang "I Saw the Moon Crying Last Night" and "I Hear the Lord Callin' for Me."

Because Neal had a girlfriend he was serious about, he was holding down a full-time job as an electrical contractor. This was absorbing most of his time and interest, and eventually he got married and moved to

Ruidoso, New Mexico. Buddy then teamed up again with Bob Montgomery, his old friend from J. T. Hutchinson Junior High, and sang with him on KDAV's "Sunday Party." Buddy and Bob's high-pitched harmonies resembled those of the Everly Brothers, who were still living in Knoxville, Tennessee, singing on their parents' C&W radio show on station WROL. But Buddy and Bob had more of a rustic C&W flavor than the Everlys and were closer to Bob Wills's western swing. Born in Kosse, Texas, in 1905, Wills produced numerous hits such as "Mexicali Rose," "Faded Love," and "Steel Guitar Rag."

"The 'Sunday Parties' were always about whoever showed up to pick," said Sonny Curtis, a multitalented musician from Meadow, Texas, a small town thirty miles south of Lubbock. Anyone who had the tenacity to come across the plains to Lubbock and the nerve to sing into a microphone was welcome at KDAV. Sonny remembers broadcasting with Buddy and Bob, singing duets with Ben Hall, and sometimes doing solos. Weldon Myrick, who turned into a "real hot steel-guitar player," was also around the "Sunday Party," Sonny told Bill Griggs in 1980.

Sonny Curtis was a good-looking youth with pixie eyes, a sexy-sounding voice that derived some of its quality from a slight underbite, and poetry flowing in his veins. "Sonny started performing when he was eight years old, playing and singing bluegrass with our brother, Dean, and me," Sonny's older brother, Pete, said in 1995. Sonny was also a songwriter and could upstage just about anyone with his hoedown fiddling. He worked at Adair Music Store in Lubbock, and after hours he'd bring "race" records to Buddy's house "where we'd spend the night listening to R&B," he says. Then they'd go out to the Holleys' Oldsmobile and listen to Gatemouth Page on the car radio until they fell asleep. When they weren't practicing in someone's garage, depriving whole neighborhoods of sleep, Buddy and Sonny drank beer and chased girls.

"Sonny Curtis was very helpful to Buddy," Larry recalled. "The boys all had lots of fun playing and learning together."

In his seventeenth year Buddy grew to five-foot-eleven but still weighed only 145 pounds. Just after he started his junior year, he and Bob Montgomery told Dave Stone that they were ready for their own radio show. It was a brash announcement that Buddy offset with impeccable manners. When Buddy turned on his charm, radiating sincerity and deference, "Pappy" Stone was impressed. Auditioning Buddy and Bob and pronouncing them "very good," Pappy booked them into their own 2:30 P.M., thirty-minute segment on KDAV's "Sunday Party." "The Buddy and Bob Show" went on the air in late 1953.

"I had a bit of an ulterior motive," Stone later admitted. As Lubbock High students, Buddy and Bob were sure to increase KDAV's audience among local youths, who were demanding raunchier songs. When Buddy and Bob sang the sexually explicit R&B tune "Work With Me, Annie," which clearly describes a couple in the throes of passion—the man instructing the woman to give him plenty of "meat"—West Texas teenagers flipped. "They were hits almost immediately from the time they went on," Stone said. "Believe me, they didn't any more than get that show started when the phone would start ringing off the wall."

Most of the callers wanted more songs like "Work With Me, Annie." Buddy was completely in tune with a generation that was rapidly tiring of Perry Como, Eddie Fisher, and Patti Page and demanding music that was as raw and wild as their own feelings.

Chapter Three

A Girl Named Echo

When Roy Orbison, a homely, bespectacled kid from Wink, Texas, 125 miles south of Lubbock, heard Buddy on KDAV, it altered his life. Roy had had his own TV show, but was convinced he'd never succeed on stage because of his glasses. After he met Buddy, he thought, *If this guy wears glasses and is going to try to make it big, maybe I can too.* "I would go to see Buddy's shows and he would go to see mine, back and forth there," Orbison later recounted. "Buddy was a very bright boy, very dedicated. He wasn't uppity, or as we'd say in the business, 'flashy.' He could tell jokes. We had a relationship that developed."

Buddy helped Roy with lead structures on some of the songs Roy was trying to write at this time. It was Buddy who showed Orbison the lick that would become so popular years later when Roy recorded "Pretty Woman." Buddy took it from "Brave Bulls," a song often played at bullfights.

Hi Pockets offered Buddy and Bob some sage professional advice after he learned they'd been providing free entertainment for a Lubbock man who invited them to his parties. They'd eat all they wanted, but the man paid them nothing. "That ol' party boy is using you," said Hi Pockets, who recounted his conversation with Buddy years later on a radio show entitled "A Celebration of Buddy Holly: The Legend Moves On."

"Well, we always get fed," said Buddy.

"Look," said Hi Pockets. "I'm willing to be your manager."

"Fine," said Buddy. "What does that mean?"

"You need to beef up the act. Get someone on bass. Maybe Larry Welborn. We'll organize a trio—Buddy, Bob, and Larry."

"Where we gonna get a bass fiddle?" Buddy asked.

"I'll have to buy you a bull fiddle to get you started," said Hi Pockets.

Larry Welborn was a timely addition to the Buddy and Bob act, which was experiencing some strain. "I feel that I was just a little too close to him," Montgomery commented in *Reminiscing* magazine in 1981. "I knew that he was a very talented guy. He was doing some very original licks and he had a great sense of rhythm, but as a singer in our early times, he

never really impressed me that much." Just how much Montgomery impressed Holly is not known. No doubt the two were highly competitive
and critical of each other. According to biographer Philip Norman,
"Montgomery remembers him as 'a real ugly guy,' skinny and awkward
with worse-than-usual teenage acne and 'West Texas teeth,' stained
brown by the overfluorided water."

Around this time Buddy fell in love with a classmate named Echo
Elaine McGuire. She was the kind of girl every boy in the fifties wanted
to be associated with—she was attractive and had a good reputation. Her
pious, churchgoing, middle-class family owned a string of dry-cleaning
stores in Lubbock. Respecting such a girl's virtue could be painful. Boys
in the fifties usually ended up a date with aching testicles, known as "blue
balls." It was an all-too-familiar stigmata of the decade's paradoxical and
confusing sexual mores. Girls gave confusing signals. Their form-fitting
sweaters, wasplike waists, and pointed bras said one thing—*ravish me*—
but their demure Peter Pan collars and pert little scarves flashed a stern
warning: *I'm pure—keep your distance*. Buddy solved the dilemma, according to some observers, by dropping his steady girlfriend off after a
date and then driving by Tom Halsey's Pharmacy, where more willing
girls could always be found.

He also enjoyed abundant sexual release with a girl in school, though
he did not love her as he did Echo; the relationship was strictly physical.
The girl felt the same way about Buddy: they weren't going anywhere as
a couple but they certainly enjoyed each other's bodies. She loved to
hang out at a local juke joint and play R&B records. Some say Buddy got
her pregnant and completely disrupted her life. To avoid disgrace, her
family was said to have moved to another town. One source said the child
she had by Buddy was a boy; another was less certain of the gender; still
another said she had a girl. Bill Griggs, founder of the now-defunct Buddy
Holly Memorial Society, doubts that it happened at all, though he's
known about the allegations for more than twenty-six years, he revealed
in a 1994 letter. Sonny Curtis denies it outright, stating in 1995, "Buddy
never said a word to me about having a kid." Whatever the truth, Echo
McGuire remained Buddy's steady, though his brother Larry was skeptical
of their chances from the start. Echo was a devout member of the Church
of Christ, and Buddy was a Baptist. "I went with a Church of Christ girl
for nearly a year myself, real steady, and really thought a lot of her," says
Larry. "But I was not intendin' to marry her. She was pretty and nice. I
was in love with her, but finally we broke it off. Baptist and Church of
Christ kids will marry each other if they don't watch out and in each
case they end up not having a very good spiritual life thereafter. For
some reason Church of Christ kids have the idea that people who are

not Church of Christ are not gonna go to heaven. That just infuriates Baptists."

Though Echo was undoubtedly important to Buddy, she was never his top priority, falling somewhere below music, God, beer, and sex. "If Buddy had a choice of going out on a date or playing his guitar, he'd play his guitar," Niki Sullivan later told Griggs. "Music was more important to him, though he and Echo did go steady."

The only kind of music Buddy and Echo had in common was the harmless stuff they sang as members of the high school choir, such as Brodszky's "I Walk With God" or Christmas carols at the annual Yule Assembly. Church of Christ girls didn't listen to risqué songs like "Big Long Slidin' Thing" or dance to them, either. "They had hair all over their legs," says Tinker Carlen. "Their mamas wouldn't never let 'em shave their legs." According to Sonny Curtis, "Echo was not a knockout like my girl Jean Cates." In Megargel, the small Texas town I grew up in, 170 miles east of Lubbock, Church of Christ women wore long-sleeved dresses and thick stockings. Though I was a Methodist, I attended the Church of Christ because we were too poor to own a car, and Church of Christ folks would give you a ride. The sermons, shrilled by a hysterical preacher, left me cold, but I loved the part of the service when the congregation was invited to participate. People would stand up, release their pent-up angers and frustrations, and sing the Lord's praises. Sometimes, in the grip of the Holy Spirit, they would dance and shout. In time, I noticed that fewer Church of Christ people had nervous breakdowns than the Baptists and Methodists in town, whose participation in church was restricted to an occasional amen or hymn singing.

For religious reasons, Echo McGuire couldn't share Buddy's passion for R&B or rock 'n' roll. This proved a disadvantage because Buddy liked to check out the clubs, listen to the music, and pick with the musicians.

Larry Welborn, the bass player Hi Pockets had recommended, was a few years younger than Buddy, still attending Carol Thompson Junior High when Buddy recruited him for the Buddy and Bob act. "I was playing a little dive—I was so young I wasn't supposed to be there," Welborn remembers. "Buddy showed up one night and said, 'I came out because I heard you were playing bass.'

"Is that so? Hope you're enjoying yourself."

Buddy nodded and said, "You're closer to my age than the other musicians playing clubs around here. How would you like to work with me and Bob Montgomery on KDAV?"

"Well, at least it would be legal."

Retaining top billing for themselves, Buddy and Bob ordered business cards that read BUDDY AND BOB—WESTERN AND BOP, consigning Larry to smaller type at the edge of the card and listing Hi Pockets as their business manager, in care of KDAV. Later in 1954, Larry Welborn dropped out of the act. Buddy, Bob, and Don Guess then formed the Rhythm Playboys. "I'm going to draw up a contract on you where anybody that uses you will have to come through me," said Hi Pockets. "That will save you doing any more free parties."

Bookings began to come through, as well as cash. They performed during remote broadcasts at store openings, sang at high school assemblies, and did community shows and car-lot sales. Still being underage, for the present they played no honky tonks, bars, or dances. The trio also became a popular attraction at the Lindsey Theater, playing before Saturday midnight previews. "If we played thirty minutes and got fifty bucks, we thought we was in pretty good shape," said Hi Pockets, who did not charge the boys for his services. If he sold one of their remote broadcasts, he received a commission, and he was also paid whenever he performed as their emcee.

Busy with so many musical breakthroughs, Buddy neglected his schoolwork. He no longer had time for things like civics and algebra. Midway through his junior year, his mother told him to start bringing home some books. "It's going to be harder now," she said. But it wasn't, not for Buddy. An able researcher and writer for his age, he dashed off succinct, interesting papers. Years later, when his tests and term themes were auctioned at Sotheby's, the *New Yorker* magazine reviewed his book report on Robert Frost and pronounced it—by homework standards—"a masterpiece." His writing style, like his later song lyrics, was direct, simple, and powerful. He was indeed a natural.

In 1954 Buddy met Waylon Jennings, who was ten months younger than Buddy and just as ambitious. Having grown up picking cotton, Waylon once said, "You'll do anything to get out of West Texas. . . . It's either music or pull cotton for the rest of your life." A high school dropout at fourteen, Waylon lived in Littlefield, Texas, thirty miles northwest of Lubbock. He grew up raising hell with his brother Tommy and was "always into some damn trouble," Tommy later said. They burned down a government storage grainery and a truckload of cotton, according to Waylon's biographer R. Serge Denisoff. The Littlefield High School coach was sorry to lose Waylon, who was full of promise as a place kicker. He held a number of jobs—in a grocery store, a "dry goods" store, a lumber yard, and delivering freight. He'd won first prize—a table-top radio—on Hi Pockets Duncan's KSEL "Saturday Jamboree" when he was only twelve. "He came from a poor family," Hi Pockets said. "He was kind of on his own when he was a kid."

By the time Waylon met Buddy, at seventeen, Waylon had developed his dazzling good looks and a resonant and expressive voice. Songwriter May Boren Axton would later refer to his "deep brown eyes and a beautifully crooked grin." The title of Waylon's first song, written when he was fifteen, was "Big Time Ladies Man." Indeed he would come to be known as "the cowboy Warren Beatty." Years later, groupie Pamela Des Barres called him "honestly crude and crudely honest." After she and Waylon had sex, she says, Waylon apologized "for being so steamed up, and kissed me on the forehead, calling me a 'sweet angel.'" Des Barres revealed this in her 1987 book *I'm With the Band*, adding that he started to get up but then returned to bed, "with a vengeance, saying, 'I'll tell you what, you really know how to please a man, baby.'"

Back in 1954 Waylon would occasionally drive down to KDAV and catch Buddy on the "Sunday Party" or they'd run into each other at amateur contests held on Saturday afternoons at movie theaters around West Texas. "Sometimes the same band would win it two or three weeks running," Waylon told author Peter Guralnick in 1974. "We were still playing country—Buddy, too—hell, there wasn't anything else, really. We worked a lot of shows together."

Buddy frequently lent his sonorous Gibson J-45 acoustic guitar to Waylon, who moved to Lubbock in 1955 and became a DJ. One day they were loitering at the Lubbock bus station with Sonny Curtis, Weldon Myrick, and Roy Orbison. Standing in front of a beat-up jukebox, Buddy said, "Who's got a quarter? We gotta hear this Chet Atkins record."

Everyone was broke but Sonny Curtis, who sacrificed his last quarter. "That's all we had," Waylon recalls.

"I wish we could take in the Sonny James–Jim Reeves show," said Orbison.

"I know," said Waylon, "let's sneak in."

All five managed to crash the show. Sonny James and Jim Reeves fascinated them as C&W singers who crossed over into pop, something the boys all wanted to do. Sonny James had scored a No. 1 crossover hit with "Young Love." Reeves's "Four Walls" and "He'll Have to Go" appealed equally to hillbillies and international fans.

Somewhere around 1953 or 1954 a representative of Columbia Records heard Buddy and Bob, raising their hopes for a recording contract. They rounded up Sonny Curtis, Larry Welborn, and Don Guess and drove to Wichita Falls, Texas, two hundred miles east of Lubbock, to cut a demonstration record, or "demo", at the Nesman studio. The songs they recorded were Bob Montgomery's "Gotta Get You Near Me Blues" and "Flower of My Heart." Although they never heard from the Columbia man again, the Nesman tapes did survive. They are flat-out, free-flying hillbilly romps that stand up today as pure and timeless, despite Mont-gomery's odd dismissal of them as "embarrassing." Sonny Curtis's zesty hoedown fiddling is outstanding.

Soon the Buddy and Bob band was playing the West Texas honky-tonk circuit. One night in San Angelo they were heckled by oil-field roustabouts in the audience. Buddy finished the show barely able to con-ceal his rage. According to Larry Welborn, someone bought them a six-pack. "Of course we couldn't buy it at the time ourselves, being too young," says Larry. Driving out to the country, they popped open their beers, and started rehashing the performance. After a few beers Buddy said, "Well, less go back. I wanta whip them son of a bitches that didn't like us."

"He was ready to go back and get after it with them," Larry Welborn recalls. "He'd have that little bit of mean streak to him. He was just standin' up for his own self. He wouldn't let anybody tear him down. If he thought anybody was goin' to say anything, he just beat them to the punch. Buddy believed in hisself, stood up for hisself."

Sonny Curtis also found Buddy to be aggressive and reckless. "Though in appearance Buddy was very neat and always wore *tapered* jeans, he was *not* shy," says Sonny. "He was a drinker—loud, a smart aleck, head-strong." Jack Neal remembers being in a car with Buddy one time when he pulled a crazy stunt. Jack was driving and Buddy was sitting next to him, being very quiet. Suddenly Buddy decided Jack wasn't going fast enough and stomped on Jack's foot, sending the accelerator to the floor-board. "Scared me half to death," Jack recalls.

One day at Lubbock High, Buddy got into a violent fight with another student in Robert Knight's distributive education class. The boys flew at each other and fought their way across the room until they were hanging out of a third-floor window. "I had to grab them both by the collar," recalls Knight, who hauled them in and let everyone cool down. Only a few years older than his students, Knight didn't take the boys to the principal's office.

"Buddy was cocky, but he had a lot to be cocky about," says Knight. "He was aggressive, what experts in interpersonal relations call a 'bipolar 8.' He was very self-confident and got things done. Students who weren't that self-confident were irritated by him and took the attitude: 'I'll knock your head off.' Buddy was a visionary young man and had difficulty with them."

The brawl in Knight's class demonstrated that Buddy thought of him-self as almost invincible. He had the kind of determination known only to heroes and fools—he was willing to fight to the death. Though he was not brawny—nor particularly healthy due to his ulcer—bullies knew he wasn't to be messed with and left him alone.

The distributive education (DE) program at Lubbock High allowed students from poor families to attend classes in the morning and work at outside jobs in the afternoon. Buddy took a job at Smith Printing Company and became one of the outstanding DE students during his junior and senior years, holding an office in the DE club and helping put on dinners where employers could mingle with students and faculty members. He also traveled around with state with Robert Knight, entertaining at DE functions.

Knight found Buddy to be "unusually thoughtful, especially for a teenage kid. When I had the mumps, I was laying in bed and couldn't do anything. Buddy and Bob came over when they got off work at four-thirty or five to entertain me for a couple of hours. I brought out my dominoes and we sat and played a game of 42."

Rock 'n' roll had become more dominant on the airwaves during Buddy's senior year, 1954–55. The most popular jukebox hits were the Crew Cuts' "Sh-Boom" and the Penguins' "Earth Angel." "Buddy started playing rock at the hops," remembers Robert Knight, who chaperoned the dances in the gym. "Buddy got up there in his Levi's, a white shirt, and loafers, or sometimes in Bermuda shorts. Buddy and Bob were so exciting playing the new rock 'n' roll songs that I jumped up and danced with the kids."

When the class of '55 received its class ring—a tasteful gold band with a lariat encircling Lubbock High's Romanesque facade and campanile— Buddy gave his ring to Echo McGuire, who placed it on a chain and wore it around her neck. In photographs, they are a happy looking couple. By then Buddy had filled out. He had broad shoulders, a narrow waist, and slender hips. In profile, his least attractive angle, he looked strangely Martian, but when he faced the camera he was handsome, with a big, heroic forehead, gull-wing eyebrows, a squared-off chin, and a strong jawline. Standing next to Echo, he towered over her by at least a foot.

Shortly before graduation, he registered for the draft. He signed in on May 6, 1955—the same day an atomic bomb was exploded in the Nevada desert. For young men facing military service, it was a grim, nervous time: everyone expected an imminent attack by Russia. The feeling, exemplified by Alfred E. Neuman in Mad magazine, was counteracted by a giddy materialism, even in West Texas. Flashy, gas-guzzling cars, dubbed "arrogant chariots" by the New Yorker, grew to record-breaking size and sprouted soaring tail fins. Impressive new interstate highways were built during the terms of President Eisenhower, their opening ending the preeminence of two-lane highways like Route 66. Record sales shot sky-high when the new 45-rpm disks replaced the bulky old 78s in the same way that CDs have rendered vinyl out-of-date. The recently invented transistor radios filled the air with music as never before.

Though Buddy didn't own a car, he drove the family's new 1955 Olds-mobile to school. He told everyone that it was his graduation present. One of his classmates called his mother and asked if the car was actually Buddy's. To save her son embarrassment, Mrs. Holley answered that the car was certainly Buddy's whenever he was in the driver's seat. Before long, Buddy wrecked the car while showing off in front of Lubbock High. Waving to friends, he rear-ended the car in front of him, and the Holleys' Olds had to go into the shop for expensive repairs.

On his graduation day—Friday, May 27, 1955—Buddy Holley was not asked to sing, despite the fact the commencement exercise included sev-eral musical numbers, such as "I Believe." Following the ceremony, a prom was held downtown, atop the Dunlap Store.

In the fall, Echo went away to college, enrolling in a religious school in Abilene, Texas, 165 miles southeast of Lubbock. From then on, she and Buddy would see each other only on weekends.

"Buddy brought her over to my house some," says Larry Holley, "and I felt like he might marry her." But despite Larry's opinion, the separation from Echo marked the beginning of the end of their relationship. From this point on, her name would resonate more in melody than in actual life.

Chapter Four

Elvis Meets Buddy

When Elvis came to town, Buddy found him a girl," says Larry Holley. "She was not anyone you'd find on this side of town." Though there are still friends of Buddy's in Lubbock who claim to have seen him showing Elvis around town, fixing him up with a girl, and even bringing him to the high school one day, Sonny Curtis, who played on the same bill with Buddy and Elvis in 1955, shrugs and says, "Elvis could get pussy where I couldn't get drinking water."

Despite varying opinions regarding Buddy and Elvis's personal relationship, what is certain beyond any doubt is that when Elvis Presley hit Lubbock in 1955, he transformed all the C&W pickers in Buddy's circle into rockers. "Without Elvis," Buddy once said, "none of us could have made it." Though rock 'n' roll had burst on the world of West Texas the previous year with Bill Haley's "Shake, Rattle, and Roll," it was Elvis who whispered freedom into the ears of embattled Baptist boys like Buddy and unleashed a new generation of rockabillies. Though Elvis would not emerge as a national celebrity until the following year, he'd already been a sensation in Texas since playing his first gig in the state on August 21, 1954, in the small town of Gladewater. He appeared in Lubbock several times in 1955, and on one of his shows, Buddy and his group opened for him.

Hi Pockets once said that he was the first promoter to book Elvis into Lubbock. In the beginning, Elvis's fee was $25. He had two musicians, Scotty Moore and Bill Black, but he told Hi Pockets that he'd be glad to add to his band if Hi Pockets could guarantee them a regular dance gig. Hi Pockets kept booking them until Elvis soared out of his league. "Buddy and all those boys were out there listening," Hi Pockets remembered. "Man, they didn't miss a thing."

Sam Phillips had put Scotty and Bill together with Elvis the previous year at Sun Records in Memphis, Tennessee. Winfield Scott Moore III was a lean, stone-faced guitarist with a ski-jump nose. William P. "Blackie" Black, who drove audiences wild when he straddled his big bull fiddle and started humping it, regarded the world from slitty Roy Rogers eyes that beamed bright smiles. Bill had previously worked for Firestone Tire and Scotty was a Tennessee farm boy fresh out of the Navy. Their initial session with Elvis at Sun Records produced "That's All Right, Mama," Elvis's first commercial release. For a while, Scotty was Elvis's manager, later yielding to Bob Neal, who in turn would be replaced by Tom Parker.

As Larry Holley remembers it, Elvis was terribly late the night he was scheduled to appear at Fair Park Coliseum in Lubbock in 1955. In Elvis's absence, Buddy and his front band blew the roof off the coliseum, playing until Elvis came on. Many people in the audience preferred Buddy to Elvis, Larry proudly recalled, although Buddy was still a beginner.

Elvis billed himself as "The Hillbilly Cat, King of Western Bop." In the Deep South, where Elvis came from, "Cat" denoted a black man. Elvis's style was hillbilly music with a Negro spin—rock 'n' roll, as it would soon come to be known. "Elvis looked like a motorcycle headlight coming at you," says Sonny Curtis. "White buck shoes, red pants, and an orange jacket." When he rotated his hips in rhythm, the audience went berserk.

Tom Parker, the corpulent medicine-show promoter who'd made a star of C&W singer Eddy Arnold, was in Lubbock, scouting for talent. Both Buddy and Elvis intrigued him, but Parker focused on Elvis. Hi Pockets hobnobbed with Parker and admired his flair for promotion, which he felt was responsible for Elvis's superiority as a showman. "But as far as actual talent goes, I'd put Buddy Holley up against Elvis Presley," Hi Pockets said.

To Bob Montgomery, who also saw Parker in Lubbock, it was clear that Parker was intent on signing Elvis, but nevertheless saw great promise in Buddy. In fact, he would have put Buddy under contract had it not been against his policy to take on two performers at the same time. So impressed was Parker that he decided to recommend Buddy to Eddie Crandall, an important Nashville talent agent. Crandall didn't act on the tip immediately; but he didn't forget it, either.

After Elvis's performance at Fair Park, Hi Pockets urged everyone to go out to the Cotton Club, Lubbock's major dance hall, and put on another show. "We opened for Elvis," says Sonny Curtis. "Bales of cotton were stacked around the stage to protect him from the audience. The most beautiful girls in Lubbock were trying to climb the bales to get at him. That's what impressed us as much as the music. We'd been hillbillies, but after the Cotton Club we were rockers like Elvis."

Attempting to exit the parking lot after the show, Elvis almost got beaten up. "Somebody was wantin' to whip Elvis outside the Cotton Club—Elvis was stealin' his girl or somethin'," Larry Welborn remembered. Elvis and the girl managed to escape unscathed. According to Larry

Holley, "Buddy and Elvis got along pretty good. They went out after the show."

Buddy became such an ardent Elvis fan that he made a leather case for his J-45 guitar just like the one Elvis used on his Martin D-28. "I wish he had done one for *my* guitar," Sonny Curtis later told writer William Bush. "I had a brand-new Martin D-28 and Buddy put pick scratches all over the face. It really pissed me off."

"I Forgot to Remember to Forget" was Buddy's favorite Elvis Presley song. Buddy recorded it at radio station KLLL, whose DJs played it for years. Mrs. Holly loved Buddy's version so much that she said it was superior to Elvis's. Unfortunately, the cut has not survived. Once Buddy began to release professionally the following year, he was required by contract to withdraw his amateur records from circulation.

In a conversation with Waylon Jennings, Buddy confided that Elvis was now his favorite singer. Waylon said he liked rock 'n' roll but was also wary of it, confessing to Buddy that he was afraid he was going to be left behind as a C&W singer. "I wish I could be more 'with it,' " Waylon said. "If I could sing rock 'n' roll better, I would."

"Let me tell you something, man," Buddy said. "You can go into several fields. Don't sweat it."

Waylon remembers that Buddy was the only person, outside his immediate family, who took Waylon seriously as a singer. Elvis "changed Buddy," Waylon later told Peter Guralnick. "It was the beginning of kids really starting to think for themselves, figuring things out, realizing things that they would never even have thought of before."

Elvis's band, which eventually included a drummer, Dominic Joseph "D. J." Fontana, provided the guidelines for West Texas musicians such as Buddy Holley and Roy Orbison, who were trying to produce the rock 'n' roll sound. "We got a drummer, and I think it's a matter of instruments that defined whether you were playing C&W or rock," said Orbison, who did not add drums until he formed his second band, the Teen Kings. Buddy's first drummer was Jerry Allison, who he'd known since J. T. Hutchinson Junior High. One night Buddy dropped into the 16th and J Club, where Allison was performing with Cal Wayne and the Riverside Ranch Hands. Buddy said he'd show them the knack of playing rock 'n' roll if they'd let him sit in with them for a while.

Allison spoke to Cal Wayne, who said it was all right for Buddy to join them. Buddy talked to them briefly and demonstrated how to rock the music. They tore into "Rock Around the Clock" with explosive force, salvos of sound ricocheting around the room and jarring the audience from its lassitude. Jerry was an instant convert. Until Buddy, they'd been drifting along, playing Hank Thompson and the Texas two-step. Now they swung into "Forty Cups of Coffee," and suddenly everyone was up and bopping. Though Buddy and Jerry were not standing especially close to each other, they moved and communicated as if they were locked in an embrace. Their synergy was palpable, their sound a special syncopation all their own.

In the days that followed, Jerry moved forcefully into Buddy's circle. Strongly in Jerry's favor, as far as Buddy was concerned, was Jerry's whole-hearted conversion to rock 'n' roll. Bob Montgomery and Sonny Curtis were less committed to rock 'n' roll than Jerry was, according to what Jerry later told writer William Bush. Jerry invited Buddy to come to his house, where they could rehearse uninterrupted as long as they wanted to. Jerry set his drums up in his bedroom, and Buddy brought over his latest guitar, a gold-top Gibson Les Paul. Later Buddy complained that the Les Paul was too heavy and soon replaced it.

Buddy and Jerry played the roller rink as a duo, and those who saw them there say that they seemed to make more noise than a whole band. "We'd both play the same rhythm lick that somehow made our music sound fuller," Jerry explained. They also made some records with Bob Montgomery in Wichita Falls, including "Down the Line," but they couldn't find a record company to release them.

When Elvis came back to Lubbock in 1955, he offered to help Buddy get on "The Louisiana Hayride" if he'd come to Shreveport, where the show was broadcast every Saturday night over station KWKH from the Municipal Auditorium. Elvis was a regular on the "Hayride," appearing on the show fifty times between late 1954 and 1956. Chasing Elvis's pot of gold, Buddy and his friends set out for Shreveport, 512 miles southeast of Lubbock, driving the '55 Olds. It proved to be a wild goose chase; "Elvis was supposed to get us on and he wasn't there," Larry Welborn told Griggs in 1986.

Thanks to Sid King, who had a bluegrass band called the Five Strings, Buddy and his pals had better luck with "The Big D Jamboree," Dallas's famous Saturday-night C&W radio show. In Lubbock one night, King let Buddy, Bob, and Larry Welborn sit in with his band at the Cotton Club. Known for his bluegrass arrangement of "Blue Suede Shoes," King liked Buddy's group so much that he offered to get them on the "Jamboree" if they'd make the drive to Dallas, 323 miles east of Lubbock. In no time at all, the boys showed up on King's doorstep in Dallas, completely un-announced. King had not counted on putting the trio up without con-siderable notice. Somewhat resignedly, he told them that they could stay with him for one night, and he'd try to get them on the show the following day. King was as good as his word. The next day they sang "Down the Line" on KRLD, and King remembered that Buddy was virtually a carbon copy of Elvis Presley. Buddy "idolized" Elvis, he told King.

The turning point in Buddy's career came when he and Bob opened for Bill Haley and His Comets at the Fair Park Coliseum in October 1955. "Pappy" Dave Stone arranged the gig and told Eddie Crandall, the Nashville talent agent who was in the audience that night, to pay special attention to Buddy. Later the same month, Buddy and Bob opened for Eddie Crandall's client Marty Robbins, who was about to hit the charts with "A White Sport Coat (And a Pink Carnation)." Marty Robbins's comment to Crandall was that Buddy Holley had "what it takes." In the end, Colonel Tom Parker, who was still enthusiastic about Buddy but totally preoccupied with Elvis, convinced Eddie Crandall to take Buddy on. Crandall secured exclusive right to represent Buddy on December 2, 1955, and started trying to get him a recording contract in Nashville. Instead of approaching record companies directly, he turned to the most influential man in C&W music, Jim Denny, the former manager of "The Grand Ole Opry," who was now an artists' manager and owner of Cedarwood Music, a publishing firm. Denny agreed to give Buddy an audition. As Mel Tillis once put it, "Every young songwriter and singer in town wanted to get in to see Jim Denny." In the years before Tillis hit the top of the charts with "Detroit City," he was never able to get past Denny's wife, Dollie, "the pretty redheaded receptionist" at Denny's publishing firm. With Eddie Crandall's help, Buddy managed to break through to Denny and in doing so acquired a foothold in Nashville, the southeastern recording center of the United States.

From his Nashville office at 319 Seventh Avenue North, Crandall wired Pappy Stone at KDAV with instructions for Buddy to cut demos of four original songs and forward them to him "as soon as possible airmail." The prospect of a recording contract galvanized Buddy's songwriting abilities and he immediately went to work, turning out four new tunes. Two of them, "Love Me" and "Don't Come Back Knockin'," he cowrote with a Lubbock songwriter named Sue Parrish. The other two, "I Guess I Was Just a Fool" and "Baby Won't You Come Out Tonight," were his first solo efforts as a songwriter.

"Baby Won't You Come Out Tonight" is a hard-driving rocker. The singer urges his girl to go-go-go, to rock 'n' roll, a far franker euphemism for sex than the kiss me, hold me supplications of forties and early fifties lyrics. The rock ballad "I Guess I Was Just a Fool" is the first sign that Buddy was also capable of exploring deeper feelings and emotional states with insight and depth. In this song, the story of a man who has lost a relationship but is glad to know he's at least capable of experiencing love, Buddy seems to be drawing on his ill-starred love for Echo McGuire. From these first creative efforts, it was clear that Buddy Holley was a songwriter to be reckoned with.

Accompanied by Bob and Larry, Buddy cut the audition tape for Decca on acetate at KDAV, according to Pappy, and then forwarded it to Denny in Nashville. Denny peddled the demos up and down Sixteenth Avenue South, known as Record Row. Columbia got a crack at Buddy but rejected him. Decca was shrewder; Paul Cohen, prestigious director of the company's country-music division, was in the market for an Elvis Presley clone and was sufficiently intrigued to ask what Buddy looked like, wondering if he could be promoted as a sex symbol. "I don't care how they sing," a record mogul once told Waylon Jennings. "If they're not good looking, don't bring them around."

Pat Pinkston, Pappy Stone's wife, answered the telephone when Denny called Lubbock asking for a description of Buddy. She made no claims for him as a potential matinee idol but said he was a good Christian boy and with that Buddy Holley was one step closer to a recording contract. Denny "asked to have the boys come to Nashville for a recording session" at Decca, Pappy recalled in 1983. Decca specified they were interested in Buddy as a solo act, not as part of the singing duo Buddy and Bob. Loyal to his friend, Buddy reminded Decca that he was part of a singing team.

"Well, you can bring him along if you want, but he can't sing on the records," Denny said. "We want one singer, not two." Buddy threatened to turn down the deal unless Nashville relented and cut Bob in. When Bob Montgomery realized what was going on, he graciously bowed out, telling Buddy that this was his big chance and he should go for it. Hi Pockets was equally magnanimous, tearing up the personal-appearance contract he had with Buddy. "I wasn't able to travel with him," Hi Pockets later told Griggs, "and I did not want to hinder his success in any way." Making the first big mistake of his career, Buddy let Hi Pockets go. In the treacherous days ahead, he would need a devoted and honest manager as the breaks started coming fast. In January 1956, Hank Thompson signed Buddy for a two-week tour of the South. Buddy had attracted Thompson's attention at the Cotton Club in 1955, when he'd played intermissions for Thompson's Brazos Valley Boys. Waco-born Thompson was famous for his hit records "Humpty Dumpty Heart" and "The Wild Side of Life," better known as "I Didn't Know God Made Honky Tonk Angels." He expected Buddy not only to open his show but to play backup for other stars on the bill, including George Jones, Hank Locklin, Glen Reeves, and Justin Tubb.

Buddy had to assemble a band quickly, not only for the tour but for the recording session that would immediately follow it in Nashville. Don Guess agreed to play bass fiddle. He couldn't afford to buy the instrument, so Buddy rented one from the Lubbock public school system for $6 a year, signed up Sonny Curtis to play lead guitar, and began to rehearse his new band, often working at Lubbock High. Jerry was always around, playing drums, but he was still in school and wouldn't be able to go on the road.

After a rehearsal at the high school one afternoon, Buddy rushed out of the band room with his guitar in one hand and his amplifier in the other. He bumped into a blond beauty, knocking her to the floor. Peggy Sue Gerron, baton twirler and first-chair alto sax player in the high school band, was never out of Buddy's life for long after that. In the days that followed, he thought of her often and scribbled her initials "PSG" in his notebook. Unlike Echo, Peggy Sue listened to rock 'n' roll and loved to dance. She also liked to spend time with boys who were fun-loving and had entertaining personalities. Born in Olton, Texas, forty-five miles north of Lubbock, Peggy Sue moved to Lubbock when her father, a serviceman, was stationed at Reece Air Force Base. She first met Jerry Allison at R. W. Matthews Junior High School, when Jerry was dating her best friend. It was the beginning of one of the most important—and troublesome—relationships of her life.

Peggy Sue soon got a crush on Jerry and often stood in the band room, watching him play his drums. "I thought he was absolutely darling," she told Griggs in 1987. In high school she called Jerry "Jivin' Ivan." Eventually Jerry dropped her friend and started dating Peggy Sue. When Echo McGuire came home on visits from Abilene Christian College, they'd double-date with Buddy and Echo. Peggy Sue described Echo as "Buddy's first crush," adding, "for a brief time he was just wild about her. She was a darling thing, just precious."

Peggy Sue and Jerry soon quarreled and broke up. "Our relationship was stormy from the first," she said in 1994. "I started going with Doyle Gammill, the drum major in the band. I performed as a twirler in state competitions and was the only sophomore to make it into the senior band."

When Peggy Sue and Jerry later resumed their relationship and started going steady, her parents disapproved, considering her much too young at fifteen to be serious about a boy. They threatened to send her away to a parochial school in California. Her mother was very protective of Peggy Sue, believing she'd had a touch of polio as a child. "It was probably lupus, not polio," says Peggy Sue today. "I have lupus now, so my childhood sickness was the first sign."

Peggy Sue often saw Buddy outside the Hi-D-Ho Drive-in, standing beside his car and kicking the tires. In her father's Ford Fairlane, she and her girlfriends spent "a lot of time driving around the Hi-D-Ho in circles, hanging around, checking out the cars," she says. "When the boys didn't have anything else to do, they'd kick their tires." Waylon Jennings was the first in Buddy's crowd to get married. Under the impression that he'd gotten his girl, Maxine Carrol Lawrence, pregnant, he married her in 1956 only to discover, several hours after the wedding ceremony, that she wasn't pregnant after all. Their son, Terry Vance Jennings, was born one year later, followed by a daughter, Julie Rae, in 1958. "This is something that should not have happened in the first place," Hi Pockets observed. "He was always in desperate need of money." But Waylon refused to give up his musical ambitions and was still determined to escape West Texas at any price. Waylon's cousin, Anita Shipley, started dating Sonny Curtis during this period.

As Buddy completed his preparations for the Hank Thompson tour in late 1955 and early 1956, he and Echo continued to hold on to their tenuous relationship, but it must have been clear to them both that the end was near. His emotions were on a roller-coaster ride—heartbreak over Echo and excitement over his forthcoming Decca recording session, set for January 26, 1956. His most pressing need was to find original song material to record if he expected to score a hit recording, and he definitely expected at least one hit out of the session—not to mention a lot of money and instant fame.

Shortly before Buddy left Lubbock, Ben Hall called him and offered "Blue Days, Black Nights," a song he'd just completed. Hall no longer lived in Lubbock but returned specifically to give the song to Buddy. They arranged to meet and rehearse the song at one of the local radio stations. Although it was a winter day, the sun was shining and it was warm enough for them to go outside and work on the lyrics. They found a shady spot and sat down. Ben showed him how to sing and play the song, explaining that he'd written it about a hard time, when he couldn't find his direction. His days had been bad, and his nights worse. Buddy loved the song so much that Ben decided he'd never show it to anyone else; it was Buddy's.

Before leaving town, Buddy appealed to his brother Larry for money, confidently stating that he was about to become a star and could hardly make his debut with beat-up equipment. Assuring Larry that the family was soon going to be very proud of him, he asked for $1,000. Thunderstruck, Larry said "Why don't you just ask for the moon?" But somehow he managed to rake up the grand. Impressed that Buddy was determined to make it as a professional musician "or bust a gut," Larry says, "he blew six hundred of it on a Fender Stratocaster."

Actually, Buddy purchased the Strat for $249.50 at Harrod Music on Avenue Q in Lubbock. Though the Strat was popular with C&W musicians, having sprung from the steel guitar, it was not considered a rock 'n' roll instrument until Buddy made it famous. The futuristic-looking Stratocaster, featuring a tail-fin design that made it look more like a car than a guitar, was invented by a bespectacled Californian named Clarence Leo Fender. Among the Strat's innovations was a built-in vibrato that enabled musicians to come up with shimmering musical nuances. But the Strat's greatest attraction for Buddy as a rock musician was that it was *loud*.

After acquiring the Strat, Buddy went shopping for a red sport coat but found nothing of interest in Lubbock, where hip clothes were as scarce as hen's teeth, unless you wanted a cowboy look. Determined to outfit themselves as rockers, Buddy, Sonny Curtis, and Don Guess set out for Oklahoma City, 357 miles northeast of Lubbock, in search of the proto-Punk garb—pegged pants and turned-up Billy Eckstine collars—that Elvis Presley had found at Lansky Brothers on Memphis's Beale Street. "That's how we ended up being Buddy Holly and the Two-Tones," Sonny explains. "We bought white trousers, but one of us got a blue shirt and one got an orange one—hence the Two-Tones."

With what remained of the $1,000 loan from Larry, Buddy bought a Pro Amp for his new electric guitar. Finally the trio pulled out of Lubbock, Don's bass fiddle strapped on top of the Olds. The boys made it out of town just in time. A collection agency was after the car because Buddy's parents had turned the payments over to him, and he hadn't been making them. Buddy's hasty exit from Lubbock marked the end of his apprenticeship and the beginning of his life as a professional singer. He was well prepared for the challenges that lay ahead in the demanding world of show business. Solidly grounded in bluegrass and country singing, he'd learned rock 'n' roll from the master himself, Elvis Presley, and was ready to conquer the airwaves and jukeboxes as the latest rock sensation. He took it as a good omen that he and Elvis were going to be in Nashville at the same time. Elvis had moved from Memphis when Sam Phillips sold his Sun Records contract to RCA in November 1955, and now both Elvis and Buddy were scheduled for Nashville sessions in January 1956. At RCA, where Chet Atkins had the good sense to say, "Just go on doing what you been doing," Elvis sailed through his first session, which produced the No. 1 hit "Heartbreak Hotel." At Decca, Buddy's mentors would prove less amenable to the new music; in fact, they hated rock 'n' roll.

Chapter Five

The Hillbilly Backlash

Unfortunately, Buddy's initial forays into professionalism—the Thompson tour at the beginning of January 1956 and the Nashville recording session at the end of the month—were out-and-out disasters. The C&W establishment had been thrown into panic by the sudden ascendancy of rock 'n' roll and Buddy caught the full impact of the hillbilly backlash, an explosion of C&W paranoia and rage. On the road as a backup player, he immediately clashed with hard-drinking C&W recording star George Jones, who poked fun at Buddy's and Glen Reeves's loud clothes and boozily denounced rock 'n' roll. Buddy took it for a while and then struck back, informing Jones that he'd probably like rock 'n' roll if he were capable of singing it. One night Buddy broke into a rock beat as he accompanied Jones, who was singing his Top 10 C&W hit "Why Baby Why." Like all singers in the middle of a performance, Jones was at the mercy of his accompanist. Somehow Jones managed to complete the number as a rocker.

The situation didn't improve when Buddy arrived in Nashville and found the conservative hillbilly capital reeling from the onslaught of rock 'n' roll, which was decimating C&W on the charts. The old guard resisted rock 'n' roll with all its might. Buddy was immediately embroiled in the growing conflict between C&W and rock 'n' roll; eventually country music would be split down the middle, RCA and at least half of the C&W establishment fleeing to rockabilly—the term that was universally applied to the new rock 'n' roll hillbilly style—and the other half remaining straight country singers. The rockabillies adopted Elvis's style and mannerisms. The traditionalists took their lead from Hank Williams, Sr. Decca's Paul Cohen and Owen Bradley, instead of recognizing Buddy Holley as a potential rockabilly star, tried to force him into a C&W mold, completely disregarding his wish to sing rock 'n' roll. Buddy resisted, and Cohen got nasty, sniping, "You don't have the voice to be a singer. You should forget about a musical career." Jim and Dolly Denny had their hands full restraining a volatile and combative Buddy until the miserable session could be completed.

Of the four songs he cut on January 26 at Bradley's Barn, a quonset-hut annex to Bradley's house at Sixteenth Avenue South, "Midnight Shift" and "Love Me" come off best, but the beautiful "Blue Days, Black Nights" was wasted, vitiated by inferior sound engineering and an arrangement that was hard-edged where it should have been soft and tender. (Ben Hall's own performance of the song in Paul McCartney's BBC-TV special *The Real Buddy Holly Story* demonstrates how affecting it can be when properly delivered.) For Buddy, the only redeeming feature of the Decca fiasco was the after-hours fun he, Sonny, and Don had in Nashville. Marty Robbins let them have the run of his office, and evenings they hung out downtown and "chased chicks," says Sonny.

As if Buddy's relationship with Decca weren't bad enough, the company misspelled his name on his contract, dropping the "e" in Holley. Buddy decided to go along with the error, changing his name to Holly when he signed the contract, back in Lubbock, on February 8, 1956. The same month marked the beginning of the civil-rights movement, when a bold and defiant black woman, Rosa Parks, refused to move to the back of the bus in Montgomery, Alabama, kicking off a massive bus boycott. Whites, in embracing rock 'n' roll, were appropriating a huge chunk of black culture, but they were no closer than ever to accepting blacks as equals.

"Blue Days, Black Nights"/"Love Me," Buddy's first single, was released on April 16 and sold nineteen thousand units, a sale so dismal that it's a wonder the world ever again heard of Buddy Holly. In its review, *Billboard* failed to spot him as a future star and damned the record with faint praise, writing, "If the public will take more than one Presley or Perkins, as it well may, Holly stands a strong chance."

Buddy's next Decca session was set for late July. Determined not to repeat the same mistakes, he decided to practice and record demos of his new material, which included a hauntingly beautiful song he'd written called "Because I Love You" as well as another Ben Hall number, "It's Not My Fault." He went to Clovis, New Mexico, ninety-one miles northwest of Lubbock, which had a state-of-the-art recording studio owned by a man named Norman Petty. Hi Pockets Duncan was frantic when he heard that Buddy was about to hook up with Petty. "Whatever you do, don't go to Clovis," Hi Pockets pleaded. "Norman Petty has a bad reputation for taking advantage of kids."

Now that Buddy was in the big time, he dismissed Hi Pockets's counsel and went ahead to Clovis. Petty, a handsome man, somewhat resembling Jack Paar, the TV talk-show host, was immaculately clean, sometimes showering twenty times a day. He was devoted to his dog, Speedy, a Mexican Chihuahua. "We feel our studio has its own sound," Petty once said. Acoustical engineers had helped him "tune" the walls with built-in rounded baffles. "We have perhaps the only live echo chamber in the entire Southwest," he added.

Sounds from the studio were piped through a speaker system into an echo chamber located next door in a gas station. Once inside the chamber, sounds were picked up by another microphone and relayed back to the tape machine in the studio. When Petty sat at his control board, spinning knobs, he looked like a wizard. He was also a bravura, pyrotechnical organist who'd scored a minor hit record, "Mood Indigo," recorded with the Norman Petty Trio, an instrumental group that included his wife Violet Ann ("Vi"), who was a pianist, and guitarist Jack Vaughn. Nor Va Jak, Petty's independent record label and music-publishing firm, was named after Norman, Violet Ann, and Jack.

The Pettys' relationship was more business than pleasure; though few knew it at the time, Petty was gay, Vi bisexual. Their assistant, Norma Jean Berry, was a lesbian. All three, of course, were secretive about their sexual orientations. When the Pettys were outed in the *London Daily Mail* in 1994, Sonny Curtis, who knew everyone at the Clovis studio, remained skeptical. "If Norman was gay, he never put a shot on me," Sonny said in a 1995 interview. "Even if he was gay, what the heck?" However, Niki Sullivan, another key player, confirms the report.

Buddy recorded seven demos in Clovis, using Sonny, Don, and Jerry as sidemen. It was immediately apparent that the Clovis cuts possessed a fluid, full-bodied sound that no one at Bradley's Barn had been able to catch. "Changin' All Those Changes" and "Rock-A-Bye Rock" are early Holly gems. The plaintive "Because I Love You," the song Buddy had just written, suggests the emotional pain he was going through as Echo drifted away from him in 1956. In the lyric, the singer expresses his fear that his girlfriend has found someone else and states he would rather die than go through the rest of his life without her.

Around this time, Buddy sent some important business Norman Petty's way when he met a talented young athlete and songwriter at West Texas State College in Canyon, Texas, fifteen miles south of Amarillo, where Buddy and Roy Orbison were playing a student dance. During a break Buddy Wayne Knox, the jock-songwriter, who was twenty-three at the time and majoring in accounting and psychology, came up to Holly and Orbison, told them he'd written a song called "Party Doll," and asked how he could go about recording it. Knox said he'd written it "behind a haystack" on the farm outside Happy, Texas, where he grew up. Buddy Holly and Roy Orbison suggested that Buddy Knox go over to Clovis and record "Party Doll" at Petty's studio.

Knox heeded their advice, recorded "Party Doll" in Clovis—and beat both Holly and Orbison to the charts, becoming the first singer-songwriter of the rock era to score a No. 1 hit record. Knox's coup at this juncture must have added to the mounting frustration of Buddy Holly, who couldn't get anyone to play his record on the radio, let alone hit the charts. Finally, near despair, Holly stalked into radio station KLLL and asked DJ Bill Pickering, "Could I get you to play my record?"

"Well, let's see. Let me play this other one, then we'll put yours on the turntable and audition it and see how it sounds," Pickering replied. He allowed Buddy to introduce "Blue Days, Black Nights." Later, when asked if this was the first time the record had been been played anywhere, Pickering replied, "Yes, Buddy told me it was the first time." Unfortunately the record stirred no response from the listeners. As a Decca recording artist Buddy had expected to be rich by now, but instead he was destitute.

Appealing to Hi Pockets, who'd left KDAV and opened the Clover Club in Amarillo, 123 miles north of Lubbock, he asked, "Can you do anything for us?"

"Yeah. I'll put you into the Clover Club on Friday night for a teenage dance and we'll close the bar as far as beer is concerned," Hi Pockets said.

That night over a thousand kids poured into the Clover Club, ready to rock. When Buddy's band struck up "Midnight Shift," everyone hit the dance floor, *including* the parents who were chaperoning their children. Hi Pockets ordered all grown-ups from the floor, knowing from experience that if cops suddenly appeared and saw adults dancing, they'd automatically assume that liquor was being served and bust the place. It was a dry county, but liquor was readily available from bootleggers, who worked in cahoots with the musicians.

Back in Lubbock, Buddy started playing the Bamboo Club. "He was packin' out that little old Bamboo Club and all the youngsters, they liked him," says Larry Holley. "He could go into a little old dive that had been just as dead and not having any crowds, and play there a few nights and they'd just be packed." On May 10 Buddy and the Two-Tones—Sonny Curtis and Don Guess—opened for Faron Young at the Bronco Stadium in Odessa, Texas, a one-horse town deep in the stark Permian Basin, 120 miles southwest of Lubbock, and then toured for a few weeks with Sonny James, Faron Young, and Wanda Jackson. Returning to Lubbock, Buddy went to the movies one night with Sonny Curtis and Jerry Allison and got the title for the song that would change his life. *The Searchers*, a John Ford western, ran in Lubbock from May 31 to June 20, 1956. At one of the showings, Buddy, Sonny, and Jerry sat in the refrigerated darkness of the State Theater on Texas Avenue and watched the story of Ethan Edwards unfold. Played by John Wayne at his cantankerous best, Ethan returns to Texas after the Civil War to discover that a tribe of Comanche Indians has massacred his brother and sister-in-law and kidnapped their daughter, played by Natalie Wood. In the course of his long search for the lost girl, Ethan often expresses his exasperation with the human race by grumbling, "That'll be the day."

The phrase stuck in Buddy's mind, perhaps reflecting his aggravation over his hapless romantic and professional fortunes. A few days later he was working up a new tune at Jerry's house when he suddenly turned to Jerry and suggested that they compose a song together.

"That'll be the day," Jerry said, echoing John Wayne's skepticism. Buddy thought he was suggesting a song topic and said, "Yeah. That sounds like a good idea." The pessimism and doubt inherent in the phrase mirrored the overall frustration Buddy was feeling that summer. Echo was headed for Nebraska and college in the fall, transferring from Abilene Christian. Both physically and emotionally, she was getting farther and farther away from him and there was nothing he could do about it. If driving 165 miles to see her in Abilene had been a drag, journeying 700 miles to Nebraska would be a nightmare. Their relationship made less sense every day, but, to paraphrase the lyrics, they couldn't stop loving each other. That a major recording company had released one of Buddy's records made it clear to Echo that he was launched on a musical career and would never give it up for her. Echo's religious convictions would never permit her to accept such a life.

Buddy poured his bitterness, tinged with acid wit, into this song that would be legendary, "That'll Be the Day." For a pop tune, a genre notorious for its tendency to support the soppiest romantic delusions of mankind, it was unusually tough-minded and realistic about the vicissitudes of love. While Jerry remembers he "didn't have any idea it was ever going to be called a classic," Buddy did see it as a possible ticket to fame and recorded it at his next Decca session, which was held at Bradley's Barn in Nashville on July 22, 1956, with Sonny, Don, and Jerry accompanying him.

The session didn't go any better than the first one. Owen Bradley, their producer, had his heart set on going waterskiing and was eager to leave the studio. When they showed up for the session without a bass—the one they'd been renting from Lubbock High was no longer available due to summer vacation—Bradley gave them "a big hassle," Sonny Curtis later told John Goldrosen. Bradley ordered them to come up with a bass in twenty minutes or the session would be canceled. They rushed to radio station WSM and borrowed a bull fiddle from Lightning Chance, a well-known session man.

At 10:30 P.M. they finally began recording. They made a complete mess of "That'll Be the Day," partly, Jerry later told Griggs, because "it was a real serious record deal" and they were trying "real hard," and partly because their Decca mentors, intent on getting a country song, urged Buddy "to sing so high, which was out of Buddy's range at that time,"

Jerry added. This mopey early version of the song can be heard on a British LP that was released many years later, *Buddy Holly: The Nashville Sessions.* Despite the mauling of "That'll Be the Day," the session was not a total wash. "Rock Around With Ollie Vee," written by Sonny Curtis, and "Girl on My Mind," by Don Guess, are full of innovative guitar licks, classic ones that would help define and solidify the new rock 'n' roll genre. Buddy's vocals on both cuts introduce many of his trademark sounds, including glottal twitches and fractured syllables.

Though it should have been clear to everyone present that Buddy was a startlingly original new singer-songwriter, Owen Bradley called "That'll Be the Day" "the worst song I've ever heard." Paul Cohen said Buddy was "the biggest no-talent I've ever worked with." Other than Buddy, the only person in Bradley's Barn who pegged the song a hit was the janitor, who said, "Man, I like 'That'll Be the Day.' " Decca couldn't seem to get anything right—the executives suggested that the band change its name from the Two-Tones to the Two Tunes, but since there were three of them—Sonny, Don, and Jerry—they made it Buddy Holly and the Three Tunes.

Decca had no intention of releasing "That'll Be the Day" or any of the other new cuts and refrained from doing so, at least for the present. Expecting his option to be dropped, Buddy was surprised when he was told to return for a third session in November. Before leaving Nashville, he and his buddies had some fun in the dives on lower Broadway, in the tenderloin district, which were full of hungry housewives dreaming of becoming C&W singing stars. "I don't remember the chicks, but I remember chasin' 'em," Jerry commented in 1993.

Back in Lubbock, Buddy's friends got the impression that he was no longer seeing Echo. He started dating other girls, including one named Sue Poff, and hanging out with the carhops at the Hi-D-Ho Drive-in. Jan Fulton, one of the carhops, found Buddy to be quiet when he was around girls, except when he was playing his guitar or beating on the dashboard of his car as he tooled around Lubbock. At the Hi-D-Ho, according to Jan Fulton, Buddy "played on the roof, outside, inside, everywhere."

When Little Richard played the Cotton Club on August 24, 1956, Buddy was in the audience. Little Richard, twenty-four, was riding high on the success of "Tutti-Frutti," "Long Tall Sally," and "Slippin' and Slidin'." During his performance the previous evening in Amarillo, officials complained that Richard's performance was not "altogether what we thought it would be." When Richard refused to "change his act somewhat," Bill Griggs later stated in *Reminiscing* magazine, Richard was booked on a vagrancy charge, although he was carrying $2,669. The real issue was Richard's uninhibited music, which, in critic Greil Marcus's memorable description, "disrupted an era, broke rules, created a form, gave shape to a vitality that wailed silently in each of us until he found a voice for it."

The next night in Lubbock, Buddy attended Richard's show at the Cotton Club with Jerry Allison. During the performance they stood directly in front of Richard, yelling "*Hey, all right!*" as Richard sang hits like "Tutti-Frutti." The audience was an uneasy mixture of five hundred whites and Latin Americans, many of them dancing the dirty bop. R. L. Lowe, manager of the Cotton Club, "stopped the blaring beat of the Negro pianist's band," according to a newspaper account headlined ROCK-'N'-ROLL DANCE IS SHUT DOWN AFTER DISTURBANCE HERE in the following day's Lubbock *Avalanche-Journal*, when the dancers overflowed into the concession area and the restrooms and violent fights broke out in the parking lot.

According to Little Richard, Buddy brought him home for dinner with the family. "They got to be good buddies," says Jerry. When Buddy tried to bring Little Richard into the Holley home, L. O. Holley "wouldn't let me in," says Little Richard, who was not only black but a self-described "glaring homosexual." In Texas in the fifties, gays were completely in the closet; there were no gay bars, there was no gay culture, and the word *gay* itself was not yet in use as a description of homosexuality. It was indeed "the love that dare not speak its name," and when it was spoken, usually by punks spoiling for a fight, the word used was *queer*. Shunned by straight society if they dared betray any sign of "deviance," threatened with prison if they were caught making love, and damned by the church as sinners, gays led lives of desperate secrecy. On rare occasions, homosexuality would burst forth in the public prints, such as the inevitable scandals that erupted when prominent figures, supposedly heterosexual, were murdered by hustlers.

Blacks, like gays, were expected to remain invisible if they wanted to survive in Texas in the fifties. Blacks were restricted to their own sections of town and forced to ride in the back of the bus when they ventured into the white world; they were not permitted in white theaters, churches, or restaurants. And when they shared the same department stores and train stations with whites, they used separate drinking fountains and restrooms. Whites were never seen in the company of blacks in public; it was unthinkable. The attitude of people who called themselves "good Christians" was that blacks should be treated with the same courtesy and humanity afforded to whites *as long as* blacks knew their place and stayed in it. In breaking through these barriers, Little Richard was displaying incredible bravery, and Buddy appreciated his valor.

"If you don't let Richard in," said Buddy, "I'll never come back to this house again."

L. O. Holley finally relented, but Little Richard balked on the doorstep. As Little Richard would later tell Phil Donahue, "I didn't want to go in there, because I felt that if it was happening like that on the outside, I better not go *inside*." In *The Life and Times of Little Richard: The Quasar of Rock*, written by Charles White but copyrighted by Richard Wayne Penniman (Little Richard's full name), White, and Robert A. Blackwell, Little Richard stated that the Holleys "weren't too happy. I'll bet they washed them dishes I ate off of about twenty times after we'd gone."

In my 1992 interview with Larry Holley, I ask, "What about Little Richard saying that when Buddy brought him home, your folks wouldn't let him in?" Larry understandably leaped to his parents' defense and denied it. "That's another fictitious lie," he said. "Mother would never not let Little Richard in."

"And he came there and had dinner?"

"I'm sure he did if he came over there."

Meeting Little Richard was a rich and resonant experience for Buddy. Richard opened Buddy to a new sense of sexual curiosity and adventurousness. "We had some great times together," said Richard during an autographing session for *The Quasar of Rock* in 1984. "He was the greatest." Richard was mainly drawn to heterosexual males, he revealed in *Quasar*. At the time he was what is known in the gay world as a "size queen." Nothing turned him on like "a big penis," Richard said in *Quasar*. He was adept at setting up orgies, usually involving his band men. Though he unequivocally stated in *Quasar* that "Buddy Holly was a wild boy for the women," Richard routinely seduced such straight men, using voluptuous girls as bait. He'd see "some big guy" and invite him to his room while the girl said, "Yeah, c'mon. I'd like to see what you got there." Should the man's equipment satisfy Richard's requirements, he'd then produce a wad of money, he stated in *Quasar*, and bribe the man to fornicate with the girl. He would eventually invite Buddy Holly into such a situation, somewhat later on, when they played New York together.

The special affinity between Buddy and Little Richard was fired not really by sex but by a deeper passion—a kind of masochistic religious agony. Both were doomsday Christians, damned by their church's curse on rock 'n' roll and perhaps secretly savoring the conflict. "We always had that feeling that rock 'n' roll wasn't really worthy and had no socially redeeming value," Jerry Allison said in 1989. Little Richard believed that "if you want to live with the Lord, you can't rock 'n' roll it, too. God don't like it." Born into a devout Seventh-Day Adventist family in Macon, Georgia, Richard was disowned when his father (who sold sourmash whiskey on the side) discovered that Richard was gay.

In associating with the black, gay, and altogether outrageous Little Richard, Buddy made his most defiant statement yet against the vicious, narrow-minded dogmas of his church. Even today the religion from which Buddy sprang would be appalled. "The homosexual should be punished by civil government . . . along with murder and kidnapping," writes E. L. Bynum, the current pastor of Tabernacle Baptist Church. "Homosexuality has been instrumental in destroying a number of civilizations."

Little Richard represented another step in Buddy's liberation from the racism and narrow-mindedness of Texas. As their friendship demonstrates, rock 'n' roll was one of the forces breaking down race barriers and pointing to a new identity that would encompass both black and white. Many of the young people who listened to, sang, and danced to this hybrid black music in the fifties would go to the barricades for integration in the freedom marches, sit-ins, and street fights of the sixties. A primary reason the new music was so hated and feared by the white establishment was that it was bringing about the racial mixing that white supremacists had feared for centuries. A white backlash against rock 'n' roll began in 1956, but was powerless to stop either rock or the social changes it helped to instigate. Before the decade was out, integration would be enforced by law.

Increasingly now, Buddy found himself at odds with the mores of West Texas. Race was only one of the issues troubling him. He loved to party and drink, which went against his mother's religious scruples and eventually led to a showdown between them. If his mother was anything like mine—a fundamentalist Methodist of the same generation, geography, and economic background as Ella Holley—she was smotheringly overprotective, sitting up at night waiting for her cherished son to come home from dates, smelling his breath for signs of alcohol and tobacco when he finally came in. And if Buddy adored his mother as I did mine, and clearly he did, the burden of guilt was intolerable and resulted in further rebelliousness.

Melba Montgomery, a C&W singer, once stated that in those days, "a lot of the singers would put away a fifth or two of Jack Daniel's a day." On one occasion, Buddy got falling-down drunk with some musicians shortly after returning from another Hank Thompson tour in the autumn of 1956. When he staggered home that night, he made so much racket that he woke up his mother. One look was enough to tell her that he was drunk. Buddy said, "Mom, I'm sorry."

"I wasn't really mad at him," Mrs. Holley recalled years later. "I was mad at those fellows in the band." Her words demonstrate the depth of her denial about Buddy's drinking; she was too proud to admit that a son of hers might have an alcohol problem. As long as she could blame someone else—the fellows in the band—she could blind herself to his drinking, a serious issue for anyone but a potentially fatal one for ulcer sufferers. Then there was the matter of Buddy's smoking. "We were against drinking alcohol or smoking cigarettes," she said, adding that Buddy had no such compunctions about either vice. For years Buddy tried to conceal his smoking from his parents, but they knew he smoked "on the sly," Mrs. Holley said. One day she caught him smoking and told him to stop trying to hide it, to light up right in the middle of the living room if he wanted to.

One of the stressful issues that might have been driving Buddy to drink in 1956 was the unresolved situation with Echo McGuire. After she left Texas to go to college, he made the long trip to Nebraska to see her. She told him he was leading the kind of existence "I couldn't be part of," Echo said, according to Buddy Holly biographers John Goldrosen and John Beecher. She could see the path he was taking, and "it just wasn't what I wanted for myself," she added. She stopped wearing his class ring around her neck. Buddy never went back to Nebraska to see her again.

After they stopped going steady, Buddy appeared "not to care who he went with much," his mother observed. She later confided to John Gold-rosen that Buddy dated many girls "who didn't have too good a reputation. I wouldn't have wanted him to marry them, I know that."

Girls weren't the only problem. "He run with some pretty rough guys," Larry reveals in a 1992 interview. "Run with a rough crew." One of Buddy's friends rode a motorcycle and carried a chain. "Any time anybody tried to beat up on Buddy, he would take his chain and whip them, you know," Larry recalls. He was a beloved and invaluable ally, since Buddy had resentful local rednecks to contend with—ambitious Lubbock pickers who weren't good enough to cut a record and hated anyone who had. "Buddy liked everybody, but everybody didn't like Buddy," Larry continues. "Nowadays everybody who knew him says they was his good buddies, you know, but at that time it was a different story. He had his enemies and his friends. There was a lot of people in Lubbock who didn't like him. There must have been a hundred musicians here that could play a little bit—this little band and that little band—and they were all jealous of each other. It was a vicious little circle.

"There's so many musicians in Lubbock and they're all vying. Buddy was strugglin' for the top notch. This was a very jealous town and there was always some guys that wanted to beat up on him, because he was popular with some of their girlfriends. They'd make remarks. There was a lot of jealousy among Texas boys against anybody in their area that is famous or drawing some attention. That's just the way Texans are. There were a few times that me and Travis had to go to the roller rink and see if Buddy was getting into trouble."

Larry Holley believes that sinners are in imminent danger of God's retribution. "It's scary if you're out of God's will and you're a Christian," he says. "I know I used to be pretty wild and I flew around in my own airplane. Nearly crashed it several times. If you do wrong and keep on doing willful sins, the Lord will take you out of the picture. He beat me down to a nub. He'll whup you until you get back in line. If you don't, He'll finally turn you over to the devil for the destruction of the flesh. You cannot live a life and entertain the world and the worldly crowd who could care less about the Lord, you cannot do that and be a Christian and just keep going on and on—the Lord will take you on to be with Him."

Larry at last decided to speak to Buddy about the trouble he was getting into and the way he was treating his parents. "He was about nineteen at the time," Larry recalls. "Mother and Buddy had it around and around quite often because he liked to stay out nearly all night." In addition, Buddy's friends were complaining. "Lot of people said they didn't like Buddy's attitude," comments Larry. Mrs. Holley scolded Buddy for bossing his musicians around, even yelling at them. "He was pretty snobbish and felt like he was better than others in a lot of cases," Larry remembers.

One day in 1956, Larry took Buddy out to his car for a long talk. "Now, Buddy, if you're going to be a musician and make it in the world, you're gonna have to learn to be friendly with ever'body you run into and just treat them nice whether they're poor or whether they're rich or whatever," Larry said. Buddy sat very still, listening but saying nothing.

"Another thing," Larry continued. "I want you to start treatin' mother better. She's come to me several times cryin' and tellin' me how impudent you talked to her. She's my mother too and I love her and I'm just talkin' to you like a big brother and I want you to start actin' like you're gonna have to—you're liable to go some place in this world and you're gonna change your ways."

"Thank you," Buddy said. Since Buddy respected his brother and had always sought his approval, Larry's influence prevailed. In a few days, Larry recalls in 1992, Mrs. Holley told him, "I don't know what you said to Buddy but he's a different person since then." Says Larry today, "Buddy was just a wild kid, baby of the family, spoiled . . . and he did pretty much as he pleased. He had some goals and he wouldn't let nothin' stand in his way until he reached them. . . . When I sat down and talked to him, he thought that I hung the moon."

On October 23, 1956, the *Lubbock Avalanche-Journal* took notice of Buddy, writing, "Lubbock now has its own answer to Elvis Presley. . . . He plays an electric standard guitar and wears 'fancy' sports coats . . . singing rock 'n' roll exclusively." Jack Neal came back into Buddy's life in time to supply him with some new material before he went to Nashville for his third Decca recording session in November 1956. One night Neal and Buddy were at Don Guess's house when Don started kidding Buddy about being as big a cocksman as Don Juan. Neal, who later told Griggs that Buddy Holly was generally thought to be "a ladies' lover," had been working on a song called "Modern Don Juan," was having trouble with it, and wondered if Buddy and Don would help him.

Buddy liked "Modern Don Juan" enough to take it to Nashville with him on November 10. Unfortunately, he didn't get Neal's permission to record it, which would later create complications. As usual, everything went wrong in Nashville. It wasn't just Decca's continuing insensitivity to his talent and total mismanagement of his recording career. Buddy's life was falling apart, both personally and professionally. It takes money to hold a rock 'n' roll band together, and Buddy was unable to pay his musicians. Sonny Curtis did not come to Nashville this time, nor did Jerry Allison. Only Don Guess accompanied him when he went into Bradley's Barn on November 15, 1956, to record "Modern Don Juan" and a Don Guess song, "You Are My One Desire." He also rerecorded Sonny Curtis's "Rock Around With Ollie Vee," but this cut was no more likely to make it to the charts than the version he'd recorded in Nashville the previous summer. Though Boots Randolph's sax solo was terrific, the recording lacks a raw rockabilly edge and sounds thin and anemic.

No hits emerged from this session, but both "You Are My One Desire" and "Modern Don Juan" contained glimmers of Buddy's genius. "Modern Don Juan" is the story of a virile teenager who is a victim of his own promiscuity. With half the girls in his neighborhood gossiping about what a stud he is, the one girl he really cares about is unimpressed when he says he's fallen in love with her. Indeed, the song might be called a clever rock 'n' roll *Don Giovanni*.

On the other side of this recording, Don Guess's "You Are My One Desire," Buddy's voice quivers with an intensity that's weirdly arresting. Nashville session-man Floyd Cramer pounds out his inimitable staccato on the piano. When Buddy lowers his voice to a lover's purr on this cut, he's at his most appealing. Unfortunately, he was singing too high on the other cuts, following the advice given to him by Decca C&W star Webb Pierce. Years later Owen Bradley attempted to explain how Nashville ruined its opportunity with Buddy Holly: "He needed somebody else to help him, not us. He wanted to make things not as country, as we were instructed to do it, but he didn't fight it that strong." Bradley had received his marching orders from boss Paul Cohen to make a country record and was simply trying to survive. It was his job, as he saw it, to keep Paul Cohen happy, he later told Goldrosen. It all came down to office politics: Cohen was Bradley's "benefactor" as well as the Decca official who'd signed Buddy, so Buddy also felt constrained to satisfy Cohen, according to Bradley, who later claimed there was no friction between him and Holly. Indeed Bradley characterized Buddy as friendly and cooperative. But the game they were playing would do neither of them any good. Had

Decca turned Buddy loose in the studio, as RCA continued to do with Elvis a few blocks away, they'd have had the string of hits that Buddy later produced at another studio.

Though Elvis Presley's film *Love Me Tender* was the runaway box-office sensation of the year, Decca in 1956 still thought of rock 'n' roll as "a passing fad," according to Decca producer Dick Jacobs, who later worked with Buddy. "Decca had been a middle-of-the-road company and was not surviving well during the rock 'n' roll era." No wonder. When Decca had been offered Elvis Presley, Decca's national sales manager, Sydney Gold-berg, had said, "We got the best country label in the world. Who's gonna buy a record by a guy named Elvis Presley? We pass." During those years of the mid- and late 1950s, Decca, grounded by its success in the past, lacked the vision to see where American music was heading.

Decca's hillbilly bias was the undoing of Buddy's record debut. Right down to the final take at Bradley's Barn, they were still trying to turn him into a C&W warbler. And his troubles were just beginning. "Modern Don Juan," for which he hadn't secured a release from its author, Jack Neal, was to be issued as a single almost immediately, on December 24, 1956. A tense confrontation with the songwriter awaited Buddy as soon as he returned to Lubbock, Neal later revealed in an interview with Griggs. Buddy shoved some papers at Neal and ordered him to sign them. Bristling, Neal inquired why. Buddy nonchalantly related that he'd just recorded "Modern Don Juan" at Decca. Digging in his heels, Neal said, "No, I ain't signing no papers." He had Buddy over a barrel. If Neal didn't consent to the recording, Decca could sue Buddy for breach of contract. Neal was in a strong negotiating position, to say the least, but, good friend that he was, he finally relented and signed the release without changing any of the terms.

When "Modern Don Juan" was released on Christmas Eve 1956, with "You Are My One Desire" on the B-side, Decca lost the opportunity for a rock 'n' roll hit when it was classified as C&W, destroying its chances in the burgeoning rock market. Despite a good *Billboard* review, neither record stores nor DJs knew what to do with the record. Though "Modern Don Juan" was no great loss to the world, it's unfortunate that the sexy and hypnotic "You Are My One Desire" was a casualty of Decca's marketing gaffe.

Jack Neal attempted to cheer Buddy up, reminding him that at least he had a new record on the jukeboxes. Designed and manufactured by Wurlitzer, jukeboxes in the fifties were elaborate consoles with glowing rainbow lights and bubbles rising in transparent tubes, all surrounding a selection of approximately one hundred recordings which were displayed under glass and chrome. One play for a nickel, five plays for a quarter, and once the coin was dropped and the selection made, an ingenious robotic arm would pluck the designated disc from a chrome rack and deposit it on the turntable. Excellent bass and volume boomed from the bellies of the jukeboxes, filling the cafés and lunchroom diners of the time with big sounds like Gogi Grant's "The Wayward Wind" and the Four Lads' "No, Not Much." The diners ranged from brightly lit, shiny chrome Pullman cars to the austere pillboxes of the White Tower chain.

After Buddy settled his differences with Neal, he double-dated with him and his future wife that winter, though Buddy was without a steady girl. *Love Me Tender* was playing at the Lindsey, while *Hot Rod Girls* and *Girls in Prison* was the double bill at the Red Raider Drive-in, which advertised in-car heaters. When they went out with their girls, Buddy was so talkative that Jack had to interrupt Buddy's interminable monologues to get a word in edgewise. Years later Neal told journalist Philip Norman, "He could be quiet as a mouse one minute, then cut up and do something crazy."

Except to scorn them, the city of Lubbock took little note that two of its young citizens had a record in national release on a major label. According to Bob Church, brother of local musician Terry Noland, Ben D. Johnson of Tabernacle Baptist Church deplored the fact that his congregation was becoming infested with rock 'n' rollers. Noland later told Griggs that the church nonetheless accepted Buddy's generous donations. Buddy's passive acceptance of their condemnation is typical of the behavior of some ulcer victims. Gastrointestinal specialist Dr. M. Michael Eisenberg believes that "ulcer-prone people are oral-dependent and passive in situations where more active and open aggression is more appropriate. Ulcers may be caused by a kind of inner-directed hostility or discontent stemming from a strong childish need to be looked after and loved, a need that may be rejected or denied." Unfortunately, the more abusive Buddy's church became about his music, the more he drank and the worse his ulcers got.

His Nashville failures and his church's disapproval might have undermined his hopes for a recording career had it not been for the moral support and financial help of Larry Holley, who urged him to go to Clovis and keep on making records. Buddy was too broke to maintain a band, but Larry Welborn and Jerry helped him cut "Brown-Eyed Handsome Man" and "Bo Diddley" at Petty's studio at the end of 1956. "I really didn't get any session money or anything for it," Welborn told Griggs in 1986. There was an unspoken understanding among the friends that they would back each other up musically anytime they were needed.

But without money, the band's days were numbered. Occasional gigs like the one they played on November 22, 1956, at the American Legion Hall in Lubbock barely kept them in cigarettes and beer. The new year, 1957, brought the most demoralizing news Buddy Holly would ever receive: Decca was not renewing his option. The record royalties he'd expected would never materialize. He was insolvent. His band, Buddy Holly and the Three Tunes, was on the skids. His musicians began to leave him in rapid succession.

The first to go was Don Guess, who found some of Buddy's expectations to be unrealistic. Buddy had been nagging Don all year to purchase a stand-up bass fiddle, as if this expensive instrument were something a destitute rocker could afford. Don couldn't even buy a decent car and went around Lubbock in a secondhand hearse. Finally, according to Jerry, Don told Buddy, "Well, I'm not cut out to be a bass player."

Sonny Curtis was the next to go. He had both personal and musical issues with Buddy. Musically Sonny wasn't as committed to rock 'n' roll as Buddy 'and could sometimes be fondly dismissive about rock. In the beginning, Sonny was a better guitarist than Buddy and had played lead. But Buddy quickly caught up with him and demanded to play lead in addition to singing, consigning Sonny to rhythm guitar. Personality clashes were inevitable between two such gifted musicians. Sonny, who eventually would write the hit song "I Fought the Law," was really too talented to play second fiddle to anyone, especially if he wasn't being paid for it. "The main thing was that there wasn't any money coming in," Sonny asserted in 1993. He quit Buddy Holly and the Three Tunes, left Lubbock to tour with Slim Whitman, and later joined the Philip Morris Country Music Show in Nashville. Sonny faced some lean times after leaving Lubbock. Philip Morris made him pay his own expenses on the road, so every time he'd go into a café, he'd total up everything before he ordered to make certain the bill didn't exceed a dollar. He moved to Colorado Springs in 1957, then to California, writing songs all the while, and finally came home to work on his father's farm in Meadow, Texas, to replenish his depleted bank account before going to New York at the end of the decade to record for Dot Records. When Griggs asked him in 1980 whether he regretted his decision to leave Buddy Holly just before the Crickets became a sensation, Sonny said that it would have been interesting "to contribute my influence," but he had no regrets. In Sonny's opinion, "everything works out for the best."

Without a band, Buddy considered giving up his singing career. He was never as confident as later portrayed in legend, Mrs. Holley told Griggs in 1979, after the release of Gary Busey's film about Buddy, and "came darn near quitting for a time or two," she revealed. But underlying all the failures was a quiet certitude about his destiny that was as strong as his faith in God. As a last resort, he drove to Clovis to see Norman Petty. He intended to cut some demos to show to record companies and asked if he could make them in Petty's studio. Petty was concerned about Buddy's clothes, Levi's and a T-shirt, which were disdained in the Southwest as lower-class garb until the movie *Urban Cowboy* made them fashionable decades later. Cronies of Petty's, local businessmen, criticized him for attracting "a hillbilly like Buddy" to their town. Though Petty defended him as "a diamond in the rough," he turned Buddy down, advising him to go home, get himself a band, make some arrangements, and put together an act.

It was bizarre advice to give to Buddy Holly, who would shortly score million-selling records as a solo recording artist, but Buddy followed it, returning to Lubbock and working with a new group of musicians, all of whom wanted to make records. Jerry stayed with him from the old crowd, but the others were new faces: June Clark, Niki Sullivan, June's cousin Gary Tollett, and Gary's wife, Ramona. All of them were dreaming of having a hit on Roulette, the label behind the phenomenal success, "Party Doll." June was the kid sister of Don Lanier, who'd cut "Party Doll" with Buddy Knox and Jimmy Bowen. Don and June had a sister named Teddy who worked at Roulette and felt she could get their demos heard by Roulette's Phil Kahl, since she'd brought "Party Doll" to the label. Practicing at the home of June and Nig Clark in early 1957, they built themselves into a tight band and backup singing group. They recorded Gary Tollett's songs at Petty's studio, but nothing came of them.

One night at June and Nig Clark's house, Buddy, who'd been drinking, had a seizure, possibly a reaction to alcohol poisoning. "He went out to the yard and starting swinging his arms around," Niki Sullivan remembers. "Finally, it was Jerry, I think, who calmed him down."

Shortly afterward, Buddy made his fateful decision to rerecord his Nashville turkey "That'll Be the Day" in Clovis. This time, he went into the studio with a well-rehearsed group that had defined and honed their sound. Buddy, Larry Welborn, Niki Sullivan, Gary and Ramona Tollett, and Jerry Allison looked and sounded like a winning team. Decca was still sitting on the recording Buddy had cut of this song in Nashville the previous July, exactly seven months before. In retrospect, Decca's neglect of "That'll Be the Day" sums up the country establishment's dismissal of Buddy Holly as a failure. Decca's lack of vision did nothing to diminish Buddy's faith in the terrific song he'd written, which he knew could hit the charts if recorded as an all-out rocker.

Chapter Six

The Clovis Sessions

I'm advising you again not to go to Clovis," said Hi Pockets Duncan. Buddy had just informed him that he was thinking of rerecording "That'll Be the Day" in Petty's studio. Hi Pockets had known Petty for years and didn't trust him. He cautioned Buddy that Petty would steal the songwriting credit for any of Buddy's songs recorded in Clovis, but Buddy was so obsessed with the fact that Buddy Wayne Knox's "Party Doll" had come out of Clovis that he again ignored Hi Pockets's warning. He was so desperate that he was willing to sign over a share of his songwriting royalties if Petty could make him a star. In Clovis he told Petty, "If you can get a hit for that Buddy, you can get a hit for this Buddy."

"It's the talent, not the studio," Petty said, promising nothing. But he was flattered that Buddy had followed his instructions and formed a tight vocal group and a good band, one that included Jerry Allison and Larry Welborn. He let them move into the studio and begin rehearsals for a recording session.

The Clovis version of "That'll Be the Day" was recorded on February 24, 1957. It was a cold Sunday evening, the temperature hovering around thirty degrees, when Buddy and his entourage set out for Clovis in two cars. Most of them held down jobs and hadn't been able to leave until after work. In Buddy's car, he frantically put the finishing touches on "I'm Lookin' for Someone to Love," which was the A-side to be recorded that night. The rerecording of "That'll Be the Day" was the B-side.

After stopping on the road to visit relatives, they approached Clovis around nine P.M., shortly after crossing the Texas–New Mexico border. In 1992, on a chilly day around Easter, I made the same trip. It's difficult to stay awake during the ninety-mile drive because of the unrelieved flatness of the terrain, the monotonous, unwavering straightness of the road between Lubbock and Clovis, and the absence of visual relief save a few houses and an occasional herd of cattle. This is New Mexico's milk pail; dairies are open twenty-four hours a day, operating nonstop. Some four thousand cattle are brought here daily, fattened up, slaughtered, and shipped all over the U.S. Portales, twenty miles to the south, is peanut country, supplying the nation's ballparks. The land rises imperceptibly but steadily as you reach Clovis, your ears popping from the 4,300-foot elevation. Located on an old Comanche trail, at first the town looks like nothing more than a few scattered low buildings at the edge of a cattle pasture. But then you leave the highway and in a few minutes reach the downtown area, a couple of streets with neat two-story brick buildings that were probably put up in the twenties. I visited the town on a winter day in 1992. Though a few cars and pickup trucks were parked diagonally to the curb, there was no one to be seen on the streets and absolutely no traffic. I had the disorienting, dreamlike feeling that I was standing in the middle of a painting by Magritte.

Billy Stull, a Chuck Norris look-alike, was managing the Norman Petty Recording Studios in 1992, Petty having died some years before. We met at El Charro Restaurant, where the owner, Mr. Muscato, remembered that Norman Petty "used to come in here and eat—Norman was very quiet." Later, Billy Stull gave me a guided tour of Petty's two studios in Clovis. The original building is located a few blocks from the heart of town, at 1313 West Seventh Street. It looks like a 1930s gas station. Inside, the small, ten-by-twenty-two-foot studio is virtually unchanged since Buddy's day, full of gleaming instruments and vintage jumbo microphones. There's not a scratch or a cigarette burn on Petty's huge electric console organ, a testament to the respect and love he must have earned from a generation of rough-hewn rockabillies. "Norman was a tremendous musician," Billy Stull says. "In most sessions he would try to upgrade the musical abilities of the people in the studio . . . because he had such a tremendous knowledge of music, a great ear, a great imagination, a sense of experimentation."

Stull may very well be right, but few who were present that February evening in 1957, when Buddy's band and backup singers filed into the studio and began rehearsing "I'm Lookin' for Someone to Love," would agree. Jerry told Griggs in 1982 that Petty was a first-rate engineer and that he granted them complete freedom in the studio, but Jerry minimized Petty's role as a producer, declaring emphatically that Petty did nothing but select and arrange the microphones and run the control board. In 1983 Griggs interviewed Gary Tollett, who said that Buddy "ramrodded" the entire session, making it clear that he was the star, that this was *his* performance, that everyone was there to do the record *his* way, because he was the boss. Whatever Petty's contribution, he clearly deserves credit for his behavior at this key moment in the history of rock 'n' roll: he let Buddy be himself, which no one at Decca had been willing to do.

They worked until midnight on "I'm Lookin' for Someone to Love" and then recorded "That'll Be the Day" almost as an afterthought, getting it in two takes. On the second take, the one that ultimately was released and became a hit, they weren't playing together at a certain point in the last chorus, which sounded a bit ragged. They knew they could do it more professionally, but it was only a demo to send to New York, or so they thought, and no one dreamed it would be released. As it turned out, its charm is in its rawness and spontaneity, which might have been lost had they done another take.

Rockabilly has been defined as taking a country song and rocking it. Recorded only seven months after the Decca catastrophe, the Clovis rockabilly or "Tex-Mex" version of "That'll Be the Day" is so far superior to its Nashville antecedent that it's virtually unrecognizable as the same song. The most obvious improvements are Buddy's cocky self-assurance and the peppier pace, which give the cut a feeling of untamed animal energy. Perhaps more than any other song of the fifties, the Clovis "That'll Be the Day" captures the spirit of an era when music had just burst out of the garage and was still fun. With this cut Buddy introduced his unique sound, one that combined the heart and soul of C&W with the joy and edgy irreverence of rock 'n' roll. And at the song's flinty core is a profound diffidence about romantic love. The attitude in the song is identical to one expressed by Larry Holley: that Buddy never permitted any girl to come between him and his career.

At one point during the session, Petty called everyone together in the control room and struck his deal for the recording. "I'll give you the acetate, and you go peddle it and that will be five hundred dollars," he said. "Or," he added, "I'll go get you on a record label and for that I want the publishing rights. It's your choice." Petty also demanded part song-writing credit for himself. He assured them he was claiming co-authorship only because DJs knew him and would play the record if they saw his name on it. Jerry was the first to object to such blatant dishonesty. How could Petty claim authorship of "That'll Be the Day" when it had already been written—and recorded at Decca—as a Holly-Allison song?

But Buddy was adamant, irritably pointing out that they were quibbling over money that might never materialize and insisting that at this low point in their careers Petty's contacts were absolutely vital to the band. Letting impatience override common sense, Buddy agreed to a deal that would eventually cost him a fortune. In the 1950s people were not as quick to consult lawyers as they would become toward the end of the century. As Elvis once put it, "Colonel Parker knows the business and I don't." But from Buddy Holly to Billy Joel, who would become entangled in legal controversies with his manager, artists who trust others with their affairs often live to regret it.

On February 25, 1957, sometime after three A.M., Buddy's weary troupe finished "That'll Be the Day" and headed for their cars to start the long drive back to Lubbock. With the temperature in the mid-thirties, they stood shivering as Buddy spoke briefly with Jim Robinson, a songwriting friend of Waylon Jennings's from Littlefield. Robinson remembers introducing Buddy to his wife and remarking on a scraggly Van Dyke goatee Buddy had at the time. Buddy told them he was not going to cut if off until he scored a chart-topping record. Then he got in his car and headed out to the highway. Watching him drive off, Robinson's wife, Bonnie, shook her head and said, "Well, that poor little darling, poor thing." Robinson was somewhat more sanguine and told his wife that Buddy was going to be a star someday.

In the following days Buddy concentrated on holding together the band he'd assembled for the Clovis session. He enlisted Niki Sullivan, who'd sung backup on "That'll Be the Day," to play rhythm guitar in his new band and he wanted to keep Jerry as his drummer. Larry Welborn, the bass player, was getting tired of working for no pay—especially since he never received any recognition for his contribution.

There were other problems with the band. Between Jerry and Niki, the nucleus of what would shortly become the Crickets, there was no love lost, Petty later confided to interviewers Skip Brooks and Bill Malcolm. Jerry made Niki feel unwelcome, perhaps because Jerry found it difficult to share Buddy with anyone, man or woman. Also, Niki was good looking, had stage presence, and attracted adoring glances from the girls. Though Niki stayed on, he would never be included in the special camaraderie Buddy and Jerry enjoyed.

Larry Welborn was the first to cut out. He and Buddy were "getting cross" with one another, Jerry later told Griggs. Welborn returned to a Lubbock group called the Four Teens. A few days later Buddy and Jerry dropped in on a Four Teens dance at the boxing arena on First Street. Besides Welborn, Jerry Allison knew another musician in the band, a pint-sized, Nordic-looking blond whom Allison used to cut study hall with to smoke cigarettes. His name was Joe Benson Mauldin, though everyone called him "Joe B.," and he was the Four Teens' bass player. Between sets Buddy approached Joe B. and asked him if he wanted to play in Buddy's band. Joe B. would be glad to, he said, if it didn't create any conflicts with the Four Teens.

The next day—March 2, 1957—Buddy and Jerry roused Joe B. out of bed and asked him if he wanted to play a gig that night in Carlsbad, New Mexico. What sort of performance would be expected of him, Joe B. inquired. Buddy assured him that he would be allowed to express his feelings freely. Joe B. liked the sound of that and told Buddy to count him in. Later that Saturday, in gloriously typical Texas spring weather— sixty-two degrees—they drove 181 miles west to Carlsbad, site of the famous limestone caverns. Like Clovis, the town is nondescript, engulfed by endless space and sky, but the gaping black hole that leads into the apparently bottomless cave is an awesome sight, especially at sunset, when a million bats fly out for the night. That evening the as yet unnamed Crickets played their first gig together, a four-hour dance at the Elks Club, for $65. It was the defining moment not only in their lives, which would be inextricably entwined from now on, but, to an extent, in the history of rock 'n' roll, for this was the prototypal band that helped invent the sound of rock. Slapping his King acoustic bass, Joe B. pulled the Crickets sound together, cushioned it, and added a new depth. What he left out was as important as what he put in. "I was very basic in what I played, usually just hitting on the first and third beats—you know, half notes," Joe B. later told William Bush. Gone was the jagged edge of Buddy and Jerry's visceral rockabilly, but Buddy now had the professional sound he'd dreamed of.

They rocked Carlsbad that night, launching into the risqué "Birthday Song." Like Elvis Presley, Niki had an educated pelvis and could be quite uninhibited onstage. "It brought the house down," Niki says.

On the drive back to Lubbock, Buddy attempted to persuade Joe B. to join the band as its permanent bass player, painting a rosy picture of the success they were going to achieve as big-time recording artists. Joe B. had heard that kind of bragging from a lot of musicians around Lubbock and wasn't impressed. Personal ambition was beyond his ken. He expected to end up a shoe salesman. But when Buddy kept promising big money, Joe B. finally asked him how long it was going to take to break into show business. Buddy uttered the magic words *Elvis Presley*, pointing out that stardom had come fairly quickly for Elvis, and Joe B. finally relented. That night Joe B. informed his mother he was joining a rock 'n' roll band. Her response was typical of middle-class contempt for rock at the time. She told Joe B. that she hoped he would have to work his "fingers to the bone" for the remainder of his days and that he was going to regret his decision for as long as he lived.

The Crickets' lineup was now complete—two guitars, bass, and drums; it would serve as the model for rock bands for decades to come. Buddy said he needed a name for the group, something to put on the demo of "That'll Be the Day" before he sent it off to Roulette Records in New York. He would have put his own name on it, but by contract he was forbidden from rerecording "That'll Be the Day" as Buddy Holly. He called Paul Cohen and asked Decca to waive the clause, but Cohen refused.

Buddy and Jerry considered several names for the band, including the Scoundrels. Ideally they wanted something blue-collar and gritty, a name that would announce the arrival of a new generation with radically different values from those of their parents. The World War II generation had dreamed of glamour and romance, two-stepping to the strains of Guy

Lombardo and His Royal Canadians and jitterbugging to the Andrews Sisters. Buddy wanted something that would reflect the up-front, let's-fuck attitude of R&B records like "Sixty Minute Man"—impudent, down-to-earth, proletarian, and, above all, black.

"Witchcraft," a record by the Spiders, was a favorite of Buddy's, and he suggested they find a name like the Spiders—some kind of insect. Finally they consulted an encyclopedia at Jerry's house. Niki remembers that someone proposed the Grasshoppers and then the Beetles, but Jerry complained that beetles were the kind of bug people like to squash. Jerry later denied that they ever considered the Beetles; they chose the Crickets, he told Griggs in 1982, because they were insects that made noise. Niki's memory of the episode is more colorful; he told Goldrosen that Jerry liked crickets because they "make a happy sound by rubbing their legs together."

On March 12, 1957, they made their first recording as the Crickets, cutting a couple of tunes to send to Roulette along with "That'll Be the Day" and "I'm Lookin' for Someone to Love." One of the cuts was "Maybe Baby," a song Buddy wrote in collaboration with his mother. Though it was a promising tune, the Clovis cut of "Maybe Baby," unlike the hit version made later at Travis Air Force Base, didn't come off any better than the Nashville cut of "That'll Be the Day." It fell flat, especially the ineffectual backup vocals. They also recorded a song composed by Joe B., "Last Night," a jilted lover's lament, heavily influenced by the Platters' 1956 hit "My Prayer."

Finally Buddy dispatched the 78-rpm demo of "That'll Be the Day" and the other songs to Roulette, hoping to fare better with Gary Tollett's connections there better than Tollett himself had. In New York, Roulette's Morris Levy promptly turned down "That'll Be the Day" and added insult to injury by trying to acquire "That'll Be the Day" for Buddy Knox to cover. Buddy Holly said no, even though almost any record by Buddy Knox at this point would have been a surefire hit; in March Knox's "Party Doll" passed the million mark and continued to outsell every other record in the United States. Roulette's attempt to preempt the song for Knox underscored Holly's certainty that the song contained the magic and the energy that would propel him to the top of the charts if only he could continue to hold on to it and get a reasonably decent rock 'n' roll version of it on tape. Obviously Holly valued his integrity and sense of responsibility toward his talent and career above money.

When the Roulette deal fell through in early 1957, Petty offered to take the demo to New York himself and offer it to his contacts at the record companies. His terms were exorbitant, as usual: Petty wanted a cut of writer's royalties in return for sharing his New York contacts. "We couldn't lose," Buddy later told DJ Freeman Hoover. "We were about as far down as you can get already." As Petty departed for New York, Buddy told the Crickets that stardom now lay just ahead. None of them believed him. Niki says no one in the band expected "That'll Be the Day" to go over the top—except for Buddy.

Petty arrived in New York and began to pitch the Crickets to the industry's artists and repertoire men, the record-company executives whose job is to scout new material and artists. He called on Columbia Records' Mitch Miller, the bearded A&R man who'd been responsible for signing Petty's "Mood Indigo." Rock 'n' roll was about as welcome in his office as dog meat. Though his A&R job had once been exciting— matching artists like Frankie Laine with material like "Mule Train"— rock 'n' roll had radically diminished his role. A rock group like Buddy's wrote its own material and did its own arrangements, leaving A&R executives like Miller, who'd once dictated material and reigned over recording sessions, out in the cold. The joke in the industry was that A&R now stood for Arguments and Recriminations. Miller was out of touch with new trends. Recently he'd passed on Connie Francis. "The girl has no distinctive sound," he said, according to Connie's autobiography, *Who's Sorry Now*. Shortly thereafter she became the richest female singer in the world. Predictably, Miller turned down "That'll Be the Day."

Though Petty later denied it, Atlantic's Jerry Wexler and RCA's Joe Carlton were the next industry wise men to pass up the Crickets, according to the authoritative *Rolling Stone* history of rock 'n' roll, *Rock of Ages*. Having run out of all the majors except for Decca, who'd already fired Buddy Holly in Nashville, Petty finally appealed to Murray Deutch of Peer-Southern, the music publisher who'd handled the Norman Petty Trio's song "Almost Paradise." Petty's Nor Va Jak music-publishing firm was affiliated with Peer-Southern, which acted as sole selling agent for Nor Va Jak, handling all its sheet-music sales and promotion of record releases. Deutch wanted a fifty-fifty split on the publishing rights of "That'll Be the Day" if he could swing a record deal for the Crickets. Though the terms were gluttonous, at least Deutch had the gumption to spot "That'll Be the Day" as a winner. He rang Bob Thiele, Teresa Brewer's husband and the A&R director of Coral Records, a Decca subsidiary. According to Thiele, Deutch called him and offered the demo, explaining that although it had been rejected by RCA, Columbia, and other companies, he thought Deutch would like it. Thiele invited Deutch to bring the demo in and play it. Afterward, Thiele received a call from Norman Petty. Years later Thiele revealed in *Reminiscing* magazine that Petty pleaded with him, saying, "Please, I don't want any money for it. Just get this record released." Petty could have obtained a better deal for Buddy by not showing his hand. As soon as Thiele finished listening to "That'll Be the Day," he said, "Let's go! It's great!" Petty practically gave it away, selling the demo for "$150 per side and a royalty on every record sold," Petty later admitted to writer Helen Betty in *New Mexico* magazine in 1960.

What did Thiele see in Holly that all his colleagues in the record industry had missed? In an interview with author and record executive Joe Smith, Thiele said, "I like to think of myself as maybe different from Milt Gabler, Mitch Miller, and those guys. I honestly don't think I've ever made a record I didn't personally like."

Petty couldn't believe that Thiele was willing to release the demo and insisted on going back to Clovis and putting together a good master recording of "That'll Be the Day." Thiele wouldn't hear of it—the record was perfect, he said. Petty kept arguing that it was merely a demo. But Thiele steadfastly maintained that he had exactly what he wanted "right here on this tape." Petty finally left the demo with Thiele and returned to his hotel room to wait for the contract. "Unfortunately, it wasn't that simple," Thiele revealed in his liner notes for the album *Buddy Holly*. The minute he tried to get the approval of his Decca superiors, president Milton Rachmil and vice president Leonard Schneider, he ran into a brick wall of opposition. They scorned "That'll Be the Day" as "junk," dismissing it as "a joke," Thiele later stated in Goldrosen and Beecher's *Remembering Buddy*. Coral, the Decca subsidiary Thiele worked for, was better at handling artists such as the McGuire Sisters and Lawrence Welk, the Decca brass argued. Brash rockers like the Crickets might offend Coral's roster of stars.

Recalling the controversy, Dick Jacobs, another Decca executive, said that Decca's top officers considered Thiele to be insane for trying to sign up an artist who'd already been fired by Decca's Nashville office. But Thiele wielded sufficient clout at the company to get his way. In his interview with Joe Smith, Thiele said that, in the crunch, he sometimes put his job on the line, saying, "Fuck it . . . fire me, but I'm going to make that record." Finally Decca told him that he could put the Crickets on Brunswick, a kind of trash-basket label in which Decca dumped its undesirables.

Petty returned to Clovis in triumph, acting as if he'd pulled off the deal of the century. Though he did not tell the Crickets, he left the impression in New York that he was already in complete control of Buddy and the band. He struck Deutch as officious, as someone with a stranglehold on his clients, whom no one could talk to without first going through Petty.

When Buddy learned that his new label, Brunswick, was a Decca subsidiary, he chuckled and said it was "kind of like going out the front door and coming in the back door." Hi Pockets and Jack Neal were appalled when Buddy confessed that he'd cut Petty in on songwriting credits. Neal angrily exclaimed that Petty was usurping credit for Buddy's songs. Buddy shrugged it off as the price he had to pay for a shot at stardom. When the stakes are big, he told Neal, you always have to invest some of your own money. There was some truth to this but also more than a little youthful gullibility. Petty misled the Crickets into thinking he'd give them a share of his company if they produced a hit record. On hearing this, Joe B. glanced around Petty's studio, which was crammed with expensive equipment, and assumed that he was now a shareholder, that he'd finally arrived. Joe B. let Petty take equal songwriting credit, which Joe B. would later regret.

Excited over his new Brunswick contract, Buddy dropped in to KSEL to share the news with DJ Jerry Coleman. Buddy often came by KSEL to listen to and study its extensive collection of Little Richard and Fats Domino records. On this occasion he appeared at eleven P.M. "He sat there for hours and sang along with Little Richard and Fats Domino," recalls Coleman. Buddy, who was now twenty, complained to Coleman about his acne. "He had a terrible complexion," says Coleman. Like his chronic nervous stomach and his ulcer, his skin condition was exacerbated by alcohol consumption, smoking, and a rich diet. "He liked pizzas real well," Ella Holley told Griggs in 1977, adding that when he came home late, around midnight, she'd always fix him a peanut-butter sandwich. Steak was another favorite food of Buddy's, but the dish he loved above all others was okra dipped in a cornmeal batter and then fried in grease. Though it was a typical diet for a Texas boy in the fifties, before people realized the danger of eating fat, it was not one designed to soothe a digestive tract already traumatized by ulcers. Buddy told Coleman he'd heard about a scraping process that would smooth out his acne scars, and he decided to undergo the operation as soon as he could afford it.

On Coleman's nineteenth birthday, Buddy returned to the station with the Crickets and presented Coleman a sterling silver lighter engraved, "To Jerry from Buddy Holly & the Crickets." Though DJs as a group were doing nothing at this time to promote Buddy's records, Buddy cultivated them because he liked them and knew their goodwill would one day pay off.

The Crickets received their contract from Brunswick on March 19, 1957; it was simply a letter of agreement giving the company the masters of "That'll Be the Day" and "I'm Lookin' for Someone to Love." In effect, Buddy was now an independent producer, free of studio interference and in complete artistic control of his sessions. It sounded good, but in reality it left Buddy and his band penniless, with only a promise of royalties if the record sold. To make matters worse, Petty strong-armed them into donating a whopping 40 percent of the royalties on their first record to the Baptist church. They all joined hands and prayed before signing the contract.

Larry Holley helped the Crickets out of their financial bind, hiring them as construction workers. He put Buddy, Jerry, and Joe B. to work grouting—filling the spaces between tiles with white cement. Showing up on the job unexpectedly one day, Larry discovered everyone goofing off except Buddy. Jerry was lolling on a slab of cardboard, and Joe B. was beating out a rhythm on a box. Larry told them he was firing them, but Buddy convinced him to give them all one more opportunity, and they'd promise to do better. Larry always found it difficult to say no to Buddy and agreed to put them to work digging a storm cellar. After a few days, the Crickets developed blisters on their hands and started sloughing off again. Hearing of their plight, Petty gave Buddy some indoors work, lining the walls of the large echo chamber next door to the Clovis studio with ceramic tiles.

Construction work made Buddy acutely aware of his physical limitations. Determined to build some muscles, he joined a gym and started lifting weights. Though still slender, he eventually developed well-defined pectorals, biceps, stomach muscles, and powerful thighs and calves. As he grew stronger, he was able to take a job as a truck driver in Larry's business. According to Larry, Buddy knew how to handle a truck. During a long haul to San Angelo in an eighteen-wheeler, Buddy and Larry decided to stop for a hamburger just outside the city limits. Not until they were seated in the restaurant did they realize that they'd stopped in the black section of town. The customers as well as a small band playing blues music were all black. Buddy, who was wearing Levi's, T-shirt, and moccasins, talked to the band during a break and ended up playing "Sexy Ways" with them. News quickly spread through the community that some "ofay cat" was fracturing his fuse box. Soon the joint was packed. Buddy later told Larry that this was the moment he decided to devote the rest of his life to entertaining people.

On the strength of that conviction, new creative energies poured through Buddy and he started working on one of his most memorable songs, "Words of Love." The Crickets were rehearsing one day at June and Nig Clark's house when a tornado alert was announced over the radio. A twister was tearing through the South Plains near Lubbock. They dashed to a neighbor's cellar and stayed there for two hours as the tornado bounced around the prairie. Recognizing the musicians, some of the neighbors started complaining to them about all the noise they'd been making, especially the drummer. Confined in such close quarters, Buddy and his musicians had little choice but to promise to stop making so much racket. Subsequently, they asked Petty if they could use his studio to practice in from now on. Petty agreed, and soon they were practically living in Clovis, using the little apartment in the rear portion of the studio, which had all the comforts of home—refrigerator, stove, couch, and a fireplace. With its Scandinavian decor—blond wood furniture and Scotch plaid upholstery—the apartment was the fifties version of a bachelor pad.

The Crickets often crashed there after working all night. Buddy was an inveterate night owl, and so was Petty. Their metabolisms were synchronized, reaching their peak from three to six A.M. From a technical standpoint it was the best time to record—there was less traffic noise from the eighteen-wheelers that hauled feed during the day to cattle on the grazing fields around Clovis.

If the studio was booked by other musicians when Buddy arrived, he'd play as a sideman on their records. His voice and guitar can be heard on the recordings of Jack Huddle, Jim Robinson, Fred Crawford, Ray Ruff, and many other musicians in the Tex-Mex circle. Soon they were all helping each other during their recording sessions in what Petty once described as a big, joyous Tex-Mex family.

Reporting for work in the morning, Norma Jean Berry, Petty's secretary-assistant, often found the Crickets sprawled over the sofa and chairs. They'd rub their eyes, rouse themselves, drink their morning coffee, then swarm into the studio to record the brilliant songs Buddy was composing in early 1957. He was on a fantastic creative roll, turning out "Everyday," "Words of Love," "Listen to Me," "Tell Me How," and "Peggy Sue" in six months.

Petty expected them to keep the place in order, including weeding the rose garden and mowing the lawn in back of the studio. Working and sleeping together, the Crickets grew to be as close as brothers. Though Buddy was indisputably the star, he was generous and egalitarian to a fault, insisting on an equal split when Petty introduced the subject of record royalties. "Share and share alike. There's four Crickets so everybody gets the same cut," Buddy said, according to Maria Elena Santiago, the girl he'd marry the following year. Petty reminded Buddy that *he* was the star; the others were only sidemen who could be put on salary. Buddy said he would never treat his musicians like dogs; they would all get equal shares of their earnings, and that was that.

Suddenly altering his strategy, Petty conceded the four-way split on live performances but held out for a better deal for Buddy on the recordings. Most artists hire musicians for recording sessions, paying them union scale and excluding them from participation in royalties, Petty pointed out. Finally Buddy agreed on a 65–35 percent split, in his favor, on records. Petty continued to demur, implying that hacks could easily be enlisted on a per-session basis for recordings. Buddy refused to budge, and the Crickets' percentages remained intact.

Ray Ruff, a musician who recorded in Clovis, once said that Buddy was so generous he would give you the shirt off his back if you asked him for it. According to Ruff, enjoying life and having fun were more important to Buddy than money. Women were quick to recognize and appreciate Buddy's aura of virility, which promised sexual stamina and a good time in bed. Unlike many of his peers in the uptight fifties, he never had to struggle for sex; women came on to him. One of them was Vi Petty, Norman Petty's wife. Often Norman was absent from the studio, making out, according to Niki Sullivan, with a male lover who was a business associate. One night, when the Crickets had been recording late, Norman suddenly left the studio with no explanation. After a while, Vi smiled provocatively and motioned for Buddy to join her in the Pettys' apartment nearby. Later, when Buddy returned to the studio, he told Niki, "I can't believe it. I made love to Vi." In a 1995 interview, Sonny Curtis called the story "ludicrous. Guys tell each other things like that, and I would have known about it." Though Sonny was familiar with the Clovis scene, he was not, at this particular time, a Cricket.

As Buddy worked on "Words of Love" that spring, he spent many nights listening to a hypnotic recording called "Love is Strange," a 1956 hit by Mickey and Sylvia; he wanted "Words of Love" to have the same mesmerizing quality. His mother would call him in to dinner, and he would eat his meal as if in a trance. Then he'd go out and sit in his car for hours, letting the lyrics to "Words of Love" form in his mind. Finally he'd go back in the house, head straight for his room, pick up his guitar, and perform whatever portion of the song he'd just composed. When people heard him sing the finished work, they were speechless, caught in the spell of a great song. At once sensual, meditative, and spiritual, "Words of Love" is an enduring love song, most likely inspired by intimate exchanges between Buddy and Echo in their years together. The lyrics, mellow and beguiling, suggest the late-night murmurs of lovers who've just been inside of each other—body and soul.

The Crickets recorded "Words of Love" on a sunny, warm day in April 1957. The marathon session began on Wednesday the seventeenth and continued well into the next day. On Thursday morning a fatigued Joe B. put down his bass, assuming they'd finally finished. Not quite, according to Buddy, who announced he wanted to try something new. He started overdubbing his vocal, using a second machine, harmonizing with himself. Due to the loss of fidelity with each successive generation of dubbing, Jerry's drums came through as a faint but compelling background pulsation. They spent more time on "Words of Love" than on any song they'd ever recorded, and it was worth it. Buddy's vocal stands out in high relief over distant but still distinct and strangely compelling sounds, recalling the Mickey and Sylvia hit that inspired it but at the same time achieving a quality all its own.

Joe B. found the process by which the song gradually evolved into a masterwork nothing short of miraculous. Rock critic Richard Goldstein once said that to hear Janis Joplin sing "Ball and Chain" is to have been "laid, lovingly and well." Buddy's meltingly warm delivery of "Words of Love" indeed has the same effect.

Though exhausted, they remained in the studio long enough to slap together the flip side, "Mailman, Bring Me No More Blues," getting it in three takes. Buddy did it as a favor for Bob Thiele, his champion at Decca, who'd written it expressly for Buddy, with Ruth Roberts and Bill Katz. Buddy and Deutch had needed to humor Petty into making the record. Thiele once told Griggs that Buddy was a sensitive artist who would have preferred fewer business pressures.

In "Mailman" Buddy stretches the intensity of the blues past the breaking point. He begs, he pleads, he's down on all fours, he's out for the count, but the cut is a tour de force, staggering in its ambition and difference, not at all like any other song. Niki Sullivan calls it "horrible" and says that if it had been the Crickets' first record, they'd have been washed up as recording artists. "Mailman" anticipates wild-eyed crack-up songs like the Rolling Stones' "Scattered," Joplin's "Piece of My Heart," and Four Non-Blondes' "What's Going On?" and established Buddy as rock's foremost vocal contortionist. His bizarre performance wrecked the neat conventions of establishment pop and the slick sentiments they represented.

Instead of sending "Words of Love"/"Mailman, Bring Me No More Blues" to Bob Thiele at Brunswick, Petty dispatched the demo to Deutch at Peer-Southern, which would prove to be a costly mistake. Although "Words of Love" was the superior cut, it was "Mailman," according to Niki, that finally convinced Southern Music that the Crickets were an important group and that they should put all their clout behind Buddy Holly. As a result, Buddy would not score a hit with "Words of Love." Someone at the publishing company gave the song to a rival group, the Diamonds, who'd just had a million-seller with "Little Darlin'." The Diamonds' cover of "Words of Love" was rushed out; it would clobber Buddy's original the following summer. Deutch and Peer-Southern collected their royalties no matter who recorded their songs.

Months passed and still there was no word from New York regarding a release date for "That'll Be the Day." In New York, Bob Thiele ran into one obstacle after another from Brunswick Records' parent company, Decca, which was reluctant to associate itself with rock 'n' roll. Murray Deutch kept pressuring Thiele to make at least a token release so that Peer-Southern could begin collecting royalties. Decca finally agreed to let Brunswick press a mere one thousand units.

Meanwhile, the Crickets were broke and had to go back to gigging around Lubbock to survive. Despite his penury, Buddy managed to acquire a used red Cadillac, having worn out the Olds while driving the Crickets around Texas and Tennessee. Larry helped Buddy secure financing to purchase the car by cosigning the loan papers. The Crickets were as hard on the Cadillac as they'd been on the Olds. Larry maintains that the car held up only three months under the beating it received from Buddy, Jerry, and Joe B. before it started falling apart. Buddy returned the Cadillac to the used-car lot, parking it when the owner wasn't looking. The next day the owner showed up on Larry's doorstep, demanding the rest of the payments. Larry says his hair started turning gray as he tried to keep Buddy and his friends, all of whom were starry-eyed with ambition and not very realistic or responsible, out of harm's way. In the end, Larry made the payments so Buddy could keep his Cadillac.

On May 11, 1957, Buddy was scheduled to audition at 3:45 P.M. at KFDA television studios in Amarillo for the *Arthur Godfrey Talent Scouts* TV show. Godfrey was a redoubtable starmaker, responsible for the discovery of Julius LaRosa, Pat Boone, Patsy Cline, Shari Lewis, the McGuire Sisters, Carmel Quinn, and June Valli. The public loved Godfrey's deep, warm voice and his relaxed, low-key, straightforward manner; his shows accounted for twelve percent of CBS's television revenues. But in the fifties, the wracking pain he suffered as a result of injuries sustained in a 1931 automobile accident led to a series of on-camera outbursts that cost him his reputation. His treatment of LaRosa, whom he fired in the middle of a telecast, and musical director Archie Bleyer, whom Godfrey also fired, seemed unduly abusive and branded Godfrey as a difficult neurotic with a mercurial and explosive temper.

The Godfrey office instructed the Crickets to perform one nonoriginal song and to have plenty of additional material rehearsed and ready to perform if necessary. They were also told to provide one eight-by-ten glossy photo. Dreaming of national television exposure, the Crickets made the three-hour drive up the Panhandle to Amarillo. When they went before the judges, they performed a Little Richard song and some of their own compositions. When they finished, the Godfrey scout uttered a mild expletive and expressed concern for the future of music. If it was any consolation, Godfrey and his scouts were hardly infallible; they'd rejected Elvis in 1955. As values and styles rapidly changed in the late fifties, Godfrey and his pop-oriented show seemed increasingly old hat. His popularity on the wane, he made a tearful farewell speech and retired from television in 1959.

In May 1957, the Everly Brothers made their debut on Cadence Records, which had been formed by Godfrey rejects Archie Bleyer and Julius LaRosa. "Bye Bye Love" dominated the charts for weeks. Buddy became a fan of the Everlys and managed somehow to contact Don. He was aware that Don was deriving some of his arrangements from Bo Diddley, Buddy said, and offered to write a song called "Not Fade Away" for the Everlys, utilizing Bo Diddley's distinctive jungle beat. Beautiful singers but not the shrewdest judges of material, Don and Phil Everly turned down "Not Fade Away." Later Don attempted to justify the goof, saying that he was afraid people would say the Everlys sounded too much like Bo Diddley. Besides, Don added, Felice and Boudleaux Bryant had just given them a terrific song called "All I Have to Do Is Dream," so who needed "Not Fade Away"? Even so, says Don, "it was nice of Buddy to do that for us." In fact, Don came to view the episode as a feather in his cap, telling journalist Philip Norman in the 1980s, "Buddy wrote 'Not Fade Away' for us. It burns me up when I read *reportedly* written by Buddy Holly for the Everly Brothers."

Far from envying the Everlys their breakthrough, Buddy took it as a good omen: when Buddy sang, he *sounded* rather like Phil Everly, and when Buddy overdubbed his own voice and harmonized with himself, he sounded like both Don *and* Phil.

Rehearsing the Crickets day and night in 1957, Buddy rented an office on the south side of Lubbock for daily practice. One night they participated in a "Battle of the Bands" contest at a local theater. "Ever'body had their clique there, and the one that clapped and hollered the loudest was determined the winner," Larry Holley related in 1992. "Buddy was the last on the show. He had somebody with him, but I don't remember if Joe B. was there. Jerry Allison might have been playin' drums. Before Buddy came on, a guy named Jimmy Peters imitated Elvis and did a real good job of it and got a lot of applause. Then Buddy came out. He was dressed up, not just his Levi's but real nice, like a professional musician." As soon as Buddy appeared onstage, a group at the back of the theater started booing.

"There comes old turkey neck," someone yelled.

It must have hurt Buddy, but he didn't let it show. "Lubbock is a very jealous town," Larry observes. "I didn't think he was going to win after hearing all them other guys. They was booin' and hollerin' and carryin' on, but Buddy didn't let it bother him at all. Of course, I was there and it made me mad, but Buddy got up there just as professional-like and started playin' and it wasn't any comparison to them other guys. He started shufflin' across the floor, not like Chuck Berry where he gets down and squats, but just shufflin' along like he was playin' for the King of England and could care less what they thought. He was goin' to do the best he could, and the crowd went wild, and he won. That's when I knew that Buddy had the quality that it would take to overcome the hecklin' and whatever it takes to make it."

On May 16, 1957, Buddy received an agreement from Coral Records for "Words of Love" and "Mailman, Bring Me No More Blues." Coral, a

Decca subsidiary considered more prestigious than Brunswick, had pegged Buddy as a solo singer. Decca had not deemed the Crickets good enough for Coral and kept them on Brunswick, but Buddy's vocal on "Words of Love" was clearly a star turn. From now on Buddy's recordings would be released alternately on Brunswick and Coral: Brunswick when the Crickets' contribution was obvious, Coral when Buddy dominated the record. Buddy's generosity again asserted itself; on his Coral releases, he gave the Crickets their usual pay.

He finished writing "Everyday," and recorded it in Clovis on May 29. Between takes he wandered through the studio and came upon what appeared to be a toy piano but was in fact a keyboard xylophone—a celesta. Though it's widely thought that Vi Petty played the instrument on "Everyday," Norman Petty later informed Bill Griggs, "Vi only showed me how since I couldn't read music, but I'm the one who played the celesta on 'Everyday.' "

Expertly and delicately played, the celesta was the cut's lead instrument, and its gentle nursery-like chimes would give the record its endearing, soft-textured appeal. Instead of lust and rebellion, the usual ingredients in rock, "Everyday" dwells on the youthful belief that love is right around the corner. Though tender, the song has a relentless, inexorable drive, underscored by Jerry's subtle but tenacious percussive effects, which were accomplished not by drums but by Jerry slapping on his knees. The resulting sound, a delicate pitter-patter, insistent as the ticking of a clock, drives home the song's message: that love is not so much a revelation, or something you fall into, as it is a gradual unfolding. In rock critic Jonathan Cott's words, "Holly's deepest, wisest, and seemingly least complicated songs express the unadorned confrontation of beauty and love with time."

"Everyday" also embodies Buddy's dogged faith that Echo, the "good girl" of every fifties boy's dreams, or a girl very much like her, would eventually become his wife and the mother of his children. The song always remained one of his personal favorites. Unfortunately, he couldn't sign his name to it, since he feared that Cedarwood Music would nail him on a technicality that might result in litigation. Cursing the day he'd ever set foot in Nashville, he was forced to use the pseudonym Charles Hardin. Eventually Petty went to Nashville and hammered out a deal transferring publishing rights from Cedarwood to his own Nor Va Jak publishing operation.

The only reason Buddy recorded "Not Fade Away," which he also cut on May 29, was because the Everly Brothers had rejected it. The Everlys' loss is our eternal gain: "Not Fade Away" is one of his best performances. Cocky and brash, it explodes like a string of firecrackers. Jerry performs his customary magic, again eschewing drums, this time in favor of a pasteboard box. Syncopated background vocals, overdubbed by Buddy, Niki, and Jerry, turn Bo Diddley's jungle rhythm into a rockabilly riot. Unlike the lover of "Everyday," the singer in "Not Fade Away" orders his girl to make love to him, promising she'll get something bigger than a Cadillac. The relationship of the couple in the song follows the same up-and-down, off-and-on course as Buddy and Echo's affair, or Jerry and Peggy Sue's: the singer chastizes his girl for rejecting him, but by the final verse, he's regained his confidence and is able to assert that the only love that doesn't die is one grounded in honesty and trust. For a pounding, danceable rocker, the song packs a tremendous amount of meaning.

"Only thing I minded about Norman," Sonny Curtis said in 1995, "was that he grabbed some songs he didn't help write. J.I. was coauthor of 'Not Fade Away' and Norman grabbed credit and kicked J.I. off." J.I. was Jerry Ivan Allison, Buddy's drummer and the true collaborator on "Not Fade Away."

The demos of "Everyday" and "Not Fade Away" were sent to New York, but neither Brunswick nor Coral announced plans for releasing this pair of classics. Buddy was deluging his record company with tremendous material but Decca executives, oblivious to the gold mine they were sitting on, played it safe. They opted to wait and see how "That'll Be the Day" fared in the marketplace when they finally released it on May 27, 1957. Obviously they hadn't spotted "That'll Be the Day" as a winner or they'd have been pressing follow-up records and albums, which they easily could have done, considering the brilliant demos Buddy kept pelting them with throughout the spring and summer of 1957. At first there was so little action on "That'll Be the Day" that they wrote it off as a clunker, doing nothing to promote or advertise it.

But nothing could stop the creative roll Buddy was on in 1957. He lived for the hours he could spend in Clovis, where the songs surging through him could be caught on tape. The Crickets were back in Petty's studio a few weeks after the "Not Fade Away"/"Everyday" session, this time to record "Ready Teddy" and "Valley of Tears." Niki was sitting on a sofa in the back room, repeatedly playing a catchy refrain, when Buddy wandered in and stood listening to him, fascinated by the riff Niki was working on. "Tell me how," Buddy said, and a song grew from that simple sentence. Though Niki inspired the song, it was Petty who'd share the writing credit with Buddy and Jerry. Buddy's vocal seems to dance over the lyrics in "Tell Me How," pleading for love from a girl who keeps it locked in her heart. Though the Moog synthesizer was not yet in use, there are some unidentifiable, synthesizer-like sounds, due to Jerry's percussive virtuosity and Petty's bewitching inventiveness.

"Ready Teddy" was written by Robert A. "Bumps" Blackwell and John Marascalco and recorded by Little Richard in 1956. Elvis also sang it in

1956 on his first *Ed Sullivan* appearance, and it came to be known as an Elvis song. Such formidable precedents not only failed to intimidate Buddy but spurred him on to a powerful rendition. No one could be fiercer than Buddy, so gentle in his ballads, when he wanted to go hell-for-leather in a gutsy rocker. In "Ready Teddy," he infuses the word *ready* with a gripping carnality. Yelping, growling, delighting in his voice as an instrument of seemingly infinite inflection and suppleness, Buddy proved that he could hold his own with the wildest men in rock.

Buddy's poignant, uniquely C&W-flavored style reinvents Fats Domino's little-known "Valley of Tears." Petty, at his Baldwin electric organ, provides a searing accompaniment.

On June 14, 1957, Buddy Knox returned to Texas to celebrate the chart-topping success of "Party Doll." Holly and a carload of Lubbock musicians, including the Tolletts, drove up the Panhandle to Dumas, Texas, to appear in a show feting Knox and his group, the Rhythm Orchids. Buddy Knox remembers sitting on the front porch of his house and talking through the night with his chums from Lubbock. Soon Knox was recording in Clovis again. Holly was around the studio constantly, Knox recalls. Often Holly would play rhythm guitar on Knox's cuts, and Knox would play on Holly's records whenever needed. In terms of good fellowship and creativity, Clovis was part of rock's Southern axis, a prairie version of Sam Phillips's Sun Records in Memphis, where Elvis, Johnny Cash, Carl Perkins, Roy Orbison, and Jerry Lee Lewis all sparked each other.

When "Words of Love" was released on June 20, it came nowhere near the Top 40. The Diamonds' cover of "Words of Love" had completely stolen Holly's thunder. The record-buying public also ignored the stunning oddity of "Mailman, Bring Me No More Blues." Holly desperately needed some good news, but Decca kept him completely in the dark about the sales of "That'll Be the Day."

Unbeknownst to its performer at first, "That'll Be the Day" was flying out of the stores in July 1957, thanks largely to flamboyant disk jockeys in Buffalo and Philadelphia. Georgie Woods of Philadelphia's WDAS, a black station, played the record so continuously that it became a regional hit, according to Deutch. A Buffalo DJ named Tom Clay, broadcasting on WWOL under the name Guy King, played "That'll Be the Day" consecutively for twenty minutes one day. Afterward he decided to call Lubbock and talk with Buddy on the air. As Clay subsequently related to DJ Jerry Rio, Clay told Buddy that he might very well have a hit.

"That'll Be the Day" climbed onto *Billboard*'s regional best-seller list for upstate New York, Boston, and Cleveland. According to Tom Clay, it was not major metropolises like Manhattan or Los Angeles but second-rank cities such as Buffalo and Cleveland that accounted for the initial success of rock 'n' roll. Still awaiting confirmation from Brunswick that the record had broken out, Buddy drove to Clovis that July in 103-degree heat to cut "Peggy Sue," "Oh Boy," and other gems from his early-1957 songwriting binge, surely one of the most prolific in the history of popular music.

Originally, "Peggy Sue" was entitled "Cindy Lou," named after Buddy's niece, the infant daughter of his sister Pat Holley Kaiter. Before the song metamorphosed into "Peggy Sue" while being recorded in Clovis, "Cindy Lou" had a Latin beat, somewhat similar to Harry Belafonte's 1957 calypso hit "Banana Boat (Day O)." During the session they realized that it was a dud, puny and lacking both style and commercial flair. Jerry suggested a drumroll like the one in Jaye P. Morgan's "Dawn," but when they tried it, Jerry drowned out everything else on the tape. Bill Pickering, who had formed a singing trio called the Picks, who'd later work with Buddy, said Jerry "beat the tar out of those drums. He had the fastest hands I've ever seen, faster than Wyatt Earp."

Realizing that they had to get the drums outside the studio, Norman Petty told Jerry to move his instruments into the hallway. Resituated in the reception room, Jerry used the loudspeaker system and headphones to communicate with Buddy. It was decided that Jerry should play paradiddles, a basic exercise used by drummers. The result was the unbroken drumming sound that would ultimately pull the recording together. But first Jerry asked Buddy if they could change the song's title from "Cindy Lou" to "Peggy Sue." Jerry and Peggy Sue Gerron had recently feuded and broken up. "Jerry wanted to do something to get me back," Peggy Sue revealed in 1994. That would take some doing, since Peggy Sue's parents, convinced she and Jerry were getting much too cozy, had moved her to Sacramento, California, enrolling her in Girl's Catholic School.

As Peggy Sue later told Dick Clark, Buddy struck a bargain with Jerry: if Jerry could sustain the steady drumming throughout the cut Buddy would agree to the title change. The instrument Jerry used was "a snare drum with the snares off," he told Griggs in 1978. When they tried the new beat, the song was completely transformed. At first the change in tempo threw Buddy off. When the time came for the lead break, he discovered it was physically impossible to switch from the rhythm position to the lead position on his Fender Stratocaster. The studio became a scene of frenetic activity as Buddy instructed Niki to kneel at his feet and throw the switch of his Strat the instant Buddy gave him the signal (a nod of Buddy's head). At close range, Niki discovered that the reason Buddy's guitar playing sounded so lush was that Buddy played all six guitar strings continuously, unlike the majority of guitarists, who usually deal with one or two strings at a time. On "Peggy Sue" he used nothing but downstrokes, refined during years of playing the mandolin. Soon, Buddy's downstroke

strumming technique would become a rock legend; author Jimmy Guterman's 1992 book *The Best Rock 'n' Roll Records of All Time* refers to "Peggy
Sue" as the "source of the greatest rhythm guitar solo in all rock 'n' roll."

Petty was busy in the control room, pushing the on and off signals to
the echo chamber in time with the music. Petty also jiggered the volume
on Jerry's mike, which gave "Peggy Sue" its erotic throbbing sensation.
Niki was so occupied with helping Buddy out that he finally gave up
trying to play his guitar. On the first cut, Jerry made a mistake and either
Buddy or Norman told him to shape up or they'd reinstate the title "Cindy
Lou." They got "Peggy Sue," one of the most exciting and durable cuts
in rock 'n' roll, on the next take. Only twenty minutes had elapsed since
they'd begun. Years later, in his book *Rock 'n' Roll: The 100 Best Singles*,
critic Paul Williams wrote:

> There is something *perfect* about the sound of "Peggy Sue." It gets
> into the blood. Buddy Holly could have been a country singer, or
> pop crooner, could have and probably would have fitted his talent
> to whatever music was happening in the world when he came
> along. It happened to be rock 'n' roll. But it only fully became rock
> 'n' roll the day Buddy Holly started singing it.

Though Petty horned in on the "Peggy Sue" songwriting credit, Niki
later told Griggs that Buddy and Jerry cowrote it. In all the collaborations
in the studio, Buddy generated the song ideas and contributed the most
to their composition, Niki added in Goldrosen and Beecher's *Remembering
Buddy*. Norman Petty, in a long interview in 1983 with Brooks and Malcolm, did his best to minimize Buddy's contribution and inflate his own,
claiming that Buddy dropped off the first part of "True Love Ways" one
day on his way to Portales, New Mexico, to visit an aunt with his mother
and father. According to Petty, Buddy told him to write some lyrics and
a bridge. The Crickets tolerated Petty's attitude because, according to
Niki, they were vulnerable, unsophisticated youths and didn't concern
themselves with business since it never occurred to anyone they'd score
a hit.

The same late June–early July sessions that produced "Peggy Sue" also
brought forth "Listen to Me," "Oh Boy," and "I'm Gonna Love You Too."
From the opening riff on "I'm Gonna Love You Too," Buddy's vocal
encompasses a remarkable succession of situations and feelings. The singer
enumerates the delicious things his girl is going to do to him, even though
another boy has stolen her. The song carries a powerful message to teenagers lost in their own confusion and sadness. Here's a guy who could be
wailing the blues but instead he's rocking out, overflowing with good
humor and joy.

As the Crickets recorded "I'm Gonna Love You Too," a real cricket trapped in the echo chamber started chirping. They went into the echo chamber and tried to rout the cricket, but it managed to evade them. Finally they gave up. The cricket can be heard quite clearly near the fadeout of "I'm Gonna Love You Too" on the LP *Buddy Holly* (MCA Records-25239) and the cassette *Oh Boy* (MCA-20425).

A more deliberate auditory innovation occurs in "Listen to Me," another Holly song influenced by Mickey and Sylvia's "Love is Strange." Buddy somehow makes his guitar sound like a plugged-in harpsichord. Overdubbing his vocal, he sings a duet with himself and achieves some memorable pyrotechnics. His voice rises suddenly over the eerie instrumental, whispering urgent intimacies. The effect is at once startling and moving. At exactly one minute and fifteen seconds into the cut, the same cricket heard on the previous song starts chirping again—in tempo. ("Listen to Me" is on the same LP and cassette mentioned above.)

In "Oh Boy," a tune by Sonny West and Bill Tilghman, Buddy introduces some of rock 'n' roll's most familiar sounds, his falsetto trills and feral growls. Originally entitled "Alla My Love," "Oh Boy" opens with the exuberant boasts of a red-hot lover, bursting with animal pleasure. Both of the song's composers were deliriously happy when they first heard Buddy's cover. "Oh Boy" was so effective in its spontaneity that Petty decided to leave the take completely intact, including Buddy's cough, which is audible just after the guitar break, at one minute and twenty-three seconds into the cut (on the MCA-20425 cassette *Oh Boy* and the Coral 57279/757279 LP *The Buddy Holly Story*).

By early July, Buddy was anxious and depressed. He was working with Larry on a city health unit building on the outskirts of Lubbock. The midsummer heat was blistering. Around three P.M. Larry noticed that Buddy was dejected and asked him what was the matter. Buddy replied that he was revolted by the whole process of making records, that it had been almost two months since his exhausting labors in Petty's studio, and he despaired of ever hearing from Brunswick. He was still convinced that he had the ability to go all the way to the top, but he felt that luck was against him.

Larry suggested they knock off work for the day and call the record executives in New York and threaten to withdraw the record unless it was released immediately. When they got home and made the call, someone at Brunswick excitedly blurted that Buddy should see what was going on in New York. "That'll Be the Day" was going to be a million-seller; people were humming it on the streets of Manhattan. According to Bob Thiele, no sooner was the record issued than Philadelphia snapped up sixteen thousand copies, a sure sign of a monster hit.

If the record was such a big success, Buddy said, Brunswick could afford to forward him a check for $500. He explained he needed it to cover some urgent expenses. When Buddy got off the phone, Larry asked him which song they'd been talking about, and Buddy replied that "That'll Be the Day" was taking off. But surely that was the B-side, Larry said, reminding Buddy that he'd spent much more time on "I'm Lookin' for Someone to Love," which was supposed to be the A-side.

When "That'll Be the Day" had been released on May 27, *Billboard* failed to recognize the future hit, according it a low 72 rating and a tepid review, noting, "Performance is better than material." Gary Tollett's record "Pretty Baby" came out at the same time and *Billboard* rated it 76, just four points behind "That'll Be the Day." This was proof positive, Tollett reflected, that critics didn't know how to spot a winner.

One morning after a long session, Petty woke the Crickets at eight A.M. and informed them he had some amazing news. He read them a congratulatory wire from Murray Deutch, who said "That'll Be the Day" had sold fifty thousand copies and that Petty should get the Crickets ready to fly to New York. The Crickets had scored a bull's-eye with their first record. Buddy tried to share his excitement with them, but, according to Niki, they were too groggy and tired to display any emotion; they all turned over and went back to sleep.

Though "That'll Be the Day" sales were promising, the Diamonds' cover of "Words of Love" beat it to the *Billboard* chart, zooming into thirteenth place. Buddy had dreamed of stardom as a singer but his first hit was as the songwriter of "Words of Love."

Offers started coming in. The Crickets were in demand for tours, record-store promotions, and TV and radio appearances. When Petty advised them to hire a manager, Buddy said, "We've got a manager," Petty later told Brooks and Malcolm.

"Oh? Who is it?" Petty asked.

"You are," Buddy replied.

Later Petty patronizingly referred to managing the Crickets as a "glorified babysitting job," but he was so eager to take control of their lives that he immediately exceeded his authority, demanding to know if the Crickets were dating girls and warning them that if they wanted to be major rock stars like Elvis Presley, they'd better not get serious about anyone and certainly not get married. Such intrusions were unsolicited and resented by the Crickets. Later Petty admitted that he had been too strict. But in a profoundly disturbing sense, Petty was exactly what they'd been looking for. Overgrown children in many respects, they often depended on Buddy's father to tote them around to gigs and recording sessions. Buddy had always been surrounded by people who enabled him to avoid the responsibilities of growing up; first his family—and now Norman Petty.

They might have been playing "That'll Be the Day" on the streets of New York, but they certainly weren't playing it in Lubbock. Other than the $500 he'd finally managed to extract from Brunswick, there was no visible evidence in Buddy's world that he'd cut a great record. Snuff Garrett, a DJ on Lubbock's KDUB at the time, claims to have been one of the earliest DJs to spin "That'll Be the Day" on the air. Snuff played it as soon as he received the demo. It didn't catch on at first with most DJs, which meant that there was more than a little hyperbole in Bob Thiele's claim of instant success. As the summer of 1957 wore on, "That'll Be the Day" languished in the record bins, at least in the stores of the American Southwest. If Buddy had depended on his hometown, or even his home state, to jump-start it, "That'll Be the Day" would have died a quick death. Like the blue northers that swept down the plains from Canada, fame would descend on him from the north.

Chapter Seven

On the Road

Buddy Holly entered show business in the heyday of the great rock 'n' roll and R&B package tours. Nothing like them exists today. Planned and mounted like military campaigns, these all-star caravans swept across the country in buses, playing as many as seventy cities in eighty nights, featuring rosters of recording stars such as Clyde McPhatter, LaVern Baker, Eddie Cochran, Frankie Lymon and the Teenagers, Gene Vincent, Paul Anka, Jerry Lee Lewis, and on and on. Each performer would do a fifteen-minute turn and then clear the stage for the next act. To grasp how extraordinary this was, one only need imagine a tour in the 1990s including Red Hot Chili Peppers, Crash Test Dummies, U2, Pearl Jam, Metallica, and Van Halen. Other considerations aside, no one could afford to mount such a show. But in 1957, rock 'n' roll was new and the performers seized the opportunity to sing the controversial new music in public, often enduring harsh and abusive conditions on the road and working for a fraction of what rock stars receive today.

The Crickets' first tour was an all-black package that played the "Around the World" circuit, a string of theaters in eastern U.S. cities that catered to black audiences and featured R&B acts. Their inclusion on such a tour, where they were not welcomed at first by either their black co-stars or their New York audience, was a managerial gaffe of colossal proportions on the part of Norman Petty. He failed to advise them that they were the only whites involved, leaving them completely unprepared for the inevitable crises that awaited them when they began three-week-long engagements at black theaters in Washington, D.C., Baltimore, and New York City in August 1957. Petty delivered them into the hands of Irving Feld, the tour promoter. The Crickets remained unaware that the black audiences in the theaters they'd be playing—the Howard, the Royal, and the Apollo—were expecting to see black acts and might be out for the scalps of any honkies who dared show up on their stages. For Buddy, the tour was a catastrophe.

It was also a bust financially. The Crickets received $1,000 per week. After Petty's commission and the union's cut, each Cricket received a little more than $200, hardly a princely sum, considering travel expenses. In Petty's next managerial mistake, he advised the Crickets to discard their punk attire—the jeans that Buddy's mother had been pegging—in favor of square-looking suits. When they emerged from the Lubbock dry-goods store Petty took them to, they looked like a two-bit lounge act, Buddy in gray trousers and a white linen jacket and the Crickets in funereal gray suits. On the threshold of a major recording career, they needed and deserved a big-league agent and instead they got a nanny. As they boarded the 6:30 P.M. flight from Amarillo to New York on July 28, 1957, to face the hard-boiled, greedy world of professional showbiz, they were armed with a list of instructions from Petty to carry $30 or $40 in cash and the rest in traveler's checks and to take along copies of their record, plenty of clean underwear, twenty-four Dramamine tablets, twenty-five feet of extension cord, a shoe-shine kit, telephone and hotel credit cards, and a Bible. Not bad advice, but the sinister implications in the final suggestion in Petty's nineteen-point memo—to forward all their earnings to Clovis—would not become evident to them until it was too late. Sending money to Clovis was like dropping it in a bottomless well, for all the Crickets would ever see of it again.

In New York they stayed at the Edison, an inexpensive hotel off Times Square. They were due in Washington a day or two later. For years the only documentation of their New York stay was a telegram from Petty, sent from Miami Beach, in which he congratulated them on their arrival in the big city, signing the telegram "Papa Norman." Then, in a 1995 interview, Niki Sullivan provided an account of the Crickets' first experience of New York City. They took a look at the Brill Building at 1619 Broadway, the fabled headquarters of tunesmiths and song pluggers, and then ate at Jack Dempsey's Restaurant in Times Square. "The Crickets had their first drink together at Jack Dempsey's," Niki says. "Cocktails—bourbon and Coke, which drew howls from the waiter and bartender. Coming out of a dry county, we had no experience in drinking anything but beer, at least legally. We were over our heads in New York, totally green, but we snickered and made fun of everything around us."

The trip was planned by their music publisher and record company as a "kind of a heros' welcome," Niki explains, "to meet everyone who'd had a hand in what we were doing. There was a writer and artist at our publishers, who showed us how songs are plugged at a publishing house." Next they went to their record company. "We were introduced to the head of Coral Records, Bob Thiele," Niki continues, "and he invited us to his home in upstate New York, a beautiful place with two-inch-thick carpeting. There were about six to ten people at the party, including Steve Lawrence, but mostly Coral-Brunswick. Met Teresa Brewer, who was pregnant, a dainty, cute, wonderful, polite, sincere person—a doll; we all fell in love with her. We were asked to perform and did a four-piece vocal of an old song. Norman Petty had given us this barbershop quartet song, something like 'O Baby Mine,' just to prove that we were a group and could sing together. We did it without any instruments. Whole bunch was nice people, so comfortable and pleasant, but New Yorkish, elite enough to be upstate for relaxation."

Before beginning their tour, they went to Philadelphia for an auto-graph-signing session at a record store. Then, reporting to Washington's Howard Theater to begin performances on August 2, they were taken aback when the Cadillacs, who were also on the bill, told them about a black Bronx group called Dean Barlow and the Crickets, some of whom were now in the Cadillacs, since Barlow's group had broken up after having a hit record, "Fine as Wine." Earl "Speedy" Carroll, the Cadillacs' lead singer, had sung one of rock's most famous lyrics on the 1955 hit record "Speedo," pointing out that his nickname was "Speedo" but people usually called him Mr. Earl. Buddy tried to explain to everyone at the Howard that the Crickets had attempted to find a name that hadn't been used before, but obviously they'd goofed.

Some of the black performers put Buddy and the Crickets down as one-hit wonders and predicted they'd soon be washed up, like so many white boys who tried to sing black music. Others, however, such as Clyde McPhatter, the headliner, befriended the boys from Texas, Joe B. recalled. In Niki's recollection, the black audiences liked them, but the situation was so fraught with ambivalence that Buddy came down with a case of "nerves" and lost his voice. Diagnosed with laryngitis, he told Niki to go on for him.

None of the Crickets professed to be singers, and Niki was scared out of his wits over the prospect of singing, adding that he wasn't yet much of a guitarist, either. When Petty joined the tour and learned that Niki had succeeded in putting over Buddy's songs, he commented, with his usual condescension, "Anyone can sing those songs." Petty noticed that Niki and Jerry's personalities clashed and that Niki felt alienated from the group, but he did nothing to alleviate the conflict. He knew that Buddy, the most important member of the group, would always side with Jerry in any row with Niki. Eventually, according to Petty, everyone wanted Niki out. To make matters worse, Niki's Gibson electric was sto-len during the tour and he had to dash out and buy a new one between shows.

In Baltimore the Royal audience was famous for draining wine bottles and then tossing them at the performers. During one show a drunk in the balcony heaved a bottle at a black girl group called the Hearts and cut one of the singers, who left the stage bleeding.

The next stop was New York, where they were to play Harlem's fabled sixteen-hundred-seat Apollo Theater beginning August 16. Still standing today, the Apollo is a neoclassical three-story gray brick building. The large plate-glass windows on the upper floors make it look more like a garment-district building than a theater, but, as Billie Holiday once noted, "Uptown, the Apollo was what the Palace was downtown." A towering fifteen-foot sign, flashing the Apollo's name in purple neon letters, lights up the ghetto sky nightly. Since 1934, its huge marquee had announced the noblest names in black entertainment, including Bessie Smith, Charlie Parker, Billie Holiday, Lena Horne, Sammy Davis, Jr., and Ray Charles. Accustomed to genius, the Apollo audience was the most exacting this side of La Scala. Blacks often said, "If you can work the Apollo, you can work anywhere in the world."

Buddy Holly faced this challenge in a state of near collapse. When he visited Bob Thiele at Brunswick, he seemed a nervous wreck. An unguarded remark, Thiele felt, could shatter what little equanimity Buddy had left. Another Decca executive, Dick Jacobs of Coral, Buddy's solo label, thought Buddy looked like a Lone Star lout, with his eyeglasses in unfashionable silver frames and a mouthful of gold fillings. After they talked for a while, however, Jacobs was smitten by Buddy, calling him a miracle of gentleness and kindness, a great soul. The Crickets walked in on Murray Deutch at Peer-Southern wearing jeans and T-shirts, striking Deutch as country bumpkins, fresh from Podunk, Texas. But Buddy won him over with a deference that was as courtly, and as full of yes sir's and no sir's, as Elvis Presley's. They gave Deutch a humorous jingle they'd recorded to the tune of "That'll Be the Day," thanking him for having launched their recording careers and referring to him affectionately as the "Dutch boy."

Their hotel, the legendary Theresa, stood at Seventh Avenue and 125th Street, resembling a smaller, grimier version of the Hotel Plaza in midtown Manhattan. On the Theresa's ground floor, there was a handy Chock Full o' Nuts, where they could buy the best coffee and powdered wholewheat donuts in town. Within a few years, in 1960, Cuban premier Fidel Castro would choose to stay at the Theresa, occupying a ninth floor suite. Conveniently for the Crickets, the hotel was near the Apollo, which is located at 253 West 125th Street between Seventh and Eighth avenues. Just north of Central Park, Harlem covers six square miles of Manhattan. Though it had once represented the ultimate expression of the black spirit in America, especially in the 1920s, its streets ringing with music, laughter, and uninhibited gaiety, by the fifties Harlem was on the way to becoming an angry ghetto. Few whites ventured there unless they were drunk and looking for "poon." The Crickets were too innocent, according to Joe B., to realize they might be in danger.

To blacks, the Apollo Theater, bearing the name of the Greek god of music, retained the status of a holy shrine. When Elvis Presley visited the theater two years previously, Bo Diddley spotted him from the stage and later recalled, "I didn't know who the heck he was, but him were there." Known as the "black Vegas," the Apollo represented the ultimate night on the town for the residents of Harlem. In the fifties they dressed conservatively, meticulously conking their hair, straight as a shingle, or marcelling it into shiny, precise waves. Elegant black women in spike heels glided past the tiled walls of the narrow foyer, which was decorated with photographic murals and mirrors. Mary Johnson's refreshment stand offered candy, peanuts, ice cream, and potato chips.

Inside the auditorium, the interior reflects the Apollo's infamous past as a burlesque joint. The rear wall is covered with three nude paintings of fleshy women in baroque frames, one of them reputedly Cleopatra. The wallpaper design is made up entirely of nudes. Several roomy boxes flank the stage. On Wednesday nights the C Box on stage right was always reserved by a gaggle of flamboyant black transvestites in gaudy drag.

Backstage before the show, the Crickets climbed to their dressing room on the top floor. Anthony Gourdine of Little Anthony and the Imperials once said, "I don't care if you had nine hit records, when you first came to the Apollo you were nobody." Like any other new act, the Crickets had to walk four flights down to the stage. Contrary to the 1978 movie *The Buddy Holly Story*, which stated that the Apollo management thought the Crickets were black and didn't discover the truth until they showed up for work, the Schiffman family, who owned the theater, was aware that the Crickets were a white act. Frank Schiffman's sons, Bobby and Jack, had both caught the Crickets' act at the Howard Theater in Washington earlier in the month. The Apollo's then-manager, Leonard Reed, said that Frank Schiffman's policy was never to hire an act without knowing all about them. According to Atlantic's Ahmet Ertegun, Schiffman was regularly fed information about hot new acts by industry A&R men. Nor were the Crickets the first white faces to be seen on the Apollo stage, as *The Buddy Holly Story* also implied. Although Jack Schiffman personally informed the film's producers that Buddy Rich, Woody Herman, and other white musicians had preceded the Crickets, the producers elected to disregard the fact, said Schiffman. Unlike the other theaters on the black tour, which were shocked when the Crickets turned out to be white, the Apollo deliberately booked them because of their proven appeal to black record-buyers, who were sending "That'll Be the Day" high up the R&B charts.

On opening day, Friday, August 16, Murray Deutch sent the Crickets a telegram, assuring them that they were going to be a smash. The matinee began at 10:20 A.M. "They were wide awake early in the morning," Billie Holiday, who started at the Apollo for $50 a week, once commented.

"My knees were shaking so bad the people didn't know whether I was going to dance or sing. . . . One little broad in the front row hollered out, 'Look, she's dancing and singing at the same time.' "

At curtain time, the house band hit its warm-up and then the MC announced, "It's showtime at the Apollo!" When the Crickets' cue came, they took their places behind the crimson curtain. Anyone would have been apprehensive about following Clyde McPhatter, whose high-pitched, silky renditions of his hit records "Have Mercy, Baby" and "Without Love (There is Nothing)" always elicited the audience's roaring approval. Performers at the Apollo were also anxious to impress the booking agents—GAC, Universal, William Morris, and Associated—all of whom sent representatives to the Friday openings to scout for new talent. Also in the audience for the first show of the week were Apollo regulars Ed Sullivan, Milton Berle, and Joey Adams.

Dwarfed by the cracked and chipped imitation marble proscenium arch, the Crickets faced the audience and prepared to begin their set. Suddenly a woman in front started heckling them, leaning forward in her seat and yelling threateningly that they'd better sound *exactly* like the recording or else. Another heckler yelled, "What is this?" Watching from the wings, Ted Scott of the G-Clefs, who had a hit record called "Ka-Ding Dong," thought the Crickets put on a show that could be mentioned in the same breath with Chuck Berry, Muddy Waters, and the best artists of the Chess/Checker labels. But that didn't stop the audience from booing them, Scott recalled in 1983, and Niki, the following year, confirmed that they were a miserable flop; the audience hated them, derided their music, and was not impressed that they had cut a promising record. After two days, the Crickets were demoted to the bottom of the bill. They retreated to their dressing room, which was dirty, smelly, drafty, and roach-infested. Taking stock of their predicament, they realized, according to Niki, that they weren't up to the standards of the Apollo audiences, who'd heard the best headliners in show business and had found them wanting.

Luckily for Buddy, it was a tradition at the Apollo for the performers to monitor each other's acts and offer constructive criticism. Once his black colleagues realized how different he was from Pat Boone and other white recording artists who were covering R&B records, they accepted him as one of their own. Ted Scott realized that Buddy wasn't the type to lurk around R&B artists in order to rob them of their material. Buddy's performance had an authentic bluesy quality, Scott later told interviewer Bill Floyd.

On August 19, four days before the end of the run, "That'll Be the Day" finally showed up on the *Billboard* chart. Just before they went on-stage at the Apollo that day, Buddy suddenly told the band, "Let's open with 'Bo Diddley.' " They hadn't rehearsed it and were forced to improvise, but they caught the primal rhythm of "Bo Diddley," which at last galvanized the Apollo audience. From that performance on, the blacks accepted them and cheered their sets. To Jerry it seemed that the blacks viewed them as a novelty, but he was delighted that their Apollo engagement turned out to be a happy one.

Leslie Uggams saw Buddy at the Apollo and later described the experience to author Ted Fox. Uggams had been performing at the theater ever since making her debut on Amateur Night at the age of seven. Throughout 1957 she'd been buying Buddy's records, thinking, "Hey, another brother out there doing his number." She was under the impression that Buddy was black. At the Apollo, when the Crickets came on stage, the people around her murmured, "Oh, that's Buddy Holly!" Turning to one of them, she remarked, "He's *white*, isn't he?" Recalling Buddy's performance years later, Uggams told Ted Fox, "He was terrific . . . sexy and wonderful . . . and that's what made it happen. It wasn't that they didn't want any white acts. . . . As long as they do a great show, that's all the audience cared about."

Now that they were a hit, the Crickets relaxed and began to enjoy the Apollo's ribald backstage scene, which was "better than the show out front," Uggams recalled. Hookers masquerading as exotic dancers offered the stars "anything you could want from matzo balls to matrimony," said Chuck Berry, who frequently played the Apollo. Harlem characters drifted through hawking wristwatches, soul food, and dope. "There were drugs back in those days, mostly marijuana," Ted Scott recalled in 1983.

After the Apollo run, the Crickets went directly into Alan Freed's Labor Day rock 'n' roll extravaganza at the 4,400-seat Brooklyn Paramount, located at the corner of Flatbush and DeKalb avenues. A popular DJ on radio station WINS, Freed was rock 'n' roll's first czar. Ever since 1955, hip New York teenagers had been religiously attending his stage shows, which were held on Easter, Labor Day, and Christmas. Rehearsing for the Labor Day show, Buddy again ran into Little Richard, who was the headliner.

"I loved him dearly," said Little Richard years later. "I still love him." In *The Quasar of Rock*, Richard remembered that Buddy "used to idolize my music" and would go onstage and sing Richard's songs before Richard had a chance to. Richard used voluptuous girlfriends to lure Buddy and other straight-looking men into bisexual encounters. On one occasion he invited all the Crickets to come up to his dressing room. As they entered, an orgy was in progress. Niki recalled in the *London Daily Mail* in 1994 that the revelers ignored them and "carried right on with what they were doing." The only whites in the room, the Crickets stood against the wall, gaping. "This was definitely not our territory," Niki said in 1994. Rock star Larry Williams was making love to a woman while she gave Richard oral sex. "Everyone else was watching, like us," says Niki. After Richard and his partners were finished, Richard closed his robe and walked over to the window. For a while he stood looking out at a nearby building, a home for senior citizens. Then, according to Niki, he said he'd been wondering if the old people would would appreciate it if he paid a visit and offered to conduct a prayer meeting.

Larry Williams was a dashingly handsome, mustachioed twenty-two-year-old singer from New Orleans. In 1957 he was scoring a string of Little Richard–type hits such as "Short Fat Fanny" and "Bony Moronie." "I brought him to fame," Richard said. Later, when Richard purchased some cocaine from Williams and failed to pay for it, Williams showed up at his house with a gun to collect. Though Williams's career suffered when he was arrested for narcotics possession, he continued to grow and develop artistically over the years. *Rolling Stone* rates him among the greats, writing, "His red-hot version of 'Heeby-Jeebies' stands up to Little Richard's own smoking version." Eventually Williams committed suicide, shooting himself in the head. At his funeral, Richard sang a moving a cappella version of "Precious Lord."

Little Richard himself described the 1957 orgy with Buddy in somewhat more detail in *The Quasar of Rock*. His account differs significantly from Niki Sullivan's, but it's possible there was more than one such episode, so both Niki and Little Richard may be telling the truth. According to Richard, Buddy appeared in his dressing room while "I was jacking off," said Little Richard, adding that a girl was "sucking my titty." Instead of leaving, Buddy stayed and quickly became aroused. After watching Richard and the girl for a few minutes, Buddy unzipped his pants. "He was ready," Richard remembered. "She opened up her legs and he put it in her." While Buddy and the girl had intercourse, she "was sucking me," Richard continued. Suddenly, with all of them at the height of passion, they heard Buddy's name announced from the stage. Had Buddy been less determined, the tryst would have turned into a case of coitus interruptus, but Buddy went for a spectacular finish and "he made it, too," Richard said. "He came and he went!" As Buddy greeted the audience he was still zipping up his fly. In Little Richard's account, he identifies the girl, but the girl denies participating in such an orgy.

September 5, 1957, the final day of the Brooklyn Paramount run, was also publication day for Jack Kerouac's beat generation novel *On the Road*. The *New York Times* hailed it as a "historic occasion." The *Times*'s regular book reviewer, square, conservative Orville Prescott, had gone on vacation, so his replacement, Gilbert Millstein, who was excited by the emerging beat literature, got a chance. In this odd way, a legend was born.

Shortly the book went onto the *Times* best-seller list and created a national sensation.

Though beatniks preferred jazz, their true musical counterpart was rock 'n' roll, for both the beatniks and rock forced upon the world a convulsive new freedom in which outmoded moral and artistic constraints were smashed. Like Buddy Holly, Kerouac at heart wanted to be a Negro. In *On the Road* he wrote, "At lilac evening I walked with every muscle aching amongst the lights of 27th and Welton in the Denver colored section wishing I were a Negro, feeling that the best the white world has offered me was not enough ecstasy for me, not enough life, joy, kicks, darkness, music, not enough night." He could have been speaking as well for Buddy Holly.

One bright autumn day in 1957, the Crickets climbed to the roof of the Brooklyn Paramount to pose for the cover photograph of their first album, *The Chirping Crickets*. Their exultant smiles make it clear that the Crickets were intoxicated by recent triumphs. In the last few days they'd made their network television debut, performing on Freed's *Rock 'n' Roll Show* on ABC-TV and Dick Clark's *American Bandstand*, an after-school rock danceathon. For the Clark show they went to Philadelphia on Monday, August 26, the same day the Ford Motor Company unveiled the Edsel, which retailed for $2,400. *American Bandstand* would soon become the major showcase for rock groups in the United States; its success turned Philadelphia into a busy recording center. "Everyone you met was raging and racing, twenty-four hours a day, seven days a week, and existed for nothing but hype," Phil Spector observed. "A real glee was involved." Scheduled to go on the *Bandstand* at 2:30 P.M., the Crickets entered the studio carrying their garment bags and were cordially greeted by the twenty-seven-year-old Clark, who radiated a clean-cut Young Republican handsomeness. Rock was not a passion with him but a means to wealth and power; his own musical taste ran to easy-listening discount classics, the kind advertised on TV, like "Stranger in Paradise," based on Borodin's "Polovetsian Dances." "There were no skeletons in his split-level closet, just a lot of two-button jackets and ties," wrote Richard Goldstein. The Crickets hurried to their dressing room to get ready for the show.

The set for *American Bandstand*, a hot, brightly lit area, was smaller than it looked on TV. Just before showtime, two hundred teenagers filed in and sat on the bleachers, eager to hop up and dance at the first opportunity. A signboard listed the week's top hits, headed by Debbie Reynolds's "Tammy," Elvis's "(Let Me Be Your) Teddy Bear," Paul Anka's "Diana," the Coasters' "Searchin'," and Pat Boone's "Love Letters in the Sand."

At the start of the telecast, Clark stepped onto a makeshift podium and introduced the Crickets. As soon as they struck up "That'll Be the

Day," the bleachers emptied out and the teenagers started dancing. All across the United States, twenty million kids sat glued to their sets, as entranced by the sight of other teenagers dancing as they were by the lip-synched performance of the Crickets. One of the dancers, fourteen-year-old Kenny Rossi, had become a full-fledged celebrity in his own right, with 301 fan clubs, far more than the musicians had who appeared on the show. Rossi was a jet-haired, fair-skinned Philadelphia dreamboat, and when he took his favorite partner, a winsome blond named Justine Corelli, in his arms and started to dance, he upstaged everyone on *American Bandstand*.

After their performance, the Crickets sat at an autograph table, signing their 45-rpm records, and then returned to New York. Immediately following the Brooklyn Paramount run, they were to leave on promoter Irving Feld's eighty-day, seventy-city rock 'n' roll package tour with many of the biggest stars of the day, including the Everly Brothers, Buddy Knox, Paul Anka, Chuck Berry, Frankie Lymon, and Fats Domino. One day before their departure, Petty came to the Crickets' room at the Edison and discovered Buddy and Jerry sitting on the bed with all their money spread out around them. They were playing with it. Petty suggested that it would be a good idea if he opened a Crickets account and placed their money in it. Joe B. was curious to know exactly how the account would be set up and whether individual Crickets would be able to withdraw sums without getting approval from the other members of the band. The officious Petty immediately made it clear that *he* was the sole party who'd have access to the account, proposing that they each retain $100 from their $1,000 weekly pay and send the rest to him. He promised to bank it and pay their bills.

The arrangement proved unsatisfactory from the start. Anytime the Crickets inquired about their bank balance, Petty grew vague and evasive. When pressed, he said that if the Crickets had bothered to keep proper records, they'd know that they'd gone through everything. His secretary, Norma Jean Berry, backed him up, saying the Crickets wasted all their money on expensive baubles. Norma Jean served as an effective mouthpiece for all of Petty's operations and even wrote fulsome stories about him in the *Clovis News-Journal*, crowing that "Norman Petty has put Clovis, New Mexico, right smack dab in the spotlight in the music world." An obvious promotional piece for Petty's studio, Norma Jean's story stressed how difficult it was "to break [into] the big time" and claimed that Petty could "make the way easier for . . . rising stars in the entertainment world by aiding them in the climb to stardom."

The Crickets were still very young—Joe B. was eighteen, Jerry was nineteen; and Niki and Buddy were twenty—and all too often they acted their age. Relinquishing their money to a man like Petty was but one example. Horseplay that sometimes seemed to careen out of control was another. Niki and Jerry had a water-squirting contest that turned into a fistfight. Niki punched Jerry in the eye. Though Jerry dismissed the altercation as jejune high jinks, a cut under his left cheek was bad enough to show up in the cover photo on *The Chirping Crickets*. They could also be very close and affectionate. There is a touching photo showing them celebrating Jerry's birthday in their cramped hotel room: the Crickets are kneeling beside a bed on which a big birthday cake is surrounded by a sunburst arrangement of lollipops. Jerry's middle name, Ivan, has been spelled out underneath the cake in what appears to be sugared candle holders. The display had obviously been created with great care and love. As the boys posed for the photographer, Joe B. grabbed Jerry in a close hug, pressing his cheek to Jerry's temple. Buddy and Niki form the other close unit in the photo, and they appear to be very proud of their handiwork.

Norma Jean Berry's charge that the Crickets wasted their money had little basis in fact. They did some shopping in New York, but many of their expenditures involved essentials such as stage clothes. Don and Phil Everly thought the Crickets looked atrocious, comparing them to gauche provincials. Don and Phil had been in Manhattan a few times more than the Crickets and were feeling very urbane when they arrived for the Irving Feld "Biggest Show of Stars" tour and started practicing in a basement rehearsal space. (In some interviews Don says they didn't meet until Montreal, where the tour would play on September 15.) Eyeing the Crickets' old-fogey clothes, Don chided them for wearing gray Texas business suits that looked weird in New York. Don recalled, "They saw what we were wearing and said, 'Gee whiz!' The only publicity picture they had then was of them all down in Lubbock, Texas, in T-shirts, settling tiles on the roof." Don marched them over to Phil's Men's Shop, a Third Avenue emporium frequented mostly by gay males and hip musicians. The Crickets and the Everlys purchased sleek Ivy League single-breasted three-button suits and trousers with buckles in back. "We got to be very close friends with Buddy Holly and the Crickets," Don told *Rolling Stone*'s Kurt Loder in 1986, "because we all had the same kind of country-blues background."

The Everlys' second single, "Wake Up Little Susie," was on its way to the top of both the pop and C&W charts. The boys were so dashing that the groupies who chased them everywhere they went referred to them as "the Foreverlys." Don and Phil advised Buddy to get rid of his "old-fashioned" clear-plastic-and-silver eyeglasses, showing him where to find thick horn-rim frames like the ones Steve Allen popularized on *The Tonight Show*. Phil says they became best friends, spending all their time together, and that he helped Buddy adjust to big-city ways.

As the other stars of the tour arrived in New York in September, their circle expanded to include Buddy Knox, Eddie Cochran, Chuck Berry, Gene Vincent, Dave Somerville, and Jimmy Bowen. Buddy Holly's closest friends among the new arrivals were Cochran and Somerville. Like Holly, Cochran was a product of the Southwest, born in Oklahoma City in 1938. He grew up in Albert Lea, Minnesota, and got his start in Bell Gardens, California, singing in a C&W brother act with Hank Cochran (no relation), who went on to become a C&W star. Holly's other new friend, Dave Somerville, was the handsome lead singer of the Diamonds, the group that had covered "Words of Love" and scored two more hits in 1957, "Silhouettes" and "The Stroll." Buddy Knox christened the clique the Young Rockers. Frequently they'd all grab their guitars, take a cab down to Greenwich Village, and invade a nightclub called the Village Gate, located at the corner of Bleecker and Thompson streets. Holly, Knox, Cochran, and Vincent would pick with each other until last call at four A.M. Some of these singers would not join the forthcoming tour until it reached the West Coast.

One day Chuck Berry took them all to Lindy's Restaurant at 51st Street and Broadway, just above Times Square, for their first taste of New York cheesecake. Times Square, where Seventh Avenue and Broadway meet between 42nd and 47th streets, is the place people mean when they say Broadway. In the evening it became the Great White Way, a jumble of flashing neon signs and a surge of restless people, moving beneath a fifty-eight-foot-tall cigarette billboard from which a smoker blew perfect smoke rings. The latest news dispatches circled the Motogram on the Times Tower. There were thirty theaters in the area, including the Palace, the Winter Garden, the Music Box, the Shubert, the Booth, the Mark Hellinger, and, of course, the Paramount, though it would shortly fall victim to the wrecking ball. Lindy's would also pass from the scene, but in the fifties, the aroma of corned beef and kosher dills greeted customers as they entered. Tourists were shown to the left, regulars—an assortment of Damon Runyonesque characters—sat on the right. Holding forth almost daily at Table No. 1 were comics Milton Berle, Red Buttons, George Jessel, Henny Youngman, Jack E. Leonard, and Buddy Hackett, who specialized in cutting each other to pieces with gags like "If Moses saw you, he would have invented another commandment."

Refering to the joys of dining out in Manhattan, Don Everly said, "We all got into that real quick." None of the Young Rockers had ever traveled before, and suddenly they were at the crossroads of the world, their pockets full of money, surrounded by gifted friends. They all found it thrilling. "There was a real camaraderie there at the beginning of rock 'n' roll," Don said.

Buddy's Knox's room at the Edison became their headquarters as they waited to leave on the eighty-day Feld tour. There was always a poker game going on, usually involving Holly, Jerry, Joe B., Don Lanier, Jimmy Bowen, and Don Kirshner. Knox remembers Kirshner as an ambitious person who always trailed along in their wake, attempting to persuade them to record his tunes. Later Kirshner became a power in the music business, launching Neil Sedaka and the Monkees, and hosted the seventies TV show, *Don Kirshner's Rock Concert*, a pioneering forerunner of MTV.

On occasion Eddie Cochran would pull up at the Edison in a long white limo and join the poker game in Knox's room. Endowed with sultry bedroom eyes and deep dimples, Cochran rivaled Elvis as the best-looking of the first-generation rock stars. According to his sideman Dave Shriver, "drinking beer and playing with the girls" occupied Cochran's offstage time. The "Okie chicks," five groupies who'd latched on to Cochran in Tulsa, followed him like a sultan's harem, servicing his every need. Says Niki Sullivan, "Everybody had a good time whenever Eddie Cochran was around."

The Everlys considered Cochran the biggest make-out artist among them, someone who could pick up a girl just by looking at her. Phil Everly noted that Cochran didn't even have to come up with a line when he approached a girl, didn't have to utter a single word. Phil once saw Cochran seduce an airline stewardess in midflight. "Got her in the back of the plane," Phil later told journalist Kurt Loder. Associating with good-looking teen idols like Cochran and the Everlys motivated Buddy to improve his physical appearance. During the following winter, beginning December 14, 1957, he would pay a dentist $600 to cap his front teeth, removing the unsightly brown stains left by Lubbock's water. He consulted a dermatologist about his acne. Though Buddy had naturally wavy hair, he got a permanent from an overzealous Manhattan barber who "kinked" it, getting it too tight. Nevertheless, Buddy scored regularly with eastern girls. One day he and Niki were walking in midtown Manhattan when Buddy suddenly ducked into an apartment building, explaining that he had a date with a girl songwriter who'd promised him a "quickie." Niki waited outside on the street for the assignation to run its course.

During the Crickets' stay at the Edison, Buddy Knox's room was trashed. Knox was taking a shower when he heard a commotion in his bedroom and ran out, naked, to see what was going on. The Crickets, Petty, and Ray Ruff had come by to invite Knox to go to the movies. Knox decided to join them. Hastily pulling on his clothes, he forgot to turn off the shower. When they returned from the movies they saw fire-trucks in front of the hotel, which they soon learned had been flooded. Knox's room was totaled, and the whole floor had been turned into a swamp.

A favorite pastime of Holly's that autumn was visiting Manny's Music Store in Manhattan. He spent hours inspecting the guitars and discussing their relative merits with clerk Henry Goldrich. Holly first came in with Buddy Knox in 1957, Goldrich recalls. Holly lifted a Les Paul guitar with some difficulty and said it was far too weighty; so was the Stratocaster, for that matter, but Buddy said it was his own fault, laying the blame on his lean build. Over the following year, Holly became one of Goldrich's best customers, purchasing a Gibson J-200 acoustic, two white Stratocasters, a Guild F-50 Navarre acoustic, a Magnatone Custom 280 amp, and a Gibson Stereo GA series amp.

The "Show of Stars" tour party set out for Pittsburgh on September 6, rolling across the George Washington Bridge at three A.M. in a pair of Greyhound buses. The towers of the 3,500-foot-long suspension bridge, which has linked the island of Manhattan to the U.S. mainland since 1931, looked like a magnificent doorway to America, arching high above them as they passed over the mighty Hudson River. Filled with a sense of adventurous possibility, they were going into the country, many of them for the first time. They would discover their newfound stardom while exploring their homeland "from sea to shining sea," from the mountains of Pennsylvania to Los Angeles on the roaring Pacific Coast.

According to evidence recently discovered by Bill Griggs, including hotel receipts and a contract, Buddy and the Crickets remained behind in New York for three days, camping out at the Brooklyn Paramount. They missed the tour's first engagements, scheduled for Pittsburgh and Norfolk, and later caught up with the tour buses, which were packed with all-star passengers including the Everly Brothers, LaVern Baker, Paul Anka, Frankie Lymon, Clyde McPhatter, Jimmy Bowen, the Drifters, and the Bobettes. Guitars, drums, and amps were jammed in among the performers, many of whom brought aboard sacks of fried chicken and then left the picked bones under their seats. The buses rumbled across the American continent, crossing the Blue Ridge Mountains and the Shenandoah Valley of Virginia, passing battlefields commemorating the Civil War that had torn the country apart less than a century previously. A long night's run of almost 400 miles on September 9–10 took them northwest into Ohio's Appalachian Plateau for a show at the Akron Armory on the tenth, then across the fertile Ohio plains for appearances at the Cincinnati Gardens on the eleventh and the Veteran's Memorial Auditorium in Columbus on the twelfth. Backtracking to Hershey, Pennsylvania, home of the famous chocolate candy bar, they played the Sports Arena on the thirteenth before heading north into Canada.

Before one of their shows, Jimmy Bowen, who'd hit the charts with "I'm Stickin' With You," stood backstage watching Buddy and the Crickets just before their set. Buddy seemed remarkably composed, far less nervous than the others on the tour. "For someone that age, he had his shit together," Bowen told Griggs in 1980. The Crickets went on and roared through "Blueberry Hill," "Roll Over Beethoven," and "Brown-Eyed Handsome Man." Though their set was brief, approximately ten minutes, they remained onstage throughout most of the show, accompanying the other acts. Buddy was delighted when it became clear that the Crickets were the audience's favorite. Every time they got an encore, Buddy would say, "Wasn't that fun?"

One-night stands meant traveling all night and arriving in the next town barely in time for the show. The stars caught what sleep they could sitting up in their seats or sprawled across the aisle, like LaVern Baker, who used her suitcases as a makeshift bed. Phil Everly said everyone loved LaVern, the great R&B singer whose hits included "Jim Dandy," because she could always be counted on to patch up your jacket or sew your buttons on.

Buddy, who'd just turned twenty-one on September, 7, 1957, shot craps in the back of the bus with Chuck Berry. Bus driver Tommy Tompkins, who thought of Buddy as a clean-cut, well-mannered boy, watched a game one night and was shocked at Buddy's expertise at throwing dice; no one, Tompkins later told interviewers Nick Rossi and George Block, was shrewder or more streetwise than Buddy. When not shooting craps, Chuck Berry passed the time by writing the lyrics to "You Can't Catch Me," later adding the melody during dressing-room jams or "in lonely afternoon hotel rooms with the guitar as a guide," Berry related in his autobiography. After a sizable royalty check caught up with Berry at one of their stops, he bought a Cadillac. Joe B. had become friendly with Berry and hitched rides in the Cadillac, a luxurious first-class treat compared with the squalor of the bus. At thirty one, Berry was about ten years older than the others on the tour, and Joe B. often went to him for advice. Berry would stop whatever he was doing and invite Joe B. to relax and tell him his problems.

"It was a bus loaded with everybody in the Top 10," Phil Everly later recalled. An amazing group, it contained the future of rock 'n' roll. Frankie Lymon was the life of the party, getting everyone to sing and make up songs, partying all night during long bus rides. Unfortunately, he was bombing onstage. Though his adolescent soprano voice had charmed audiences on a previous "Show of Stars" tour, his voice was changing and audiences didn't like it. His decision to drop his group the Teenagers after their hit "Why Do Fools Fall in Love" was a mistake; success eluded him when his label, Gee, tried to groom him as another Sammy Davis, Jr. Only fourteen years old, Lymon was shooting up heroin and sleeping with a leggy showgirl twice his age. He was busted during one of the tour's Canadian stops in what Niki Sullivan describes as a carefully planned police raid. After staking out Lymon's drug connection, the police broke into his hotel room, but he was released in time to continue with the tour. On the bus, Lymon's racy language offended Tommy Tompkins, who said that Lymon showed no respect for the younger members of the tour, such as the Bobettes, a girl group whose hit record, "Mr. Lee," was named after their principal at P.S. 109 in New York. Lymon was ordered off Tompkins's bus, but Carl Vesterdahl, the driver of the other Greyhound, came to his rescue.

Popular music had never had to deal with such situations before; rock 'n' roll saw the emergence of very young performers, some not yet fifteen, which represented a complete break from the past, when singers like Perry Como, Frank Sinatra, and the Andrews Sisters were thought of as very mature—and were. Paul Anka had just turned sixteen and had the No. 1 hit, "Diana," which he'd written about his siblings' baby-sitter. Described as "a billion volts of energy" by Niki, Anka was goofing backstage during Buddy's performance when he kicked a plug out of a socket, killing the sound. Striding offstage, Buddy cursed so loud that the packed auditorium overheard him. Nevertheless, Buddy respected Anka's songwriting gifts; the two entered into an agreement to write songs for each other. In Anka's native Canada, where they played the Montreal Forum on September 15, thirty thousand teenagers jammed the two sold-out performances, and police had to turn away hundreds of ticket seekers.

"Peggy Sue"/"Everyday," Buddy's first Coral solo record, released while they were in Winston-Salem, North Carolina, on September 20, was hailed by *Billboard* as a rockabilly record that could "cop plenty of pop and C&W coin." "Everyday" was a cross-over tune "with a folkish flavor," the reviewer added. *Cash Box* saluted Buddy as "a newcomer who's broken into the star category." He had indeed. On September 23, "That'll Be the Day" hit No. 1 on the *Billboard* chart. Niki later couldn't remember exactly where or when they heard the news, except that it was on the road in autumn of 1957. The Crickets rushed to a phone booth near the theater where they were playing and tried to cram themselves inside. They called Clovis and talked to Petty, who got Decca executives from New York and Los Angeles on a tie line and asked them to confirm that the record had sold a million. It was true; their first record was a monster hit. Dashing back to the theater, they ran onstage and breathlessly shared their triumph with the audience, announcing their million-seller. The crowd burst into a thunderous ovation. The Crickets did four encores that night, the only group on the show that was called back so many times.

The tour entered the white-supremacist Deep South at about the same time Arkansas exploded in racial violence. At the beginning of September 1957, Governor Orval Faubus, rabid opponent of integration, had defied U.S. federal law and ordered state militia to Little Rock to stop black students from enrolling in Central High. President Eisenhower summoned Faubus to a meeting and ordered him to obey the U.S. Supreme Court's integration ruling. On September 25, Ike sent in federal troops, who pointed their bayonets at fifteen hundred white agitators while escorting nine Negroes into Central High. Though the integrated rock 'n' roll tour of which Buddy was a part did not play Arkansas, trouble awaited them as soon as they crossed the Mason-Dixon Line. In Louisiana and Georgia, the whites and blacks on the bill couldn't drive in the same cars or buses and had to book separate hotels. In New Orleans, racist laws even prohibited them from performing on the same stage together. The Crickets, Paul Anka, the Everlys, and the other whites had to leave the show until it finished the southern portion of the tour.

While the blacks carried on, the Crickets enjoyed a three-day break. The tour had been especially difficult on Niki, who later said he didn't care for the "lifestyle." Basic routines such as trying to eat three meals a day and going to the Laundromat were all but impossible on a tour of one-night stands. It was an unhealthy and exhausting way to live. The hazing and horseplay that the Crickets reveled in were an anathema to Niki, who had grown up as an only child and a loner. Besides the petty arguments and fisticuffs among the Crickets, he disliked the way they took out their frustrations on him, he later disclosed in Goldrosen and Beecher's *Remembering Buddy*. One day they went into a restaurant for dinner, and everyone ordered steaks except Niki, who loved waffles and often ate them at lunch or dinner. The Crickets picked on him throughout the meal for eating a breakfast food at dinner. To Joe B. it was all in fun, but it grated on Niki, who was also dissatisfied with his peripheral role in the band. As its rhythm guitarist, he wasn't miked on some of their records, since Buddy's virtuosic attack on the guitar provided both lead and rhythm. Niki started thinking about leaving and getting his own record deal. When he dropped hints about his intentions, no one in the band tried to dissuade him.

The tour regrouped and resumed regular performances in Tulsa on September 28. On the same date, the Norman Petty Trio was playing the Officers Club at Tinker Air Force Base in Oklahoma City, 104 miles west of Tulsa. Since the Crickets needed some more tracks to fill out their first LP, *The Chirping Crickets*, which was to be released in December, Petty arranged for them to record in a corner of the main room of the Officers Club. The acoustics at Tinker AFB were fantastic, far superior to many of the studios they'd recorded in.

One of the Tinker cuts was "An Empty Cup and a Broken Date," a desolate tune by Roy Orbison about a boy who's been jilted in a drive-in. Though Orbison resented Buddy's success and had been making snide remarks such as " 'Blue Days, Black Nights' sounded just like Elvis," he began to court Buddy once "That'll Be the Day" hit the top of the charts. He hoped Buddy would record some of the songs he'd been writing. As a singer, Roy had become discouraged, partly due to a sour experience with Norman Petty. Roy recorded "Ooby Dooby" at Petty's studio but had to sue in order to break free from an unfair contract in which Petty grabbed "half the writer's share and all of the publishing," Roy confided to Odessa attorney John R. Lee. After extricating himself from Clovis, Roy went to Memphis and rerecorded the song at Sun Records. This time "Ooby Dooby" was a hit, though Roy's subsequent efforts at Sun proved unsatisfactory.

Moving to Nashville, Orbison concentrated on songwriting and pitched "Claudette" to the Everly Brothers. Luckily for Roy, they put it on the B-side of their No. 1 record "All I Have to Do Is Dream" and Roy collected $25,000 in royalties. It was around this time that Buddy recorded Roy's "An Empty Cup" at Tinker AFB, along with another Orbison tune, "You've Got Love," written in collaboration with Little Johnny Wilson, a member of Orbison's band the Teen Kings. "You've Got Love" has a typically self-abnegating Orbison lyric about how worthless and incomplete he felt without a woman. Claudette Frady, the beautiful girl in "Claudette," was dating Little Johnny Wilson, who, though only five-foot-two, was considered the sexiest of the West Texas rockabillies. Roy was infatuated with Claudette and eventually persuaded her to marry him. Although he wrote the immortal "Pretty Woman" for her, their relationship was a calamitous one, marked by infidelity, divorce, Claudette's fatal motorcycle accident, and the deaths of two of their small children by fire.

"You've Got Love" would not be one of Buddy's successful records, but in a later version recorded by Little Johnny Wilson, who added "Peanuts" to his name when he became a Brunswick recording artist, it became a rockabilly classic, along with the B-side, "Cast Iron Arms," another Orbison-Wilson collaboration.

The pièce de résistance of Buddy's Tinker AFB session was "Maybe Baby." This was his second attempt to record the song, and at Tinker he got it right at last. Unlike the flat Clovis version, the Oklahoma City "Maybe Baby" soars with the same intensity and rhythmic abandon as "Oh Boy." *Rolling Stone* places it among the all-time "rock classics." Buddy's mother deserves part of the credit for "Maybe Baby." For some time Mrs. Holley had been trying to persuade Buddy to record one of her songs, but he always found them too sad and dreamy and advised her to write lyrics that were perkier and more fun. When she gave him a few lines of

"Maybe Baby," he smiled and told her she was on the right track. He finished the lyrics and wrote the music, using the drum beat from Little Richard's "Lucille." As a member of Tabernacle Baptist Church, Mrs. Holley preferred not to have her name on a rock 'n' roll record and asked Buddy to keep her contribution a secret. Joe B. said he also participated in the composition of "Maybe Baby," but he was elbowed aside by Petty, who, as usual, appropriated cowriting credit with Buddy.

Carl Perkins and Buddy met in Oklahoma City, spotting each other backstage, Perkins later told British DJ Stuart Coleman. In conversation Perkins found Buddy to be humble and soft-spoken, but the minute he went onstage, "he was *fire*," Perkins remarked to interviewer Wayne Jones in 1980. Buddy was aware, Perkins added, that he'd invented his own sound, one that was quite different from the Sun sound, and he was intent on developing it and growing as a songwriter.

Perkins was having a hard time in his personal life in 1957, following the success of "Blue Suede Shoes" the previous year. "You can't take the strain without a crutch," Perkins said. "For me it was booze—I've seen the bottom of a lot of bottles. I was a mess, a wreck for years."

The Feld tour came within 209 miles of Lubbock when it played Wichita Falls, Texas, but, amazingly, Lubbock didn't book the show. As Clyde McPhatter once said, "You can't even draw flies eating watermelon around your hometown." Waco, with a population well under one hundred thousand—about half the size of Lubbock's—managed to get the show in October, as did numerous other Texas cities, including Fort Worth, Dallas, San Antonio, Corpus Christi, Houston, Austin, and El Paso. Larry Holley has some scathing observations on Lubbock's indifference to its most famous son:

"There's nobody in Lubbock that's interested in him. I'll tell you the actual fact—if Buddy was to be alive right now [1992] with his fame and we decided to have a concert here in Lubbock, and they did not let anybody know about it but the people in Lubbock, there wouldn't be a thousand people comin' to it. It's just Lubbock, this area—they could care less. They'd rather go to a basketball game or a rodeo. Now if there was going to be a [tribute] concert with everyone he influenced [for example, the Beatles, The Rolling Stones, Clapton, Dylan, Ronstadt], and they let the word get out to the world, they'd come in from every direction. But if it was just exclusively for Lubbock, they wouldn't have a thousand people. I wish you'd put that in your book."

While they were in Waco for an appearance at the Heart of Texas Fair, Buddy and Niki discovered that they were third cousins. "There were about thirty-five people in the audience for the afternoon show and they were all related to me and Buddy," Niki recalled in a 1995 interview. "We treated it like a jam session. No one was at the matinee because of school, I guess. But they showed up for the evening show, which was packed."

"Peggy Sue" hit the charts while they were in Texas in October 1957, making Buddy the only star on the tour with two smash records. Oddly, the Crickets were still hurting for money. "Norman Petty was actually taking their money," Larry said in 1992. "Buddy told me, 'I can't even tithe because I don't have any money for the church.' Norman told Buddy, 'Well, I'm tithing with ya'll's money here at our church and it goes to the same place.' Which it don't. Norman kept them broke all the time, havin' to ask for money. He got all the money in, did what he wanted to with it. He built that big pipe organ in that church up there [in Clovis] with some of the money."

Niki confirmed, in a 1984 interview with Jack Miller, that their financial issues were one of the factors behind his quitting the band. Niki's father tried to get to the bottom of it, going to Clovis and asking to audit the Crickets' account. Petty said the books were with his accountant. Niki's father returned to Clovis with the same request, but Petty again found some excuse to conceal the books from him. Following Mr. Sullivan's inquiries, Petty made no efforts to shore up Niki's position, which was already shaky due to personality conflicts in the band, according to Petty's interview with Brooks and Malcolm in 1983. Niki later told interviewer Steve Bonner that he saw the handwriting on the wall before the end of the tour and that the only thing he missed about being a Cricket was getting to meet people like Chuck Berry, one of his favorite performers.

After Texas, the tour moved west, bound for California. The road unwound endlessly as they crossed the New Mexico and Arizona wastes, where the spaces are so immense and empty that, on a perfectly clear and sunny day, you can see a weather system miles ahead as it bumps into a mountaintop and cascades down the ridges, spewing rain and hail. As Tom Snyder writes in Michael Wallis's *Route 66: The Mother Road*, "By the time we reached the rimrock country of New Mexico and Arizona . . . everything seemed connected in some intangible way. I sensed something resonant in the cliff faces, in the sky, in the endless run of highway beneath. Something that seemed to be in me, too."

Don Everly received tragic news when they played the Catalina High School Auditorium in Tucson, Arizona, on October 10. His wife, Mary Sue, had given birth to their daughter, Mary E. Everly, but the infant died on the same day and was interred in the Everly family plot in Central City, Kentucky. Ironically, at the same time, the Everlys' "Wake Up Little Susie," released over the objections of producer Archie Bleyer, who warned that the record would be banned because it sounded like Susie and her boyfriend were making out at the drive-in—hit No. 1. "Wake

Up Little Susie" went on to become their second million-seller, but, sadly, there would be no waking up little Mary Everly.

When they reached the West Coast, major changes were made in the cast. The Bobettes, the Spaniels, and Johnnie and Joe dropped out. Eddie Cochran, Buddy Knox, and Jimmy Bowen and the Rhythm Orchids took their places. Cochran's friend Johnny Rowe later revealed in Alan Clark's *Tribute to Eddie Cochran* that Frankie Lymon and Buddy were the performers Cochran was especially drawn to in the "Biggest Show of Stars for 1957" package. Connie "Guybo" Smith, Cochran's stand-up bass player, remembered riding on the same bus with Holly and Cochran and was present when they jammed during off-duty hours on several occasions. Cochran was happiest when surrounded by musical friends, trying out lyrics and arrangements for new songs or simply picking together. Afterward, he would stay up late with his friends, talking and flexing his wit and intellect, like bright young people have always done. Buddy later told his mother that he and Cochran became intimate friends and made some recordings together, though these tapes have never been released.

Both Holly and Cochran carried pistols. For Cochran, it was just a matter of fun; he liked to practice his draw when he got bored during tedious tours. For Buddy it was a practical matter; he acquired his gun when he started collecting the Crickets' performance fees directly from the promoters, some of whom were shady characters and might require coercion. It was a not uncommon practice among performers in the fifties. Brenda Lee, who toured with Elvis, Chuck Berry, Patsy Cline, and J. P. "The Big Bopper" Richardson, once said that you must always get a "first count"—that is, go to the box office for your money before the show— or the promoter would slip out the back and you'd never be paid.

Buddy proved more efficient at collecting the Crickets' money than he was at distributing it, doling out cash to his musicians at whim. Inevitably the Crickets' finances ended up in a mess. In his own way, he was acting rather like Norman Petty, but Jerry later insisted to Goldrosen and Beecher that Buddy was too decent to have been capable of exploiting or cheating the Crickets. Nonetheless Jerry also stated that Buddy probably owed them money; he withheld their share at times, but at other times they received an amount in excess of their exact percentage. Financially, it was a pretty hopeless situation.

On the road, Buddy concealed his .22 in his shaving kit. Cochran, a crack shot, was bolder, brandishing his gun in hotel rooms. "He was . . . into quick-draw and loved to practice out on the desert," Eddie's sister, Pat Hickey, told *Albert Lea Tribune* reporter Lauri Winters in 1994. While on tour, Cochran would often stand in front of a bureau mirror, joking about how he could beat himself to the draw. He gave a gun to Jack Scott, a musician who toured with him, and the two of them tried to outdraw each other. Scott confirms that Cochran was probably the fastest gun in rock 'n' roll.

Playing with guns was the undoing of another rock pioneer, twenty-five-year-old Johnny Ace, who shot himself in the mouth during a game of Russian roulette at a Houston concert in 1954. His posthumous hit "Pledging My Love" became one of rock's first anthems. In the early 1950s young people had no idols, and Johnny Ace was the first in a succession of blood-smeared heroes who made death look cool. With twenty-four-year-old James Dean's fatal car crash just one year after Johnny Ace died, a strange cult developed. Danger and death became essential ingredients of the rock-generation ethos from the start, infusing young people with a sense of tragedy. Until the great liberations of the sixties, death seemed the only exit from the conformist, materialistic world of the fifties, which seemed to snuff out the sensitive and gifted, like poet Sylvia Plath, or drive them to nervous breakdowns, like Seymour Glass and Holden Caulfield, the doomed fictional heroes of J. D. Salinger's novels and short stories.

Besides their penchant for guns, Buddy Holly and Eddie Cochran had many other traits in common. They were both homeboys who loved their mothers' cooking, and they'd probably have gone rabbit hunting together under circumstances less confining than the tour. Cochran referred to his mother, Alice Cochran, as "Shrimper," and each time a tour ended, he'd call her and say, "Shrimper, I'm coming home. Put on the pan of corn-bread and beans," Mrs. Cochran remembered in 1991. Like Holly, Cochran at first struck many people as socially recessive, listening quietly at parties as people revealed themselves to him. He wasn't shy; he was simply deciding whom he wanted to focus on. Once he liked someone, he let them know it in subtle, quietly endearing ways. As Dick Clark put it, "Reserved, intense, he can stare you down with a look that, I'm told, makes a girl's knees go weak."

In buses caked with desert dust, the tour party approached the sprawling, arid basin of Southern California in October. They arrived in Los Angeles on the fourteenth and were greeted by hot Santa Ana winds that blew grit into their eyes. In the fifties, L.A. was a collection of seedy towns like Hawthorne, where the future Beach Boys were growing up, and Pacoima, where young Ritchie Valens was still singing Mexican corridos at gang dances. The corridos were traditional folk ballads, updated to embrace contemporary themes. Around L.A. Valens was known as the "Little Richard of the San Fernando Valley."

The fledgling L.A. rockabilly scene included Ricky Nelson, Lorrie Collins, Wanda Jackson, and songwriter Sharon Sheeley. Earlier in 1957 Ricky had become a teen idol, singing and promoting his record "I'm Walking" on his parents' TV show, The Adventures of Ozzie and Harriet.

Ricky had fallen in love with Lorrie Collins, who, with her little brother Larry, sang rockabilly as the Collins Kids on the popular L.A. Saturday night *Town Hall Party* C&W television series. Ricky and Lorrie wanted to get married, but Lorrie was only fifteen, Ricky was seventeen, and their parents objected. The romance ended abruptly when Lorrie married a man nineteen years her senior. Ricky was devastated. "Rick Nelson was like the heartthrob of the world," Lorrie said. "Poor me. I just adored him. It was pretty awful, and it was my fault." Buddy Holly and Ricky Nelson would meet later on, and Ricky would cover many of Buddy's songs, including "Rave On" and "True Love Ways."

Buddy knew Wanda Jackson, a brunette beauty, from the Hank Thompson tour the previous year. She had been one of Elvis Presley's girlfriends, and Elvis had urged her to sing rock 'n' roll. In 1957 she returned to L.A. to record "Let's Have a Party," "Fujiyama Mama," and other rockabilly classics. "West Coast rockabilly found its fullest female expression in Wanda Jackson," wrote authors Mary A. Bufwack and Robert K. Oermann. "With her snarling, powerhouse singing, Wanda Jackson captured the elemental, low-class wildness of this music better than any other female of her day."

The L.A. that Buddy and the "Biggest Show of Stars" tour discovered in 1957 was at its height as a supermarket of cockeyed metaphysical urges; a neon sign on La Brea advertised "Car Wash and Mind Control." It was also Shelley Winters and Marilyn Monroe lunching at Schwab's Drug Store; Frances Fay headlining on the Sunset Strip; Mildred Pierce–type restaurants with hostesses who showed you to numbered booths; and nice apartments on Holloway Drive that could be rented for $227 a month. The glamour of the fabled movie studios was quickly vanishing; the ground beneath them was now worth more than their productions and would soon be turned into real estate. The movie executives of the future would not be studio chiefs in the tradition of Louis B. Mayer and Darryl F. Zanuck, but builders of plastic palaces for kids, like Disneyland, which opened in Anaheim on July 17, 1955.

Buddy checked into the Hilton Hotel with the tour party and played the Shrine Auditorium the following night. Standing backstage, songwriter Sharon Sheeley fell in love with Cochran at first sight. To Sheeley, Cochran was a golden-haired Elvis Presley who projected a ripe sensuality. Phil Everly told her to get over Cochran as quickly as possible, mindful of Cochran's prodigious sex life. It was useless; she was hooked. She became Cochran's girlfriend and co-wrote his hit "Somethin' Else" as well as Ricky Nelson's first No. 1 hit, "Poor Little Fool."

The tour's in-crowd included Gene Vincent, who sparked much of their fun, especially in New York and Los Angeles. Vincent's second record, "Hula Love," went to No. 9 in the fall of 1957. The gimp-legged, alcoholic Vincent, one of the most talented of the first-generation rockers, best known for "Be-Bop-A-Lula," was a last-minute addition to the Irving Feld tour. The strenuous pace—seventy one-night stands in three months—took a heavy toll on the original cast, some of whom succumbed to physical and nervous exhaustion.

The tour promoter, Irving Feld, was about forty at the time. "Irving and Izzie Feld were druggists and sold records retail and then toured rock," Frank Fried, a concert promoter who'd later handle the Beatles and Frank Sinatra, said in a 1994 interview. Feld had been president of Super Enterprises before founding General Artists Corporation (GAC) with two business associates. The rock package shows of the fifties were largely Feld's innovation; their all-rock-star rosters distinguished them from their British counterparts. In England, where there were fewer rockers at the time, rock tours were made up of traditional music-hall variety acts with perhaps a single rock attraction on the bill.

Nevertheless GAC would come in for severe criticism in the following decades for its treatment of rock 'n' roll performers. "The executives of the company didn't like rock music," Frank Barcelona, a former GAC agent, revealed in Robert Stephen Spitz's *The Making of Superstars: Artists and Executives of the Rock Music Business*. "The way the agency treated rock performers was a crime. . . . They didn't like rock performers, knew nothing about the music, couldn't relate to the audiences . . . it was too unimportant for them to be bothered with."

GAC assembled the original rock package tours and turned them over to promoters such as Dick Clark, who called his package the Dick Clark Caravan of Stars. "If you had seven hundred fifty or eight hundred dollars, and you decided you wanted to be in show business, you could become a promoter," Barcelona explained. "You'd call the agency. . . . We'd try to sell you an act for as much as we could possibly con out of you, you'd try to put on a dance or a hop at the local high school, and that was it. . . . Clark paid as little as he possibly could. . . . He treated his acts like a meat market. . . . *All* the acts went on the bus. But it was a joke. No one made money."

Despite harsh conditions, the tours were a powerful force in the spread of rock 'n' roll. As the tours approached each city, DJs played the artists' records repeatedly. "It was almost a guarantee that if you were on the show, you were going to get your record played for at least the duration of the tour," said Barcelona. "It was quite important to the performer and also to the record companies." The package tours had far-reaching consequences. They presaged the rock tours of today. Even more significantly, they were a key link in the creation of the youth culture that would come to dominate postwar America.

On October 18, when they played Sacramento, Peggy Sue Gerron, now a student at Girl's Catholic School in Sacramento, heard "Peggy Sue" for the first time. In my interview with Peggy Sue in 1994, she recalls how the nuns at the school had forbidden her to listen to rock 'n' roll. When Buddy saw her in Sacramento he laughed and said, "Here comes 'Song.' " Peggy Sue and Jerry had broken up, but they were to reconcile in Sacramento. "Buddy played Cupid," says Peggy Sue, explaining that it was Buddy who'd allowed Jerry to change "Cindy Lou" to "Peggy Sue." In Sacramento Buddy asked her if she was keeping up her interest in music. "Yes, I'm twirling in California," she replied. "How are you, Buddy?"

"I love writing and hate touring," he said.

With the Crickets still on the road, Petty mixed their album, *The Chirping Crickets*, in Clovis, using the Picks to provide background vocals. Buddy admired the Picks and welcomed their participation. The Picks made a significant contribution to many of the cuts, particularly "Oh Boy," lending their unique mixture of C&W and do-wop. "Oh Boy" was released as a Crickets single in October, with "Not Fade Away" on the flip side. Twenty years later, rock critic Dave Marsh called both sides "classics," but on release they were ignored in the United States. It was a different story overseas, where "Oh Boy" hit the charts in the United Kingdom.

Rock 'n' roll's port of entry to Europe was Liverpool, England, which was closer to America than any other city in Britain. Buddy's recordings started showing up there in 1957, carried to Liverpool by sailors—known as "Cunard Yanks"—who worked on the shipping lines and often shopped for records and souvenirs when they docked in New York. Back home, as the records circulated, "That'll Be the Day," "Peggy Sue," and "Oh Boy" became familiar to Liverpudlians, including future Beatle John Lennon, who'd just enrolled in Liverpool College of Art that fall. Rock 'n' roll was banned on the BBC, but John and millions of other young Britons listened to it every night at eight P.M. on Radio Luxembourg, a privately owned radio station on the Continent that was powerful enough to reach Central Europe and England. Buddy's popularity spread throughout England in late 1957, as Coral officially released his records overseas. In September, "That'll Be the Day" showed up on the *New Musical Express* charts and threatened to knock Paul Anka from the No. 1 spot, where "Diana" had racked up a triumphant run of nine consecutive weeks. Soon, both "Peggy Sue" and "Oh Boy" were rising on the charts in England and Australia.

In frigid Vancouver, British Columbia, on October 23, 1957, during a backstage interview in the Georgia Auditorium with Canadian DJ Red Robinson, Buddy revealed that he wanted to go home, where, he diplomatically observed, the temperature wasn't so "cool" and the skies were considerably "drier." Still unaware that he was setting the Thames on fire, he was pessimistic when asked to predict the future of rock 'n' roll. He gave it about half a year, doubting it would survive Christmas 1957. Enervated from singing his guts out in nightly rock shows, he longed for a radical change in musical trends, confessing that he'd rather sing songs that didn't require him to scream and shout. Critical of "That'll Be the Day," he felt he'd made substantial progress with "Oh Boy."

By the time the tour reached Denver on November 1, "Peggy Sue" was bounding up the *Billboard* chart. In an interview in Cochran's room in the Albany Hotel, a local radio personality asked Buddy if he was going to make a movie. Suddenly turning to Cochran, who was lounging nearby, Buddy gave his friend a plug, revealing that Cochran had already broken into the movies. Jokingly, Buddy added that he was going to butter him up and see if he could get the Crickets a Hollywood contract. Cochran's film was *Go, Johnny, Go!* a low-budget Hal Roach programmer featuring Alan Freed and Jimmy Clanton, with musical interludes by Chuck Berry, Ritchie Valens, Jackie Wilson, and Cochran. Like all the other rock 'n' roll exploitation films, including Jayne Mansfield's *The Girl Can't Help It*, this was just another dumb jukebox movie. Even the glimpses it affords of rarely filmed legends such as Cochran and Valens are ruined by clumsy intrusions of the inane plot.

Cochran evidently tried to get the Crickets in *Go, Johnny, Go!* During the shooting, Freed's manager Jack Hook called Petty and offered the Crickets a cameo—for no pay. The publicity they'd derive from appearing in a Hollywood film should be pay enough, said the filmmakers. Jerry didn't agree, according to Petty, who later claimed that Jerry said the movie people could go to hell if they weren't paying. Not true, said Jerry, who laid the blame on Petty and added that the Crickets were dying to see themselves in a movie; Petty's bungling of the deal helped turn them against him, Jerry said.

When the Feld tour played Omaha, Nebraska, on November 4, Buddy found himself not far from Echo's college but made no effort to contact her. In late 1957 she'd begun dating a classmate. She was over Buddy. If he was heartbroken, there was little sign of it in his interview the next day, November 5, on radio station KTOP in Topeka, Kansas, during which he gleefully ticked off his recent triumphs on the U.S. record charts.

His accomplishments abroad were just as impressive. On November 2, "That'll Be the Day" seized the No. 1 position on the British charts. It remained the best-selling single in England for three consecutive weeks, selling 431,000 copies. "Peggy Sue" and "Oh Boy" were almost as successful, going to No. 6 and No. 3, respectively. All three records were No. 2 hits in Australia. The British rock scene that Buddy now dominated had just begun to coalesce the previous year. "Skiffle"—an easy, do-it-yourself music using kitchen washboards, kazoos, tin cans, and bass fiddles made out of wire and a broomstick—had coincided with the Elvis Presley phenomenon to touch off the first "youthquake" in British history. Before rock, the word *teenager* hadn't even existed in England. In September 1957 a major concert was held at London's Royal Albert Hall, featuring both rock 'n' roll and skiffle. Lonnie Donegan, whose skiffle hits included "Rock Island Line" and "Does Your Chewing Gum Lose Its Flavor (On the Bedpost Over Night)," was on the Royal Albert bill, along with Terry Dene and Nancy Whiskey.

John Lennon's band, the Quarry Men, which did not yet include Mc-Cartney, Harrison, or Ringo Starr, was just beginning to play in Liverpool, at places like the St. Peter's Parish Church Youth Club in Woolton and an open-air party in Rosebery Street. Until they heard Buddy Holly, they were mostly performing Lonnie Donegan skiffle records, though for some time they'd been bored with skiffle and longed to play rock 'n' roll, if only they could figure out how. "In late 1957," wrote Beatles biographer Philip Norman, "American rock 'n' roll gave struggling ex-skiffle groups in Britain their first friend. His name was Buddy Holly. . . . Among the new performers thrown up after Presley, Buddy Holly was unique in composing many of the songs he recorded, and also in showing ability on the guitar, rather than using it merely as a prop. He gave hope to British boys because he was not pretty, but thin and bespectacled, and because his songs, though varied and inventive, were written in elementary guitar chords, recognizable to every beginner. . . . John Lennon, though he had always tinkered with lyrics, had never thought of writing entire songs before. Egged on by Paul—and by Buddy Holly—he felt there could be no harm in trying. Soon he and Paul were each writing songs furiously, as if it were a race."

In a few short months Buddy had gone from total obscurity to stardom in his own country and enormous influence abroad. His impact on the coming generation of rock stars in England would carry his distinctive sound well into the next decade, when the Beatles would usher in the golden age of rock.

Part Two

Stardom

Chapter Eight

Ed Sullivan

The ultimate accolade for a performer in the fifties was appearing on *The Ed Sullivan Show*, a weekly TV variety program with an audience of fifty million viewers. The Crickets were summoned to New York to make their prime-time network debut on the show on December 1, 1957. From its inception on CBS in 1948 as *Toast of the Town*—Sullivan changed the name in 1955—the show was more than a hit; it was an American institution. Every Sunday night at eight o'clock Sullivan seemed to turn the United States into one big family. An unlikely looking MC, he slouched onstage, moving like a sleepwalker and sounding strangely addle-brained and inarticulate. Even his closest associates sometimes called him the Toast of the Tomb. Nonetheless, the whole world seemed to light up with anticipation every time he announced, "Tonight we have a really big show."

During the 1950s, Sullivan presented Elvis, Louis Armstrong, Red Skelton, Phyllis Diller, Totie Fields, Sophie Tucker, Connie Francis, Teresa Brewer, Fats Domino, Bill Haley and the Comets, Gene Vincent, and Frankie Lymon, not to mention the Italian mouse Topo Gigio, talking dogs, plate spinners, foot jugglers, boxing great Joe Louis, the Jujiwara Opera Company from Japan, Miss America, Fidel Castro, Judith Anderson as *Medea*, the Harlem Globetrotters, Mickey Mantle, Maria Callas as *Tosca*, and circus elephants. Just when you felt you'd seen everything, out would come the entire cast of a Broadway show, such as Julie Harris, Ethel Waters, and Brandon de Wilde in *Member of the Wedding*. Sullivan was able to cram so many performers into his one-hour format because he permitted no act to exceed the length of a commercial, convinced, rightly, that the public preferred fast-paced entertainment. As Mark Leddy once joked, Sullivan filmed the Crucifixion but only gave Christ three minutes.

At the time of the Crickets' appearance in 1957, Sullivan was fifty-five years old. He had come up through journalism as a New York sportswriter and gossip columnist, later turning vaudeville MC and TV star. His dour demeanor won him the nickname the "Great Stone Face." "Ed's the only man who can brighten up a room by leaving it," comic Joe E. Lewis observed. The Crickets would have agreed with Lewis wholeheartedly; though they got off to a good start in their relationship with Ed Sullivan, it soon soured. In fact, Buddy Holly hated Ed Sullivan and ended up feuding with him. So had many others, for Sullivan was not the genial fellow he appeared to be on the TV screen. Over the years, he clashed with Woody Allen, Sid Caesar, Nancy Walker, Joan Crawford, Marlene Dietrich, Walter Winchell, Bo Diddley, Jackie Mason, Dinah Shore, Nat "King" Cole, Fred Allen, Henny Youngman, Hedda Hopper, Soupy Sales, and Jack Paar. After Paar's tiff with Sullivan, Paar quipped that NBC's trademark was a peacock and CBS's was now a cuckoo. Who else but Sullivan, he asked, could "bring to a simple English sentence such suspense and mystery and drama?" Paar was referring to the awkward way Sullivan sometimes introduced his acts, such as vocalist-guitarist Jose Feliciano, about whom Sullivan said: "Let's hear it reeely big fer singer Jose Feliciano. He's blind—and he's Puerto Rican."

Niki dismisses the Crickets' Sullivan appearance as a total farce. Instead of getting a week's break in the tour, which was what the band needed, they had to backtrack and fly to New York, where the Feld tour had begun. They were shocked to learn the pay was so paltry on the most popular TV show in the world that they were actually going to lose money on the deal. They received $1,600 but had to pay $1,800 to various unions, coming out $200 in the hole. Both the dress rehearsal—and the telecast the following day—were held at Studio 50 (later renamed for Sullivan and since 1993 the home of David Letterman's *Late Show*) in Times Square. Thanks to deceptive camera angles, Ed Sullivan's studio audience always looked vast on the TV screen, but the Crickets were astonished to discover that the theater was dumpy and rather small, seating about 250 people. The cramped performance area was jammed with circus acts, jugglers, acrobats, and singers; the dressing rooms were grim cells.

The Crickets went to their hotel after the rehearsal and returned to Studio 50 for the telecast the next day. Other acts included Sam Cooke, whose recording "You Send Me" was the current No. 1 hit, and *Collier's* all-American football team, who completely dwarfed the Crickets as they stood together backstage. One of the jocks "petrified" them, Niki recalled, when he asked Buddy who they were and Buddy replied that they were the Crickets; the jock then wanted to know what the Crickets did, and Buddy answered, simply, "That'll Be the Day," which ended the exchange.

Niki was depressed by their performance on the first part of the show, which he later described as a "letdown." They were better in the second half, when Ed Sullivan brought them back to sing "Peggy Sue." "Buddy

Holly, Buddy, Buddy, Buddy, come back here," said Sullivan, who proceeded to quiz Buddy about the ages of each of the Crickets. Buddy explained that two of them were eighteen, one was twenty, and Buddy was
twenty-one. As he spoke, the crew was hastily shoving Jerry's drum platform into the wings, clearing the stage for the next act. But Sullivan
obviously liked Buddy and drew him out about Lubbock and whether
they still went to school. Buddy's demeanor—confident but respectful of
his elder—completely won over Sullivan, who had not previously been
a rock 'n' roll fan. Their unlikely rapport seemed to surprise and delight
both men, so different in taste, age, and outlook. Visibly relaxing during
their chat, Sullivan asked him about the origins of the Crickets and
whether they were an overnight sensation. Buddy assured him that they'd
had their share of "rough times" but felt lucky to have made it to the
Sullivan show this quickly. Obviously pleased, Sullivan called Buddy
"Tex," said he'd enjoyed their conversation, and asked the audience to
give the boys a big hand.

All their records on the charts at the time leaped ten points within
two weeks of the Sullivan show, Niki calculated. *Cash Box* named them
the most promising vocal group of 1957, based on a national poll of
jukebox operators. Technically the Crickets were not a vocal group, since
Buddy was the only singer. Unfortunately, the Crickets' excellent vocal
group, the Picks—whose work on *The Chirping Crickets*, released on December 1, was a crucial element in the Buddy Holly sound—received no
recognition.

After the tour folded in New York in early December 1957, the Crickets flew back to Texas, their first visit home since becoming international
recording stars. As if it had undergone a mass lobotomy, Lubbock took
no official notice of their homecoming, though Buddy was the only famous person the city had ever produced. It didn't matter so much to
Buddy that neither the mayor nor a brass band showed up at his plane,
but he was at least looking forward to seeing his folks and hearing their
reaction to the extraordinary events of the past few months. As if to prove
he was a star, he rented a limo for the drive from the airport to his parents'
humble dwelling. Gazing out the limo window, he saw that nothing had
changed in Lubbock, except that the town was dressed up in all its Yuletide bunting. He was disappointed when he arrived home and found no
one there, his mother later told Griggs. Dejectedly, he dismissed the limo
driver and went inside. When his parents finally returned he complained
that the large fee he'd paid for the limo had been completely wasted.

The first thing his mother wanted to know, according to Goldrosen
and Beecher, was what he thought about all the "Negroes" on the tour
and how he'd managed to get along with them. Buddy replied that he

was a Negro, too; he *felt* black, he said. Larry told Buddy that he was beginning to sound like a New Yorker and warned that he should never lose his Texas accent. Buddy promised that he wouldn't become a Yankee.

Noticing that Buddy looked terrible, Larry commented that the tour must have been an ordeal. Month after month of one-night stands had left Buddy completely depleted; he went to bed and slept for three days. For weeks he was still recovering from the rigors of the road. The fact that his parents hadn't caught his *Sullivan* appearance could hardly have improved his morale. Mrs. Holley once confessed that she'd seen Buddy on stage three or four times but never on TV.

During the 1957 Christmas holidays the first royalty check, $192,000, arrived from Coral/Brunswick. Though it seemed like an enormous amount, upon investigation the Crickets discovered that it should have been much more, because the $192,000 represented only "That'll Be the Day" record sales and a fraction of "Peggy Sue" sales. Where, they wondered, were their $50,000 songwriting royalties for "That'll Be the Day," which should have been split three ways between Buddy, Petty, and Jerry, and their BMI earnings (fees collected by Broadcast Music Incorporated for each air play of a song on radio and television)? When pressed, Petty said they'd spent it all, but he offered no records to prove his contention. Years later, Hi Pockets Duncan revealed in a radio special on Buddy that Petty had been siphoning 90 percent of their earnings until an attorney entered the picture much later on.

While he was still recovering his strength, Buddy went on a fishing trip to Ballinger, a town in central Texas, 160 miles southeast of Lubbock, with his father and Larry. On the way back, while Buddy was asleep, they decided to stop for coffee. "That'll Be the Day" was blaring over the roadhouse jukebox. L.O., trying to impress the waitress, said that the song's composer was asleep in his truck. When she ignored him, L.O. feistily announced that he was going to prove it. He went to the truck and brought Buddy back inside, but the waitress still didn't believe him.

Success had not, despite the use of the limo, turned Buddy's head. He tended to view success as an episode rather than as a state of being. After two years in the recording industry, he told his mother, he'd be washed up; popularity was an ephemeral thing that could vanish with the newest fad. But while it lasted he intended to share his good fortune with everyone who'd helped him over the years, beginning with his family; he paid Larry back the $1,000 he owed him. He promised his parents a home, according to DJ Larry Corbin, and gave them a red-and-white Impala. "I really respect a guy like that," Corbin later told Griggs. He was also good to his friends. He owed money to "just about everybody" in Lubbock and though many of his benefactors had written off their loans as losses, Buddy dropped in and reimbursed them, Corbin added. "I appreciate your carry-ing me," Buddy said, and paid them back double.

Inexplicable and baffling as it seems, the Crickets continued to work with Norman Petty. None of them wanted to bother with business deal-ings, contracts, and the like, but they would pay dearly for such flippancy. Volunteering for more abuse from Petty, they went back to Clovis on December 17. The song they cut that day, "(You're So Square) Baby I Don't Care," is, in Waylon Jennings's estimation, the best example of the Buddy Holly sound, which he attributes to the symbiosis achieved by Buddy on guitar and Jerry on drums.

Niki, the only member of the Crickets who'd never fit in, finally quit, walking out during an emotional scene in Clovis. According to Joe B., Buddy's attitude was: If Niki wants to go, let him. Later Niki returned to Clovis and asked Petty how he was going to collect his royalties now that he was no longer a Cricket. Unbeknownst to the other Crickets, Petty promised that if Niki would give up every other claim, he'd see that Niki received 10 percent of all proceeds from their No. 1 hit "That'll Be the Day." Niki agreed but Petty went back on the deal, costing Niki hundreds of thousands of dollars. Later, as a goodwill gesture, the Crickets gave Niki $1,000. In a 1994 interview, Niki said he bore no ill will toward Jerry and Joe B., adding that they "get along perfect." He told Goldrosen in 1975 that he blamed Petty for the split; Petty could have patched up Niki's differences with the Crickets and somehow held the act together, Niki felt. It was a manager's responsibility, he contended, to tell feuding musicians to sleep on their problems and discuss them the next day, when everyone had calmed down. Petty didn't see it this way at all. He revealed to Goldrosen that Buddy, Jerry, and Joe B. had all told him they wanted Niki out.

"Peggy Sue" soared to No. 3 in America in late December, selling over a million copies, and it was still a hit in the United Kingdom. When "Peggy Sue" reached No. 1 on the popular TV show Your Hit Parade, Dick Jacobs, a Decca executive who was also the show's musical conduc-tor, admitted they didn't have any rock singers to perform it. Finally Alan Copeland, a Hit Parade regular, attempted to imitate Buddy's hiccups and nasal cooing, and "Peggy Sue" remained on the show for nine weeks.

The Crickets returned to New York on December 23 to play one of the world's most exalted venues—the 3,650-seat Paramount Theater in Manhattan, where legendary stars such as Frank Sinatra, Peggy Lee, Benny Goodman, Johnnie Ray, and Dean Martin and Jerry Lewis had made entertainment history. The Crickets never replaced Niki; from now on, they would perform as a trio. For a while life in the band was more peaceful, though time would prove the respite to have been nothing but the proverbial calm before the storm. Musically, Niki's exit had no effect on the band. By Niki's own admission, Petty hadn't miked him in the studio as a way of reducing possible mistakes on their one-track recordings. Onstage his principal contribution had been his swivel-hipped, Elvis-inspired theatrics. Why had Buddy kept him around? one might wonder. Niki told Goldrosen that Buddy liked his company, both in the studio and when they finished sessions at two A.M. and hit the lonely streets of Clovis, New Mexico.

Christmas 1957 found the Crickets on the rising platform stage of the nation's No. 1 showplace in the heart of Times Square. Their co-stars on Alan Freed's 1957 "Holiday of Stars Twelve Days of Christmas Show" were Fats Domino, Jerry Lee Lewis, and the Everly Brothers. They had indeed arrived. The *New York Times* estimated that twenty thousand teenagers started forming a line five-deep in Times Square at five-thirty in the morning in bone-chilling fifteen-degree temperature. The line stretched west on 43rd to Eighth Avenue and south to 42nd. The overflow crowd made the Christmas show at the Radio City Music Hall a few blocks north seem like a scout jamboree.

Stage shows at the Paramount were held every two hours, six times daily, between screenings of a grade-B British movie, *It's Great to Be Young*. While the surging crowd waited outside for the show to begin on opening day, a backstage battle was going on between the stars. Jerry Lee Lewis had launched a last-minute campaign to steal top billing from Fats Domino. The Crickets were fourth-billed, under Domino, Lewis, and the Everlys. "I'm the king of rock 'n' roll," Jerry Lee informed Freed, according to Jerry Lee's wife, Myra. "I want to close the show."

"Yeah," replied Freed, "says who?"

"I can blow Fats Domino off the stage. Why do I hafta go on before him?"

"Because he's had six No. 1 hits and you've only had two in the Top 10."

"Yeah, but who's got the hottest song right this minute?"

"You," said Fred, who could not deny that Jerry Lee's "Whole Lot of Shakin' Going On" was the current No. 3 hit. Nevertheless, Domino's contract clearly specified, "*Fats on top*," meaning Fats was entitled to close the show every night. When Buddy got wind of the billing war, he fired a few shots of his own, informing Freed that if anyone was the star of the show, Buddy Holly was, pointing out that "Peggy Sue," "Oh Boy," and "Everyday" were all charting simultaneously. The sly Freed knew that the way to Buddy's heart was money and offered him a raise. At $5,000 per week the Crickets were already the highest-paid act in the show. "I'll get you more money if you keep quiet and stay put," Freed told Buddy. The strategy worked. A Depression baby, Buddy always went for the money. With the Paramount's demanding schedule, there was little opportunity to spend it. Instead, Buddy dreamed of the cars and motorcycles and boats he'd buy one day, if the touring ever stopped.

At curtain time, the orchestra played Chuck Berry's current hit, "Rock 'n' Roll Music." Freed, resplendent in a garish tartan jacket similar to the one popularized by Bill Haley, appeared on the slowly ascending stage. "Hello, New York, and hello all you old friends of WINS," Freed said, "Great to see all of you out tonight. We've got the biggest, the brightest, the hottest rock-'n'-roll show you've ever seen. I'm not gonna waste another minute, so if he's ready, please put your hands together and welcome Terry Noland singing 'Patty Baby.' "

The audience greeted the Lubbock newcomer politely but saved their cheers for later. They'd come for one reason: to hear current chart champions pitch their Top 40 hits. Paul Anka sang "I Love You, Baby," followed by Danny and the Juniors, whose "At the Hop" got everyone up and dancing. Buddy and the Crickets then played a frenzied twenty-minute set and were brought back for an encore. The Paramount, built in 1926, had a gigantic balcony, and there were reports that the ceiling, walls, and floor were shaking. The audience's tumultuous roar "supported Buddy's contention that he deserved to close Freed's show," according to Freed's biographer John A. Jackson.

When the crowd at last permitted the Crickets to leave the stage, the Everly Brothers appeared, dressed identically right down to their guitar straps. They mellowed everyone out with cool, immaculate mountain harmonies. Then Jerry Lee got everyone excited again, sticking the microphone between his legs, crouching at the piano, and singing "Whole Lot of Shakin'." When he stripped off his maroon sharkskin jacket, girls in the orchestra section rushed the stage. Police halted the show for ten minutes to restore order. The cops' overreaction to the incident, which seems innocent enough today, reveals how desperately the establishment feared any threat to the status quo in the 1950s. Rock 'n' roll had thrown down the gauntlet of sexual freedom and society was running scared.

By the start of Fats Domino's set, many in the audience had left or were on their way out. After the show, when Fats told Freed he'd never again follow Jerry Lee, Freed immediately changed the bill, making Lewis the headliner. Had Norman Petty been doing his job at this juncture, Buddy would have become the headline attraction, rather than remaining fourth-billed, under Lewis, Domino, and the Everlys.

Running through January 5, 1958, the Freed show was the biggest hit in town, breaking the attendance record set by Sinatra fifteen years previously. The scene at the stage door was pure chaos. Shrieking, pushing, stamping fans mobbed the rock stars, ripping their clothing to shreds.

Running for his life, Terry Noland noticed that the girls were so hysterical that they were attacking the stagehands and anyone else who emerged from the backstage entrance. Bristling with macho magnetism, Don Everly was the darling of the fans. New York cops, who disdained rockers as juvenile delinquents, stood by idly while Don was jumped on by a gang of girls determined to tear off pieces of his flesh as souvenirs. Though Don could have been killed, the police laughed and refused to intervene, an Everlys biographer, Consuelo Dodge, wrote in 1991. Don and Phil's clothes were destroyed so regularly that they had to keep identical outfits on hand.

Joe B.'s memories of the Paramount run center on Eddie Cochran. The Crickets, who were rooming with the Everlys and Terry Noland, stayed at a hotel directly across the street from the theater. Between shows, they partied in Cochran's suite. When it was time to go on, they left Cochran's room in plenty of time to get to the theater. Cochran always waited until the very last minute, having calculated the precise amount of time required to walk from the hotel to the stage door. He'd be drinking and talking with Buddy, glance at his watch, and remark that it was time to head for the Paramount. Then he'd reconsider and announce that he had another thirty seconds. They'd talk some more and finally Cochran would rise and say he was going to work. Joe B. made the trek from the hotel room to the Paramount stage with Cochran a couple of times. Cochran never broke his stride from the moment he left the hotel elevator. As he entered the backstage area, the announcer was just finishing his introduction. Cochran proceeded to the microphone and began his act, wowing the stagehands with his perfect timing.

The Paramount show was the pinnacle of Freed's stormy professional life, which was about to take a disastrous plunge as a result of the payola scandal that would burst into the headlines the following year. Payola was a practice by which radio DJs accepted money and other favors from record manufacturers and distributors in return for playing their artists' new releases. Indeed, some record companies were so corrupt that they gave DJs cowriting credit on recordings for promising sufficient radio airplay to boost those records onto the Top 40 list. Though Freed's name appears on hit recordings such as "Sincerely," "Nadine," and "Maybellene," he had no more role in their composition than Norman Petty had for "Peggy Sue." When Freed pushed Chuck Berry's "Maybellene" for two hours one night on his "Rock 'n' Roll Party" radio program in 1955, the record shot to fifth place on Billboard's pop chart and sold over a million copies. Not until Berry received his first royalty statement did he realize that Freed "had written the song with me," Berry later remarked in his memoirs.

Like Freed, many of the performers on the Paramount bill, including Terry Noland, Jerry, and Joe B., regarded the show as the culmination of the their careers. All his life Joe B. had been told he'd never amount to more than "a cotton farmer from Lubbock, Texas," he related to Bill Griggs, but now "we were on Times Square in New York and it was Christmastime." Nowhere is Christmas observed with more panache than in Manhattan, where, in Rockefeller Center, a block-long row of silver angels trumpets their welcome all the way from Sak's Fifth Avenue to the huge Christmas tree in the skating rink underneath the RCA Building. In the windows at Lord & Taylor's department store, animated puppets re-create familiar fairy tales and Yuletide stories. Well-heeled shoppers flock to Tiffany's, Cartier, Bendel's, Bergdorf-Goodman, and Brooks Brothers. Parents take children through the ultimate toy store, F.A.O. Schwarz. Flagship department stores like Macy's and Bloomingdale's transform themselves into winter wonderlands. Midtown street vendors hawk succulent roasted chestnuts in front of the Public Library, where regal stone lions sport red Christmas wreaths around their manes. Salvation Army Santas stand on every corner, soliciting contributions for the needy. Skyscrapers sparkle late into the evening as workers celebrate their annual office-party revels. Up and down Fifth Avenue, the *Messiah* wafts gloriously from churches. Thousands of worshipers pack the city's Gothic cathedrals, St. Patrick's and St. John the Divine, for midnight services. In 1957 Abercrombie and Fitch, now long gone, still offered pricey items such as a leather-upholstered hippopotamus for the person who had everything, while the economy-minded shopper could seek out bargains at Korvette's (the forerunner of Kmart), Gimbel's, B. Altman's, and Stern's, now also gone. At City Center, a venerable mosque-turned-theater, the New York City Ballet staged its spectacular *Nutcracker* before its move in the sixties to the Lincoln Center for the Performing Arts.

Catching New York's Christmas spirit, Buddy bought himself the present of his dreams, going into Manny's and selecting a Guild F-50 Navarre acoustic guitar with a sunburst spruce top. The Guild sound was big and bright. It can be heard on "Well All Right," recorded by Buddy the following year. Some of his guitars were only briefly in his possession. He enjoyed giving them away to young rockers who couldn't afford them. Joe B. says that Buddy was the most generous person he'd ever encountered. One day at the Paramount a youth approached Buddy and said he really admired Buddy's guitar. "Here, man, you keep it," Buddy said, adding that he already had his eye on another one at Manny's. According to Joe B., Buddy felt that his goal in life was to bring happiness to the world wherever he could.

But he was no longer as much fun as in the old days, both Jerry and

Joe B. later told Goldrosen; fame had altered him somewhat. Buddy seemed moody and egotistical. He wouldn't horse around anymore. Up to his old shenanigans, Jerry once almost knocked Buddy's glasses off. Buddy told him to cut it out. During a pillow fight that involved three bands—the Crickets, Dickie Doo and the Don'ts, and Danny and the Juniors—Buddy ordered everyone to behave themselves. As in the lives of all celebrities, a chasm had opened between the new star and his lesser-known associates that nothing would ever bridge. Buddy's musicians could indulge in asinine antics to their hearts' content and no one would notice or care. But Buddy was in the spotlight, a position he'd sought all his life, and he quickly embraced it, relishing the dignity and perquisites of stardom.

A complete physical makeover was one of his first priorities. He underwent plastic surgery to remove his acne scars. According to Jerry Coleman, the Lubbock DJ, "When Buddy went to New York he had his face redone with acid or scraped." Dermabrasion, the medical term for scraping, is a painful process, resulting in inflammation and swelling. A rotating wire brush is used, and the procedure lasts one hour, causing a few days' soreness. The other treatment for acne is known as chemosurgery, involving application of a caustic solution, phenol, which creates a mild burn. The skin sloughs or peels off, revealing smoother skin underneath. The fee for chemosurgery, in 1990, was $1,640; in the fifties it was probably more like $750.

Whatever the cost, it was worth it to Buddy, who was in the process of reinventing himself for stardom. He was more and more in demand for public appearances and television shows. On December 28, he appeared with the Crickets on NBC's *Arthur Murray Party*, a variety show named after the founder of a chain of dancing schools. When the band arrived backstage before the show, they mingled with the star-studded cast, which included theater legend Tallulah Bankhead, movie stars Farley Granger, June Havoc, and Gloria DeHaven, jazz singer Sarah Vaughan, television personalities Gertrude Berg and Paul Winchell (with puppet Jerry Mahoney), actor Walter Slezak, and screen-siren Hedy Lamarr. Hostess Kathryn Murray scurried about, greeting the lineup for her sixty-minute special. Dressed in elegant tuxedos, the Crickets had a new, soigné look. An impudent spit curl in the middle of Jerry's forehead offered a daring foretaste of punk, though it also made him look like a member of the Addams family. Fortunately a kinescope survives of the Crickets' performance. Buddy maintains an attitude of regal cool while pounding the audience with the potent and intoxicating sounds of "Peggy Sue." The frenzy and momentum of rock 'n' roll were new to the Arthur Murray dancers, who'd just completed a waltz and remained on stage in full view.

Still as statues, they clutched their hands in front of them, quietly grooving.

On New Year's Eve the Crickets were still in the middle of their run at the Paramount Theater, located directly across the street from the Times Tower, the focal point of the biggest New Year's celebration in the world. Buddy, Jerry, and Joe B. stood on top of the Paramount and gazed down at the multitude in Times Square. At ten seconds before midnight the giant ball on the facade of the Times Tower began to descend. In a moment it was 1958. In one sense, Buddy's life was already completely fulfilled—all he'd ever wanted, as he'd often stated, was to make his mark and be remembered. Before him lay a privileged existence as one of the world's elite, loved and revered by the remarkable generation that he helped to define. *Time* magazine called them the Silent Generation, but they were far from silent—indeed, had anyone ever turned the volume up higher? Born in the Depression, they were bent on liberation, and in their music there was a blossoming sense of people coming into their own. Though it has never been so christened, surely this was the Rock Generation. Black and white, they were creating the anthemic music of our time. By 1958 it was growing more popular daily and had already leaped the Atlantic and Pacific oceans. Rock 'n' roll was civilization's wake-up call, and its pioneers, like James Joyce's Stephen Dedalus, were—wittingly or unwittingly—forging in the smithy of their souls "the uncreated conscience" of their race. But its immediate future in 1958 was rife with so much hatred and hostility from society that it's remarkable that rock 'n' roll managed to survive at all.

On the deepest level of his life Buddy was troubled and unfulfilled. Like many in his circle, he was headed for misfortune. Cochran would soon come to grief. Don and Phil would hit bottom from drugging and drinking. Little Richard renounced rock 'n' roll to become a Seventh-Day Adventist minister. Jerry Lee would be drummed out of England for marrying a minor, his thirteen-year-old cousin and child bride, Myra. In the coming year Corporal Elvis Presley would make a pass at a ninth grader, Priscilla Beaulieu, and give her Dexedrine pills, beginning a relationship that would end in frustration and divorce. For Buddy, life on the road offered no opportunity for meeting the kind of girl he wanted to marry. Echo McGuire was now engaged to the Nebraska classmate she'd been dating, although the breakup with Buddy hadn't been easy for her. Echo still loved Buddy—indeed, she would never stop loving him. She simply could not see herself as the wife of a rock 'n' roll star. Buddy, the young man who genuinely loved "good girls," found such girls even tougher to meet as a famous rocker.

He began the new year as Decca's leading recording artist. The company that had gone to such lengths to disavow any association with him, consigning him to obscure subsidiaries, announced that his next release, "You Are My One Desire"/"Love Me," would bear the Decca label. The company's top executives regularly showed up backstage at the Paramount, courting his favor. One of them was Dick Jacobs, Jackie Wilson's producer, who suggested that Buddy make a recording with violin accompaniment as a way to propel himself out of the rock 'n' roll market and into the pop mainstream. Like many people, Jacobs did not yet accept that rock had replaced pop as the mainstream music, but his idea of a string session would lead to some of Buddy's best recordings. Though mixing violins with rock 'n' roll was a radical idea, Jacobs had already punched up Jackie Wilson's R&B hits "To Be Loved" and "Lonely Teardrops" with lush strings. Buddy loved Wilson's big, rich sound and was fascinated to learn from Jacobs that violins had played a substantial role in its creation. In the coming months, when Buddy and Petty were in and out of New York, they would often joke about doing a session with a violin section.

If Buddy had any resistance to violins, it was because Petty had been nagging him to jettison rock 'n' roll and start cutting pop records. Rock stars, Petty kept harping, were dumped by the public and the record companies after two years. He advised that Buddy change his singing style and get accepted in a more durable market so his career wouldn't vanish with the demise of rock 'n' roll, which Petty warned was imminent. Ultimately he envisaged Buddy as a Vegas nightclub act, crooning to drunks and gamblers, and cutting Sinatra-type lovers' albums. "Naw," Buddy said, "I don't dig it."

With simultaneous hit records, he could now be more confident about rock's future. Just a few months ago, it had appeared that rock 'n' roll was in a decline. Only three rock records had been in the Top 10—Presley's "Teddy Bear," the Everlys' "Bye Bye Love," and Marty Robbins's "White Sport Coat." Then a confluence of events—the Everlys' four-week chart-topper "Wake Up Little Susie," Jerry Lee Lewis's stunning debut, and Buddy's string of hits—had injected a shot of propulsive energy, enough for the new music to rock on, possibly forever.

For many people the new year brought bad news—Elvis was inducted into the Army; Khrushchev threatened to bury capitalism; Elizabeth Taylor escaped death in the air crash that killed her husband, Mike Todd, when she decided to stay home with a cold; Governor Orval Faubus shut down the public schools in Little Rock, Arkansas; and the world's scientists warned of nuclear holocaust—but for Buddy Holly, 1958 began auspiciously. "Peggy Sue" and "Oh Boy" remained in the Top 10 in the United States, England, and Australia. Fans throughout the English-speaking world were clamoring to see him in person. International tour offers were beginning to materialize. It was the last full year that he would live.

Brilliant new singles rolled out one after the other. The hard work he'd done in Clovis in the first six months of 1957 was paying off. Before fame he'd written and recorded enough hits for a lifetime. His assault on the charts in 1957 made him the darling of the music press. Critics heaped praise on his newest single, "You Are My One Desire." How quickly the review press changes! Critics are like lemmings. Having ignored the obvious signs of genius in his early work, they automatically endorsed everything he did once success bestowed its imprimatur. "Kid'll flip over this one," rhapsodized *Cash Box* on January 4, describing "You Are My One Desire" as "an emotional love story chanted with great feeling." The B-side, "Love Me," *Cash Box* endorsed as a "swinging rock-a-billy jumper."

On January 8, the Crickets set out on another Irving Feld–GAC tour, but this one, lasting only seventeen days, was less grueling than the 1957 marathon. Another improvement, for the Crickets at least, was their salary: $1,200 a night as opposed to the $1,000 per week they'd been paid on the fall tour. The tour reunited them with old friends such as the Everly Brothers, Paul Anka, Danny and the Juniors, and Jimmie Rodgers. Around the time they were playing Hazelton, Pennsylvania, a groupie came up to the Everly Brothers, took off her blouse and bra, according to Phil, and asked them to sign her breasts—one for each brother. Reporters from the establishment press often witnessed such scenes and resented them. Throughout the fifties the press remained largely as conservative as the Eisenhower administration and scorned any deviation from the norm. Probably motivated by envy, reporters regularly ridiculed these new stars.

"They thought you were outlandish because of your long hair, you dressed different, and they threw you out of town," Phil later stated in the *Kansas City Star*. One reporter set up a photo shoot that was deliberately designed to impugn the manhood of Buddy and the Everly Brothers because they'd let their hair grow out. Calling the boys together with a girl group on the tour—the Shepherd Sisters, three bouncy blonds who had a hit called "Alone"—the photographer posed all of them in profile, which seemed odd. The reporter accompanying the photographer asked only one question: How were the singers going to make a living after the death of rock 'n' roll? Buddy and the Everlys thought there was something suspicious about the shoot and, sure enough, when the picture was published, the caption said: "The Only Way You Can Tell the Difference Between Rock-'n'-Roll Boys and Rock-'n'-Roll Girls Is the Boys Have Longer Hair."

Don later complained to interviewer Floyd Mattson that the press was fixated on "the length of your hair" and determined to show "how the guys looked like the girls. . . . And it wasn't that long anyway." First-generation rockers "were fighting the current," added Phil. "All . . . kinds of pressures and fears . . . contributed to a lot of the hard times." Don told Mattson that rock 'n' roll at first "wasn't respectable at all. . . . They really wondered if you were outside stealing hubcaps between shows." Quipped Phil, "And we all did, occasionally."

The Everlys' experience reflects the anti-rock sentiment that was rampant in 1957–58. The *New York Times* quoted a psychiatrist who called rock 'n' roll "cannibalistic and tribalistic." The *New York Daily News* spurned it as "a barrage of primitive, jungle-beat rhythms." From an Alabama lowbrow who said rock 'n' roll was the "means by which the white man and his children can be driven to a level with the niggers" to the usually sane pundit Dwight Macdonald, who denounced rock in the *New Yorker*, the establishment recoiled from the new music in a manner that smacked of both racism and paranoia. Journalists warned that rock 'n' roll would lead to a wave of youth crime, but what they really feared and resented was rock's violation of society's taboos against racial mixing. As Robert Palmer later wrote in *Rolling Stone*, "Much has been made of sixties rock as a vehicle for revolutionary social and cultural change, but it was mid-fifties rock 'n' roll that blew away, in one mighty, concentrated blast, the accumulated racial and social proprieties of centuries."

In an even deeper sense, rock 'n' roll went against white America's ingrained fear of sex and pleasure, a joyless legacy of the country's puritan origins. In the forties and early fifties there'd been a sense of safety in the mid-tempo ballads of Doris Day, Joni James, and Patti Page; all that was completely undermined in 1955 by the steady beat and rhythmically heavier style of rock 'n' roll, which was derived from the R&B backbeat. The wanton body language of Elvis Presley, the surrender to lust in Buddy's "Oh Boy," the contagious eroticism of Little Richard promised more joy than a oppressed, inhibited society could absorb in its initial reaction to rock 'n' roll. A new, youth-led rock apostolate, sneered at by rednecks, disdained by intellectuals, and infinitely small in comparison with the rock counterculture of the sixties, alone supported rock 'n' roll and kept it alive, buying recordings, listening to the radio, and faithfully braving the winter winds to attend the rock-package shows.

After their Pennyslvania gig, Buddy and the others stars of the January 1958 GAC tour left for Rochester, New York, which was in the middle of an icy upstate winter. During two shows in the Rochester Auditorium, Buddy befriended a young Brunswick recording artist named Jerry Engler, who had become a target of Communist witch-hunters because of his new record, "Sputnik (Satellite Girl)." Engler had been employed at Kodak in Rochester on October 4, 1957, when the Russians sent their Sputnik satellite into orbit around the earth. Commemorating the event, Engler wrote "Sputnik" in thirty minutes while on duty at Kodak and made a recording of it with his band the Four Ekkos. As Buddy Knox had done before him, Engler asked Buddy Holly where he should record, and Buddy advised him to go to Clovis. Engler then asked Holly how he should cope with charges that he was a Communist. Buddy told him not to worry— "Sputnik" was such a danceable rocker that no sane person would mistake it for political propaganda. Engler's record was only one of a flock of novelty tunes that proliferated in the wake of Russia's stunning techno-logical coup, which frightened Americans into beefing up the science curricula of their universities in 1958, lest the U.S.S.R. wrest control of outer space.

As the GAC tour neared its completion in late January, Buddy drowned the pain of losing Echo with the amorous delights of the road. Though he was far from being the best-looking star in the package, he attracted more girls than he could handle and sometimes passed them on to colleagues who might have been handsomer but lacked his magnetism. "Buddy Holly put me to bed with a girl," Phil Everly told writer Philip Norman in 1982. "And he *laughed.*" Buddy was drinking heavily, Phil added, and asked Phil to tuck him in—alone.

The Crickets returned to New York on January 25 to begin work on their new single, "Rave On." Six months earlier, Decca executives hadn't considered the Crickets worthy enough to grace their label, but now Decca was urging them to record in New York, where the executives could court them and control them, rather than in Clovis. The same fickleness and hypocrisy that Decca showed in 1958 holds true today not only in the record business but throughout the entertainment world, which is slow to recognize talent but quick to fawn over it at the first sign of success. The familiar spectacle of executives vying to take credit for the latest hit suggests nothing so much as a pack of hyenas tearing at a joint of meat. In 1994, rock historians Dave Marsh and James Bernard de-nounced the major labels as "gutless and greedy, disdainful of artistry in the face of the bottom line" and "notorious for not paying artists what they owe them."

Bob Thiele, who'd championed Buddy from the time he was a complete unknown, was already planning a second LP, *Buddy Holly,* and he made no secret of his wish to personally produce "Rave On," which was needed to fill out the new album. He naturally wanted the Crickets in New York to maximize his influence over them and urged Buddy to cut "Rave On" at Bell Sound Studios on West Fifty-fourth Street in Manhattan. Pre-dictably, Petty immediately objected, and Buddy told Thiele he'd give the matter some thought. At this point he considered firing Petty outright and hiring his brother Larry. "He called me from New York and asked if he should do this or that," Larry said in 1992. "He wanted me to be his manager. He offered me a tremendous sum of money just to go with him everywhere and keep him out of trouble, sorta like a bodyguard, but I couldn't leave. I was running the [tile] business."

Buddy also called Hi Pockets, saying he was furious at Petty and sorry that he hadn't followed Hi Pockets's counsel the previous year and avoided Petty. Though Petty had originally said he was only putting his name on the records to attract airplay, he demanded full royalties once the records hit, insisting that the money be divided exactly as specified in the contract. Buddy was "steaming mad," he told Hi Pockets. In re-taliation Buddy collected and held all income the Crickets received from live performances and told Thiele that he was going to cut "Rave On" in New York instead of Clovis. As a sop to Petty, Buddy let him play the piano on "Rave On" when they recorded it at Bell Sound in January.

Songwriters Sonny West and Bill Tilghman, the same team that had given Buddy "Oh Boy," had originally conceived "Rave On" as a song about a domestic fight. They'd heard the phrase on a car radio while driving through Tilghman's hometown, Levelland, Texas, twenty miles west of Lubbock. Petty rejected the first draft and told them to rewrite it as a love song. Two weeks later Sonny West recorded the revised version in Clovis and sent the demo to Atlantic Records, which accepted it, put West under contract, and released "Rave On" in early 1958. West's ver-sion flopped. Buddy's cover, a blazing dash of musical gusto, was recorded at eight P.M. on Saturday night, January 25. He got it in three takes.

"That's My Desire," a slow ballad that sold a million for Frankie Laine in 1947, proved to be Buddy's Waterloo. His worst recording, the song was ill-suited to Buddy's voice and style. He struggled through two false starts with a backup group called the Jivetones before getting a track down. At two A.M. Sunday, January 26, he completed his second unsat-isfactory take and gave up, telling Decca not to release the cut. Thiele thought better of moving Buddy to New York. Perhaps he was better off in Clovis after all.

Later the same Sunday, the Crickets returned to *The Ed Sullivan Show* to promote "Oh Boy." Since the Picks had sung backup vocals on the record, Buddy asked Sullivan to bring them to New York so that the TV audience would hear the same sound as the recording. Unfortunately, the Picks didn't belong to the musicians' union, a requirement for appearing on the show, and neither Sullivan nor Petty was willing to pay the union fee. By the time Buddy got to the studio he was dejected and in no mood for yet another setback. During dress rehearsal, Jerry and Joe B. started goofing around as usual and missed their cue. Exasperated, Buddy went onstage without them. Sullivan demanded to be told where Buddy's mu-sicians were. Buddy shrugged; he didn't know or care.

Originally they were to do two songs, but Sullivan cut them down to one, adding that they must *not* sing "Oh Boy" because it was too vulgar for his show. Anti-rock bias was so strong that just the previous week, on January 20, radio station KWK in St. Louis, Missouri, banned all rock music from the air; KWK staffers stormed through the station library, systematically destroying the entire rock 'n' roll collection. In the freer air of the nineties it seems impossible that the repressiveness of the fifties could have reached such violent extremes, but it did, and it was by no means limited to harebrained hooligans from the Ozarks. Rock 'n' roll had laid bare the moral hypocrisy of fifties society, striking a blow against its racial double standard and its paradoxical attitude toward sex. As reflected in the oblique and tortured plays of Tennessee Williams, the gay writer who held up a mirror to the mendacity of the time, the public was sex-obsessed and lecherous on the one hand and, on the other, secretive and guilt-ridden. To a conservative like Ed Sullivan, "Oh Boy," which promises the best orgasm anyone ever had, was rock 'n' roll at its most seditious, surging with powerful rhythms that could arouse uncontrollable passions.

When Jerry and Joe B. arrived at Studio 50 and prepared to go on the show with Buddy, Sullivan asked what they'd decided to substitute for "Oh Boy." Buddy explained that his friends at home were expecting to hear his current hit and if he couldn't sing "Oh Boy" he was going to walk out. Customarily deferred to because of his power throughout the entertainment industry, Sullivan resented Buddy's defiance. He had an animal act waiting in the alley on Fifty-third Street, at the side entrance to the studio, for just such an emergency. A vengeful man, he struck out at any performer who dared to challenge his authority. In 1955 he ordered Bo Diddley to sing the Uncle Tom-ish "Sixteen Tons." When Bo refused and sang his current hit "Bo Diddley" instead, Sullivan cheated Bo out of the $750 fee they'd agreed on.

As soon as the Crickets went before the cameras and struck up "Oh Boy," everything seemed to go wrong. First the sound went dead. Buddy tried to compensate by turning up the volume on his guitar. The sound came back on but not nearly at the volume required by rock 'n' roll. Then the overhead lights went out. The Crickets looked and sounded like a bush-league combo. Backstage Sullivan was perpetrating the fiasco, ordering sound and lighting technicians to wreck the performance. Despite these harassments, the response to the Crickets was so overwhelming that Sullivan had to swallow his pride and invite them back for a third guest shot. When Buddy received the offer, he turned it down. CBS then doubled its offer. Buddy told them to shove it.

His contretemps at CBS can be seen as a classic struggle between art and commerce, Sullivan representing the corporate giant who tries to preempt a new art form in order to dilute it into something bland enough for mass consumption. The temptation for an artist to compromise in the face of a platform as impressive as Sullivan's—an audience of fifty million—must have been powerful. Buddy's resistance to Sullivan demonstrates not only that he was growing and maturing beyond the ingenuous youth who'd sold his soul to Norman Petty only half a year ago, but that he now had the courage to remain on the cutting edge of musical and cultural change. CBS didn't have enough money, he finally told the studio, to buy the Crickets.

Chapter Nine

Life Beyond the United States

Buddy Holly left the United States for the first time in 1958, carrying rock 'n' roll—the music as well as its highly subversive message of freedom—to the world at large. Though he appears to have had little interest in politics, his music planted the seeds of a larger cultural revolution everywhere he went—from Nashville to Australia, from London and Liverpool to the North Sea—laying the groundwork for the social and political upheavals rock 'n' roll was instrumental in fomenting in the following decade. The fact that the Crickets' influence spread so rapidly overseas was remarkable.

Bound for Sydney, the Crickets began a ten-thousand-mile trek on January 26, 1958, leaving New York aboard a Pan Am Constellation prop plane—international jet service would not begin until October—stopping in Los Angeles to pick up Jerry Lee Lewis and his entourage, which included Jay Brown, his bass player and the father of Jerry Lee's thirteen-year-old bride. Sitting next to Buddy, Brown started cracking jokes. Buddy, unamused, withdrew into himself.

Across the aisle, Jerry Lee sat next to Paul Anka, referring to him as "Anchor." Trying to be friendly, Anka showed Lewis some lyrics, including the ones he'd written for "Diana." Jerry Lee scorned them, deciding he didn't like "Anchor" or his No. 1 hit. Jerry Lee preferred the company of fellow Southerners like Elvis Presley, with whom he shared an Assembly of God background and a penchant for booze and outlandish pranks. Before Elvis's induction in the Army, Jerry Lee once confided to record executive Joe Smith, Elvis and Jerry Lee took a naked motorcycle ride at 2:30 A.M. in Memphis, "only for thirty-five or forty seconds, 'round the corner and back," Jerry Lee said. "Anchor," still sixteen and a teetotaler, did not seem a likely partner for such high jinks on the tour.

Though young, Anka was shrewd and fiercely competitive. He quickly seized the stellar position over the older stars in the package by agreeing to take a cut in his regular fee. Petty was present on the tour, but, unhappily for Buddy, he was not as wily a negotiator as Anka's manager, Bill McCadden. Once again Buddy was the ranking star in terms of current chart hits, but Petty, instead of protecting Buddy's interests in the dog-eat-dog world of show business, acted like a greenhorn tourist, snapping pictures from the plane window and enjoying a paid vacation, courtesy of the Crickets. It was increasingly evident that Petty would never be able to provide Buddy the kind of aggressive, combative management essential for survival in the top-heavy all-star rock packages.

The first stop was Hawaii, which was not yet a state of the Union. The Constellation landed on Oahu, and the group checked into a hotel at Waikiki Beach, overlooking the Pacific Ocean. Their concert at the Civic Auditorium attracted such a large crowd—ten thousand—that the Crickets felt overwhelmed. Anka was the only singer on the show who impressed the *Honolulu Star-Bulletin* critic, but Buddy felt good enough about the Crickets' performance to write his sister and brother-in-law, Mr. and Mrs. J. E. Weir, in Lubbock, stating that he'd gone over better than expected. He was delighted to discover that Hawaiians liked rock 'n' roll as much as U.S. mainlanders did. He played a free show, open to the public, at Oahu's Schofield Barracks, the U.S. Army post immortalized in James Jones's haunting 1951 novel *From Here to Eternity*. Elvis Presley's conquest of Hawaii would not occur until 1961, when he filmed *Blue Hawaii* on location and gave a benefit concert at Pearl Harbor's Bloch Arena for the U.S.S. *Arizona* national-shrine memorial fund, raising $62,000. The movie would prove to be one of his most popular, and in 1966 he would return to the Islands, filming *Paradise, Hawaiian Style*, in Oahu, Kauai, Maui, and along the Kona Coast.

In 1958, Ritchie Valens briefly joined Buddy's tour in Honolulu, performing at the Civic Auditorium. His appearance was arranged by local promoters Ralph Yempuku and Earl Finch, who'd been putting on rock shows in Hawaii for the past few months. Only sixteen, Ritchie was a shy *guero* (light-skinned Mexican), the first rocker to emerge from the Chicano community, a striking youth with hazel-green eyes and thick dark brown hair styled in a waterfall with a ducktail in back. Even his pudginess was an asset, lending a teddy-bear appeal to his aggressively masculine appearance. His repertoire at the time included Little Richard's "Jenny, Jenny" and Chuck Berry's "Sweet Little Sixteen," but when he sang them he substituted his own lyrics, improvised on the spot. Likable and enthusiastic, he seemed to have no ego whatsoever and plied the established singers with intelligent questions but appeared to have made no impression on Buddy at this time.

Leaving Oahu, the tour party flew 5,844 miles to Australia aboard a Pan Am Constellation that had sleepers in first-class, a far cry from the more primitive Greyhounds of the previous fall. Jerry Lee and Paul Anka started a pillow fight that got out of hand, and the stewardess even cleared everyone else out of the area and told Lewis and Anka to go ahead and clobber each other.

There was an altercation between Buddy and Norman Petty when Jerry Allison disclosed his decision to get married. Peggy Sue Gerron had accepted Jerry's proposal. Petty, his own love life closeted and complex, suggested to Buddy that they fire Jerry and hire an unmarried drummer, since unwed rockers attract more fans. Turning to Jerry, Buddy said that, by the same token, they ought to fire Petty, a married man, and hire a single manager. Petty's domineering attitude was becoming intolerable. Buddy would have married Echo had she been willing, but now she was irretrievably out of his life: after a brief engagement she'd married her college classmate in Nebraska. Though Buddy's own marital plans were dashed, he staunchly defended Jerry's right to personal happiness. If he ever had to choose between Jerry and Petty, Petty would go. Jerry had been with Buddy from the start and the connections between them, both personal and musical, ran deep.

The Crickets landed at Sydney Airport in New South Wales on January 30 and checked into the Chevron Hotel before starting a week of engagements in Australia. The man behind the tour was Lee Gordon, one of the fifties' legendary rock impresarios, who the previous year had brought Bill Haley, the Platters, Little Richard, Gene Vincent, and Eddie Cochran to Australia. The Crickets again experienced difficulty playing to an arena-sized crowd—stadium rock was still ten years in the future for the United States. Australian rocker Col Joye later told Damian Johnstone, vice president of the Buddy Holly Appreciation Society of Australia, that Buddy was "electric—a fantastic performer," yet others were unimpressed. Alan Heffernan, codirector of the Lee Gordon organization, who introduced all the acts from an offstage microphone, revealed that Buddy, like many American rockers at the time, was "overwhelmed" in his initial confrontation with eleven thousand hysterical fans. Buddy froze the first time he faced the big Sydney crowd.

Nor was the subsequent tour by any means a progression of uninterrupted triumphs. Roger Covell, the *Brisbane Courier-Mail* reviewer, found Buddy to be obviously "ill-at-ease" and "inexperienced." Jerry Allison later acknowledged that they were not always at their best in Australia, especially during the first few shows. Since it was January, Australia was in the middle of its summer season. Allison cooled off by hitting a pub in Sydney with Anka and Jerry Lee where strong lager was served in foaming buckets. A nondrinker, Anka abstained, pointing out that, as the headliner, he had to remain sober for the evening performance. Bristling at the mention of the word *headliner*, the emulous Lewis encouraged Anka to have a beer. A few buckets later, as Lewis's ex-wife Myra relates in *Great Balls of Fire*, Lewis drove Anka out to the bush and said that he despised headliners and was going to kill him. Upset and ill, Anka missed the performance that night. According to Myra, Anka scrupulously avoided the Killer from then on.

Johnny O'Keefe, a handsome young singer whose recording "Wild One" was the rage of Australia, didn't care for Jerry Lee, either, but considered Buddy "a great fellow [with] an intangible quality as a performer." O'Keefe was known as "the Wild One" because of his abandon on stage and his hit record of that title. Jerry Allison liked O'Keefe's record and covered it later on, changing the title to "Real Wild Child." Allison's voice has a funky, freaky appeal—not in the least melodic but so catchy and engaging that it's unfortunate he hasn't done more solo work as a singer.

Following two Sydney performances, the tour was transported by bus to Newcastle, 105 miles northeast of Sydney, for two shows at the Stadium on January 31. The *Newcastle Morning Herald* reviewer wrote that the audience "rocked in the aisles and stamped their feet" but noted that the riots incited by Little Richard in Newcastle the previous year did not recur. After the performance, DJ Pat Barton from radio 2KO Newcastle asked Buddy how he got into rock 'n' roll. He and Jerry were old friends, Buddy said, and they'd performed together for five years; Joe had joined them the previous January. Since they recorded on two labels, were there two sets of Crickets? Barton asked. It was the same band on both Brunswick and Coral, Buddy replied. Asked if he wrote all their songs, Buddy replied that all the Crickets were songwriters. Then Barton wanted to know if Buddy's favorite singer was Elvis Presley. "I guess he's one of them," Buddy said, adding that he'd once known Elvis "quite well."

Was there any truth to rumors of conflict between the singer and his band? Barton queried. Buddy denied it, though he did admit that Niki had "stayed behind." As for Jerry and Joe B., Buddy stated categorically that he'd never split with them. The truth was perhaps too painful for Buddy to acknowledge, even to himself. His band was unstable. The Crickets were threatened from within by immature behavior that Buddy would increasingly have less tolerance of. Even more serious was the issue of his fast-growing fame, so disproportionate to Jerry and Joe B.'s that it would eventually threaten the continued existence of the Crickets.

By the time they played the Sydney Stadium on February 1, the group was accustomed to the large crowds. Jerry Lee later told Goldrosen that Buddy was the true star of the show and always left the Aussies in shock. Ken Taylor, an Australian record executive, christened Buddy and the Crickets the first gentlemen of rock 'n' roll. In Brisbane, 310 miles northeast of Sydney, where they played the Cloudland Ballroom on February 3, Lee Gordon put them up at the luxurious Broadbeech Hotel fifty miles

outside the city, on the gold coast of Queensland. The Australians appreciated Buddy's "innate decency" and "ascetic" nature, Taylor later
wrote in his autobiography *Rock Generation*. According to Myra Lewis,
Jerry Lee insulted the natives by saying they were so dumb when inebriated that they couldn't tell the difference between piss and beer. To prove
his point, he urinated in an empty beer bottle in a Brisbane bar, placing
it directly in front of an unsuspecting customer. The hapless man picked
up the bottle and took a swig. Spitting and wiping his mouth, he yelled
that he was going to murder the son of a bitch responsible for this outrage.
Jerry Lee, an artful dodger, somehow made it out of the bar alive.

From Brisbane they flew 1,250 miles to Melbourne, where they were
scheduled to appear at the Stadium (later renamed Festival Hall) on
February 4. Buddy checked into Melbourne's Chevron Hotel in St. Kilda
and went into the foyer to have morning coffee with Melbourne's only
rock 'n' roll DJ, Stan "The Man" Rofe. Since no one seemed to be waiting
for him, Buddy settled in a little lounge off the lobby and ordered his
coffee. Rofe later told Nigel Smith and Damian Johnstone of the Buddy
Holly Appreciation Society that he did not recognize Buddy, and for half
an hour they sat within fifty yards of each other, wondering if they'd been
stood up. When they finally connected, they got along so well that Buddy
returned with Rofe to 3KZ Radio and helped him broadcast his "Platter
Parade" program, chatting for ninety minutes on the air, reminiscing
about Eddie Cochran, and spinning the Top 40. Johnny O'Keefe popped
in just as Rofe was playing two versions of "Oop Poop A Doo" back to
back, one by O'Keefe and the other by Jessie Hill. Buddy committed a
faux pas, dismissing O'Keefe's version as "pretty horrible." Rofe hastily
advised Buddy that the recording artist he'd just insulted was sitting next
to him. Laughing it off, the good-natured O'Keefe looked at Buddy and
said, "You're hysterical."

At the end of "Platter Parade," Rofe and Buddy shared a taxi to the
West Melbourne Stadium, where Rofe, who had a large teenage following,
emceed the 6:15 P.M. show. After introducing Buddy, Rofe went backstage, but there was so much excitement in the audience that he went
back out front to catch Buddy's phenomenal set. The reviewer for the
Melbourne Herald wrote on February 5 that Buddy "shook the stadium"
with "Oh Boy" and "Rip It Up," emerging the "undoubted star" of the
tour. All of this was remarkable in Melbourne, a city with a prim Vic-
torian heritage that was far more repressed in its taste and sensibility than
Sydney to the east.

Though O'Keefe never caught on with U.S. fans, he was idolized in
his native Australia. Several years later, O'Keefe met Sonny Curtis during
a visit to the U.S. They went partying in Tijuana and when they decided
they'd had enough and started to cross the border back into California,

O'Keefe said, "There's just one problem, Sonny. I don't have any citizen-ship papers."

"Oh, no," Sonny said. "Well, just say, 'I'm from Omaha, Nebraska,' and maybe they'll let us through."

Recalled Sonny in 1993, "It worked. We got back into California and breathed a sigh of relief."

Back in 1958, before leaving Melbourne, the tour party recorded a Colgate Palmolive radio show for the Macquaire Radio Network at the Nurses Memorial Center on St. Kilda Road, which had the best acoustics in town for recording a big live concert. There was no audience except for the doctors and nurses who wandered through the performance area and paused for a few minutes to listen to the rockers from America. MC Geoff Manion, the breakfast announcer at radio station 3AW, com-plained that Jerry Lee disrupted the rehearsal by banging on the piano with his feet while the show band tried to rehearse. Buddy, on the other hand, impressed Manion as unassuming and likable, qualities Manion had not previously noted among touring celebrities.

Buddy's latest recording, "I'm Gonna Love You Too"/"Listen to Me," was released back in the States during the Australian tour and received a *Cash Box* "Pick of the Week" designation. After noting that Buddy's songs had been on the charts continuously for the past six months, the reviewer praised "Listen to Me" as "thrilling," describing it as a C&W-inflected rock ballad with a Latin tempo. The B-side, "I'm Gonna Love You Too," also received high marks. The reviewer lauded Buddy's multiple-track performances on both sides, concluding, "Chalk up an-other hit for Holly."

Unfortunately, *Cash Box*'s prediction was wide of the mark. Though "Listen to Me" is one of Buddy's best records, it was undermined by an untimely release. Decca never should have issued another Holly single when he already had so many hits in circulation. DJs are reluctant to play consecutive records by the same artist, so they sacrificed "Listen to Me" in order to go on playing Buddy's more familiar Top 40 releases. Had Decca waited for his 1957 hits to run their course, "Listen to Me" prob-ably would have succeeded. Though both sides eventually showed up on the U.K. charts—"Listen to Me" cresting at No. 16 in England and "I'm Gonna Love You Too" making it into Australia's Top 40—neither reached a wide U.S. audience. Buddy's uninterrupted winning streak on the *Billboard* chart was over—due not to a decline in quality but to an embarrassment of riches.

On February 6, the tour party began the long journey home, stopping over once again in Hawaii. On February 9, Buddy paid a series of visits to Honolulu DJs to promote his records. In a color picture Petty took of Buddy in his room at the Kaiser Hotel, Buddy is shown gazing out over the blue Pacific, his expression reflecting a new maturity and content-ment. If he was savoring his moment at the epicenter of pop, he was doing so with remarkable calm and apparent humility.

During the return flight, one of the Constellation's engines blew a valve and stalled over the Pacific Ocean, as if an omen of things to come. The pilot made an emergency landing on the remote island of Canton, where Jerry Allison wrote a letter home complaining about the delay.

On Monday, February 10, 1958, aboard Braniff Airlines flight 39, the Crickets finally set down in Lubbock. After the summer heat of Australia, the 40-degree temperature seemed arctic. As usual Lubbock took no no-tice of its world-class celebrity. At some point in that year, Buddy went shopping for a new Cadillac. Mindlessly, he let his father talk him into buying a Lincoln, which he regretted at once. He drove to Clovis on February 12 to cut "Well All Right," a hard-edged indictment of cynical, jaded grownups who dismiss young love. Jerry's ride-cymbal figure is the perfect accompaniment to Buddy's tense, insistent vocal. The Tinker AFB version of "Maybe Baby" was released on February 12, with the equally felicitous "Tell Me How" on the B-side. "Maybe Baby" entered the *Cash Box* chart the same month. Brash, turbocharged, and cocky, with a unique "dot-ditty-ot-dot" backup riff by the Picks, "Maybe Baby" is perhaps the definitive Holly song, a breezy seesaw ride, alternating doubt and hope.

The Crickets were back in the Clovis studio two days later to cut "Take Your Time," "Think It Over," and "Fool's Paradise," working with a new vocal group called the Roses. Robert Linville, a member of the trio, later described Buddy to Bill Griggs as "a skinny guy with a pack of cigarettes rolled up in his T-shirt sleeve." They rehearsed everything they were going to cut that day, but when the session started, the Crickets performed without their backup singers. Not until later did the Roses overdub their vocals, which include some of the most inventive doo-wahs to be heard south of the Bronx. Though the Roses' contribution is crucial in "It's So Easy," "Think It Over," "Lonesome Tears," and "Fool's Paradise," they were paid only $65 each per session.

George Tomsco, a young musician from Raton, New Mexico, who had a band called the Fireballs, was around the studio in 1958. One day Buddy picked up Tomsco's new Fender Jazzmaster and started playing it. Tomsco, who didn't recognize Buddy, started to complain, but when Petty in-formed him of Buddy's identity, Tomsco's attitude suddenly changed from irritation to gratitude. He remembers being "spellbound" that day as he watched Buddy record.

The Clovis sessions did not always go smoothly. While Buddy was recording "Take Your Time," Petty inserted some awkward lyrics that Buddy kept tripping over. Far-fetched and pretentious, the lyrics attempted to evoke an improbable image of hearts and strings. It was an unsingable line and Buddy said it was going to take all night to get it right. On the unreleased tape, Vi Petty can be heard in the background snapping, with mock patience, that they had plenty of time. Buddy warned that he was going to "crap out." Later, as they recorded another song, "Think It Over," Vi vented her anger by violently pounding the keyboard during the piano break. When they played it back they realized it was a first-rate boogie-woogie piano solo. Buddy was so pleased that he made Vi an honorary Cricket. It was about time; her contribution in the studio was essential. Since none of the Crickets could read music, she was perpetually on call to play tunes from sheet music until everyone learned them.

"Think It Over" epitomizes Buddy's "who needs you?" attitude toward women and perhaps life in general. After his relationship with Echo, he developed a thicker emotional skin. Though he maintained a polite fa-çade in public, he became outspoken and sometimes rude with girl fans, whom he and Jerry Allison referred to as "chicks." On the road, a careless remark from a pushy girl could raise his hackles. Jerry recounted in Gold-rosen and Beecher's *Remembering Buddy* what happened when an unlucky fan asked Buddy why he wore such large eyeglasses. "Hey, forget you," Buddy said, and kicked her out. Both Buddy and Jerry Lee Lewis, who'd become friends during their shows at the Paramount and in Australia, were sometimes cruel to rock's first-generation groupies. Jerry Lee punched some fans in the eye when they annoyed him backstage. Those who grabbed at him during performances sometimes got their hands crushed and their arms kicked at. "Animosity toward Jerry Lee's allegiants," wrote Myra Lewis, "was the first of many amazing self-contradictions indicating the workings of a troubled mind."

Phil Everly observed the same ambivalence in Buddy and later de-scribed it to interviewer Margaret McNie. On one of their tours together, Buddy was entertaining Phil and a groupie in his hotel room. The groupie wanted to go to bed with Buddy, but Buddy winked at Phil and started playing games, telling the girl that, as Phil's friend, he had to be mindful of Phil's feelings. But it was Phil's impression that Buddy was staging the whole scene as a joke on Phil. "If I asked her to leave," Buddy said, staring at Phil, "you'd go along, wouldn't you?" When Phil said that of course he would, Buddy perversely insisted that *Phil* tell her to leave. Phil, who'd been looking forward to partying with the girl, cussed Buddy out. Sud-denly Buddy started laughing, stood up, and threw the girl out of the hotel room himself. He was torn between the natural urgings of a youthful and vigorous sex drive—so easily satisfied for a popular rock 'n' roller—and his yearning for the good girls of home, like Echo, who was now lost to him forever. He longed to establish a home and start a family, but not with the groupies who flocked to him.

At home between tours he discussed his religious conflict with his brother Larry. As they sat in Buddy's Lincoln Continental, he asked Larry what he should do about his life, which he felt had veered off course. He'd surfaced from agonizing religious raps with Little Richard extremely disturbed. Richard was now studying to become a minister at a theological college in Alabama. Was it possible, Buddy wondered, to be in touch with God's will and pursue a career as a rock star at the same time? Larry did not answer him directly but pointed out that no higher power could be effective in anyone's life unless spirituality came first, even above career and ambition. God does not take a backseat to anyone or anything, Larry said. The next Sunday, Buddy dropped a sizable check in the collection plate at Tabernacle Baptist Church and had a serious talk with Reverend Ben D. Johnson. Later he told Larry that he was going to record some religious albums as a way of remaining a singer and a Christian simultaneously and that he intended to keep pouring money into the church.

But he couldn't buy the church's approval, and so his religion turned the thing he loved most, music, into a curse. No wonder his life would be increasingly stressful and reckless in the few precious months that remained of it. Sadly, despite all his parents' support of him, he sensed that they, too, withheld their approval. Since he was still young enough that their opinion mattered, he never quite convinced himself, despite his hit records and superlative reviews, that he had truly arrived. He existed in a state of tension and expectation, wondering how to top himself, how to prove himself to his parents. It wasn't enough to be creating music and releasing records on a national label; everything he recorded had to be a hit.

In this spiritual crisis, it is to be hoped that Buddy, who knew the Bible well, did not overlook God's grand synthesis of music, flesh, and the spirit, which is described in the Old Testament, in *The Song of Solomon:*

> The voice of my beloved! behold, he cometh leaping upon the mountains, skipping upon the hills. My beloved is like a roe or a young hart. . . . Rise up, my love, my fair one, and come away. For, lo, the winter is past, the rain is over and gone; the flowers appear on the earth; the time of the singing of birds is come, and the voice of the turtle is heard in our land. . . . Arise, my love, my fair one, and come away. O my dove, thou art in the clefts of the rock, in the secret places of the stairs, let me see thy countenance, let me hear thy voice; for sweet is thy voice, and thy countenance is comely. Take us the foxes, the little foxes, that spoil the vines: for

our vines have tender grapes. My beloved is mine, and I am his; he
feedeth among the lilies. Until day break, and the shadows flee
away, turn, my beloved, and be thou like a roe or a young hart
upon the mountains . . .

So many of the conflicts that vex mankind—and bedeviled Buddy
Holly—come from religion, not from spirituality or God.

Buddy's forthcoming trip to England, set for March 1958, at first seemed
to him quite the most important event of his lifetime. The challenge of
translating rock to the Old World both excited and frightened him. But
in a conversation with Larry, he said that nothing would ever be as meaningful to him as the day he was baptized. He reminisced about that time
in his youth: he had still been in adolescence but he was already getting
into "all kinds of jams," he said, just beginning his brush with juvenile
delinquency. Then one day he realized that although he would never be
flawless and could never attain perfection, he qualified as a son of God
and he could always trust Jesus to take care of him. He had turned his
life and his will over to the care of God on the day of his baptism. Since
then, he had not felt that he was leading his life so much as walking in
God's shadow, or trying to.

Unlike many who achieve early stardom, Buddy retained his humility,
though he worked hard to do so. Despite being a headliner, he could
always be counted on to provide musical backup any time a show-business
colleague needed it. On the "Big Gold Record Stars" tour of Florida in
February 1958, just before his departure for England, Buddy helped the
Everly Brothers out of a bind. They lacked a band of their own, and
the booker in Florida had assigned them three high school students. The
Crickets opened the show and received a tumultuous ovation. Watching
from the wings, the Everlys almost panicked. How could they, with their
raggedy band, possibly appear on the same bill with the fabulous Crickets?
Their predicament only worsened when Jerry Lee Lewis followed the
Crickets and reduced the audience to a state of quivering hysteria. At last
it was time for the Everlys to go onstage and close the show, which could
be nothing but an anticlimax with their high school band. In desperation
they appealed to Buddy, who immediately offered to back them up. A
grateful Phil later revealed that "only by the grace of God and Buddy
Holly" had the Everly Brothers managed to survive that night. With the
Crickets behind them, they came on and created "pandemonium," Phil
added.

A reviewer who attended the second of their two Fort Lauderdale performances in February wrote that although Jerry Lee received a "solid
reception for his wild act . . . the top scorers" with the audience of 3,000
at the War Memorial Auditorium were Buddy Holly and the Everly

Brothers. Charging through "Peggy Sue," "Oh Boy," and "That'll Be the Day," Buddy proved to be "adept at his medium," the critic noted, his "slim frame present[ing] a touch of humor . . . as he struts around the stage bobbing his head back and forth to the rhythm of the music." Unimpressed by the Royal Teens, who had only "Short Shorts" to "crow about," the reviewer said they "failed to get into the same league" with Buddy and the Everlys and panned their "fairly nondescript offerings."

When they played the National Guard Armory in Jacksonville, Florida, Buddy almost had a run-in with Mae Boren Axton, the cowriter of "Heartbreak Hotel," the No. 1 hit that propelled Elvis from regional stardom to international idol. Axton, who was handling the publicity for Buddy's Jacksonville appearance, was upset when he failed to appear for a TV program that had been scheduled just before the first Armory show. "Impulsive that I am," Axton later wrote in *Country Song Roundups*, "I was inclined to berate young Holly somewhat, until I saw the hurt look in his eyes, and heard the quick defense by his companion artists, Don and Phil Everly." None of the singers had been advised by the tour promoter that they were expected at the TV station, the Everlys told Axton. "Our high esteems of young Holly continued because of Don and Phil's true friendship of him," Axton concluded.

After the Florida tour, "Holly and his group rushed to the Miami airport to make connections for their first trip to England," a reporter wrote. Buddy's arrival at London's Heathrow Airport on March 1, 1958, marked a watershed in the history of rock 'n' roll. The twenty-five-day British tour inspired and molded a generation of English musicians—among them John Lennon, Paul McCartney, Keith Richards, Eric Clapton, Graham Nash, and Elton John—who would spearhead the British Invasion of the 1960s. They would add distinction and depth to rock and take it to a level of cultural influence, political power, and personal wealth scarcely dreamed of by its West Texas pioneer.

England was ripe for Buddy Holly in the late 1950s; Britain's underemployed and resentful working-class youth had grown restive under an antiquated and repressive caste system which marked people for life according to their lineage and locution. Though London was an elegant and sedate city of green parks, double-decker buses, spotless taxicabs, scarlet telephone booths, and immaculate white town houses, the society seemed as stagnant and arcane as its cumbersome currency system, the last in the world to resist decimalization. The government-owned BBC was the only TV and radio network. Wimpy's was the sole fast-food chain. Bars serving room-temperature ale and stout closed their doors promptly at eleven P.M., and there was no nightlife; the Underground (subway) closed at midnight. Stores stopped doing business at noon on Saturday and didn't open again until Monday morning. England was a land still recovering from the trauma of war thirteen years before, and poverty was widespread.

Voices of change were just beginning to be heard. In the mid-fifties Colin Wilson's ground-breaking study *The Outsider* heralded a generation of dissidents. Then came the Angry Young Men of the West End theater, led by John Osborne, whose play *Look Back in Anger* galvanized young people fed up with the sclerotic establishment's culture, manners, snobbism, and hypocrisy. From the publishing world came John Braine's sizzling novel *Room at the Top*, which announced the arrival of a dynamic working-class hero. Rock 'n' roll was the next step in the emancipation of the British from years of stiff-upper-lip stodginess, and Buddy Holly was its standard-bearer.

The Crickets were under contract to Lew and Leslie Grade, two brothers whose power was felt throughout show business in the United Kingdom. Lewis Grade, later to become Lord Grade, was described in 1988 by John Lennon's biographer Albert Goldman as "the fat-cat, cigar-sucking boss of the British entertainment industry." He owned ATV, the Associated Television Corporation, England's major independent producer of TV programs. Leslie Grade, Lew's brother, ran the largest theatrical agency in England, handling stars such as Laurence Olivier and also packaging movies, television shows, and stage attractions. In the sixties, the agency attempted to sign the Beatles, by then the most valuable act in the world, and failed. In retaliation, ATV seized controlling interest in Northern Songs, the Lennon-McCartney publishing company, in a hotly contested takeover. A third brother, Bernard Delfont, was a theater owner and controlled many of London's West End stage productions. Unlike Lew and Leslie, who had changed their names from Winogradsky to Grade, Bernard preferred the tonier-sounding Delfont.

At Heathrow, accompanied by the Crickets and Norman and Vi Petty, Buddy complained to a *Melody Maker* reporter that he was paying two managers and a booking agent. According to *Melody Maker* he could well afford to, having received $2,000 per night on his last tour. Wally, the British road manager, "stuffed" the Crickets onto a bus along with the "motley crew" that made up the rest of the package: comedian Des O'Connor, a juggling act, the Tanner Sisters, Ronnie Keane, and a fourteen-piece band. After the star-studded casts of the Feld tours, the Crickets were astonished to be the sole rock band on the bill. But it was fun from the start, Jerry said years later in Paul McCartney's TV documentary *The Real Buddy Holly Story*. Tired of the American road, they welcomed the enormous change that England represented for them.

One reporter informed Buddy that more than one million English teens had purchased his recordings. His reply struck the journalist as "very cautious"; Buddy said the band had been together for a year but he still wondered "how long it's going to last." He was grateful that the public "seems to like us" and felt they'd survive if they didn't "make any mistakes." Though Buddy was a man of true humbleness, both he and Elvis Presley realized the value of a public display of modesty. Indeed, they made it the style of early rock 'n' roll; soon it would be replaced by the surly cockiness of sixties rock.

He was apprehensive about how the British were going to respond to a bunch of country boys from Lubbock, which was more like Liverpool than he could ever have imagined. He needn't have worried. Forty-five hundred fans came to the Trocadero, Elephant and Castle, for the Crickets' debut on Saturday, March 1, 1958—fifteen hundred at the first show and three thousand at the second. One critic saluted the Crickets as "one of the breeziest packages to be imported into Britain." The reviewer also listed some reservations: their set was too short—only twenty minutes—and the ticket price too steep at 10s.6d. "Shortweight is hardly forgivable," wrote the critic. Reviewing them on March 8, *Melody Maker* said Buddy was "obviously out of his depth" when he imitated Elvis's movements and elicited "scornful laughs" from a few in the audience, but the hecklers were drowned out by "screams from the usual bevy of teenagers." On a more positive note, the reviewer praised Buddy's "Peggy Sue" as "every bit as good as on the disc" and concluded that Britain's "outdated variety halls could learn a lot from these teenage coast-to-coast tours."

Jerry remembered the elation they felt on being cheered by the British, who have a reputation for being restrained and highly discriminating. Bill Haley was the only rocker who'd preceded them to England; many in the audience were experiencing rock 'n' roll for the first time. The Crickets were so stimulated by their favorable reception in England that they started leaping around on the stage, vying to see who could be the most audacious. Joe B. reclined on the stage, lowering his bull fiddle to his body as he might a woman, and plucked away. Buddy squatted over him, singing into a microphone that was attached to the bass. When the Crickets noticed that everyone was "marvelin'," as Jerry put it, they thought "aren't we the ones!"

Since Lew Grade owned ATV and personally produced *Val Parnell's Sunday Night at the London Palladium*, the most widely viewed television program in England, the Crickets were guaranteed a slot on the show. Their live TV appearance at the Palladium on March 2, 1958, some say, became the bedrock on which English rock 'n' roll was founded. Still children or teenagers in 1958, the future leaders of the British rock movement watched the show on their families' or their neighbors' TV sets.

As Buddy boogied the audience in the venerable, gilt-crusted Palladium on Argyll Street, near Oxford Circus, seventeen-year-old John

Lennon leaned toward his TV screen in Liverpool, gaping at Buddy's
Fender Stratocaster, the first he'd ever seen, and studied Jerry's paradiddles
in "Peggy Sue," which he'd never understood before. Later Lennon would
call Buddy the innovative master of early rock 'n' roll.

•Paul McCartney, fifteen, had recently joined Lennon's band the
Quarry Men. He later said that he acquired his technical "info" as
a rock 'n' roll guitar player by watching Buddy's Palladium performance, studying his fingers to discover how he performed the
"Peggy Sue" solo and if he used the capo. Paul scrutinized the guitar itself, the weird but cool-looking Fender. From then on, Paul
"always loved Buddy's music" and regarded him as a major influence.
•Keith Richards was a fifteen-year-old living at 6 Spielman Road in
Dartford, a small industrial town sixteen miles southeast of London, where his father worked as a foreman in an electronics factory in Hammersmith. He'd first met Mick Jagger, a Dartford
neighbor, when they rode their tricycles around Denver Road and
later attended Wentworth Primary School. In 1955 Keith's
eleven-plus examination landed him in Dartford Technical College. With his soprano voice, he sang in the school choir and
later at Westminster Abbey during the coronation of Queen Elizabeth II, performing the "Hallelujah" chorus from Handel's *Messiah*. Then, in 1958, "rock 'n' roll hit England like Hiroshima,"
Richards later told interviewer Charles Young. He talked his
mother, Doris, into buying him an acoustic Rosetti guitar for
seven pounds. Among his first musical influences were John Lee
Hooker, Muddy Waters, Chuck Berry, and Buddy Holly. Richards
respected Buddy because he was "self-contained, wrote his own
songs, had a great band, and didn't need anyone else." The Rolling Stones would derive their sound from Buddy's "Not Fade
Away," which also provided them with the "extra provocation,"
Richards said, to compose their own material.
•Eric Clapton, thirteen, was living in Ripley, a village in Surrey,
where he was considered a weirdo, at the time of Buddy's
Palladium telecast. He'd been listening to a Saturday-morning
radio program since he was ten or eleven that featured a DJ
named Uncle Mac, whom Clapton later described as "a very old
man with one leg. . . . He'd play things like 'Mule Train,' and
then every week he'd slip in something like a Buddy Holly
record."
Clapton first heard of the blues when he read the liner notes

on one of Buddy's album covers and "greatly admired the style, the look, the individuality of Buddy Holly," according to biographer Ray Coleman. For Clapton's fourteenth birthday, he asked his grandparents, Rose and Jack Clapp, who were raising him, for a guitar. He picked up a $35 acoustic from Bell's instrument shop in Kingston and smiled all the way home. Years later he told Philip Norman that his grandparents paid for the guitar "on the HP [hire purchase or time payment]—a [double cutaway] Kay. It wasn't cheap and flash; it was expensive and flash." Practicing the guitar became Clapton's overriding obsession, and the turning point of his life occurred when he discovered he could get an echo effect like Buddy Holly's by playing in the stairwell at home. "It sounded like a record," Clapton said later, "and I thought, 'Yeah, this could be. . . . The world had better watch out.'"

•Elton John was an eleven-year-old growing up in Metroland, Buckinghamshire, and still known as Reginald Kenneth Dwight. He was so impressed by Buddy that he started wearing glasses "not because he needed them," wrote Philip Norman, "but in homage to Buddy Holly, rock music's first four-eyes. At thirteen Elton John imagined himself to *be* Buddy Holly."

•Denny Laine, the future linchpin of Wings, was twelve at the time of Buddy's tour and had been "listening to Buddy Holly a lot. He was my first real inspiration," recalled Laine. "In fact, the guitar lick on 'That'll Be the Day' made me want to learn to play." Later on, McCartney produced Laine's solo LP *Holly Days*, ten tracks of Buddy Holly songs including the seldom covered "Lonesome Tears" and "Look at Me."

Obviously oblivious to the impact he would have on the coming generation of musicians, Buddy engaged in a fervent backstage colloquy at the Palladium with comedian Bob Hope, the British-born star of U.S. wartime radio and films. In a lengthy letter to his parents, Buddy proudly recounted their talk as one of the high points of the trip. The tour party left London on March 3, bound for Hampshire, where it played the Gaumont Theater, then went north into Yorkshire and east to Stockton-on-Tees, by the North Sea. Outside London, the audiences were punctilious, polite, and comparatively subdued. At first the Crickets thought they were bombing, but everywhere they went, hundreds of silent, well-mannered fans, including both teenagers and adults, queued up for their autographs, sometimes standing in the rain.

Occasionally the Crickets ruffled the feathers of a provincial critic, like the Bradford, Yorkshire, *Telegraph and Argus*'s Peter Holdsworth, who deplored the "fanatical reception" accorded Buddy, then referred to him as a "screeching guitar player." Seventy percent of lyrics "which issued from the lips of this foot-stamping, knee-falling musician" were indecipherable, according to Holdsworth, who couldn't understand why the kids didn't prefer a more "articulate vocalist." He concluded his fulmination with the question, "Where on earth is show business heading?"

Their hectic itinerary allowed no time for sightseeing, Buddy complained in a letter to his mother. They were in Birmingham, a city whose industrial grittiness contrasted with the majesty of London, to play Town Hall on March 10. With a population of one million, Birmingham was, like Liverpool, poorer—its teenagers more like those in Lubbock. Writing on the stationery of the Alexandra Hotel, Buddy reported that he'd been suffering from a cold for the past four days. Still sick and feverish the following morning, he boarded the bus and rode twenty-five miles to Worcester, where he managed to complete two shows at the Gaumont. Joe B. later told Griggs that they were homesick and full of complaints about the cold, damp weather. Expecting to freeze any moment, they yearned for the warmer climate of Lubbock.

Despite exhaustion and chills, when they returned to London for two shows at Croydon's Davis Theater on March 12 and two more at the East Ham Granada on the thirteenth, they received a rave review from the *New Musical Express* critic, Keith Goodwin, who praised their high spirits and unrestrained fury and predicted that they were destined for a long and exciting career. According to Goodwin, their success in Britain was due to the fact that they sounded as good in person as they did on their recordings. "This is rock 'n' roll like we've never heard it before in Britain," Goodwin concluded.

In London, Buddy must have slipped away from his Texas colleagues long enough to sample the sartorial splendors of Saville Row, for in photographs taken after the British tour it is clear that the kid from Lubbock had gone shopping in this bastion of the aristocracy. With the innate taste and style that had led him to wear Levis in Texas when everyone else was in baggy gabardines, Buddy selected some elegant clothes, perhaps including the overcoat with a fur collar, cravats, and Turnbull & Asser shirts in which he was later photographed. He also picked up a mod jacket somewhere, possibly in Carnaby Street. His shopping spree would have reverberations throughout the 1960s, first in the neo-Edwardian styles of British rockers and later throughout Anglo-American culture, when men rebelled against traditionally staid masculine dress codes and adopted the "peacock look."

The tour set out once again from the British capital, zigzagging across the island country with stops in Ipswich, Leicester, Doncaster, Wigan, and Hull. On March 20, the group arrived in Liverpool, the center of a burgeoning rock movement, to play Philharmonic Hall. By this time the Crickets had four records in the British Top 30—"Listen to Me," "Oh Boy," "Peggy Sue," and "Maybe Baby"—and were responsible for a boom in guitar sales in every town and city they played. A foggy, sooty seaport city of five hundred thousand, Liverpool was the birthplace of British rock. John Winston Lennon, a school boy whose adolescence parallels Buddy Holly's in remarkable detail, grew up a shoplifter, juvenile delinquent, gang member, and garage-band organizer who favored drainpipe trousers and wore eyeglasses. About eight months prior to Buddy's arrival, Lennon and McCartney met through a mutual friend named Ivan Vaughan. Lennon's group, the Quarry Men, was playing a local church fair. McCartney was invited to join the group and the Quarry Men's evolution into the Beatles took a great leap forward.

It was Buddy's look as much as his music that inspired the Beatles, who'd previously been drawn, McCartney later revealed, to "really good-looking" performers such as Cliff Richards and Elvis. Buddy's glasses intrigued them. Like the bespectacled Roy Orbison, who'd feared he'd never succeed as a performer until he saw Buddy Holly, the Beatles assumed that singers who wore glasses could never expect stardom. Said McCartney in 1986, "Until Buddy came along, any fellow with glasses always took them off to play." Suddenly Buddy's bold, unashamed appearance before the British public in thick horn-rims gave them hope, especially John Lennon, who was legally blind but stumbled around onstage without his glasses, afraid he'd be ridiculed. After seeing Buddy, Lennon adopted "the Buddy Holly Look," McCartney later told Lennon's half-sister Julia Baird, wearing "big thick black glasses" onstage and off; he could "see the world for once," said McCartney, adding, "anyone who really needed to wear glasses could then come out of the closet." John and Paul soon started cutting classes at school and hiding out at Paul's house, where they'd take out their guitars and compose songs for hours on end, attempting "to figure out how Buddy did it."

Lennon became such a Crickets fan after their two Liverpool shows that he wrote to Jerry Allison's mother in Lubbock, inquiring how Jerry and Buddy had formed the Crickets, how they'd broken through to success, and how John and his band could launch themselves. Years later Lennon explained to California Buddy Holly fan Jim Dawson how he selected the name the Beatles for the band. Mindful of the Crickets, Lennon started casting about for another insect name and finally came up with the Beatles. He intended for the name to be taken as a double entendre, signifying insects as well as music with a distinctive beat. Still another factor, according to Mark Hertsgaard's 1995 book *A Day in the Life: The Music and Artistry of the Beatles*, was the motorcycle gang in Marlon Brando's movie *The Wild One*, which was called the Beetles.

After Liverpool the Crickets returned to London, traversing 175 miles on March 21 and staging two shows the same day in Walthamstow's Granada Theater. Afterward they continued south, driving eighty miles to Salisbury, where they played the Gaumont on the twenty-second and then repaired to the Old George Hotel for a warm, cozy night. Petty and Jerry lounged in front of a roaring fireplace, analyzing a dream of Petty's in which all his teeth had fallen out. Overhearing them as he sat nearby, composing a letter to his mother which was later published in Griggs's magazine *Reminiscing*, Buddy wrote, perhaps only half jokingly, that Petty seemed to be getting decrepit. In the same letter he complimented his parents for making improvements on their house and signed off with love, promising to call them when he arrived in New York at the end of the month. The amenities at the Old George delighted them. "The ladies fixed us hot chocolate at night," Vi Petty later recalled. Such respites were rare. None of them got a really good look at England, according to Vi, who said that the Crickets were awake all night or trying to grab an hour's sleep, "just piled all over each other in the bus."

After playing Colston Hall in Bristol and the Capitol Cinema in Cardiff, they concluded the tour in London with two shows at the Hammersmith Gaumont on March 25. It was a dreadful day for the Crickets. The same horseplay that had driven Niki from the group erupted again in Hammersmith, threatening to destroy the band. Buddy was relaxing in the dressing room after the first of their two shows when Joe B. walked in, chomping on a stogy, which he threatened to light up. Joe B. later told Griggs, "Jokingly, both J.I. and Buddy said that I was *not* going to smoke that cigar in the dressing room." Buddy was beginning to get ready for the final performance and probably feared that Joe B.'s cigar smoke would damage his vocal cords.

But Joe B. was adamant. He struck a match, lit the cigar, and began to puff on it furiously, deliberately attempting to turn the room into a smoke box. Buddy and Jerry lunged at him and tried to wrest the cigar from his mouth. Buddy secured Joe B.'s left arm while Jerry pinned down his right, hoping to keep Joe B. still long enough to grab the cigar. Joe B. struggled violently, swinging his head and trying to hit Buddy in the stomach. Later Joe B. told Goldrosen that he wanted to strike Buddy hard enough to knock the breath out of him. Then he intended to "take care of J.I.," he added in a 1980 interview with Griggs. In the upshot, Joe B.'s forehead slammed into Buddy's mouth instead of his stomach, and the caps on Buddy's two front teeth broke off and went flying. Reeling from the blow, Buddy immediately called off the show and said they'd forgo their fee; he could hardly go onstage in snaggle-toothed disarray. Professionally, it was a potential wipeout. As Joe B. himself later said in *Rem-*

iniscing magazine, the cancellation would jeopardize the Crickets' career; he described it as a "very traumatic incident."

Petty, who never seemed to appear in time to prevent trouble, promptly materialized the minute his meal ticket was threatened. He persuaded Buddy to go on after all. A wad of chewing gum concealed his exposed stumps. The show they put on was "hideous," according to Joe B., whose forehead had sustained an injury serious enough to scar him for the rest of his life. When they returned to the dressing room, Petty, with his usual lack of finesse, told them that they had just put on the "worst" performance of their career.

Such was the end of the Crickets' historic British tour. Despite the career strides they had made in England, it was clear by the time they boarded the plane to return to the United States that nothing short of a miracle could save rock 'n' roll's premier band. Buddy must have been disgusted by the debacle at the Hammersmith Gaumont. Back in New York, he became absorbed in personal matters that monopolized all his attention, especially his courtship of a pert, petite girl behind the receptionist's desk at Peer-Southern. He met her one day when he dropped in to see Murray Deutch and immediately started flirting with her. She was not altogether unresponsive.

Her name was Maria Elena Santiago. Slightly older than Buddy, she was a Puerto Rican young woman who had come to New York to live with her aunt, Provi Garcia, in the 1940s. Hundreds of thousands of Puerto Ricans had gone north to New York in the following decade, forever altering the cultural face of the city and bringing a new vitality. The most distinguished musical of the 1950s, *West Side Story*, epitomized, if not stereotyped, the character of this historic migration, and the musical was currently playing at the Winter Garden, featuring a chorus of Puerto Rican girls, including one named Maria, singing an impudent, spirited song about the wretchedness of San Juan and the dubious advantages of America.

"He came in with the other two Crickets, Jerry and Joe B.," Maria Elena said in our 1993 interview. "He introduced himself and said he was going to see Murray Deutch—he had an appointment. I said, 'All right.' I called in and Murray said for him to wait a few minutes; he had another client in there. In the meantime, while Buddy was waiting, he started a conversation, just to get my attention, I guess. That was when he asked me if I wanted to go out to dinner with him."

Maria Elena regarded him with interest, not only because he was a rock star, but because his forward behavior struck a responsive chord in her. She was already then a tempestuous, passionate woman. Buddy appeared to be sinewy and vigorous, and women were often quick to sense that a veritable "Superman" lurked beneath his "Clark Kentish" exterior. Recalling the moment in 1993, Maria Elena's voice waxes warm and intimate. "I liked him. I liked him right away," she confides. "As quiet and shy as he appeared to be, when he made up his mind, *that was it.*"

Though she seemed hesitant, Buddy grew even bolder. Her luminous eyes contradicting every word, she explained that she "was not allowed to go out with anybody that was a client here. My aunt is one of the executives here. I live with my aunt. She doesn't want me to go out with musicians. She feels that they are not 'all there,' that they're mostly crazy people." She was charmed when Buddy attempted to speak Spanish with her. Later, she told Griggs that Buddy said, "How are you, Señorita?"

Murray Deutch summoned Buddy into his office. Having had a significant hand in launching Buddy's career, Deutch remained a close adviser. They greeted each other fondly and rehashed Buddy's profitable tours of Australia and England. Everywhere Buddy had appeared in the United Kingdom, fans had flocked to the stores, sending his records up the charts. In March 1958 "Maybe Baby" was No. 4 in England, No. 15 in Australia, and No. 17 in the U.S. "Listen to Me" was No. 14 in England, where Paul McCartney would later tell John Tobler that it was his favorite Holly tune, "a really great track." Though *Rolling Stone*'s David McGee would one day hail "Listen to Me" as a brilliant tender-tough ballad, one of Buddy's "best-conceived efforts," in 1958 the single was hopelessly lost in a U.S. record market glutted with Holly hits.

Also disappointing were sales on Buddy's new solo album, *Buddy Holly*, which Coral released in March. Though the LP included the immortal "Rave On," later hailed by *Rolling Stone* as "one of the great rock-'n'-roll songs," "Rave On" bombed in the United States on release. *Cash Box* didn't even mention it as one of the cuts on the LP in its March 15 review. When Decca released "Rave On" as a single in April, it at last hit the Top 40, despite flak from easy-listening radio stations, whose DJs identified "Rave On" as the cause of juvenile delinquency. Still, it crested at No. 37 in America, faring far better in the United Kingdom, where it soared to No. 5 in England and No. 29 in Australia.

Neither of Buddy's LPs—*The Chirping Crickets* and *Buddy Holly*—made the *Billboard* Top 40 in America, where rock 'n' roll had peaked and was beginning to decline. Years later, rock critics would place both albums near the top of their all-time best LP lists. In England, in the wake of Buddy's tour, his LPs sold briskly from the beginning. *The Chirping Crickets* shot to No. 5 and *Buddy Holly* went to No. 8. "The British were certainly warming to rock 'n' roll," Ed Ward later wrote in *Rock of Ages: The Rolling Stone History of Rock 'n' Roll*. "When *Billboard* noted that fifteen of the top twenty records in Britain were American, they were talking about

BUDDY (*third row, third from right*) in the Tom Lubbock High School chorus. Buddy was in the class of 1955, but he was not asked to sing during the musical portions of the commencement exercise. (*Westerner*)

JERRY IVAN ALLISON, future drummer of the Crickets, as a schoolboy in Lubbock. His steady drumming sparked the early rock classic "Peggy Sue," inspired by classmate and girlfriend Peggy Sue Gerron. (*Westerner*)

Future Cricket **SONNY CURTIS**. From Meadow, Texas, Sonny was the most talented and articulate of Buddy's musicians—skilled with both fiddle and guitar, and a gifted singer and songwriter. (Pete Curtis)

LESTER FLATT (*left*) and **EARL SCRUGGS**, kings of bluegrass music in the 1940s, were an early influence on Buddy. (Alan Clark Archives)

"Buddy brought her over to my house some," says Larry Holley, referring to Buddy's girl **ECHO McGUIRE** (*with Buddy, left*), "and I felt like he might marry her." But it was not to be. (Buddy Holly Memorial Society)

The **HI-D-HO** was a popular spot for Lubbock youths, and Buddy once dated a carhop. One night, the Crickets climbed on the drive-in's roof and gave an impromptu concert. (Collection of Bill Griggs)

Above: Texas honky-tonk singers like **LEFTY FRIZZELL** inspired Buddy and a generation of Texas rockers. Both Buddy and Roy Orbison admired Frizzell's intimate, sexy C&W style. (Alan Clark Archives)

Right: Buddy's rise was swifter than **ROY ORBISON**'s, which made Roy jealous, but he admitted that he'd never have had the courage to go onstage wearing glasses if Buddy hadn't done it first. (Wink High School)

Roy Orbison
To lead a Western Band
Is his after school wish
And of course to marry
A beautiful dish.

When Buddy, Don Guess, Jerry Allison, and Sonny Curtis drove to Nashville in 1956 to cut "That'll Be the Day" at Bradley's Barn, they chased girls and hung out with **MARTY ROBBINS**. (Alan Clark Archives)

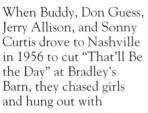

BUDDY WAYNE KNOX wrote "Party Doll" in Happy, Texas, but didn't know how to get it recorded. Holly and Orbison met him in 1956 and advised him to go to Norman Petty's studio in Clovis, New Mexico. Knox became the first singer-songwriter of the Rock Generation to hit No. 1. (Alan Clark Archives)

"Without **ELVIS**," Buddy once said, "none of us could have made it." When Elvis played Lubbock in 1955, Buddy opened for him—and fixed him up with a girl, according to Buddy's brother Larry. (UPI/Bettmann)

Buddy toured with **HANK THOMPSON** and the Brazos River Boys in 1956. (Alan Clark Archives)

Buddy thought of calling his band the Scoundrels, but chose the Crickets instead because they make a happy sound by rubbing their legs together. *Left to right:* **NIKI SULLIVAN, JOE B. MAULDIN, BUDDY**, and **JERRY ALLISON** in 1957. (Alan Clark Archives)

In New York to begin their first tour as "That'll Be the Day" crept up the charts to No. 1, the Crickets drank at Jack Dempsey's Bar in **TIMES SQUARE** and ate cheesecake with Chuck Berry at Lindy's. (AP/Wide World)

Above, left: Buddy recorded on the Coral label, which was run by **BOB THIELE**. Niki Sullivan says Buddy and the Crickets got a teenage crush on Thiele's wife, Teresa Brewer, when the Thieles invited them to dinner. (AP/Wide World)

Above, right: Buddy starred in rock czar **ALAN FREED**'s spectacular holiday stage shows in New York and went on the road with Freed for months at a time. (AP/Wide World)

Above: According to Niki Sullivan, the Crickets walked in on an orgy in **LITTLE RICHARD**'s dressing room— and left. But Richard says Buddy joined in on one of his orgies wholeheartedly. (Alan Clark Archives)

Left: **LARRY WILLIAMS**, who also starred at the Paramount. (Alan Clark Archives)

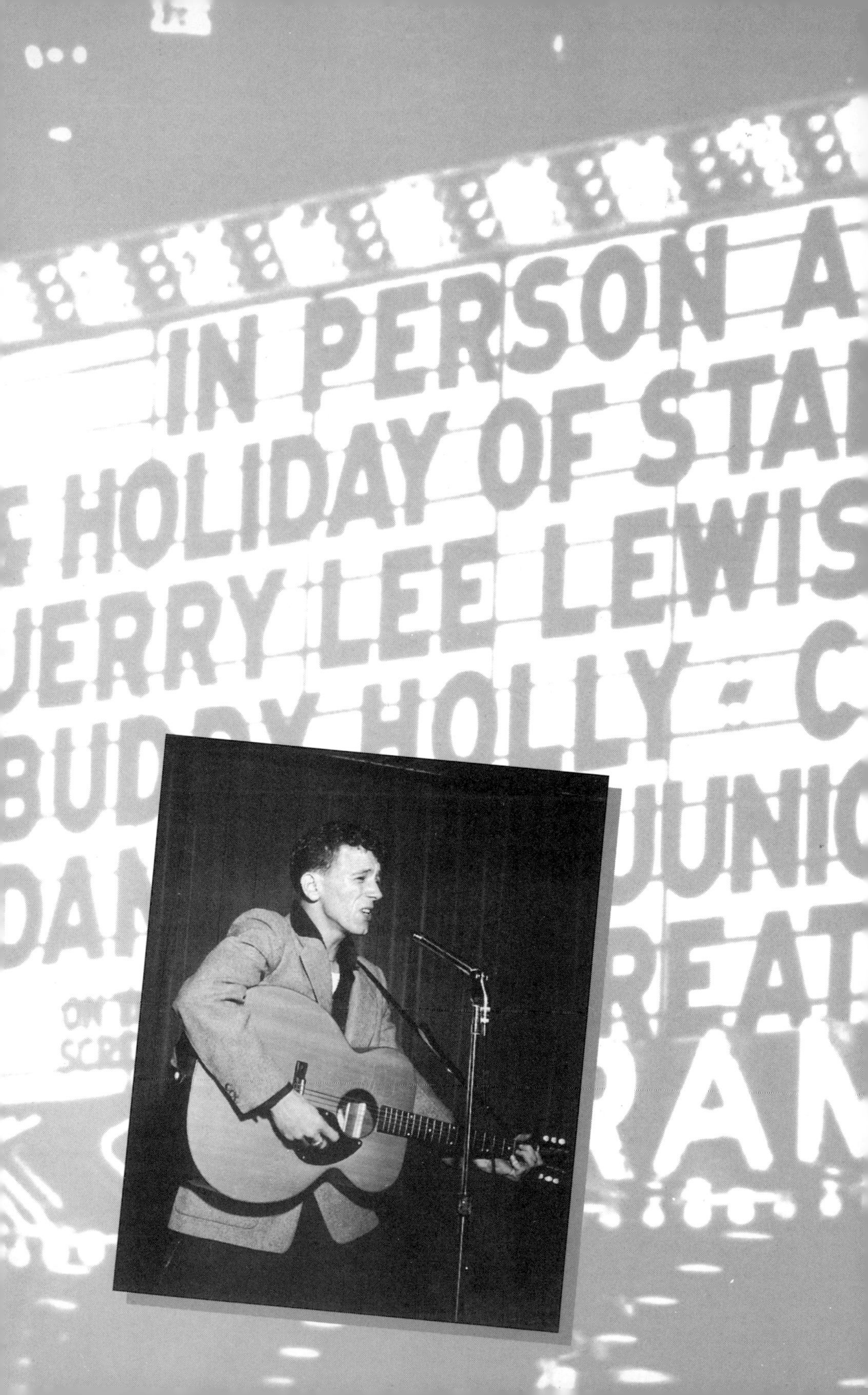
IN PERSON
HOLIDAY OF
LEE LEWIS
HOLLY

Background: The Young Rockers kicked endlessly at Alan Freed's stage shows in Brooklyn and Manhattan. (Collection of Bill Griggs)

Above: Buddy and **JERRY LEE LEWIS** became friends while touring together in America and Australia in 1957–58. (Alan Clark Archives)

Opposite: **GENE VINCENT**, whose "Be-Bop-A-Lula" became an early rock classic, frequented the Village Gate in Greenwich Village with Buddy Holly, Eddie Cochran, Jimmy Bowen, Buddy Knox, and the Everly Brothers. (Alan Clark Archives)

Dynamic **EDDIE COCHRAN**, whose "Summertime Blues" was one of the first rock anthems, liked to play with guns and girls. (AP/Wide World)

Buddy cursed a blue streak when sixteen-year-old **PAUL ANKA**, whose "Diana" was No. 1, kicked the mike plug out in the middle of the Crickets' set on the "Biggest Show of Stars for 1957" tour. (Alan Clark Archives)

Buddy became a major star during the eighty-day, seventy-city Irving Feld rock tour when both "That'll Be the Day" and "Peggy Sue" hit the charts. (Alan Clark Archives)

R&B queen **LAVERN BAKER** of "Tweedlee Dee" and "Jim Dandy" fame.
When the tour reached the Deep South, Buddy had to drop out, since it was
against the law in 1957 for blacks and whites to appear together on the same
stage. (Alan Clark Archives)

Fourteen-year-old **FRANKIE LYMON**, who scored a million-seller with "Why Do Fools Fall in Love?" pictured at the London Palladium, which Buddy later played. In 1957, Holly and Lymon endured a long U.S. bus tour together. (AP/Wide World)

Above: Buddy sang "It's So Easy" on **DICK CLARK**'s *American Bandstand.* Clark embraced the new rock 'n' roll music because it was popular, but preferred "easy-listening" music for his own pleasure. (Alan Clark Archives)

Right: Buddy looked in on the L.A. rockabilly scene in 1958. There he met **RICKY NELSON** in the Everly Brothers' room at the Hollywood Hawaiian Hotel. Ricky later covered Buddy's "True Love Ways" and "Rave On." (Alan Clark Archives)

rock-'n'-roll records, for the most part, and about Buddy Holly and the Crickets."

While Buddy and Murray were talking at Peer-Southern that day in March 1958, Maria Elena Santiago was plotting her way around her aunt, Provi. Despite Provi's strictures, Maria Elena had no intention of missing a date with Buddy Holly. Too smart to defy Provi openly, Maria Elena enlisted the support of an important Peer-Southern associate her aunt could scarcely afford to ignore—Jo Harper, Murray Deutch's secretary. After Jo Harper's intercession, Murray Deutch himself rang Provi in Buddy's behalf, explaining that "Buddy is a very nice boy and it will be okay for you to let Maria Elena go out with him."

Recalls Maria Elena today, "That still didn't sit very well with my aunt."

Maria Elena, who was born in Puerto Rico, had lost her mother when she was eight. At that point her father had sent her to live with Provi in Manhattan, where Provi had moved years before. Since 1898, when the United States had seized the colony of Puerto Rico from Spain in the Spanish-American War, two million Puerto Ricans had already immigrated to America, fleeing an overpopulated and undernourished island. Between 1950 and 1956, the Puerto Rican population of New York alone escalated from 245,880 to 577,000, alarming some New Yorkers, including blacks, who foresaw a drain on the already scarce job market. The new immigrants—"PR's," New Yorkers derisively called them—were scorned as the lowest of the low. "I like *los Estados Unidos*, but is sometimes a cold place to live," says a character in Piri Thomas's *Down These Mean Streets*, "not because of the winter and the landlord not giving heat but because of the snow in the hearts of the people."

Most Puerto Ricans settled in the squalid tenements of what would become Spanish Harlem between Fifth Avenue and the East River. The smoldering Latino temperament lent an aura of romance to the ghetto, which Puerto Ricans called *el barrio* (the place). Songwriters soon celebrated it in sumptuous wall-of-sound recordings such as "A Rose in Spanish Harlem," "Up on the Roof," and "In the Ghetto." The teeming *barrio* was a world away from the high-rent district in Greenwich Village that Maria Elena Santiago and her well-heeled aunt called home. Even before Provi paved the way for her to work at Peer-Southern, Maria Elena had held a variety of jobs in New York. Her breezy air of friendliness and efficiency enchanted Buddy, as did her Hispanic lineage, which would have kept most Caucasian boys at a distance in the fifties. Perhaps like Marlon Brando, who was romantically involved with Rita Moreno for nine years, Buddy must have sensed that a Latin woman would understand him better and be a more unrepressed lover.

By midafternoon, following Murray Deutch's call to Provi about Buddy Holly, Provi reached Maria Elena on the phone at Peer-Southern. "Buddy's very nice," Maria Elena assured her. "I like him."

"You know, I really don't believe you should get involved," Provi said. "I don't think you will be very safe with those people."

Maria Elena was a smart, tenacious girl. Half an hour later, Provi agreed to let her go out with Buddy and said, "There's just one condition. I want you to come home early, at least by twelve, not later than that."

Buddy took Maria to dinner at P. J. Clarke's, the popular and even then fashionable pub on Third Avenue that had been used in the filming of *The Lost Weekend* in the 1940s. "That happened the same day," Maria Elena remembers. "That evening we got to the place and he sat down and ordered drinks." Clarke's was, and remains, one of the most lively bistros in the world. You enter a long, narrow bar with an antique, white-tiled floor, walk past a crowd of noisy ad men and models unwinding after a day's work, pass through a small, cozy dining room, and finally arrive at the main room in back, which has an open kitchen with a blazing grill. This is where Buddy Holly and Maria Elena Santiago fell in love.

She wanted to be an actress. "José Quintero ... *The Iceman Cometh* ... I saw that," she recalls in 1993. "I used to be in that circle because I wanted to be a singer-actress-dancer. I was always around there. They really had something going." Quintero, a fellow Puerto Rican, was the most highly regarded theatrical director in New York. Almost single-handedly he'd launched the off-Broadway movement, reviving modern classics such as Tennessee Williams's *Summer and Smoke* and Eugene O'Neill's *The Iceman Cometh* at a Greenwich Village theater, Circle in the Square. He'd discovered some of the major dramatic stars of the day, notably Geraldine Page, George C. Scott, Colleen Dewhurst, Peter Falk, and Jason Robards, Jr.

Buddy told her that he wanted to be an actor, too, "exactly like Tony Perkins," he said, Maria Elena recalls. Perkins was then a leading matinee idol of the fifties, both in movies such as *Friendly Persuasion* and on Broadway, where he was currently starring in the Pulitzer Prize–winning hit, *Look Homeward, Angel*. "How do you learn about acting?" Buddy asked, and she told him that she'd heard Lee Strasberg was a good teacher. Buddy wanted to know all about Strasberg, the renowned exponent of the Stanislavsky Method acting technique and head of the Actors' Studio, where Shelley Winters, James Dean, Marilyn Monroe, Paul Newman, and Marlon Brando all studied. Though the studio was for working thespians, Maria Elena felt sure that she and Buddy could get into Strasberg's private school.

It was all very stimulating. Buddy had never known a girl who was so simpatico. She was worldly, self-possessed, and evidently not the slightest bit domestic. That was okay: He wasn't looking for his mother or another Echo McGuire. "My aunt and I—we always ate out," Maria Elena says in the 1993 interview. "We never cooked! Aunt Provi was always busy, so we went out to all these places for dinner. We loved Luchow's, a German restaurant on 14th Street. And O'Henry's had sawdust on the floor. I told Buddy about the time my aunt and I went to the Café Luna; that was in Little Italy. 'About five minutes after my aunt and I walked out, the Mafia killed everybody there,' I said.

" 'You just missed it!' Buddy said.

" 'Yeah. We never went back there again.' " She loved living in the Village and had even been to the notorious Club 82 over by Second Avenue, where female impersonators cavorted nightly. The more she chatted, the more Buddy must have adored this surprising, vivacious girl. Years later she still recalls how he suddenly rose from the table and said, "Excuse me a minute, Maria Elena. I'll be right back." When they'd entered the restaurant they'd noticed a flower vendor standing on Third Avenue, just outside the door. Buddy now went to the vendor, selected a red rose, and hurried back inside.

"This is for you," he said, "and would you marry me?"

Though Norman Petty would later contest Maria Elena's claim that Buddy proposed to her on the first day they met, it would not have been uncharacteristic of Buddy, considering his impetuous, sometimes reckless nature, especially at this time. The gap in his life since the loss of Echo, and the fact that he did not ultimately respect groupies, had left him lost and adrift emotionally. Maria Elena knew none of this and burst out laughing at his rash proposal. "Oooh, sure!" she said. "When do you want me, now or later?" Over three decades later, she muses, "Of course, you know, I had just met this guy, and this is our first time out. I thought he was just kind of kidding around. I sort of took it as a joke. I said to myself, *My aunt is right. These people are crazy*. For him to come out, you know, right away. . . . *This is not really happening*, I thought. I just took it as a joke."

"I'm serious about this," Buddy said.

Suddenly she stopped laughing. "Well, I guess you are," she murmured, gazing at him pensively. "I'll tell you what you need to do. Tomorrow morning you come over to my aunt's apartment, and you tell her that you want to marry me."

After they said good night, part of her mind remained skeptical. "I was still taking it as a joke," she recalls. "I thought, *This guy is not going to come*." But for Buddy it was anything but a joke. He'd found, in his typically impulsive way, the girl he wanted to marry, someone with whom he could share what he called true love ways—dining out, exchanging hopes and dreams, laughing, and being romantic and intimate together.

No doubt he went to sleep that night happier than he'd been in years. "The next day, Saturday, at nine o'clock sharp he was there to see my aunt, to my surprise," says Maria Elena.

Purposefully striding into the stately building at 33 Fifth Avenue, at the corner of Tenth Street and Fifth, Buddy instructed the doorman to ring Maria Elena's apartment. Upstairs, as she received the announcement, Maria Elena thought, *My goodness! Ummm, this can't be*—but sure enough, the doorman brought Buddy up.

"My aunt is still in bed," Maria Elena explained. After a while, Provi joined them. Maria Elena made the introductions. "Of course, she knew of him," Maria Elena says in our 1993 interview. "She asked questions, who he was, what he was, what he did. I guess he told her, but she knew quite a bit about him." After filling in a few personal details about himself and his family, Buddy came directly to the point.

"We want to get married," he said.

"He asked her, told her, not asked, *told* her that we wanted to get married," Maria Elena recalls in my interview with her. "My aunt almost went through the floor. Because I didn't tell her anything. I'd just said, 'He's a nice guy, a nice person. I like him a lot.' When he came in and said 'We want to get married,' she said, 'Well, uh, don't you think you should wait a little bit longer? Make sure that this is what you want?'

" 'No, no, no,' he said. 'I don't have time for this courting. I know that I want to marry Maria Elena. I know she wants to marry me.' Buddy was very decisive. Nothing stood in his way. That's the way he was. My aunt said, 'Well, if that's what you people want, I couldn't say no, because no matter what I say, it would be worse if I say no and you just go right ahead and do it.' "

They immediately proceeded to discuss Maria Elena's trousseau and the wedding. "My aunt traveled quite a bit for the company," Maria Elena recalls. "She had a trip coming up and she could not be around to help me get ready so she said, 'Okay, here's my credit card. Go out and get whatever you need.'

" 'No,' Buddy said. 'Maria Elena doesn't have to have your card. I'll give her some checks and she can buy—' . . . After he proposed he spoke to his mother on the phone."

According to Larry Holley, Buddy didn't break the news to his mother until he'd first consulted with Larry. Interracial marriages were repugnant to proletarian WASP Texans. To make matters worse, Maria Elena was four years older than Buddy (five, according to Peggy Sue). In the fifties, women who went with younger men were accused of "robbing the cradle." Larry backed Buddy up, but Ella Holley opposed the union on religious and racial grounds. L.O. would easily be won over by the pretty Maria Elena when they met later on.

Petty was aghast. He opposed the marriage from the start, not so much, as he claimed, because it would cost Buddy his fans, but because he regarded Maria Elena as a rival in the music business and a threat to his position as Buddy's manager. Years later, in a 1983 interview, Petty was still trying to undermine her, stating that she and Buddy had known each other before they started dating. Indeed, Maria Elena herself would state in an early 1959 issue of 16 magazine that they'd initially met in January 1958, according to Alan Mann's A–Z of Buddy Holly. Archivist Alan Clark reprinted the 16 article in 1989 in his booklet, Buddy Holly. Entitled "A Farewell to Buddy Holly: The Young Bride of a Favorite Young Star Bids Him a Last Goodbye," the story is presented as a first-person narrative by Maria Elena, who says that she and Buddy had often seen each other around Peer-Southern and she'd begun to think that he was so shy they'd "never get beyond the point" of greeting each other and kidding around.

The article goes on to state, in Maria Elena's voice, that they finally connected when she and a friend encountered him at Howard Johnson's one day. He was dining with Petty and the Crickets and invited them to sit down. After she'd left, Buddy turned to Petty and bragged, "You see that girl? I'm going to marry her." Some months later, after a tour, Buddy took her to a record session, followed by "a quiet dinner." Later, as he dropped her off in a taxi, the car made a sharp turn and threw them together. "Before either of us realized it, we were sharing our first kiss," Maria Elena said. They continued to stay in touch by phone while Buddy was on the road. Not until June 1958, the 16 account continues, did Buddy and Maria Elena decide that they wanted to get married, after talking with each other on the phone "two or three times a day" over a period of months.

Whatever the truth, it was typical of the vengeful Petty that he was determined, twenty-five years after the fact, to discredit her account of their courtship as a "whirlwing [sic] thing," which he dismissed as a sentimental myth. He was categorically right about one thing only—she was a rival, and she was a threat.

Chapter Ten

The Decline of Early Rock

Escorted by Sonny Curtis, who was visiting New York, Maria Elena Santiago attended Buddy's opening when Alan Freed launched his new forty-four-day "Big Beat" package tour in Brooklyn in March 1958. No one in the audience was aware of the tense maneuvering that had been going on backstage at the Brooklyn Paramount as the performers vied for top position on the bill. Once again it was clear that Buddy needed a better manager; he was not even a serious contender in the billing war that raged among members of the starry cast. The principal combatants for the closing spot on the show were Chuck Berry and Jerry Lee Lewis. When Jerry Lee stated his case for top billing, Alan Freed refused, reminding him that Berry had seniority. Jerry Lee reluctantly agreed but vowed to upstage Berry on opening day.

The issue was still unresolved at one P.M., March 28, when they began the first of their five daily shows. As Chuck Berry later recalled in his memoirs, most of the performances were attended by seven thousand kids screaming at the tops of their voices. "Never before had I confronted more than a thousand people watching me perform," Berry wrote, "and I had never seen the inside of a theater as enormous as the Brooklyn Paramount." Though Buddy and the Crickets were seasoned veterans of stadium rock and should by rights have closed the show, Petty failed to provide the aggressive representation they required. Buddy was at the peak of a fame that would, like high barometric pressure, soon wane, largely due to Petty's managerial incompetence and passivity as well as the decline of rock 'n' roll's first, pioneering phase, which would soon be coming to an end. The notorious events that occurred during this Freed tour, culminating in a melee in Boston, would change forever the way that rock 'n' roll was perceived, and the establishment would set out to destroy the rock movement.

At the opening performance in Brooklyn Jerry Lee, having lost out to Chuck Berry in the billing imbroglio, stormed onstage and threw a Coke bottleful of gasoline on his piano and set it afire. After driving the audience to an orgiastic ecstasy, he sauntered backstage and told Berry, "Follow *that*, nigger," according to Nick Tosches, author of *Hellfire*, a biography of Lewis. As Berry would note about Lewis on another occasion, "He wouldn't have known where he was if the Bells of St. Mary had rung in his ear. . . . He was bombed." No one could top Berry with his duck walk and his scoots and splits. Years later, the two men became friendly enough to jam together at a music festival in Schelsen, Germany.

Those who saw the Crickets at the Brooklyn Paramount testify that Buddy and his band more than held their own, rocking the SRO crowd with "Rave On" and "Not Fade Away." Buddy was such a personal sensation that ambitious young singers throughout the metropolitan area began to seek him out for advice and help. Though a star, Buddy made himself accessible to newcomers, adopting a policy that was unusually generous and nurturing. Indeed, it would prove to be mutually beneficial and mark the beginning of a new direction in his career, one that would eventually lead to record producing.

His first protégé was a young New York Italian, Lou Giordano, who could croon like Sinatra but had never made a record and was desperate for a break. He came to Buddy's attention through Joe Villa, who'd had a 1956 hit entitled "Blanche," singing with a group called the Three Friends. Joe Villa switched to the Royal Teens and scored a No. 3 smash, "Short Shorts," which was recorded at Bell Sound Studios in New York with two teenage girls their manager found hanging around in the lobby. The Royal Teens promoted the song on Dick Clark's *Saturday Night Beechnut Show*, wearing short shorts, the fifties version of hot pants, although it was a cold, snowy night. Buddy had shared a bill with them during his Florida tour earlier in 1958.

Joe Villa invited Buddy, Lou Giordano, and Don and Phil Everly to his home in Brooklyn one day during the Paramount run, promising them a dinner cooked by his mother. Sitting at Mrs. Villa's table that night with some of the most powerful and popular rock stars in the world, young Giordano suddenly burst out with a touching plea for help. "I can make a record," he said, according to Joe Villa, who recalled the scene in 1981. Buddy must have been touched, remembering how eager he'd been for the same kind of break not long ago. The likable Giordano managed to attach himself to Buddy, Don and Phil Everly, and Joe Villa despite his amateur status, largely on the basis of his considerable personal charm. He somewhat resembled the tough, lovable Dead End Kids. Soon Giordano was tagging along everywhere they went, and they all grew fond of him. Finally, both Buddy and the Everly Brothers assured Giordano that they'd help him make a recording. Buddy explained that he couldn't do it immediately, since he was touring until May; he'd return to New York and help him later. They could use the Beltone Studios and Buddy would be his producer. It was Buddy's first deal as a record producer, a career that would shortly gain momentum when he introduced Waylon Jennings to the world as a recording artist.

Before departing on the Freed tour, Buddy confided some of his concerns about Norman Petty to Maria Elena. Thanks to her job at Peer-Southern, she was knowledgeable about his business affairs. She never tired of talking with Buddy about his music and his career; her favorite Holly songs, she later told Griggs, were "Maybe Baby," "That'll Be the Day," and "Everyday." "I'm not happy with Norman," Buddy said, Maria Elena recalled in a 1993 interview, "because Norman does not want to spend money on publicity. He never wants to put money out to promote us."

As she recalls today, Maria Elena realized that "Norman didn't want to spend a red cent because he didn't want the money to get out of his hands. I don't care what anybody says, you need to be promoted. I don't care how good, how wonderful you are, you need that exposure. And, sincerely, the man never did that. Buddy was not happy with it. Everybody else was always out there, and Buddy always had to struggle to make sure that people knew about him. Of course, he was lucky that he was actually recognized because of his talent . . . but otherwise Norman [did no promotion]. . . . Even [Buddy's] pictures were taken by Norman. . . . I was the one who [suggested] promoting him [and doing] PR work."

Buddy made it clear to her that he "wanted to break with Norman even before he met me," Maria Elena added in 1993. As an employee in the office of Buddy's music publisher, with inside information about Petty's business dealings at her fingertips, including details regarding negotiations and royalty payments, Maria Elena was in a unique position to help Buddy. All of Petty's Nor Va Jak titles published by Peer-Southern in Latin America went through Maria Elena's Aunt Provi. Today, when Maria Elena discusses Petty's handling of the Crickets' money, she sums it up as "not a very kosher situation." She was also close to Jo Harper, who worked for Murray Deutch and served as Petty's and Buddy's secretary at Peer-Southern. "Norman . . . knew that I knew a lot about him and what he was doing," says Maria Elena, "so he certainly did not want me to be around because he knew what was going to happen. He knew that the minute that we got married things were going to turn different, which they did."

It was grossly unfair, she felt, for Norman to "put his name on every song that Buddy wrote," she said in 1993. The falsity of the situation, she pointed out, "was proven by the fact that the first 'That'll Be the Day' record . . . came out and the publishing only had 'Buddy Holly.' The second time around when it came out it had Norman Petty as a writer. I see Norman never wrote any other songs that he put his name on. It is also very clear that after Buddy died, Norman didn't write any songs."

To Maria Elena, Buddy seemed to be trying to crowd several lifetimes into one. "Buddy talked to me a lot about all the things he did before and what he planned to do," she says. She had an eerie feeling "that Buddy was not going to be here a long time, because everything was happening so *fast*."

"Music is my life," he told her. "I want people to feel wonderful and great when they hear my music."

After concluding the Brooklyn Paramount run, the Crickets played Loew's Paradise in the Bronx on March 31 and the New York Coliseum in Manhattan on April 2, then set out across the country. The "Big Beat Show" was the most extensive tour Alan Freed had ever mounted. For Buddy, almost burned out due to unrelieved touring and mismanagement by Petty, it was another demanding series of one-night stands, encompassing nineteen states and eastern Canada and lasting for forty-four days, from March 28 to May 10. He returned to many venues familiar to him from previous tours, such as the Baltimore Coliseum; the Windsor, Ontario, Arena; the Cincinnati Gardens; and Oklahoma City's Municipal Auditorium. There were also many new stops along the way, such as the Central High School Auditorium in Kalamazoo, Michigan, and the State Theater in Hartford, Connecticut, where, on March 30, the audience included Bill Griggs, who later remembered, "The lineup at the State was Alan Freed, Jerry Lee Lewis, Frankie Lymon, Chuck Berry, Buddy Holly and the Crickets, the Diamonds, Danny and the Juniors, Billy and Lillie, Larry Williams, Screamin' Jay Hawkins, the Chantels, and Jo Ann Campbell. All this plus two movies for 90 cents!"

Reminiscing about the tour a few months later, Alan Freed and Buddy remembered flying almost "every kind of plane there was," Freed said, noting that the DC-3 flights were particularly dicey. When Freed reminded Buddy how they'd almost gone "right through the ceiling," Buddy made some *wump-wump-wump* sounds like a plane in trouble and started laughing. Buddy must have been relieved and grateful to have graduated from the Irving Feld bus tours, but the hazards of flying from one town to the next were dramatically brought home to them in April, when they landed in Cincinnati shortly after a helicopter had crashed on the runway. Always impatient of any delay and eager to get on to the next gig, Buddy was the first to urge taking a plane, according to Freed, who'd later say, "We toured together for forty-four days. He was a bug for flying."

Danny Rapp, whose "At the Hop" was the biggest single of 1958, later described in *Reminiscing* magazine how Buddy, an "all-around great guy," gambled large quantities of cash to take his mind off the jarring bumps and altitude drops they encountered in stormy skies as they flew from one gig to another across America, practically living on the plane. Soon

Buddy was gambling compulsively. What struck Rapp most about Buddy was his enormous enjoyment of life, never more evident than in their backstage crapshoots during the tour, when Buddy would get so excited he'd sometimes wager as much as $3,000 (the most Rapp ever ventured was $5 to $10). He was also impressed with Buddy as an artist, noting that Buddy was "way before his time," the model for "what the Beatles came out with" several years later. Constant stress would eventually prove too much for Danny Rapp, who died of an apparently self-inflicted gun-shot wound in Parker, Arizona, in 1983. Chuck Willis, whose "It's Too Late" Buddy had recorded in 1957, was another casualty of rock's pio-neering days; he collapsed during a stomach-ulcer attack in 1958 and died at the age of thirty. His last record, ironically entitled "What Am I Living For?" went gold after his death.

When the Freed tour played the Keil Auditorium in St. Louis, Missouri, on April 15, Buddy's favorite guitar, his Fender Stratocaster, was stolen. A replacement had to be flown in from Manny's in New York. By the time the entourage reached Iowa in late April, everyone was exhausted and testy. Though Jerry Lee had given manic, show-stopping perform-ances early in the tour, totaling several pianos and even shoving a bat-tered piano into the audience, his early show in Cleveland was so perfunctory that the promoter had to beg him to resume the mayhem his fans had come to expect. Two pianos sat backstage at Cleveland's Public Hall, specifically earmarked for destruction by the Killer. Jerry Lee rose to the challenge, and business picked up. *Billboard* reported that one of Freed's Cleveland shows raked in a "smashing $17,000." Altogether the "Big Beat" tour grossed $150,000 in the first ten days on the road.

Then business began to fall off. Attendance was sagging for all three of the traveling rock shows that spring. Irving Feld was surviving, but "The Rhythm and Blues Cavalcade of 1958" would be pulled on April 27. Surprisingly, when the Freed show arrived in Waterloo on April 22, 1958, fifteen hundred tickets had been sold in advance for the 3:30 P.M. performance in the Hippodrome Auditorium, setting a local record. The afternoon performance was a disaster. Jerry Lee failed to show up alto-gether, which could hardly have pleased the restive crowd. The lead singer of Dickey Doo and the Don'ts aggravated an already dangerous situation by getting into a fight with a member of the audience. Bouts of shoving and hair-pulling broke out in the auditorium.

On that sinister note the tour pressed on for Boston, where Freed had been busted by the police in 1956. At that time Freed had referred to the cops as "a bunch of rednecked old men." Boston officials retaliated by banning rock 'n' roll in the city after a 1957 Freed show allegedly caused a violent incident in the subway. Shortly before Buddy arrived with the tour on May 3, 1958, Mayor John B. Hynes at last lifted the ban and the

"Big Beat Show" was allowed to go on. The seventy-two-hundred-seat Boston Arena was located downtown in the sleaziest section of the city. "The dregs of society lived there," said Jack Hooke, Freed's business associate. Just before the show, as *Time* magazine would later report in a story headlined "Rock-'n'-Roll Riot," five thousand "hip kids" were milling around the arena. Several girls were accosted and raped by gang members. Fifteen beatings and stabbings were reported before paddy wagons arrived and hauled the offenders off to jail. The fighting spread to Roxbury and Back Bay, where stabbings and store lootings were reported.

Inside the arena, a riot was about to erupt. The bigoted Boston audience resented black R&B stars and had been spoiling for an opportunity to disrupt an integrated show. According to R&B musician and historian George Moonoogian, who was seventeen years old when he attended the Boston Arena show that night, the audience was 60 percent white and 40 percent black. Racism and riots in Boston were a tradition that extended back to the days of the abolitionists in the 1830s, when the poor Irish felt threatened. As former *New York Post* journalist Cy Egan puts it, "Boston always had a lot of 'donkeys'—flannel-mouthed Irishmen with great skills at talking but no brains and filled with prejudices and resentments." Violence broke out at the Freed show after a black vocal group began their set. A Caucasian girl leaped onstage, grabbing the crotch of one of the singers. No longer able to restrain themselves, the kids in the audience left their seats and started dancing. Freed dashed onstage and tried to restore order. Appearing suddenly from the wings, a policeman confronted Freed and snarled, "We don't like your kind of music here."

Chuck Berry attempted to finish the show, but gang members wearing colored head bandanas started throwing objects from above. These were the years just before the Freedom Marchers and only two and a half years after Rosa Parks. As chairs and other objects rained down, Chuck Berry had to run for cover behind his drummer. Security forces took over and expelled the crowd from the arena. On the street, a pitched battle broke out between the fans and the cops. Freed, Buddy, and the other performers retreated to the Hotel Statler and remained incommunicado until noon Sunday. They boarded a plane for Montreal at two P.M. Boston Mayor John Hynes again banned all rock shows. District Attorney Garrett H. Byrne denounced "rock-'n'-roll paganism." Freed was indicted for inciting a riot by a Suffolk County, Massachusetts, grand jury, which cited the state's antianarchy law and claimed that Freed intended to overthrow the government. Massachusetts State Senator William D. Fleming introduced a bill to ban rock from all government buildings.

Their remaining gigs, including Troy, New York; New Haven, Connecticut; and Newark, New Jersey, were canceled. Though Freed was in no way at fault, the Newark promoter, who had sold every seat in the

Newark Armory for the May 10 show, went berserk and burst into Manhattan radio station WINS while Freed was on the air, pulling a gun and threatening to shoot Freed. The management of WINS, outraged by bad publicity, fired Freed, effectively ending his career as a DJ and tour packager. Die-hard promoters like Irving Feld would continue to mount smaller rock 'n' roll package tours and Buddy Holly would continue to go on them. As he discovered on the 1959 "Winter Dance Party" tour, they could be shoddy, ill-planned, and dangerous.

Sensing that the time was ripe for administering the coup de grace to rock 'n' roll, the guardians of the public weal joined the attack. The Boston Archdiocese condemned rock 'n' roll. From the nation's capital FBI director J. Edgar Hoover warned that rock was a "corrupting influence on America's youth." In the end, the combined forces of the establishment—the police, the government, the church, the courts, and even the press—waged all-out war on rock 'n' roll. The *New York Herald Tribune* editorialized, "There was a time when cities boarded their gates against the plague. . . . Musicians are not generally thought to be dangerous [but] now another pied piper seems to have turned up. Most communities still try to keep known thugs at bay." After showing a clip of Jerry Lee's antics at the "Big Beat" Detroit performance, *Today Show* host Dave Garroway shook his head in dismay.

One of the few voices raised in rock's defense at this time was that of Jack Kerouac, spokesman of the beat generation, who wrote in the March 1958 issue of *Esquire* that "the Korean postwar youth emerged cool and beat," describing them as "characters of a special spirituality . . . staring out the dead wall window of our civilization . . . prophesying a new style for American culture. . . . The new Rock'n'Roll youth" whose records were being played on "jukeboxes from Montreal to Mexico City, from London to Casablanca" were, Kerouac believed, the first sign of the "Second Religiousness that Oswald Spengler prophesied for the West . . . a generation of crazy, illuminated hipsters suddenly rising and roaming America, serious, curious, bumming and hitchhiking everywhere, ragged, beatific, beautiful."

The rockers were the standard-bearers of a new freedom on society's horizon, but the establishment had reacted by branding them as subversives and revolutionaries. The sensitive, usually well-behaved and law-abiding young rock singers were astonished that the music they'd invented for their own amusement in Texas garages and on Bronx street corners was now regarded as seditious. Conceivably they could be prosecuted for treason. Though all charges against Alan Freed were dropped when Boston officials failed to produce sufficient proof of insurrection, the damage had been done. Suddenly Freed's "Big Beat" concerts were too hot for show business and the tour was blackballed by timid theater owners. The heyday of the rock-package tour was over.

And the first, innovative stage of rock 'n' roll approached its concluding days. The aftershocks of the Boston riot were extremely damaging to the way rock 'n' roll was viewed around the world. It was now subversive, if one listened to the FBI and J. Edgar Hoover, and just about everybody did in the 1950s. All of this Buddy Holly had unintentionally—or perhaps more intentionally than we know—helped to foment. The late fifties was an increasingly dark time. As the conservative sector of the public plunged into paranoia over rock 'n' roll, a response that would be repeated periodically, right up to the 1990s flap over rap, the world was also in despair over the worsening Cold War. The inevitability of a nuclear holocaust that would destroy all life on the planet was a given for Buddy's generation. He was now twenty-one, and like other young men facing the draft, he must have felt the melancholy certainty of death or disfigurement by loathesome radiation on an atomic battlefield. So universal was the feeling of gloom and doom by the end of the decade that one of the most emblematic films of the time, On the Beach, starring Ava Gardner and Gregory Peck, was a bleak depiction of the end of the world that nonetheless had everyone whistling its memorable theme, "Waltzing Matilda." According to film historian Leslie Halliwell, On the Beach was "about the most downbeat production ever to come from Hollywood." William Golding's pessimistic novel Lord of the Flies was even gloomier, portraying mankind's reversion to savagery following a nuclear war.

Buddy's draft notice finally arrived from Selective Service's General Hershey on May 28, 1958, ordering him to report for a physical examination. For once in his lifetime his fragile constitution proved to be an asset. Buddy escaped the draft due to a "stomach ulcer," his mother later told fan Dave Skinner. Buddy's poor vision was also a factor in his exemption.

It was an opportunity for a rare period of rest and relaxation, and he seized it, returning to Lubbock for a vacation, riding an English Ariel Cyclone 650cc motorcycle he bought as soon as he deplaned in Dallas. He'd wanted a Harley Davidson ever since he'd seen Marlon Brando play Johnny, the prototypical Hells Angel, in The Wild One in 1954. For a while he'd owned a Triumph, but when the Crickets landed at Love Field in Dallas on May 13, 1958, he made a beeline for the Harley showroom, his pockets filled with $5,000 in cash. Pointing to a shiny new model, he asked the owner to tell him the price. Jerry later told Goldrosen that the owner sized the Crickets up as feckless teenagers, laughed, and said they could never afford a Harley and he wasn't going to waste his time talking to them. A typically insular Texan, out of touch with the world beyond the Lone Star State, he failed to recognize the international celebrities under his nose. According to Bill Griggs, whose article "Buddy's Motorcycle" appeared in *Reminiscing* magazine in 1983, the owner asked Buddy Holly and the Crickets to leave his shop, blowing the easiest $3,000 cash sale he'd ever have made.

Determined to ride three motorcycles out of Dallas, regardless of model or make, they took a cab to Ray Miller's Triumph Motorcycle Sales at 3600 West Davis, today known as the Big D Cycle Shop. Miller instantly recognized Buddy and the Crickets and welcomed them to test-ride any bikes they fancied. Buddy chose the Ariel and a black leather wardrobe to go with it. Joe B. bought a Triumph Thunderbird, and Jerry selected a Triumph Trophy. Buddy shelled out over $3,000, then they roared down the highway to Lubbock, 323 miles west of Dallas, barely missing the hail, tornadoes, and rainstorms pounding most of West Texas that day. In their matching motorcycle caps with silver eagle insignias, they looked like the biker gang from hell, especially Buddy, who was wearing black sunglasses.

In the following days the Crickets tooled around their neighborhoods on their bikes and hung out on the sidewalk in front of their parents' homes. Jerry's brother James Allison photographed them with his home-movie camera. In one shot, Buddy sits leaning on his handlebars, looking cool in shades and leather cap. In another scene, a bare-chested Jerry Allison mugs for the camera, looking like he could use some exercise and home cooking. As Jerry leaves for a spin on his Triumph, Buddy places an affectionate hand on Joe B.'s shoulder, both young men looking happy and relaxed. Joe B. later recalled in Douglas Brooker's television documentary *Reminiscing* that Buddy was the "big brother" he'd always wanted, that he "really loved" Buddy's companionship, and that their times together made his life "really enjoyable." Buddy called Joe B. "Buyus," later explaining the nickname to Alan Freed. According to Freed, Joe B. was always cadging sodas and candy, saying, "Buy us a Coke, buy us a candy bar."

"Buy us somethin'," Buddy added.

The summer of 1958, Buddy told Freed, gave the Crickets an opportunity, after the uninterrupted touring of the previous year, to enjoy the fruits of their labor for the first time. Buddy reunited with old friends such as Bob Montgomery, who was still playing gigs around Lubbock, singing C&W and going to Clovis to learn everything he could about the record business. Montgomery can be seen in the background, on someone's front lawn, in James Allison's home movie of Buddy and Jerry playfully reenacting the knife fight from *Rebel Without a Cause*. Jerry played Buzz Gunderson, the gang leader who'd been portrayed by Corey Allen in the movie. Buddy was Jim Stark, the archetypal fifties adolescent immortalized by the late James Dean, whose death in 1955 presaged Buddy's own four years later. (Maria Elena, addressing the Buddy Holly Memorial Society in 1984, said that James Dean and Anthony Perkins were Buddy's favorite movie stars.) As James Allison's camera rolled, Jerry seems to be charging at Buddy, holding a small object that appears to be a pocketknife. Possibly remembering his disastrous clash with Joe B. in London, Buddy went to his motorcycle and revved up the engine. "It was an English Ariel," Larry Holley said in a 1992 interview. "It shifted on the road side, brakes on the opposite side. Everything was backwards. It was a pretty motorcycle. I rode it a little bit, but I was getting used to dirt bikes."

Buddy's family was glad to see him, but they seemed oddly unimpressed by the developments in his career. He tried to convey the extent of his fame to them. Larry Holley later told members of the Buddy Holly Memorial Society that Buddy said the English accepted him "with open arms"; he enjoyed the British tour so much that he found he couldn't "say enough about it," he told Larry. At last his family seemed to grasp what the world outside Texas had long known. They had a star in the family. They finally "realized it after he went to England," Larry told Griggs. "I don't think we realized it before that." Even the handful of people in Lubbock who were cognizant of Buddy's achievements affected a bland indifference, too ornery to admit that one of their own had made it in the world beyond Texas. No doubt nothing could have been more disappointing for Buddy, who valued praise above money and who'd hoped his hometown would at last come through with the recognition and love they'd so long withheld. To his barber, Jake Goss, he seemed irritable and abrupt when he came into the shop with the Crickets the day after he'd swept into Lubbock on the Ariel. The boys were loud and boisterous, as noisy as their motorcycles, Goss later told Griggs.

Plopping down in a barber chair, Buddy ordered Goss to restore the natural wave to his overpermed hair. As Goss struggled with his locks, Buddy contemplated what style to try next. It was more than vanity on Buddy's part; hair was gradually becoming the radical "freak flag" of rock 'n' roll. Buddy kept trying different styles, going in for extreme changes on at least three or four visits to the shop; none of them satisfied him. Though Goss took pride in his work, calling it "personality styling," cutting and shaping a customer's hair to suit his face and profession, and even throwing in a shampoo—all for $5—he found Buddy anything but appreciative, describing him as hurried, impatient, fidgety, domineering, and moody. "I usually felt ill at ease when I was styling his hair," Goss told Griggs. "He really wasn't very talkative."

Buddy's taciturnity was attributable, at least in part, to his neighbors' stolid refusal to acknowledge his accomplishments over the previous ten months. In contrast to Lubbock, Jerry Lee Lewis's hometown—Ferriday, Louisiana—accorded Jerry Lee a hero's welcome when he returned from the same Alan Freed tour on May 17, awarding him the key to the city. Lubbock did nothing to honor Buddy, though he continued to score one hit record after another. That summer the Crickets' new single "Think It Over" went to No. 27 in the United States and No. 11 in England. Years later *Rolling Stone* reflected on the song's profundity: "The adolescent confidence of . . . 'Think It Over' conveys Holly's magical notion that the insistent repetition of one's wishes is in fact the fulfillment of the wish itself," wrote Jonathan Cott. "As in ritual, the rapture of song becomes the proof of this magic and, in the end, the magic itself."

Buddy had another classic tune on the drawing board. At the end of May he recorded "It's So Easy," the song he sometimes referred to as "It's So Greasy to Fall in Love." No small contribution to the record is the flowing, coherent lead guitar playing of Tommy Allsup, one of Petty's staff musicians. A native of Tulsa, Allsup had been the lead guitarist in a western swing band led by Johnnie Lee Wills, Bob Wills's brother. Allsup was drawn to Clovis, like so many musicians in 1958, by Petty's reputation as the genius behind Buddy Holly. "Petty had 'em lined up at the door," Allsup told writer William J. Bush in 1982. Petty's house band now scheduled sessions with a different singer every night.

Larry Holley noticed that Buddy was "flush with money" that summer. The Crickets had been holding back as much of their pay as they could from Petty and justifying it to him as expenses. Petty realized he'd lost control of them when they angrily objected to being kept on salary despite their fame and substantial earnings. From that point on they discontinued forwarding money earned on the road to the Crickets account in Clovis. It was, of course, the smartest financial move they'd ever made, but unfortunately they stopped short of making a clean break. Jerry later acknowledged in the TV film *Reminiscing* that they "weren't taking care of our business like we should have been." They were "just a bunch of kids" who liked the excitement of being entertainers but had absolutely no interest in looking over their contracts, Jerry added.

While at home, Buddy went on a fishing trip to the Brazos Box Canyon in northern New Mexico, taking along his brother Larry, his father, his cousin Sam, and Bill Edwards, a friend of Larry's. Maria Elena remained in New York all this time, where she had been since Buddy departed following his New York engagements in early April. When quizzed about this in 1993, she said, "I remember that he had to go somewhere, and he wanted me to come with him, but I couldn't go because my aunt would not let me. In between that time [and their August wedding] I prepared to get ready to go to Lubbock."

Accompanied by his relatives, Buddy hiked through the rugged wilderness until they reached a trout stream that poured from a crack in the mountains. Sheer cliffs jutted a thousand feet overhead. The fishing was excellent and they roasted their catch over an open fire. At nightfall, bedrolls were unfurled and they slept out under the stars. When they left the next day, toting heavy backpacks, Buddy surprised Larry by leaving the others far behind. It was a ten-mile hike, and Buddy beat everyone else back to the car by several hours. He was still growing, and he was getting stronger physically every year.

Back in Lubbock, Buddy strolled downtown, stopping at a shoeshine stand to get his boots polished. Robert Linville, one of Buddy's backup singers, later told Griggs that when the black shoeshine attendant admired Buddy's wristwatch, Buddy gave it to him with a smile, commenting that he liked it more than Buddy did, so he deserved it.

The Crickets felt that they could now afford an apartment in Clovis, so they wouldn't have to make the daily drive from Lubbock to cut their records. The quarters they leased were located on Main Street, near Petty's studio. Buddy was a hero around Nor Va Jak the way he would never be in Lubbock. His string of hits had turned Petty's modest establishment at 1313 West Seventh Street into one of rock's premier studios, second only to Sun Records. Roy Orbison continued to record in Clovis whenever he visited the Southwest, finding it more amenable than Memphis or Nashville. Charlie Phillips's "Sugartime" originated in Clovis, with Buddy playing guitar, before the McGuire Sisters covered it and sold a million records. Buddy was in the studio daily, cutting his own songs or playing guitar for, among others, Trini Lopez, Buddy Knox, Carolyn Hester, and Terry Noland. Whether he was working on his songs or those of his compadres, to Buddy Holly the studio had become a sacred place where magical things happened. Though his only tangible contribution was as session guitarist, his powerful presence informs Fred Crawford's "By the Mission Wall," Jack Huddle's "Starlight," Jim Robinson's "Whole Lotta Lovin'," and the Norman Petty Trio's "Moondreams."

One day he rode his Ariel Cyclone up to Shaw's Jewelry Store in Clovis to buy a present for Maria Elena. The clerk, a Clovis woman named Maxine Nation, told Bill Griggs in 1984 that Buddy was wearing a black leather jacket when she noticed him standing at the diamond counter, studying gems. She assumed that he was an ordinary biker until she noticed that his hands and fingernails were immaculate, very different from the greasy paws of the bikers who regularly roared through Clovis. He was making a Manhattan girl his bride, he told Maxine, and he was shopping for a gift to express his love. As Maxine displayed an array of jewels, she was struck by Buddy's politeness and charm, though she still didn't recognize him. Buddy finally selected a diamond pendant, said he'd prefer to pay by personal check, and offered to cover the cost of a long-distance call to Lubbock should Maxine need to ring his bank. Smiling, Maxine assured him the store would absorb the cost of the call. When he volunteered the information that he was in Clovis to make records at Petty's studio, Maxine did a double-take and asked him if he was really Buddy Holly. Later she told Griggs that Buddy laughed and said, "I guess so." They chatted and Maxine told him that in person he had the same radiance as he had on his recordings. She offered him respect and admiration, which was rare for him in the Southwest.

Around this time, realizing that his fame had availed him nothing on his home turf—the place that mattered most to him—he began to redefine his values. The desire for worldly recognition had motivated him and energized his climb to stardom, but now he began to see that public opinion, applause, performing, and touring—all the razzle-dazzle of show business—had no effect on one's self-esteem. He formulated new dreams: producing, publishing, and owning his own recording studio and record label. Unfortunately, each time he tried to implement these plans, Petty proposed another tour or promotion trip.

It was at Petty's urging that the Crickets went to San Francisco in June to appear on Ted Pandall's KPIX-TV show, promoting their records. Afterward Buddy flew down to Los Angeles to see his old friends the Everly Brothers, who were staying at the Hollywood Hawaiian Hotel. While Buddy was visiting the Everlys, Eddie Cochran's girlfriend Sharon Sheeley dropped in. With her was the new teenage idol Ricky Nelson, whose recording of a song she'd written, "Poor Little Fool," was a hit. Later they all went to see Cochran at the Knickerbocker Hotel, where he was staying with Gene Vincent, drinking liquor out of a flask, and celebrating his No. 8 smash "Summertime Blues." They took in a party in Jerry Lee Lewis's suite at the Knickerbocker, but Ricky left in a huff when Jerry Lee pissed in the corner.

Buddy returned to Texas briefly and then departed for New York to cut new singles. This time, he left the Crickets behind. His movements during this period reflect the fact that his life and talent were pushing forward in new directions. There was the increasing influence of Maria Elena and, with Maria Elena there, the lure of New York City—where the professionals were. One can also sense the coming demise of the Crickets. He was feeling the need to branch out and grow, and Decca had offered him the run of its New York studios. Petty, suspicious that Decca executives were once again trying to subvert his influence, decided to tag along when Buddy went east.

In New York, Dick Jacobs suggested that Buddy knock out a quick cover of a Bobby Darin song, "Early in the Morning." It was a good idea, resulting in a return to the charts for Buddy, hitting No. 32 in the U.S., No. 17 in England, and No. 22 in Australia. "Early in the Morning" was a Ray Charles–type mix of gospel and R&B—someone called it "rock 'n' soul"—and it marked Buddy's transition from a rockabilly singer to a versatile rock star. Though he missed Jerry and Joe B., the session at last freed him to make the quantum jump he'd been yearning to. Buddy must have been enormously pleased in the summer of 1958 to be on the charts both as a solo performer and as a member of a group; the Crickets' "Think It Over" was a simultaneous Top 40 hit, going to No. 27 in America and No. 11 in England.

"Early in the Morning" was recorded on June 19, 1958, at Coral Records Studios in the Pythian Temple, a building then owned by the New York Institute of Technology. Jacobs says that every time they saw each other following the session, Buddy told him that "Early in the Morning" was the finest recording he'd ever made. With the Crickets back in Texas, he found it stimulating to work with New York professionals, including guitarists Al Chernet and George Barnes, drummers David "Panama" Francis and Philip Kraus, Sam Taylor on alto saxophone, and Ernest Hayes at the piano. He worried about hurting the Crickets' feelings, confiding to Petty his apprehension that Jerry and Joe B. would consider him disloyal if he continued to make records without them, but when "Early in the Morning" became a worldwide hit, Jerry graciously said he did not resent Buddy's solo success.

Buddy now looked increasingly to New York—and specifically to Dick Jacobs—for guidance. Petty refused to acknowledge the deterioration of their relationship, pointing out that he was present in the control room at the Pythian Temple sessions. While granting that Dick Jacobs was Buddy's new producer, Petty insisted that he was still the manager of the Crickets and Buddy Holly. He could not face the fact that Buddy had evolved beyond the Clovis/Tex-Mex ethos. Years later, in an interview with Skip Brooks and Bill Malcolm, Petty still found it difficult to address why he hadn't been more supportive of Buddy's need to experiment and grow as an artist; Petty admitted he had lacked vision.

While in New York, Buddy purchased a gold chain for the diamond pendant he'd bought Maria Elena in Clovis. Petty was aware of Maria Elena's hold on him and knew that she had told Buddy he could get along perfectly well without the Crickets and that he no longer required the services of Norman Petty. Petty struck back with adder-tongued viciousness. As Maria Elena later revealed to Goldrosen, Petty circulated malicious lies about her, telling Buddy that she was a "cheap girl" who flirted with all the singers who visited Peer-Southern, that she liked to be "picked up," that she went around with numerous men. Petty's source was supposedly an executive at Peer-Southern. After Buddy repeated Petty's slander to Maria Elena, she summoned the executive who'd allegedly maligned her and confronted him in Petty's presence. Was he responsible for the lies? she asked. The executive denied everything. Petty was hope-lessly out of his league every time he squared off with Maria Elena Santiago.

Rock 'n' roll's future continued to look precarious in 1958, partially due to a recession that cut into teenagers' buying power but also because of continuing attacks, such as the one from the NBC division responsible for radio advertising. "Rave On" was singled out by NBC Spot Sales as an example of the kind of music the network did not want its stations to play. The wave of protest continued when *Contacts*, the Catholic Youth Organization's periodical, warned teens to censor the music played at hops and "smash the records . . . which present a pagan culture."

Perhaps skeptical about his future as a rock performer, Buddy became more interested in songwriting as a profession and attempted to supply other stars with material. He wrote two songs, "Love's Made a Fool of You" and "Wishing," both composed in collaboration with Bob Mont-gomery, for the Everly Brothers, who were on a run of seven Top 40 hits in 1958, including "Devoted to You" and "Bird Dog." Buddy envisaged the new songs as the A and B sides of the Everlys next single. After recording the demos in Clovis, Buddy delivered them to the Everlys' manager, Wesley Rose, head of the powerful Nashville publishing firm Acuff-Rose. Rose refused to permit anyone outside his stable of song-writers, even Buddy Holly, to write for the Everlys. As long as he could restrict the Everlys' choice of material to in-house tunesmiths such as Felice and Boudleaux Bryant, who wrote Everly Brothers hits such as "Wake Up Little Susie" and "Problems," he could collect royalties from both the singers and the songwriters. According to British fan Dave Skin-ner, who interviewed Buddy's parents in 1969, Ella Holley said that Rose listened to "Wishing" but turned it down, saying that the Everlys could never put it over as effectively as Buddy. Rose also declined Buddy and Bob's "Love's Made a Fool of You." Don later told Kurt Loder that he rued having lost these songs, blaming his contract with Acuff-Rose.

While in Nashville, Buddy ran into Roy Orbison, who was about to give up singing and was now employed as a staff songwriter at Acuff-Rose. "I was in a restaurant in Nashville one time with the Everlys having lunch," Orbison remembered. "Buddy Holly came in and said he'd just been to England and it was magnificent. So the Everlys said they'd go, and it was magnificent. At the same time, other people had gone and it was a disaster. (I won't say who.) So I didn't really want to go." Orbison was deluding himself. At the time he was still a couple of years away from the kind of stardom that Buddy and the Everly Brothers already enjoyed. In 1958, major bookers weren't seeking Roy Orbison for tours, either at home or abroad. Chet Atkins hadn't been any more successful with Or-bison at RCA's Nashville studio than Norman Petty had been in Clovis or Sam Phillips at Sun. It would take two more years—and the collaborative input of songwriter Joe Melson, with whom Roy would write "Only the Lonely"—for Orbison to emerge as a star.

Before leaving Nashville, Buddy met DJ Ralph Emery. "Buddy Holly came to visit me on 'Opry Star Spotlight,' my all-night show," Emery stated in his 1992 autobiography *Memories*. "I told him I could not play any of his records, because I had none." Obviously nothing had changed in Nashville, but Buddy's songwriting efforts there in 1958 were symptomatic of his determination to emerge as an individual rather than a tool of record promoters and tour packagers. Nevertheless, he needed money and so, in July 1958, he set out on the "Summer Dance Party," which charged through Iowa, Indiana, Illinois, Michigan, Minnesota, and Wisconsin, playing one-night stands in godforsaken outposts such as Decorah, Oelwein, and Wausau—a veritable blitzkrieg of the Upper Midwest. This is Grant Wood country, the American heartland, and, in summertime at least, it's fertile, green, uncrowded, and full of breathtaking sights.

The "Summer Dance Party" was strictly a Buddy Holly tour, not another all-star rock 'n' roll package show in the Alan Freed–Irving Feld–Dick Clark tradition. The only other act on the bill was Tommy Allsup and his Western Swing Band, who opened each night for the Crickets. They traveled in Buddy's Lincoln and the band's DeSoto station wagon, carrying their equipment in a U-Haul trailer. For once they didn't have to lug Joe B.'s bull fiddle; Joe B. started playing an electric bass that summer, using a Fender Precision purchased at Manny's in New York.

Even in 1958, Iowa invariably spelled trouble for Buddy. On the "Big Beat" tour the previous April, a near-riot had broken out in the Hippodrome Auditorium in Waterloo. When he returned to the area for a July 8 show, another crisis developed, one that put his life in jeopardy. What started as a day of recreation for the Crickets turned into a nightmare after they rented a boat and went waterskiing on Cedar River, near Waterloo. All went well until the Crickets started horsing around. Buddy had been drinking on this tour, and his judgment may have been impaired when, together with the Crickets, he decided to walk some logs floating in the river. Later, *Des Moines Register* reporter Larry Lehmer described the resulting emergency as Buddy's "unplanned dip in the river." The logs started turning and dumped the musicians in the water, fully clothed. Luckily, no one was hurt.

A few days later, Buddy found himself in another dangerous situation. After their July 12 performance in Wausau, Wisconsin, he stayed up all night, drinking and listening to records with a group of fans, recalled Bob Oestreich, the drummer with the Roustabouts, who opened for Buddy at Wausau's Rothschild Pavilion. The next day, though he was tired and possibly hungover, he tried to swim across a cold lake in the North Woods, near Rhinelander, Wisconsin. The day was chilly and gray, and a harsh wind made the water choppy. According to Lehmer, when Buddy was halfway across the lake, trying to fight the wind and currents, he drifted off course. He looked up and failed to see the shore, became confused, and almost panicked. Barely managing to control his terror, he kept swimming. Finally he reached land and dragged himself out of the water, pale and gasping for breath. Onlookers rushed to him with blankets and steaming coffee. Suffering from exhaustion and possibly hypothermia, he couldn't stop shivering. They carried him to a house and put him in a hot shower. Finally he rallied and said he felt like he could go onstage that night.

People came from miles around to hear Buddy at the Crystal Rock in Rhinelander on July 13, unaware that he'd almost died a few hours before. He felt so sleepy and weak he barely made it through the first set. At the break he went outside and curled up in the backseat of the Lincoln, falling fast asleep. Unfortunately, the fans wouldn't let him alone. One of them was seventeen-year-old Neale Winker, who'd driven with five friends from Tomahawk, a town twenty miles southwest of Rhinelander. Years later, in a 1993 interview, Neale recalled how he and his friends peered through the Lincoln's backseat window and recognized Buddy snoozing inside. They were thrilled to be close to their favorite rock star. "We knocked and woke him up," says Neale. "Someone came out of a side door and told us to get our butts out of there."

When it was time for the show to resume, Buddy reluctantly climbed out of the Lincoln, went back inside the Crystal Rock, and splashed water on his face. He trudged onstage and tried to summon the energy to sing rock 'n' roll. Suddenly, a kid in the audience started yelling. It was one of the boys in Winker's party. At first annoyed, Buddy soon realized the guy was only requesting a song. "Hey, Buddy," he yelled, "I'll buy you a beer if you play 'Rave On.'" Buddy smiled and felt a surge of energy. He boogied the house down with "Rave On" and still felt so charged up after the show that he ducked into a bar across the street for a nightcap. There he spotted Winker and his friends sitting in a booth and went over. "I'm here to collect my beer," Buddy said. Recounting the incident in 1993, Winker recalls, "Buddy made my friend buy him that beer."

Back home in Lubbock, Jerry noticed a change in Buddy. Once he'd been so ambitious he'd said yes to everyone who wanted to hear him sing. Now he was more selective. After the "Summer Dance Party" was over, the last thing he wanted was another round of one-night stands. Accustomed to the old workaholic Buddy, Jerry still expected him to leap at every offer. One day Buddy and Jerry were cruising through downtown Lubbock on their choppers. When they stopped at Sixth Street for a smoke, Buddy told Jerry about a lucrative tour offer Petty had just received. Jerry was all for accepting it immediately, he later recalled in Paul McCartney's *The Real Buddy Holly Story*, but Buddy wanted to lay off for a while and simply enjoy life. What if their records stopped selling and the tour offers dried up? Jerry asked. They ought to grab work while they could. Buddy said he had some money and could buy Jerry whatever he wanted, including a Cadillac. Then Buddy said something strangely prescient. How sad it would be, he told Jerry, if they were suddenly killed without ever savoring the riches they'd earned. They turned down the tour.

Waterskiing became Buddy's favorite sport, Ella Holley revealed in 1977. Larry Holley adds in a 1992 interview that the Crickets found Buffalo Springs Lake, eleven miles east of Lubbock, to be an ideal setting. Buddy and Joe B. jointly purchased an Owens outboard with a thirty-five-horsepower Evinrude motor, completely equipped with skis and ropes, reported Zenon Bilas in *Waterski* magazine in 1992. As usual, Buddy plunged into the sport, heedlessly attempting feats beyond his experience and ability. As Jerry and Joe B. pulled him across the lake, Buddy tried to negotiate the Lubbock Ski Club's formidable jump. In the ensuing wipeout, he lost his wallet and eyeglasses, which sank to the "bottom of the lake," Mrs. Holley later told Griggs, and were not recovered until several years later, after his death. Workmen who were dredging the lake, which was being enlarged, recovered them. The billfold still contained Buddy's driver's license and some cash, "crisp as if they had been burned," said Mrs. Holley.

Recalling the seemingly innocent summer of 1958, Larry Holley later told Bill Griggs that Buddy was bursting with fun, laughter, and rowdiness. Larry remained what he'd always been to Buddy, a reliable and caring older brother. Buddy became so unruly that summer that Larry had to caution him, just as he'd done in Buddy's adolescence. In some ways Buddy had never changed; he was as "salty" as ever, Larry noticed, and still had "a lot of fire" anytime he decided to relax and play. He'd been working out with weights and developing some really defined muscles that he was proud of. By August his bodybuilding regimen and karate classes paid off in an unexpected way: He was not only more muscular, but there was a change in his face as well. For the first time since his reign as King of the Sixth Grade, he could be described as handsome.

He and his fiancée Maria Elena were looking forward to a double wedding with Jerry and Peggy Sue. Jerry began to push for an early date, but Buddy was still uncertain how to handle his mother's resistance to the prospect of an interracial marriage in the family. Finally he informed her that he was bringing Maria Elena to Lubbock in August. According to Goldrosen, Mrs. Holley said, "Oh, no." Ella Holley wasn't the only obstacle Buddy and Maria Elena faced. Petty continued to voice strenuous objections to both Buddy's and Jerry's marriages, protesting, Jerry later told Goldrosen, that they were neither old enough nor sufficiently mature. Petty was probably correct on both counts, Jerry later conceded. Peggy Sue said in a 1994 interview, "There is a warm side to Jerry. Our relationship was extremely stormy, and it was from the very beginning. There's nothing wrong with the fact that we can all make a decision that is not especially good for us."

Before long, Buddy and the Crickets were flat broke. They had to go to Petty for every cent. It was, time and again, a way for Petty to tether his boys as if they were children. Jerry later told Goldrosen that he would never have been able to tolerate the idea of his wife going to Petty for money.

Maria Elena at last arrived in Lubbock in August 1958, and Buddy braced himself for inevitable flak. His Baptist neighbors felt the marriage had two strikes against it from the start: race and religion. Buddy settled the issue with his mother first, displaying the forcefulness that he was sometimes capable of. According to Goldrosen, he said his mother "might as well not say anything because I've made up my mind, and I'm going to marry her."

Buddy was literally penniless. "He didn't have a red cent," Maria Elena disclosed in 1993. "Buddy did not have a red cent in his name. Norman controlled all of the monies. . . . He paid for everything. Buddy would send him whatever needed to be paid, even the cars that they bought were paid for by Norman. Any money you got you had to go through Norman."

Petty later characterized his relationship with Maria Elena as hostile and jealous. His gravest miscalculation was dismissing her as someone who was naive and inexperienced about the music industry. Nothing could have been further from the truth: She had worked in New York at the center of Tin Pan Alley and had kept her eyes open. At Peer-Southern she probably gained a more comprehensive knowledge of deals and negotiations than any outlander from Clovis could ever hope to possess. Petty mistakenly figured that the threat to his position as Buddy's manager came from the A&R men at Decca when in fact it was closer to home; his only adversary was Maria Elena, but he persisted in fretting over Dick Jacobs, who, he later confided to Goldrosen, appeared to be undermining his clout with Buddy.

"Norman did not want Buddy to get married because he felt like his fans would find out and that would take away something from the popularity," Maria Elena said in 1993. "Of course, that was the belief of everybody at that time, that they'd lose their popularity. It turned out that marriage really didn't affect popularity at all." Petty also failed to realize how determined a man Holly was—neither racial prejudice on the public's part nor Petty's warnings would deter him. Petty even raised the specter of scandal, saying that the press would be outraged if Buddy Holly wed a Puerto Rican. The adverse notoriety of Sammy Davis, Jr.'s, marriage to blond May Britt, Brando's co-star in *The Young Lions*, demonstrated that Americans were unready to accept mixed marriages. What Petty failed to take into account was that the careers of both John Wayne and Marlon Brando had survived interracial marriages; by society's double standard, Caucasian males were allowed to marry outside their race.

As Maria Elena and Buddy approached their August nuptials, Petty made one last attempt to turn Buddy against her. "Norman said that Buddy should not marry at that time," Maria Elena recalled in 1993. "First of all, he knew about my aunt. . . . Norman knew that once I got involved, I would be finding things that he didn't want me to find or Buddy to find and that once I was in the picture, things would turn around."

Though a joint ceremony with Jerry and Peggy Sue had long been Buddy's desire, Jerry and Peggy Sue finally decided they could wait no longer and went to the Lubbock County Courthouse on July 21 for their marriage-license affidavit. They eloped the following day. Both were eighteen years old. On July 22 they drove 320 miles to Honey Grove, a tiny town on the Texas-Oklahoma border, where Jerry's uncle, a minister, performed the ceremony. Despite her hasty departure, Peggy Sue's bridal attire was appropriate, including a white tiara-type hat with a short veil, long white gloves, and a form-fitting white short-sleeved dress that displayed her shapely, wasp-waisted figure. Jerry wore a dark single-breasted three-button jacket and Slim Jim tie. Years later he told Goldrosen that he was much too young to realize "what I was doing."

After the ceremony they drove to Dallas and pondered how to break the news to Buddy, who was bound to be disappointed that they hadn't waited. Jerry called him on July 23 and, as Peggy Sue later told Griggs, admitted "jumping the gun." Peggy Sue then got on the line and Buddy made her promise to postpone their honeymoon until he and Maria Elena were wed. Buddy had made up his mind that they were all going to Acapulco and announced he'd plan the entire trip, right down to making the reservations.

Meanwhile, at the Holley home, Buddy's parents and future wife were getting used to each other. According to Goldrosen, Buddy's father liked Maria Elena, recognizing a certain logic in this match between an assertive girl and his son. First Buddy had been a mama's boy, L.O. said, then he was manipulated by Petty. Now at last, he'd "come into his own," L.O. told Maria Elena. Perhaps he was still unaware of the power she was beginning to exert in the management of his professional affairs. Maria Elena later told 16 magazine that Buddy's "mother and father were so wonderful," giving her "the same warmth and affection" that she'd received from Buddy.

The editors of the Lubbock Avalanche-Journal, evidently uninformed that a world-renowned singing star was in their midst, misspelled Buddy's name and misstated his fiancée's hometown in the routine marriage notice they buried in the back pages after Buddy and Maria applied for their license in August: "Buddy Charles Halley [sic], 21, and Miss Maria Elena Santiago, 25, both of Lubbock [sic]," it began, as if an addled Linotypist had set the notice. It had been taken from the court docket and no supplementary information was offered by the couple; Petty's paranoid horror of massive fan defections was allowed to spoil much of the fun of their wedding.

"There wasn't a proper announcement or anything," Maria Elena comments in 1993. Buddy wanted to buy her a large diamond ring, but Petty wouldn't hear of it. " 'One karat is enough,' Norman said. He didn't like me at all, so I got a one-karat ring," she recalls. "It didn't make any difference to me. The wedding was at the Holleys' home, performed by the minister of the Tabernacle Baptist Church [Ben Johnson]. There were some of Buddy's cousins and relatives, his sister, brothers, nephews. And Jerry, Peggy Sue, and Joe B., who was not married at that time. Jerry was, to Peggy Sue. Just members of the family. Nobody from the outside."

It was a hot day, the temperature hitting 97 degrees. Maria Elena wore "a short—not even to the calf—white dress with a veil, nothing ostentatious, a simple dress," she remembered. Buddy wore a dark suit. He had on his dark sunglasses because he hadn't yet replaced the regular glasses he'd lost waterskiing in Buffalo Springs Lake. The bride gave the groom a gold wedding band. After the ceremony, Jerry played Buddy's record "Now We're One," a bouncy, upbeat Bobby Darin tune that Buddy had recorded at the Pythian Temple. He tipped pastor Johnson $100, paying by check. Bill Griggs revealed in Rockin' 50s magazine in 1991 that Buddy maintained a checking account under the name "Charles Holley." He was so secretive about it that not even Maria Elena knew of its existence. When asked in 1993 if Buddy had "no bank account, no money in his name," she replied, "No. Just Norman, and he handled that as he saw fit." But there is ample proof of the account's existence in the form of canceled checks that turned up at a Sotheby's auction in New York in 1990.

After their wedding, Buddy and Maria Elena flew to Mexico for a double honeymoon with Jerry and Peggy Sue, which would prove less than blissful for some of the newlyweds. Acapulco, nestled among the Sierra Madre Mountains, lies along the curve of an aquamarine bay. Villas and plush hotels are stacked on cliffs overlooking the Pacific Ocean. Tourists relish long cool drinks at bars on the beach, ride in horse-drawn carriages

streaming colorful balloons, and shop for silver in the Mercado de Ar-
tesanias. Watching the divers plunge each day from La Quebrada cliffs
into a narrow cove 130 feet below is de rigueur, but Peggy Sue reveals in
1994 that they skipped this attraction. There was too much tension between Peggy Sue and Jerry for it to be a very happy honeymoon. "It was
uncomfortable," Peggy Sue recalls in 1994. As for Buddy and Maria Elena,
when Griggs asked Peggy Sue in 1987 whether Buddy's behavior altered
after marriage, her answer was intriguing. Buddy was indeed different, she
replied, adding that the Buddy she'd previously known so well had always
been "a happy person." Griggs attempted to dig deeper, asking again if
Buddy acted differently after getting married. "I don't think that Buddy
was real happy," she said. Later, in the 1994 interview, she also mentioned
the differences in background and age between Buddy and Maria Elena.

They all stayed at Las Brisas at the beginning of the honeymoon but
soon moved to El Cano, "which was closer to town," recalled Peggy Sue
in 1994. "El Cano" means "the ghetto" in Spanish, which indicates that
their first hotel, Las Brisas, a well-known money-shredder, had proved to
be too expensive and that they'd moved to El Cano in order to economize.
An aficionado of waterskiing, Buddy discovered that the bay and lagoon
were perfect for water sports. They rented a boat and skiis. Peggy Sue
later stated in *Waterski* magazine that Buddy taught her how to waterski.

On their way back to the States, they stopped over in Mexico City
and checked into the Hilton. "We spent the night and had our picture
taken there," Peggy Sue recalls in 1994. In the photo, Jerry and Maria
Elena are beaming at the camera while Buddy and Peggy Sue appear
somewhat subdued. Peggy Sue is wearing a drab jersey shift that does
nothing for her excellent figure, while Maria Elena is chic in a stylish
tropical outfit: an airy white dress with a low, ruffled neckline. Jerry was
not as happy as he appears in the photo. Like Peggy Sue, he was "uncomfortable," he later revealed in McCartney's film *The Real Buddy Holly
Story*. "All of a sudden it wasn't Joe B., Buddy, and I hanging out," he
said. Naturally he wanted to spend time with his wife and Buddy wanted
to be with Maria Elena, which created a "weird" situation, Jerry added.
He and Buddy longed for the old camaraderie, which was now impossible.

Upon returning to Lubbock, Buddy and Maria Elena, in abject poverty,
had to move in with Buddy's parents. They couldn't even afford to buy
groceries. In desperation, Maria Elena called Provi. "My aunt was the one
supporting us when we got married," Maria Elena said in 1993. They
appealed to Petty for money, but he turned them down. With current
recordings on both sides of the Atlantic, Buddy knew that he'd earned
more money than he'd yet collected, but Petty refused to budge. "Norman
said, 'No. I have to get together with the accountant,'" Maria Elena
added. "After we got married, Norman was furious."

Buddy's father looked on Maria Elena as his daughter, he later told Goldrosen. L. O. Holley heaped extravagant praise on her, telling her that her marriage to his son was the most beneficial thing that had ever occurred in Buddy's life. L.O. seemed to be under the impression that Maria Elena was capable of working some magic in the improvement of his son's character. She had unleashed Buddy from Ella Holley's apron strings, L.O. proclaimed; marriage was transforming Buddy into a real "*man*." Not everyone agreed. "She was running Buddy's life," says Jerry Coleman, the KSEL DJ, in a 1993 interview. "When she hollered jump, he jumped. The only thing I ever heard Norman Petty say something almost bad about was Buddy's wife. 'Well, we don't get along,' he said."

Maria Elena does not deny that she assumed a decisive role in Buddy's business affairs, nor that she alienated some of his friends and associates in the process. "Jerry and Joe B. felt a little bit intimidated by the fact that I was there and that Buddy didn't do very much without my being involved," she remarks in 1993. "I guess Jerry more so than Joe B. felt uncomfortable with the fact that I was making decisions." Her low opinion of Norman Petty was all the evidence Buddy needed that his wife possessed a shrewd and penetrating grasp of human character. She was not going to let him be exploited anymore.

For most people marriage is a personal matter. For Buddy Holly it was also a professional partnership. Mixing pleasure and business is risky at best. For Buddy it would bring a season of long-delayed fulfillments as well as drama beyond his wildest imaginings.

Chapter Eleven

Breaking Up Is Hard to Do

Voices from every establishment stronghold, including evangelistic crusader Billy Graham, had been condemning rock 'n' roll since the Boston riot, and finally the music industry itself seemed to turn against rock. Tin Pan Alley songwriters felt threatened by performers such as Buddy, Little Richard, and Chuck Berry, who wrote their own songs and didn't need ASCAP hacks for material. Muckraking author Vance Packard told the Senate Subcommittee on Communications that rock had been imposed on unsuspecting teens and that this "cheap music" was "largely engineered, manipulated for the interests of BMI. . . . The public was manipulated into liking rock 'n' roll." Frank Sinatra denounced rock singers as "cretinous goons" who seduced teenagers with "the most brutal, ugly, desperate, vicious form of expression it has ever been my misfortune to hear." Oscar Hammerstein, smarting over the disappearance from the charts of his Broadway show tunes, charged that rock 'n' roll could not be sold to the public without payola.

A congressional investigating committee, formed the following year, exposed 207 DJs in forty-two states for taking $263,000 in payola. "Clean up this whole mess," President Eisenhower ordered. The conservative *New York Herald-Tribune* exulted ghoulishly, editorializing that rock 'n' roll was "so bad that it's almost a relief to learn they had to be paid to play it." The record industry began a purge that rivaled Hollywood's Communist witch hunt in its maniacal search for scapegoats. Label owner George Goldner said he had paid Tom Clay, the first DJ to champion Buddy Holly, "approximately" $100 a month for a year to play records. Now working at Detroit's WJBK, Clay admitted that DJs were regularly given percentages of songs and even pieces of record companies as inducements to play certain records on the radio. After Clay defended such practices as "the backbone of American business," he was fired from WJBK. Across the United States, other DJs' heads began to roll. "If somebody sent you a Cadillac," Alan Freed was queried, "would you send it back?" His brazen reply sealed his fate. "It would depend on the color,"

Freed said. He was blackballed in the music business and died a few years later, according to his biographer John Jackson, "awash in a sea of alcohol and staggering legal fees and facing . . . federal tax-evasion charges."

Despite the payola scandal, the recording industry was faring better than ever: record sales went from $189 million in 1950 to $600 million by the end of the decade. Though mass consumption of rock 'n' roll was solely responsible for this dramatic growth, the founders of the music were rapidly passing from the scene. Little Richard was studying to become a Seventh-Day Adventist minister at Oakwood College in Huntsville, Alabama. Elvis, given speed to stay awake on Army maneuvers, was abusing drugs while stationed in Bad Nauheim, Germany. Jerry Lee's reputation never recovered from the scandal over his child bride. Chuck Berry would eventually serve time in a federal penitentiary in Springfield, Missouri, a victim of fifties prudery and prejudice. Both Buddy Holly and the Everly Brothers were close to burnout from the strain of constant touring and the pressure to score hit records.

The Crickets' albums had never sold well and now even their singles began to slip. The megahit records of the second half of 1958 reflected the adult public's growing disenchantment with rock 'n' roll and a resurgent taste for novelty, cha-cha, and "rockaballads," including Sheb Wooley's "Purple People Eater," Perez Prado's "Patricia," Domenico Modugno's "Volaré," and Conway Twitty's "It's Only Make Believe." The charts still reflected a fair rock 'n' roll showing, with No. 1 hits by Elvis Presley, Ricky Nelson, the Elegants, and Tommy Edwards, though it was nothing like the previous year, when every No. 1 hit, with the exception of Perry Como's "Round and Round" and Debbie Reynolds's "Tammy," had been rockers, including four by Elvis as well as the Crickets' "That'll Be the Day." By mid- to late 1958, the American music scene was becoming what Nicholas Schaffner, author of The British Invasion, called "a teenage wasteland," partly due to the adult world's suppression of the burgeoning youth culture and also because, according to Rolling Stone's Ed Ward, "people kept waiting for the rock-and-roll fad to pass and the bands to come back."

Neither Buddy's "It's So Easy" nor the flip side, "Lonesome Tears," succeeded in the United States or England in 1958. "It's So Easy" did reach No. 8 in Australia, where it remained on the chart for nineteen weeks, but there would be no more gold records, at least in Buddy's lifetime, though in a later cover by Linda Ronstadt "It's So Easy" would shoot to No. 5. For someone who'd been as obsessed with recognition and fame as Buddy, he accepted his decline as a recording artist with surprising equanimity, perhaps because he was already well into a second career—this one as a record producer and music publisher.

All that was stopping him from constructing his own recording studio in Lubbock was Petty, who refused to release the necessary cash. Nevertheless, Buddy went ahead and had plans drawn up for the studio. It was to occupy one wing of a home he was planning to build for his parents and would include a publishing company, both grouped under the name of Prism Records. Buddy was president, Ray Rush was promotion manager, and Bob Montgomery and Snuff Garrett were also to have some involvement. Petty was named sales manager, in charge of day-to-day operations. Obviously Buddy was finding it hard to break with Petty despite the bitter complaints he was making to Maria Elena. Clovis was no longer Buddy's artistic home. Lubbock radio station KLLL, where twenty-year-old Waylon Jennings was a DJ, became the new focus of Buddy's professional life. Until Buddy showed up at KLLL in September 1958, Waylon was "just sitting around listening to my hair grow," Waylon told *Guitar Player* magazine's William J. Bush in 1982. Waylon was being modest; his show was "immensely popular" with young listeners, Sky Corbin told *Cash Box* magazine. Sky, KLLL's high-strung, demanding station manager, had hired Waylon away from KVOW for $75 a week for two shows a day. The station's format was "hillbilly Top 40." Its studios were located on the twentieth floor of the Great Plains Life Building, the tallest structure in Lubbock.

Hi Pockets Duncan, Buddy's earliest mentor, had returned from Amarillo after his fling at running highway clubs and restaurants and now had a daily thirty-minute program on KLLL. Corbin described Hi Pockets in *Cash Box* as a "top C&W DJ in this area" for the past fourteen years. During bull sessions at the Great Plains coffee shop, which was located one floor below KLLL, Hi Pockets "began to pitch Waylon to Buddy," Waylon's biographer, R. Serge Denisoff, wrote in 1983. "He reintroduced the two. Waylon had been playing Holly's records, and Holly was grateful." By now Waylon was so popular at KLLL that young women were flocking to the station, guitarist Tommy Allsup said, according to Denisoff, " 'to see the swingingest guy around.' " Supporting his wife and children had become "a burden" for Waylon, Denisoff added. "Maxine stayed at their Fifth Street home taking care of the kids, reading movie magazines, and drinking large amounts of Coca-Cola."

Like Buddy, Waylon would eventually enjoy a racially integrated love life. He would not be afraid to flaunt his preference for black women, Randal Riese wrote in *Nashville Babylon* in 1984. "I've been with some pretty foxy little black chicks," Waylon said, "and the devil had nothing to do with the first time, and the second time, the third time, the fourth time, it was all mine."

"Buddy liked Waylon," Hi Pockets said. Buddy advised Waylon on how to improve his image, taking him to his barber and having "his hair cut the way he thought it should be cut," Hi Pockets added. Since Waylon was always broke and consequently rather seedy looking, Buddy went to a department store with him and had Waylon outfitted with a natty new wardrobe.

Every day, Buddy would arrive at KLLL carrying his guitar and ready to perform, compose music, or simply hang out. Don Bowman, a DJ at the time, described in the video biography, *Waylon: Renegade, Outlaw, Legend,* how they'd write songs, play them in the control room, and make their demos at KLLL. Sonny Curtis, one of the "local pickers" who was drawn to the station, said they must have "got in the way" but the station personnel "never made us feel that way." KLLL had been on the air under Sky Corbin's ownership and programming policy since May 1, 1958; in his stable of "personality DJs" were his brother Ray "Slim" Corbin and "Mr. Sunshine," a well-known West Texas country-gospel DJ. Other regulars at the station included Jerry and Joe B.; Terry Noland , who was recording on Brunswick; the Four Teens, Challenge recording artists; and Sonny Curtis and Niki Sullivan, both now recording on the Dot label. Sky Corbin affectionately referred to them all as "Lubbock boys, and we're proud of 'em."

When practicing or recording at KLLL, Buddy, Waylon, and the Corbin brothers liked to work in the back room to keep out of the way. Frequently their jam sessions lasted all night. At the time Buddy was smitten with Ray Charles and played his record "My Bonnie," singing along with it, until he wore it out, according to Ella Holley, who sometimes joined in and made it a trio. Waylon later told William J. Bush that Buddy adored Ray Charles's material and was "looking for the guy" who did Charles's arrangements, which Buddy intended to use "for guitars, or around guitars."

Waylon often recorded KLLL's commercials while Buddy sang in the background or pounded on trash cans. KLLL's practice of broadcasting jingles as station IDs was initiated by Waylon. On September 1, 1958, the station owner came in and told everyone to clear out of the back room so he could cut some commercial jingles. Buddy asked if he could try his hand at a few of the commercials. Accompanying himself on the guitar, he cut a promotional jingle advertising "KL Double L" to the tune of "Everyday" and another to the tune of "Peggy Sue."

The Great Plains coffee shop became the social center for hip young Lubbock musicians, including Sonny Curtis and Tommy Allsup. "All I got out of the coffee shop was a divorce from the secretary on the sixth floor," said Don Bowman. "God, I spent a lot of time [there]. I should have spent more time at home." Waylon later referred to his days at KLLL as "best times of my life," characterizing them as a "free-for-all, with a lot of personalities on the air."

Hi Pockets later recalled how he had just finished broadcasting one day and was walking across the parking lot to his car when Buddy and Maria Elena drove down the street in Buddy's "big old Lincoln" and pulled over. After Buddy introduced them, Maria Elena told Hi Pockets that Buddy had often spoken of him but she couldn't remember exactly what role Hi Pockets played in Buddy's past. Buddy turned to her and said, "Let me put it this way. If it wasn't for him, I wouldn't have you," Hi Pockets later told Griggs. Unchanged since the days when he'd discovered Buddy, Hi Pockets was still promoting young singers, and Waylon was his latest enthusiasm. Hi Pockets booked both Buddy and Waylon to appear in a concert he was staging for the golden anniversary of the town of Spur, Texas, located sixty miles east of Lubbock. Waylon sat in that night as Ray Price's bass guitar player, marking the first time Waylon attempted to play the bass. The Crickets, Sonny Curtis, and June Carter also appeared in what was probably the liveliest hoedown ever to hit tiny Spur, population 1,690.

Waylon later told William J. Bush that Buddy's father admired Waylon's singing and urged Buddy to take Waylon seriously as a potential recording star. "His dad said to Buddy, 'I want you to listen to this boy,'" Waylon recalled, "and Buddy did." Buddy told Waylon about Prism Records and offered him a job as a regular staff musician. Other West Texas instrumentalists Buddy intended to hire for his proposed recording studio were guitarists Tommy Allsup and George Atwood, but his interest in Waylon went beyond using him as a sideman. Maria Elena revealed in a 1993 interview that Buddy finally told Waylon that he was willing to produce Waylon's first record.

"When Waylon Jennings wanted to get involved with rock 'n' roll Buddy said, 'No, not rock 'n' roll. You're country,'" Maria Elena remembered. "Waylon kept insisting, 'I want to be a rock 'n' roller.' Buddy said, 'No, no, no. I'll tell you what. We'll record you with this song first, which has a beat to it,' which was 'Jole Blon,' a Cajun song. 'If you don't feel comfortable then there's always time for you to change and do rock 'n' roll, but you'll find out I'm right.'"

Maria Elena agreed that Waylon was talented. In fact, his singing thrilled her so much, Waylon later told William J. Bush, that it gave her "goose bumples." Added Maria Elena in 1993, "Buddy knew always that Waylon would be a country [singer]. Buddy was really a very, very astute person." Waylon told Bush in 1982 that Buddy was a major influence on him both as a human being and as a singer ("he was *smart*, man"). As Buddy began to produce Waylon's first record, he decided to go to southern Louisiana, some seven hundred miles to the southeast, just across the Sabine River from Texas, to study Cajun music and culture. Unfortunately, Petty wouldn't provide the financing for the trip, so Buddy selected the Cajun warhorse, "Jole Blon [Pretty Blonde]," a French folk song that had been a hit record for Harry Choates in 1946. Buddy planned to record Waylon at the next Clovis session. According to Bob Montgomery, Waylon was the first artist Buddy signed.

The session was scheduled for September 10, 1958. On September 7, Buddy celebrated his twenty-second birthday. He traded his orchid-colored Lincoln for a Cadillac at the Alderson dealership on Nineteenth Street in Lubbock. Larry referred to the color of the new car as "pink" but Buddy called it "taupe." Though Buddy had previously owned a used Caddie, the one Larry had ended up paying for, this was his first new Cadillac, a 1958 60 Special Sedan. In the fifties and sixties, long before the Mercedes craze hit the United States, the Cadillac was the ultimate American status symbol. On September 10, Buddy drove the Cadillac to Clovis to record Waylon's "Jole Blon" as well as his own new single, "Reminiscing," with saxophonist King Curtis, who wrote the song. Though KLLL's equipment sufficed for jams and personal tapes, Buddy still needed Clovis and Norman Petty for demos of the highest professional quality.

Fellow Texans, Buddy and R&B tenor saxophonist King Curtis had met at an Alan Freed show in New York. *Rolling Stone* critic David McGee later wrote that "King Curtis helped define the spirit of early rock-'n'-roll/R&B with his honking, stuttering tenor-saxophone solos." Another *Rolling Stone* writer, Ed Ward, added that Curtis's "distinctive, almost hillbilly-tinged sax line" sparked the Coasters record, "Yakety Yak," the "teenage classic of social commentary . . . that would set parents and school authorities against rock and roll." Years later, in his memoirs, *Rhythm and the Blues*, Atlantic Records' Jerry Wexler lavished praise on King Curtis's "lickety-split barnyard tenor sax" and the "riotous tone" it set for "Yakety Yak," which became the No. 1 R&B record of 1958.

Just before the Clovis session, Buddy called Curtis in New York to hire him to come to Clovis. "That'll be five hundred dollars and plane fare," Curtis said.

"Ain't that a little high?" Buddy asked.

"You're making yours all the time and I gotta make mine," Curtis replied. "You send the money up to New York."

"No," Buddy argued, "if I was to send you five hundred dollars and the plane crashed, I'd lose my money and my sax player."

"Mr. Holly, just send the money and don't talk like that."

He paid Curtis a total of $600, determined to capture a sound for his new record that would be startlingly different from anything Holly fans had heard before. Larry Welborn, who saw Buddy in Lubbock at this time, subsequently told Goldrosen that Buddy was finding the effort to be unique with every record increasingly difficult.

The session was truly "an event," Sonny Curtis later reported. Most of

Buddy's friends crowded into the Clovis studio, including Sonny, Bob Montgomery, Jerry Allison, George Atwood, Tommy Allsup, Bo Turner, Waylon Jennings, and Waylon's brother Tommy.

"Reminiscing" is the story of a jilted lover licking his wounds, but the bluesy lyric is far from melancholy; the song's effect is sensual in a funky, groovy way. Curtis's nimble, eloquent saxophone provides a witty and deft counterpoint to Buddy's swirly, hiccuping vocal. Though he didn't play on the session, Waylon was in the studio, "just marveling a whole lot," he recalled in *Guitar Player*, as Buddy and Curtis took rock 'n' roll into an exciting new dimension.

King Curtis, whose real name was Curtis Ousley, eventually became Atlantic's full-time sax man, arranger, and in-house bandleader, working with Aretha Franklin and Cissy Houston, before recording his own albums, *Live at the Fillmore West* and *Blues at Montreux*. His untimely death in 1971 shocked colleagues throughout the recording industry. A vagrant stabbed him to death in front of the building he owned at West Ninety-sixth Street in New York, ending a brilliant solo career. At his funeral, Aretha Franklin sang "Never Grow Old." Eulogizing Curtis as "an integral conveyor of the Atlantic sound," Jerry Wexler said Curtis "loved to eat, shoot dice, record, ride his bike, and make shrewd record deals."

At the same time Buddy recorded with Curtis that day in 1958, he officially began his career as an independent record producer, having finalized an agreement with Brunswick Records to produce a specific number of masters each year. Waylon's "Jole Blon" was his maiden effort. Buddy had intended to cut Harry Choates's Cajun standard himself, but he gave it to Waylon because he was motivated by a desire "to see his friends make it," Sonny Curtis observed in the video *Waylon*. In a 1993 interview Sonny added that he felt "privileged" to be at the session. Waylon said in his authorized video biography that "Jole Blon" was "Buddy's idea" and added that Buddy "thought it might be a pop hit." The original French lyrics describe "Jolie blonde," a fickle heartbreaker who has spurned the singer and run off with another man, wrecking all hope of happiness. Though Waylon was "scared," he remembered the session as "a lot of fun."

Singing the song in Cajun may not have been the wisest decision for Waylon's recording debut. Neither Buddy nor Waylon understood Cajun dialect and had had to play the Choates record over and over, painstakingly transcribing the words. Although Waylon's backwoods sound on the record is authentically rustic, there is little sign of the major star that Waylon would one day become. "I wasn't near ready to start recording then," Waylon later told Serge Denisoff. Trade reviews were tepid, one critic noting that the singer "acquits himself to listenable effect. . . . It has a chance," and another referring to "Jole Blon's" "interesting, infectious issue . . . lots of rock snap and could show up." But the record was not a commercial success when it finally came out the following year. Buddy's instinct about Cajun's potential, however, placed him at the forefront of the late fifties "country Cajun" trend. Singer-fiddler Doug Kershaw and his brother Rusty scored a huge hit with "Louisiana Man," which combined rockabilly and Cajun influences to produce a classic of southwest Louisiana swamp life.

Waylon later described what Buddy Holly was like as a record producer: "An upper, happy all the time, really matched his music . . . a lot of energy." To William J. Bush he added that Buddy "laughed a lot," but always stressed that an artist should never "compromise about your music: Do what you feel. Seemed like he was trying to tell me everything he could in a short period of time." Buddy advised him to "leave while you're ahead," Waylon remembered. If a singer retires while he's still on top, Buddy explained, critics will overrate him, but if he hangs around until he starts repeating himself, they'll base their judgment on his final performances and dismiss his entire career as insignificant.

Throughout September 1958, as Buddy worked with Waylon, the Clovis studio was rife with intrigue. Behind Buddy's back Petty was busily trying to turn Buddy's friends against him. Maria Elena was luring Buddy to New York, Petty said. Vi and Norma Jean made snide remarks about Maria Elena's accent, trying to destroy her influence with Buddy any way they could. Petty attempted to spook the Crickets into thinking that they'd be exploited and robbed by unscrupulous New York record executives if they let Buddy convince them to move east; Joe B. says Petty "hyped" them on the idea that even very successful bands ended up broke if they permitted the New York offices to control their affairs.

The Crickets accompanied Buddy when he went to New York on September 23 for an Alan Freed TV show. Once again, Buddy met with Lou Giordano, the young singer he was considering signing for Prism Records. Louis Patsy Giordano (pronounced in four distinct syllables), born June 23, 1929, in Brooklyn, was the fifth of ten children born to Italian immigrant parents, Filomina and Dominick Giordano, Sr. Known to family and friends as Louie, he grew up listening to Vic Damone and Frank Sinatra, developing a smooth crooner's style. His credits were almost nonexistent: a few radio programs, some USO shows, and a gig or two with someone named Joe Coniglio at the G.I. Pipesmokers Club on Avenue S in Brooklyn. One day at Joe Villa's house Buddy played a new song he'd written, "Stay Close to Me," and gave it to Giordano, offering to produce his first record. Phil Everly rounded up some more material to fill out the session, and at Beltone on September 30, 1958, Phil gave Lou a new tune he'd just completed, "Don't Cha Know," for the flip side of "Stay Close to Me."

When the record was released some months later, it received good if not exceptional trade notices. *Cash Box* gave Giordano a "B-plus" on both sides, praising the "larks" singing behind him on "Don't Cha Know" for their "effective . . . vocal bits." The "larks" were Buddy, Phil, and Joe Villa, warbling in soprano tones. They'd do "anything to make music," Phil later remarked to interviewer Margaret McNie. *Cash Box*'s critic termed Giordano's performance "first-rate teen ballad work." Though Giordano attracted a loyal following—a fan club was established in New York by a girl named Karen Oretti—no sales pattern developed for the recording. His soft, mellow voice was alluringly erotic but must have seemed relatively tepid in comparison with the power hitters of the time—Connie Francis with "Who's Sorry Now" and Frankie Avalon with "Venus."

While in New York, Buddy drank too much at a party with the Everly Brothers and Eddie Cochran in Cochran's suite at the Park Sheraton Hotel, a few blocks below Grand Central Station on Park Avenue. Phil later described the Park Sheraton to Kurt Loder as the "hot hotel" favored by the first generation of rockers. It had never taken much alcohol to get Buddy high; according to Phil, he "was having a drink, and he asked me to make sure he got home that night, and I did." Everly denied that they were "a bunch of drunks" but added that occasionally they'd "tie one on."

Despite Everly's disclaimer, Buddy's inability to navigate on his own indicates he was blacking out, which Alcoholics Anonymous identifies as the sign of a drinking problem. Don and Phil were also headed for trouble with substance abuse. Ritalin got Don "strung out," he told Loder, describing his life on drugs as a "disaster." Like Buddy, the Everly Brothers were drained from battling a greedy and domineering manager. When Don and Phil finally broke free from Wesley Rose's stranglehold and demanded more autonomy in the matter of song selection, Rose cut them off from Boudleaux and Felice Bryant, their source of hit material. Phil said that the people who were exploiting them for money drove them too hard. They they deserved a "long rest," Phil added, but they were kept so busy performing that they never got around to taking it.

If blond, blue-eyed Phil Everly was the boy every girl wanted to take home and make happy, dark-haired, gray-eyed Don was the sort you'd "be afraid to take home—he was, well, all male," according to the Everlys' biographer Consuelo Dodge. Don was described by Kurt Loder as "rootless, restless, mercurial," a gourmand with a weakness for Beaujolais and gorgeous girls. He and Buddy grew close in late 1958 in New York, frequently dropping into Manny's Music Store, sometimes with their wives. If the girls became impatient, the boys told them to go shopping and buy anything they wanted. Clerk Henry Goldrich later said that Buddy and

Don remained at Manny's for four hours on one occasion, playing "every guitar I had in stock."

Though Buddy was tired of touring, Petty had frozen his money and he had no choice but to go back on the road. No matter how he tried, he could not get away from the domination of managers who did not have his best interests at heart. Patsy Cline, another innovative artist of the late fifties, was suffering the same kind of abuse. Early in her career, her recordings were restricted to songs controlled by her producer. Later, like Buddy, she had a string of hits but was always strapped for money. Such exploitation was typical of this era, before agents took control of their stars.

Together with the Crickets, Buddy signed up for a General Artists Corporation all-star tour of the Northeast and Canada in the fall of 1958, headlining a bill that included Bobby Darin, Dion and the Belmonts, Frankie Avalon, and Clyde McPhatter. In certain cities they'd be joined by Eddie Cochran, Paul Anka, the Everly Brothers, Connie Francis, Jerry Lee Lewis, Ritchie Valens, and Frankie Lymon. The tour party rehearsed at two P.M. on October 2 at the Nola Studios in Manhattan. As the star, Buddy had sufficient clout to demand and get a backup vocal group. He chose the Roses, who were flown up from Texas. He was also able to secure private dressing rooms, one for the Crickets and another for the Roses. Others on the bill "had to go to the gym and change," Bob Linville, one of the Roses, later told Bill Griggs. Tommy Allsup came along as Buddy's lead guitarist. The final and most controversial addition to Buddy's entourage was his wife.

Immediately they faced the issue of whether to live openly as man and wife on the road or conceal their marriage in deference to Buddy's fans, as Petty wished. In a 1993 interview Maria Elena recalled, "I did not say that I was married to him when I was on tour. I always said that I was the secretary of the group. Buddy really did not care for that and said, 'No! You're my wife. I'm going to say that you're my wife. I don't care what everybody says.' I felt like, I don't want people to start hounding me or him about our marriage or him being married or whatever. It was mostly me, not him."

Buddy had always traveled with the Crickets, but now, with his wife along, that was clearly out of the question. While the Crickets and the Roses followed behind them in a DeSoto station wagon, pulling all their equipment in a trailer, Buddy and his wife enjoyed the luxury of the Cadillac. The arrangement displeased the Crickets. Years later Joe B. told Goldrosen that he felt Buddy was acting like a "bigshot star" but admitted the real issue was his jealousy of Maria Elena. He felt that Buddy wasn't his "brother," as in the past. Obviously the difference in Buddy's marital status required growth and adjustment all around, but the Crickets balked at the prospect of change. Hurt, confused, and demoralized, they hit the bottle, sometimes drinking during working hours, which Buddy, a consummate professional, found obnoxious.

As the tour crossed the blazing October landscapes of Massachusetts and Connecticut, Maria Elena decided that show business was "not glamorous at all. I can vouch for that," she said in 1993. "I did a lot of washing: underwear and shirts. You have to set everything up yourself and pick it up yourself, and go and collect your money sometimes under very strange circumstances." When asked whether Buddy carried a gun, she replied, "Yeah. You had to at that time." Did he use it? "While I was with him usually I would do the collecting," she said. "I didn't fool around. I said, 'Okay, pay me now.'"

Maria Elena's bravery was clearly an asset. The directness and spontaneity that went with it sometimes led to drama, such as the incident at the Canadian border as they reentered the United States following engagements in Ontario and Quebec. The Roses' Bob Linville later told Griggs that when a customs official asked if they had anything to declare and whether they were American citizens, Maria Elena said, "No. I am from San Juan, Puerto Rico." The guard immediately asked to see her papers. According to Linville, she didn't have any with her. Other guards appeared. They were detained, and all of them were questioned. Buddy was "irritated with Maria Elena" and "chastised her for that," Linville added. As soon as the guards realized they were professional entertainers in Canada on legitimate business, they waved them on.

Relations between Buddy and the Crickets were strained. Jerry complained that the only time the Crickets saw Buddy was when they were onstage performing. In the old days they'd hung out together after work; now Buddy unwound with his wife. Buddy pointed out that Jerry and Joe B. were drinking too much. Jerry later disclosed in *Remembering Buddy* that occasionally he and Joe got loaded before noon and remained inebriated throughout the day. After a show one night, Buddy called a meeting and read the riot act, telling them that he objected to their boozing "all the time." The Crickets blamed everything on circumstances, refusing to correct, or even to acknowledge, their own character flaws. They lost all interest in performing. According to Jerry, they started "shucking it." Buddy threatened to fire them if they persisted in goofing off. Anyone who expected to be in his band, he warned, had better demonstrate more enthusiasm and interest in performing music. At last Jerry and Joe B. realized Buddy was right and promised to "tighten up a little bit," Jerry later told Goldrosen.

Since Maria Elena didn't have a driver's license, she couldn't take turns at the wheel and Buddy had to drive constantly, without anyone to relieve him. The long distances between one-night stands soon left him tired and testy. In mid-October 1958, following a performance in upstate New York and late for a show in Scranton, Pennsylvania, Buddy floorboarded the Cadillac as soon as they pulled onto the turnpike. The needle on the speedometer climbed steadily from seventy to ninety. Just behind the Cadillac, in the band's car, Bob Linville noticed that Buddy was getting too far ahead and decided to catch up, although it meant breaking the speed limit. As their speedometers hovered around ninety-five, the sound of police sirens split the night air and suddenly the highway was full of flashing lights. They all stopped and waited for the inevitable confrontation. Did Buddy have any idea how fast he was going? the policeman inquired. Buddy made a wisecrack and got hauled into the station house. Later, under a bright light at the sergeant's desk, the cop looked at Buddy, did a double take, and asked him if he was a performer.

Buddy irritably informed the cop that he was in Alan Freed's "Biggest Show of Stars" tour. At that point the cop smiled brightly and asked for his autograph. Buddy looked at his watch. If they left immediately, they could make the Scranton show—maybe. The signature he scribbled on a piece of paper as he dashed from the station house was utterly illegible. They made it to Scranton's Catholic Youth Center without a second to spare.

Toward the end of the tour Buddy told Jerry and Joe B. that he was firing Petty and moving to New York. One can only speculate about what finally pushed Buddy over the edge, but everyone involved seems to agree that it was his marriage to Maria Elena. Petty objected to her so viscerally that it became impossible for Buddy to continue his association with Petty. Also, Maria Elena was filling Buddy's ears with "things that [Petty] didn't want me to find or Buddy to find," such as all those not very kosher business practices of Petty's, of which Maria Elena and Aunt Provi had proof.

Buddy expected Jerry and Joe B. to go along with him on both decisions: Petty's firing and the move to New York. Joe B. was against it. He was still under the influence of Petty, who had convinced him that he would be cheated by Yankee record executives. Jerry went along with Buddy on the understanding that he'd receive a share of Prism Records. Jerry then informed Petty that they were leaving Texas and resettling in Manhattan. For the present, no one told Petty that he was being fired.

After the tour, Buddy's relations with the Crickets remained tenuous. They did not perform with him during the October 21 Pythian Temple "string session" in New York that produced, in three and a half hours, what writer Mark Steuer has called "the most inventive music of 1950's rock": "True Love Ways," a song Buddy had just written, and "It Doesn't Matter Anymore," which was composed expressly for Buddy by Paul Anka. In his book *The Best Rock 'n' Roll Records of All Time*, Jimmy

Guterman cites Buddy's recording of "It Doesn't Matter Anymore" as "perhaps the only instance of a great version of a song written by Paul Anka," though Frank Sinatra, who would make Anka's "My Way" his signature song, would hardly agree.

A number of Buddy's friends were present in the studio, including Peggy Sue. "I met them after the Canadian tour right before the Pythian Temple session," Peggy Sue recounted in 1994. "Maria Elena was there, as were Jerry, Joe B., Norman and Vi Petty, and Jo Harper from Peer-Southern." Hal Buksbaune, Decca's art director and session photographer, also attended. Dick Jacobs produced the session, though it had come about as a result of a conversation between Buddy and Petty, who advised Buddy that the new songs he'd been writing, such as "True Love Ways," would be more effective with violins. In view of Buddy's recent differences with the band, he feared that the Crickets would assume he was "going against them," Buddy said, but Petty assured him that no one was trying to break up the band.

According to Dick Jacobs, Petty wanted to wean Buddy from rock 'n' roll and turn him into a pop singer. Every time Petty visited Decca's offices in New York, he continued to promote the idea of a string session. Finally Buddy admitted that the more he thought about violins, the more he liked the idea. "Buddy was growing up, and so, perhaps, was rock and roll," *Rolling Stone's* Ed Ward later wrote. Buddy was the first major Caucasian rock star to use a string session, Jacobs later told Wayne Jones. There is no question that Buddy's decision was instrumental in expanding the vocabulary of rock 'n' roll.

Journalist William J. Bush wrote in *Guitar Player* in 1982 that the violinists for Buddy's string session were recruited from the New York Philharmonic and the old NBC Symphony, which had been founded for Arturo Toscanini's radio concerts and survived as the American Symphony under the baton of Leopold Stokowski. Buddy selected four songs to record with the violinists and told Jacobs to create the orchestrations. One of the songs was dropped when Paul Anka's "It Doesn't Matter Anymore" became a last-minute addition. The others were "Raining in My Heart" by Boudleaux and Felice Bryant, "Moondreams" by Petty, and "True Love Ways" by Buddy. Referring to "Raining in My Heart," Don Everly later told Kurt Loder that the song had been written for the Everly Brothers by the Bryants, but Don and Phil didn't think it was "right" for them and decided to give it to Buddy.

Several hours before the Pythian Temple session began, Buddy rushed into Jacobs's office carrying his guitar. Paul Anka had just finished writing a song and presented it to Buddy on an exclusive basis, Buddy informed Jacobs, and Buddy was determined to cut it during the session. It was impossible, Jacobs said; they were scheduled to go into the studio in three hours, at eight P.M. Buddy kept insisting that the Anka song was "fantastic," Jacobs later told Wayne Jones. Finally Jacobs relented and asked Buddy for the lead sheet. Buddy looked at him blankly and admitted that he didn't have one but would be glad to sing the song for Jacobs's copyist. As Buddy sang, Jacobs devised the "pizzicato arrangement for the strings," Jacobs later explained. By eight P.M. they were ready to start recording, beginning with "It Doesn't Matter Anymore." At the last minute Paul Anka burst into the studio. Years later he still recalled the moment with pride, telling TV host Phil Donahue in 1977, just before singing "It Doesn't Matter Anymore" on Donahue's show, "I wrote this song for the late Buddy Holly."

When Peggy Sue entered the Pythian Temple studio that day in October 1958, the atmosphere was heavy with excitement and tension. She was awestruck by the sight of the full orchestra, waiting for Buddy to take charge. The prospect of some of the finest classical musicians in New York working under the direction of a Lubbock rocker who couldn't read a note of music was as incongruous as it was funny, though there was no laughter, at least at the beginning of the session. The musicians included violinists Sylvan Shulman, Leo Kruczek, Leonard Posner, Irving Spice, Ray Free, Herbert Bourne, Julius Held, and Paul Winter. David Schwartz and Howard Kay played violas, and Maurice Brown and Maurice Bialin were the cellists. Doris Johnson played harp; Al Caiola, guitar; Sanford Bloch, bass; Ernest Hayes, piano; Clifford Leeman, drums; and Abraham "Boomie" Richman, a veteran of Tommy Dorsey's orchestra, played tenor sax. Peggy Sue would later tell Griggs that the violinists at first were "real snobbish" and made it clear that they disdained rock 'n' roll, but Buddy "didn't let anybody shake him up," she added.

Before they started to work, Buddy posed for a photo with the musicians in the background. According to Peggy Sue, he then indicated that he knew exactly the sound he wanted and that the recording would be "the way he heard it or it wasn't going to be." Describing the moment to Griggs in 1987, Peggy Sue noted that rock 'n' strings, as the new subgenre could be called, "had not been tried before, and there was a lot of prejudice against rock music at the time." She lauded the "maturity" that twenty-two-year-old Buddy displayed in taking charge of the orchestra. He handled them "beautifully," she said. Dick Jacobs later told Griggs that as they did a quick run-through of the arrangements, Buddy appeared "very apprehensive" but his conduct was "untemperamental" and later "completely relaxed."

His extraordinary collaboration with the string section would take rock music into heretofore uncharted territory, with far-reaching consequences for the rock ballad, later perfected by Roy Orbison in grand opuses such as "It's Over" and "In Dreams." The Pythian Temple session would also have an impact on C&W music, though that impact would not be felt until the early 1960s, when Owen Bradley, who had failed Buddy in Nashville, added lush Holly-type string arrangements to Brenda Lee's No. 1 hit "I'm Sorry" and Patsy Cline's "True Love" and "So Wrong."

After the playback of take one of "It Doesn't Matter Anymore," Buddy and the musicians looked at each other and broke into broad smiles, realizing they'd achieved a perfect recording on the first try. A grateful Dick Jacobs, who was expecting at least a three-hour session, predicted that at the rate Buddy was going they'd be finished in "one hour flat." He was amazed that Buddy recorded the Anka tune exactly as rehearsed, changing nothing.

"It Doesn't Matter Anymore" has more in common with Paul Anka's weightier compositions, such as "My Way" and "(You're) Havin' My Baby," than it does with earlier Anka standards like "Diana" and "Lonely Boy." With perception and power, the song lays out the successive stages of grief that one goes through at the end of a love affair: denial, anger, acceptance, and hope. Buddy offsets the seriousness of the song by giving it the same propulsive force that made "Maybe Baby" so zesty and stirring. Jacobs later told Griggs that Paul Anka "flipped out" when everyone in the studio agreed that Buddy had scored a surefire hit on take one; Anka walked around grinning, deliriously happy.

Jacobs found that it wasn't necessary, as it was with all the other artists who recorded at the Pythian Temple, to place Buddy in an isolation booth or have him wear earphones. Those measures were normally taken in order to prevent "leakage" of the soloist's voice and to ensure that the orchestra wasn't picked up by the performer's mike. Buddy sang quietly, and all Jacobs had to do was turn up the "gain" on his mike to achieve an ideal mix of voice and instrumentalists. Buddy stood "out cold in the studio, in front of the orchestra, just like the singers with the old dance bands," Jacobs later revealed in *Rockin' 50s* magazine.

They recorded "True Love Ways" next. Its serene and haunting melody was inspired by one of Buddy's favorite black gospel hymns, "I'll Be All Right," as recorded by the Angelic Gospel Singers on Nashboro Records. Though "True Love Ways" would never make Billboard's Top 40, it reached No. 25 in England. The song seems to glide along as if in perpetual motion, slowly enough to look back upon itself and admire its perfection. The singer portrays love as a state of being or a condition of the soul, compounded of joy, sighs, and tears. Along with happiness always come conflict and the necessity for acceptance. The term "true love ways," like all the phrases Buddy coined—"it's so easy," "not fade away," "words of love"—sounds so right that it seems always to have been part of the language.

A powerful feeling that Buddy wrote "True Love Ways" about and for Maria Elena comes over me when I meet her and spend some time with her in 1993. In a way, Maria Elena Holly reminds me of Janis Joplin, someone who is completely up-front, but she's also very much a lady. When I ask her to pose with me for a photo, she smiles and puts her arms around me, as if we've known each other for years. With her love of show business and her ability to take "better to the touring than some others," as she put it to Goldrosen in 1975, it's easy to imagine the fun she brought to the marriage. When Maria Elena was by his side, it was because she was exactly where she wanted to be, whether they were in New York or on the road. If she'd had her way, there would have been no more lonely nights for Buddy, ever. What neither he nor she could have foreseen was that her pregnancy, which occurred soon after their marriage, would prevent her from accompanying him on tours and taking care of him as she had on the autumn 1958 trip.

At the string session, after recording the Bryants' "Raining in My Heart" and Petty's overripe but not unappealing "Moondreams," Buddy expressed his satisfaction with all the cuts but added that he was worried about how the rock market would greet his experiment with violins. Maria Elena reassured Buddy, telling him that although he wrote neither "It Doesn't Matter Anymore" nor "Raining in My Heart," they were among her favorite Buddy Holly performances.

During the session Peggy Sue announced that she liked everything Buddy had recorded that night equally, but years later, like Maria Elena, she decided "It Doesn't Matter Anymore" and "Raining in My Heart" were the best. Dick Jacobs preferred "Raining in My Heart" but added that he loved Buddy so blindly that he accepted everything Buddy recorded as perfect. Buddy himself favored "Raining in My Heart," later telling his brother Larry that it would eventually be regarded as the "best record I've ever put out." It took Buddy's mother to spot the classic among the songs recorded that night. She singled out "True Love Ways," and she was absolutely right.

When the triumph of his string session finally registered on him, Buddy grew more confident in his dealings with Decca and told Dick Jacobs that he wanted to record a Ray Charles album as his next project. Decca was receptive to the notion, considering Buddy to be "as good a ballad singer as anyone in the business," Jacobs told Bill Griggs. Though Jacobs had recorded Louis Armstrong, Jackie Wilson, and Steve Lawrence and Eydie Gorme, he told Griggs he ranked Buddy as the "most un-temperamental artist of them all." Decca executives were inclined to accommodate his every wish, including a new idea he had for an album with a Count Basie sound, for which he'd require a full brass section and several saxophone players. Bob Thiele, the chief executive at Coral, Buddy's label at Decca, agreed to the big-band recording, with stipulations. Buddy promised to make the record in New York and to use Thiele as his producer, overriding the objections of Norman Petty, who'd not yet been told he was fired. But Petty sensed the worst and returned to Clovis, resentful, bitter, and determined to break up the Crickets. If he couldn't keep Buddy, he could at least keep Jerry and Joe B. Petty would sue, if necessary, to retain the Crickets' name and money. As far as Petty was concerned Buddy Holly was finished in show business unless he got back in line.

Petty is not without his defenders. "I'm not championing Norman but I feel he's been treated unfairly," says Peggy Sue, who was engaged in 1995 in writing a book about Petty and Nor Va Jak, according to Bill Griggs. "Doing business in Clovis, New Mexico, when rock 'n' roll had just started, they were all learning, including Norman Petty," adds Peggy Sue. "He was paid for what he did, it's true. If Buddy had been in L.A. or New York he could have walked into a studio and paid scale to musicians and an A&R director and had them do the same thing, but none of them was there. And no one in Clovis was that sophisticated at that moment in business. If Mr. Petty had a fault, it was that he cared and loved too much, like a father. He had a very protective attitude toward Buddy, Jerry, and Joe B." The only hole in the father-figure theory is that Petty was only nine years Buddy's senior; even Peggy Sue concedes that "Mr. Petty wasn't that much older." Petty was more like an envious sibling than a protective parent. Perhaps their relationship had more in common with the Old Testament story of Cain and Abel, in which Cain murders his brother, out of jealousy, when Abel's offering proves more attractive to God.

It was with little joy in her voice that Peggy Sue recalled, in a 1994 interview, those late autumn days in 1958 that she and Jerry spent with Buddy and Maria. "They say husbands and children are your karmic lessons, and I have to truly say that one was," says Peggy Sue, referring to her marriage to Jerry Allison, which was wrong from the start. In New York in 1958, Peggy Sue, then only eighteen years old, felt out of her depth among the savvy, fast-talking Brill Building pros, so different from the gang at the Hi-D-Ho. The Crickets were now surrounded by celebrities. Peggy Sue had been a fan of Phil Everly's and when she found herself rubbing elbows with him in Manhattan, it was somewhat disconcerting. The insecure young girl from the provinces needed someone to lean on and no one was there.

When Peggy Sue was asked shortly after arriving in Manhattan what she wanted to see in the big city, everyone expected her to say the Statue of Liberty or the Empire State Building. Instead, she asked to be shown Carnegie Hall. Still proud of the standing she'd achieved in the Lubbock High School Band as its first-chair alto sax player, Peggy Sue knew that

Carnegie Hall was the world's top musical venue. Jerry and Joe B. took her to Fifty-seventh Street for a look at the imposing tan-brick concert hall, which has several flights of perilously steep steps leading up from the crowded sidewalk. In 1958, posters advertised concerts by the New York Philharmonic, Eugene Ormandy and the Philadelphia Symphony Orchestra, and the great operatic soprano Vittoria de los Angeles. A few doors down from Carnegie Hall is the red-plush-and-brass Russian Tea Room, which keeps Christmas decorations up all year. Across Fifty-seventh stands the stately flagship showroom of Steinway Pianos, with a gleaming black concert grand behind a plate-glass window. Art galleries, auction houses, a Horn and Hardart automat, a Chinese restaurant, an art cinema, and a huge Schrafft's restaurant completed the lineup of establishments along the elegant and bustling thoroughfare of West Fifty-seventh Street.

When she returned from her midtown jaunt, Buddy asked her why on earth she'd chosen to go to Carnegie Hall. Peggy Sue later told Bill Griggs that she replied, "That's where we're gonna play. Buddy Holly and the Crickets are going to be in Carnegie Hall someday." Buddy laughed and told her that Carnegie was far too distinguished a venue ever to "accept" him. Indeed, Tchaikovsky himself had conducted there shortly after its opening more than sixty years before. They'd never welcome Buddy Holly. Oh, yes, they would, Peggy Sue insisted, because the Pythian Temple session proved that he was taking rock 'n' roll in the right direction. Her observation was prophetic. A few years later, when rock 'n' roll had gained a semblance of respectability, the Beatles played a doubleheader at Carnegie, making their American debut.

One evening, Buddy, Maria Elena, Jerry, and Peggy Sue all went out on the town, beginning with dinner at Mama Leone's, a tourist mecca in Times Square, and going on to a glamorous movie premiere. Among the chic, understated New York women, Peggy Sue struck Jerry as painfully conspicuous, she later told Griggs; her clothes were as inappropriate as her conversation, Jerry complained. She ought to get some fashion tips from Maria Elena, he said, and instructed Peggy Sue to round up Maria Elena and buy some New York clothes.

To Peggy Sue, Maria Elena was "attractive" and "very polished," but she "was not a girl," she later told Griggs. Maria Elena was "five years older than Buddy," said Peggy Sue, and she'd been brought up in Manhattan, the polar opposite of Lubbock. Moreover, Peggy Sue pointed out, "Buddy only knew her about a month." On their shopping spree, Peggy Sue selected a skirt that was too tight and spike heels that made her teeter precariously when she attempted to walk in them. Later, her idol Phil Everly and his girlfriend Jackie joined the two couples at Mama Leone's. Peggy Sue was upset when her pocketbook strap, a solid one, struck a cabinet in the powder room and broke. After dinner, struggling with the unfamiliar tight skirt and high heels, she stumbled as she emerged from their car at the film premiere. One of her heels got stuck in a subway grate and broke off. She fell on the street in front of a glitzy New York crowd. She was mortified. All the signs were there that this Texas girl just did not belong in New York.

She looked to Jerry, but he seemed as embarrassed as she. Peggy Sue lay there chastising herself, wondering why her life was just one awkward impasse after another. Her friends seemed to have matured faster and left her behind. Sometimes she thought she was the only one in the group still searching for her identity. When Buddy saw her predicament, he rushed to her side to help. The solution he proposed was clever and expedient: She should remove her slippers and walk into the theater barefooted. Peggy Sue scanned the dressy gathering under the marquee and protested that she couldn't possibly do such a thing. She was ready to creep back to the hotel alone when Buddy picked her up and told her she was "going to the movie and that's all there is to it." She made it through the evening, thanks to Buddy's kindness and resolve. Recalling the incident in 1994, Peggy Sue says, "Buddy was gifted with the white light of Christianity."

Had Buddy lived beyond 1959 he might have written a sequel to "Peggy Sue Got Married" and called it "Peggy Sue Got Divorced," for that's what happened almost eight years later. In a 1994 interview Peggy Sue sums the marriage up as a mistake but adds, "There's always a reason. My first marriage was a karmic lesson, let's put it that way." She and Jerry had no children and eventually divorced. Later she married a man named Lynn Rackham and lived in an opulent house overlooking the American River in Sacramento. She and her husband owned the Rapid Rooter plumbing company until their divorce in 1993, after which Peggy Sue returned to her home in Slaton, Texas, to care for her ailing mother and work on her book. Today she is an attractive, gracious, soft-spoken woman, and after talking with her for only a few minutes, it's clear why Buddy Holly was moved to write two of the best love songs of the rock era to her, "Peggy Sue" and "Peggy Sue Got Married."

In late 1958, while Petty was in Clovis plotting their downfall, the Crickets continued their East Coast swing, making two appearances on national television in October. On the first, *The Dick Clark Saturday Night Beechnut Show*, Buddy sang "It's So Easy." The telecast was taped in Manhattan's Little Theater in Times Square on October 25 with an all-star lineup including Buddy, Frankie Avalon, Don Gibson, Bobby Day, and Robin Luke. Buddy was getting along better with the new friends he met in New York, especially Robin Luke, than he was with his fellow Texans, which helps explain why he was being drawn more and more to the city.

Luke, a young Los Angeles–born singer who'd scored a million-seller on Dot with "Susie Darlin'," later told Holly fan Steve Vitek how he treasured his brief, intense encounter with Buddy on the Dick Clark show. They spent hours together in Buddy's dressing room, where Buddy gave Luke a marathon, hour-and-a-half guitar lesson, demonstrating how he blocked the strings with his right hand to get the muted guitar sound on "Peggy Sue."

On Tuesday, October 28, this time accompanied by the Crickets, Buddy went to Philadelphia to appear on Clark's *American Bandstand*, performing before an audience of 8.4 million viewers. In a kinescope that survives of the show, Clark introduces Buddy first as a solo act, heralding him as a wunderkind who writes and performs his own songs. When he asked Buddy how many tunes he'd composed, Buddy replied "fifteen, twenty songs." Affable and relaxed, he said, "Okey dokey," when Clark announced that he was ready to bring on the Crickets.

They lip-synched their way through "It's So Easy," which has a sudden, abrupt ending that caught Clark completely off guard. Muttering, Clark complained that the Crickets did him "a lot of dirt" every time they sang "It's So Easy." Before they left the stage, Clark asked Jerry if he was returning to Lubbock. Jerry replied that they were "eager" to go home "just as soon as we can fly out of New York."

Buddy told Clark that he was "taking a three-day journey back in the car," adding that the Crickets had "to fly in because I won't let them ride with me." He meant it as a joke, but the separate travel arrangements remained a sore point between him and the band. Jerry and Joe B. were not pleased when Buddy told them he was moving to Manhattan "where I can be close to record companies and publishers. I hope you guys will go along." Joe B. seemed confused and uncertain but Jerry agreed to move to Manhattan and "start our own publishing company." Jerry and Joe B. then left to catch their plane, while Buddy and Maria Elena started driving to Texas. Buddy was under the impression that they would all reunite in Lubbock and go together to Clovis to fire Petty jointly. But something went wrong with the plan. Joe B. began to feel that Buddy was being "headstrong" in insisting on moving to New York, he stated later in McCartney's *The Real Buddy Holly Story*. Moreover, as Joe B. would confide to Goldrosen, Petty still had him convinced that the record executives in New York would rob him if he didn't have Petty around for protection.

Despite their agreement to wait for Buddy, Jerry and Joe B. went to Clovis without him. "The boys went to see Norman to get some money as soon as they got back," Larry Holley says in a 1992 interview. The Crickets' Clovis bank account contained $50,000, but only Petty was authorized to draw on it, and he refused to release any money until he knew where he stood. He extracted the information he needed from Jerry and Joe B., who revealed that they were leaving Petty and moving to New York with Buddy. In a later conversation with Larry Holley, Buddy said that Petty tried to turn the Crickets against him. According to Larry, Petty said: "Buddy ain't ever'thing. He's just hoggin' the show. Ya'll don't need Buddy Holly. He's never been fair to ya'll. You can make it on your own. Stay in Texas and work as the Crickets. When he don't have ya'll, well, ya'll see how far he goes. You stay with me and we'll get another singer and . . . let him do what Buddy's doin.' "

Implying that he could make recording stars out of them, Petty offered to produce Jerry and Joe B., assuring them that they could continue calling themselves the Crickets, even without Buddy. In reality, they had about as much chance of stardom as the Wink Westerners without Roy Orbison, but they fell for Petty's blandishments. Petty said he had Buddy's money locked in the bank, Joe B. later told Goldrosen. In a 1983 interview with Skip Brooks and Bill Malcolm, Petty disclosed that he told the Crickets that Buddy "would produce himself in New York as Buddy Holly." Petty's next words, which Joe B. quoted to Goldrosen with chilling exactitude, show that Petty had Buddy Holly's blood on his hands. "We'll starve him to death," Petty said.

Buddy and Maria Elena pulled into Lubbock a few days later and attempted to round up the Crickets for the prearranged trip to Clovis. When Buddy called Jerry's house, according to Goldrosen, he discovered that Jerry and Joe B. had not waited for him but had gone on to Clovis without him. Unable to believe that the Crickets would confer with Petty behind his back at such a sensitive time, he turned to his mother, Larry Holley revealed in 1992, and asked, "Where's Jerry and Joe B.?"

"They went over to Clovis," his mother said. "Buddy just got livid mad," Larry added. Buddy immediately drove to Clovis with Maria Elena, who confronted Petty in front of the Crickets, Vi, and Norman Jean. Maria Elena described the scene in a 1993 interview. "We went to Clovis one day to get our money," says Maria Elena "Norman definitely said, 'No. I am not ready. I've got to get to the facts and account to the other two boys. I cannot let you have the money." Petty later alleged to Goldrosen that Maria Elena announced she and Buddy could "do better" and felt Petty was "not fit" to manage the Crickets. In 1993, Maria Elena revealed that Vi and Norman Jean started making fun of her accent. Buddy leaped into the fray. "He got mad and told Vi and Norma Jean where to get off," Maria Elena says in 1993. In an earlier interview with Goldrosen, Maria Elena said she told Vi to try communicating with her "in Spanish." When the monolingual plainswoman remained speechless,

Maria Elena pointed out that she could speak Vi's language, "but you
don't know a word of mine. You think you're so sophisticated, but I know
more than you ever will."

Petty demanded an explanation—what had he done that was so bad
that he deserved to be fired? In Petty's recollection, Maria Elena asserted
that it wasn't what he'd *done* so much as what he *hadn't* done that was
the source of all the trouble. Petty then turned to Buddy and asked him
if he'd definitely made up his mind to terminate their association.

Buddy continued to press for their money and assured Petty that he
would give the Crickets their share. At that point, Petty dropped his
bombshell. The Crickets were leaving Buddy and staying with him; *he*
would pay Jerry and Joe B., as their manager. Buddy felt "betrayed,"
stabbed in the back, Maria Elena later told Goldrosen. Once again she
confronted Petty. In a 1993 interview she recalled, "I said, 'Well, Norman, you need to let him have at least part of his money. We need to
live on something.'

"He said, 'No, he cannot have his money. You have to wait until I get
all the accounting done.' Of course I knew that he was doing that on
purpose. Jerry and Buddy got upset and Norman said, 'Well, to be honest
with you, I don't have to pay anything until I'm ready.' Buddy said, 'Well,
you know, give me my money or you're going to be in some kind of a
problem.' Buddy was really very upset. 'Oh,' Norman said, 'I'll tell you
what. I'd rather see you dead first before I give you any money now.' That
was said in front of me. So I said, 'Buddy, let's go.' Buddy was going to
sock him. I said, 'Let's go. Let's get a lawyer when we get back.' And
that's exactly what we were doing. We put the things in the hands of a
lawyer. But of course we needed some money and my aunt was taking
care of us."

They left the studio, and Buddy and the Crickets went out to the car.
Buddy was disappointed and wished the Crickets would reconsider and
stay with him, Jerry revealed in *Remembering Buddy*. When they declined,
he warned them, according to Jerry, that they were going to regret their
decision. They were welcome to the Crickets' name, he said. Buddy had
long ago established a separate identity and had less need of it than they.

Once he was alone with Maria Elena, he broke down. Searching her
memory over three decades later, Maria Elena says, "Buddy got real hurt
when they did this. He cried, thinking that the boys had betrayed him,
staying with Norman." Back in Lubbock, he was so distraught that he
told his parents and Maria Elena that he might give up his singing career.
"Listen, Buddy," Maria Elena said, "they were the ones that left you and
you have a lot of talent of your own and you'll do well." Though Maria
Elena found him to be "real perturbed and real upset," she revealed in
1993, by dawn he regained his confidence and knew that he could get

along without the Crickets. "Of course, everybody knew that he still missed the guys, you know," says Maria Elena. "That was obvious. He really cared for those two boys. They made good music together."

Jerry is brief and to the point when asked in 1993 to explain the Crickets' breakup. "Really the reason we split was because we decided to stay in Texas," he says. "We wouldn't have decided to stay in Texas, but Norman Petty talked us into staying there and working as the Crickets."

The disastrous consequences of the breakup were felt at once. Buddy's life, never in the best fiscal shape, became totally unmanageable. Without money, it was impossible for him and his wife to remain in Lubbock; they could count on Aunt Provi to support them in New York and made plans to move east. But even if they'd been able to support themselves in Lubbock, Maria Elena could never have endured the Texas attitude toward "blacks and Mexicans," she told Goldrosen and Beecher. Though Maria Elena was fearless and quite beyond being intimidated by anyone, Buddy loathed Lubbock's bigoted thinking; he still couldn't fathom how supposedly religious, churchgoing, Bible-thumping people could flout Jesus's admonitions to love everyone, judge no one, and treat others exactly as one wished to be treated one's self.

When they said good-bye to Buddy's family, Buddy gave his brother Travis his Guild F-50 Navarre acoustic. DJ Snuff Garrett later told Bill Griggs that Buddy stopped in Wichita Falls to visit him while Snuff was in the middle of a stay-awake marathon at radio station KSYD. Outside the building, a crowd had gathered to watch Snuff, whose stunt to publicize his sponsor, Fred Jones's Lincoln Mercury dealership, had already lasted five days. Buddy remained with Snuff throughout the night, chatting, spinning records, and playing "4-5-6 Dice." While Buddy was in the station, Maria Elena tried to get some rest in the Cadillac, which was more comfortable than the studio. Buddy told Snuff that he was changing the name of his recording company from Prism to Taupe Records and his publishing company would be known as Taupe Music. Taupe was the color of his Cadillac, which he adored so fervently that from now on he was going to name *everything* after it (*Webster's II* defines taupe as "brownish-gray to a dark yellowish brown"). Before Buddy left, he took the mike and announced a station break for KSYD, "the station that other stations listen to."

A few days later, following another long drive in the Cadillac, they arrived in Manhattan, glad to have the Southwest behind them but wondering how they'd cope and where they'd live in New York. The most urgent priority, however, was to obtain legal counsel for the financial chaos that the Clovis fiasco with Petty and the Crickets had plunged them into. As they were destitute, Aunt Provi again came to their aid. Buddy's new single was not a money-maker. The Latino-styled "Heartbeat" was released on November 5 but stalled at No. 82 in the United States; it went to No. 30 in England, evidence of the United Kingdom's continuing love affair with Buddy Holly. The B-side, the hard-edged "Well All Right," one of Buddy's best tender-tough records, failed to chart significantly in either America or England, though Australians responded to its power and urgency and sent it up the chart to No. 24.

Buddy and Maria Elena found an apartment in New York in Provi's neighborhood, Greenwich Village, on Fifth Avenue. On their first visit to Apartment 4H, No. 11 Fifth Avenue, they stood in a spacious high-ceilinged room, then walked out onto a terrace, gazing down at the teeming life of the Village. This was the age of bohemians and Kerouac; the Village was crawling with hipsters, beatniks, pale actresses in black leotards and heavy eye makeup, and drunken abstract-expressionist painters. Tatterdemalion folk singers were just then beginning to congregate a few blocks away, around the fountain in Washington Square, just beyond the majestic Arch designed by Stanford White, honoring the first president of the United States. The center of American bohemianism since the 1890s, Greenwich Village was the very antithesis of the provincialism of Lubbock and Clovis that had proved so inhospitable to them both. Villagers were characterized by tolerance and defiance of middle-class standards, including those that prohibited crossing ethnic barriers as Buddy and Maria Elena had done. The Village "stood for a fresh start . . . for liberty," wrote Emily Hahn in *Romantic Rebels: An Informal History of Bohemianism in America*. "It stood for fun . . . Those who stayed . . . were usually people who would have felt chilly and displaced anywhere else." Buddy and Maria Elena looked at each other and knew they'd found their home.

Chapter Twelve

Sunset and Evening Star

Mark Twain was seventy years old when he moved to what would become modern Greenwich Village. Despite personal and financial problems, he experienced a great creative flowering, spilling out a five-hundred-thousand-word autobiography that made him rich again. Five decades later, on the same spot on lower Fifth Avenue, in similar financial straits, Buddy Holly wrote "Peggy Sue Got Married" and other classic songs that rivaled his stunning roll of Clovis hits in 1957. From our vantage, knowing the tragedy that was about to befall him, the winter of 1958 seems full of foreboding, but for Buddy, the few months he still had to live were a time of ferocious creativity, producing the last outpouring of great Holly songs, the apartment tapes. December 1958 through January 1959 was an incredible, yet short-lived period of fecundity few artists have since matched in so brief a period. These new songs reflected a new depth and maturity, especially "That Makes It Tough," "Learning the Game," and "Crying, Waiting, Hoping." But the most famous of the apartment tapes was "Peggy Sue Got Married," which he recorded on his Ampex tape machine on December 5, 1958. Years later, *Rolling Stone* critic Jonathan Cott eloquently singled it out as a "masterpiece":

> With Peggy Sue he created the first rock-'n'-roll folk heroine. . . .
> In "Peggy Sue Got Married," he continues his complicit arrangement with his listeners, half-pleading with them, and with himself, not to reveal something which he himself must hesitatingly disclose. . . . He has become one of his own listeners as Peggy Sue vanishes, like Humbert Humbert's Lolita, into the mythology of American Romance.

L. O. Holley had suggested the song. Since the original "Peggy Sue" was doing so well—eventually it sold ten million—L.O. advised Buddy to write a sequel. Though "Peggy Sue Got Married" is one of Buddy's best performances, the demo remained in a Scotch Magnetic Tape box in his apartment long after he cut it. Obviously no one at Decca was pushing for a new recording session. Buddy could certainly have used the money. Without Provi's help, they couldn't even meet the rent. "We were paying nine hundred dollars a month," recalls Maria Elena, which was an astronomically high rent, even in New York, in 1958. Buddy still did not have "a red cent," she adds. "It was very expensive at that time. Carmine De Sapio lived there in the upper floors. You pay as you go up."

Carmine De Sapio was the boss of Tammany Hall, the County Democratic Executive Committee, which had its headquarters in Greenwich Village. At the time, De Sapio was one of the most powerful men in U.S. politics. Occasionally they would see him in the elevator: an imposing figure in tinted eyeglasses and a pompadour. Another Village neighbor, then a community organizer named Edward I. Koch, the future mayor of New York, called De Sapio "the boss of bosses," a man who "had controlled Village politics since before anyone could remember."

Once Buddy and Maria Elena settled in, Buddy immediately started making improvements. "It was a corner apartment with a wraparound terrace," Maria Elena recalls. "It was a very prestigious address because the apartment complex had been built on the site of Mark Twain's house." Maria Elena recalled that Buddy Holly had read Mark Twain, "the basic stories that we read in school. There was a big hoop-te-do there in Greenwich Village because at that time Twain's house wasn't a landmark and I don't know what happened to it. I think somebody transported the house somewhere. Where Mark Twain used to sit and write, this apartment building went up and a lot of big wheels lived in that complex. It was very exclusive."

During our interview in 1993, when Maria Elena mentions that the number of their apartment was 4H, I ask, "H as in Helen?"

"No, H as in Holly," she ripostes.

Buddy designed cabinets for the kitchen as well as a bar that opened out onto the terrace. If he couldn't make it as a singer, he told his wife, he could always earn a living as a draftsman or engineer. His mother had always been proud of how skilled and resourceful Buddy was, how he could fix anything that went wrong around the house, how he could draw professional blueprints and excel at any task he tried.

As winter came on, Buddy and Maria Elena bundled in warm sweaters and began to explore the bohemian neighborhood that surrounded their luxury building, a neighborhood that was one of the most colorful in the world. They took walks "late at night or early in the morning," Maria Elena remembers. "Buddy and I were like night owls. We couldn't sleep. Both of us were hyper. We just felt like walking. We kept on the move. We went to coffeehouses and listened to poetry readings. He *loved* the poetry readings and the folk singers in Greenwich Village. I remember one coffeehouse we went to that had beers from every country in the world."

That was the winter that New York was full of poets, who were flocking to the Village from San Francisco, Paris, and Morocco, many of them with Allen Ginsberg's *Howl*, the beat generation manifesto, sticking out of their jeans pockets. Ginsberg and fellow poet Frank O'Hara sat squeezed into a tiny booth at the Cedar Tavern on University Place and Eighth Street, where, O'Hara later wrote in "Larry Rivers: A Memoir," "we often wrote poems while listening to the painters argue and gossip." Kerouac, who'd just published *The Dharma Bums*, was reading poetry around the coffeehouses and reciting it, to saxophone accompaniment, on Dot Records. Often drunk, he was bashed by Village punks outside the Kettle of Fish bar on MacDougal Street and sought refuge in the apartment of novelist Joyce Glassman. Allen Ginsberg, like most of the future counterculture leaders converging on the Village at this time, looked on his tiny apartment at 170 East Second Street as "a silent castle for sleeping, balling, cooking and writing" and made it available to all his friends as a crash pad. Buddy and Maria Elena's apartment would also become a home away from home for Waylon Jennings and other rockers passing through New York.

Folk music had become dominant in 1958, emanating from the coffeehouses off Sixth Avenue like the Gaslight, Phase 2, Café Wha?, the Bitter End, and the Café Bizarre. Earlier that fall, the Kingston Trio's "Tom Dooley" had sold 3.5 million records and launched the folk movement, paving the way for sixties singers such as Joan Baez, Bob Dylan, Peter, Paul and Mary, John Denver, and Gordon Lightfoot.

Among the many reasons Buddy loved New York was its musical and artistic ambiance. Ginsberg once wrote that the floodlit skyscrapers looked "as if they were manufacturing cosmic jazz." Like Paris, which nurtured the creative renaissance of the 1920s, New York in the fifties spawned half a dozen artistic movements, from abstract expressionism to the New York School of Poets and avant-garde breakthroughs like *The Connection* at Julian Beck's Living Theater. Musically, New York was the cradle of formidable achievements ranging from fifties Broadway musicals (*Guys and Dolls*, *My Fair Lady*, *West Side Story*), to the folk movement, to Buddy Holly's apartment tapes, to Brill Building rock 'n' roll (spearheaded by Neal Sedaka, Carole King, Jerry Leiber, Mike Stoller, and Phil Spector's "wall of sound"). It was one of the city's most romantic and glamorous eras, unforgettably evoked by Truman Capote in his 1958 bestseller *Breakfast at Tiffany's*.

The Greenwich Village alleys and byways that Buddy and Maria Elena haunted that winter are very different from the rest of Manhattan's ledgerbook grid. Originally a farm in colonial times, later a thriving town known simply as Greenwich, and by the mid-nineteenth century the fashionable residential area of Henry James's *Washington Square*, Greenwich Village was settled long before the checkerboard pattern of Manhattan was designed in 1811. Positioned often diagonally to the rest of the city, Village streets, which have names like Gay, Jane, and Washington Mews, are like a maze; they contain numerous surprises, such as the completely illogical intersection of West Tenth and West Fourth streets near Sheridan Square.

"Buddy loved the jazz places," Maria Elena says, mentioning the Five Spot, the Half Note, and the Village Vanguard. At Max Gordon's Vanguard, a narrow cellar on Seventh Avenue, they could hear Thelonius Monk, John Coltrane, Gerry Mulligan, and Cannonball Adderley, as well as a gaggle of "sick" comedians, such as Robert Clary, Mort Sahl, and Lenny Bruce. "Johnny Johnston had a jazz club downstairs on Ninth Street," says Maria Elena. "Buddy *really* loved to go there." Jazz was enjoying unprecedented popularity in the fifties. Buddy, as a singer adept at inventing and embellishing as he performed, would have related profoundly to the freedom and spontaneity of jazz. You could walk from club to club and hear Count Basie at Birdland, Red Allen at the Metropole, Carmen McRae at Basin Street, Red Norvo at the Embers, Mabel Mercer at the RSVP Room, and Marian McPartland at the Hickory House. For Dixieland you hailed a cab and went downtown to Eddie Condon's in the Village, where you could also catch Kaye Ballard, Felicia Saunders, or Sylvia Syms at the Bon Soir on Eighth Street.

"We were always around the Village Gate," Maria Elena remembers with fondness. In 1958 the Gate resounded with the sounds of R&B. Buddy, Eddie Cochran, Jimmy Bowen, Don and Phil Everly, Gene Vincent, and Buddy Knox had long been regulars there. Knox later told Griggs that they "were probably the only ones in the place at the time. Later it became a huge commercial place."

Recalling the one occasion when they went to the movies, Maria says, "The only movie Buddy and I saw together was *Mister Roberts*. Buddy had no time for anything but his music and getting things together. And so was I, trying to get things organized, get things established. He had so many plans in mind." Not the least of his concerns was how to support himself and his bride. He visited booking agencies but had no professional portraits to leave with them. Petty's amateurish snapshots were completely unacceptable in New York. Finally Buddy posed for a show business photographer and acquired a decent portfolio. "The first pictures that were suitable for promotion were the Bruno portraits, which I suggested," recalls Maria Elena. "As soon as we were able to get his money in his hands, we were going to do some real promotion."

Unable to afford clerical help, they answered fan mail personally and tried to get some fan clubs started. In reply to a letter from fan Jeff Speirs, Buddy wrote that, although there would not be a third album from the

Crickets, he hoped Speirs would enjoy his current single, "It's So Easy." He enclosed a photograph, as requested, and thanked Speirs for being such a conscientious collector of his records. "We were working night and day," Maria Elena says in 1993, "trying to establish all these things that he wanted to do. For instance, Buddy said, 'You know, I want to learn acting.' " Once again Buddy referred to his favorite actor, the gangly Tony Perkins, whose recent films then included *Fear Strikes Out*, *Desire Under the Elms*, and *The Matchmaker*. "Buddy always watched Anthony Perkins," says Maria Elena. " 'I want to be like Anthony Perkins because I'm kind of tall and lanky, like him. I want to do a movie. Not only act in it—I want to write the score of the movie.' "

As Buddy's career required so much time, Maria Elena was unable to pursue her own ambitions to be a dancer-singer-actress. "After we got married, he said, 'No, no. You don't need to do that,' " she remembers. Without any hint of bitterness or regret, she adds, "He wanted me to be around."

One day Buddy told her, "I want to do a classical score."

"Well," Maria Elena replied, "you want to do it, go ahead."

She marveled at the many-faceted nature of his genius. "All the ideas that Buddy had at that time!" she says. "He wanted to open studios in different areas, like London." His flagship recording studio, which would concentrate on Texas talent, would be in Lubbock, with branches in California, New York, and London. The Lubbock studio would include a retail record store to be managed by L. O. Holley.

"Phil Everly came into town," Maria Elena remembers. Phil was still single, though he would later marry Jacqueline Alice Ertel, Archie Bleyer's stepdaughter. In 1958 Phil was a frequent visitor at the Holly apartment. One evening they all wanted to experience a "completely different" cuisine, Maria Elena recalls, and went out to a restaurant. The young stars were anonymous on the Village streets. Among the bohemians and beatniks, rock 'n' roll was not the rage that it was in the outer boroughs or New Jersey, where Buddy Holly and Phil Everly would have been mobbed. "We went to a Spanish flamenco place, somewhere around Sheridan Square," adds Maria Elena. During the floor show Buddy was immediately caught up in the drama and excitement of flamenco guitar playing. After the show, he invited one of the musicians over to their table. Later Buddy told Maria Elena, "I want to learn classical guitar and do some kind of classical score for the Spanish guitar."

With Maria Elena's Latin heritage came a love of flamenco music; she owned a large collection of flamenco records, which she brought out for Buddy when they returned to the apartment that night. "He started listening to them and said, 'Oh, I could do that, easy,' " she says. "He started playing his guitar and soon he picked it up. He was into perfection and said, 'Who do I call?' " Maria Elena knew a teacher in the neighborhood. Buddy started taking flamenco lessons and soon was buying all of Andres Segovia's albums.

Phil Everly and Buddy took long walks and talked about their careers and the direction rock 'n' roll was taking. Phil later told John Goldrosen how he and Buddy lived in suspense each time they released a record, hoping they wouldn't be written off as one-hit wonders. The Everly Brothers' string of megahits in 1957–58—"Bye Bye Love," "Wake Up, Little Susie," "All I Have to Do Is Dream," "Bird Dog," and "Problems"— did nothing to allay this fear. Phil complained that he couldn't find anyone in the music industry who knew enough about rock to be trusted as a mentor. The genre was changing so fast there seemed to be no standards, just fads that kept coming in rapid succession, like the speeded-up walla-walla-bing-bang nonsense in "Witch Doctor" and the trilling of the chipmunk Alvin in David Seville's "The Chipmunk Song," the hit of the 1958 Christmas season. Obviously record executives were mindful of the number of Baby Boom families after World War II.

"Rock 'n' roll is being integrated into popular music," warned DJ Bill Randle of Cleveland's WERE. "It's no longer a novelty. Rock 'n' roll was an earthy, virile influence, but the authentic artists were destroyed by the gimmick imitators. . . . There's a point to which you can't cater to the mediocre any longer." According to Consuelo Dodge's *The Everly Brothers,* Phil Everly said, "People were always asking you what were you going to do when it's over?" Phil considered Buddy to be one of the few persons on the rock 'n' roll scene with some stability. Despite the doubts Buddy had expressed in 1957 about rock's future, he now felt that rock 'n' roll had solidly established itself and advised Phil that he could look forward to a lifetime career in rock if he wasn't averse to experimentation and change.

There were difficult moments that winter, shared with Phil Everly, when Buddy despaired over his absence from the charts. After "Think It Over" and "Early in the Morning," which both hit in August 1958, *Billboard* reported nothing more of Buddy Holly's in the Top 40 during his lifetime. He was drinking over it. Years later Phil Everly told Philip Norman, "I can remember him [one] night playing me all of his songs and asking me why he couldn't get a hit record, he was so low. Then he said, 'Will you put me to bed?' "

Casting about for ways to produce some income, he tried to capitalize on his celebrity by endorsing commercial products. In late 1958, Buddy asked the Guild guitar company to manufacture a Buddy Holly signature model. Guild agreed and Buddy began designing a blond electric Buddy Holly guitar. He was to receive a percentage of the profits. At the same time, Don and Phil Everly, who used Gibson's J-200 acoustic, entered into negotiations with Gibson. Don cut out the pick guard shape he preferred and forwarded it to the Guild factory in Kalamazoo. By 1963 the Guild catalogue would advertise the Everly Brothers Signature Guitar: J-180, described as "a special guitar, capable of creating a strong rhythm . . . An unusual concept in jumbo flat-top guitars, designed and developed in close cooperation with the Everly Brothers." Actually, according to Eldon Whitford, David Vinopal, and Dan Erlewine, authors of the book *Gibson's Fabulous Flat-Top Guitars*, the Everly Brothers guitars were just "black J-200s with large and white double pick guards, in mirror image, one on each side of the sound hole." Subsequently Gibson's smaller J-185, a discontinued model, was substituted in order to avoid competition with the ever-popular J-200. The J-185 was dressed up with ten pearl stars inlaid on the rosewood fingerboard and an eleventh pearl on the peghead, just under the Gibson trademark. The double jumbo pick guards were made of mock-tortoise shell. The maple back and sides and spruce top combination "emphasizes the punchy sound while lessening overall sustain," wrote Whitford, Vinopal, and Erlewine.

Don Everly once referred to Buddy as "a thinking man," someone eternally expanding the parameters of rock, introducing innovations such as the string section and the saxophone duet with King Curtis. Eventually the Everly Brothers would break up, and the end would be as ugly as Buddy's and the Crickets'. In a 1973 outburst Don would tell the press that he was fed up with being an Everly Brother. When he showed up drunk at a gig, an infuriated Phil slammed his guitar to the floor and walked out.

At one point during the winter of 1958, Buddy decided to learn Spanish. Maria Elena taught him by singing Latin American songs to him, beginning with "Maria Elena," a Lorenzo Barcelata song written in 1933 for the wife of Mexico's president, which was a million-seller for Jimmy Dorsey and Bob Eberle back in 1941. Buddy and Maria Elena recorded a few tapes together, but Maria Elena didn't consider them good enough to be taken seriously.

Another new project was an LP with Ray Charles. In a 1993 interview Maria Elena says, "He wanted so desperately to do a gospel album that he said, 'You know, I'm going to try to get Ray Charles and talk to him about doing a duet with him.' Guess what happened later along the line? Paul McCartney went with Stevie [Wonder, 'Ebony and Ivory'] and Michael Jackson ['We Are the World'], a lot of the stars went with each other to record. When that happened I thought, my god, look at this. That man was really ahead of his time."

He also told her, "I love Mahalia Jackson. I love gospel," she reveals in the 1993 interview. The legendary singer made an unlikely film debut in 1958, appearing in a Lana Turner tearjerker, *Imitation of Life*, in which Mahalia belted the Twenty-third Psalm from a pulpit. *St. Louis Blues*, a dour and listless biography of W. C. Handy, also failed to capture Mahalia's essential vibrance. According to Goldrosen, Buddy wanted to cut a sacred album as a tribute to Mahalia and present it to his parents.

He never stopped thinking and talking about new musical challenges and ways to diversify and expand as an entertainer, Maria Elena comments in 1993. His favorite part of the day was when he settled down in front of his hi-fi to listen to other artists' recordings or play his various guitars. Despite his breech with the Crickets, sagging record sales, and no income, this was a happy time, thanks largely to Maria Elena and her generous Aunt Provi. "Buddy was a twenty-two-year-old going on fifty," says Maria Elena. "He was very relaxed and easygoing, but he had this drive and his mind was so sharp. It was going all the time." He was bursting with so many ideas that he'd wake up in the middle of the night and want to talk.

Buddy's parents came to New York for a visit and stayed with them in the Village, Larry Holley revealed at the 1981 Buddy Holly Memorial Society Convention in Lubbock. The Holleys were likely surprised by the complete absence of domestic routines in their son and daughter-in-law's household. There was no set time to eat, a habit Buddy had picked up on the road, which Maria Elena did nothing to discourage. "He didn't eat much and neither did I," she says. "I tried to cook. Buddy liked steak. You can't mess that up too much. But I tried to cook just little things that I started learning."

Soon she and Buddy were dining almost exclusively in restaurants. "There was a Mexican place on Fourth Street," she recalls. "They were Cuban, but they had Spanish food. They had only about four tables. That's where we went to eat some of our meals because they were so inexpensive. It was downstairs, and they had a bar and a couple of tables. People would make reservations for two weeks in advance. I met the owners and they were from Cuba. We always had a place there. They used to sometimes give us our meals free, because of Buddy."

In order to pursue his theatrical ambitions, Buddy soon realized that he needed professional training if he expected to find work on the New York stage or in TV and movies. "He was going to . . . get himself some acting experience," says Maria Elena. They made plans to enroll in Lee Strasberg's private school. Maria Elena urged Buddy to learn how to dance, an essential skill if he ever expected to appear in a Broadway musical. Complaining that he had "two left feet," Buddy tried to beg off, but she kept at him. Finally he agreed to enroll for lessons at a dance studio, as if he didn't already have enough irons in the fire.

When no job offers were forthcoming, Buddy turned again to composing and wrote "That's What They Say." Using his Ampex tape machine, he recorded it in the apartment on December 3. In the lyrics, it's poignantly clear that the singer has failed to find love. Instead of irony or bitterness, Buddy's voice conveys a patience that is touched with spirituality. Though the song includes an element of hope, it is not held out as strongly as the conviction that faith is its own reward. Keep waiting, the song seems to say, and you'll find joy in the process of living; serenity, which may in the end be preferable to romantic love, will come your way. Touching and melodic, this is American lieder of the highest order. Buddy had begun his career as a good songwriter. By this juncture, he had apparently become a great one.

On the same day, December 3, he recorded "What to Do," a tune about the end of an affair, when all that's left is memories. Proms, long walks, and drugstore dates, the song's simple images, suggest that Buddy was writing from his own experience, his high school romance with Echo McGuire. Though buoyantly tuneful and almost bouncy, Buddy's delivery is charged with the empathy and compassion so characteristic of the apartment tapes.

He frequently composed in Provi's apartment, using her piano, Maria Elena later told Goldrosen. As he wrote, he alternated between the piano and guitar, composing at the piano and then playing his Gibson J-200 and singing the song to see if it worked. He wrote the music and lyrics simultaneously. Maria Elena recalled that he would come up with the first version of the lyrics fairly quickly and then spend hours in meticulous revision. Then he would turn to her and ask if the song was any good, invariably adding that he didn't yet have it exactly right. She would listen attentively, but just as often she'd pursue her own interests around the apartment, which sometimes clashed with his. One day he stormed out, snapping that he'd return shortly. After stalking around Washington Square, he came back home, somewhat calmer. Resuming his work, he called out to her after a few minutes and played what he'd written. He was fortunate to have found a girl who loved his music so much that she was willing to draw on an apparently bottomless well of interest and patience.

On her birthday in December 1958, Maria Elena persuaded Buddy to drink "a couple of glasses of champagne," she later stated in Goldrosen and Beecher's *Remembering Buddy*. He became seriously ill. As an ulcer sufferer, he was playing with fire. [Ulcers can be fatal; another famous American entertainer, one from of an earlier era, silent-film star Rudolph

Valentino, died in agony from a perforated stomach ulcer at the Polyclinic Hospital in New York in August 1926. He was thirty-one, just nine years older than Buddy Holly at the end of 1958.] According to Maria Elena, Buddy was ill for the entire day following the champagne fiasco. Contrite, she swore that never again would she encourage him to drink.

As the New York winter set in, Buddy kept writing songs, the new tunes spewing out like an eternal fountain. On December 8, he recorded "That Makes It Tough," a blues number that dissects a broken heart with unflinching honesty. The performance is as impressive as the composition; Buddy's multi-note variations and subtle inventiveness reflect his continuing development as a singer.

"It's So Easy," which Brunswick released on December 9, continued to sit in the stores, shunned by record buyers in the United States and England. The widespread impression that "It's So Easy" was a huge hit is due to the 1977 Ronstadt album it sparked, *Simple Dreams*, which was an almost instant million seller. But Buddy's original version was completely overshadowed in December 1958 by the Teddy Bears' No. 1 smash "To Know Him Is to Love Him" and Ritchie Valens's No. 2 hit "Donna." Buddy's only pass at the *Billboard* chart in December was "Heartbeat," which held on for four weeks but stalled at No. 82. On England's *New Musical Express* chart "Heartbeat" bobbed into thirtieth place but vanished after a single week. His customarily discerning and loyal Australian fans ignored "Heartbeat" altogether but redeemed themselves by sending the B-side, "Well All Right," to No. 24.

Despite declining sales, he continued cutting the magnificent apartment tapes. As Christmas approached, on December 14, he recorded the eloquent "Crying, Waiting, Hoping." Buddy's voice gently probes the poignancy of every line, uncovering nuances of truth and emotion that lift the song to universal significance. "Learning the Game," relentlessly tragic in its view of romance, was the last of the apartment tapes, recorded on December 17. His voice is edged with bittersweet irony as he drives home the truth that romantic love is the cause of most human suffering. There is something deeply comforting, even healing, in the way Buddy defines heartache as the common lot of mankind. The promise of earlier songs like "Listen to Me," which hinted at the wisdom he was capable of, is fully realized in these December songs—twilight melodies, in a way—in which the interior life is touched and resonates darkly.

At last a job offer came through. Irving Feld wanted him for another tour, hardly an inviting prospect. After the Boston riots, rock 'n' roll package tours had all but disappeared. Dick Clark had dropped out of the business altogether. Among the few packagers left was GAC's Feld, who was organizing a January-through-February 1959 bus tour of the Midwest. Feld had teamed up with Buddy Howe and Tim Gale of General

Artists Corporation to co-sponsor rock stage shows to be emceed by local DJs across America. They signed more than a hundred artists to go on a series of tours over a ten-month period, leaving July and August free. They offered Buddy a deal to headline the first of these tours, which would be known as the "Winter Dance Party." After having spent most of the past eighteen months on the road, Buddy hated the idea of another tour, especially on a bus in the dead of winter, and rejected the offer. Then he reconsidered. He'd had no other job offers for a while. Decca was not clamoring for another session, since his singles weren't selling, and his albums still hadn't caught on. He needed money to support himself and his wife, who was now pregnant. Reluctantly, he accepted Feld's offer and left for Texas a few days before Christmas to put together a new band. The bittersweet memories of his brief few months in Manhattan would remain frozen in time—as if an entire era of innocence and youth would be preserved during that frenetic autumn of 1958.

At no time was the duality of his situation more underscored than during that Christmas visit. On the one hand, his heart still resided in West Texas. He was happiest when he stood in radio station KLLL's quarters atop the Great Plains Building, gazing down at the vast tableland of pastures and fields that spread out from the city in all directions. He dreaded his imminent departure for the frigid north. On the other hand, his audience was in the north, his recording studio in New York. The Lord pulled him home, while the power of money and fame drew him north and east. In the end, at least in his lifetime, the Lord would not prevail.

By the end of 1958 Buddy Holly's life had become all but unlivable. His funds were frozen in New Mexico, largely as a result of having given Norman Petty power of attorney over his business affairs. Bankruptcy had forced him to accept a dangerous bus tour in one of the worst midwestern winters on record. While in Lubbock, he confided to both his mother and brother that he didn't want to go on the tour. Larry revealed in a 1992 interview that Buddy told him, "It's sure gettin' to be a grind. I'm gettin' tired of having to run constantly and be in the limelight. I can't lead my life like I want to. I'm gettin' fed up with it. I'm not fed up with music in general—I like producing and writing songs. But as far as touring and being in front of the public eye constantly, that really gets to be a drag."

He showed Larry the insane schedule for the "Winter Dance Party," which packed far too many dates into twenty-four days, with no time off for rest. Zigzagging all over the upper Midwest, the itinerary looked as if it had been planned by a blindfolded idiot throwing darts at a wall map. "Look at this!" Buddy exclaimed, according to Larry. "It's pathetic, the way they're pushing me. Every night in a different town." He called GAC and tried to break the contract, Ella Holley told Griggs in 1981. His mother said he "begged" GAC to release him, but they refused, treating him like an employee. "It was not really an appropriate tour for Buddy, who was already established," Maria Elena observes in 1993. "It was a tour for people starting out, like Ritchie Valens, who'd just had his first hit, and J.P. ["The Big Bopper" Richardson]. Of course, they needed a headliner and that was Buddy."

Painful as it was to replace the Crickets, he started trying to assemble a new band to back him on the tour. He told his family he was devastated over Jerry and Joe B.'s defection and how hard it was to start over from scratch. Mrs. Holley later lamented "he didn't have any group . . . any Crickets." Maria Elena disclosed to Goldrosen that he'd attempted to call the Crickets before leaving New York, hoping to line them up for the tour, but the boys had not been at home. They were in Clovis with Petty, though their new relationship was predictably to sour as well. Despite the rosy picture Petty had painted for Jerry and Joe B., the Crickets "had not got any engagements," according to Goldrosen and Beecher, since breaking up with Buddy three months before. Petty was trying to record them, using a singer named Earl Sinks, who'd opened for Buddy on the 1958 "Summer Dance Party," and Sonny Curtis, who'd rejoined the Crickets. On their recording of Buddy and Bob's song "Love's Made a Fool of You," Sinks tried to ape the Buddy Holly sound, but his impersonation of Buddy was almost comic. On Vi Petty's "Someone, Someone," Sinks stepped out of his role as a Holly clone and emerged as an exciting vocalist. "Someone, Someone" should have been a hit but went nowhere on release.

Buddy tried to sign up Larry Welborn for his new band, but Larry was content to remain in Lubbock, working at KLLL and performing occasionally with the Four Teens. Terry Noland was also contacted, but nothing came of it. For the time being, Buddy suspended his efforts and concentrated on enjoying Christmas with his family. He had borrowed enough money to act like a rich man whether he was one or not, drawing freely on the $2,500 advance from GAC to shower his family with expensive presents, which the financially strapped Holleys appreciated. For years to come, Larry Holley would look back on the 1958 holiday season as a glorious Christmas.

The temperature on December 25 reached a high of forty-nine, dropping to twenty-three toward evening. The *Avalanche-Journal* carried a picture of carolers on the front page with the headline CHRISTMAS AR-RIVES QUIETLY OVER AREA. Another story told of Miss Yvonne Skinner, twenty-one, Lubbock's "Maid of Cotton," who was preparing for her trip to Memphis to compete in the 1959 National Maid of Cotton contest. Though Buddy Holly's visit was by far the most newsworthy event to occur in Lubbock that Christmas, the paper made no mention of him. Throughout his career, his hometown paper, either through reportorial oversight or in deference to its Bible Belt readership, ignored him, despite hit records and a triumphant world tour.

The weather turned warmer on December 28—62 degrees—which was perfect for the fishing trip Buddy hosted for his father, brothers, and cousin Sam. He took them all to a sporting-goods store and had them completely outfitted at his expense. "We had some good times," Larry reminisced. "It just didn't last long enough." Back in Lubbock, Buddy called on old friends, sang his latest songs for them, and encouraged any beginners who sought him out.

Larry was with him one day when they visited someone who lived on the outskirts of town, near the Lubbock city limits. Buddy suddenly picked up his guitar and announced he was going to perform his next song, which he called his personal favorite. It was "Raining in My Heart," one of the numbers from the Pythian Temple string session. Larry agreed it was the best thing Buddy had ever done. Much later, when Larry heard the recording, with its luscious symphonic quality, he still liked it, he revealed in a 1992 interview, but he always preferred the simpler version he'd heard Buddy sing in Lubbock. Buddy's voice had never been more tender or appealing than in this Felice and Boudleaux Bryant ballad, which tells of a lover's brave, vain efforts to hide his broken heart. Above all, the recording evokes the sweetness of the singer: Buddy Holly's power to evoke our love is uncanny.

One afternoon Buddy and Larry sat in the family car talking about God. Buddy once again asked how he could simultaneously serve the Lord and be a rock star. He rehashed the discussions he and Little Richard had about God. Larry was not easy on Buddy, reminding him that God wouldn't "play second fiddle in anybody's life."

Ken Johnson, who had gone to school with Buddy, was now associate pastor of Tabernacle Baptist. According to Johnson, Buddy did not feel good about having drifted from regular church attendance. Though Buddy's religion had condemned his very livelihood, he was ineluctably drawn back to Tabernacle Baptist Church; the roots of fundamentalist dogma in his life were as deep as they were tenacious. Brother Ben D. Johnson was still thundering venomous denunciations of rock 'n' roll, according to Terry Noland, who later told Griggs that Ben Johnson would stand in the pulpit and inform the rockers in his congregation that they were "going to hell."

Nevertheless, Ben Johnson was willing to accept sizable donations from rock-star Buddy Holly, though they came through his associate, Ken Johnson, who looked up from his desk one day during the Christmas season and saw Buddy in the doorway. "He came in and brought us a very generous offering to give to the church and to help in the building fund," Johnson reveals in a 1993 interview. "He said, 'I've got to get out of this. I want to get into a business that is much more acceptable in being able to work for the Lord. As soon as I can make enough money to get into my own business, that's my plan.' That was the direction of his whole thinking. He knew the Lord as his Savior. People are not aware of that because only the secular aspect of his life has been popularized. But Buddy was very knowledgeable of his need of the Lord and the need of spiritual guidance in his life. He was conscientiously seeking the right direction for his life, though a lot of people did not know that inwardly Buddy was that dedicated."

On that same visit to Lubbock, Buddy's father found him to be in a carefree, happy-go-lucky frame of mind, like someone who really "had it made," said L.O. For a lark, Buddy did a no-fee remote broadcast for KLLL from the Morris Fruit and Vegetable Store. As usual, Lubbock wasn't clamoring for a Buddy Holly concert, and Buddy didn't encourage it. He told his father he'd never be able to stand it if he flopped in his hometown. Nonetheless, when Slim Corbin introduced the subject of a major Lubbock concert, Buddy authorized him to set it up for the following summer. It was planned as a big Buddy Holly homecoming concert.

Waylon Jennings and the other KLLL DJs atop the Great Plains Life Building always played Buddy's records as soon as they received advance acetates. Although KLLL was emphatically a C&W station, rock 'n' roll was still viewed as hillbilly music in 1958. The impressionable Waylon was sometimes nervous working "up a building higher than any I've been in my life," he told Larry Corbin in 1973. Buddy embraced old friends Hi Pockets Duncan and the Corbin brothers—Ray ("Slim"), Larry, and Sky—and was interviewed on the air during the holidays. One day Buddy told Waylon and Slim he was trying to complete a new tune called "You're the One." He wondered if they'd help him. They did, though Waylon remembers contributing only one line, and it was finished in fifteen minutes. Then, as Buddy recorded "You're the One" in the back room of the studio, Waylon and Slim stood by, clapping their hands to provide percussive effects in lieu of a drummer. Buddy's performance of "You're the One" is an air-cushioned skyrocket ride in the same league as "Maybe Baby." It's one of his love-me-hurt-me songs: In one breath he berates his girlfriend for abusing him and in the next asks for more, truly a prisoner of his own obsession.

After producing Waylon's first record, the unremarkable "Jole Blon," which would prove a disappointment upon release the following year, Buddy continued to encourage Waylon, producing his recording of "More and More" and even, according to Griggs, playing the guitar accompaniment as Waylon sang. Buddy also offered him a job in the band he was forming for the "Winter Dance Party" as electric-bass player, to replace Joe B. Waylon said he'd love to but didn't know how to play bass very well. Buddy assured him that he could live with Buddy and Maria Elena in New York and Buddy would teach him how to play the instrument before the tour in January.

This was the break Waylon had been waiting for. His wife Maxine was pregnant and predictably raised objections but, as Waylon's brother Tommy pointed out, "An artist . . . will give up everything for that shot." Understandably Maxine was "pretty tore up," Tommy said, but Waylon proceeded to ask Sky Corbin for a leave of absence from KLLL. Sky was reluctant—Waylon's popular afternoon show pulled a 60 percent share of the audience—but eventually Sky granted the leave. Maxine was "awful disgusted," Tommy later revealed. She disliked "the idea of him being gone all the time." Buddy and Maria Elena immediately invited Waylon to stay with them in their Greenwich Village apartment. As a couple Buddy and his wife were so compatible, their lives so intertwined, and their goals so identical that Maria Elena didn't have to think twice before agreeing to such arrangements.

Buddy saw other old friends in Lubbock. He and Jack Neal, his original singing partner, met for a meal at the Nightowl Restaurant, Neal later told Griggs. Excitedly, Buddy described the recording studio he was going to build immediately following the "Winter Dance Party." There were so many gifted musicians in Lubbock, Buddy said, that he was going to make the city his world-wide production headquarters. Buddy promised that Jack was at the top of the list of the local musicians with whom he was going to work.

Airplanes were another new passion of Buddy's. Maria Elena "got mad," she later told Goldrosen, when she discovered that Buddy was taking flying lessons. "I *always* go commercial," Maria Elena said in 1993. Nonetheless, Buddy completed one thirty-minute session at Champs Aviation at the Municipal Airport in Lubbock. According to Griggs, Buddy piloted a Cessna, wing number N9274B, paying $9 for the lesson. Larry was also becoming a pilot. Buddy took the lesson "behind my back," Maria Elena revealed. When she uncovered his deception she admonished him not to fly in small aircrafts because it frightened her. However much he wanted to become a pilot, her terror of single-engine planes "should be reason enough" for him to avoid them, she said, according to Goldrosen.

Years later, Waylon discussed "Buddy's flyin" with talk-show host Mike Douglas, disclosing that Buddy "had several hours to be a pilot . . . and he was gettin' me into that, too. . . . We'd fly . . . to Odessa and here and there and everywhere." Odessa, which is located 125 miles south of Lubbock, in the middle of the West Texas oil fields, was the scene of Buddy's

1959 New Year's Eve celebration. He brought in the new year pounding on drums in a honky-tonk where Tommy Allsup and his dance band were playing, according to Ray Rush, one of the Roses. Buddy told Allsup about his midwestern tour, opening in Milwaukee on January 23, and hired him to play lead guitar. Now all Buddy needed to complete his new band was a drummer. He told Allsup to "get ahold of that kid," Ronnie Smith's drummer, whom he'd met in Clovis. Fortuitously, Carl "Goose" Bunch was playing around Odessa with Smith and his band, the Poor Boys. Though Buddy "didn't even remember my name," Bunch later told Griggs, Buddy hired him immediately, a sign of the pressure he was under. The newly reconstructed Crickets were now ready to go.

Tommy Allsup later recalled in an interview with William J. Bush that during the New Year's dance in Odessa, Buddy told Allsup that he admired Moon Mullican, who was playing piano in Allsup's band. Mullican was one of the most respected and influential personalities in southwestern C&W music. Buddy said he was "dyin' to gig" with Mullican and would be willing to sit in on drums if Tommy's regular drummer would let him. Tommy's drummer readily relinquished his sticks to Buddy Holly for the next two hours.

Aubrey "Moon" Mullican, born on March 27, 1909, in Corrigan, in the heart of the East Texas piney woods, fascinated Buddy not only because of Mullican's well-known recording of "Jole Blon" but because of his legendary status as an innovator of Texas honky-tonk boogie-woogie piano playing, which reached its zenith in the 1940s with Mullican's recording "Cherokee Boogie." The style evolved out of blues licks that Mullican had first heard performed by Joe Jones, a black guitarist who labored on the Mullicans' sharecrop farm in Corrigan when Mullican was growing up. At sixteen, Mullican played barrelhouse piano in the brothels of Houston and the port towns along the Texas Gulf Coast, where, said Mullican, prostitutes sat next to him on the piano bench and fanned him as he worked. He played so hard that the beer bottles bounced on the tables. Along with Floyd Tillman and Ted Daffan, with whom he worked in the Blue Ridge Playboys, Mullican became a seminal figure in the flowering of western swing in the thirties and forties. In the fifties Mullican emerged as a husky-voiced C&W singer, scoring hit records such as "I'll Sail My Ship Alone" and "Sweeter Than the Flowers."

Jamming with Moon Mullican that night in 1958, Buddy Holly chose not to steal the spotlight and remained anonymous throughout the set. No one in the Odessa audience recognized him. Besides the pleasure it gave him to play with Mullican, the drum practice would soon come in handy; he'd be required to wear many hats during the forthcoming "Winter Dance Party," including that of drummer.

Before leaving Texas, Buddy made arrangements for Allsup, Bunch, and Waylon to come to New York for a week of rehearsal in January 1959 prior to the tour. Though Buddy had given the Crickets' name to Jerry and Joe B., his new band, for legal reasons, would also be known as the Crickets. In view of anticipated litigation, it was advisable for Buddy to retain the name as a possible way of claiming monies being held by Petty. As Jerry and Joe B. faded into the past, the new year marked the birth of Buddy's new band: Waylon Jennings, Tommy Allsup, and Carl Bunch.

The night before they all left on the "Winter Dance Party" tour in January, Maria Elena had a frightening dream, which is recounted in both *Remembering Buddy* and *Rolling Stone*'s history of rock 'n' roll, *Rock of Ages*. In the dream, Maria Elena watched in frozen horror as a huge fireball came hurtling at her. Though it roared by, just missing her, it plowed into the ground and dug a huge crater. She woke up screaming. When she described the nightmare to Buddy, he looked at her strangely. He'd just had a similar dream, he said, in which he was flying in a small plane with Larry and Maria Elena. Larry, who was at the controls, ordered Buddy to get rid of Maria Elena, but Buddy refused, saying, "Anywhere I go, Maria comes with me." Larry landed the plane on top of a skyscraper and kicked Maria Elena out. "Don't worry," Buddy cried as they took off. "I'll come back and get you."

At breakfast the next morning with Tommy, Waylon, and Carl Bunch, Maria Elena and Buddy described the terrible dreams, Tommy later told Goldrosen.

Waylon was staying in the apartment with Buddy and Maria Elena, earnestly trying to learn the unfamiliar electric bass in the short time remaining before the tour. Waylon later told Bush that Buddy was accustomed to the smooth professionalism of Joe B. "and all of a sudden he's stuck with me." In fact, Buddy treasured his relationship with Waylon, forged over the years in talent contests and at radio stations and recording studios. "He intended to make me more or less his protégé," Waylon later told Larry Corbin. "He taught me a lot." Accustomed to playing an acoustic six-string guitar, Waylon quaked at the prospect of mastering the formidable electric bass, but Buddy bought him one and told him to learn to play it in fourteen days. Buddy also gave Waylon his albums *The Chirping Crickets* and *Buddy Holly*, and told him to study them because he'd be expected to perform all the songs on the tour. Waylon obediently committed to memory "everything he had ever recorded."

In practice sessions, Buddy struck Waylon as a perfectionist. Eventually Waylon had to appeal to Tommy Allsup for help, and Allsup agreed to tutor him. As shaky about singing rock 'n' roll as he was about playing the bass, Waylon said that if he "could sing rock 'n' roll better, I would." He remained with Buddy and Maria Elena in the apartment "a week or so before going on the tour," Maria Elena recalls in 1993. "They were rehearsing, and Buddy kept trying to show Waylon how to play the bass guitar." The two most essential assets of an outstanding guitarist, Waylon learned, are rhythm and stamina, Waylon recalled in 1982. Even when playing ballads, Buddy never lapsed into a "lazy sound," Waylon noticed.

Sometimes Waylon switched from bass and borrowed Buddy's Fender Stratocaster. When they practiced Little Richard's "Slippin' and Slidin'," Waylon used Buddy's big acoustic Gibson J-200. The most valuable thing Waylon learned from Buddy was syncopation; Buddy's rhythm "really turned me on," Waylon later told Bush, adding that he also adopted Jerry's paradiddle sound from "Peggy Sue." In January 1959, they taped "Slippin' and Slidin' " on Buddy's Ampex recorder in the apartment. The opening guitar lick, probably by Waylon, is identical to the stunning lick that kicks off the Everly Brothers' rip-snorting "Bird Dog." Years later *Rolling Stone* rated Buddy's vocal on "Slippin' and Slidin' " among his most inspired creations. On the apartment tapes, Buddy planned everything in meticulous detail, Waylon explained in his interview with Bush. Buddy recorded as if he were in a studio, using everything he had ever learned and working with total seriousness and concentration. Waylon "was learning as I went along. . . . I had to be driving him nuts." Buddy was always "harder on himself than anybody else," Waylon said.

The "Winter Dance Party," which would become the most famous tour—perhaps the most notorious—in American music history, was scheduled to begin on January 23, 1959. Buddy established the final set list and rehearsed the band in a rented hall in New York. Waylon sang harmony on "That'll Be the Day" and other songs written by Buddy. Other composers were included in the set list. Waylon later told Bush that he and Buddy together worked on "Gotta Travel On," a song based on a nineteenth-century British tune and adapted by the Weavers but never recorded by Buddy Holly. In a recording by Billy Grammer, it entered the charts in December 1958 and by early 1959 it was the nation's No. 4 hit record.

One evening after a full day of rehearsing and taping in New York, Buddy, Maria Elena, and Waylon discussed what to have for dinner. Maria Elena recalled in 1993 that she said, "I'm going to cook some rice and beans and make some steaks." Buddy looked at her in surprise. Maria Elena made no claims for her cooking and often admitted she didn't know how to cook very well. Dinner that evening was inedible. "The beans came out horrible," Maria Elena recalls. "They were awful; they were burned." Buddy avoided them. Waylon, who'd never tasted Maria Elena's cooking and didn't know any better, took a heaping spoonful of red beans, swallowed them, and started choking. "Oh, my—" he sputtered, Maria Elena remembers, but Buddy kicked him under the table to shut him up.

"Aren't they good!" Buddy exclaimed, lying. "You did a good job, Maria Elena!"

Waylon stood up and excused himself. "Well, I'm full," he rasped, hurrying from the room. When Maria Elena recounts the episode thirty-four years later, she observes, "Buddy didn't want to hurt my feelings. He knew I was trying. I just didn't know how to cook. He wouldn't hurt my feelings for anything."

Before leaving on the tour, Buddy assured Waylon that afterward he'd devote himself intensively to Waylon's career. He intended to establish a studio band at his new Taupe Recording Studios, and the band's primary purpose would be to back up Waylon, whom Buddy envisaged as Taupe's first star. The band would also back up Buddy and other Taupe recording artists such as Terry Noland and Lou Giordano. Buddy invited Noland to come to New York and record on the Taupe label directly following the "Winter Dance Party," Noland later told Bill Griggs. The Taupe studio band was to include steel guitars and fiddles, a sign that Buddy was returning to his C&W roots, prefiguring the fusion of rock 'n' roll and C&W that would occur in the sixties with the Byrds' *Sweetheart of the Rodeo* and again in the seventies with the Eagles' *One of These Nights*. Other influences were also beginning to gel: as a result of his exposure to jazz in Greenwich Village in 1958–59, he also intended to explore the uses of jazz in his own recordings once he opened his studio.

These plans had to wait because Petty was holding on to something like $50,000 to $80,000 of Buddy's money. "In mid-January 1959 Buddy sent a registered letter to Norman Petty asking Norman to send him his publishing money," Bill Griggs states in a 1995 interview. Petty did not send the money. "I'm going to Clovis and break everything in sight, including Norman's back," Buddy said. He was forced to spend what remained of the $2,500 advance from GAC to establish a payroll for the new Crickets. He paid his band well. The most experienced musician, Tommy Allsup, received $250 a week, a lot of money in 1959, Waylon and Carl Bunch somewhat less (Waylon's biographer Serge Denisoff says Waylon received $200 a week). Allsup appreciated Buddy's largess; his last job had paid $80 a week.

In Buddy's absence, his pregnant wife would remain completely dependent on her aunt. "Buddy was very concerned with the fact that my aunt was supporting us," Maria Elena comments in 1993. "We were married, and he felt terrible about it."

Before leaving New York in late January 1959, Buddy went to the Blair House Restaurant for lunch with Dick Jacobs, who was now head of Artists and Repertoire at Coral Records. At one point during the meal, Buddy handed over some demos and told Jacobs they contained the material he intended to record at a future session. For some reason, none of his great apartment tapes was included. He and Jacobs then discussed instrumentation and arrangements for his next session. Jacobs remembered it as a "very nice" meeting, he told Wayne Jones in 1985, and pinpointed the time as several days before Buddy's departure on the tour.

Buddy met Maria Elena for lunch at the St. Moritz on Central Park South, according to Owen Bradley, who was lunching at a nearby table with Buddy's old bête noire from Decca, Paul Cohen. Bradley was the Nashville producer of thirteen early Holly recordings, including the botched first version of "That'll Be the Day." In an interview years later, Bradley remembered that they "went over and talked for five or ten minutes. . . . We had a very nice conversation." Since they all worked for the same label, Buddy probably figured he needed to get along with them, but was no doubt relieved when they returned to their table so he and Maria Elena could enjoy their farewell lunch. Despite her pregnancy, Maria Elena told Buddy she wanted to go on the tour, she recalls in 1993. Three weeks of one-night stands would be too hard on her, Buddy pointed out. They could have taken the Cadillac, as they'd done the previous autumn, but the Midwest was undergoing a horrendous winter that made driving dangerous if not impossible.

In the last moments before Buddy's departure, Maria Elena had a premonition that he would fly in a small plane during the tour. "I had found out that I was pregnant and I was not feeling very well," she says in 1993. "It was just starting. That's why I didn't go even though I was planning to. I went to the door with him." One last time, she asked if she could come along. "No, this is just a very short tour," Buddy said, "and you're not feeling well."

"Up to that minute," recalls Maria Elena, "I was out there trying to go because I knew that if I were there Buddy would not have anything to do with planes—at all. No way. We always traveled commercial. I was deathly afraid of small planes."

They lingered in the doorway, Buddy holding her close. She had a strong sense that he didn't want to go. As a husband and prospective father, he wanted to be with her during her pregnancy. This was also his first tour without Jerry and Joe B. "He still missed the guys," she says. "That was obvious." Waylon also noticed Buddy's distress. "The only reason Buddy went on that tour was because he was broke—flat broke," Waylon stated years later. "He didn't want to go, but he had to make some money. I ain't saying the person's name that was the reason he was broke. But he knows who he is." There can be little question that Waylon was referring to Petty.

Finally Buddy kissed Maria Elena good-bye. In 1993 she recalls his final words to her: "Buddy said, 'I want you to take care of yourself and my baby.' "

Chapter Thirteen

"There's Nobody Else to Do It"

I n late January 1959 all the members of the ill-fated "Winter Dance Party"—Buddy, Ritchie Valens, the Big Bopper, Dion and the Belmonts, Frankie Sardo, Waylon Jennings, Tommy Allsup, Carl Bunch, and road manager Rod Lucier— met in Chicago and checked into their hotel. It was the beginning of rock's most famous tragedy, and predictably the weather was already bad. Much of the city was snowbound, but they made it to their rehearsal on schedule. As Tommy revealed at the 1979 convention of the Buddy Holly Memorial Society, Buddy seemed upset. Tommy assumed it was because the tour marked the first time that Buddy and his bride had been separated. It was obvious that Buddy missed the comfortable home he'd established with Maria Elena.

Buddy was also apprehensive about meeting Ritchie Valens, who was then only seventeen and might prove as troublesome as sixteen-year-old Paul Anka had on a previous tour. Valens wasn't the only potential problem; as soon as Buddy heard them play, all the other musicians struck him as amateurish. Buddy was the only singer who'd brought his own band. At rehearsal, accompanying themselves on the guitar, the others sounded impossibly tinny. Taking charge, Buddy announced that his band would shoulder the responsibility of backing up all the acts. Carl Bunch later told Griggs that they accompanied "everybody"—the Bopper, Valens, Dion and the Belmonts, and Frankie Sardo.

Ritchie turned out to be nothing like Buddy had imagined. Quiet, shy, and unpretentious, Ritchie was reserved but responded warmly to friendly overtures. There'd been no time in Hawaii for Buddy to get to know him. Valens had grown up among gangs in Los Angeles and was discovered while singing with a group called the Silhouettes. He was so good-looking he was being called the "new Elvis." Maria Elena relates in 1993 that Buddy telephoned her and said, "Ritchie Valens and I really hit it off well." One reason for the affinity Buddy and Ritchie felt was the Hispanic background that Ritchie and Maria Elena had in common. Another was that the two young men were both successful recording artists who'd seen little of the money they'd earned. Despite Ritchie's current record, with a hit on each side—"Donna" and "La Bamba"—he hadn't yet received his royalties.

While Buddy's rise had been slow and torturous, Ritchie's was meteoric. Their meeting proved opportune for both. Ritchie, the new rock star, looked on Buddy as an experienced headliner who could give him much-needed guidance, while Buddy, who was always on the lookout for new talent to produce, sized Ritchie up as a brilliant newcomer who could put Taupe Records over the top with a string of Chicano-rock hits. Recalls Maria Elena in 1993: "Buddy was talking to Ritchie. Ritchie asked Buddy if he would record him and produce him. He had a few ideas to do some of the Spanish songs." In just six months, Buddy had shaped up as a future mogul of the recording industry, attracting talents such as Waylon Jennings and Ritchie Valens, who would both be worth millions.

As the tour members became acquainted with each other in Chicago, Waylon was drawn to the Big Bopper, whose real name was Jiles Perry Richardson, though everyone called him "Jape" or "the Bopper." Waylon would later tell TV interviewer Dick Cavett that he found the Bopper to be "a straight shooter." They liked to go out after rehearsals and unwind with a few beers or shots of vodka. The Bopper was a big, crew-cut bruiser with a slaphappy smile and 190 pounds on a five-foot-nine-and-a-half frame. On stage he favored zoot suits and floppy hats. He spoke lovingly of his wife, a doe-eyed Cajun girl, Adrianne Joy Fryon, whom he sometimes called "Teetsie" or "T.C.," and their young daughter. Like Maria Elena, Adrianne was pregnant when her husband said good-bye to her in January. Their second child would be a son, Jay P., due in late 1959. The Bopper acquired his famous nickname while working as a DJ on radio station KTRM in Beaumont, Texas. He announced on the air one day, "Bee-bop's big and I'm big, so why don't I become the Big Bopper?" The name stuck.

As a DJ the Bopper's antics rivaled the most bizarre excesses of that 1950s breed of bug-eyed, daredevil radio announcers. On his KTRM "Disc-A-Thon" in May 1957 he'd stayed awake for six days, spinning 1,821 records, dropping thirty-five pounds from his then-240-pound body, and collecting $746.50 in overtime. Proud of having established the world's record for continuous broadcasting, he was still, on the "Winter Dance Party" a year and a half later, wearing the watch he'd been given, which was inscribed: KTRM CHAMPION DISC-A-THON, 122 HOURS, 8 MINUTES, J. P. RICHARDSON, 5-4-57.

He was discovered as a recording artist by Houston's Harold "Pappy" Dailey, who ran Mercury-Starday Records. "Chantilly Lace" was recorded on such a shoestring budget that jingle bells were used to represent a ringing telephone. A routine, somewhat sexist 1950s perception of women, the song is a racy ode to girls, extolling their wiggly walk, giggly chatter, pony tails and, especially, their transparent Chantilly lace lingerie. Made of silk with an outline of coarse thread, Chantilly lace originated in the Middle Ages in a village twenty-five miles from Paris, near the Forest of Chantilly. When the Bopper sang about it, he made the material sound as delicately appealing as his wife Teetsie, who was described by their friend Gordon Baxter as "little bitty cute . . . soft and pretty and stood beside him all the time and didn't say anything."

According to columnist Bob Rogers, both Buddy and the Bopper were scheduled to tour Australia later in 1959. "I once asked [the Bopper] why he left his safe, sane job as a deejay in Texas to go on tour," Alan Freed would recall in May 1959, "and he answered, 'Cause it's a ball. 'Cause I'm getting to see the country. I'm a traveling salesman. I'm selling 'Chantilly Lace.'" The record had been the third most-played song of 1958, going to No. 6 on the *Billboard* chart, but its sequel, "Big Bopper's Wedding," had barely cracked the Top 40. On the tour the Bopper was pluckily trying to salvage his fading stardom. His friend Gordon Baxter said that everyone loved the Bopper "because there wasn't a mean bone in his head."

When Buddy wasn't with Ritchie during the tour, he could usually be found with Waylon or Dion DiMucci, the Bronx-born, street-smart lead singer of the Belmonts. Riding high on a string of Top 40 hits including "I Wonder Why" and "A Teenager in Love," Dion idolized Buddy. "I dug Holly's lean, sparse Texas sound," Dion stated in his 1988 autobiography *The Wanderer*, adding that he admired Buddy's artistic freedom from record-company control. "But most of all I admired how together he was," said Dion. They "hit it off right away" despite being from widely divergent backgrounds. Dion described in his memoirs how he'd grown up shooting heroin on Crotona Avenue and 187th Street. He was addicted to heroin, marijuana, pills, and alcohol, but heroin was the "silent partner in everything I did," he wrote, "a way to regulate and control a hectic scene." A weightlifter since his youth, Dion had developed a bodybuilder's physique and regarded himself as the "hippest, handsomest, most together cat on the block, the best dancer, the sharpest dresser." Heroin, his "secret lover," gave him "instant courage." Like Buddy, Dion had fooled around with gangs. He joined the Fordham Daggers and survived enough rumbles, zip gun fights, car crashes, and stab wounds to graduate to a tougher gang known as the Baldies.

Nothing in Dion's background, however funky, had prepared him for the "Winter Dance Party," which set out for the Million Dollar Ballroom in Milwaukee, Wisconsin, on January 23, 1959, in a vehicle none of them would have spat on at home. Everyone was crammed into what appeared to Dion to be a "converted school bus." When they felt like going to bed, "we slept where we were sitting," Dion wrote in *The Wanderer*. To Tommy

Allsup, the tour was a disaster from the start. "It snowed on us from the time we left Chicago," Allsup said in 1979. "I don't know why we got such lousy buses, such lousy *old* buses." Transportation for the tour had been arranged in Chicago, where the job had gone to the lowest bidder. Unsurprisingly, the lowest bidder had the worst buses. "Usually the heater wouldn't work," Tommy added.

Shivering and miserable, the performers realized too late that the tour was a "third-class operation," Dion recalled. The booker, General Artists Corporation, was responsible for the precarious situation the hapless artists found themselves in. Discredited by riots and controversy, rock 'n' roll packages were considered passé, and the promoters were signing artists and then abandoning them to abominable conditions in far-flung territories like the upper Midwest.

The bus's worn-out engine frequently stalled, usually when they were thirty miles from the closest service station. To ease the tension, Buddy and Dion played "dueling guitars," wagering to see who could make his Fender Stratocaster ring the longest. Dion's Fender was solid white, Buddy's had a sunburst. Ritchie joined the fun, lolling beside them with his feet in the aisle. He serenaded them in Spanish, strumming his acoustic and singing songs like "Mama Long," which he'd made the rage of Pacoima Junior High. Biographer Beverly Mendheim later revealed in *Ritchie Valens: The First Latino Rocker* that "Mama Long" was a group song and each person had to make up a verse about Mama Long, an outrageously foxy girl. As the verses became progressively risqué, Ritchie punctuated them with the *grito*, the cry he made famous in "La Bamba." Dion later recalled that Ritchie "played the meanest rhythm guitar" of them all. When Ritchie's Latin sound "filtered through pure rock 'n' roll . . . it knocked me out," Dion added.

Buffeted by freezing winds, they continued north from Chicago to Milwaukee, skidding and sliding along Lake Michigan for a hundred miles. When they began to fall asleep, some of them climbed into the luggage racks, where they stretched out and began to snore. Others sat and watched their breath turn to bluish vapor. The bus's heater was woefully inadequate. By the end of the journey, noses were running and sneezes were exploding up and down the aisle. Piling out, they rubbed their hands and stamped their feet—all except for Carl Bunch, who could hardly walk. His feet were numb, a dangerous sign of frostbite. The musicians peered into the ghostly air and braced themselves against the snow blowing in from awesome Lake Michigan, which is 300 miles long, 118 miles wide, and 925 feet deep; winter ice moves in around November and usually stays until spring.

They checked into their Milwaukee hotel briefly, then they took a cab to the Million Dollar Ballroom. It was so cold in the cab that

Tommy had difficulty breathing. Would anyone come out to a rock concert in such weather? they wondered, according to Waylon's biographer Serge Denisoff. When they arrived at the dance hall, a long line of teenagers trailed around the corner, waiting for the January 23 show in twenty-five-below-zero weather. Even in the 1950s, there were enough Midwestern kids who worshiped rock 'n' roll to fill the "Winter Dance Party" venues to capacity. As the cold seared their lungs, performers and fans regarded each other in the gray winter light, beginning to feel the transcendent sense of community that typifies the rock experience. After performing in the same area many years later, Bruce Springsteen said in Dave Marsh's *Glory Days*, "There's a very different feeling that happens when you get out there in the Midwest, really out there where there's nothing for miles and miles around. The thing we got the most from was touring, getting people to come out, to leave their houses and come down to the show."

Just before curtain, Buddy called Maria Elena. "I'm going onstage now," he told her, she recalled in 1993. "I'm leaving the phone off the hook. I want you to hear something." Then, Maria Elena remembers, "he sang 'True Love Ways,' which was our song. It became a ritual. He called me every night from wherever he was."

The Million Dollar Ballroom audience accorded the Crickets' debut "a *great* reception," Tommy later told Bush, adding that the musicians found it necessary to turn their amplifiers up to top volume in order to compete with the cheering. Waylon struggled with the unfamiliar bass and tried to keep up with master guitarists Holly and Allsup. On four occasions during the performance Buddy turned to Waylon and told him something, but the sound was so loud Waylon couldn't hear him. Finally Buddy walked over to Waylon and shouted in his ear, "*Turn that goddamn bass down!*" Waylon later confided to Bush. On the *Mike Douglas Show* in 1975 Waylon admitted that he was "probably the world's worst rock 'n' roll bass player. I was playin' country bass behind a rock 'n' roll singer."

The Crickets looked sharp in tasteful new outfits: gray slacks with black jackets and silver ascots. When those became soiled, they would switch to their other uniform: brown slacks, brown tweed jackets, and golden ascots. The brown jackets sometimes looked maroon because of the poor stage lighting. Tommy recalled in 1979 that the only lighting provided for the shows was a bulb or two "hanging over the bandstand." The sound, though equally primitive, was viscerally exciting. If the venue had a PA system, they hooked their Fender guitars into it. Each musician used his Fender amplifier "and that was it," Tommy said. "Things have changed a lot. It takes all day just to set up the equipment today, but back then it was fun and it sounded good. I think it sounded better then than it does now."

Tommy also revealed that, after the show, he, Waylon, and the Bopper decided to go out and sample Milwaukee's famous beers, hitting a few of the city's 1,650 bars. Tommy had noticed Buddy's drinking in the past and was surprised that he wouldn't join them on their pub crawl; Buddy was homesick, yearning to return to his bride. From Milwaukee they backtracked, driving fifty miles south to Kenosha, Wisconsin. The tires on the old bus squished sideways in gale-force winds from Lake Michigan. It was so cold inside the bus that Carl Bunch's feet seemed to be freezing. The symptoms he described—tingling and numbness—sounded more and more like frostbite. He pulled on several pairs of socks and hoped for the best.

Buddy and Dion huddled together to keep warm. "I got to know Holly pretty well," Dion recalled in *The Wanderer*. "Maybe I was always after someone to look up to, but I remember him as being a lot older than me, even though I was nineteen and he was only twenty-two." Buddy was someone Dion could respect and learn from. He reminded Dion of Bobby Darin, who'd long been Dion's role model.

All the musicians on the bus generously shared their musical expertise with each other. They sang and picked continually, mostly as a way to keep their minds off the cold. Everyone sang a Hank Williams song, even city-bred Dion, who'd been singing "Hey, Good Lookin'" for years to kids on Bronx stoops. Like Buddy, he'd studied Hank Williams's "bent notes" and learned to emulate the "plaintive catch in his throat," he wrote in *The Wanderer*.

On January 24 they played the Eagles Club in Kenosha, a small predominantly Italian community in Wisconsin of some fifty thousand people, many of whom were employed at the local American Motors automobile plant, manufacturer of the popular Rambler. The stars posed for photographer Tony Szikil: Buddy in a shawl-collar sweater is draping his arm around Frankie Sardo, a sensuous Frankie Avalon look-alike whose record "Fake Out" was selling briskly along the tour route. Beside them in the photo the Bopper clowns in a simulated leopard-skin jacket, which was nicknamed "Melvin."

After they finished the show at midnight, Buddy collected their pay. According to Waylon, Buddy cleared about $500 a night, after expenses. Tommy gave him a gun when he realized how much cash Buddy was carrying, Tommy later told Griggs. The .22-caliber "Vest Pocket" revolver was German-made, bearing the serial number 6K5313. The existence of Buddy's gun was also reported in April 1959 in the *Mason City* (Iowa) *Globe-Gazette* and has been verified by reporter Larry Lehmer of the *Des Moines Register*. Buddy kept the gun, fully loaded, in the bottom of his toilet kit.

It was now the early morning hours of Sunday, January 25, and they were expected in Mankato, Minnesota, 350 miles northwest of Kenosha, on the same day. The real deprivations experienced by the musicians have over time helped create the legendary status of the tour. During the long ride over icy roads in the days before the advent of eight-lane interstates, Ritchie sat with Buddy and rapped about the notorious "girl" songs they'd both been having so much success with. Buddy had virtually invented the genre with "Peggy Sue," while Ritchie was now scoring the hit of the year with "Donna." Peggy Sue had already entered the vernacular; Ritchie had mentioned her in "Ooh My Head," a song he performed in Alan Freed's movie Go, Johnny, Go!

When they arrived in Mankato, a rural community sixty miles southwest of Minneapolis, Buddy telephoned Maria Elena from the Kato Ballroom. He was still excited about producing Ritchie, who was standing next to him, waiting to talk to Maria Elena. Maria Elena stated in a 1993 interview that Buddy told her, "I want to do some Spanish songs myself, with English lyrics." Ritchie then took the receiver and introduced himself. Speaking in Spanish, he said that Buddy was going to produce his records, adding, "Maria Elena, I'd like to come to New York with Buddy after the tour and stay with you in your apartment," Maria Elena recalled in 1993.

En route to Eau Claire, Wisconsin, all they had to eat was what musicians call "jungle food": pretzels, sardines, cheese, and potato chips— mostly snacks that could be extracted by coin or brute force from bus-stop candy machines. Ritchie sat down next to Buddy on the bus and said he was tape-recording a message to his mother, Concepcion "Connie" Valenzuela, who'd played a significant role in his career. In January 1958, she'd used the $65 mortgage payment that was due on her squat clapboard house at 13327 Gain Street to rent the $57-a-night Legion Hall in Pacoima for Ritchie's debut. He was such a hit that Concepcion made a profit of $125, taking in tickets while her neighbor, Angela Hernandez, checked coats and ran the concession stand.

Ritchie had not been an easy child to raise. After his father Joseph Steven Valenzuela died in 1951 from diabetes, when Ritchie was ten, the boy ran wild. Concepcion couldn't provide for her children on Joseph's $140-a-month pension; she remarried, then divorced and went to work as a domestic. The north end of the San Fernando Valley was a tough neighborhood and Ritchie had his share of troubles with the law. Finally Concepcion confided to her cousin Henry Felix that she was ready to give up. "I tell him to be a good boy, but he doesn't listen to me," she complained. Felix told her to turn Ritchie over to him and he'd "see that he gets straightened around." After a few months of rigorous discipline, Ritchie returned home, a hell-raiser no more.

On the tour bus, Ritchie went from seat to seat, asking all the musicians to tape record a greeting to Connie. Fred Milano, one of the Belmonts, later told interviewer Wayne Jones that they "all talked on the tapes, including Buddy," saying "hello to Ritchie's mother." Justifiably proud of the fact that he'd bought his mother a new home on Remmington Street in Pacoima, Ritchie intended to treat Connie to a Hawaiian vacation. He was a devout Catholic and had taken the Bopper to midnight mass with him a couple of months ago when they'd both played Alan Freed's Christmas show at Loew's State in New York. Ritchie had wanted to say a special prayer for Connie. According to Freed, the Bopper "wasn't very religious," but, like Ritchie, he was homesick, and going to church helped him get through the holidays away from Teetsie. "I never saw anyone so pleased as the Bopper was," Freed later told reporter Jim Hoffman.

It was 25 below zero outside the Fournier's dance hall when they pulled into Eau Claire on January 26, 1959. An eager crowd rushed inside and immediately filled the wooden seats and pine bleachers. Buddy roared through seven songs: "Gotta Travel On," "Peggy Sue," "That'll Be the Day," "Heartbeat," "Be Bop a Lula," "Whole Lot of Shakin' Goin' On," and "It Doesn't Matter Anymore." After the show, Buddy, Ritchie, and the Bopper ate dinner at Sammy's Pizza, Don Larson, a fan, recalled in a 1993 interview. Carl Bunch discovered that he'd lost his gray and black stage clothes, which meant the musicians would now have to wear their one remaining costume—the brown tweed—until their clothes were filthy.

They boarded the bus and set out for Montevideo, Minnesota, 250 miles away, to play the Fiesta Ballroom on January 27. Aboard the bus, Buddy motioned to Waylon. "Come here," Buddy said, Waylon later recalled in *Guitar Player* magazine. "We're going to do 'Salty Dog Blues' together." They rehearsed the song and decided to add it to the set list. A country tune by Charlie "Papa" Jackson, "Salty Dog Blues" is yet another indication that Buddy was pioneering a merger of C&W and rock. "We did country songs onstage," Waylon told Goldrosen. "We did 'Salty Dog Blues,' and that's as country as you can get." Moving through the audience after their performance one night, Waylon heard a teenager say, "Man, that 'Salty Dog Blues' is what's happening."

At the height of the Montevideo show, someone snapped a photo of Buddy, Waylon, and Tommy on stage. Crowding the mike, rocking out with fierce energy, they define the very essence of aggressive, vital rock 'n' roll, but backstage Buddy felt like collapsing. Reaching Maria Elena by phone in New York, he described the tour as "awful" and the buses as "dirty and cold," adding that the promoters had reneged on all their promises. Maria Elena divulged in 1993 that she and Buddy spoke "every day, maybe twice, depending on how much time he had, usually in the evening before he performed." In 1975 she told Goldrosen that Buddy instructed her, in the event Jerry or Joe B. called, to tell them that he

was returning to New York in two weeks and wanted to propose a reconciliation. He intended to maintain two separate bands in the future;
the original Crickets would tour with him, and the other band would be
session musicians at Taupe Recording Studios in Lubbock, playing for
Ritchie, Waylon, Lou Giordano, and other artists on Buddy's label. Later
in the week Buddy rang Niki Sullivan but was unable to reach him. Niki
says Buddy was planning to get the original Crickets back together.

Maria Elena remembers that "Jerry called me at home and asked me if
I knew where they were and I did tell him where they were at the time,"
she revealed in 1993. "I gave him the phone number of the place and
the venue that they were performing in. As I understand, Jerry tried to
but they were going onstage, so Jerry said he was going to try again."

Not all insiders agree that a truce between Buddy, Jerry, and Joe B. was
imminent. When asked in 1992 if the original Crickets were intent on a
reconciliation with Buddy, Larry Holley simply said, "I think that was
another fictitious thing." Petty also pooh-poohed the notion that Jerry
and Joe B. "wanted to go to New York and join Buddy again," pointing
out that "there were things that were in the works at the time that would
lead me to believe otherwise. They were going to stay with me and I was
going to produce them as the Crickets."

After playing the Prom Ballroom in St. Paul, Minnesota, on January
28, the "Winter Dance Party" dipped south into Iowa. Bound for Davenport, they ran into drizzly weather, a harbinger of the cold front that
was creeping down the plains from Canada. On Thursday, January 29,
the temperature kept dropping, and the trickle of heat from the old bus
heater failed to keep out the chill. Unpacking their bags, they swaddled
themselves in loose clothing and drew close to each other, passing bottles,
gulping straight shots of liquor to ward off the cold. Ritchie's favorite
drink was "Silver Satin wine," which sometimes plunged him into black-
outs, a former musical colleague of Ritchie's, Freddie Aguilera, later told
Beverly Mendheim, a Valens biographer. Ritchie also loved speed, which
he called "whites," Aguilera added.

Later on January 29 they pulled into Davenport, a small town situated
on a bluff over the Mississippi River, fifteen miles from Buffalo Bill's
birthplace. During their performances at the Capitol Theater, the temperature continued to plummet, winds howled, and the rain turned to
sleet. Roads in the area glazed over and cars began to skid and pile up.
Several accidents were reported around Davenport. All flights were canceled out of the Quad-City airport. Weather forecasters warned that the
sleet would turn to snow during the night. In northwest Iowa, where the
tour was due for a show in Fort Dodge the following day, a four-inch
snowfall was expected.

Despite suicidal driving conditions, they left Davenport in the early morning hours of January 30. Between them and their destination, Fort Dodge, lay two hundred miles of sparsely populated plains, scattered farmsteads, and small towns. Locals rarely ventured out under such conditions, knowing that weather was their master in the winter, and they its slaves. Several miles out of Davenport, the heater completely conked out and everyone started turning blue. Carl Bunch complained that the coordination in his feet was "shot." During performances, he no longer had any stamina. Drummers play both the bass drum and the hi-hat with their feet, so he worried about how he'd ever manage to complete the tour. None of them yet realized how close they were to frostbite—to gangrene and death. Dion and Buddy discovered a way to pool their body warmth. "Holly and I used to climb under a blanket together to keep warm," Dion recalled in his memoirs. Buddy asked him to sing "A Teenager in Love." "I could always get a laugh out of Buddy—soft and low like his drawl," Dion said.

Waylon and the Bopper huddled together, sipping vodka and collaborating on a song they were crafting specifically for their mutual idol, George Jones, called "Move Over Blues." "I don't know if it was any good," Waylon later recalled, but it was "real country." Though the Bopper would never have a No. 1 record, two of the songs he wrote, "White Lightning," recorded by George Jones, and "Running Bear," recorded by Johnny Preston, both went to the top of the C&W charts later in 1959.

The bus crept along at twenty-five miles an hour, sliding over the sheet ice covering the old roads. Forty miles out of Davenport, they reached the town of Tipton (population 2,800) and pulled into Mac's Shell Station around noon for fuel and repairs. Punchy and stir-crazy, they made a dash for Al's Meet and Eat Café. It was the lunch hour and Al Hendricks's small hamburger shack was packed with workers on their break. Waitress Esther Wenck later told reporter Larry Lehmer that Ritchie went over to the jukebox and asked her if she'd like to hear him sing his "famous" recording.

She assumed he was joking but went along with the ruse and told him to go ahead and play it if he wanted to, though rock 'n' roll "wasn't my kind of music," she added. Ritchie played "Donna" and sang along with it, giving the small-town folk a free concert. Esther still assumed he was "goofin'," she recalled. Ritchie was in a euphoric mood during the tour, according to his California friend Gail Smith, who later told Mendheim that Ritchie said, "When I get back, I'm gonna get my T-Bird." He'd already decided he wanted a blue one.

As they ate that day in Tipton, several members of the tour party began to talk about deserting the bus and chartering a plane. Describing the scene to interviewer Wayne Jones years later, Fred Milano said, "If you're going to live in a bus for twenty-eight days it should at least be comfort-

able. Well, it wasn't. So a couple of the guys said, 'Let's take a plane.'"
The idea caught on among the musicians, though GAC disapproved of
charter flights as too dangerous, according to Tim Gale, who originated
the dance-party tours with Irving Feld at GAC.

The Bopper had recently flown in a small plane piloted by his friend
Gordon Baxter in Texas. "I took J.P. up . . . and he asked me what causes
airplanes to crash in bad weather," Baxter later told interviewer Jim Thomas. Baxter gave the Bopper a frightening demonstration, telling him to
close his eyes, Baxter sent the plane into a "graveyard spiral." Though
they were plunging earthward, the Bopper thought they were climbing.
Baxter's point was that a pilot can become so disoriented in heavy
weather that he can easily crash the plane. Despite the risks of flying, the
Bopper was willing to do anything to escape the agony of the GAC bus.
He wanted to get back to Texas, buy a radio station with the money he'd
made on the tour, and continue writing songs for C&W artists, according
to reporter Carol Gales.

Buddy considered chartering a four-seater for himself and his band, but
"Tommy Allsup wasn't making enough money to pay his share," Fred
Milano later told Jones. "And Ritchie Valens was," Milano added. But
Ritchie was afraid of flying, his friend Gail Smith later revealed. He was
also strangely drawn to it, even in hazardous weather. He'd never been
in a small plane before and was eager to try it, Tommy Allsup later stated.
Sadly, there were no responsible adults around for Ritchie to go to for
advice. "Our managers were never around," Bo·Diddley, a veteran of
many grueling tours, once said. "No one cared about the performers. You
should've seen the old bus we had to travel in. It was sheer chaos. And
that doesn't happen if a manager is thoroughly involved, totally committed to his clients. The road trips were a nightmare of inefficiency and
confusion." Buddy was now without management, but even when Petty
had represented him, Buddy had been subjected to exhausting conditions
on previous GAC tours.

As they finished their meal in Al's Meet and Eat Café, the bus driver
came in and told them he was ready to go. No more was said about
chartering a plane—at least not for the present. On the way to Fort
Dodge, the bus was so cold that once again they were in danger of frostbite. Carl Bunch's feet were no better; he could be facing amputation and
a loathsome death from gangrene. An intensely religious youth to whom
God and the devil were palpable entities, Carl was convinced that "Satan" was hounding the "Winter Dance Party." In a 1981 interview with
Griggs, he'd refer to Buddy as the musical point man of a "massive rebirth"
of Christ consciousness throughout the world. Satan, fearing Buddy's
power over millions of fans, was determined to stop the tour, Carl was
convinced; the devil was coming "to kill, to steal, and destroy," he said.

The perilous 210-mile trek across the Iowa plains, from Davenport to Fort Dodge, was taken at a time of year known as "winterkill." Snow falls on this oceanic expanse in November and crusts over with ice, often remaining until spring thaw. Winterkill destroys the bacteria in the soil so that Iowa's rich crops of corn, wheat, and soybeans can flourish. Though good for the economy, winterkill makes the area difficult for humans.

Nebraskan Theodore C. Sorenson once called the Midwest "a place to come from or a place to die." His comments were particularly apt for the "Winter Dance Party" tour. Nobel Prize–winner Sinclair Lewis, who was born in Sauk Centre, Minnesota, wrote novels about the Midwest's isolation, stupefying provincialism, and smugness. Minnesota-born author F. Scott Fitzgerald dreaded the "icy breath of death rolling down low across the land."

The "Winter Dance Party," despite the deprivations that winter brought on, made it to Fort Dodge and played the cavernous Laramar Ballroom to an avalanche of applause. They were fatigued, unwashed, malnourished, and, except for Buddy, disheveled in their dirty, smelly suits. This was the first night Buddy sported the alternate gear he'd brought along. He had never looked better; he'd at last discovered a style that suited him. He introduced Edwardian fashions to rock 'n' roll during this tour, years before they became popular in the sixties. He wore an ascot and a greatcoat with a fur collar, displaying a style that was radical, even unthinkable in an era of Brooks Brothers sack suits and button-down collars. The "peacock look" men would embrace in the following decade can be traced to the clothes Buddy wore in 1958–59, although he avoided the flash that would characterize sixties fashions. Tasteful and vaguely aristocratic, his new image was romantic and subtly effete, presaging the androgyny of Mick Jagger. Through tireless and shrewd experimentation with cosmetic surgery, dental reconstruction, permanent waves, and hair dyes, Buddy had repeatedly reinvented himself until finally achieving a sort of beauty. Duane Eddy, whose twangy guitar made him rock's No. 1 instrumentalist, saw Buddy at this time and described him, in Griggs's *Reminiscing* magazine, as an impressive sight—tall, powerful, and strikingly handsome.

The tour party blew off some steam after the Fort Dodge show. In his black Levi's suit with silver studs, Ritchie was the favorite of the groupies. Dion took on all comers. "Dion had his groupies, only they had a less flattering name for the girls back then—TFFs, Top Forty Fuckers," Sue Butterfield, Dion's future wife, told ex-groupie and author Pamela Des Barres. As the "Winter Dance Party" tour would prove in 1959, the real Top Forty Fucker was GAC. Leaving Iowa on January 30, the group headed north, driving 350 miles to Duluth, Minnesota, the remotest inland port in America. Their next few gigs would take them through winter badlands, where even the place names—Thunder Bay, Copper Harbor, Beaver Bay, Iron County, Porcupine Mountain, Caribou Island, Brute River—seemed to suggest the severity of nature. The bus broke down just as they pulled into Duluth. While it was being repaired, they took a look at the city that novelist Gore Vidal once described as a place "where cars skid and pelvises and femurs snap on the ice-slick pavements." In Duluth, North Woodsmen congregate at the Classy Lumberjack Bar. Another favorite haunt, Black Bear Lounge, got its name when a bear smashed through the window and romped inside. Locals, trying to be philosophical about the worst weather south of the polar ice cap, joke about Duluth's "nine months of winter and three months of poor sledding."

The city clings to the clifflike shores of ice-bound Lake Superior, the largest single body of fresh water in the world—350 miles long, 160 miles wide, and 1,333 feet deep. In *Moby Dick*, Herman Melville described Superior's "dismasting waves as direful as any that lash the salted wave. They have drowned many a midnightship with all its shrieking crew." In late 1958, shortly before the arrival of the "Winter Dance Party," the 729-foot-long ore vessel *Edmund Fitzgerald*, later immortalized in Gordon Lightfoot's "The Wreck of the Edmund Fitzgerald," churned out of Duluth on her maiden voyage. Sixteen years later, in a November northeaster of unimaginable force, the ship ran into a "white blob," a thirty-foot-high wall of water that slammed her onto a reef and broke her to pieces, wadding her up like tinfoil. Superior swallowed her dead without a trace. Such is the fury of the region into which this band of roving musicians wandered, with no more protection than secondhand school buses that were overdue for the junkyard.

"I saw Buddy Holly in Duluth, at the Armory," Bob Dylan later told *Rolling Stone*'s Kurt Loder. In 1959 the future folk-rock idol was still known as Bobby Zimmerman, a middle-class Jewish boy from Hibbing, Minnesota, about fifty miles northwest of Duluth. He wore Hush Puppies, played in a high-school garage band, and had a girl named Echo Helstrom, who proved as elusive as Buddy's Echo and whose memory, according to some observers, Dylan would one day enshrine in "Girl From the North Country." Commenting years later on Buddy's Duluth show in *Rolling Stone*, Dylan said, "Buddy was great. Buddy was incredible." Tickets for the January 31 show at the National Guard Armory cost $2, and the MC was a man named Lew Latto. More than two thousand teenagers attended what the local paper would later describe as "one of the biggest dances in the history of Duluth."

Jimmy Bowen, playing clubs in the Midwest after his stint with Buddy Knox in the Rhythm Orchids, also caught the Duluth show and visited with Holly, who told Bowen that he was happy with his bride and that his life had settled down considerably since his single days. They spent an hour together, having a "nice little rap," Bowen later told Griggs.

The bus required extensive repairs. As they waited, Ritchie Valens reintroduced the subject of a charter flight. "Tell everybody I'm flying," he said to a Duluth newspaper reporter. But a replacement bus arrived at the last minute. Ritchie called his manager Bob Keene, who was dining at Jack's on the Pier Restaurant in Santa Monica, California. "It's thirty-five degrees below back here. I'm freezing," Ritchie said, Keene later told a *Modern Screen* interviewer. According to Mendheim, Keene advised Ritchie to "finish that evening and then come home if things were that bad."

"No," Ritchie said, "I just wanted to tell you. Tonight I got two curtain calls! How about that!" Keene said he was proud of Ritchie and intended to cut a new album as soon as he returned to the West Coast.

They began the 330-mile trip to Appleton, Wisconsin, rumbling along the shores of Lake Superior, where ice floes were colliding like battering rams. They were entering the North Woods, land of the fox and the fur trapper. The heater was no match for icy blasts from the lake, but it was all that stood between them and cruel exposure. They stayed on U.S. 2 for a hundred miles, crossing the Brute and Iron rivers before entering the Chequamegon National Forest, a mournful region of lakes, loons, and gloomy woods. Somewhere around Ashland, Wisconsin, a town on Chequamegon Bay, the heater heaved its last puny puffs and died. The loose, rattling windows let in the cold and frost. Though the engine was knocking and missing, the bus continued on U.S. 2, traversing the Bad River Indian Reservation and the Whitecap Mountain Ski Area.

At Hurley, a town of 2,015 on the Wisconsin-Michigan border, they left U.S. 2 and turned south onto U.S. 51. Appleton still lay two hundred miles to the south. It was past midnight, February 1; later the same day, they were expected to perform a matinee in Appleton and an evening performance in Green Bay, Wisconsin. Fifteen miles out of Hurley, disaster struck. They were going up a hill when the engine froze and stopped. "The bus finally broke down, out there in the middle of the wilderness," Carl Bunch later told Griggs. They were stalled on the highway, in a bus with no heater. "It was cold," Tommy recalled. "Really cold."

As Iron County garage mechanic Gene Calvetti would later tell *Iron-wood Daily Globe* reporter Ralph Ansami, the piston had gone completely through the engine block. The tour party was on U.S. 51, a mile north of Pine Lake, Wisconsin, in the rugged North Woods, not a place where anyone would want to be stranded at one-thirty A.M. on February 1, 1959, during the coldest weather in memory. In these northern highlands, tearing blizzards and wind-driven snow can plunge the temperature to 50 below with startling suddenness. The low in Hurley on February 1 was

25 below, but out on the road it was more like 40 below. At this time of year, birch and pine trees snap in the wind, their ice-laden limbs crashing onto the highway. Snow, slanting in the wind, often piles up six feet deep.

The bus driver was no stranger to the outdoors. Leaning toward the windshield, he peered into the woods beside the highway. He could "feel" bears out there around Pine Lake, he said, writer Mark Steuer later reported in *Voyageur: Northeast Wisconsin's Historical Review*. At least the musicians had the protection of the bus, but even that would soon be denied them. According to Tommy, they burned "newspapers in the aisle to keep warm." When they ran out of newspapers and began to freeze, they were forced to go outside, hoping to hail down a car. They stood in the middle of the highway, where the wind keening down from the north was as sharp as splintered glass. The surrounding forest and the Great Lake beyond the trees seemed full of menace. This was the area Henry Wadsworth Longfellow wrote about in *The Song of Hiawatha*, referring to Lake Superior by its Indian name:

> *On the shores of Gitche Gumee . . .*
> *Dark behind it rose the forest, rose the*
> *black and gloomy pine trees.*

In the early morning hours, traffic in these North Woods was all but nonexistent. The tour party was far less prepared to survive this wilderness than the French explorers, wearing buckskin and moccasins, who'd discovered it in the 1600s. "We didn't know enough to be afraid, or what a mid-winter night by the side of the road really meant," Dion wrote in *The Wanderer*. It was an hour, Tommy later told Buddy's fans at a 1979 convention, before a big semi truck came thundering through the snow. They all started waving frantically. Obviously the driver had no intention of stopping "and tried to get around us," Tommy added. As the truck disappeared into the enveloping snow, they trudged back to the bus. "We just sat there and froze," Tommy recalled.

Freezing is indeed one of the more gruesome ways to die. Human tissue deteriorates at temperatures below 32 degrees. By now the temperature in the bus was 40 below. Carl Bunch couldn't use his feet. Victims of frostbite experience a pins-and-needles sensation as their tissues begin to die. In the next stage of frostbite, blood vessels freeze and complete numbness sets in. The skin turns white and is cold and hard to the touch; finally it becomes red and swollen. In advanced or "wet frostbite," bacterial infection develops and gangrene sets in, giving off a foul odor as it spreads. The gangrenous area oozes pus. When it thaws, the dead tissue is black as tar and must be amputated, along with all adjacent tissue. Like the leper, the frostbite victim watches his body decompose and fall apart. Ideally, the sufferer should be treated promptly—sheltered from the cold and told to remain very still. The damaged parts should be immersed in lukewarm water at 110 degrees. In hospitals the patient is placed in a hyperbaric chamber at once, where he can breathe highly concentrated amounts of oxygen to help heal the damaged tissue.

Marooned in the unforgiving backcountry, Carl Bunch was at maximum risk. Exposure time necessary for frostbite varies. For someone who is dry and protected from the wind, it could be eight to twelve hours. For anyone in wet socks and exposed to the wind, it can strike in two to three hours. Carl had on all six pairs of socks he'd packed for the tour, but he had been exposed to subzero temperature for most of the two hours that had elapsed since the bus had left Duluth. To make matters worse, his right leg was especially vulnerable because of a severe football injury he'd sustained at the age of thirteen that later required surgery for bone cancer. Told by his doctors he'd never walk again, he was hospitalized for over a year and later confined to a wheelchair. Refusing to give up, Carl had learned how to play drums, hoping the footwork required by the bass and the cymbal would promote healing in his leg. The novel therapy succeeded; ironically, it also led to his present, life-threatening crisis.

Elsewhere on the bus, Buddy and Dion shared their blanket, telling each other the stories of their lives, talking "through the dark hours while we waited for something to happen," Dion recalled in 1988. Ritchie, who was the type to cheer people up when they were down, jumped into the middle of the aisle and started a jam session. They all grabbed their guitars and joined in. Buddy's proto hard-rock attack blended with Ritchie's Latino rhythms and the Belmonts' intricate harmonies, creating a music that had never been heard before. "And never heard again," Dion added.

It took two hours for help to arrive. According to Tommy, the truck driver had gone on into Hurley, where he stopped and alerted the Iron County sheriff's department to their predicament. A posse came out to get them in jeeps. They returned to Hurley in the predawn darkness of February 1 and were deposited at the Club Carnival Café on Silver Street, a former striptease joint. As if they hadn't already suffered enough, the management of the café refused to serve the black bus driver. The musicians ordered his food and carried it to him at the Iron County Garage, where the bus had been towed.

Unable to walk, Carl Bunch was rushed to the Grand View Hospital, which is located halfway between Ironwood and Bessemer, Michigan, seven miles east of Hurley. Diagnosed with frostbite in both feet, Bunch was immediately hospitalized. For Carl, the "Winter Dance Party" was over, for the next few days at least. For the others, worse was yet to come. Their road manager, Rod Lucier, no doubt reported their circumstances to GAC, who offered little comfort. Though it was clear they'd never make it to Appleton, Wisconsin, in time for that day's scheduled matinee, which had to be canceled, GAC expected them to perform that night in Green Bay, despite the ordeal they'd just been through.

At 11:30 A.M., February 1, the party pulled out of Hurley on a Chicago-Northwestern train, bound for Green Bay, an oasis of football madness. On their arrival in the city of the Packers, the first thing the Bopper did was dash into a store and purchase a sleeping bag. He'd picked up a terrible case of the flu. At the Riverside Ballroom that night, Ritchie substituted for Carl Bunch, playing drums during Buddy's set. One of the Belmonts played drums when Ritchie sang his set, and Buddy was the drummer when Dion and the Belmonts went on. Whenever necessary, Buddy never hesitated to "jump out there and play drums to fill in," Tommy later said. Sometimes Buddy alternated the job of drumming for Dion with Frankie Sardo.

The Riverside Ballroom's two-hundred-thousand-square-foot dance floor was packed with two thousand teenagers boogying under a gigantic sunburst ceiling. Some of the girls wore ballet slippers and skintight "stem" skirts; others had on balloon layers of petticoats. Bouffant hair stylings (back-brushed and back-combed) were popular, though many girls looked pert in ponytails and Peter Pan collars. The boys wore their hair crew-cut or DA and preferred dirty white bucks, boots, or Florsheim loafers.

One fan, Sandy Stone Blaney of Ashwaubenon, Wisconsin, later told writer Mark Steuer how she edged her way to the front of the stage and reached up to Buddy, who "held my hand and sang a song to me," she said. "And Dion held Sharon Larscheid's hand and sang a song to her. We were in love with those guys." Buddy was amazed that the kids knew the lyrics to his songs, including recent releases, well enough to sing along with him. After the show he rang his mother in Lubbock. He spared her the details of the bus breakdown but shared some news that may have been just as unwelcome. Chicano Ritchie Valens was coming to Lubbock to stay with them as their guest the following summer, Ella Holley later revealed in a 1964 letter to German fan Gerd Muesfeldt. Though Buddy was happy living in New York, obviously he was still thinking of Lubbock as home—and no doubt the point of inviting Ritchie to Texas was to produce Ritchie's records at Taupe studios.

Though the tour party was supposed to have the following day off, GAC had a last-minute offer for a February 2 booking from Carroll Anderson, the thirty-nine-year-old manager of the Surf Ballroom in Clear Lake, Iowa, 350 miles to the southwest of Green Bay. It was an unusual request; customarily the Surf used local bands or simply held record hops presided over by local DJ Bob Hale. Interviewed by Griggs in 1977, Hale explained that Anderson first called him shortly after the tour set out from Chicago in January 1959. According to Hale, Anderson knew who Buddy was but had to inquire about the Bopper and Ritchie. Hale assured him that "if he could get those three on one show," they'd break the Surf's attendance record. Anderson himself told Wayne Jones in 1977 that Buddy was "the star of that show" and the only real draw because Clear Lake "hadn't heard of" the Bopper and Ritchie.

When Buddy discovered that GAC had greedily filled their one open date, he was distraught. As Anderson would later observe, Buddy by this point was "just a high-class bum being kicked around on the road." In order to make it to Clear Lake, the tour party would have to depart immediately following the Green Bay show, with no time to take a shower or have their laundry and cleaning done in Green Bay. Buddy felt responsible for the morale of his band, which was at an all-time low after its ordeal in the North Woods. The tour was "really clicking good," Tommy said in 1979, except for the torture of the freezing buses. Then, Norman Petty began to hound them, sending a telegram to Green Bay on February 2 warning them, according to Bill Griggs, to "stop using the name the Crickets because the Crickets are Jerry and Joe B."

For the trip from Green Bay to Clear Lake, they were expected to use the same wretched GAC bus that had stranded them in the wilderness. Two hours after they'd left Hurley on the train the previous morning, a wrecker had arrived in Hurley, carrying a replacement engine for the bus. After it was installed, the driver delivered the bus to Green Bay. Altogether, they'd ridden in seven different buses since the tour started. Tommy later said that they considered flying but "something happened" and the idea was dropped, possibly because Waylon "was afraid of small planes," Tommy added.

Expecting the worst, they boarded the bus in minus-25-degree weather with their road manager Rod Lucier. They left for Clear Lake, where they were scheduled to arrive at four P.M. for an eight o'clock show, but the bus kept breaking down all the way across Wisconsin and northeastern Iowa. Finally they ditched the bus, leaving it on the highway, according to Tommy, and finishing the trip in a rented school bus. At least they "did stay warm that time," Tommy added.

In a 1993 interview Maria Elena said, "Buddy called from the tour and said how unhappy he was." She asked him, "Why don't you come home?" she recalled in a 1988 article in the *Chicago Tribune*. Buddy replied, "Maria, you know me. I have to finish." And there was another motive: "We needed the money," Maria Elena recalled. They had a baby on the way. A February 1 audit of one of Petty's accounts showed that only $5,000 was due the Crickets, a far cry from the $50,000 to $80,000 they'd been expecting. Buddy was "infuriated," Tommy later told Goldrosen. Petty's audit may well have been as inaccurate as those of the Hollywood movie studios, long notorious for their so-called "creative bookkeeping."

Ritchie was as fed up with the tour as Buddy and considered chucking it. Fearing his tour mates would call him chicken if he quit, he hesitated to "skip out," Mendheim later revealed. He knew that some of the performers were still talking about chartering a plane; perhaps that would solve his problem. Though he was terrified of flying, he was so concerned that his fatigue from the bus rides would damage his performances that he decided to go along if they flew from Iowa to Minnesota, where they were due on February 3, 1959.

The thirty-six-hundred-acre lake that gives the north central Iowa village of Clear Lake its name was frozen solid for the winter of 1958–59. The white cottages surrounding it looked as if they'd been shuttered for months. Snow and ice blanketed everything, including the empty sidewalks. Tourist-board promotional leaflets boasted of winter sports such as ice fishing, snowmobiling, and cross-country skiing, but there was little evidence of human habitation.

By the time they bumped and skidded into Clear Lake, which then had a population considerably less than its present seventy-five hundred, Buddy knew he couldn't endure another long bus ride. They arrived at the Surf Ballroom at 7:30 or 7:45 P.M. and were due on stage at eight o'clock. A line of teenagers, many with their parents, extended from the box office all the way to the end of the sidewalk.

It was almost five hundred miles to their next gig in Moorhead, Minnesota. The thought of climbing back on the bus in a few hours was intolerable. Buddy made up his mind to charter a plane to Fargo, North Dakota, which had the nearest airport to Moorhead. They would leave immediately after the show. According to Tommy, Buddy told the other performers he'd take their dirty laundry and dry cleaning and have it ready for them by the time they arrived in Moorhead on the bus the following day.

The *Clear Lake Mirror-Reporter* later disclosed that Buddy told Bob Hale, the MC at the Surf, that he "didn't want to take a chance in the bus since it had broken down while traveling from Green Bay, Wisconsin, to Clear Lake."

Thirty-four years later, in February 1993, I found Clear Lake to be little changed, still nothing more than a wide place in the road. Winter light, which makes the air turn white, had made my landing at nearby Mason City extremely hazardous. Though our small plane came down in broad daylight, visibility was a frightening, blinding zero. The downtown area is only a minute's drive from busy Interstate 35, which slices through the United States' midsection from Texas to Canada. The only halfway edible food I found was at a big truck stop, where the "broasted chicken" had been fried in a pressure cooker, presumably to ensure maximum infusion of grease. The four-inch-high meringue on the "chocolate silk" pie looked promising, but the chocolate filling underneath had curdled into a black, rubbery clabber. In my Army days in the fifties, stationed at Fort Dix, New Jersey, I used to think that drab little towns like Brown's Mills and Wrightstown were the last places on earth I wanted to be. I was wrong; it's Clear Lake, Iowa, in the winter.

At some point during the evening of February 2, 1959, Buddy, Ritchie, and the Bopper ate dinner at Witke's Restaurant, joined by Carroll Anderson and his wife Lucille, who worked with him at the ballroom, and Bob Hale. In 1980, now sixty years old, Anderson told interviewers Mike Oestreicher and Pat Kennedy that he always attempted, as a matter of policy, to make entertainers playing one-night stands in Clear Lake "feel as if that was their home" for the evening. Though tired, the stars struck Bob Hale as courteous, warm, "classy young men," he told a *Chicago Tribune* reporter in 1988. Hale was then a DJ at radio station KRIB in Mason City.

The temperature outside Witke's Restaurant that night was eighteen degrees. In warmer months, Buddy was assured, Clear Lake was a bustling resort. The Methodist Camp, the Girl Scout Camp, and the Open Bible Camp are all located on the lake's south shore. Imagining how scenic Clear Lake would be in the springtime, Buddy's mind turned to his favorite sport, waterskiing. Bob Hale later told *Des Moines Sunday Register* reporter Ken Fuson that "they talked about coming back to Clear Lake for a spring concert and going waterskiing."

Anderson agreed to book the stars for a return engagement and said he'd finalize the deal later that week. Bob Hale hastened to invite them to dinner in his home when they returned in the spring, Hale later told Griggs. Leaving Witke's they walked across the street to the Surf Ballroom, a relic of the big-band era that looks like an airplane hangar except for its box office and marquee. The glory of the Surf, which still stands today at the same location, 460 North Shore Drive, is the 6,300-square-foot rock-hard maple dance floor, which is darkly luminous, like a lake in the moonlight. Overhead an arched ceiling of midnight blue comes alive with drifting clouds, projected from a custom-made machine. Several tiers of art-deco wooden booths accommodate most of the ballroom's twenty-two hundred patrons. Built in 1948 after the original Surf, which opened in 1933, was destroyed by fire, it was supposed to resemble a "Florida beach club."

Buddy used a pay telephone inside the lobby, next to a cavernous coat-check room, to call Maria Elena, who later described their conversation to John Goldrosen. The promoters had fulfilled none of their pledges, Buddy said, and everyone was disgusted. He was going to Moorhead, Minnesota, ahead of everyone else to take care of laundry and cleaning. Why, she wanted to know, should *he* have to be the one to go?

"There's nobody else to do it," he replied.

As Ritchie telephoned his family in California, Buddy went into Anderson's office to arrange the charter flight. "Will you find out what can be done?" Buddy asked, Anderson recalled in 1980. The Bopper joined them, Anderson later revealed to Wayne Jones. "It was the Big Bopper and Buddy that set this up," said Anderson. They told him they wanted to reach the Fargo airport in plenty of time before the Moorhead show in order to have their clothes cleaned and enjoy "a good night's rest, too. That was the main objective," Anderson added. Fargo, North Dakota, was just across the Red River from Moorhead, Minnesota, where they were booked to play the Armory the following night. With a population of about seventeen thousand, Moorhead was too small to have its own airport and depended on the facilities at Fargo, which was only ten miles away. Clear Lake also had no airport.

"How far is the airport from here?" Buddy asked, Anderson recalled in 1980.

"It's only a mile and a half," Anderson replied.

It was Anderson's impression that they needed a third passenger to cover expenses; Buddy and the Bopper may have "encouraged Valens to go with them. Valens didn't want to go at first," Anderson said in 1977. Evidently Ritchie had got cold feet once he realized that the flight was about to become a reality.

Anderson attempted to reach Jerry Dwyer, the owner of the charter company, to book the flight, but Dwyer had left his office to attend a meeting of the Mason City Chamber of Commerce. Someone at Dwyer's Flying Service in Mason City told him the fare—$108 for a four-seat plane, $36 each for three passengers—and said they'd call back in a quarter of an hour, as soon as a pilot could be found.

The pilot who took the assignment was Roger Peterson, an employee of Dwyer's Flying Service. The twenty-one-year-old Clear Lake pilot was exhausted, having worked nonstop for possibly the past seventeen hours, Civil Aeronautics Board investigator Van R. O'Brien later estimated. The last thing young Peterson wanted to do was fly to Fargo that night. He had the following day, February 3, off, and he'd been looking forward to getting home to his attractive bride of four months. Now those plans were shattered. The Fargo flight would not start until 12:30 A.M., following the conclusion of the show at the Surf. Then Peterson would have to fly to North Dakota and back—a seven-hour round trip—before getting any sleep.

Perhaps he should have said no, given how fatigued he was, but

Peterson was a Buddy Holly fan, Bruce Wilcox and Bill Griggs discovered in 1981, and he probably couldn't resist the idea of flying the singer to his next gig. Maria Elena stated in 1993, "The young man was so impressed that he was flying all these stars and he insisted on doing it." But only minutes after Peterson accepted the job, he evidently had second thoughts and tried to get out of it. Prodded by his conscience, he called a qualified pilot, Duane Mayfield, who was also chief deputy sheriff of Cerro Gordo County. Mayfield subsequently told *Mason City Globe-Gazette* reporter Jeff Tecklenburg that Roger Peterson asked him if he "wanted to take these singers" to Fargo. After Peterson ticked off the illustrious passenger list, Mayfield, unimpressed, said no, thanks, he was "more of a Lawrence Welk fan" himself.

Later, Peterson's mother vigorously defended her son's decision, saying that it had been characteristically selfless of Roger to undertake a flight "in the middle of a winter night." When anyone faced an emergency, she added, Roger "was always there to do what he could." Everything about Roger Peterson was appealing except for the fact that he was not qualified to fly under that night's conditions. A wholesome Iowa farm boy, he was the oldest of Arthur and Pearl Peterson's four children, born on May 24, 1937, in Alta, Iowa, a hamlet 105 miles southwest of Clear Lake with a population of fifteen hundred. By the time he reached high school, he was quite handsome—blond, well-built, and athletic. His steady date at Fairview Consolidated School was a pretty, intelligent girl named DeAnn Lenz. His mother described him to Bruce Wilcox in 1980 as "very popular" with "many friends," a "good Christian," an athlete who was nearly six feet tall and excelled at basketball. "A thoughtful, considerate boy," he'd always helped his parents on the farm while growing up.

Art Peterson, Roger's father, was such an avid aviation buff that he'd constructed a hangar and a runway on their farm. From the age of sixteen, Roger piloted the family's Piper Cub J-3. His younger brother Ron eventually became the chief jet pilot for Gate City Steel in Omaha, Nebraska. Following an Army hitch, Roger worked as a car mechanic. He married DeAnn on September 14, 1958, and appears to have been the husband of every woman's dreams, a macho jock who was sensitive and even loved to cook. His mother said his cakes were "superb." DeAnn took a job to help with expenses.

Roger had received his pilot's license from the Ross Aviation School in Tulsa, Oklahoma, and worked at the Graham Flying Service in Sioux City, Iowa. In late 1957 and early 1958, Peterson underwent eight hours of training from Lambert Fechter, a flight instrument instructor from Hartley, Iowa. According to Fechter, Peterson could hardly control the plane. He began to experience vertigo and let the aircraft "go into a spiral to the right." When Peterson became more experienced, such "tendencies grew less and less," Fechter added.

Vertigo is characterized by a tangled, disoriented state of mind; dizziness sets in, as well as a sensation that everything is whirling around, including one's self. During flight instrument training, most pilots learn to cope with vertigo: above all, the pilot must abide by his instrument reading regardless of his own feelings. According to Fechter, even pilots with many hours of flight time occasionally experience vertigo, but they always maintain trust in the instruments, Fechter later stated in a CAB investigation. Unfortunately Roger Peterson had failed his instrument flight check on March 21, 1958, according to Federal Aviation Administration general safety inspector Melvin O. Wood, who conducted the test. During the flight, Peterson descended below his assigned altitude and went into a dive. He managed to recover and climb back to his assigned altitude, but Wood canceled the rest of the test because it was obvious, Wood later stated in a CAB investigation, that Peterson was incapable of establishing "a proper holding procedure."

Moreover, Peterson's Airman's Certificate, dated November 4, 1958, specified that "holder does not meet night-flight requirements." In permitting Roger Peterson to fly, all the government agencies that are supposed to protect the public had inadvertently set the stage for disaster.

Peterson applied for work as a charter pilot at Dwyer's Flying Service in Mason City and was hired by Jerry Dwyer in July 1958. With Roger working at Dwyer's and DeAnn employed in the accounting department of KGLO-TV in Mason City, the newlyweds were able to establish a comfortable home in Clear Lake at the Armsbury Cottages on North Shore Drive. They attended Redeemer Lutheran Church in nearby Ventura. Dwyer was so pleased with Roger that he made him a flying instructor. By February 2, 1959, when his path crossed Buddy Holly's, Peterson had accumulated 711 flying hours—not an inconsiderable amount—including 128 in the Beechcraft Bonanza, the plane that would be used to fly Buddy to Fargo.

Jerry Dwyer didn't learn of the flight until Peterson reached him by phone at the Chamber of Commerce. Dwyer left the meeting at once and met Peterson at the airport to help prepare the plane, a single-engine four-seater, for the three-and-a-half-hour flight. It was hardly ideal weather for flying—eighteen degrees with snow flurries—but Peterson was bent on seeing the rock 'n' roll stars. The Fargo hop would be the last flight out of Mason City that night, leaving at about one A.M. on the third of February.

On the evening of February 2, Rod Lucier, the "Winter Dance Party" road manager, heard of "a gathering Midwest snow storm," the *Lubbock Avalanche-Journal* later revealed, and became convinced that the troupe should not travel that night. He decided to call GAC and express his concern.

Under the Sword of Damocles, the faintest of hopes began to flicker.

Top: Relaxing in a hotel room with the **EVERLY BROTHERS** (*Don, left; Phil, third from left, standing*). Buddy produced the debut of young **LOU GIORDANO** (*in striped shirt, seated*), "Stay Close to Me." (John Buzzell, photographer. Collection of Bill Griggs)

Above: Buddy was effortlessly successful in love. **PHIL EVERLY** (*right*) was impressed by Buddy's ability to attract women. (John Buzzell, photographer. Collection of Bill Griggs)

BUDDY's 1958 cosmetic makeover included dental work to remove brown stains caused by Lubbock's water; a bridge to replace the front teeth that Joe B. Mauldin knocked out in London; plastic surgery (a scraping process to remove acne scars); and a permanent wave. (AP/Wide World)

3rd SHOW of STARS
ONE NIGHT ONLY

- **Paul ANKA**
- **Jerry Lee LEWIS** AND HIS BAND
- **Buddy HOLLY**
- **The CRICKETS**
- **Jodie SANDS**

TOM MOFFATT, M.C.

CIVIC AUDITORIUM

Monday, January 27

**2 SHOWS · 6:30 & 8:15 P.M.
PRICES: $1.50 · $2.50 · $3.50**

Although Buddy was the ranking star when he played Hawaii's Civic Auditorium in 1958, he lacked aggressive management. Paul Anka seized top billing by taking a cut in his regular fee. (Alan Clark Archives)

September 1958: The great tenor sax man **KING CURTIS** flew to Clovis to cut "Reminiscing" with Buddy. Many years later, Curtis was stabbed to death on a New York street. (Alan Clark Archives)

Above: **BUDDY** and his bride **MARIA ELENA** (*far left*) honeymooning in Mexico City with **JERRY** and **PEGGY SUE**. (Collection of Bill Griggs)

Opposite: Buddy and Maria Elena settled in **GREENWICH VILLAGE** in 1958. They loved the jazz joints, the Village Gate, and poetry readings in the coffeehouses. (AP/Wide World)

Opposite: The 1959 "Winter Dance Party"—the most notorious and perhaps most poorly run rock tour in history—ended in tragedy for its three headliners. (Alan Clark Archives)

Left: **RITCHIE VALENS** planned to record with Buddy in 1959 and stay with Buddy and Maria Elena in New York and Lubbock. Buddy was organizing his own record company, Taupe Records, named after the color of his Cadillac. (Alan Clark Archives)

DION DIMUCCI (*center*, with the Belmonts) and Buddy Holly shared a blanket on the frigid "Winter Dance Party" bus to keep warm. (Alan Clark Archives)

Left: **THE BIG BOPPER**—Jiles P. Richardson—a DJ from Beaumont, Texas, hit the charts with "Chantilly Lace" and joined the "Winter Dance Party" tour in 1959 with Buddy, Waylon Jennings, Dion, and Ritchie Valens. The Bopper caught the flu and begged Waylon for his seat on the ill-fated airplane. (UPI/Bettmann)

Below: **WAYLON JENNINGS** worried about singing rock 'n' roll, but Buddy always knew—according to Maria Elena Holly—that Waylon would be a great country star. In 1976, with *Wanted: The Outlaws*, Waylon became the first C&W singer to sell a million records. (Waylon Jennings Collection)

The "Winter Dance Party" played Kenosha, Wisconsin, on January 24, 1959:
FRANKIE SARDO (*left*); **THE BIG BOPPER** (*center*); and **BUDDY** (*right*).
"Buddy was laid back and just said 'hi,'" photographer Tony Szikil recalled in
1995. (Tony Szikil)

Top: **RITCHIE VALENS** rocked the Eagles Ballroom in Kenosha, Wisconsin, on January 24, 1959, as **WAYLON JENNINGS**, Buddy's bassist, accompanied. (Tony Szikil)

Above: **WAYLON JENNINGS** (*far left*) and **RITCHIE VALENS** in Kenosha. Rock Generation boys wore neckties (older teens in the background wore open-neck shirts and T-shirts). Girls favored sweater sets, stem skirts, and butterfly eyeglasses. (Tony Szikil)

"Winter Dance Party": Midwestern kids were among the first, and most ardent, supporters of rock 'n' roll. Here, in Kenosha, Wisconsin, on January 24, 1959, they interacted with **RITCHIE VALENS** (*extreme left*), **FRANKIE SARDO** (*kneeling*), **DION DIMUCCI** (*dark sweater*), and **THE BIG BOPPER** (*leopard-skin jacket*). (Tony Szikil)

DION DIMUCCI (*left*) on the "Winter Dance Party" tour in Kenosha, January 24, 1959. "We would tell each other stories. [Buddy] about Lubbock. Me, about the Bronx. I could always get a laugh out of him—soft and low like his drawl." (Tony Szikil)

Above: "Winter Dance Party": **WAYLON JENNINGS**, **TOMMY ALLSUP**, and **BUDDY HOLLY** at Fournier's dance hall in Eau Claire, Wisconsin, on January 26, 1959. (Don Larson)

Right: **ROGER PETERSON**, the twenty-one-year-old pilot of the doomed Beechcraft Bonanza. (Collection of Bill Griggs)

Buddy's death made banner headlines in Lubbock, Clear Lake, and Mason City.

Top: Three records mark the spot where Buddy died, which the author uncovered in 1993, as he trudged through hip-deep snow to find the crash site near Clear Lake, Iowa. (Photo by the author)

Above, left: The post-Holly Crickets: **JOE B. MAULDIN** (*bottom*), **SONNY CURTIS** (*center*), and **JERRY ALLISON** (*top*). (Pete Curtis)

Above, right: Buddy's statue, shown with sculptor **GRANT SPEED**, stands at the center of Lubbock. (UPI/Bettmann)

Top: Buddy's namesake, **THE HOLLIES**, were among the leaders of the British Invasion of the 1960s. **GRAHAM NASH** (*left*) went on to an even bigger career in Crosby, Stills and Nash. (Alan Clark Archives)

Middle: Shown with **ED SULLIVAN**, in 1964, **THE BEATLES** revived Buddy's music and spearheaded the British Invasion of America. (UPI/Bettmann)

Above: **THE ROLLING STONES** made their American recording debut with Buddy's "Not Fade Away" in 1964. (UPI/Bettmann)

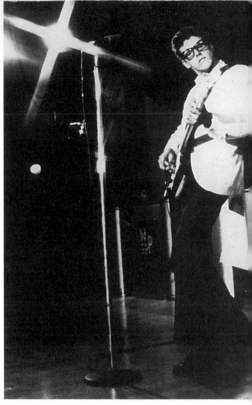

Above: **DON McLEAN**'s "American Pie" became the anthem of Christmas 1971, immortalizing February 3, 1959, as "the day the music died." (AP/Wide World)

Right: **GARY BUSEY** was originally slated to play Jerry Allison but ended up in the title role of *The Buddy Holly Story,* receiving an Oscar nomination for his performance. (AP/Wide World)

Buddy's original tombstone in Lubbock was stolen. Later it was replaced by a gravestone that included his Fender Stratocaster but reverted to the pre-rock-star spelling of his name. (Collection of Bill Griggs)

Winterkill

I t was after eight P.M. and the first of their two shows that night was going to begin late. In the Surf's communal "Backstage Band Room," a shantylike affair annexed to stage left, Buddy listened to the stirrings of the crowd of thirteen hundred and "said he was worried about girls . . . pulling his hair," Carroll Anderson recalled in 1980.

"I don't think you need to worry about that at all here because security is pretty heavy," Anderson said. Also, 125 to 150 parents were in attendance at the first show, Anderson added, and no doubt their presence would keep the kids on their best behavior. Fred Milano stood next to Buddy as they changed their clothes before going on. He noticed that Buddy wasn't wearing an undershirt, he told Wayne Jones years later. The drafty old ballroom still used gas turbine heaters and was quite chilly, so Milano asked Buddy why he wasn't more warmly dressed. Buddy replied that he never wore undershirts because if he wore them for several days and suddenly took one off, he'd "catch a cold," he explained, as if he always was defying the elements. His nakedness was a constant theme of his life—a desire to expose himself directly to danger, whether through the music that he introduced to Lubbock or the challenge that he took on when he told Norman Petty to go packing.

Fred then inquired about the charter flight that everyone in the tour party was talking about. Buddy repeated that he'd take everyone's laundry and it would be ready for them on arrival, Milano recalled. The flight would be over in "three or four hours," but the bus trip would require "at least ten hours," Milano added.

In its planning stage, the manifest for the flight to Fargo underwent numerous changes, which began around showtime February 2 and ended after midnight, when the passenger list was finalized just prior to takeoff. According to Waylon Jennings, Buddy leased the plane strictly for himself and his band, but other eyewitnesses, such as Anderson and Milano, later claimed that the Bopper was on the list from the beginning. Early on the evening of February 2, the Bopper somehow lost his seat, possibly when

Buddy realized that his own sidemen, Waylon and Tommy, were entitled to first dibs.

Though Tommy Allsup stated in 1979 that he was on the passenger list from the outset, Fred Milano told Wayne Jones in 1977 that Tommy could not afford to make the flight. Dion revealed in 1988 that he saw Buddy going from musician to musician, soliciting passengers, saying he needed more people to share the charter fee. Dion liked the idea of flying but declined, calculating that it would cost him the equivalent of a month's rent.

That was when "Holly rounded up Ritchie," Dion wrote in *The Wanderer*. But if Ritchie made it onto the manifest before midnight, he didn't stay on it for long. The final seat on the plane went to Tommy. At showtime the manifest read: Buddy Holly, Waylon Jennings, Tommy Allsup, and Roger Peterson, pilot. Maneuvering for seats on the plane was far from over, however. It would resume after the performance. During these vacillations, Rod Lucier was still hopeful of reaching someone at the agency and canceling the Moorhead gig.

At some point after eight P.M., Bob Hale stepped on stage and noticed that the ballroom was "filled to the rafters." The spaciousness of the hall belonged to another era—the age of the big bands and mammoth ballrooms like Roseland and Danceland and the Avalon—but now it was a rock venue and the kids were wearing not suits and formals and corsages but jeans and swirling felt skirts with cutout poodles on gold-chain leashes. The crowd's anticipation ran high as they awaited their favorite recording stars. Half a dozen floorwalkers dressed in dinner clothes cruised the dance area, the tiers, and the promenade, surveilling the crowd for rowdies.

According to Carroll Anderson, Sardo and Dion and the Belmonts performed for thirty minutes for "dancing and listening" before the star attractions came on. Among the teenagers on the dance floor were Karen Lein and her future husband Jack, both seniors at Mason City High School. "I had my jeans rolled up, saddle shoes, and a big white shirt with a scarf around my neck," Karen recalled in 1995. "We entered the jitterbug contest and danced up a storm." Frankie Sardo opened the show with "Fake Out," his ABC Paramount record that was gaining in sales as the tour progressed through the Midwest. Twenty-year-old Sardo had been acting, singing, and dancing with his parents in Italian theaters in the United States since he was five years old. He attended P.S. 108 in New York and Fork Union Academy in Virginia. With his matinee-idol appearance—fair skin, dark hair, and chiseled Michelangelesque features—he had his heart set on becoming a movie star but, as a *Hit Parader* article put it in 1959, "he can't help it if it's his singing voice that's launching him into stardom."

Kicking off the main part of the show, Ritchie Valens sailed into "La Bamba," transfixing everyone with his ability to go from a soft, almost childlike attitude to a gritty impudence. Then, with Buddy backing him on drums and Waylon and Tommy playing their guitars, Ritchie sang "Donna," giving it the same stately cadence and compelling gravity of Phil Spector's "To Know Him Is to Love Him." As *Rolling Stone* would later note, "It had the perfect creeping tempo for slow, passionate dancing." According to Billie Rose, then a student at Clear Lake High School, "Everybody was out on the dance floor." Though February 2 was a Monday—a school night—very little homework was done on the evening of the "Winter Dance Party."

Ritchie had learned from Bob Keene that he would receive his gold record for "Donna" as soon as he came home. Ironically, he was having far more success with the recording than with the real Donna, a high-school classmate he'd met at an Igniters gang dance in LA, according to Mendheim. Though Donna Ludwig was going with another boy, Ritchie said "Hi, blondie!" every time they passed in the hallway at San Fernando High, Donna later recalled. They danced together at noontime school hops and, according to Donna, necked whenever they ran into each other at hangouts like the Big Boy in Mission Hills or the Rainbow Roller Rink in Van Nuys.

Donna later revealed to Mendheim that her father disapproved of his blond, blue-eyed daughter dating a Chicano. Though for a while Donna sneaked out to meet Ritchie at the roller rink, their relationship proved too much of a "hassle" for her and they broke up. *Sixteen* magazine would state in July 1959 that a sore point between them was Ritchie's jealousy, which provoked many of their fights. "You flirt too much," he growled at her before they split up. On the rebound, Ritchie dated Donna's girlfriend (and later stepsister) Cathy Brown, but he still loved Donna and wrote the song to get her back, according to Donna herself as well as Doug Macchia, the twenty-year-old San Fernando High graduate who brought Ritchie to the attention of record producer Bob Keene.

In September 1958 Ritchie called Donna and began, "Donnie . . . Listen, I'm really sorry what happened." Cool at first, Donna melted into tears when he told her he was writing a song about her, according to a 1959 article in *Modern Screen*. Suddenly he started singing, and the song told of how she'd left him and how devastated he was. "Well, he began to cry," Donna later told *Photoplay*. In another interview, in August 1959, she added, "We'd broken up about a year ago—but not really." As a beautiful sixteen-year-old, Donna never lacked for dates, but according to mutual friends who observed them at the time, whenever Ritchie came home to L.A. from one of his tours, he could usually be found "walking

Donna Ludwig to her next period class, carrying her books, an arm thrown affectionately over her shoulders or around her waist."

On February 2, 1959, after Ritchie completed his set at the Surf Ballroom, the Bopper came on next and titillated the crowd with "Chantilly Lace," in which a lecherous lover enumerates the unmentionable acts his girlfriend is willing to perform on him. "I remember the Bopper," says Jim Weddell, who was seventeen and had driven with two friends from Clarion, Iowa, forty-five miles southwest of Clear Lake. "The Bopper was the biggest thing to me," Weddell adds. Karen Lein recalls in 1995, "The Bopper was really good." Carroll Anderson added in 1980 that the Bopper had everyone "screaming." But it was Buddy, Anderson said, who "almost blew the roof. They didn't want to let him go."

The break between the two shows that night fell at 10:30 P.M. Anderson reminisced years later in *Rave On!* magazine about how he escorted Buddy from the stage "and we came right down on the little brick wall there and he signed autographs." Ritchie and the Bopper "didn't give near as many," Anderson recalled, "because Buddy was the big star." With only a few minutes remaining before the late show, Buddy joined the other musicians in the band room. Bob Hale arrived to interview them for his DJ show on KRIB. Though Hale had dined with Buddy at Witke's, he failed to recognize Buddy as the drummer during Ritchie's performance and asked who was the "guy with the glasses playing drums."

"My name is Mr. Holly, Mr. Hale," Buddy replied.

Amused, Ritchie began to extol Buddy's latest record, "It Doesn't Matter Anymore," and told Hale that Buddy was the first rock star to record with a full violin section. Ritchie joked that Buddy should be performing in a cutaway with tails and predicted he'd be leading the philharmonic before the end of the year. They all sat around drinking Cokes and coffee and having an impromptu party. A reporter from the *Clear Lake Mirror-Reporter* came in and found the stars "full of pep, reacting joyously to the big crowd of young people." The Bopper and Ritchie "playfully Indian-wrestled backstage between acts," he added.

Anderson recalled in 1980 that while Sardo and Dion began the second show, sometime after 10:30, Buddy spoke to him about the charter flight. "Let's confirm that," Buddy said, Anderson related in *Rave On!* They rang Dwyer's Flying Service again and were advised that the plane would be ready for them around midnight.

When Buddy began his set after the break, the Belmonts' bass singer Carlo Mastrangelo sat in on drums; Carl Bunch was still in the hospital in Bessemer, recovering from frostbite. Buddy had planned to hire another drummer, "but something happened," Tommy said in 1979, and they never got around to it. Buddy sang "Gotta Travel On," a song that evokes the free but melancholy life of a rolling stone, one who bums around little towns and periodically decides it's time to hit the road again, usually at the first sign of winter. Buddy could have been singing about himself and the "Winter Dance Party" troupe, who'd never spent more than one night in the same town and still had to play Moorhead, Sioux City, Des Moines, Cedar Rapids, Waterloo, Dubuque, Spring Valley, Chicago, Peoria, Springfield, Louisville, Canton, and Youngstown before wrapping on February 15, less than a month after they'd started.

People in the audience began to call out the titles of Buddy's hit records. Charging into "Peggy Sue" at full throttle, he ignited the ballroom in seconds. Even the boozers lurking in back were stirred. "We drank beer and gin," says Jim Weddell. "We went to a bootlegger before the show. There was always somebody who'd buy your booze for you." Weddell put aside his drink and started bopping to Buddy's driving attack in "Peggy Sue." For Weddell and many others that night, the "Winter Dance Party" prefigured latter-day rock festivals such as Monterey Pop and Woodstock and would live just as vividly in memory.

It also marked the end of an era. With its major stars in decline and the upcoming congressional auto-da-fé that would wipe out tour packagers and DJs, fifties rock was celebrating its final night. As Rolling Stone's Robert Palmer would write from the perspective of 1990, "It is a measure of fifties rock's genuine revolutionary potential (as opposed to the revolution-as-corporate-marketing-ploy so characteristic of the sixties) that while sixties rock eventually calmed down, was co-opted or snuffed itself out in heedless excess, fifties rock 'n' roll was stopped. Cold."

Dion, Ritchie, and the Big Bopper had warmed the Surf audience up, but Buddy took the show to a higher level of excitement, bombarding them with one relentless rocker after another, from "That'll Be the Day" to "Rave On." Then "Heartbeat" and "Everyday" bound the whole crowd together in blissful fellowship. Bob Hale later described it as "fantastic . . . just one big surge" around the bandstand. Dion, who was watching from the sidelines, later wrote that Buddy had founded rock's avant-garde and that his absence from the charts in 1959 was no more than a temporary setback: "He'd made it this far because he knew exactly where he wanted to go. To the top." Though Buddy was the veteran star on the bill, Dion reflected that Buddy "was only at the beginning of a career that had already changed music."

Years later, when asked what he was thinking during Buddy's Surf performance, Jim Weddell says, "I dunno—I was just out there a-boppin'." Buddy Holly had ironically and unknowingly achieved his purpose: a generation was up and dancing, and the world would never be the same. The rest of the century would bear his stamp.

The evening was not an unqualified success. When Buddy, Ritchie, and the Bopper attempted to sing together, they weren't exactly the platters. "Thank God they never went into a recording studio," Hale later told Griggs. It was all offered in a spirit of fun, and they left their audience in ecstasy. "There would never again be a time when the land was rocking in harmony," *Rolling Stone*'s Ed Ward observed, almost thirty years later. Russ Rippon of nearby Rock Falls, Iowa, later told *Rave On!* that the final number performed at the Surf that night was Ritchie Valens's "La Bamba." The show ended at 11:55 P.M.

Following the performance, Anderson paid the road manager, who was still trying to reach GAC to cancel the next show. The troupe was paid its base rate of $850 plus an extra $250, thanks to the "60 percent privilege" clause they had in their contract. Anderson later explained that 60 percent of the box-office net that night "was greater than the guarantee," hence the $250 bonus. As Anderson counted out the money to the road manager, Buddy came into the office and said, "I'm down to only $19 or $20," Anderson recalled in 1980. Lucier handed Buddy approximately $300, which Buddy "just rolled . . . up and stuffed . . . in his pocket."

Anderson offered Buddy and his musicians a ride to the Mason City airport in his station wagon. As they started to leave, the Bopper approached Waylon and said he was suffering from the flu. "He was a big man," Waylon said, explaining that the Bopper couldn't rest on the bus. According to Tommy, the Bopper wanted to reach Moorhead early in the morning so he could visit a doctor and get an injection. The Bopper offered to leave his new sleeping bag with Waylon if he could take Waylon's place on the plane.

Waylon's reply to the Bopper, Waylon later told Sky Corbin, was: "It's all right with me, if it's all right with Buddy. You go ask him." Buddy raised no objections. Waylon was relieved to be off the flight, according to Tommy. For Waylon, the fun and camaraderie of the bus far outweighed its dangers. It was the beginning of an addiction to the road that would eventually be detrimental, driving Waylon "to drugs," according to the video *Waylon*.

Ritchie began to wonder if there was any way he could talk Tommy Allsup out of the last seat on the plane. He, too, was suffering from a cold but again hesitated to plead illness out of fear that the older stars might say he couldn't "take" the hardships of touring. Instead, Ritchie said he needed to get to their next gig in time to have his hair cut, Alan Freed later told writer Jim Hoffman. Ritchie remained ambivalent about flying, according to his sister-in-law Ernestine Reyes. On his final night in Los Angeles, he'd gone to the Guardian Angels church on Laurel Canyon Boulevard with his friend Gail Smith and prayed for a safe journey. He was afraid of airplanes, he told Gail, according to Mendheim, but he was getting used to them and might even take one at some point during the "Winter Dance Party." Gail warned that it was snowy and storming in the North and asked, "What'd you do if you crash?"

"I'll land on my guitar," Ritchie said.

His mother told him she'd had a premonition, writer George Shetlock later disclosed in *Teen* magazine. "She didn't want him to go," Shetlock wrote, "but she couldn't bring herself to stand in the way of his career." Ernestine Reyes drove from her home at 13812 Judd Street in Pacoima to give him a lift to the airport. Shortly thereafter, she told Concepcion that just before boarding the plane, Ritchie had said "he wished he didn't have to fly," Hoffman revealed in *Photoplay*.

At the Surf, despite these qualms, Ritchie asked Tommy for his seat on the plane. Tommy said no, explaining that he "was starting to freeze every night, too."

"I have never been on a small plane before," Ritchie begged, according to Mendheim. "Please let me go instead." Tommy shook his head and left the ballroom with Buddy, the Bopper, and Anderson. They went to the parking lot and dumped their belongings in the back of Anderson's station wagon. Anderson's wife Lucille and their eleven-year-old son Tom joined them for the ride to the airport. Suddenly, according to Tommy, Buddy asked him to "go back" and make sure they hadn't left any amplifiers or other equipment behind. Returning to the ballroom, Tommy again encountered Ritchie, who was surrounded by fans clamoring for his autograph. One of them, Cindy Johnson, recalled in 1989 that she and her friends lacked pencil and paper so Ritchie accommodatingly signed their hands. Spotting Tommy, Ritchie decided to make one last play for the seat. "You going to let me fly, guy? Come on. Flip," Ritchie said, according to Tommy. Reaching in his pocket, Ritchie produced a 50-cent piece, Tommy stated in a 1979 interview. "Let's flip a coin," Ritchie said.

Tommy told him to go ahead and flip it "if you want to go that bad." But if Tommy lost, he later told Goldrosen, he wanted to use the Bopper's sleeping bag on the bus. Evidently that wasn't possible; in 1979 Tommy told a meeting of Holly fans that the Bopper promised the sleeping bag to Waylon "and no more was said about that." If the coin came up heads, Ritchie would go on the plane; tails and it was Tommy. Ritchie flipped the coin. It danced in the dim light of the empty ballroom and landed in Ritchie's palm with a soft splat. His big dimpled face broke into a wide smile as they peered down into his hand. "You won the toss," said Tommy.

"What do you know? This is the first time I've ever won," Ritchie said, Alan Freed would tell Hoffman a few months later.

Then Ritchie and Tommy went outside and spoke briefly with Buddy, explaining the latest change in the manifest. Tommy asked Buddy to pick up a registered letter from his mother, which she'd sent to the post office in Fargo. Some identification would be necessary, Buddy pointed out, and he asked Tommy for his driver's license. "Here, take my wallet," Tommy said. Buddy stuffed the wallet in his pocket and climbed into the station wagon with Ritchie and the Bopper.

Tommy left to join Waylon, Sardo, and Dion and the Belmonts, who were boarding the bus. At exactly midnight, Angelo D'Aleo of the Belmonts started celebrating his nineteenth birthday, inside the bus; it was February 3, 1959. All the members of the tour party were gathered in the parking lot, ready to leave for Moorhead, some by bus, others by plane. A light snow began to fall, and suddenly it was a scene as sad and star-crossed as the third act of *La Bohème*. Bob Hale and his wife stood in the darkness, saying good-bye to the three stars of the tour, who were sitting in Anderson's station wagon, waiting to go to the airport. At 12:05 A.M. Anderson started the car and they headed for Mason City.

The rest of the tour party sat on the bus, peering out the frosted windows at the snow. Just as they started to leave for Moorhead, a carload of fans pulled up. They chatted with the musicians and mentioned that some of their friends were going to the airport to see the stars off. Someone on the bus told them that they'd never be admitted to the airport. But a fan named Billie Rose was already on her way there, accompanied by friends. The snow made driving on the highway dicey, according to another fan, Jim Weddell. Anderson noted that "it was spitting a trace of snow," as he later told Wayne Jones. Back in Clear Lake, Bob Hale considered it far more than a trace. As he and his wife returned to their lakeside cottage, it was snowing "like mad," he later told Bill Griggs. He felt sure that Buddy's plane would never take off in such weather and took it for granted that the stars would spend the night in a hotel in Mason City and fly out the following day.

Jim Weddell confirmed in 1993 that the weather had turned nasty. "We were on our way home and it was a snowstorm, really blowing," he said. "I can't say that the snow was coming down that hard, but it was really blowing across the road. I remember the wind. That was the reason that we stayed at the Holiday Lounge in Clear Lake for a long time."

Mason City, which the stars now approached in Anderson's station wagon, bears the name of the Freemasons who wrested the area from Indians in the nineteenth century. Its population numbers thirty thousand. Buildings designed by Frank Lloyd Wright, the most influential architect of the century, can be found throughout the town, including the City National Bank and the Park Inn Hotel, both completed in 1909 and both classics of Wright's Prairie School style, featuring his trademark terra-cotta brick trims, flat roofs, and jutting eaves. During the ride to the airport, the rock stars rehashed the Surf show. " 'We had as much fun as the kids did,' they said," according to a story in the *Lubbock Avalanche-Journal* later the same week.

At the airport, Anderson deposited them at Dwyer's Flying Service. He later stated that it was 12:15 and their mood was "jubilant" because they were relieved to be flying out of the area despite the weather. When Anderson was quizzed by *Rave On!* in 1980 about a delay that developed at the airport, he explained that Peterson was having the flight "charted through the CAA." Though Anderson noticed "snow blowing across the runway," he looked up at the sky, noted that it was clear enough to see stars, and so failed to warn the young men of the danger of flying in such weather. Buddy asked about the distance to Fargo and was told it was 350 miles. Anderson later remembered that there was a pencil hanging by a string from a large wall map. Ritchie, the Bopper, and Buddy each measured the distance from their homes to Fargo—nine hundred miles for Buddy; one thousand miles for the Bopper; and almost two thousand miles for Ritchie.

Back in Clear Lake, Rod Lucier was still hoping to get the Moorhead show called off, but time was running out if he expected to stop the flight. The stars paid their fares, got back in the station wagon, drove onto the airfield, parked on the runway, and carried their luggage to the red and white Bonanza, which sat on runway 17, buffeted by the wind and looking more like a fragile child's toy than an airplane. With Roger Peterson's help, they crammed their bags into the small cockpit until it was cramped and uncomfortable.

The single-engine airplane, N3794N, had been in constant service for eleven years, with 1,238.20 hours of flying time, according to researchers Sue Frederick and Bill Griggs. A typical four-seat Beechcraft Bonanza model 35, it weighed 1,599 pounds empty and could carry 992 pounds. Its maximum speed was 184 miles per hour. Beechcraft had delivered it to the airplane sales division of the Butler Company of Chicago on October 23, 1947. N3794N was purchased on the same day by Dwight Rohn, who operated a flying service in Peoria. It had passed through four more owners by 1954, when Robert Stout of Des Moines bought it for $6,243. Two years later Stout sold it for $4,425. It would have three more owners before ending up in Dwyer's hangar at the Mason City Municipal Airport, Frederick later reported in *Reminiscing*.

N3794N was in perfect condition, Dwyer's mechanic, Charles McGlothlen, later told CAB investigator Van R. O'Brien. Since a recent overhaul, the plane had accumulated only forty hours' engine time, McGlothlen added. Cerro Gordo County Deputy Sheriff Duane Mayfield had taken it up three days previously and pronounced it "fit," Jeff Tecklenburg later revealed in the *Globe-Gazette*. As the musicians climbed aboard the aged aircraft, Anderson noticed "little spiffs" of snow, but again he raised no objection to the flight, even though such flurries often presage blinding storms. Sheriff Mayfield later confirmed that "snow showers" occurred on the night of the flight. As Alan Freed would later observe, "That Buddy Holly. . . . If you tied two orange crates together, put a wing on it, and said it would fly, he'd climb in and take off. He always wanted to get someplace ahead of the others."

Suddenly Billie Rose and the other fans who'd tailed them from Clear Lake pulled up and started yelling and waving. According to *Globe-Gazette* reporter Douglas Hines, they were trying to "stretch their evening with the stars a little longer." Billie Rose later described to Hines how the three singers prepared to board the plane as the kids yelled "like crazy teenagers." The fans shouted "Hey, thanks for the show" and the stars "waved and yelled back," Rose recalled.

Anderson later stated in *Rave On!* that the pilot was the first to enter the cockpit. Since the door was on the right front of the aircraft, Peterson crawled over to the pilot's seat on the left side and said, "Holly, why don't you ride abreast from me in the co-pilot's seat." Suddenly Buddy realized that he'd forgotten his briefcase. According to Anderson, he and Buddy went back to the station wagon and "picked it up." At some point Buddy observed, "Who knows how long I'll be on top," Anderson later told interviewers Mike Oestreicher and Pat Kennedy. The stars finally shook hands with Anderson and then climbed into the cockpit. The Bopper sat behind the pilot, Ritchie was beside the Bopper, and Buddy was in front.

Leaning from the plane, Peterson exchanged a few words with Anderson, who was standing on the runway. If later reports are correct, there were several problems that should have ended the flight before it began. Peterson was completely ignorant of two alarming weather advisories, according to Goldrosen and Beecher. Visibility was going to be poor due to snow and fog in Iowa. It wasn't any better in North Dakota; they were heading straight into a band of snow there. Additionally, Peterson was not as familiar with the plane's instruments as he might need to be, given the poor weather that night. This was especially true since he had failed his latest instrument flight check test in 1958. Also, Griggs would report in 1989 that Peterson's Airman's Certificate stated unequivocally, "Holder does not meet night-flight requirements."

Billie Rose later described the "beautiful snow" to reporter Douglas Hines but found it "really strange" when she considered "how treacherous" the skies were that night for flying. Despite these omens, Carroll Anderson closed the door and bid them "good luck," Anderson later told UPI correspondent Dan Wilinsky. The clearance was given, and the plane taxied down the runway. According to the *Chicago Tribune*, Jerry Dwyer stood in the control tower. He was waiting for Peterson to call in his flight plan by radio, according to Griggs. Dwyer was under the impression that his pilot "had taken a nap" during the afternoon and was competent to fly, he later testified before the CAB. He and Peterson had checked weather conditions several times together before takeoff, Dwyer added. The wind was from the south, gusting at 35 miles an hour, Dick Mettler, manager of the Mason City Municipal Airport, later stated. The temperature was 18 degrees, the dew point 11 according to an investigation conducted later by Coroner Ralph E. Smiley, M.D. Peterson would never have taken the plane aloft "if there had been any doubt in our minds about the weather conditions," Dwyer later told the CAB.

As the plane continued to taxi, Billie Rose pulled away in her car and sped off, heading for the Half Moon Inn, she later told Hines. On the runway, Peterson radioed the tower for additional information about the weather en route but received a briefing that was tragically "incomplete," both the CAB and Sheriff Mayfield subsequently confirmed. Unaware of the danger ahead, Peterson told the tower that he would file a flight plan after he was in the air. Airport files revealed in 1993 that takeoff occurred at "0040-0100"—about one A.M.—Tuesday, February 3, 1959, from runway 17. Dwyer, in the tower, and Anderson, on the ground, both saw the red light of the plane turn and begin a northwest course, toward Clear Lake.

"Ironically," a reporter from the *Lubbock Avalanche-Journal* later wrote, Rod Lucier, who was aware of the coming snowstorm, "telephoned the group's agency Monday night trying to call off the next appearance. Meanwhile, the plane carrying the singers took off."

Anderson climbed into his station wagon and drove away with Lucille and Tom. In the tower, Dwyer waited with mounting anxiety for Peterson to file his flight plan as promised. All that greeted him, as the coroner would shortly disclose, was radio silence. Two minutes after takeoff, Dwyer saw something he couldn't believe. " 'It looks like it just went down,' Dwyer reportedly said," according to the *Chicago Tribune*. "The other man in the tower said no, it was just an optical illusion."

But it wasn't. The plane was going down, though Peterson thought it was going up, according to *Globe-Gazette* reporters Jeremy Powers and Jeff Tecklenburg. Larry Holley, a licensed pilot, later told Griggs, "In any Beechcraft Bonanza with a 'V' tail, if you have the nose down even slightly, it'll pick up speed so fast that you'll be going down before you know it."

Peterson had encountered the weather front, which closed in on them just outside Clear Lake. As he flew into the snow, he may have lost visual reference. Though there were farmhouses in the fields below, nothing was visible but snow and eerie winter vapors. They were caught in a "terrible snowstorm," Powers and Tecklenburg wrote.

In such cases, the pilot "can either go above or below the snow showers," Sheriff Mayfield, a licensed pilot, later observed. The Bonanza "had an automatic pilot" and had Mayfield been flying the plane, he'd "have turned it on and climbed on top of the snow," he said. But Roger Peterson "probably wound up underneath the snow shower and found himself too low," he added.

Peterson looked at the gauges and tried to interpret them, according to a CAB report. His chronic vertigo may have compounded his confusion and caused him to read the gyroscope backward, so he thought he was accelerating up just as he went into a power dive. They were going to crash under full power. Down below, a few farmers stirred in their sleep, recognizing the sounds of a plane in trouble. Reeve Eldridge noted, "Woke out of a sound sleep by motor roar. Sounded smooth but pulling, as though climbing." Another farmer, Delbert Juhl, said the "motor was working pretty good and he had it going pretty good, and that was the last we heard of it." What these witnesses were hearing was a plane struggling to gain altitude. Peterson had perhaps realized his mistake too late and was trying to correct it, according to both Sheriff Mayfield and the current director of aviation at the Mason City Municipal Airport, Jerome J. Thiele.

Inside the cabin, there was likely a moment of nauseating panic as the ground rushed up at them. The young stars, idols of a generation, were more sure of their invincibility than ordinary mortals, but the unthinkable was happening. There was perhaps a second to blurt frantic prayers. They were facing one of the least desirable of ends; *The Book of Common Prayer* states, "Good Lord, deliver us from lightning and tempest, from earthquake, fire, and flood, from plague, pestilence, and famine, from battle and murder and sudden death."

The plane came in level, Sheriff Jerry Allen later told Griggs. It hit the pasture at cruising speed, according to Bob Booe, a KCRG-TV employee from Cedar Rapids, Iowa, who would view the wreck later that day. The recommended cruising speed was 172 miles per hour, Sue Fredcrick reported in her article, "The Airplane—N3794N." At that speed, everyone on board must have died instantly. The landing gear was still retracted, according to FAA investigator Eugene Anderson. The position of the wheels offers strong evidence that Peterson was unaware that the plane was going down; and, therefore, that the crash was not an emergency landing. Upon impact with the ground, the fuselage split open instantly, Booe later told interviewer Kevin Terry. Buddy and Ritchie shot from the wreck like circus performers blasted from a canon, flying seventeen feet, according to the coroner's report, and striking the ground with what must have been sickening thuds.

The crash was by no means over. The Bopper was still in the plane, which bounced out of the crater it had dug and continued across the field. The left wing snagged the ground and dug a furrow fifty feet long before crumpling off. The plane then cartwheeled and skidded through the stubble and snow until it was reduced to a ball. Five hundred and seventy feet from the point of impact, it finally crashed into the fence line, hurling the Bopper "40 feet from the wreckage, across the fence in a picked cornfield," Coroner Smiley later noted. Only Roger Peterson remained in the plane.

Buddy's head had slammed against the ground with such force that his skull cracked open from his forehead to his crown. Half of his brain tissue seeped down onto the rough stubble field. According to his death certificate, blood gushed from both ears. His face was disfigured by deep, jagged gashes. So many of his ribs were pulverized that the consistency of his chest was soft. His left forearm was fractured, his right elbow broken, and both of his thighs and legs had multiple fractures. "There was a small laceration of the scrotum," wrote the coroner.

The bodies remained out in the snow for ten hours after the crash. As I discovered researching this book, some people in the area were aware of the accident shortly after it happened—including at least one police officer—but, no doubt, they could not search the countryside for wreckage in the dark. As the coroner would later write in his report, it snowed through the night, and drifts formed around the bodies. "Some parts of each body had been frozen by the ten hours' exposure in temperature reported to have been near 18 degrees during that time," Dr. Smiley added. Scattered all about them were Buddy's pistol, eyeglasses, and diamond-studded Omega, the Bopper's dice, and Ritchie's crucifix. Ritchie had landed on his face, close to Buddy. His brains and most of his skull were gone. His features were flattened beyond recognition. His right eye socket was empty. Both arms were shattered.

The Bopper, like a tenacious cowpoke on a bucking bronc from hell, had stayed with the plane until it hit the fence, which threw him into the adjoining field. He came down on his head, his skull splitting clockwise from his eyes to his crown. His brain was almost completely eviscerated. The right side of his face was misshapen and mangled beyond recognition. The bones in his arms, legs, and chest were practically pulped.

Trapped and enmeshed in the instruments he'd never learned to read, Roger Peterson was sticking upside down in the wreckage, one foot jutting crazily into the night sky. His body was wrapped around the instrument panel and bound to it by a spiky thicket of wires, cables, broken glass, and twisted metal. Roger Peterson looked as if he were disappearing into the jaws of a giant predator. His skin had been flayed from much of his body. His brain stem had been destroyed. His aorta was severed. His heart, lungs, liver, spleen, and right adrenal gland were ruptured and lacerated, and there were "multiple traumatic fractures" in his skull, sternum, six-teen ribs, pelvis, arms, right elbow, wrists, knees, and legs, and his right thumb had been amputated.

All four men died of gross trauma to the brain, the coroner later de-creed. Had any of them survived, they would have perished in the sub-freezing weather, though their bodies lay just 5.4 miles north of Clear Lake. At last, shortly before dawn, the Mason City Municipal Airport is-sued an alert. The reason given for the delay in finding the bodies was "early morning fog," the *Globe-Gazette* reported in its issue of February 3.

The crash raises serious questions about private aviation and the gov-ernmental agencies that regulate it. The real tragedy of February 3, 1959, was that it didn't have to happen. The Civil Aeronautics Board even-tually laid much of the blame on an incomplete weather briefing and the pilot's unfamiliarity with the plane's instruments.

Jim Weddell, who attended the Surf dance, first heard about the crash between three and four A.M. on February 3, approximately six hours *before* the authorities recovered the bodies, he revealed in a 1993 interview. Weddell and his two friends were driving home after the show when they decided to pull into an all-night truck stop in Belmond, Iowa, thirty miles out of Clear Lake. Someone from the Mason City area came in and said, "There's a plane down." Adds Weddell in 1993, "No one knew who the victims were until the next morning."

"What you're saying alters the historic record," I point out. "John Goldrosen, Bill Griggs, all the Holly experts are under the impression that no one knew about the crash until Dwyer discovered the bodies the next morning, around nine-thirty."

"I know," says Weddell, "but we heard about it at three or four o'clock in the morning at that truck stop."

While inspecting the files of the Mason City Airport Commission, I came across reporter Douglas Hines's 1989 article in the *Globe-Gazette*, which seems to corroborate Weddell's testimony. Billie Rose, the fan who'd driven to the airport, went to the Half Moon Inn, a supper club, after waving good-bye to the stars. While she and her friends were eating, a policeman came in and told everyone that Buddy, Ritchie, and the Bopper had been killed in the plane crash. "It really blew our minds," Rose told Hines. "We thought it was a pretty sick joke." Contacted in 1995, Cindy Florer, who works at the Half Moon Inn, which is still in business, two blocks from the Surf (on the renamed Buddy Holly Ave-nue), said the restaurant usually remains open until about two o'clock in the morning.

Throughout the night, Dwyer attempted to reach control towers in Iowa, Minnesota, and the Dakotas, according to Goldrosen and Beecher, but no one had heard from N3794N. February 3 dawned a hazy, chilly day with a low overcast. Dwyer at last went looking for his plane, flying a two-seat Champ, sometimes as low as twenty-five feet from the ground, Bob Booe later told Terry. At 9:35 A.M., eight and a half hours after the crash, Dwyer spotted the wreck, he later told CAB investigators. But in the official report of Cerro Gordo County Coroner Ralph E. Smiley, the time was placed at "about 9:00 A.M.," and, later, Chief Deputy Sheriff Mayfield told the *Globe-Gazette* reporter Jeff Tecklenburg that it was around 8:40 A.M. when dispatcher Esther Cook rang him with news of the crash. These discrepancies lend credence to the possibility that the people in the area knew about the crash before Dwyer spotted it. Elwin L. Musser, the *Globe-Gazette* photographer who photographed the crash site later that day, reveals in a 1995 interview that he heard the news "just after I got to work at 8:15."

As Dwyer flew over the wreck that morning, Buddy's yellow leather jacket was the one bright spot in the carnage. The coroner later noted that the force of the impact was so horrendous that all four seams in the jacket were split from collar to hem. Dwyer radioed the location to authorities. Booe later told Terry, "Jerry said, 'They're in a pasture . . . I think they're all dead.'" A ham radio operator overheard Dwyer and leaked the information to the local station, scoring one of the scoops of the decade. (The only event comparable in the world of music occurred over two decades later, when John Lennon was killed in New York City outside the Dakota, his apartment building, in 1980.) After the leak that morning in 1959, the news of the plane crash was broadcast around the world.

In New York, Lou Giordano telephoned Maria Elena. Later, in a 1993 interview, she was asked, "When did you lose the baby?"

"When I got the news," she replied. "I was sick in bed that day. As soon as I heard, the following day I lost the baby."

"Was it too early to know whether it was a boy or a girl?"

"It was too early. I was just starting out."

Lou Giordano tried to break it to her gently, asking her if she had her radio on or was watching TV. As soon as Lou determined that Maria Elena had not yet heard, he hung up and left for her apartment. Puzzled and curious, Maria Elena went directly from the phone to the TV and turned it on. It was a brutal way to hear. (In the months following the tragedy, no longer would the names of accident victims be broadcast before notification of next of kin.) Fortunately for Maria Elena, she was not alone in her apartment. Aunt Provi entered the room during the newscast. The cause of Maria Elena's miscarriage was attributed to psychological trauma, according to *Parade* magazine.

In Lubbock, Ella Holley screamed and collapsed in sobs, Ken Johnson, associate pastor of Tabernacle Baptist Church, later stated. A well-meaning but insensitive neighbor had called her on the phone. "Put the radio on," she said, Griggs later reported. "There's some news about your son." According to Ken Johnson, the announcer mentioned "an airplane crash in Iowa," but Mrs. Holley instinctively turned the radio off to keep from hearing the worst. Just then she looked around and saw a contingent from the Tabernacle Baptist Church arriving on her porch that included Ben D. Johnson and Ken Johnson. "Oh, no! It can't be true," she cried, Ken Johnson said in 1993. The ministers calmed her and then prayed with her.

Later both preachers stepped out on the back porch for a word with Buddy's brothers, Larry and Travis. "Maybe it was just the Lord's will to take him before he got so deep in rock 'n' roll," said Ken Johnson in 1993. "Otherwise his testimony would have been rock 'n' roll rather than the Lord Jesus Christ." Larry Holley's statements in a 1992 interview indicate that he agreed with Johnson. "The Lord figured He could probably get more actual witnessing to a bigger group of people through me and some of the rest of us that were left," Larry said. But Carl Bunch, also a deeply religious person, told Griggs, "God doesn't go around killing people. He's not a murderer. God gives but He doesn't take away."

Carl learned of Buddy's death when his mother called him long-distance at the hospital in Michigan. Medicated with painkillers for his frostbitten feet, Carl was resting in bed when a nurse put him in a wheelchair and took him down the hallway to a pay phone. People were staring at him strangely, and he couldn't decide if the weird feelings coming over him were due to their curiosity or the drugs.

"Honey, what are you going to do now?" his mother asked, Bunch later recounted in *Reminiscing*.

"Mom, I'm going to be okay," he said, misunderstanding her. "My feet are just fine."

"No, honey. I mean, what are you going to do *now*?"

"Well, Mama, just as quickly as I can get thawed out, I'm gonna join Buddy out on the road."

"No, darling. You just don't understand."

After she explained it to him, he returned to his room, grieving and frightened. Back in bed, he looked up and saw three schoolgirls in the doorway, crying. One said her name was Rose. They had stayed out of school that day because they'd heard the late Buddy Holly's drummer was in the hospital. Carl thanked them and said they made him feel "special." Though he'd often been onstage, playing with rock bands, he'd never felt like an exceptional human being before. In gratitude, he tried to cheer the girls up but then started crying himself. "It's so strange," he told Griggs in 1981. "It's hard to believe that it really happened, that they all died out there that way."

"A cult is a phenomenon built on collective will, a confirmation that something of significance has occurred and must be kept alive," writes David Dalton in his landmark biography of James Dean, *The Mutant King*. A cult is also a form of denial, a refusal to let go of a beloved icon. The legend of Buddy Holly was born the day he died, when fans like fourteen-year-old Don McLean began to mourn him. Delivering newspapers on his route that morning in New Rochelle, New York, McLean cut open a bale of papers and read the horrifying dispatch. "That was a miserable day for me," McLean recalled in *Reminiscing*. And in a *Life* interview, he said, "Buddy Holly was the first and last person I ever really idolized as a kid." A dozen years later McLean's "American Pie," the biggest record of 1972, identified February 3, 1959, as the day early rock 'n' roll passed into history.

Future C&W star Ronnie Milsap heard the news while a student at the Governor Morehead School for the Blind near Raleigh, North Carolina. He'd been a fan of Buddy's since first hearing him on the radio. "He sounded so sincere," Milsap recalled in his autobiography *Almost Like a Song*. "And he wasn't that much older than I was! It was like being hit with a tow sack full of wet cement the day they told me that Holly and the others had died. It was like losing a member of the family. . . . His music, and that of other pioneer rock 'n' rollers, had unleashed the anger of America's parents. . . . Buddy must have undergone harassment similar to what I received from the Morehead music teachers. So I felt close to him." Milsap and a friend decided to stage their own private wake for "our fallen heroes," playing and singing all their hits in the Governor Morehead music building. They were discovered by their overly strict music teacher, who was so outraged to find them singing rock 'n' roll that both boys were banned from all future music programs at the school. Later, Milsap went on to score thirty-five C&W chart toppers, including "A Legend in My Time," "Happy, Happy Birthday Baby," and "Lost in the Fifties Tonight (In the Still of the Night)."

In the Midwest, the reaction to Buddy's death on the morning of February 3 provided another sign that Buddy was quickly ascending to the realm of myth and legend. "I mean, I'll never forget the image of seeing Buddy Holly up on the bandstand," Bob Dylan, who'd caught Buddy in Duluth on January 31, later told *Rolling Stone*'s Kurt Loder. "And he died—it must have been a week after that. It was unbelievable." Dylan added, in *Newsweek*, "The music of the late Fifties and early Sixties when music was at that root level—that for me is meaningful music. The singers and musicians I grew up with transcend nostalgia. Buddy Holly and Johnny Ace are just as valid to me today as then."

After Jim Weddell and his friends left the Belmond truck stop where they'd first learned of the crash, they drove the remaining fifteen miles home, to Clarion. "We didn't have school that day because there was so much snow," he recalls in 1993. "We heard the names of the victims about midmorning. I was just shocked, really. Being there, and somebody getting killed the same night."

Bob Hale, the Surf MC, was spinning records on the morning shift at radio station KRIB in Mason City. Blood drained from his face as a telephone caller told him the news. "I just lifted the needle off the record and told everybody," he later said to Ken Fuson of the *Des Moines Sunday Register*. Within an hour, stunned teenagers flocked to the station in their cars, driving back and forth in front of KRIB with their radios on, hoping to hear a retraction.

DeAnn Peterson was at work at radio station KGLO in Mason City when her husband's obituary came over the wire machine, according to Carroll Anderson. "I was young and he was gone," DeAnn later told the AP. Her life was "shattered," she said; she'd "never get over" Roger's death. DeAnn was twenty-one. Eventually she would move to Minneapolis, get a job in the personnel department of Northeast Orient Airlines, and remarry. She never forgot Roger, however, and stayed in touch with his parents. Pearl Peterson, Roger's grief-stricken mother, blamed the crash on the rock stars, telling the AP that Buddy, Ritchie, and the Bopper should have taken the bus to Moorhead with the rest of the tour party.

In Lubbock, Sonny Curtis tried to shake Jerry Allison out of a deep sleep. "Hey, man, I've got something real bad to tell you," Sonny said, according to Jerry Allison. It was ten A.M. on February 3. Sonny had slept on the living-room couch at Jerry and Peggy Sue's place after their return from Clovis the previous night. A woman who lived across the street had broken the news to Sonny. Jerry refused to accept it. "I thought that there might have been a plane crash, and that Buddy might have been around it, but he couldn't be dead, he couldn't possibly be," Jerry later told Griggs. Joe B. convinced himself it was all a publicity stunt. His sister kept trying to convince him that the news was real and finally said, in exasperation, "No, no, go out and get the newspaper and look at the headlines."

It was Jerry who told Norman Petty. In a 1978 interview, Griggs asked Petty for his reaction and Petty uttered a single word: "Catastrophic." Robert Linville, one of Buddy's backup singers, describing the scene in Clovis that morning, said he rushed to the Pettys' upstairs apartment and found both Norman and Vi weeping. All three of their telephones were ringing and the callers were saying, pleadingly, "It's not true," but Norman, Vi, and Linville kept telling everyone, "Yes, it is. New York just called." Linville remembers remaining at the Pettys all day "and the phones never stopped ringing."

DJ Snuff Garrett hastily rounded up the Crickets and Petty for telephone interviews on KSYD in Wichita Falls. Petty was characteristically evasive and defensive when Garrett asked if Buddy Holly fans could look forward to any unreleased tapes. "It depends," said Petty. He mentioned the possibility of litigation and refused to discuss the matter further.

At Decca Records in New York, Dick Jacobs sat at his desk planning Buddy's next Coral session. He hadn't yet seen the Associated Press account in the *New York Daily News*, which was replete with photographs of Buddy, Ritchie, and the Bopper as well as a staff artist's map detailing the projected flight from Mason City to Fargo. The *Daily News* ran the story inside the paper, but the editor did at least assign it three columns and a thirty-six-point bold headline, 3 STARS OF ROCK 'N' ROLL KILLED. The page-one significance of Holly's death would only be realized over time.

"Did you hear the news?" one of Dick Jacobs's colleagues inquired, advising him to sit down. Buddy had been Jacobs's favorite artist on the label. Now he found himself unable to speak. He sat at his desk and burst into sobs. Later he closed his office for the day and went home. "It wasn't a question of losing an artist," he later told Wayne Jones. "I had lost a friend."

Over at Alan Freed's *Big Beat* television show, Freed observed before he went on camera, "Crazy, isn't it, that his new hit is called 'It Doesn't Matter Anymore'? I know it matters to me and to all those kids who loved him . . . and to his wife, Maria Elena." Then Freed walked into the studio and requested a minute of silent prayer. Roy Hamilton, the powerful Georgia baritone whose "Unchained Melody" was the best-selling R&B record of 1955, sang "You'll Never Walk Alone."

GAC's reaction was characteristic of its behavior toward the performers throughout the tour. "We always fought against the idea of any of them chartering their own planes," said Tim Gale. Mindful of the bottom line, Gale decided that the decimated "Winter Dance Party" "would be continued to its conclusion." On Tuesday morning, February 3, Waylon, Tommy, Dion, the Belmonts, and Frankie Sardo were still en route to Moorhead, unaware that they'd lost their headliners and that GAC would expect them to go on as if nothing had happened.

In Los Angeles, at James Monroe High School, kids were standing in groups around the playground between the second and third period classes. Rock 'n' roll was blaring from several transistor radios but suddenly

there was an announcement and then all the radios were turned off.
Everyone looked over toward Donna Ludwig, who was sitting on a bench
apart from the others. When one of her friends approached, she glanced
up and smiled. Then she noticed that the girl had tears in her eyes. Donna
stood up and asked her what was the matter.

"You'd better sit down, Donna," she said, according to an article in 16.
"Ritchie is dead. We just heard it on the radio." Donna couldn't believe
it and rushed to a pay phone to call Concepcion Valenzuela. Ernestine
Reyes answered the phone. "Pray for us, Donna," she said. "Pray for
Ritchie." Then Concepcion came on the line and said, "Will you come
over after school, Donna? I want to see you."

Back in Clear Lake, at roughly the same time that morning, the cornfield
was finally abuzz with activity both around the bodies and in the air
overhead. "The macabre fascination that surrounds violent death in general and that of celebrities in particular descended on Clear Lake," Douglas Hines later wrote in the *Globe-Gazette*. A half mile from where the
bodies lay, Wallace Johnson, a farmer, was rattled by buzzing airplanes.
"It was like a war zone," he told Hines. At first he couldn't figure why
"fifty or sixty airplanes" were circling the area, and then he heard the
news on the radio.

Cerro Gordo County Sheriff Jerry Allen was away in St. Louis on a
criminal investigation, but Allen's deputy Duane Mayfield took charge
and set up roadblocks. Deputy Sheriff Bill McGill pulled up to the wreckage, accompanied by patrol cars carrying reporters, photographers, and
television cameramen. *Life* magazine had already requested photos. By
9:45 A.M., curiosity seekers were getting out of hand. Souvenir hunters
wanted to dismantle the plane and carry it away in pieces, Mayfield later
told Tecklenburg.

At 11:15 A.M.—ten hours and fifteen minutes after the crash—black
Cadillac hearses advanced across the field, bumping over the cornrows
covered by the previous night's snowfall and finally nosing up to the
corpses. It could have been a scene from an early Robert Altman film.
Carroll Anderson arrived to assist with identifications, but even with his
help it was impossible. The boys were disfigured beyond recognition. Further confusion developed when five billfolds were found—and only four
bodies. Buddy had been carrying Tommy Allsup's wallet in his pocket.
Anderson later told Wayne Jones that one of the patrolmen brought the
wallet to him and asked if Tommy Allsup was Buddy Holly's real name?
"As far as I know, Buddy Holly is a real name," Anderson replied.
Throughout the morning the key issue was "Buddy Holly and whether
he was Tommy Allsup," Anderson said. The first UPI release listed
Tommy Douglas Allsup as one of the dead.

Photographer Elwin L. Musser's wide-angle photo of the crash site is as stark as an Ingmar Bergman winterscape. In the foreground, Stetson-hatted Deputy Sheriff Lowell Sandquist squats before a wheel that had come loose and gone wobbling across the pasture. In the background, a dozen figures hunch in the cold, staring at debris and dead bodies. They include Eugene Anderson, crash investigator; Coroner Smiley; Deputy Sheriff McGill; Walt Schreader, Dwyer's attorney; Jim Collison of the *Globe-Gazette*; Andy Anderson of the *Clear Lake Mirror-Reporter*; funeral-home directors Dick Van Slyker and Wendell Wilcox; and Carroll Anderson. To cub reporter Collison the scene was heartbreaking. "It was my first assignment," he later told Kevin Terry, "and I'd just rather forget the whole ordeal."

Elwin Musser, who had been a U.S. Navy combat photographer during World War II, remembers picking his way between the corpses and the wreckage, snapping pictures with his Speed Graphic. "The wire services were clamoring for photos," he says, but mainly he was concerned with the deadline for the *Globe-Gazette*'s early afternoon edition. Altogether he shot eight photographs, which in the coming years would prove to be the most requested prints from the *Globe-Gazette*'s morgue. Buddy and Ritchie "were lying face-down," Musser remembers, but the Bopper "was terribly broken and twisted." Buddy's coat, he recalls, was light, almost shiny. After a while, Musser left the scene, walking back to the road with Deputy Sheriff Lowell Sandquist.

Morticians Van Slyker and Wilcox stood consulting with Coroner Smiley. Carroll Anderson joined them and then they "gathered Buddy up" and took his body to the morgue. "We have two morgues here and two bodies went to each," Anderson later told Wayne Jones.

The police were hesitant to touch the instruments that enfolded Roger Peterson. They decided to wait until government officials arrived that evening to conduct their investigations. Guards were posted. Hours later, according to Smiley, a crew of field representatives headed by C. E. Stillwagon of the CAB and A. J. Prokop of the FAA poked around in the debris, taking notes. Then, Smiley added, Deputy Sheriffs McGill and Sandquist, using metal cutting tools, opened a space in the wreckage and extricated Roger Peterson. It was the point where fact and legend exchanged places, and neither, like the bodies themselves, could ever be fully extricated clearly anymore.

Smiley took money from their pockets and paid himself, according to the coroner's report. From the $193 Dr. Smiley found on Buddy's body, he kept $10 for "Inquest or investigation"; 65 cents for "mileage, 7 cents per mile"; and $1 for "docket case"—a total of $11.65. He extracted the same amount from each of the bodies. Ritchie had been carrying $22.15 in cash; two $50 Hollywood, California, bank checks; a religious medal; and a bracelet with a "Donna" charm. The Bopper had been carrying $202 and a guitar pick. Peterson had $20 in cash and a check from Dwyer for $130.55.

The remains of Buddy and Roger Peterson were arterially embalmed at the G. W. Wilcox Funeral Home in Clear Lake Tuesday night, February 3–4. Ritchie and the Bopper were taken to the Ward Funeral Home. Again Carroll Anderson attempted to identify the bodies. They were unable to recognize Ritchie until they saw his tattoo, "RV.," on the underside of his right forearm. They still weren't sure about Buddy, Carroll Anderson later told Wayne Jones. Larry Holley reveals in a 1992 interview that he immediately made plans to fly to Clear Lake on Wednesday, February 4.

According to Bill Griggs, Peterson was the only one of the four victims autopsied. That the other bodies were not autopsied would later lead to various controversies, including allegations of drug use and violence and gunfire aboard the doomed plane in its final minutes. Jerry Dwyer allegedly told Kevin Terry that four autopsies were done and later reportedly implied that the autopsy reports were " 'missing,' or covered up," Bill Griggs reported in 1989. No proof of irregularities of this nature has yet come to light.

Smiley and Dr. George T. Joyce carried out the autopsy on Roger Peterson at Mercy Hospital in Mason City. Smiley's report reveals the amount of crushing that a human being undergoes in a plane crash. When slight pressure was applied to certain areas of Peterson's skin, "multiple small fragments of bone" came through. When moved, his wrist crackled and rattled. Comminuted fractures had turned some bones into powder. The jagged ends of sixteen broken ribs had virtually minced his internal organs. Peterson's family was charged a $100 autopsy fee.

In Los Angeles, after school on that Tuesday, Donna Ludwig tried to make her way through the large crowd that was gathering in Ritchie's neighborhood. Finally she arrived at the pink stucco house at 13428 Remmington that Ritchie had bought for his mother. Hundreds of students throughout the northern part of the San Fernando Valley stood in hushed groups, many of them crying, and were admitted to the house a dozen at a time to express their sympathy to Ritchie's family. The press was there in force, and flashbulbs were popping. As Donna pushed her way through the throng, she became impatient. "We finally got in with all those assholes around," she later said, according to Mendheim.

Inside the house at last, Donna found Concepcion sitting beside a small shrine she'd made to Ritchie—a table with his picture, some flowers, and his guitars: a Gibson and the turquoise green one he'd first played on. Maintaining an expression of pride and self-respect, Concepcion rocked back and forth as Ritchie's classmates and fans passed before her, sharing their love and concern. Donna was clinging to her. "I was so proud of him," Concepcion said. She spoke of the days when Ritchie was still a toddler and how, even then, he used to sing and wag his toy guitar around on the floor. "He had the music in him," she said. "There hasn't been enough time," she added, explaining that Ritchie had once rung her from Hawaii and invited her to vacation there with him some day. "We had so many places to go." She sighed.

Finally, the terrible day of February 3, 1959, ended. But a grim aftermath was just beginning. In the darkness of midnight, around one A.M., Wednesday, February 4, the police gained admittance to Wilcox Funeral Home and asked to see Buddy's body, which had already been embalmed and placed in a coffin. Duane Mayfield revealed to Tecklenburg in 1989 that they fingerprinted the bodies "while they were in the caskets." It was a "tough" job, especially at that hour of the morning, said Mayfield.

Later that morning, according to the *Mirror-Reporter*, Ritchie's body was shipped to California. Ritchie's half-brother Bob Morales and Bob Keene identified him, Mendheim later disclosed. The body was then taken to the Noble Chapel Funeral Home in San Fernando. In Donna's home at 10861 Paso Robles Avenue, she prepared to go to school, dressing in a black sweater and black skirt. Before she left the house, she placed a gold-framed photograph of Ritchie in a black tote bag and proceeded to James Monroe High School in Sepulveda. The entire school was in mourning—the flag was at half mast and a boy from the school band played taps. After school, a group of girls went to St. John de la Salle Catholic Church to pray and light candles.

The rosary ceremony took place at ten A.M. on Friday, February 6, at St. Ferdinand Catholic Church, where Ritchie had been baptized. Bob Keene said he paid for Ritchie's $7,000 funeral. Requiem Mass was celebrated the following day at ten A.M. at St. Ferdinand's. Though the day was dismal and damp, a thousand mourners attended. Several policemen stood guard, expecting the largely Chicano crowd to riot. Donna Ludwig knocked a photographer's camera from his hands when he attempted to take her picture. Though Ritchie and Donna had broken up, Donna would soon make a record called "Lost Without You"/ "Now That You're Gone." She did so, according to Mendheim, only because "my silly father went and got me an agent. . . . I seem to have been hoodwinked into that song." At the funeral, Donna comforted Concepcion, who wore a black scarf over her graying hair, a black dress, and a full, lighter colored coat. She was surrounded by her children, Bobbie, Connie, Irma, and Mario, ranging in age from seventeen to two. As fans crowded around, she described Ritchie as "a good boy . . . a praying boy" who always came to St. Ferdinand's "to light his candles."

As Ritchie's funeral began, Sharon Sheeley, Eddie Cochran's fiancée, broke down at the sight of his coffin, which writer Marcia Borie later described in *Photoplay* as a modest brown casket. It was borne by members of Ritchie's band, the Silhouettes. The officiant, Rev. Edward M. Lynch, O.M.I., offered the prayer: "O gentlest Heart of Jesus, ever present in the Blessed Sacrament, ever consumed with burning love for poor captive souls in Purgatory, have mercy on the soul of Thy departed servant." This was followed by "The Hail Mary": "Hail, Mary, full of grace; the Lord is with thee: blessed art thou among women, and blessed is the fruit of thy womb, Jesus. Holy Mary, Mother of God, pray for us sinners, now and at the hour of our death. Amen."

The burial was at the San Fernando Mission Cemetery. Concepcion stood looking over the huge floral mound that covered her son's grave, which was surrounded by elaborate funeral wreaths arranged on tall stands, including one in the shape of a cross. As the crowd dispersed, a crew-cut youth from the Drifters, a car club in the Valley, told Bob Keene that Ritchie had been an "honorary member" of the Drifters. He took a wadded piece of paper from his leather jacket and began to read a poem. Entitled "Our Boy—in Memory of Ritchie Valens," it described Ritchie as someone who'd always been as happy-go-lucky as a mockingbird; then, as sudden as a violent storm, their "dearest friend" was taken from them, and now he was in God's arms.

Following the funeral, Gil Rocha, who played vibes for the Silhouettes, went home "and cried like a baby for a very long time," he later told Mendheim. No stone would mark Ritchie Valens's grave until money was raised some time later at a memorial dance. Eventually, the stone was engraved with these words, which reflected Ritchie's dual identity as son and rock star: BELOVED SON—RICHARD S. VALENZUELA—RITCHIE VALENS—1941–1959. The dominant motif on the gravestone was a large cross with the initials IHS (the first three letters of the Greek spelling of Jesus). An engraving of a rosary with a crucifix was draped over the transverse piece of the cross. Beneath Ritchie's name were some musical notes from his first hit, "Come On—Let's Go."

*

The Bopper's death certificate revealed that his body was sent home from Clear Lake on Wednesday by private plane. He was taken to the Broussard Funeral Home in Beaumont, Texas. In her third trimester with their second child, his wife arrived from New Orleans, where she and their daughter Deborah had been visiting, according to the *Clear Lake Mirror-Reporter*. Adrianne had heard the news when it was blurted over KTRM, the station where her husband had worked. Gordon Baxter, the Bopper's colleague at KTRM, later acknowledged that it was "a horrible thing," explaining that when an important bulletin came over the wire machines, a siren went off at the station, and the announcer on duty automatically read it on the air.

The Bopper's widow later told *TV Movie and Record Stars* magazine that she was giving the Bopper's guitar to Dion, whom she singled out as the Bopper's best friend on the tour. Elvis Presley and Col. Tom Parker sent a telegram of condolence to the Bopper's mother, reporter Carol Gales would reveal on the occasion of the unveiling of a statue of the Bopper, Buddy, and Ritchie in Beaumont thirty years later. During the funeral service, an altercation broke out when a photographer from *Life* allegedly attempted to pose three weeping fans as they threw themselves over the coffin. According to writer Randall C. Hill, the photographer was "bodily ejected" from the church.

Gordon Baxter recalled that during the Bopper's sleepless Disc-A-Thon in 1957, the Bopper experienced a hallucination in which he'd foreseen his own death, later reporting that "the other side . . . wasn't all that bad." After his funeral, the streets of Beaumont were lined with fans as a long procession of cars followed the hearse to the cemetery. Baxter ran the board at KTRM, playing the Bopper's favorite songs, including "When the Saints Go Marchin' In." According to Baxter, the Bopper was "a spiritual kind of guy." The way to really understand him, Baxter said, was to "turn out the lights some night" and play the Bopper's Mercury recording of "Someone's Watching Over You." When the record was released the following month, it received a "Pick" in *Billboard*, the reviewer hailing it as "a sacred offering with simple, but effective choral backing. . . . Sure to reap heavy spins." But the Bopper would never again make the Top 40.

Roger Peterson had two funerals—one on February 5 at the Redeemer Lutheran Church in Ventura, a village of five hundred a few miles west of Clear Lake, and another on the following day at St. Paul's Lutheran Church in Alta. In attendance were his widow DeAnn, his parents Pearl and Arthur E. Peterson, two brothers, Ronald and Robert, his sister, Janet, and his grandmother, Mrs. Elmer A. Peterson. He was buried in the Storm Lake Memorial Cemetery. His grave marker bears an airplane insignia, Buddy Holly fan Bruce Wilcox reported in *Reminiscing.*

A grieving Pearl Peterson was still angry at Buddy, Ritchie, and the Bopper and would continue to blame them for her son's death, telling an Associated Press reporter in February 1988—twenty-nine years after the crash—"If it wouldn't be for those guys having to go out that night, they'd all be here today." Despite her resentment, she was gracious when Bruce Wilcox sought her out in 1980. Pearl served "a delicious lunch" of ham, cheese, home-baked bread, and a "super good cherry dessert," Wilcox recalled. Later, Pearl sobbed when she attempted to discuss her son. At least they could now listen to the radio without cringing every time a song by Buddy, Ritchie, or the Bopper was played, Art Peterson said. By 1988 he could tell the AP, "The music doesn't bother us now. We've gotten used to it."

Buddy's funeral was announced for Saturday, February 7, in Lubbock. To retrieve his body from Clear Lake, Larry chartered a plane at West Texas Aircraft and flew to Mason City on Wednesday, February 4, accompanied by his brother-in-law J. E. Weir. They went directly to the Wilcox Funeral Home in Clear Lake, where Larry was asked to go inside the chapel and view the body. Larry refused. "I just wanted to remember Buddy like he was when he was little," Larry said in 1992. "I didn't want to remember him all beat up." As Larry paused outside the chapel, trying to picture Buddy "laughing, hollering, and cutting up," J. E. Weir went inside and lifted the casket lid. He took one look and vomited. Later he told Larry, "He was so tore up. I'm glad you didn't go in there."

They drove out to the pasture, where two FAA investigators, bundled in heavy parkas, boots, and fur-lined hoods, had been collecting scraps of metal since shortly after sunrise. It was snowing, which made their work more difficult. The FAA team, Eugene Anderson and Fred Becchetti, both of Des Moines, pulled and poked at the wreckage, which now was almost half covered with snow. Dwyer said he didn't have the "faintest idea" why it had happened, according to the February 3 *Globe-Gazette.* In Dwyer's estimation, the craft had been in good condition, the pilot was competent, and weather had been good. Dick Mettler, the airport manager, conferred with the investigators but "could wind up with only one question, 'How in the world did it happen?'", Collison wrote in the February 5 *Globe-Gazette.*

Buddy's brother thought he had the answer. "We went out in the snow and saw the plane wreck," Larry said in 1992. Earlier, in a 1979 interview, he explained, "They had just installed a Sperry gyroscope on that plane, and they work just the opposite of the other ones. In one, the little airplane goes up and down in the little window, and in the other, the background changes. This kid, Roger Peterson . . . [was] reading the instruments backwards." Later, the CAB would confirm that Peterson "misread the instrument," according to Powers and Tecklenburg.

A large pile of clothes had been stacked in the middle of the field. "It was a very colorful pile, reds and greens," Larry recalls in 1992, "nice jackets and pants stacked real high."

"Do you want these?" someone had inquired. Unable to distinguish Buddy's belongings from the others, Larry replied, "Naw, I don't want 'em."

"These are Buddy's clothes," he was told. "What do you want to do with them?" Deep in anger and grief, Larry snapped, "Get rid of them. Burn them. Give them away—whatever. I don't want to see them again." Later he had second thoughts, he recalls in 1992. "Just as I was leavin', I picked up this little ol' dop kit because I had seen Buddy carrying it many times and knew it was his. It had some tooth powder that had come open and everything was white. There was a prescription or two in there for cold medicine, a razor, a comb, stuff like that."

Several fans, including teenager Gary Edward Keillor—later known as humorist Garrison Keillor—were standing around watching. The officials were cleaning up by Wednesday, Keillor recalled in a 1993 television newscast. They didn't do a very thorough job—Buddy's pistol would remain hidden in the snow until spring plowing, according to an April 10, 1959, story in the *Globe-Gazette*. The wreckage of N3794N was finally loaded on a flatbed trailer and hauled to a hangar, where the FAA disassembled it, piece by piece, Carroll Anderson told Wayne Jones. Their findings would be announced at an FAA hearing later that month.

Buddy's casket was carried to the plane on Wednesday, February 4, and he began his final trip home. Niki Sullivan, who would later serve as one of Buddy's pallbearers, described the casket as "silverish— a metallic gray plastic." The plane made it as far as Des Moines, one hundred miles south of Mason City, before it ran into bad weather and had to be grounded, Griggs later revealed in *Rockin' 50s* magazine. The following day the plane completed its flight to Lubbock. Traveling separately, Larry went straight to his parents' house as soon as he landed. "They had Buddy's music playin', they had his pictures out—I couldn't look at them," Larry said in 1992. "I couldn't listen to the music. If I heard half of one of his songs I'd start cryin'."

Tinker Carlen had been hanging around the funeral home in Lubbock ever since he'd heard of Buddy's death. "It was real sad, it was hard to take," he recalled in 1992. "I just stayed up there by Sanders Funeral Home waitin' for them to come in. I never even went home, I was just drivin' around town. I was in a daze, couldn't believe it."

Maria Elena flew from New York with Provi, arriving at 4:40 P.M. Wednesday. Ill from the miscarriage, she went into seclusion at the Holleys. At last, Buddy's body lay in Sanders Funeral Home at 1420 Main Street. Advertised as "Family Owned & Operated Since 1931," the mortuary's logo was—and remains—a drawing of a knight in full armor, wearing spurs, brandishing a six-foot sword, and holding a shield inscribed SERVICE MEASURED NOT BY GOLD BUT BY THE GOLDEN RULE. Sanders aggressively advertises "pre-paid & pre-arranged burial plans and cremation service," calling itself "your golden-rule funeral home" and promising "service you can depend on."

In death, Buddy at last got the attention of the local newspaper. The *Lubbock Evening Journal* accorded his death the lead story on the front page of the February 3 edition. The thick, black, eight-column banner headline screamed LUBBOCK ROCK-'N'-ROLL STAR KILLED. Oddly, the headline writer seemed reluctant to mention Buddy's name, consigning it to one of the smaller subheads. The story was positioned in the extreme right-hand column, which is always reserved for the most important news story of the day: BUDDY HOLLY, THREE OTHERS IN AIR CRASH/RITCHIE VALENS, J. P. RICHARDSON, PILOT ALSO DEAD. Not until the fourth paragraph were Buddy's parents mentioned, and there were no photographs of them. The story quoted "friends" who described Buddy as "probably one of the biggest entertainment celebrities ever to hail from Lubbock," a non sequitur of sorts, since the city had never produced a celebrity in the same league with Buddy Holly, nor would it to this day.

Directly underneath a two-column photograph of Buddy was a weather story about winter's frigid grip on the South Plains: On the day Buddy died, the same cold front in which he'd perished swept down the plains, chilling Lubbock and the Permian Basin. In a "killer storm" of snow and freezing rain, schools were shut down, and State Highway 302, which ran through Roy Orbison country, between Odessa and Kermit, was closed due to "heavy sheet ice." Near Graham, on U.S. Highway 88, twenty trucks were stalled on a hill after a truck and trailer "jackknifed on the ice-slicked highway." By the following day temperatures climbed to forty-one degrees, and all across the vast western stretches of the state, from the Red River Valley through the Big Bend country to El Paso, the land "began sloughing a heavy coat of ice." In the Northern Plains, however, nothing had changed; the surviving members of the "Winter Dance Party" faced a "new surge of arctic air," which plunged temperatures below zero.

As Lubbock awaited Buddy's funeral that first week in February the local paper continued to run news stories about his death and upcoming funeral on the front page as well as features on his career inside the paper. One story, headlined SERVICES PENDING FOR BUDDY HOLLY, VICTIM OF IOWA PLANE CRASH/SINGING STAR'S BODY DUE HERE TODAY, included the information that Waylon Jennings's wife and two daughters were living in Littlefield; also that some of Buddy's grandparents survived him, including his maternal grandmother, Mrs. Eva P. Drake of Lubbock, and his paternal grandparents, Mr. and Mrs. John Holley of Commerce, a small town in East Texas.

In the same edition, Larry Welborn and Bob Montgomery were referred to as Larry Wilburn and Bobby Burgess, an indication of just how unfamiliar the editorial staff was with the life and career of the city's most famous son. Jack Sheridan's otherwise fascinating feature story was absurdly headlined DEATH CUTS SHORT METEORIC CAREER FOR LUBBOCK YOUTH. Meteoric hardly describes Buddy's career, which survived a fiasco in Nashville, a firing by Decca, six months of grueling, unheralded recording in Clovis, an uneasy apprenticeship with Hank Thompson, and the hapless "black tour" before finally taking off. Sheridan's contention that Buddy rejected movie offers because he disapproved of the "hurried way" rock exploitation films were ground out probably came from Petty and is very far from the truth, in light of statements to the contrary by Jerry Allison, Maria Elena Holly, and Buddy himself, who said he was "buddying up" to Cochran in the hope of getting into Go, Johnny, Go!

But Sheridan's story contained some first-rate reporting and a number of newsy nuggets. For example, after the Crickets left Buddy he "examined his career" and decided he was "better off on his own," Sheridan wrote. Buddy and Slim Corbin were well along in their plans for Buddy's summer 1959 Lubbock concert. Sheridan also learned of Buddy's upcoming LP of "sacred and spiritual" songs, and he broke the news that Buddy and his new band were set for a four-week tour of England in March 1959. Buddy intended to fly abroad and sail back on a luxury liner, "just for fun." The labels for his new company, Taupe Records, had already been printed. Sheridan also reported that Buddy's purpose in taking flying lessons was to fly between gigs and come home to Lubbock more often.

On the day Buddy was buried, Saturday, February 7, Niki Sullivan and Tinker Carlen were working at McKissick Auto. Naturally both of them wanted to attend, but they were informed that "only one person will be allowed to go to the funeral," Tinker recalled in 1992. Then Larry Holley asked Niki to be a pallbearer. "I told Niki, 'You go and I'll work,' " Tinker revealed in 1992. After Niki left, Tinker slipped out of the shop, got in his pickup, and drove to Tabernacle Baptist Church, where a large crowd was already beginning to form. "I got paid for goin'," Tinker said.

Peggy Sue Allison went to Buddy's parents' house to commiserate with Mr. and Mrs. Holley before the funeral. She remained there until it was time to leave for the church. Along the route to Tabernacle Baptist, kids playing with Hula Hoops in their front yards stopped to watch the unusually heavy traffic heading toward the unimpressive brown shed at 1911 Thirty-fourth Street.

The church was packed with a capacity crowd of fifteen hundred. The citizens who had ignored Buddy in his lifetime, according him no honors or even a hometown concert, now grabbed every seat at his last rites and overflowed into the lobby, where loudspeakers had to be set up to accommodate the crowd, and into the parking lot. Americans indeed love a good funeral. How ironic that death begets legend—that Holly, like Elvis Presley eighteen years later, would become a true legend only in death. The legitimate mourners had difficulty making their way through the onlookers. Phil Everly later told Kurt Loder that he "flew down to Lubbock" and "sat with his parents." He was not a pallbearer, however, because he couldn't stand to see Buddy "put down in the earth." Don Everly refused to attend, he told Loder, because Buddy's death "just freaked me right out."

The closed light gray casket had a framed twelve-by-fourteen-inch photograph of Buddy atop it, according to Ken Johnson, who helped Rev. Ben D. Johnson officiate. In addition to Niki, the pallbearers included Sonny Curtis, Bob Montgomery, Jerry, and Joe B. Among the honorary pallbearers were Larry Welborn and two of the Roses, Dave Bingham and Bob Linville. During the service Niki Sullivan sat between Phil Everly and Joe B.; Jerry sat directly in front of them, Niki told Griggs in 1978. Norman Petty, despite the bitterness and near violence of his final confrontation with Buddy, was in attendance. Vi Petty, who just months before had insulted Buddy's wife, was also there.

Peggy Sue nervously scanned the packed congregation, looking for a seat but finding that all the choice ones were occupied. The spillover crowd included a "heavy density of teenagers," the *Avalanche-Journal* later noted. Peggy Sue was forced to sit by herself, at the back of the church, alone. "The thing I remember," she later told Griggs, "is that Maria Elena wasn't there." According to the *Avalanche-Journal,* "His bride of less than six months, the former Maria Ellna [sic] Santiago of New York City, was ill at the home of the Lubbock youth's parents and unable to attend the services. She came to Lubbock Thursday [sic]."

Recalling the occasion years later, Maria Elena explained in a 1993 interview, "I was in Lubbock, but I could not attend the funeral. I could

not handle that. My reasoning was I didn't want to see Buddy dead. I
wanted to keep his memory the way I saw him when he left."

The competition for seats was so hectic that even honored guests were
edged out. Ken Johnson recalls in 1993, "There was one pew that had a
vacant space in it that had been reserved for the ushers. They never did
have the opportunity to come in and take their seats. The auditorium
was filled, every seat in that auditorium, and it would seat at that time
around fifteen hundred people. There were people out on the front porch,
in the vestibule, and some even in the parking lot. We did not have an
external PA system, but the PA went into the vestibule of the church."

Seated in one of the front pews near the casket, Buddy's family appeared remarkably composed. Niki Sullivan was "surprised and amazed"
that L.O. and Ella Holley "held up so well," Niki later stated in *Rockin'
50s*. Tinker Carlen observed in 1992 that "ever'body was tryin' to put up
a good front, but the funeral was real sad. I remember seein' Phil Everly
and Norman and Vi. It was hard on ever'one." Bill Pickering sang "Beyond the Sunset," an upbeat hymn by Virgil Brock and his wife, Blanche.
The song paints a picture of life after death so appealing that not even
the most hardened atheist could resist it. The Brocks composed it after
viewing a spectacular sunset at Rainbow Point on Winona Lake in Indiana. Awestruck, Virgil turned to Blanche and asked, "What lies beyond
the wondrous sunset? What will it be like when our work is done and the
experience of heaven begun?" As described in the song, heaven is a place
free of fear and work, where the dead meet God face-to-face and find
peace of mind at last. They are reunited with everyone they've ever loved
and lost, never to be separated again.

The funeral fell flat as soon as the preachers took over. This was not
surprising in Lubbock in 1959. Buddy could have been an obscure clerk
for all the mention the clergy made of rock 'n' roll. "I don't think the
service was about a star," Niki later told Griggs. In fact, it didn't even
seem to be a funeral; it was more like an ordinary, impersonal Sunday
morning church service, Niki added. "Brother [Ben] Johnson had the
main message of the funeral," Ken Johnson related in 1993. "Mine was
the first part of the message. I read Buddy's obituary, read some scripture,
commented on it, and then had prayer for the family." Pretty uninspired
stuff for the rocker of ages. Not one of Buddy's records was played. Bill
Pickering sang another song, though later he was unable to recall the
title. "I had never heard of it before. It was a song that I had to read the
music to as I sang it," Pickering stated in *Reminiscing* in 1981.

The most appropriate musical selection was a recording by the Angelic
Gospel Singers, "I'll Be All Right," long a favorite of Buddy's. At the end
of the service, everyone lined up behind the family and passed in front
of the casket. Buddy's parents had shown no emotion throughout the

funeral, which "made it easier" for everyone else, Niki said in 1978. Joe B. still thought Buddy was alive, explaining in 1987 that, because the casket was never opened, he could continue to refuse to "accept the reality" of Buddy's death.

At the conclusion of the service, the crowd filed outside to wait for the casket to be brought from the church. The pallbearers came out with everyone else, then realized they'd forgotten the casket and had to go back inside. In a few minutes they reemerged, this time bearing their burden and depositing it in the hearse. Peggy Sue could stand no more. As soon as the funeral was over, she went home, unable to face the cemetery. What bothered her more than anything else was the large crowd, though apparently it was a perfectly orderly one. According to the *Avalanche-Journal*, the predominantly teenage throng had "sat mostly in silence as the Rev. Ben D. Johnson, pastor of the church, delivered the oration."

Leaving the parking lot, the funeral procession wound through Lub-bock, likely passing the places—Tom Lubbock Senior High, the Hi-D-Ho Drive-In, the roller rink, the radio stations, and the theaters—that had defined Buddy's world and provided its limits until a brief eighteen months ago. The Lubbock City Cemetery is far out on the east side of town, just beyond a vast automobile junkyard. Buddy's casket was placed at the grave site, relatively near the entrance. Ben Johnson spoke briefly. "There were some tears," Niki later told Griggs, but again Niki noted the equanimity of Buddy's parents. Terry Noland, who had attended Taber-nacle Baptist Church with Buddy, approached L. O. and Ella Holley and gave them the letter in which Buddy had invited Terry to come to New York and live and work with him after the tour. Terry's brother Bob would tell Griggs in 1982 about Rev. Ben Johnson "hating rock 'n' roll because of all the rock 'n' rollers that were coming out of his church." In the same interview, Terry would expose the church's hypocrisy, revealing that after Buddy became successful and lavished money on the church, "that changed everything."

Just as Maria Elena had avoided the funeral, she also stayed away from the graveside service. "Up to this date I refuse to see his grave," she said in 1993. "I won't do it." To her, Buddy is still a living presence, she his eternal bride. "I want to leave the morbid parts out," she told *Mason City Globe-Gazette* reporter Kevin Baskins in 1992.

Buddy's parents were able to draw stupendous strength from their faith, which was the kind described in the hymn "How Firm a Foundation," addressed "to you who for refuge to Jesus have fled": "When thro' the deep waters I call thee to go, the rivers of sorrow shall not overflow." According to Larry, "They definitely felt that they would get to see Buddy again," he later stated in *Reminiscing*. Such belief in a literal resurrection of body and soul echoes the theology expressed in Protestant hymns like "When the Roll Is Called Up Yonder (I'll Be There)," "In the Sweet Bye-and-Bye," and "Beautiful Island of Somewhere." Egos and personalities will be completely intact, ready to resume worldly relationships exactly where they'd been left off. In fairness to the hymns, no one has yet disproved their vision.

Buddy's casket was lowered into the ground, and the mourners dispersed. Some of them gathered at the home of Buddy's parents. "Maria Elena come over there with her aunt," Tinker Carlen remarked in 1992, "and I remember Phil Everly was out there in the front yard and we's a-talkin', and I remember Larry Welborn was there and Bob Montgomery. There was a bunch of 'em." Niki Sullivan summed up one of the saddest days any of them would ever experience: "We all then went home and spent a quiet afternoon," he told Griggs in 1978.

A few weeks after Buddy's burial, Ella Holley approached Ken Johnson, who recalled their conversation in a 1993 interview. "Brother Johnson, I want to apologize," Mrs. Holley said.

"What for?" Ken Johnson asked.

"Well, the way I acted when you and Ben D. Johnson were up there on my porch and I heard the terrible news about my son."

"Mrs. Holley, you don't need to apologize about that. There's not many things that are a heavier burden than a mother losing her son."

"I'll always have a very warm place reserved for you in my heart. You and Buddy were about the same age, you know." Says Johnson today, "She was a very strong person and so was Brother Holley. They always were. You would be amazed at the graciousness that Mrs. Holley had. She was a little bitty lady. A small person, even for a woman. But she was so gracious."

Buddy's grave lies near a road that runs through the cemetery. A lone tree stands nearby. Beyond his grave looms a mammoth grain elevator with at least sixty silos. The original tombstone, an upright guitar, was stolen shortly after it was installed. The replacement stone lies flat against the earth and is more like a marker than a tombstone. The engraving is tasteful and appropriate—a Fender Stratocaster, some musical notes, and a few holly leaves. The inscription reads: "In loving memory of our own Buddy Holley—September 7, 1936–February 3, 1959."

Restoring the "e" to his surname—Holley—seems at first an odd denial of Buddy's fame as the rock star Buddy Holly. But it is consistent with the attitude that prideful and pious Texans had always taken toward him. The church had rejected his music and the locals had remained impervious to his celebrity. In burying him as Buddy Holley, they now attempted to redeem him from the clutches of the devil's music and reclaim him as "our own Buddy Holley."

Part Three

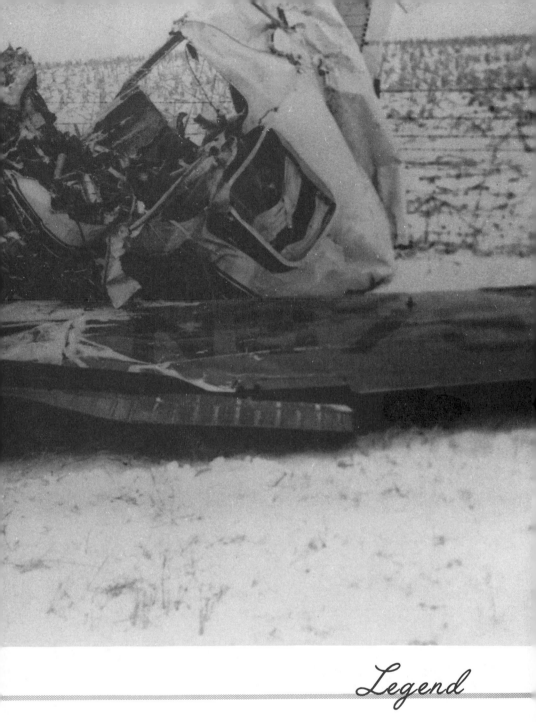

Legend

Chapter Fifteen

The Days After

In the months following Buddy's death, the CAB report laid the blame for the crash on pilot error but did little to prevent rumors of foul play, especially after Buddy's pistol was discovered at the crash site. During spring thaw, farmer Albert Juhl, who was Delbert Juhl's father, finally turned up the gun, according to the *Mason City Globe-Gazette*, "while cleaning small bits of wreckage out of his field in preparation for seeding it to pasture." When the *Globe-Gazette* revealed that two of the chambers in the six-shot pistol were empty, rumors spread that the pilot had been shot. The paper attempted to allay such speculation by reporting that "there were no shells in the remaining two chambers nor were there any empty shell casings in them." But a further complication set in when it was disclosed that the pistol had contained *no* bullets when the sheriff received it because Juhl had "fired all four bullets into the air when he found the pistol." The plot thickened twenty years later, in 1979, when Griggs interviewed Sheriff Jerry Allen, who insisted that "only one shot had been fired by Albert Juhl."

Eugene Anderson indicated that these questions were not explored in the CAB report because the investigator in charge, the late C. E. Stillwagon, was solely interested in the condition of the plane and the pilot's qualifications. Anderson concluded that the CAB report was "pretty sloppy."

Local speculation that the crash victims had been taking drugs was based on nothing more than candy wrappers which were found around the plane wreck, Bill Griggs stated in his exhaustive 1989 article on the crash in *Rockin' 50s* magazine. Though it is true that drug users crave sweets, it's far more likely that the young men were eating the candy bars for badly needed energy and body warmth in the subfreezing weather. Despite suspicion of drug use, no drug tests were performed on the bodies. Because Roger Peterson's autopsy had been carried out after arterial embalming, it could not determine drug use. Blood tests can only be done before arterial embalming.

Dwyer denied that the crash had been caused by pilot error and maintained, in a 1988 interview with Wayne Jones, that "my pilot was incapacitated in some manner." In an interview with Kevin Terry, Dwyer stated, "There was more than what appeared on the report, especially around the head area." On yet another occasion, Dwyer said, "I could tell the *National Enquirer* one hell of a story, but it would hurt a lot of people." Eugene Anderson, one of the crash investigators, told Bill Griggs in 1989 that the crash was not Roger Peterson's fault, calling into question the CAB's verdict of pilot error and opening the possibility that there had been a struggle of some sort in the cockpit in the final minutes. Despite unanswered questions, the official CAB report was adopted on September 15, 1959. It was so incomplete that it failed to make any mention whatsoever of Buddy's pistol, let alone explain why some of its bullets had been fired. The report came under fire from the FAA's Eugene Anderson, who complained that "we didn't see the report" until it had already been approved and released, and that Stillwagon had "overruled" certain pertinent lines of inquiry.

According to the wildest rumor, the pilot was shot by someone sitting in the backseat. Though Carroll Anderson saw Buddy in front and Ritchie and the Bopper in back just before takeoff, crash investigator Eugene Anderson stated that the Bopper was in front, that he and Buddy changed places during the flight. Anderson confirmed that sufficient space existed in the cockpit for "people to move around, even from back to front." The CAB report offered unexpected corroboration of Anderson's thesis; the CAB found that the heaviest person—the Bopper—was sitting in the front right seat. Incredible as it seems, the implication is that Buddy Holly shot the pilot.

Dwyer's friend Bob Booe wondered if Jerry Dwyer "simply doesn't want to admit that Roger was at fault," Booe stated in Griggs's 1989 article on the crash. Booe also dismissed charges of drug use as mere speculation. Interviewed in 1995, Jeremy Powers, a reporter who investigated rumors surrounding the crash for the *Globe-Gazette* in 1989, concluded that Roger Peterson was not shot and that drugs and alcohol played no part in the accident.

Attempting to resolve these mysteries, I visit the Mason City Municipal Airport in 1993, hoping to check the plane wreckage myself and see if there's a bullet hole in the seat behind the pilot, as reported by one Lubbock visitor to Clear Lake in 1988. Though the CAB report stated the plane was sold for scrap, an employee at the airport tells me, "The plane is out here at the airport. It's locked in a shed down here. Dwyer is going to make key chains out of the pieces. People keep asking him why he doesn't put it in a museum. He just has it locked in a shed."

No one answers when I knock on the door at Dwyer's Flying Service, which is located in the new administration building that was constructed in the sixties. The airport director, Jerome J. Thiele, sees me trying to get in and invites me to his office upstairs, which overlooks the runway where N3794N took off 34 years ago. "Why did Buddy's plane crash?" I ask Thiele, gazing over his shoulder at the long runway, lined on both sides by steep snowbanks. Some single-engine planes are sitting there, looking every bit as rickety as they did in 1959.

"It was snowing," Thiele says. "The pilot didn't have enough experience with his instruments. He thought he was straight and level in a climbing mode, but instead he was in a shallow dive."

In 1959, lawsuits developed after the crash but were suddenly and mysteriously dropped. Ritchie's mother sued Dwyer for $1.5 million, charging that the flight had been carried out in unsafe weather. The estates of all three singers reportedly were awarded $50,000 from Dwyer's insurance company. That settlement, of course, could not compensate the families for the loss nor heal their wounds.

In practical aviation terms, little seems to have been learned from the disaster at Clear Lake, despite the celebrity of its victims. "The aviation industry was growing fast and the investigative force was strained to the extreme," says veteran reporter Cy Egan, who covered air crashes in the fifties for the Standard News Association wire service. "They gave less attention to smaller aircraft, reserving time to investigate larger commercial airlines." Thirty-six years later, there were still widespread charges that commuter planes are not safe to fly. Perhaps Waylon Jennings put it best when he observed, "His loss was all for nothing."

On February 3, 1959, the fate of the surviving members of the tour—Waylon, Tommy, Dion and the Belmonts, and Frankie Sardo—was equally hopeless and, for Waylon Jennings at least, deeply traumatic. With all of its headline stars dead, the tour logically should have been canceled following the plane crash, but GAC decided to continue the "Winter Dance Party" to its conclusion. Waylon and the others did not learn of the crash until their tour bus, muddy and battered from another punishing trip through the snow, rolled into Moorhead, Minnesota, around noon on February 3. The tour manager went into the hotel but quickly came back and boarded the bus, ashen-faced. "Come outside, I want to talk to you for a while," he said to Waylon, according to an interview with Waylon published by Bill Griggs in 1981. Waylon sensed that something was wrong and refused to budge from his seat. Once again, the manager implored Waylon to get off the bus.

"No," Waylon said, quietly but emphatically. The manager wandered off. Waylon turned to Allsup. "Tommy, you go," he said. Allsup later stated on the TV program *Instant Recall* that he went up to the hotel desk and asked for Buddy Holly's room. "Haven't you heard?" the clerk said. "Those guys got killed in a plane crash." Allsup returned to the bus, his eyes bulging and his face drawn. " 'Boys, they didn't make it,' " Allsup said, Waylon later recalled in *Reminiscing*.

Years later Waylon said he "felt guilty," as if he were somehow responsible for the accident. At the time, all he wanted to do was "go home," immediately. He would carry his grief for years, finally coming to a "tough reckoning with himself about that," according to Reba McEntire in her 1994 autobiography *Reba*. After the 1991 plane crash that killed seven of McEntire's musicians and her tour manager, "I was greatly comforted by [Waylon's] words," McEntire wrote. " 'Don't you feel guilty because of the plane crash,' he told me. 'It wasn't meant for you to be on that plane or you would have been. So don't blame yourself and don't feel guilty.' "

In Moorhead in 1959, Allsup found a telephone and put through a long-distance call to his mother. Luckily she hadn't been watching the television, which for the past two and a half hours had been broadcasting news of Allsup's death, due to the discovery of his wallet at the crash site. Waylon's family was not as fortunate. His brother Tommy had been working on a tractor in a Littlefield garage when KVOW announced that the Crickets had been killed along with Buddy. "I went crazy," Tommy said. Waylon's mother was in shock. It was "two or three hours," Tommy said, before a correction was broadcast.

Back in Moorhead, Dion stepped out of the bus and wandered around the hotel, still unaware of the news. In the lobby, empty except for two pale, stooped figures hunched before the TV, he paused and listened as an announcer described the crash. "There were no survivors," the newscaster said. Dion returned to the bus, picked up Buddy's Fender Stratocaster, and sat staring at the starburst design. "All around me were their belongings," he recalled in *The Wanderer*.

Fred Milano of the Belmonts was sound asleep on the bus, exhausted from the ten-hour trip. "The plane had crashed already," Milano told Wayne Jones in 1977, "and the whole country knew about it except us. We heard it last." Waylon was packing, hoping to accompany Buddy's body back to Texas, when "the people from New York called and begged us to go on for a couple more days," Waylon later told the *Chicago Tribune*. The promoters promised to fly Waylon and Tommy to Lubbock for Buddy's funeral if they'd finish the tour. The agents also promised to pay them Buddy's share for the remaining sixteen shows, amounting to $4,000. Waylon and Tommy agreed, but GAC later reneged on their promise.

In death Buddy Holly would be instrumental in the rise of many stars, including the Beatles, the Rolling Stones, the Hollies, Don McLean, Gary Busey, and Linda Ronstadt. But the first, created before the sun set on the day he died, was Bobby Vee, who lived in Fargo, North Dakota, and had been looking forward to attending the "Winter Dance Party" on

February 3. A sixteen-year-old sophomore at Central High School, he was a Buddy Holly fan and had formed a band just the previous week. At the time he was still known as Robert Thomas Velline. Though small, Vee was classically cute: blond, smooth-skinned, bright-eyed, with a huge Mickey Rooney smile and perfect teeth.

At noon on February 3, he came home from school for lunch. His brother told him about the accident at Clear Lake. Turning on the radio, Vee heard an announcer ask for local talent to fill in for the dead stars that night. Back at school, where almost all the kids had tickets for the show, everyone was talking about the tragedy. A musician in Vee's band, bass player Jim Stillman, called the radio station and offered to fill in, Vee related in a 1987 article by Bill Griggs. The announcer instructed them to appear at the Armory at seven P.M. for an audition.

When they were added to the bill, they realized they needed a name for the band. Just minutes before they went on at the Armory that night, Vee and his band christened themselves the Shadows, Vee later stated in the liner notes for his LP I Remember Buddy Holly. "It was a very bizarre evening. There was no merriment at all," Vee told Holly fan Don Larson in 1979. Frankie Sardo murmured a few words in reference to the crash and sang Ritchie's "Donna." Many in the audience burst into sobs. Tommy Allsup seemed a million miles away, staring blankly over the heads of the dancers and the wire service correspondents who milled among them, soliciting quotes. For once, the performers were properly lit, thanks to a promoter named Bing Bingstrom, who filmed the show with an eight-millimeter camera and brought his own lights. Eyewitnesses that night gave wildly different accounts of the concert. To Fred Milano, standing on the stage, the crowd of two thousand teenagers "were trying to hold back the tears," he later told Wayne Jones. But an AP stringer reported that they "screamed, clapped, and whistled as the rock 'n' roll groups sang their best-selling numbers." At one point during every set the performers "paid tribute to the victims," the AP correspondent added.

As his turn approached, Bobby Vee looked on with increasing uneasiness as Dion, Sardo, Waylon, and Tommy wiped tears from their eyes, "and he saw the audience crying along with them," reporter Pat Williams later wrote in Movieland and TV Time. Vee finally opened his mouth to sing, his voice "a bit unsteady." Then he calmed down by thinking, This is for Buddy. It helped. He bounced through hits by the Everly Brothers, Little Richard, and Jerry Lee Lewis, captivating the crowd. It was his lucky night. He was discovered by Bing Bingstrom, who arranged other bookings. Vee subsequently debuted with "a fair-sized hit" record, "Suzie Baby," and went on to work with Buddy's friend Snuff Garrett, who recorded Vee's "Devil or Angel," a No. 6 smash. Many Top 40 singles followed, including "Rubber Ball" and "Take Good Care of My Baby," as well as the albums *Bobby Vee Meets the Crickets* and *Nothin' Like a Sunny Day.* "Our style was modeled after Buddy's approach," Vee said, referring to his vocal-and-instrumental group the Shadows. "I've never forgotten Buddy Holly and his influence on my singing style and my career."

The crowd tensed as the Crickets, minus Buddy, began their set, Waylon, Tommy, and Carl bravely trying to sing "Rave On." Though many were weeping, others focused on Waylon, whose charm and good looks were more evident now that he was in the spotlight. All started screaming and surging toward the stage. At first, Tommy assumed that the cheers were to honor Buddy's memory. "But then," Tommy later told Denisoff, "I realized they were for Waylon."

Following the Armory show, according to Waylon, the promoters announced they were subtracting from their salaries the amount that Buddy, Ritchie, and the Bopper would have received. "This, after begging us to play. Real nice people," Waylon later told Goldrosen. Though Moorhead was supposed to be a double-header, GAC canceled one of the performances in a display of decency. Although Carl Bunch had just recovered from frostbite, he reported for work the following day, Wednesday, February 4, in Sioux City, Iowa.

They were set to play the Shore Acres Ballroom in Sioux City with a new lineup of musicians, including Ronnie Smith, who arrived from Texas, Jimmy Clanton, and Frankie Avalon, who were expected to appear in time for the performance. Clanton, who'd scored five Top 40 hits in the past six months, including "Just a Dream," "A Letter to an Angel," "My Own True Love," and "Go, Jimmy, Go," had toured with Buddy in Iowa the previous July. When the "Dance Party" stars were killed, Clanton was taken off another tour and sent to Sioux City. "I always felt that they should have canceled that tour as only one act was left, and that was Dion and the Belmonts," Clanton told Griggs in 1979. After joining the troupe in Sioux City, Clanton found Buddy's guitar on a Greyhound bus parked behind Shore Acres. No one objected when he asked if he could use it that night.

Performing on the post-Holly "Dance Party" was "eerie," Clanton observed. The audience was "very somber," he told Griggs. He felt the fans came only because they were stuck with the tickets and couldn't get refunds. They had a sad, lonely aura. He found them to be disconcertingly quiet, something the Baton Rouge, Louisiana, rock star wasn't used to.

Romantic, dark-haired Frankie Avalon, one of the teen idols emerging as rock 'n' roll's pioneers passed from the scene, was on a roll of million-selling records. "Dede Dinah," "Venus," "Just Ask Your Heart," and "Why" all came out in 1958–59. In his two-toned golf sweater, white bucks, and gabardine slacks, the eighteen-year-old child prodigy from

Philadelphia looked like a juvenile version of Dean Martin or Frank Sinatra. His career had been built up on Dick Clark's *American Bandstand* but would suffer when Clark dropped him during the payola scandal of the early 1960s. Clark, who was not found guilty of any wrongdoing, divested himself of substantial interests in music publishing and record companies.

For Waylon, Tommy, and Carl, the Sioux City show was almost impossible to get through. They were "too hurt, too sad, too sick" to concentrate on their performance, Bunch recalled in 1981. Ronnie Smith assisted Waylon with the lead vocals. They went onstage and tried to play Buddy's hits, but all they could think of was their friends and the brutal way they'd died. Despite his trancelike delivery, Waylon's applause matched Frankie Avalon's. Frankie Sardo, the suave-looking Italian whose singing had improved under Buddy's tutelege, was so depressed he decided to give up rock 'n' roll. Later he told reporter Larry Lehmer that "it was a different show" after the night of the crash. Thereafter, it became "a memorial" to the fallen stars, with everyone acutely aware of "who wasn't there."

A teenager named Doug McLeod, who'd seen Buddy in Fort Dodge on January 30, attended the Thursday performance at the Val Air Ballroom in Des Moines. "Shock permeated the atmosphere," he recalled in an interview with Holly fan Hans Goeppinger. When the emcee asked for a moment of silence, it "seemed to go on forever," said McLeod. "It was hard for Buddy's band, trying to perform his songs on their own, without Buddy. I remember Tommy Allsup standing there, trying to play and sing, with tears rolling down his cheeks."

Waylon, inexperienced and on his first road trip, had been "nervous enough" even when Buddy was alive and Waylon could lean on him, McLeod noted. After the plane crash, Waylon was expected to "carry the show," but it proved too difficult. "Waylon Jennings was almost a basket case," McLeod said. All that had been keeping Waylon going was GAC's promise to fly him and Tommy home for Buddy's funeral on Saturday. But by Friday, February 6, after they played the Danceland Ballroom in Grand Rapids and still had no plane tickets to Lubbock for the funeral the following day, it was clear to Waylon that GAC had betrayed him.

The tour ended in Springfield, Illinois, on February 15. They took a bus to Chicago, transferred to a train, and finally arrived in New York two days later. Waylon was a wreck. During the trip he'd been drinking vodka and 7-Up. Tommy Allsup spiked his drink with a handful of "crosses," amphetamines that Ronnie had acquired in a Mexican border town, and Waylon was strung out by the time they reached New York. Still feeling the effects of the speed, he stalked around Forty-second Street and Seventh and Eighth avenues day and night until he finally crashed on February 20 at five A.M. "After the first one," Waylon later said, referring to speed trips, "the second one came easy."

They went to GAC to collect the promised $4,000 fee but no one at the agency would speak to them. Finally someone at GAC informed Waylon and Tommy, "We gave it all to Buddy's widow."

Then GAC offered to tour them as the Crickets in order to take advantage of the publicity surrounding the crash. Petty immediately sought an injunction, informing GAC that Jerry, Joe B., Sonny, and Earl Sinks were the Crickets. Carl Bunch later revealed that Maria Elena arranged a recording contract for him, Ronnie, Waylon, and Tommy to record as Ronnie Smith and the Jitters, but little came of it and they soon disbanded.

Waylon returned to Texas, confused, bitter, and threatening to quit show business. He felt that the people in the music industry were nothing but "flesh peddlers." According to his biographer, Serge Denisoff, "he blamed Norman Petty for Buddy's death."

Buddy Holly died intestate, leaving no will. Though Maria Elena was his sole heir, she assigned one-half of the Buddy Holly estate to Ella and L. O. Holley. At first there was nothing to split. "The only way I got money was when Buddy died and I used my lawyers," Maria Elena said in 1993. "I had to use all kinds of methods to be able to get [Petty] to cough it up. Jerry can be witness to this. We got together in New York with my lawyers—what to do about the music. Buddy never did recoup all his money."

Finally Petty paid $70,000. Over the years reporters persistently quizzed him about rumors that he'd usurped Buddy's fortune. In 1985 he promised interviewers Skip Brooks and Bill Malcolm that he'd one day explain everything in a book, but he never got around to publishing it.

Maria Elena eventually remarried, becoming Maria Elena Diaz-Hernandez, and had three children. She turned over many of Buddy's personal effects to the Holley family. According to Larry, "When Buddy died, Maria was so distraught that she said, 'Mother 'n' Daddy'—that's what she called them, 'Mother 'n' Daddy'—'Ya'll take all this stuff. I don't want to see it again. I don't want to ever hear of it again. It just brings back too many bad memories. Ya'll do what you want to with it.' " Larry says they told her, "We'd might as well." Maria Elena confirmed in *Reminiscing* in 1977 that "most of the things that I had, I gave to Mrs. Holley."

The Holleys soon regretted it. "We got tired of trying to keep them insured, and keep them hid so they wouldn't get stolen," Larry said in 1992. "A steady stream of fans were coming by, wanting to see them and hold them and have their picture made with them. It just got to be a burden we couldn't bear." Among other things, Buddy's memorabilia presented a space problem; he (or his mother) had saved almost everything he'd ever owned or written, including all of his school homework.

Even in death, the spirit and talent of Buddy Holly continued to provide for his family. Larry's fondest dream was that his parents would have no financial worries as they grew older. Thanks to Buddy, they would never want for anything. The first sign that Buddy was going to be a more lucrative "property" dead than alive came with the sudden spurt in sales of his last single, "It Doesn't Matter Anymore." Decca executives had written the record off as a flop. After the plane crash, they watched in awe as orders started pouring in. Storming the stores, record-buyers felt they could keep Buddy alive a little longer by snapping up "It Doesn't Matter Anymore," which jumped into the U.S. Top 40, becoming his first hit since "Early in the Morning" the previous August. Eventually "It Doesn't Matter Anymore" crested at No. 13. It went all the way to No. 1 in both England and Australia.

Buddy's posthumous hits offered cold comfort for his heartbroken parents. A month following his death, Ella and L. O. Holley went to Clear Lake, quietly, to see the place that had consumed their youngest child. They met Carroll Anderson at the Surf Ballroom and went to dinner with him. Inviting them to the show that night, Anderson said, "I want you to come back, be with me." In 1980 he recalled, "They said, 'If you don't mind, we'd like to be with you all evening.' I said, 'You be my guests at the ballroom and just try and visualize, if you can, when Buddy was performing here.'" In the coming years, the Holleys would keep returning to Clear Lake, including a trip in the fall of 1959, when they again shared a meal with Anderson. Being at the Surf somehow made them feel closer to Buddy.

The demand for Buddy's records continued to rise in the months after the plane crash. Coral rushed out a greatest-hits LP entitled *The Buddy Holly Story*, which shot to No. 11. Though Buddy had never had an LP on the charts in his lifetime, *The Buddy Holly Story* would be on and off the *Billboard* Top 100 for the next seven years, becoming one of the more durable albums in recording history. Spotting a trend, *Variety*'s Mike Gross wrote, somewhat morbidly, "The 'death rattle' goes on perpetuaing the performer and very often filling the record company coffers. . . . Material on Holly is kept in the active file to handle the flood of requests for photos and bio information that continually pour in."

Suddenly everyone at Decca/Coral started hounding Dick Jacobs to "get masters, get masters," Jacobs later said in *Rockin' 50s* magazine. Jacobs pulled off a coup when he acquired Buddy's priceless apartment tapes, including "Peggy Sue Got Married." On June 30, 1959, the apartment tapes were radically restructured on Coral Records' Studio A console, with Jack Hansen assisting Jacobs. Overdubbed with background vocals and additional instrumentation, they resembled Buddy's Pythian Temple string sessions of the previous year.

"Peggy Sue Got Married" was released in July 1959, with "Crying, Waiting, Hoping" on the flip side. Neither song charted in the United States, but "Peggy Sue Got Married" skied to No. 17 on the *New Musical Express* chart in England in September. The previous month a British reissue of Buddy's old Nashville record "Midnight Shift" had sailed to No. 26, starting a long and profitable series of posthumous U.K. chart successes for Holly singles, including "Learning the Game" and "Listen to Me." The British also loved his new album, *The Buddy Holly Story, Volume 2*, sending it up the chart to No. 7, and an LP entitled *That'll Be the Day*, a reissue of his 1956 Nashville recordings, which went to No. 5. The July 1960 *Hit Parade* reported that "True Love Ways" had "reached the Top 30. . . . What a great tribute it is to Buddy Holly's wonderful talent that his records are still selling well enough to get into the hit parade eighteen months after his death."

After the shock of his death wore off in America, his singles stopped selling in the United States. For years, Buddy Holly was all but forgotten in his native country. Though rock 'n' roll by no means died with Buddy—the next few years would see the release of Orbison's "Crying," Del Shannon's "Runaway," Dion's "Runaround Sue," the Four Seasons' "Walk Like a Man," and Little Eva's "The Loco-Motion," a banner era by any standards—the American rock scene paled in comparison with what was developing in England. In the early sixties, there were 350 rock bands in Liverpool alone. Young British musicians revered Buddy as a rock pioneer and also welcomed U.S. rock acts that had been floundering in the States, such as the post-Holly Crickets, who toured Britain with the Everly Brothers in 1960 at the same time that Eddie Cochran and Gene Vincent were overwhelming English audiences.

On February 4, 1959, the day following Buddy's death, Cochran, still devastated by news of the fatal crash, recorded Tommy Dee's song "Three Stars." A memorial to Ritchie, the Bopper, and Buddy, Cochran's performance is powerful and eloquent. He breaks down halfway through the record, when he gets to the part about Buddy. Cochran would never recover from his grief. He began shutting himself up in his room and playing Buddy's recordings all night, Lenny Kaye revealed in his liner notes for the album *Eddie Cochran*.

During Cochran's British tour, he continued to brood about Buddy. According to Kaye, Cochran seems to have foreseen his own death. Sharon Sheeley discovered him in his room, listening to Buddy's records. "You'll only hurt yourself, honey," she said. Writes Lenny Kaye, "Eddie replied, in a kind of dazed, far away voice, of how he thought he'd be seeing Buddy soon." Shortly thereafter, his Ford Consul blew a tire and smashed into a lamppost while he was being rushed to Heathrow Airport, with Gene Vincent and Sharon Sheeley, to catch a plane for America. Suffering massive head injuries, he was taken to St. Martin's Hospital in Bath, where Sonny Curtis, now a member of the Crickets, and Jerry Allison came to visit him. They were at the end of their British tour with the Everlys. Joe B. also wanted to visit Cochran but, knowing how terrible his injuries were, feared he couldn't handle it emotionally. He planned to go the following day but, for Cochran, tomorrow never came.

Sheeley and Vincent were also seriously injured but recovered. Cochran never regained consciousness, dying at twenty-one. Later, at the London airport, Phil Everly said, "We'll all miss Eddie, just like we miss Buddy Holly. In this kind of business, your friends aren't always people you see every day. They're people you know and you've toured with."

The Crickets had split with Petty in the spring of 1959 and signed with Coral to record in New York. Sonny Curtis wrote an excellent song for them, "I Fought the Law," an edgy commentary on the pitfalls of youthful impetuosity, but their recording of it sounds amateurish. Though Sonny's guitar lead is exciting, Jerry's drumming is lethargic and unrhythmic. Buddy's replacement, vocalist Earl Sinks, was too innocuous to carry the song to the charts. Later, "I Fought the Law" got a second chance with the Bobby Fuller Four's dynamic guitar-driven cover, which became an international hit. Success eluded the Crickets, who virtually disappeared from the music scene for years. Sonny Curtis left the band to fulfill military obligations, Joe B. vanished into the trucking business, and Jerry became a session drummer in Los Angeles. They would re-form later but would never again make a strong impression in the United States. In Europe, their popularity remained intact.

Though Buddy Holly fell into disrepute in America when early rock 'n' roll went out of style in the sixties, the demand for his records was so heavy in England that Decca advised the Holley family to round up all of his unreleased tapes and begin a program of issuing new albums on a regular basis. Petty was sitting on many of the tapes and threatened to withhold them. Buddy's parents took him back into the fold, giving him control of Buddy's posthumous releases. Hi Pockets Duncan, the man who discovered Buddy, was still active in radio, and would have seemed a more logical choice for the job. But again Hi Pockets was passed over. "I have a pair of nailclippers that was in Buddy's pocket when he was killed that his parents gave to me," Hi Pockets said.

Jerry Allison later told Goldrosen that Buddy would have been "terrifically unhappy" to see Norman Petty bobbing up again in his affairs. The Holleys, Jerry explained, distrusted New York record executives and felt safer keeping the control in Clovis. In the deal that was worked out in 1962, Buddy's record royalties were to be split between the Holleys, Maria Elena, and Petty.

Back in charge of Buddy's record releases, Petty vengefully excluded the Crickets from participating in extensive overdubbings of Buddy's un-released masters, using instead a local band called the Fireballs. Jerry felt that if anyone was going to play drums on overdubs of old Crickets ma-terial, he should have gotten the job. By now Jerry was back in the South-west, often in Clovis, but he was not summoned to the studio. Petty's preference for the Fireballs shows how sour the Crickets' liaison with Petty had become—perhaps how cursed it had been from the start. Jerry took it as a direct affront to him and Joe B., convinced that Petty was deliberately trying to wipe out their contribution by dubbing the Fireballs over their old tracks.

It wasn't that simple. Petty was now managing the Fireballs, who were a far bigger act than the Crickets had ever been without Buddy, scoring hits such as "Torquay," "Bulldog," and "Quite a Party." Jimmy Gilmer joined the band in 1961 and helped make their monster hit "Sugar Shack" the No. 1 record of 1963 (according to *Billboard*, "Sugar Shack" was the only 1963 recording to amass five weeks in the No. 1 position, followed by "He's So Fine" by the Chiffons and "Dominique" by the Singing Nun, both with four weeks at No. 1).

The first of the Buddy Holly–Fireballs LPs was *Reminiscing*, issued in 1963. A tremendous album, it includes multitracked versions of "Wait 'Til the Sun Shines Nellie," "Because I Love You," "It's Not My Fault," "Slippin' and Slidin'," and "Girl on My Mind," as well as the title song. Petty later told interviewers Brooks and Malcolm that "purists" charged that the Fireballs "adulterated" Buddy's early work. Years later, MCA, which had acquired Decca, released Buddy's originals—minus the Fire-balls' overdubbings—in an LP called *For the First Time Anywhere*, pro-viding an opportunity for Holly fans to draw their own conclusions about the rerecordings. *Rolling Stone*'s Jonathan Cott dismissed the purists' quib-bles, pointing out that the Fireballs' overdubbing of the "slow version" of "Slippin' and Slidin' " is a "sublime masterpiece, achieving a seemingly effortless clarity."

The album *Reminiscing* heralded a brief Holly revival in the United States, hitting the American Top 40 in March 1963. The following month it zoomed into the Top 5 in Great Britain, peaking at No. 2. Also in April, Buddy's version of Chuck Berry's "Brown-Eyed Handsome Man" hit No. 3 on the British chart. In July he was back in the U.K. Top 5 with "Bo Diddley." In September, "Wishing," an old demo he'd cut for the Everly Brothers, also made the English charts.

A new Holly LP, *Showcase*, came out in 1964 and featured previously unreleased oddities such as Buddy's one-minute recording of Ferlin Husky's "Gone," as well as covers of other rock standards, mostly vintage Holly demos cut in 1956. *Hit Parader* testily and not altogether accurately noted that "Blue Suede Shoes," "Shake Rattle and Roll," and "Rip It Up" "were done better by Carl Perkins, Bill Haley, and Little Richard," missing the pure rockabilly ebullience of Buddy's covers. Americans ignored the album, but British fans made it a No. 3 smash. Britons venerated Buddy in a way that would never happen in his native country in the sixties. Americans now disdained early rock as hopelessly "square" but went wild over the Beatles, failing to grasp that the Fab Four were simply putting their unique spin on Buddy Holly, Chuck Berry, Elvis, Carl Perkins, and Little Richard and playing them back to the U.S.A. England's Buddy Holly Appreciation Society, founded by John Beecher, owner of a record and book business in Surrey, attracted an enthusiastic and knowledgeable membership of three thousand. Typical of the high purpose of the enterprise was Beecher's publication of Ella Holley's partial memoirs, *The True Story*, in the society's newsletter. Mrs. Holley found writing to be "a lot of work" and in time dropped the project when she became "too busy," she told Griggs in 1977. When Beecher's fan club folded, it was succeeded by the British Buddy Holly Society, formed by Ray Needham of Rainham, Essex, and Trevor Lailey of Benson, Oxfordshire.

The rock scene finally exploded in England in the early sixties, as spectacular as anything that had ever occurred in show business and fired by a mix of the Holly Texas sound and the confidence and optimism of Liverpool youths. "Musically, the rock 'n' roll of Elvis Presley, Little Richard, Chuck Berry, and Buddy Holly dominated the repertoire of the hundreds of groups playing in clubs, which sold only Coca-Cola or Fanta, tea or coffee," wrote Ray Coleman, editor of *Melody Maker* and biographer of Brian Epstein, the Beatles' manager.

Both John Lennon and Paul McCartney acknowledged their debt to Buddy, pointing out that the first forty songs they wrote were directly inspired by Buddy. Their first record, a scratchy shellac, featured Lennon singing "That'll Be the Day" in a small Liverpool studio, McCartney revealed in 1987. "They play and harmonize in tune and tempo," writes Mark Hertsgaard in *A Day in the Life*, "but there is no real indication at this point of the glories that lay ahead." George Harrison learned to play the guitar by listening to a collection of Holly records owned by his friend Tony Bramwell, who'd once met Buddy. A $100 Hofner Futurama was the closest approximation of Buddy's Fender Stratocaster that Harrison could find in Liverpool. "Buddy Holly was my very first favorite and my inspiration to go into the music business," Harrison said in 1965. "I still think he is among the very best. He was different, exciting, and inimitable!"

The Beatles had a sound "quite unlike anything the 1962 British pop scene was accustomed to," according to Ray Coleman, later a biographer of John Lennon. "Few artists wrote their own material. There were wafts of original rock 'n' roll creativity from America (Elvis Presley, Buddy Holly, Little Richard). But in Britain, popular music was firmly dominated by carefully honed love songs from professional writers in Tin Pan Alley, virtually a music factory. . . . The Beatles hated the vapidity of this scene. Their rock 'n' roll thrust was tilted toward overthrowing the Establishment."

Buddy's most profound effect on the Beatles was on Lennon and McCartney's songwriting, Lennon later told fan Jim Dawson. The prodigious sounds Buddy could wring from just three chords convinced Lennon he could write music, and Buddy's eyeglasses reassured Lennon that he could be a rocker. Lennon told Dawson that Buddy was the first guitar player he'd ever seen use a capo, a small bar on the fingerboard of a guitar, used to change the pitch of all the strings at the same time.

Lennon suggested to Dawson that he, John Lennon, was the reincarnation of Buddy Holly. Whether Lennon was serious, the statement indicates the unique bond between Buddy and the British, beginning with his appearances in London and Liverpool in 1958, which went beyond mere influence and into the realm of myth. Perhaps what happened between Buddy and the British is best expressed in the Christian concept of transfiguration—the sudden emanation of radiance from the person of Christ on the mountain. The founder had passed the torch to his disciples, the Beatles, who would politicize and transform rock into an instrument of revolutionary social change. Though controversial at the time, Lennon's remark to Maureen Cleave in the London Evening Standard—"We're more more popular than Jesus now"—was a simple statement of fact. Through the Beatles, and indirectly through Buddy Holly, rock 'n' roll would be responsible for more positive moral evolution in society in the sixties than the church, the government, the family, and the educational establishment combined. Hearing it nowhere else, a generation looked to its musicians for the truth and found it.

When they were still known as the Quarry Men, John, Paul, and George used Buddy Holly songs for their auditions. They practiced "It's So Easy" "on the train from Liverpool," McCartney recalled in Reminiscing in 1981. They had just one guitar between them. McCartney and Harrison would stand on either side of Lennon, draping their arms about him "to look a bit like a stage act," McCartney said. Despite their catchy rendition of "It's So Easy," they "failed miserably." Though much of the music from that period sounds very dated today, McCartney added, "Buddy's songs still sound good . . . from 'That'll Be the Day' to 'It Doesn't Matter Anymore.' "

Rock manager Larry Parnes suggested they get a better name for themselves, "something . . . like Buddy Holly's Crickets," according to Beatles biographer Philip Norman. After calling themselves the Quarry Men for a while, they were briefly known as Johnny and the Moondogs before becoming Long John and the Silver Beatles, and ultimately the Beatles. "What's happening in Liverpool to beat groups now is exactly like what happened to jazz in New Orleans at the turn of the century," *Mersey Beat* publisher Bill Harry said to record-store manager Brian Epstein in 1961. "Everything is happening here, like nowhere in the world."

The Beatles' first significant break came when they performed as the Beat Brothers on Tony Sheridan's recording, "My Bonnie Lies Over the Ocean." Brian Epstein sold out every copy he could order of the Polydor record and asked where he could see the Beat Brothers in person. Lunchtime most days at the Cavern Club, Bill Harry said, directing him to a dank cellar in Matthew Street, near Epstein's Whitechapel shop. The Cavern catered to hard-core rockers and girls with teased hair who dined on cheese rolls and tea. The Beatles received 75 shillings each for their Cavern gigs.

On November 9, 1961, the glossy, well-heeled Epstein, who, like Norman Petty, was gay, found the Cavern show to be somewhat ragged. He deplored the way the Beatles smoked cigarettes while they played, but he was transfixed by the way they kicked endlessly. They performed "Shout!" as well as one of their own compositions, "Hello Little Girl." Later Epstein went backstage to congratulate the band, which then consisted of Lennon, McCartney, Harrison, and drummer Pete Best. Soon he was their manager. On New Year's Day 1962 he took them to London, where they stayed at the Royal Hotel in Woburn Place and auditioned for Decca Records. British Decca proved no more perceptive in dealing with the Beatles than American Decca had been with Buddy Holly at Bradley's Barn in 1956; they rejected the Beatles and told Brian Epstein to stick to the retail business.

By 1962 they were the most popular band in Liverpool, according to a poll of *Mersey Beat*'s five thousand readers. They dressed like Buddy, wearing Ivy League suits and skinny fifties ties, McCartney recalled. Though EMI had previously rejected them, they once again found their way to EMI's Abbey Road studios in London, where thirty-six-year-old George Martin recorded them singing "Love Me Do" and "P.S. I Love You." "Love Me Do" peaked on the national charts at 17—a minor success. Lennon then came up with "Please Please Me," basing the vocal on Roy Orbison's high, soaring style. It rocketed to No. 1 in 1963. Shortly thereafter, on October 13, the Beatles, now with Ringo Starr as their drummer, appeared on TV's *Sunday Night at the London Palladium*, playing the same venue Buddy had electrified in 1958. Two thousand screaming fans charged the theater and battled the police, launching the phenomenon known as Beatlemania. Singing "I Want to Hold Your Hand," "This Boy," and "All My Loving," they became the symbol of sixties optimism, echoing the sunniness and buoyancy of Buddy Holly.

Their American conquest lay just ahead. Sid Bernstein, an agent at the same General Artists Corporation that handled the "Winter Dance Party," presented them at Carnegie Hall on February 12, 1964, just five years after Peggy Sue Allison's prophesy that a pop group would one day play the hallowed venue. Soon the "British Invasion" of the U.S. record charts was underway, and for much of the following decade British rock groups almost completely dominated the American rock scene. Perhaps more than any other rock group, the Beatles—and, as their inspiration, Buddy Holly—assured the dominance of rock 'n' roll as the most popular and enduring musical form of the twentieth century.

David Garrard Lowe, an intimate of Brian Epstein's, recalls meeting the Beatles just before their Carnegie Hall debut. Epstein had asked Lowe to get the boys some publicity in the United States. Then an editor at *Look* magazine, Lowe used his contacts to land the Beatles a *New Yorker* spread. "The first thing the Beatles told me when they landed was that they wanted to meet Elvis," Lowe recalled in 1995. "The second thing they told me was that Buddy Holly was their major influence." Asked if there were any truth to later rumors that Epstein and Lennon were lovers, Lowe said, "Absolutely not. Brian would never mix business with pleasure that way."

Soon other British groups rode to fame singing Buddy's songs. Both Mick Jagger and Keith Richards were fascinated by Buddy's "Not Fade Away" and ultimately the song galvanized them into writing their own material. "The way they arranged 'Not Fade Away' was the beginning of the shaping of them as songwriters," said their manager Andrew Loog Oldham. Added rock historian Nicholas Schaffner, " 'Not Fade Away' fully realized, for the first time, the sound of the Rolling Stones—and British R&B generally—in all its explosive urgency." The most convincing evidence that Buddy was the key factor in the Rolling Stones' success surfaced with their first U.S. record release, which was "Not Fade Away," in 1964.

Keith Richards regards Buddy's influence as the most pervasive in all of rock. "He passed it on via the Beatles and via us," Richards said in 1987. "He's in everybody. . . . This is not bad for a guy from Lubbock, right?" In 1963, years before Graham Nash joined Crosby, Stills and Nash, he was part of the Manchester group the Hollies, who were named "after the American rocker who had such a tremendous influence on the British beat scene—Buddy Holly," wrote Schaffner. The Hollies would score many hit records on both sides of the Atlantic, including "Bus Stop" and "He Ain't Heavy, He's My Brother." Their LP *Buddy Holly* had sixteen Holly tracks, among them "Wishing," "Think It Over," and "Midnight Shift."

Eventually Buddy's oeuvre became the basic textbook of the British rock renaissance. Eric Clapton, rock's future guitar god, called Buddy "a very big early influence, particularly the way he looked, and I loved the look and the sound of his Strats." Clapton played with the Roosters in Ricky Tick clubs in Kingston, Windsor, and West Wickham and briefly with a Liverpool group, Casey Jones and the Engineers. Finally he joined the Yardbirds and landed a Crawdaddy residency and a regular job at Studio 51 in Soho in 1964. On the Rolling Stones' Christmas TV special *Rock-'n'-Roll Circus,* Clapton played "Peggy Sue" with a hastily improvised group that included Clapton on lead guitar, John Lennon on rhythm guitar, Mitch Mitchell on drums, Keith Richards on bass, and Mick Jagger, vocals. In 1968, Clapton covered Buddy's "Well All Right" in a band he formed with Ginger Baker and Stevie Winwood.

By the end of the sixties, Buddy's triumph in England was as total as his obscurity in America. Folk singer Phil Ochs was booed in Carnegie Hall for announcing that he was going to sing some Buddy Holly songs. While new Holly LPs such as *Holly in the Hills*, which highlighted Buddy's early C&W performances with Bob Montgomery; *Greatest Hits*; and 1969's *Giant* consistently climbed the British charts, they made no impression on Americans. He was voted No. 6 in England's *New Musical Express* poll as "World's Best Male Singer." He rated sixteenth in Britain as "World's Greatest Musical Personality," outranking George Harrison, Brenda Lee, and Frank Sinatra. But in his native country Buddy Holly was about to disappear into the same black hole that swallowed up so many of his peers, including Buddy Knox, Roy Orbison, the Everly Brothers, and Gene Vincent.

Sometimes it seemed that only his family remembered him. In the 1960s, long after Carroll Anderson had stopped managing the Surf Ballroom and opened Carroll's Café in Clear Lake, Anderson glanced up from his work one day and recognized Buddy's aged parents sitting at a table in his restaurant. When he asked if he could join them, Anderson recalled in 1980, "They said, 'You mean that you remember us?' "

It was the Holleys' third visit to Clear Lake. Only here, perhaps, could they relive the triumph of their son's last performance and come to terms with the terror of his final seconds. Anderson was touched by Buddy's parents and referred to them as "very fine people." No doubt they helped him deal with his own grieving. Even fifteen years later he was still haunted by the crash and its grisly aftermath. "You can't believe how hard it hits you," he said to Mike Oestreicher in 1980, "when you've got three young people . . . full of life . . . and in five minutes they're all dead . . . torn up, dismantled." He kept "some of the most gruesome pictures you've ever seen" locked up for years and finally burned them to erase the horror from his mind. He preferred to remember Buddy's last words to him, which were, "I hope our paths cross again some day."

Besides the undying love of family and friends, Buddy still commanded the respect of contemporary songwriters and poets. Waylon Jennings celebrated him in "Old Friend" and "The Stage," Benny Barnes eulogized him in "Gold Records in the Snow," and Sonny Curtis wrote the moving "Real Buddy Holly Story." They all helped keep Buddy's legend alive in America. When Buddy finally regained his popularity in his homeland in the seventies, it was largely due to a singer-songwriter-poet named Don McLean.

Chapter Sixteen

American Pie

By 1972, America was ripe for a Buddy Holly renais sance. The Beatles had broken up; Janis Joplin, Jim Morrison, and Jimi Hendrix were dead; and most of the sixties bands had faded from sight. David Bowie saluted the end of rock's creative, pioneering period in the fifties and sixties by introducing "glitter rock," which would usher in the disco and punk trends of the seventies. Chuck Berry returned to the charts with "My Ding-A-Ling." Elvis was smoking again with "Burning Love." Ricky Nelson's "Garden Party" hit the jukeboxes and Elton John's "Crocodile Rock" was No. 1. "Golden Oldies" thrived again on DJ radio stations, the Carpenters would soon be crooning sha-la-las in "Yesterday Once More," and Fats Domino and Bill Haley bounced back into the $400,000-a-year bracket with their fifties hits.

Don McLean's single "American Pie" made its initial appearance on *Billboard*'s Hot 100 at No. 69 on November 27, 1971. Seven weeks later it was No. 1. The song was full of nostalgic references to "That'll Be the Day," the grim headlines of February 3, 1959, and a host of fifties memories such as hops in the gym, danceable rock 'n' roll music, the Monotones' "Book of Love," Chevrolets, pickup trucks, carnations, beer, whiskey, and God. It mourned the passing of friendly Buddy Holly tunes and deplored what rock had become in the hands of the Rolling Stones, obsessed with Satan and drugs and abandoned by God. Sad and reverential, "American Pie" became the anthem of Christmas '71, providing an eerie glow to the holiday, like a distant reveille. Described by *Rolling Stone*'s Geoffrey Stokes as "an eight-minute chronicle of American pop inspired by the airplane deaths of Ritchie Valens, the Big Bopper, and Buddy Holly," "American Pie" went on to become 1972's biggest-selling single.

The LP, also entitled *American Pie*, was dedicated to Buddy. As "American Pie" dominated both the singles and album charts for almost two months, Buddy's own records began to sell again in the United States. " 'American Pie' became a tool to resurrect the memory of Buddy Holly and get it on track," said McLean. "It's growing all the time." The song made fifties rock so fashionable that *Grease*, a lightly nostalgic send-up of the fifties, became an all-time smash on Broadway. Then, just a year after the release of "American Pie," in 1973, a character in the popular film *American Graffiti* said, "I can't stand that surfing shit. Rock 'n' roll's been going downhill ever since Buddy Holly died."

Ironically, McLean's own career went into a slump after "American Pie." In the eighties, he made a comeback with a hit cover of Roy Orbison's "Crying" and again credited Buddy with his success. Tommy Allsup, who was one of McLean's sidemen for the "Crying" session, came to work one day and showed McLean the wallet Buddy had been carrying for Tommy during the 1959 plane crash. He told McLean the Iowa police had just returned it to him. To McLean it was "like an omen," McLean told interviewer Stu Fink in 1985. "Crying" soared to No. 5 on the charts and his career surged again "for about three years," McLean added.

Decca's response to Buddy's resurgence in the early seventies was disappointing. Instead of assembling a definitive Holly collection, Decca issued a slapdash German two-album set without liner notes. On the other side of the Atlantic Ocean, Buddy's British fans could choose from among a wide and rich variety of albums, including *Remember* in 1971, *Legend* in 1974, and *Rave On* and *The Buddy Holly Story* in 1975.

The first unmistakable sign that Buddy had regained his cult status in the United States was the establishment of the Buddy Holly Memorial Society, founded in 1975 by a Kmart employee and sometime racing-car driver named Bill Griggs, who lived in Wethersfield, Connecticut. Griggs eventually moved to Lubbock and published a Holly fan magazine called *Reminiscing*, which lasted over a decade, and promoted an annual week-long convention, held around Buddy's birthday and featuring live performances by the Crickets, Don McLean, Joe Ely, Carl Perkins, Buddy Knox, Bo Diddley, Del Shannon, Bobby Vee, and many others. Before the demise of the society around 1990, the membership roll boasted fifty-two hundred members from all fifty states and thirty-one foreign countries, including the Netherlands, Germany, Norway, South Africa, Switzerland, Japan, Greece, Zimbabwe, Finland, Korea, Egypt, Denmark, New Zealand, Belgium, Sweden, England, Australia, Ireland, and Canada. In his newsletter Griggs addressed the readers as if they were members of one big family, as in a sense they were, bound by their love of Buddy. Griggs disbanded the BHMS due to the increasing strain of his relationship with Maria Elena and disagreements with club members, among other reasons.

Other than McLean, the one recording artist perhaps most responsible for the revival of Buddy Holly was Linda Ronstadt. In 1976, her magnificently earthy cover of "That'll Be the Day" went to No. 11 on the charts. The following year she covered "It's So Easy," which soared to No. 5.

Altogether, Ronstadt's Holly covers racked up six months on the charts. Eighteen years after Buddy Holly's death, he was again a major force in American rock 'n' roll. Born in Tuscon, Arizona, on July 15, 1946, sultry Linda Ronstadt grew up, like Buddy, singing Hank Williams and Elvis Presley. She had a lush, doe-eyed beauty compounded of half-Mexican, half-German bloodlines. Despite formidable physical assets, she said, according to biographer Mark Bego, "I'm not a beautiful girl. I don't have good skin or good hair or a fashion-model figure." Real or imagined, such drawbacks did not prevent her from getting "a bad reputation even in junior high school because our skirts were too tight." Nor would they prevent her involvement with dynamic J. D. Souther and a relationship with California Governor Jerry Brown that provoked widespread rumor and speculation.

In 1964 she went to Los Angeles and fell in with Shilo, the band that evolved into the Eagles, who came to epitomize the seventies synthesis of C&W and rock. "The Eagles backed me up," Ronstadt said in record mogul Joe Smith's book *Off the Record.* "When I heard them sing 'Witchy Woman' in the living room of J. D. Souther's house, where I was living at the time, I knew the Eagles were going to make it." Peter Asher, formerly of Peter and Gordon, who'd covered "True Love Ways," got Ronstadt's career off the ground, guiding her to a mixture of oldies and contemporary songs. She would use the classics of Buddy Holly, Roy Orbison, the Everly Brothers, Willie Nelson, and Hank Williams as a vehicle to stardom. Her 1974 breakthrough album, *Heart Like a Wheel,* a No. 1 hit, included her cover of Buddy's "It Doesn't Matter Anymore." In 1976 her LP *Hasten Down the Wind,* featuring "That'll Be the Day," went to No. 3 on the album chart and garnered a Grammy for Best Pop Vocal Performance, Female. "It's So Easy" was in *Simple Dreams,* Ronstadt's 1977 album that went to No. 1 and sold 3.5 million copies. Years later Ronstadt acknowledged her debt to Buddy, appearing in Lubbock at a "Tornado Jam" in Buddy Holly Park. After she and Joe Ely sang a duet of "That'll Be the Day," both said they were fans of Buddy.

Ronstadt's immense popularity brought Buddy's music to a mass audience in the seventies that might never have heard of Buddy Holly otherwise. Don McLean had evoked Buddy's memory and propelled him up the ladder to pop sainthood, but it was Linda Ronstadt's covers of "That'll Be the Day" and "It's So Easy" that started the world singing his songs again and won him an altogether new audience of young people.

With so much money pouring into Buddy's estate, Buddy's mother had a hard time keeping track of it. Looking after her ailing seventy-four-year-old husband occupied most of her waking hours. According to Larry, Mrs. Holley tended to be too open-handed, kept no records, and ended up forgetting to pay her taxes. "Mother had got behind seven years without ever filin'," Larry said in 1992. "Daddy had his stroke and all she did was tend to him. Daddy didn't know nothin'—he was just there, he liked to listen to 'Hee-Haw' on the radio, he was happy. Mother didn't know nothin' [about money] and they just let it drift on by and here come Internal Revenue finally with about half a million dollars that was owed and there was no way to get it. We didn't want Mother to lose her house and have the fame of all this coming out that she was an income tax evader."

Larry was forced to sell off the American rights to Buddy's songs to Paul McCartney, whose MPL company is the largest independent music publisher in the world (the initials denote Paul McCartney and his wife Linda). The transaction divested the Holley estate of Buddy's birthright but enabled the Holleys to raise badly needed cash and to get everything squared away with the IRS's claim against Buddy's mother. Paul Mc-Cartney told author John Tobler in 1980 that his business advisers approached him one day and asked, "Who do you really like?"

"Buddy Holly," McCartney replied.

Somewhat later, McCartney heard that "Buddy's old songs and stuff" were up for sale. He "jumped on it," recognizing a business opportunity that also offered some fun as "a fan thing," he later told Tobler.

MPL owns many copyrights of incalculable value, including the perennials "Happy Birthday," "Chopsticks," "Autumn Leaves," and "On Wisconsin"; the Broadway musicals *Guys and Dolls*, *Grease*, *Hello Dolly*, *Mame*, and *A Chorus Line*; and the entire oeuvre of Scott Joplin and Ira Gershwin. McCartney's personal wealth is estimated at $500 million. The *Guinness Book of Records* lists him as the richest musician in history. In response to the sale of Buddy's catalogue to McCartney, Maria Elena told Griggs, "I was very happy to hear about that because I thought that Paul would be pushing record sales." In 1993 she added, "Paul McCartney bought the whole catalog but Southern still has the overseas market, and MPL has the American market."

From the start, overseeing the vast treasury of Holly classics proved for McCartney to be a labor of love. He'd been "a big fan of Buddy's" since childhood, he told Tobler, adding that Buddy was "one of the first artists that turned me on." On September 7, 1976, the fortieth anniversary of Buddy's birth, McCartney inaugurated Buddy Holly Week in the United Kingdom, featuring a huge hop in London. Norman Petty was the guest of honor at a luncheon hosted by McCartney and attended by Eric Clapton and other rock luminaries. Buddy Holly Week became an annual affair, described by McCartney as "just great" because "all the people like me love it and it brings back great memories." Also a fan of the Crickets and of anyone else who'd been close to Buddy, McCartney in the coming years would entertain Larry Welborn, Sonny Curtis, Jerry,

Joe B., and Larry Holley during Buddy Holly Week, and in 1979 the Crickets would appear with him and his band Wings at London's Odeon Hammersmith.

"I went and seen Paul McCartney in person in Birmingham, England," Larry recalled in 1992. "I went in there with him and stayed a couple of hours, him and his wife. They had a big tub of beer there. Just as friendly as they could be." That night Larry attended a Wings concert. "Except for 'Mother Mary, Let It Be' [sic], I have never heard any song I liked very much by his group," said Larry, "but he did a song at that concert that I really liked. It's never been put out in the States—something about some lake in Scotland, beautiful song. That's whenever I realized that Paul had some talent. The way the Beatles made it, they had promoters that hyped them up. I guarantee you, Buddy didn't have nothin' but Buddy and his guitar. And determination. Rock 'n' roll's gone so rank now. Some guy gets out there with a feather in his cap and a jockey strap on and paints hisself all up and screams and the audience is goin' crazy 'cause they're all on dope but that's not music."

Larry does not regret having sold off Buddy's songs. "I don't hold no grudge against Mr. Eastman [McCartney's father-in-law, lawyer, and manager]," he said in 1992. "Seems like a nice man. We did what we had to do. It's been a long, hard, sordid, tough struggle. I'm the guy that had to tend to it all, because I'm Mother's trustee."

Nevertheless, the loss of the priceless Holly songbook seems to fit perfectly into the star-crossed saga of Buddy Holly. In a kind of karmic backlash, McCartney was divested of his own birthright—the songs he and John Lennon wrote—when Michael Jackson acquired the company owning the Beatles' catalog. The sale resulted from Brian Epstein's mishandling of the Lennon-McCartney songs back in the sixties. Epstein's structuring of Northern Songs, the company that controlled the Lennon-McCartney copyrights, enabled one of his partners to sell off the company to ATV for 10 million pounds after Epstein's death. Michael Jackson then snapped up the company from ATV. "The Beatles were angry at what they regarded as a betrayal," wrote Ray Coleman in his biography of Brian Epstein. McCartney now has no more control of his early songs than the Holley family has over Buddy's classics, such as "It's So Easy," which was shamelessly exploited on a daily basis in a 1994 television commercial hawking home video equipment. Though Norman Petty had died in 1984, it almost seemed as if he were still calling the shots.

Books and movies about Buddy started appearing in the seventies, beginning with Dave Laing's analytical *Buddy Holly*. Then came Ralph and Elizabeth Peer's *Buddy Holly: A Biography in Words, Photographs, and Music*, which was a loving songbook by devoted fans. John Goldrosen's *Buddy*

Holly: His Life and Music arranged Buddy's life in coherent chronological form for the first time and included invaluable interviews. Less ambitious books included John Tobler's *The Buddy Holly Story* and Alan Mann's *A-Z of Buddy Holly*, both of British origin.

Movie producers had been interested in filming Buddy's life ever since 1960. By the following decade several projects went into development. One, *The Buddy Holly Story*, starring Gary Busey, would finally reach the public, but it would bear little relation to the facts of Buddy's life. The controversy surrounding it would eventually embroil Buddy's family in litigation and outrage the Crickets and Norman Petty, all of whom were ignored by Hollywood as if they'd never existed. But the film, which proved to be a popular and critical success, was a powerful factor in the continuing growth and emergence of Buddy's posthumous career and his influence on popular culture.

Chapter Seventeen

Buddy's Legacy: Exploitation, Distortion, and an Enduring Love

Hollywood has yet to produce an authentic portrait of the rock 'n' roll experience, though it is one of the most emblematic of the twentieth century. The moviemakers' flirtation with Buddy Holly's life is a classic example of distortion and exploitation, smoothing out the hard, jagged edges that make a life in rock 'n' roll so engaging, perilous, tragic, and archetypically modern—torn between a yearning for acceptance and a compulsion to destroy all that is false and hypocritical in society. The real Buddy Holly is to be found nowhere in the various efforts to represent him on film.

The first was written by Mark Saha in California as an ABC "Movie of the Week" and was to feature a voice-over by Paul McCartney. Petty saw the script and pronounced it "very good." The film was to include cameo appearances by all of the famous artists Buddy had worked with. As usual, producers ran into obstacles when they attempted to acquire character rights—legal releases from living persons who were to be portrayed in the film. According to Petty, Mark Saha secured releases from almost everyone except Maria Elena, but Goldrosen later wrote that Jerry, Joe B., the Holleys, and Petty himself all wanted more money and, perhaps, script approval. "We had favorite-nation clauses in all the releases so that if one person got paid, everyone got paid," Petty later told Brooks and Malcolm. "So, rather than to get involved, MCA just shelved the whole idea and it never did become a movie at Universal."

In the mid-1970s another movie about Buddy was put into the works by an outfit that called itself Innovisions. The producers, Steve Rash and Freddy Bauer, went to Florida to see Maria Elena, who had moved there from New York in 1968. Maria Elena and her husband, a Texas businessman, were raising their three children. Both of her sons, Buddy and Carlos, were named after Buddy, whose full name was Charles Hardin Buddy Holley (Carlos is Spanish for Charles). In 1975 both Maria Elena and Buddy's parents okayed the Innovisions proposal and signed contracts in return for a share of the royalties. The original title was *The Day the Music Died*.

Meanwhile, Jerry Allison was working on a Buddy Holly movie of his own, with Gary Busey playing Jerry. For all their talk during Buddy's lifetime about wanting to stay in Texas, the Crickets were gravitating to Tennessee and buying farms next to each other. Jerry's movie focused on the Crickets' 1957 "black tour," covering one month in Buddy's life and showing how the Crickets helped eradicate racial prejudice. Allison and screenwriter Tom Drake sold the script, then entitled *Not Fade Away*, to Twentieth Century-Fox but encountered solid resistance from Buddy's wife and family. The language was too racy for the Holleys, and Maria Elena didn't care for the small fee Fox suggested.

Nonetheless filming began in September 1975 with Steve Davies playing Buddy, Gary Busey as Jerry, and Bruce Kirby playing Joe B. Stephen Davies later appeared in a well-received made-for-cable film, *Philip Marlowe, Private Eye: The Pencil*, and a horror movie about killer cockroaches, *The Nest*. Permission was acquired from MCA to use Buddy's recordings. While filming on location in Mississippi, Jerry himself took a small role, playing a music-store owner. Bob Montgomery also got into the act, playing a tour promoter. Three weeks into shooting, Fox executives looked at the rushes and panicked. They were expecting *American Graffiti* but got *The Defiant Ones* instead—a story of whites and blacks chained together in uneasy alliance. Give us some laughs, Fox ordered, but the director, Jerry Friedman, refused. Fox shut the film down and shelved the footage when it was one-third completed, writing off a million dollars.

Innovisions, which had been moving ahead with *its* Buddy Holly movie, took out an intimidating full-page ad in *Variety* on October 28, 1975, warning of legal action if anyone else attempted to portray Buddy on screen. Two years later, *The Buddy Holly Story* was in the can, starring Gary Busey, who'd managed to promote himself from the role of Jerry Allison in *Not Fade Away* to the leading role of Buddy Holly in the Innovisions project. The movie, according to almost all serious critics, is a complete distortion of Buddy's life, beginning with the mountains clearly visible in scenes supposedly representing Lubbock, a city that's flatter than a pancake and light-years from the nearest hillock, and the skyscrapers in the background over the "Clear Lake Ballroom." Evidently the producers, who chose to shoot the film around Los Angeles, were unaware of the topography of the South Plains. Surely someone must have told them, though, that Buddy was not backed by a symphony orchestra in Clear Lake but by a drummer and two pickers. Far more damaging was their negative portrayal of Buddy's parents. In the movie, L.O. and Ella are depicted as wanting Buddy to give up rock 'n' roll. In real life, they were supportive of Buddy and his music. Eventually the Holleys would sue the producers for such distortion.

Most extraordinary of all, the moviemakers decided to omit Petty, Jerry, and Joe B., Buddy's closest associates, Billy Stull stated in an interview

at the Norman Petty Recording Studio in Clovis in 1992. Petty was offered $5,000 to be music consultant, Stull added, but when Petty foolishly
demanded script approval, he was completely deleted from the movie. "I
felt like a nonenity, like some very important years of my life had just
been wiped out," Petty complained to *Rolling Stone*'s Chet Flippo.

Although there was no way Innovisions could similarly erase the Crickets from Buddy's life, they did the next most expedient thing, changing
Jerry and Joe B.'s names to Jesse and Ray Bob. It was a cruel blow, typical
of Hollywood's lack of respect for artists. Jesse, the Allison substitute, was
played by Don Stroud, who'd portrayed one of Shelley Winters's gangster
sons in 1970's *Bloody Mama*. Charles Martin Smith, who'd made a strong
impression as Terry the Toad in *American Graffiti*, played Ray Bob, the
Joe B. character. Smith knew how to play both piano and guitar, though
he was unfamiliar with the bull fiddle. Although Goldrosen would later
state that Don Stroud lacked professional musical experience, Stroud
would be credited as the drummer on the film's sound-track album. The
LP also offered "Special thanks" to Ritchie Hayward, drummer for the
"Eddie Cochran" Band. In bit roles were Gailard Sartain as the Bopper
(he'd show up again in 1981, in *Hard Country*, with Jan-Michael Vincent,
Kim Basinger, and Tanya Tucker) and comedian Fred Travalena as "Mad
Man Mancuso," a pseudonym for the DJ Tom Clay, who was instrumental
in the success of "That'll Be the Day."

As Buddy, Gary Busey wanted to do his own singing, but Maria Elena
was still under the impression the musical portion of the sound track
would be taken directly from Buddy's master tapes. She was in for a surprise. A strong personality, Busey was a daredevil who rode his motorcycle
without a helmet—until an accident years later almost took his life. He
was born in Texas and grew up in Oklahoma. Regarded in Hollywood as
a supporting actor rather than a leading man, he'd appeared in *Dirty Little
Billy* in 1972, followed by light roles in *The Last Picture Show*, *Thunderbolt
and Lightfoot*, *The Gumball Rally*, *A Star Is Born*, *Straight Time*, and *Big
Wednesday*, as well as the television series *The Texas Wheelers* and the
television movies *The Execution of Private Slovik* and *The Law*.

To get in shape for the role of Buddy Holly, Busey, a large man, brought
his weight down from 240 pounds to 180. He had his long blond hair
dyed and cut to resemble Buddy's. He was not dissuaded by some Holly
aficionados who felt that Busey, at thirty-three, was a bit old to be playing
Buddy from ages eighteen to twenty-two. Fans were shocked again when
it was announced that Busey intended to do his own singing rather than
lip-synch to Buddy's records. To Maria Elena the idea of a Buddy Holly
movie without Buddy himself singing his hits was unthinkable. "It
wouldn't be any good with anyone else doing the singing," she told Griggs
on June 25, 1977. Griggs echoed the widow's sentiments, commenting in

December 1977 that the film would lose its claim to authenticity "if Buddy isn't singing the songs in it."

Despite the liberties the moviemakers took with historical fact, *The Buddy Holly Story* turned out to be disarmingly lovable, thanks largely to Busey's performance, a tour de force of acting and singing. Though vocally unimpressive (a fact that becomes painfully obvious when one listens to the sound-track album), Busey was not altogether inexperienced as a musician. As the pseudonymous Teddy Jack Eddy, he'd worked as a rock 'n' roll drummer, at one point with Leon Russell, and he knew how to handle a guitar, although he'd require off-camera assistance from a more accomplished instrumentalist for Buddy's virtuosic lead guitar parts when the sound-track was recorded live. More importantly, Busey knew how to act, turning in a performance of such sincerity and conviction that no one cared whether it resembled Buddy. No one, that is, except Buddy's intimates. Says Sonny Curtis in a 1993 interview, "Gary Busey was a good Chuck Berry, but he wasn't Buddy." Just prior to the film's release, Robert Gittler, the writer of the screenplay, committed suicide.

Lubbock, ever predictable, failed to lobby hard enough for the world premiere and lost out to Dallas, where the movie opened on May 18, 1978, at the Medallion Theater. Banners streamed from the marquee, a red carpet was laid out from the door to the street, and a line of policemen held back a throng of two thousand. A local band played Buddy's hits, and Maria Elena addressed the crowd briefly. Though Niki Sullivan had not been portrayed in the movie, he attended with his wife Fran and Holly fan-club honchos Griggs and Beecher. Other notables included Jerry, Joe B., and Sonny Curtis, who'd flown in together from Tennessee, and Trini Lopez, who told Griggs that he and Buddy had been close friends. Actor-director Ron Howard, Holly super-fan Steve Bonner, and Goldrosen rounded out the list of VIPs. The weather was "hot and sticky," Griggs later recalled.

During the viewing of the film, when Busey sings "True Love Ways," Mary Elena became distraught. Later, according to Griggs, she said that she'd "started seeing Buddy on the screen." Bursting into tears, she ran from the auditorium and into the women's room. Despite her own subsequent marriage and her children, she was still, at that moment, the young woman married to the legend.

In the lobby after the premiere, Griggs unofficially bestowed the imprimatur of the Buddy Holly Memorial Society on the film by congratulating director Steve Rash, producer Freddy Bauer, and executive producer Edward H. Cohen, comparing the film with *American Graffiti*, the ultimate fifties movie. Contradicting his statement just six months before that the film could hardly be considered a Buddy Holly movie without Buddy's voice, Griggs recanted, telling Rash, Cohen, and Bauer "that I loved the movie and was on cloud nine with the job that they did," he later wrote in *Reminiscing*. Busey mingled with the crowd and chatted with Holly fan Don Larson at the popcorn machine. They were discussing rare Holly memorabilia, Larson revealed in a 1993 interview. Busey had visited Buddy's parents in Lubbock and seen one of the photographs that Joanie Svenson had taken of Buddy, Waylon, and Tommy during the "Winter Dance Party" with her Brownie Hawkeye camera. Svenson later became Larson's girlfriend and gave him the photos. Busey asked Larson for copies.

A few feet away from the movie star, the Crickets—Niki, Sonny, Jerry, and Joe B.—observed their first reunion since January 1958. Jerry and Joe B. had been rendered nonpersons by the movie, which portrayed them but changed their names. Exploited again, the Crickets must have found it a bittersweet reunion indeed. "That movie just really rubbed me the wrong way," Allison later told Jeremy Powers. To Griggs he added, "I've got to be irritated when they say, 'Here's a guy named Jesse, and it's not me.'" Moreover, Allison and Mauldin felt that the aborted Holly film, *Not Fade Away*, had been ripped off, that information Allison had imparted to Busey on the set later turned up in *The Buddy Holly Story*, Allison confided to Goldrosen. These objections notwithstanding, the Crickets posed with Gary Busey when he strolled over to them at the premiere, and shutterbugs Don Larson and Mary Griggs captured the moment for posterity.

Following the premiere, the producers hosted a party at the Longhorn Ballroom. A C&W band played, Busey sat in with them, and Don Stroud played the bongo drums. The bandleader was Busey's brother. Joe B. disliked "the whole movie, period," he later told Griggs. The objections he mentioned seemed singularly trivial—Buddy never wore white socks, and his trousers were not as short as Busey's—until Joe B. confessed what was really bothering him: he wasn't given credit for winning his fight with Buddy over the stinky cigar in London! "J.I. and Buddy didn't get in a fight, and J.I. didn't knock Buddy's teeth out. I did," said Joe. B. He admitted that he'd wanted to produce the Holly biography himself and was glad that someone had at last figured out how to get it on the screen. "For some reason," he said, he'd never been able to start "the wheels turning."

Jerry was furious over the sullen, slovenly "a _ _ _ _ _ _" the movie made him out to be, he later told Griggs, especially in the scene where Stroud, playing Jerry, makes sexist and racist cracks about Maria Elena, which "*really* irritated the s _ _ _" out of him, fumed Jerry. The insult had actually come from an engineer rather than one of Buddy's friends, Allison told Powers in 1989. *The Buddy Holly Story*, Allison added in a 1993 interview, "was all bullshit. Don't base anything on that movie.

Wasn't anybody involved in it that knew what went on for real. They loosely took it from John Goldrosen. They spelled Buddy's name right was about the only thing they had right."

The day following the Dallas premiere, several of the VIPs who'd attended, including Goldrosen, Beecher, and Griggs, drove to Lubbock to see Buddy's birthplace. All they found at 1911 Sixth Street was an empty lot. After the house had fallen into disrepair, the city contracted with a private firm to demolish it. Later it was discovered that the house was still standing, somewhere outside the city limits. Fans started a collection to buy it back and turn it into a museum, but Ella Holley objected to the project. The effort and expense that would be required to retrieve the old house, which probably embarrassed her, would not be "worthwhile," she told Griggs. Buddy's mother convinced his fans to "drop the idea," Griggs revealed in 1978. Though the Holley house was modest, to be sure, with the proper vision it could have become the center of a thriving tourist complex or theme park. Buddy's fans were understandably disappointed, reacting pretty much as Elvis's would if Memphis announced it was razing Graceland. Griggs denounced Lubbock's insensitivity. "It was Buddy and nothing else that had put Lubbock on the map," he wrote in *Reminiscing*.

Though Lubbock had lost the premiere to Dallas, the producers decided to make a special event out of the opening of *The Buddy Holly Story* when they got around to showing it in Buddy's hometown, two days following the Dallas premiere. They were disappointed to learn from Lubbock officials that the city had erected no memorials to Buddy. The city hastily tacked up a sign on an undeveloped patch of property in north Lubbock proclaiming it to be the Buddy Holly Memorial Park. Located on a hill by a lake, it was a lovely setting but hardly a park or "recreation area," as they called it. Nonetheless, Mayor Dirk West hosted a ceremony, and Busey made a brief speech.

The sound-track album from the film was available on the Epic label, but it didn't make the U.S. *Billboard Book of Top 40 Albums*. Evidently it fared no better abroad, where British author Alan Mann wrote that the "soundtrack album died the death" and attributed its "modest" sales to the fact that the "superb twenty Golden Greats of Holly/Crickets material had rocketed to No. 1 on the album charts for three consecutive weeks and—thankfully—creamed off the main sales." John Tobler wrote that on March 25, 1978, "nineteen years after his death Buddy Holly topped the U.K. album charts for the first time. Before the compilation album *20 Golden Greats* finally achieved this feat, the closest he and his backing group, the Crickets, had been was with 1963's *Reminiscing*."

Gold and platinum records reached Lubbock from abroad in time for the May movie premiere. While in Lubbock for the occasion, Griggs and a contingent of Holly fans visited with Buddy's parents, Norman

Petty, Hi Pockets Duncan, Larry Corbin of KLLL, and Larry Holley. Bee-cher presented gold records to Ella and L.O. Holley and to Maria Elena, representing 500,000 sales of the British LP, which had the long and cumbersome title, *Buddy Holly Lives—Buddy Holly & the Crickets 20 Golden Greats*. Shortly thereafter Maria Elena told Griggs that she received a platinum record from England, representing 1 million sales.

Members of Buddy's family viewed the Busey "biopic" for the first time at the Lubbock opening on May 20, 1978. Initially they seemed pleased, even thrilled. As usual, Buddy's parents were astonished that anyone remembered Buddy at all. Though the family appreciated Buddy's talent, they never expected him to become a world figure, Mrs. Holley had told Griggs the previous year. At the screening, an emotional L.O. stood up as Busey sang "Not Fade Away," pointed to the screen, and informed the entire audience that the person being portrayed in the film was his son, according to Ed Cohen, the movie's executive producer. Buddy's mother was "proud" that a movie had been made about her son, she told Griggs on July 1, 1978. "We think it's just great," she said, adding that Busey had caught Buddy's "mannerisms . . . attitudes, and the way he stood." Mindful of Buddy's loyal British fans, Mrs. Holley expressed dismay over the film's omission of Buddy's 1958 tour of the United Kingdom. She hoped the British wouldn't be "upset." Altogether she'd seen the movie four times. She explained that on the first viewing, she "didn't even see it" because she "was expecting one thing and another came on the screen."

At first Larry Holley was "real pleased" with the movie, despite its realistic use of profanity, which clashed with his Baptist principles. Busey's portrayal "showed Buddy as the go-getter that he was," capturing the essential Buddy, which Larry summed up as "drive and determination," he told Griggs in 1978. *The Buddy Holly Story* played to standing-room-only crowds throughout Texas and to full houses when it opened simultaneously in New York on July 21, 1978, at the Criterion Theater, a sixteen-hundred-seat venue in Times Square, and at the Gemini I and II, and the Cinerama Dome in Los Angeles.

The Academy of Motion Picture Arts and Sciences nominated Busey for the 1978 Best Actor Oscar. The competition that year was Warren Beatty for *Heaven Can Wait*; Jon Voight for *Coming Home*; Robert De Niro for *The Deer Hunter*; and Laurence Olivier for *The Boys From Brazil*. "Cunning tactics by one publicist won an unlikely nomination for Gary Busey in the title role of *The Buddy Holly Story*," Anthony Holden later wrote in *Behind the Oscars: The Secret History of the Academy Awards*. Others, like Rona Barrett, the powerful television personality, vigorously championed Busey's performance. At the awards presentation at the Dorothy Chandler Pavilion in Los Angeles, Johnny Carson greeted a glittering audience and introduced John Wayne, whose emaciated appearance shocked many. Having survived a long struggle with cancer, he gratefully acknowledged the audience's standing ovation, saying, "That's just about the only medicine a fella'd ever really need." It was now twenty years since he'd muttered the lines in The Searchers that inspired "That'll Be the Day." "Believe me when I tell you I'm mighty pleased that I can amble down here tonight," Wayne told the Oscar audience. "I plan to be around for a whole lot longer." He died less than two months later.

Although Busey lost out to Jon Voight, The Buddy Holly Story won in another category: "Original Song Score and Its Adaptation or Adaptation Score." Although adapter Joe Renzetti took home the Oscar, it belonged, in a sense, to Buddy Holly, composer of the film's songs, but the Academy Awards are intended to reward movie-industry personnel.

After the picture had been in release for a while, most of the people connected to Buddy's estate turned against it. Paul McCartney complained that the The Buddy Holly Story "was hardly the true story" and started filming The Real Buddy Holly Story, which opened with Sonny Curtis singing his song of the same title. Larry and Travis Holley, Ben Hall, Jerry, Joe B., Sonny, Tommy Allsup, and Vi Petty talked directly into the camera, recalling old times with Buddy. At the end, Keith Richards delivered a ringing coda, saying that Buddy's influence could be heard in virtually every new rock song played on the radio. Working with producer Anthony Wall and director Richard Spence, McCartney crafted an adulatory documentary film, the best part of which is McCartney singing "Words of Love," accompanying himself on an acoustic guitar. It was shown on BBC-TV's Arena program in 1987.

Another TV documentary on Buddy was produced by Iowa PBS-TV and broadcast nationally on the PBS network. The one-hour show was entitled Reminiscing and featured appearances by the Crickets. Maria Elena was shown at a press conference but "she's not talking," said the narrator, "not by choice but by legal necessity." He explained that her attorney had advised her that any participation in the documentary Reminiscing could jeopardize the Buddy Holly estate's contract with Innovisions, which had agreed to pay the estate "a tidy sum" for portrayal rights. The narrator characterized the arrangement as "one more example of the complexities that have evolved from a man of such simple beginnings."

Relations between Buddy's parents and the producers of The Buddy Holly Story got even more complex in October 1979 when they sued for $300,000. Though they'd previously told Griggs they loved the movie, Ella and L. O. Holley now charged that the film inaccurately portrayed their relationship to Buddy. The suit was settled out of court for an undisclosed amount. Of all Buddy's intimates, only Maria Elena failed to criticize the movie's content publicly. Actress Maria Richwine, an elegant Audrey Hepburn type, played Maria Elena in the film.

That *The Buddy Holly Story* manipulated and exploited the Holly legend was finally discovered and exposed by *Rolling Stone*, which ran companion articles on September 21, 1978, entitled "The Gary Busey Story" and "The Buddy Holly Story." Rock journalist Chet Flippo concluded, "The movie does not seem to be about the real Buddy Holly." Compounding Hollywood's culpability was the revelation, made by producer Freddy Bauer to John Goldrosen, that the distortions were not committed accidentally or out of ignorance but with willful deliberation. Bauer told Goldrosen that he was not interested in a "true-to-life movie" but in a film that would be *"bigger* than life." Perhaps the movie should have been called *Buddy Hollywood.*

The saddest development in the aftermath of the film was the 1995 cocaine overdose of its star, Gary Busey, in Los Angeles, who in recent years had been playing villains in high-budget action movies. After his release from the hospital, the actor, now fifty years old, was served with a felony cocaine-possession and three misdemeanor charges. He checked himself into California's famous drug-rehabilitation facility, the Betty Ford Center in Rancho Mirage, but the district attorney's office stated that arrangements were being made for Busey to surrender. If convicted, he could be imprisoned for three years on the felony and six months to a year on the misdemeanors.

In 1979, after its fleeting moment in the limelight as a result of *The Buddy Holly Story*, Lubbock decided it would be a good idea to erect a statue of Buddy. To raise money for the project, Waylon Jennings and his band, the Waylors, gave a concert in Lubbock. Waylon had come a long way from the cotton patch. He was getting $15,000 to $25,000 per appearance on the road, a far cry from the $800-a-month he'd received in Buddy's band, and his convoy of two Silver Eagle buses led by a chrome-plated eighteen-wheel Mack truck was a considerable improvement over the converted school buses of the "Winter Dance Party." In 1961, Waylon and his wife, Maxine, had named their new baby son, Buddy Dean, after Buddy Holly and James Dean. Their marriage ended shortly thereafter.

Waylon had then wed Lynne Gladys Jones, a flamboyant barmaid from Pocatello, Idaho, on December 10, 1962. The marriage lasted until 1967. Next, Waylon married Barbara Rood, the beautiful daughter of a Scottsdale, Arizona, millionaire. Barbara left him in 1968. In 1969 he married Duane Eddy's ex-wife, country singer Jessi Colter. Around that time, his drug abuse caught up with him. He "wound up in the hospital—the pill habit was killing him," wrote Maureen Orth of *Newsweek.* A son, Waylon Albright, was born to Waylon and Jessi in 1979.

Waylon's drug habit would last twenty-one years, ultimately costing him "$1,500 a day" in cocaine bills, until it ended in 1984, he revealed in his authorized video biography *Waylon: Renegade, Outlaw, Legend*. In 1977, he'd been arrested on a federal drug charge in Nashville, which consumed, he revealed in *Waylon*, "$70,000 [in] lawyer fees" before the case was dismissed. In 1978, he'd played Flagstaff, Arizona, where he and his band trashed four rooms in the Little America Motel, throwing sand in the air conditioners, spreading ice from the ice machines, and tearing up curtains and light fixtures.

Despite these exploits, Waylon was the biggest star in C&W, just as Buddy had foreseen, scoring a dozen No. 1 hits between 1974 and 1979, including "This Time," "Luckenbach, Texas," and the Grammy-winning "Mammas, Don't Let Your Babies Grow Up to Be Cowboys," which helped to define the progressive country—or outlaw—movement. By 1980 his album sales soared to sixteen million. "In times I was down I could look back at what Buddy Holly told me," Waylon said. "The encouragement he gave me. He was my friend first and foremost . . . last and not least."

At the 1979 Lubbock fundraiser for Buddy's statue, Sonny Curtis, Niki Sullivan, Jerry, and Joe B. also performed, and the event turned into a warm reunion. All the Holleys were present, including Buddy's parents, Larry, Travis, and Patricia, as well as Snuff Garrett, Tommy Allsup, Larry Corbin, Jerry Coleman, and Maria Elena, who signed autographs for an hour and a half. Later, at the Lubbock cemetery, a crowd gathered to honor Buddy at a morning graveside service. As Tommy Allsup played "True Love Ways," Niki Sullivan's mother broke down, sobbing that she still had Niki but Mrs. Holley would never see Buddy again. After the benefit, Tommy Allsup returned to his home in Fort Worth, where he was running a bar called Heads Up, named after the coin toss that had saved his life.

Finally, an eight-foot-six bronze statue of Buddy by San Angelo sculptor Grant Speed was placed directly in front of the Lubbock Memorial Civic Center in the heart of the downtown area. Maria Elena and Buddy's parents helped the artist unveil the statue at a dedication ceremony held on September 5, 1980. Mrs. Holley was enchanted by the idea of a statue of her son standing in the very center of Lubbock, making Buddy the town's No. 1 citizen and official symbol. Buddy's father still proudly wore Buddy's Omega wristwatch, which had been returned from Iowa after laying in the snow throughout the winter of 1959. Waylon watched the statue unveiling from his hotel-room window in the Hilton Inn nearby, lest his presence divert attention from Buddy. Lubbock Mayor Bill McAllister addressed a gathering of 150, most of them members of the Buddy Holly Memorial Society, who were sporting Buddy Holly hats and T-shirts.

The fans who'd traveled the farthest were Nigel Smith and Adrian Rossi, who'd flown ninety-six hundred miles from Australia. Altogether, twenty-nine states were represented and several foreign countries, including England, Holland, Germany, Canada, Ireland, and France. "*En France,* Buddy is still alive," said Frenchman Michel Aphesbero. At a concert held in the Civic Center, Roy Orbison and Bo Diddley sang their hits and Waylon played rhythm guitar with the Crickets. Orbison, who said he loved Buddy and was "dedicating the whole show to him," must have been mellowing with age, since he usually spoke rather coldly of Buddy, his West Texas archrival.

Buddy's mother seemed somewhat reserved when Griggs asked her to comment on the statue. It was "real fine," she said, but she knew Buddy "a little better than the rest of you," she added. When I visit Lubbock for a look at the statue a dozen years later, I understand her reservations. It's a disappointing memorial, beginning with the location. The inner city is virtually in ruins. The Lubbock County Courthouse sits in a slum at Broadway and Texas, near "A Tribute to Cotton," a hulking replica of a bale of cotton, a sinister-looking monolith executed in solid bronze, without a trace of imagination, and dedicated "to those who made Lubbock County and the surrounding South Plains the greatest producer of upland cotton in the world." The starkness of the scene is relieved somewhat on the day of my visit when a Mexican wedding party enters the cupola bandstand in front of the courthouse, the bride in white lace and the groom in a gray tuxedo, surrounded by clouds of children in white finery.

"Everything's moved out to the malls. It's dead downtown," a woman bus driver tells me, referring to the migration to the suburbs that has also destroyed so many other once prospering midsized American cities. On Main Street, you can see a mile or two in either direction, down copious red-brick roads. There's not a moving vehicle in sight though it's five P.M. on a Saturday. Finally I come across a junkie hooker nodding off at a bus stop and another staggering out of a wig store. Then, like a scene from a Fellini film, a pickup truck comes careening around a corner, carrying a fat woman in farmer's jeans in back, cackling and screaming. Why, I wonder, did they place Buddy's statue in this Dalí-esque wasteland when it belongs at the splendid mall out on Slide Road, where the young people congregate.

I wander down Main Street, across Texas Avenue, and along Avenues J and K. The wind blows through these silent streets like the sigh of a ghost. At Main and Avenue J, I pass a familiar scene from Buddy's youth,

the Lindsey Theater, with its scalloped art deco facade, closed and abandoned right here in the middle of town. Nearby stand the stately Old
Pioneer Hotel, now a retirement home, and John Halsey's Pharmacy, in
the Medical Arts Building, where Buddy used to pick up girls. Somehow
these places survived the tornado of 1970 that went through the downtown area on May 11 like a giant lawnmower, killing twenty-six and
cutting a swath of destruction all the way to the airport.

Buddy's statue stands among the newer buildings—La Quinta Inn,
Denny's, IBM, the Sheraton and Holiday Inn motels, and the dreary convention center, which hugs the ground as if it's expecting another twister
from the darkened winter skies. These joyless structures, surrounded by
the crumbling inner city, bear no resemblance to the bustling city I passed
through as a child in 1939 with my family, traveling in a decrepit '29
Chevrolet that was hitched to a wooden trailer house. Like thousands of
families in the Great Depression, we were heading west, my parents in
search of work. Years later, in the early 1950s, I returned to Lubbock for a
football game between Texas Christian University, where I was a student,
and Texas Tech. My path may well have crossed Buddy Holley's at that
time, for he was attending high school only a few blocks away.

Now, in 1992, I walk across the downtown railroad tracks and pass Rail
House, the train station on Avenue K. Nearby is the West Texas Hospital,
where Buddy's father died in 1985. Today the area is dominated by places
like Rudy's 24 Hours Bail Bonds. The old Kress is now a Goodwill shop.
A lone black man ambles out of Snappy Shine, and I wonder if this is
the place where Buddy once gave away his wristwatch.

Buddy's statue is as lifeless as the city that surrounds it. Nothing about
this stiff, spindly, haggard scarecrow suggests music, rhythm, or rock 'n'
roll. A far better statue of Buddy, by artist Doug Clark, is in the Gates
Memorial Library in Port Arthur, Texas, Janis Joplin's hometown, on the
campus of Lamar University. Clark's sculpture group also includes Ritchie
and the Bopper, and all three young stars are bursting with the energy
and vitality of youth.

Buddy's legend continued to grow. Up in Clear Lake, Iowa, the Surf
Ballroom, scene of his final concert, jumped on the Buddy Holly band-
wagon, announcing an annual dance to be held on the anniversary of his
death. The gesture would have been more impressive had it come twenty
years earlier. The old ballroom could no longer survive on local business
and needed a gimmick to draw outsiders to slumberous Clear Lake. Radio
station KZEV donated a bronze plaque honoring Buddy, which was installed in the lobby. On February 3, 1979, twenty years after Buddy's
death, a crowd of two thousand flocked to the Surf for a Buddy Holly

dance, with music provided by Del Shannon, the Drifters, and Jimmy Clanton. It was so cold that frost covered the inside of the ballroom doors, and, outside, the temperature dropped to 24 below zero—95 below with the chill factor due to high winds. Nonetheless, the dance was such a hit that the Surf's Holly hops became a fixture for the next fifteen years. Rock dinosaurs such as Carl Perkins, Ricky Nelson, Bobby Vee, Tommy Sands, the Diamonds, the Crickets, Buddy Knox, Don McLean, and Frankie Ford all came to Clear Lake to play the annual Buddy Holly dance.

Despite these signs of a continuing Holly revival, U.S. fans still clamored in vain for Buddy's record company to issue a complete set of his recordings. In England, a definitive Holly collection came out in 1979, entitled *The Complete Buddy Holly*, a box set of six LPs containing all of Buddy's recordings, but in the United States, MCA dragged its feet for another two years before making a comparable set available to Americans, finally releasing *The Complete Buddy Holly* in 1981. *Rolling Stone* critic David McGee applauded the set, pointing out Buddy had gone from "having one of the most abysmal catalogues" of any important rock star to having "one of the very best. Until the mid-1980s stateside fans hungering for even a taste of Holly's prolific output had to search the import bins, where treasures abounded." The new box set included everything from home recordings and radio interviews to alternate takes, all confirming Buddy's status as "one of the most original musicians this country has ever produced," McGee wrote.

On May 31, 1981, the *Los Angeles Times* surveyed local teenagers to determine their favorite singers from the fifties and sixties. Subjects were blindfolded and told to respond as records were played to them anonymously. In the final tally, Buddy came out on top, followed by Elvis, the Rolling Stones, the Doors, Gary U.S. Bonds, Jimi Hendrix, the Drifters, Bob Dylan, Creedence Clearwater Revival, and Ike and Tina Turner. "I only wish Buddy Holly didn't die," said fourteen-year-old Eric Troop, one of the teenagers polled.

Buddy's legend leaped to such heights in the early 1980s that the special "Baby Boomer" edition of the board game "Trivial Pursuits" contained no less than twenty-one Buddy Holly questions, including "Who was the most famous singer to die on Albert Juhl's North Dakota [sic] farm?"; "What Buddy Holly song marked the North American debut of the Rolling Stones?"; and "What Buddy Holly hit did he almost call 'Cindy Lou'?"

By the eighties, Buddy was showing up in novels such as Robert Parker's *A Catskill Eagle* (as an intelligence agent, of all things) and Bradley Denton's science-fiction opus *Buddy Holly Is Alive and Well on Ganymede* (as a space alien broadcasting from a moon of Jupiter). P. F. Kluge's novel

Eddie and the Cruisers, unlike the popular sixties movie based on it, is set in the 1950s; Buddy's in a scene at a recording session just before the principal character dies in a car crash. In *Not Fade Away*, author Jim Dodge denounces "the promoters of the Winter Dance Party. . . . When you wrong the people who make the music, you wrong the music; and if the music does belong to the Holy Spirit, you wrong the Holy Spirit, too. You fuck-over the Spirit, you deserve what you finally get."

Buddy's name popped up in everything from the cult movie *The Rocky Horror Picture Show* to Mac Davis's hit record "Texas in My Rear View Mirror" and from the "Buddy Holly Handicap," an Australian horse race, to the Kathleen Turner movie *Peggy Sue Got Married* (which originally starred Debra Winger before the actress injured her back). In Lubbock, a couple of newlyweds reported that they'd fallen in love at Buddy's grave and danced to "True Love Ways" at their wedding. "Buddy—The Singing Piston" showed up in a cartoon in *Hot Rod* magazine. At the height of the TV series *Dallas*, a Buddy Holly lookalike contest was held at South-fork Ranch on Buddy Holly Day. In Somalia, Africa, Peace Corps workers told of natives singing "That'll Be the Day." In Yemen, fans mobbed the theater when *The Buddy Holly Story* opened in the Middle East.

As Buddy's posthumous fame continued to build in the eighties, many of the persons who'd played important roles in his life began to pass from the scene. Hi Pockets Duncan died after an illness on December 21, 1981. To the end of his days Hi Pockets had spoken fondly of Buddy, never regretting his decision to bow out as Buddy's manager in 1956. Going on the road with Buddy would have been an impossibility for Hi Pockets, he admitted, and he knew that long-distance management was worthless. At the time of his death, Hi Pockets was still active in West Texas radio, serving as general manager of station KRAN in Morton, a small town thirty miles northwest of Lubbock.

Buddy's friend Snuff Garrett, who'd become a high-powered L.A. pro-ducer working with Trini Lopez, Roy Rogers, Sonny and Cher, and Frank Sinatra, retired at the age of fifty-three and moved to Arizona. On Sep-tember 2, 1982, Decca's Dick Jacobs was stabbed by an assailant who'd gained access to his New York apartment. He recovered from multiple wounds to his abdomen and chest but only regained partial use of his right hand. On May 20, 1988, he died at the age of seventy. Another Decca colleague of Buddy's, Bob Thiele, was still "alive and well," Bill Munroe, a Connecticut friend, stated in December 1993.

Petty's long-time secretary and assistant Norma Jean Berry—never a favorite of Maria Elena's or Buddy's—died in 1984, at the age of fifty-five, after a long illness. A few months later one of Buddy's best backup singers, Billy Duane "Bill" Pickering, died at fifty-seven, having survived a severe cerebral hemorrhage by almost a decade. After singing at Buddy's funeral, Bill Pickering had stated that he wanted one of Buddy's recordings to be played at *his* funeral. Accordingly, the version of Buddy's "True Love Ways" that had been overdubbed by the Picks was played at the Central Baptist Church during Pickering's rites. Bill Griggs was an honorary pallbearer. Buddy's early musical partner Don Guess, who'd become an insurance salesman in Roswell, New Mexico, later opening the Don Guess Insurance Agency in El Paso, Texas, died of cancer of the throat at the age of fifty-five on October 21, 1992.

Other old friends of Buddy's continued to flourish, often profiting from their association with his legend. The Crickets opened their sets with a medley of Holly tunes. In the summer of 1984 Griggs caught them at the Country Club bar in Reseda in Southern California. The audience was enthusiastic, but Griggs was "a little disappointed" with "Peggy Sue" when Jerry substituted a new routine for the steady drumming so familiar from the hit record. Eddie Cochran's old girlfriend Sharon Sheeley was in the audience that night and took a bow, "still looking good," Griggs noted, "after all these years."

Dion made it back into the Top 10 with the elegiac "Abraham, Martin, and John" in 1968. He'd recovered from his drug addiction, experiencing a spiritual awakening that enabled him to express "the language of the heart," he said, using a phrase of Bill Wilson's, founder of Alcoholics Anonymous. "Angels were waiting in the wings," Dion wrote in his autobiography, referring to his comeback. "Abraham, Martin, and John," both a eulogy for America's slain leaders and an embodiment of the hope and love they symbolized, came in the midst of the Vietnam War, the Chicago riots, and the assassinations of Robert F. Kennedy and Martin Luther King, Jr., and helped a stunned nation come to terms with its grief.

Dion's friend, Fred Milano, one of the original Belmonts, who'd toured with Buddy in 1959, was still singing "Tell Me Why" and "Teenager in Love" in little clubs like Memories, in Johnston, Rhode Island, where, according to one fan, the sound equipment was terrible but Milano, now bald, was still in very good voice.

Located by the indefatigable Griggs, Echo McGuire asked "not to be interviewed as her memories of Buddy are too personal," Griggs related in 1992. Key figures associated with Buddy's final tour were still around in the eighties but reluctant to discuss Buddy. GAC's Irving Feld didn't answer letters, Griggs said. In 1994 British author Alan Mann reported that Feld "has long since retired but his son is in the music business, carrying on the family name." Jerry Dwyer declined requests for interviews from both Griggs, publisher of *Rockin' 50s* magazine, and Jeff Tecklenburg, city editor of the *Mason City Globe-Gazette*, who reported that Dwyer complained of "harassment." Jeremy Powers, a former *Globe-Gazette* reporter who investigated the crash, says in a 1995 interview, "It must have been tough to be the owner of the plane Buddy Holly died in. That's something you live with for the rest of your life."

Carl Bunch toured for a while with Roy Orbison. After serving in the Army from 1959 to 1961, Carl "bummed around the country" and married a girl while he was so intoxicated he could scarcely stand, Carl confided to Griggs. He worked as a prison guard in Georgia and married two more times before founding the "Dove Nest Ministries," which he discussed in a book entitled *God Comes to Nashville*. Before evangelist Jim Bakker was imprisoned for defrauding PTL followers of millions of dollars, Carl appeared on Bakker's *PTL Club* television show, singing Buddy Holly songs and freely inserting religious phrases in the lyrics. Had Buddy Holly lived, Carl is convinced, Buddy would have led a religious revival in the final decades of the twentieth century. "The devil knew that," Carl told Griggs. "That is why the devil killed him." Waylon Jennings, Carl's old friend from the "Winter Dance Party," arranged for Carl to tour with Hank Williams, Jr., as the drummer in the Cheatin' Hearts band. Carl has also played drums for Frankie Avalon, Fabian, Jimmy Clanton, Tommy Cash, Dottie West, Marty Robbins, Mel Tillis, and Charlie Pride.

Sonny Curtis was flying high on the U.S. charts in 1981. His single "Good Ol' Girls" was No. 15 in *Billboard* and No. 9 in *Record World*, and he had a new LP, *Sonny Curtis: Rollin'*. In charge of Sonny's affairs at Elektra/Asylum was Buddy's old friend Jimmy Bowen, formerly of Buddy Knox's Rhythm Orchids and subsequently head of Elektra's Nashville office. Later in the eighties, when Bowen took over MCA's Nashville division, he almost dropped Reba McEntire but thought better of it and assigned Don Lanier, another ex-Rhythm Orchid, to help McEntire find better material. "Ultimately, Bowen didn't agree to produce me, but compromised by mixing (electronically arranging) the album, which we decided to call *My Kind of Country*," McEntire revealed in her 1994 memoirs. The album made McEntire the queen of country and helped launch the New Traditionalist movement in C&W. Earlier in her career she had encountered another of Buddy Holly's old friends, Bob Montgomery, who had become one of the most successful independent record producers in Nashville as well as co-owner of a leading publishing company with Bobby Goldsboro. Montgomery was still writing songs; Patsy Cline recorded his "Back in Baby's Arms," and Montgomery's "Misty Blue" was the most recorded song of 1967. But when the young Reba McEntire's tape was submitted to him in 1975, "Montgomery was polite but equally uninterested in the demo of yet another unknown girl country singer," McEntire later recalled.

Another member of Buddy's inner circle, Buddy Wayne Knox, who was living in Canada, showed up at a Buddy Holly Tribute Dance at the Surf Ballroom in the eighties, driving a camper with a canoe strapped on top and looking like a rugged frontiersman in his full beard and curly hair. He'd never duplicated his early successes but was obviously enjoying life. Knox entertained twenty-two hundred fans who'd braved a snowstorm to attend the dance. Many of them had to spend the night sleeping on the dance floor or in the Surf's booths due to zero visibility, 57-below-zero temperature, and high winds. The next morning they were rewarded by Surf manager Darrel Hein, who served fried eggs and coffee in the ballroom.

Norman Petty's downfall was slow and tortured. After scoring an enormous hit in 1963 with Jimmy Gilmer and the Fireballs' "Sugar Shack." Petty made the mistake of criticizing the Beatles, fuzz-tone guitars, and psychedelia in the presence of record-industry associates and afterward was dismissed as old hat. Suddenly no one would take his calls. "In his latter years people that he started in the business, who were now in powerful positions, and began to reject his recordings," Billy Stull, one of Petty's protégés and later manager of the Clovis studios, recalled in 1992. "He'd always had tremendous respect and could get into any door, but now when Norman wanted to sell a new record, he couldn't. He couldn't see the top people anymore, or go to dinner with them. The Christmas cards and letters stopped. He would go and be turned down by the very people he had given their start, or he'd made their company a lot of money in the past. Maybe he didn't progress with the music. He stuck to his guns, a clean, crystal clear sound. That wasn't acceptable to the executives later so he felt disappointed and rejected. He'd been a great producer, so he felt some bitterness there."

By 1984 he lay dying of leukemia. "Norman never spoke of Buddy Holly," says Billy Stull. "He was more into the future, the next session, what's the next song we're going to do? He even started a book and threw it away. 'The book I'm going to write is not going to be about these other famous guys,' he told me. 'It will be about people like you, unknown musicians I've worked with.' "

Few publishers would have been interested in a book about unknowns, even one by Norman Petty. At some point the project was dropped. Throughout 1984, Petty suffered terribly as his cancer consumed him. Though his contribution as a pioneering record producer of the rock era rivaled that of Sam Phillips, Elvis's discoverer at Sun Records, there were few honors for the visionary of Clovis, who'd given the world Roy Orbison, Buddy Knox, Buddy Holly, and Waylon Jennings. Sam Phillips was one of the original inductees in the Rock-'n'-Roll Hall of Fame the following year, but the Hall of Fame ignored Petty, perhaps because he never succeeded in dispelling persistent rumors that he'd mistreated Buddy and other young musicians.

To the end, Petty refused to address such charges. "Norman was hurt by all these accusations," Stull says. "I spoke to Norman about it and he said, 'I'm not the kind of person to go out and try to defend myself. I'm hurt by what people say but it's not true as far as my owin' Buddy money.' He died an unhappy man. He wouldn't stand up and tell his side of it. He kept the hurt inside. He had plenty of money and fame, but he was unhappy. It had been some years since he'd had a hit as a producer." Indeed it had. "Bottle of Wine," a No. 9 hit for the Fireballs in 1968, was the last notable recording to come out of the Norman Petty Recording Studios.

In June 1984, Petty's final public recognition was a gold record, signifying one million copies, for Buddy's *20 Golden Greats*. Clovis Mayor Frank Murray spoke at the brief ceremony, citing Petty's "eminence in the recording business." The *Amarillo Daily News* covered the event, reporting that "Petty still waxes nostalgic about his three-year association with Holly." He died on August 15 at the age of fifty-seven.

"He died unfulfilled," says Stull. "He wanted a new record but the records quit getting released. Ironically, Petty's style is back—the alternative rock stuff, real clean, that was Norman's sound back in the early sixties. 'Sugar Shack' was in *Mermaids*, the Cher movie." Lubbock took little note of Petty's death, burying his obit on page eleven of the *Avalanche-Journal* under the headline, PETTY, 57, FRIEND, MANAGER OF BUDDY HOLLY, DIES HERE. Attending his funeral at the Central Baptist Church in Clovis were Buddy's mother and brother Larry. Buddy's mother said, "It's real sad, it really is." Clearly, the Holleys were very decent people.

Also in attendance were Jimmy Gilmer and Bill Griggs. The service included some peculiar touches—for instance, the minister compared Petty with Michelangelo and Beethoven. Wind chimes were installed in the church, and a powerful fan was trained on them, in keeping with written instructions by the deceased, a perfectionist to the end, who held that the only really pure notes were produced by wind chimes. Less bizarre was the playing of Buddy's record, "True Love Ways," which was followed by "Almost Paradise" by the Norman Petty Trio. After the service, the procession made its way through downtown Clovis, where policemen stood at every corner, doffing their hats. The cortege paused briefly on Seventh Street, in front of the original studio, and then proceeded to the Mission Garden of Memories Cemetery for the burial. Perhaps the final word belongs to Griggs, who says in 1995, "Petty took as much money [from Buddy] as he could legally. Morally— that's another matter."

Buddy's father, Lawrence O. Holley, eighty-four, suffered a stroke on

July 1, 1985, and was taken to the West Texas Hospital in downtown Lubbock. On July 7, his condition worsened and he was moved to the intensive care unit, where, on the following day, at eight P.M., he died. Obituaries identified him as "father of the late rock-'n'-roll star," a designation fully earned by L.O., who'd always been available when needed to drive Buddy and the Crickets to their early gigs. The Reverend E. L. Bynum officiated at the funeral, which was held at Tabernacle Baptist Church at three P.M., Wednesday, July 10. Among the pallbearers were his barber Jake Goss, Buddy Holly Memorial Society president Bill Griggs, and Charlie Johnson, a trustee of the church and father of Ken Johnson, the associate pastor who'd participated in Buddy's funeral.

L.O. was buried next to Buddy in the family plot. Buddy's grave was now flanked by that of his father and his nephew Lee Weir, who had died at seventeen as a result of a fall off a bridge and onto a highway while going to a Rolling Stones concert.

In 1986, the newly established Rock-'n'-Roll Hall of Fame named Buddy one of the ten original inductees, along with Elvis, Fats Domino, Jerry Lee Lewis, James Brown, Little Richard, Sam Cooke, Chuck Berry, Ray Charles, and the Everly Brothers. Cochran made the list the following year, as did Orbison, Bo Diddley, Carl Perkins, and Ricky Nelson (who had died in late 1985 in circumstances eerily similar to Buddy's). Atlantic Records' Ahmet Ertegun, Hall of Fame chairman, personally invited Maria Elena to attend the induction dinner at the Waldorf-Astoria on January 23, 1986. Over a thousand people assembled in the grand ballroom for the ceremony. Maria Elena attended with her daughter, Elena Diaz, who later reported that Fats Domino had told her, "I wish Buddy, Elvis, and Sam Cooke could be here to enjoy what's happening."

The eighties continued to be a decade of accolades for Buddy— Newsweek's 1985 Bruce Springsteen cover story placed Buddy at the top of rock's "Magnificent Seven"—but not all of them were in good taste. In 1988 the Surf Ballroom unveiled a six-foot monument dedicated to Buddy, Ritchie, and the Bopper which included the name of the pilot Roger Peterson, whose inexperience had contributed to the plane crash. According to the AP, the pilot's seventy-one-year-old parents were determined to see the world acknowledge Roger's existence and grant him equal billing with the dead rock stars. Understandably, Maria Elena objected. "Mrs. Holly, fifty-five, said it would be inappropriate to honor Peterson," the AP reported, adding that Maria Elena blamed Peterson for taking off in bad weather. Connie Alvarez, Ritchie's sister, rushed to the Petersons' defense, telling the AP that it saddened her that "someone can be so selfish and unforgiving," despite the passage of twenty-nine years. Elaborating on her earlier statement, Maria Elena explained that she did not hate Roger Peterson but felt that he was irresponsible. She wasn't the only one who blamed Peterson for the crash; the CAB had cited pilot error, among other factors.

In the end Peterson's name was included on the glum $4,000 monument, which looks exactly like a tombstone. In a photograph taken during the dedication ceremony, Jan Dilley, Roger Peterson's sister, stands at some distance from Maria Elena, as does DeAnn Anderson, Peterson's widow, who is embracing Peterson's father Arthur. Evidently Connie Alvarez had decided to forgive Maria Elena, for the two of them are joined in a big three-way hug with Bob Hale, the emcee of Buddy's last show.

Though Maria Elena once swore never to visit Clear Lake, she told the six hundred fans assembled in front of the Surf, "Now that I am here, I am seeing just how much the people here loved Buddy and the others and how they are so sad that this was the last place he ever performed." Then, smiling, she held aloft a new street sign, BUDDY HOLLY PL.

Jay P. Richardson, Jr., born eighty-four days after his father had died, was presented with the Bopper's watch, which had turned up at the Cerro Gordo County Courthouse. "It's heartwarming to take this back home with me where it belongs," he said, adding that a film biography of his father was in the works. (The film has not yet materialized.) He also spoke of his mother's reaction to the February 3, 1959, crash, revealing that she refused to talk about it for twenty-eight years. She was so hurt, he said, that "she tried to put it behind her."

Ritchie's half-brother, Bob Morales, was also present. In the 1987 movie *La Bamba*, starring Lou Diamond Phillips as Ritchie, Bob Morales was played by actor Esai Morales. Portraying Buddy was singer Marshall Crenshaw, who'd had a Top 40 hit, "Someday, Someway," in 1982. Former Stray Cat Brian Setzer played Eddie Cochran, and the East L.A. band Los Lobos re-created Ritchie's music. Like Gary Busey's Buddy Holly, *La Bamba* bore little relation to its subject's life and was yet another example of the continuing exploitation of the early legends of rock. Instead of concentrating on Ritchie, the producers focused on the relationship between Ritchie and Bob Morales until it became the film's central conflict. Yielding to ethnic clichés, the film presented Ritchie as a migrant laborer and a farmworker, which was far from the truth. The Tijuana episode in which a mysterious *curandero* gives Ritchie an amulet made of snakeskin was purely fictitious.

Appallingly, when *La Bamba*'s sound track was released on cassette tape, Ritchie's name was mentioned nowhere on the package. Hollywood people and singers got all the credit. The film *La Bamba* demonstrated once again that Hollywood seems incapable of portraying rock 'n' roll authentically. In the United States, the exploitation of legend and history and its distortion to make money seems to be almost an ingrained habit.

With the advent of the nineties, the British theater would come closer to the truth, offering the best dramatization yet of Buddy Holly's life.

Perhaps only in England, where respect and support for Buddy had often been more consistent than in his native country, could an artistically serious work about Buddy come into being. The spectacular British musical *Buddy* originated in 1989 in London and was in another class altogether from misguided U.S. efforts to portray Buddy. The creative team included Laurie Mansfield, who was responsible for the original idea, and designer Adam Walmsley, whose ingenious set for *Buddy* could switch from KDAV to Nor Va Jak to Decca to Clear Lake with remarkable dexterity and speed. When *Buddy* opened in the West End, the *Sunday Times* critic called it "an unashamed, rabble-rousing fiesta. It's got everything." The *London Telegraph-Mirror* reviewer saluted the "big cast . . . big sound, and big entertainment."

On November 4, 1990, the show moved to New York, opening at the Shubert Theater, starring Paul Hipp, whose scintillating Buddy Holly left Busey's interpretation miles behind. To celebrate the U.S. premiere, Paul McCartney moved Buddy Holly Week to America and threw a party at the Lone Star Café in Greenwich Village, not far from Buddy and Maria Elena's old address. During the party, Paul Hipp sang with the Crickets. Among the 140 guests, who stood shoulder-to-shoulder in the Lone Star, were Ahmet Ertegun and Tommy Allsup. McCartney and his wife, Linda, and Ricky Van Sheldon jumped up at the finale for an all-star jam.

Though the venerable Shubert Theater had housed some rousing shows since its opening in 1913, including Mae West's *Catherine Was Great* and Joe Papp's *A Chorus Line*, it had never experienced anything like *Buddy*, which stirred the audience to frenzies not seen in Times Square since the heyday of Alan Freed's holiday rock concerts. "Buddy has them dancin' in the aisles," wrote the *New York Post*'s critic. "The audience is elevated to joyful chaos." Hipp's portrayal won him a Laurence Olivier Award nomination for the Outstanding Performance of the Year by an Actor in a Musical. Despite its excellence and the precedence of a long run in London, the show lasted only a few months on Broadway, a reflection, perhaps, of New York's disdain for the pioneering artists of America's most popular native art form.

The show did better in the hinterlands. In 1991, *Buddy* went on a triumphant U.S. tour, including performances in Lubbock, where Buddy was played by Joe Warren Davis, and the Surf Ballroom in Clear Lake, where Christopher Eudy, guitarist and vocalist in the alternative band the Nubile Thangs, assumed the title role. "The Lubbock audience stood and cheered to an extent I have never seen before in this ultra-conservative town," wrote Bill Griggs. In the audience were the Holley family, Snuff Garrett, and the Fireballs' George Tomsco.

Five different productions of *Buddy* went on to enrapture foreign audiences throughout the world. It had all started in England, and it came as no surprise that Britain's love affair with Buddy extended all the way to No. 10 Downing Street. When Prime Minister John Major was asked by a *London Daily Mail* reporter to name the record he'd most like to have if he were stranded on a desert island, he promptly replied, "Peggy Sue."

In the 1990s, Buddy's family decided to sell off his keepsakes that they'd been storing for decades. The disposition of these artifacts revealed much about the nature of pop culture in America. Though the American public tends to trivialize the artistic achievements of the founders of rock 'n' roll, they revere the trappings of stardom with a hysteria that can extend to the stars' underwear. Ideally Buddy's memorabilia should have been preserved in a coherent collection, but much of it has been sold to the highest bidder, scattered and lost forever. In contrast, what makes Graceland such an amusing place to while away an afternoon in Memphis is the impressive number of Elvis's effects that are on display—everything from his kitschy jungle den to his gold records, jewelry, cars, and airplanes. Elvis's ex-wife Priscilla deserves credit for turning Graceland into a mecca for fans as well as connoisseurs of camp. Less known is the House of Cash in Hendersonville, Tennessee, a splendid repository of Johnny Cash's memorabilia. No similar shrine exists for Buddy, though enough material still remained in the family in the early nineties to furnish a small museum. Ample opportunity existed for someone to establish a Buddy Holly library or center, but no one did, despite all the people who had benefited from Buddy's legacy, such as the Holley estate, the city of Lubbock, the state of Texas, the Rock-'n'-Roll Hall of Fame, Paul McCartney, Waylon Jennings, Linda Ronstadt, Don McLean, the U.S. government, and the United Kingdom.

Imagine how serendipitous it would be for drivers crossing the monotonous Texas plains to come across Holly Land, a fifties theme park, a sort of rock 'n' roll Nashville or Branson. Cabarets and theaters could offer a panoply of rock 'n' roll, from the latest grunge and gangsta to golden oldies. The centerpiece and raison d'etre of Holly Land would, of course, be the Buddy Holly Museum, exhibiting hundreds of items of Holly memorabilia—guitars, clothes, manuscripts, furniture, homework, eyeglasses, records, vehicles, and documents. Among other things, it would be a boon for Lubbock, a city that has grown to its present population of 230,000 without developing a single tourist attraction.

Eventually the Holley estate decided, according to Larry, to "take everything we've got, inventory it, put it in the pile, and sell it at auction and split the money. And that's what we did." It seems unbelievable in retrospect that Lubbock and the state of Texas let Buddy Holly's possessions sit moldering for over three decades without making any use of them, evincing a total lack of pride in the region's central role in the origins of rock 'n' roll. Now, over three decades after Buddy's death, they were going to lose the most extensive Holly collection in the world. What was worse, it was going to be split up and the individual items auctioned off to the highest bidder, destroying forever the integrity of the collection. Certain important items were already gone. In November 1988 Emmylou Harris's husband Paul Kennerley bought Buddy's Magnatone Custom 280 amplifier from the family. Buddy's Ariel Cyclone motorcycle had been sold to W. Sanders of Dumas, Texas, in 1970; Sanders kept it until 1975, when an Austin man named Joe Waggoner bought it and, after a few years, put it up for sale for $10,000. Jerry, Joe B., and Sonny Curtis acquired it in 1979, for considerably less than the asking price, and presented it to Waylon Jennings on his birthday. In mint condition, the bike still had its original paint job and very low mileage. It would have been a perfect item for a Holly museum.

"Mother was losing her mind and didn't know what was going on," Larry explains in 1992. Mrs. Holley was admitted to the West Texas Hospital in 1988 after suffering a heart attack. She spent five days there, constantly assuring her family that she felt fine and was ready to go home. After her release, she lived two more years in her home in Lubbock before dying in 1990 at the age of eighty-eight. Mrs. Holley was buried next to her husband and near to the son she had supported so valiantly, despite her religion's disapproval of rock 'n' roll. "I knew her for so many years that finally I thought of her no longer as the mother of Buddy Holly but as my dear friend," says Bill Griggs, who was a pallbearer at her funeral. "Really, she was one of the sweetest and nicest ladies ever."

Referring to Buddy's possessions, Larry says, "I boxed them up and carried them down there to the lawyers and everybody who was taking care of it and made a deal with Sotheby's to sell at auction. Sotheby's just took a portion of the stuff and then they decided they'd have another sale a year later and they took another portion."

In Manhattan, Sotheby's announced the Buddy Holly auction for Saturday, June 22, 1991, as part of a massive clearance of rock 'n' roll "collectibles." There was no dignity to the occasion. Most of the pre-auction publicity centered, facetiously, on articles such as Elvis Presley's cape and John Lennon's autographed acoustic guitar. Both the *New York Daily News* and the *New York Times* considered the auction a joke. The *New Yorker*, though characteristically tongue-in-cheek, took a more affectionate attitude, terming the auction an event of interest to "ardent followers of the history of American culture." In its charmingly esoteric way, the *New Yorker* focused on Buddy's school assignments, which he and his family had assiduously saved; they were contributions to "the history of American homework," wrote the *New Yorker*.

Before the Holly items went on the block, Eddie Murphy arrived at Sotheby's and held his bidding paddle in the air throughout the entire Jimi Hendrix portion, buying everything offered for $45,000. Bidding was spirited for Buddy's guitars, his Fender Stratocaster fetching $110,000 and his Gibson J-45 $242,000. Bill Griggs explains why the Gibson was so high. "A Lubbock man was there, and he bought the Fender. When the Gibson was auctioned, Gary Busey, who was on the telephone, had to bid against the Lubbock man, and the price kept going up. The winning bid was Busey's." On the Gibson, Buddy's custom-stitched, personally crafted leather cover was still in mint condition, but Busey had to take the well-used guitar to Rick Turner in Los Angeles for repairs. It was refretted, and Turner repaired some cracks as well as the cracked braces.

The Lubbock man continued to bid throughout the auction, ultimately spending $182,000 and walking away with a significant Holly collection, including, in addition to the Fender, articles of clothing and the notebook in which Buddy had doodled Peggy Sue's initials and listed the Scoundrels as a possible name for his band. "It was a well-rounded collection," says Griggs.

Craig Inciardi, a cataloger in Sotheby's Collectibles Department, disclosed that the items in the 1991 auction had been released by the Holleys, whom he praised for retaining so many items not because Buddy was a celebrity, but "just because it was Buddy's."

The New Yorker's "Talk of the Town" reporter found it "sad" that such "relatively insignificant stuff" as Buddy's gray wool stage jacket and Arrow French-cuff shirt went for $5,225 while his homework "proved a drug on the market." Buddy's Robert Frost book report, which the New Yorker praised for its "smooth and engaging narrative," drew a top bid of $650 and had to be "brought back in," meaning that the auctioneer returned it to the Holleys, who had expected $800 to $1,200. The bids for the rest of Buddy's homework were equally mediocre, such as the $1,650 offer for lot No. 649, which included forty-five pages of homework, a signed two-page school report, and Buddy's school notebook with two signatures, which Sotheby's had expected to sell for $2,000.

Shara Shinn, the auctioneer, later explained that rock 'n' roll keepsakes were not comparable to "a Tiffany flatware service, with stable bidders and a predictable price." Moreover, their value increases the more directly they're related to music. Guitars and stage clothes are of immense appeal to restaurant and bar owners. "I noticed the Hard Rock Café people here today," noted one Sotheby official. He complained that there was altogether too much of Buddy's homework in circulation. The Holley family, he said, had started "flooding the market" the previous year and were continuing to release new batches of homework. Until someone could establish how much more of it was to come, it was difficult to place a price tag on it.

Unlike the homework, other Buddy Holly collectibles fetched far more than Sotheby's had anticipated. One lot of clothes that Sotheby's was prepared to sell for $1,800 to $2,200 brought in $5,225. His two-page handwritten letter to Terry Noland dated December 14, 1958, went for $4,950, exceeding the estimated value by $3,750. Buddy's 1956 harmonica went for $3,850, but Sotheby's had only valued it at $1,500. His birth certificate fetched $1,100; his high-school diploma, $3,300; and a lot that included his high-school ring went for $2,420. It was still a long way from what Elvis's remnants sold for in a 1994 auction in Las Vegas, where Elvis's wedding band sold for $68,000 and a jumpsuit that looked like something Bea Arthur might have worn in *Golden Girls* went for $68,500. On the auction block as everywhere else, Elvis was king.

In the early 1990s, in Clovis, New Mexico, Vi Petty continued to enjoy a generous share of Buddy's earnings and to look after Norman's estate, which included substantial property holdings. "Norman had been a big man in Clovis," says Bill Griggs. "That's why he never left." Billy Stull, who managed the studios for Vi, found her to be a "gracious widow who loved to talk about the old days [and] would spend hours and hours with anyone who came over . . . to talk about old times." To Griggs she was the "eccentric cat woman who picked up strays," he reveals in 1995. "She had thirty-seven to thirty-eight cats in the double garage by the Seventh Street studio. She'd converted the old echo chamber into a place for cats. It stank."

In 1992 Vi became desperately ill and went into the hospital, unable to digest food due to an ulcer that was blocking her intestine. "They tried to shrink it chemically and couldn't so they operated," says Billy Stull in 1992. "They had to remove part of her stomach which was ulcerated and reconnect it to the intestine, which is a pretty standard procedure, and she went through that okay. Then there was a ruptured intestine and her whole body was infected with peritonitis. She was in a coma five and a half weeks."

Vi Petty died on March 22, 1992. "The actual cause of death was liver failure," adds Stull. "She was only sixty-three." Vi was buried next to her husband and their assistant, Norman Jean Berry, "under one huge stone in the Clovis cemetery," says Bill Griggs. "The estate had assets of over $1 million."

At last, in 1993, Buddy received an appropriate memorial—the U.S. government announced that it would issue a first-class Buddy Holly postage stamp on June 16, 1993. Virtually all the articles in the *Lubbock Ava-*

lanche-Journal focused of how much money the stamp was going to make
for the city rather than on Buddy's life and music. There were no editorials
nor feature stories on Buddy's Lubbock background, his career, his influence on rock 'n' roll, his records, his concerts, the manner of his death,
or how his legend grew. No one in Lubbock was interviewed for personal
reminiscences, though his family, Bill Griggs, and many people who knew
and worked with Buddy were still residing in the city.

Instead of staging a concert of Buddy's music, the Panhandle South
Plains Fair booked C&W stars Alan Jackson and Tanya Tucker for the
Fair Park Coliseum. The post office struck a deal with a T-shirt company.
Ironically, Buddy had never been obsessed with money, only music and
recognition, but monetary considerations seemed to be uppermost in Lub-
bock's plans for celebrating the stamp. Russell Autry, president of the
Lubbock Chamber of Commerce, spoke of the "dollar value" that the
Holly stamp would bring to Lubbock "in terms of publicity and exposure."
It was time, he said, for Lubbock "to begin capitalizing" on Buddy, because
"he will benefit Lubbock for years to come as people come here to visit
Buddy's hometown." Those foolish enough to make such a trek would
get precious little for their efforts. Expecting at the very least to see Buddy's birthplace, a Washington Post reporter complained that nothing
greeted her at 1911 Sixth Street, where Buddy was born, but "a small
vacant lot, strewn with trash."

On June 16, 1993, the official release date of the Holly postage stamp,
Maria Elena and members of Buddy's family were introduced to a cheering
crowd of a thousand. Two years previously, a Parade magazine writer had
described Maria Elena as "60, divorced, and living near Dallas," but in a
three-column photograph atop page one of the June 17 Avalanche-Journal,
a smiling Maria Elena, fashionably coiffed, alluringly feminine and
shapely, appeared to be ageless. Asked to recall the first moment she met
Buddy at Peer-Southern, she said, "He came through the door and it was
like thunder coming through there," the Avalanche-Journal later reported.
She confessed her astonishment that Lubbock had at last woken up to
Buddy's greatness and decided to honor him. Both Cleveland and Santa
Monica had tried to convince her to come to their stamp ceremonies,
but she'd kept waiting and hoping that Lubbock would decide to do
something, however belatedly. "I hinted. I prayed. I kept hearing from
Cleveland, and I just hoped I'd hear from Lubbock," she said. "But I'd
never seen Lubbock get this involved."

Travis Holley was "astonished" by the city's sudden interest, after
thirty-six years of neglect. He told Avalanche-Journal entertainment editor
William Kerns that Buddy would be "proud if he were with us today."
Larry Holley added that Buddy's family had long since "given up on the
city doing anything." He pointed out that several European countries had

been honoring Buddy on stamps for years. Larry used the occasion to put
to rest any rumors of a rift between the Holley family and Buddy's widow.
The were "still kin folks," Larry said, and although they didn't always see
"eye-to-eye," he always stayed at Maria Elena's house any time he went
to Dallas, he assured Kerns.

Jerry Allison shared the family's surprise that Lubbock was "treating us
so well," he said. "I guess we've come a ways from 1956." The carnival
atmosphere of the ceremony quickly vanished when Bill Griggs spoke,
reminding everyone of the tragic origins of Buddy's legend. "We all know
what happened," he said, quoting Don McLean's famous lyric equating
Buddy's death with the end of early rock. "I prefer to call it the day the
music cried," Griggs added.

At 9:01 A.M., John Frisby, Lubbock postmaster, canceled the first stamp
and handed it to Maria Elena. Clearly visible in the distance, Buddy's
statue appeared to be bearing down on them like an avenging angel. Civic
Lubbock, Inc., had recently dropped its connection with the once-annual
Buddy Holly Music Festival. Maria Elena looked at the stamp, which
shows Buddy against a background of white acoustic tile, smiling and
playing his guitar, and told the postmaster she'd "treasure" and "display
it" in her house. She was eager to return to Lubbock the following year
if the Chamber of Commerce would arrange another "terrific" event, she
said.

The Chamber of Commerce agreed to hold an annual summer observance in memory of Buddy, but the city that was capable of booking top
C&W stars into the Fair Park Auditorium announced no plans for a major
rock 'n' roll festival, which would have been a more fitting tribute. If the
stars who regularly pay fulsome lip service to Buddy—the Beatles, the
Stones, Dylan, Clapton, Elton John, and Ronstadt—got together and
staged a concert, with proceeds going to a Holly museum, *that* would be
worth going to Lubbock for. Only an organizer with the vision and energy
of a Bob Geldof or a Michael Lang could bring it off—a veritable Woodstock of the West—and then only if Lubbock, the Buckle of the Bible
Belt, really wanted it, which seems doubtful.

At the conclusion of the stamp ceremony, fans formed a line at a
mobile-trailer postal station which had been set up next to Buddy's statue.
Altogether, 24,571 Holly stamps were purchased in Lubbock. Only fifteen
thousand of the Presley stamp sold, marking the first time that Buddy had
ever upstaged Elvis, even in his hometown.

Earlier in the 1990s, the Lubbock developer who'd won Buddy's Fender
Stratocaster at Sotheby's had seemed on the verge of realizing a brilliant
vision for Lubbock and for Buddy's memory. He offered the Holley estate
$1 million "to use Buddy's name and put up hotels all over the world,
just for the use of Buddy's name on them," Larry Holley revealed in a

1992 interview. The various beneficiaries could not get together on the offer, one of them expressing fear that the hotel might put Buddy's name on the toilet paper. The developer revised his offer, proposing a mammoth Disneyland-type Buddy Holly project to be located in Lubbock. He bought a large parcel of land around Fiftieth Street, two or three blocks long and a block wide, for a museum, a hotel, a park, and souvenir shops, with a Buddy Holly Boulevard running through it. He was buying up Buddy's memorabilia for the museum.

Again, something went wrong. The beneficiaries were too demanding, the developer complained, according to Larry Holley, one of them going so far as to demand a percentage of every soft drink sold on the property. "His plan fell through," says Bill Griggs. "He then offered to sell the collection to the city of Lubbock for $175,000." The City Council met to vote on the matter in July 1994. Griggs spoke in favor of acquiring the collection, and the council voted unanimously to do so. Michael Reeves of the Lubbock Chamber of Commerce confirmed in 1995 that the city now owned "a large collection of Buddy Holly memorabilia . . . including a guitar and a sweater."

The immediate problem for the city was where to house the collection. Lubbock proposed to build a Buddy Holly arena or "multi-event center," which, according to Michael Reeves, was to be located next to the Civic Center. The focal point of the complex would be the Holly display. The issue was put before Lubbock voters in October 1994. "The public defeated the referendum for a tax increase to build the arena," said Reeves in 1995. According to Griggs, the proposal lost by only six hundred votes. "Now there is talk of a new Fine Arts Center and a Visitors Information Center," Reeves added. "The Holly collection could go in either place. We're still looking for an appropriate place to house the display."

As a temporary measure, the collection was scheduled to go on display at the Texas Tech Museum in Lubbock on the fifty-ninth anniversary of Buddy's birth on September 7, 1995.

It seemed that Lubbock was finally showing signs of returning Buddy's love.

Epilogue: The Last Dance

By 1993, thirty-four years after Buddy Holly played Clear Lake, Iowa, the old Surf Ballroom seemed to be in its final days. As early as 1988 the Surf's manager had warned in the ballroom's *News Letter*, "As president of the National Ballroom Association, I am aware of several mid-west ballrooms that have gone down the tube, including the Prom and the Terp. Unfortunately, these ballrooms seldom reopen." It was increasingly difficult for tiny Clear Lake to keep the huge venue open. The annual Buddy Holly dance, drawing a few thousand people yearly, was the Surf's only big attraction. Other than that, the cavernous dance hall functioned as a kind of community center hosting a few polka dances as well as rock 'n' roll memorial hops such as the "Eddie Cochran Birthday Bash" in 1992. "If you want to vote, get married, look at new cars, celebrate a baby shower or the deer season, you book the ballroom," said Doris Pease, editor of *Music Dance News*, which is published by the Minnesota Ballroom Operators Association.

While there was still a chance to see the Surf, I decided to take in the Buddy Holly dance in February 1993. Bill Griggs greeted me inside the lobby at 460 North Shore Drive and introduced me to a blond young man named Chris Hughes. When I interviewed Maria Elena later she explained that Chris Hughes has a real-estate brokerage license and had worked for her part-time in early 1993. After talking briefly with Griggs and Hughes, I began to explore the Surf, walking past the phone where Buddy had called Maria Elena, past the cubbyhole office where the flight to Fargo was arranged, then down the wide, sloping ramp to the ballroom, and out onto the great maple dance floor, big enough for a circus, and finally up to the little bandstand, with the band room to one side, all the way it was in 1959. If rock 'n' roll has a holy shrine, it's the Surf Ballroom, where you can still almost hear the sighs and cries of "True Love Ways." Here early rock had its last hurrah, galvanized the young, and paved the way for the politicized music of the sixties that redefined modern society. More than in Lubbock, Memphis, or Cleveland, this is where you can feel the heartbeat of rock 'n' roll.

Year after year, Buddy's fans make their annual pilgrimage to Clear Lake, drawn by the old dance hall's magical vibrations. On the Friday morning after I arrived in 1993, I found a roomful of middle-aged Holly enthusiasts breakfasting at the Holiday Motor Lodge. They were bright, clever, and prosperous-looking, not at all like Elvis fans in their goofy hats, beehive hairdos, and polyester pants suits. Three pretty women invited me to sit at their table—Sharon Black, Cathy Gacek, and Yvonne Pearsall, all from little towns in Illinois. They tell me they're looking forward to dancing and having fun at the sock hop the following evening. Suddenly, Buddy's British fans, led by Trevor Lailey, publisher of *Down the Line* magazine, and Clive Harvey of the British Buddy Holly Society, swept into the room, sporting black Buddy Holly sweatshirts, joking and catching up with old friends.

Griggs introduced me to Hans Goeppinger, a six-foot-three farmer from Boone, Iowa, who was old enough to have been around when Buddy Holly played the Surf but could easily pass for forty. With his graying blond hair and flashing blue eyes, Hans looks like Leslie Howard, Oskar Werner, and Max von Sydow rolled into one. He was volunteering his services as a docent for the weekend, responsible for chauffeuring dignitaries and singers arriving for the festivities, including Maria Elena and the Crickets. He invited me to drive to the Minneapolis airport to pick up Sonny Curtis and Mike Berry, both flying in from Nashville. Though it's an ten-hour round trip by car from Clear Lake to Minneapolis, I seized the opportunity; as Buddy's most recent biographer, I was eager to meet Sonny Curtis, a bona fide Cricket and Holly pal dating all the way back to KDAV.

When I wondered aloud why Sonny wasn't flying into Mason City, as I had, Bill Griggs said, "If you were a Cricket, would you fly here in a light aircraft, the only thing that comes into Mason City, after what happened to Buddy?" Jerry and Joe B. weren't taking any chances, either; they were driving into Clear Lake aboard their tour bus.

Hans's new Lincoln Town Car, smooth as a magic carpet, whisked us over snow and ice and through dense fog to Minneapolis that afternoon. Settling into the cozy warmth of the sedan, I looked out over the snow-covered fields along I-35, thinking of how Buddy and his friends had suffered as the GAC bus trundled over these same roads in 1959. "The 'Winter Dance Party' came along here, didn't it?" I asked Hans.

He nodded and said, "They crisscrossed all over these parts. I'll never forgive myself. I was a brash little kid and a big rock fan. I'd often go up to touring stars and offer to take them to their next gig. That night Buddy played the Surf, I thought of coming over and giving him a ride to Moorhead, but my fraternity was putting on *Stalag 17* and I was in it. I often think how different it would have been."

At the airport, I recognized Sonny Curtis, a cool cat with a short silver beard and bright, friendly eyes. He wore Levi's and a trendy leather patchwork jacket. Mike Berry was in a long, navy-blue cashmere topcoat, very British and elegant. In England Mike was famous for his "Tribute to Buddy Holly" record. Recently he'd been starring in the hilarious television farce *Are You Being Served?*

Once we'd made it through baggage, collecting Sonny's Fender Stratocaster, which was encased in stainless steel, we drove back to Iowa, talking about Buddy the whole way. When we delivered Sonny and Mike to the Best Western Hotel in Mason City, Hans and I went to Sonny's room with him. As Sonny unpacked, Hans called the Surf and spoke with the manager, Bruce Christensen, who'd inquired if Sonny and Mike would make a brief appearance at the sock hop, even though they were not to perform until the following night. "It's not advisable to come on before you do your act," Mike Berry commented. Sonny agreed, so we skipped the hop and went out for something to eat.

At Perkins Restaurant, we chose eggs and pancakes, then wound up in the cocktail lounge at the Best Western, where the only other customer was a woman, thirty-fivish, alone and obviously sizing us up. "J.I. [Jerry Ivan Allison] wants me to go ice fishing with him tomorrow," Sonny said. Ice-fishing, he explained, is a popular local sport. "You drive out on the frozen lake, set up a tent right on the ice, bore a hole, and always catch plenty of fish."

The next day, Saturday, February 6, when Hans and I returned to the hotel to drive Sonny and Mike to the Surf for a rehearsal, I found Sonny sitting on the edge of his bed, restringing his acoustic guitar. When he finished, he sang his song, "The Real Buddy Holly Story," for us. Listening to him, it struck me that his eyewitness account of Buddy's life differed radically from the sanitized Gary Busey movie: Sonny concentrates on all the girls, fun, and booze.

"Why did Buddy die?" I asked him. "Why did he take a small plane in bad weather?"

"His alligator mouth did in his hummingbird ass," Sonny said.

"Come again?" It was Mike Berry, who'd just entered the room.

"He talked the pilot into taking the big rock stars up in dangerous weather, took on a bigger commitment than they could handle."

Sonny played something else, but I was lost in thought, pondering Buddy's final decision. He hadn't given it any more consideration, I was sure, than I had a few days ago when I'd decided to take a small plane from Minneapolis to Mason City in very soupy weather. Just like Buddy, I was doing a job, and flying's part of getting it done, or so we tell ourselves, when we're in a hurry.

Sonny was singing snatches of various songs he'd written, "I Fought the Law" and his sprightly theme for *The Mary Tyler Moore Show*. Afterward we drove to Clear Lake, and while Sonny and Mike rehearsed in the Surf Ballroom, I came upon Maria Elena and Chris Hughes in the Surfside 6 Café, which adjoins the dance hall ("Food line features breakfast roll, hamburgers, pizza, french fries, onion rings, shakes, and malts"). Maria Elena chatted briefly with a Vietnam vet in a wheelchair. Craggy and bearded, like Tom Cruise in *Born on the Fourth of July*, he asked her to sign his Iowa lottery ticket, which was currently featuring a picture of Buddy. When he left, I arranged for an interview with Maria Elena. She was delighted when I told her she was pretty, which is the truth. She is no more than five-one or five-two, but has a big smiling face. Her skin is light and smooth. She speaks English with a slight Hispanic accent, but with great fluency. Her costume—a baseball cap and black jogging togs—was hardly flattering, but it was easy to see, even three decades later, what Buddy saw in her. Her smile remains contagious, her warm eyes dance with fun, and she exudes a sense of joie de vivre. Playful about her dress and accessories, she had evidently raided her jewel box that day; every finger, including the index, was festooned with baubles. She readily posed for a photograph. When I asked for her address and telephone number, handing her a sheet of paper on which I'd written MARIA HOLLY, she carefully crossed it out and substituted MARIA ELENA HOLLY, adding the other details I'd requested in a scrupulously neat and stylish script.

At a VIP party later the same day, held in a bar across from the Surf, Chris Hughes and I talked about the Dallas Cowboys while Maria Elena again signed autographs. She was unfailingly courteous and friendly to Buddy's fans. In the nostalgic spirit of the fifties hop to be held later that evening, she had done herself up in an eye-catching outfit—a Technicolor novelty sweater, a long blue-denim skirt, and the ubiquitous baseball cap.

Standing beside me, the always personable and accommodating Chris Hughes noted that Maria Elena's glass of club soda was empty and stepped over to refill her glass. Maria Elena said she lived in Colleyville, a town of sixty-seven hundred near the Dallas–Fort Worth metroplex, which includes Irving, Texas, home of the Cowboys.

At the Buddy Holly Tribute Concert and Dance on Saturday night, February 6, in the Surf, I hung out at Maria Elena's table, which was on the promenade, a couple of steps above the dance floor. Sonny Curtis did a solo turn that was the high point of the evening, for me at least. Later, Maria Elena came alive when Frankie Ford of "Sea Cruise" fame performed a riotous medley of Jerry Lee Lewis hits. At one point the Gretna, Louisiana, rocker appeared to rip the keyboard off the piano and drape it around his neck; it took me a second to realize that he'd been pounding the keyboard through a thin silk scarf imprinted with all eighty-eight keys. Maria Elena became so excited that she did a kind of seated dance, snapping her fingers and tossing her hands over her shoulders, really grooving on Frankie Ford's expert interpretation of Jerry Lee. Then the Crickets came on—Jerry, Joe B., Gordon Payne, and Sonny—and Maria Elena stood up and left the dance hall. *Brava, Maria,* I thought.

I couldn't take much of the Crickets, either. Gordon Payne was singing off-key. To make matters worse, Jerry and Joe B. seemed to be playing at a different pace from Sonny. Later I asked Frankie Ford, "What happened to the Crickets' set?"

"There was a lot of tension between them in the band room," Frankie said. "I asked Sonny Curtis what happened when they ended one song in such a raggedy way. 'Was that a clash of wills?' I asked. 'More of a train wreck,' Sonny said."

Early Sunday morning, before flying home to sunny Key West, Florida, I drove out to the crash site, 5.4 miles north of Clear Lake, past farms where the only creatures stirring in the subfreezing air were pigs rooting around in farmyards. The crash site is difficult to find, buried deep in snowy, foggy fields, remote from the nearest house or barn. I managed to get lost, a harrowing ordeal, and it occurred to me that, if a blizzard blew up, you'd be lucky to make it back to the road. In 1988, after fans complained for decades about losing their way in the field, Ken Paquette, a shipyard worker from Portersfield, Wisconsin, constructed a steel marker: a large guitar and a set of three records, one for each star. Speaking for the W. H. Nicholas family, who own the field, Jeff Nicholas stated in the *Globe-Gazette* in 1992 that "the family allows people on the crash site as long as fans are respectful." Nicholas subsequently planted four oak trees, one each for Buddy, Ritchie, the Bopper, and Roger Peterson.

I finally had to trudge back to the road, 835 yards through hip-deep snow, and start all over, a bit further down. This time I found the stainless steel marker, which was barely visible above the snowline. I had stood at Buddy's birthplace with Griggs and later at his grave in Lubbock, and now I felt the desolation of the barren pasture in Iowa. A couple of years later, listening to the tape I made that morning, I hear in my voice a compound of grief and fear. I bravely try singing "Peggy Sue," one of the songs commemorated on the stainless steel record in the snow, but give it up for the Lord's Prayer. I remember walking away from the fenceline, down a slight depression, and finding the exact spot where the plane first hit the ground. Robert Frost once wrote a poem called "A Soldier." In it, the soldier falls in battle, but Frost says the force of his fall shoots his soul on to heaven. And so it was, I like to think, with the singers who fell so hard on this cold and merciless ground.

I recall looking up and seeing two distant figures approaching through the snow, a man and a woman. In a few minutes they introduce themselves as Pat and Marv Jurek of St. Cloud, Minnesota. "It's raw out here," Pat says. Then we speak of the dance the previous night. Buddy's music had brought a lot of strangers together for a honky-tonkin' good time, just like in '59.

The following year—1994—it was announced that the Surf Ballroom was closing. The Val Air Ballroom in West Des Moines was also for sale, possibly slated for conversion to a strip mall or lumberyard. The scuttlebutt around Clear Lake was that the Surf would be bulldozed and turned into condos as commercial progress continued its march through rural Iowa. The main problem, as expressed by manager Bruce Christensen, was lack of business during the five winter months when the whole area virtually shuts down. In February 1994 Maria Elena and most of the key figures in the Buddy Holly legend showed up for the last dance. Don McLean, Peggy Sue, Tommy Allsup, Ritchie's girlfriend Donna Fox, Niki Sullivan, Jerry, and Joe B. were all present. Maria Elena once said that she'd never let go of Buddy, that everything she went through after his death was like walking in her sleep. She'd never changed from the girl Buddy knew and loved, she said, because she "froze" on February 3, 1959.

Peggy Sue shook hands with fans who wanted to meet the girl behind the famous song. Tommy Allsup revealed that he'd played as a session man or recording artist on fifty-five hundred records and added that coming to Clear Lake for the first time since 1959 had proved to be a healthy catharsis and that he was leaving feeling good. "My favorite of the whole bunch would be Donna Fox by about ten yards," writer and PR man Jeremy Powers said in a 1995 interview. Powers at the time was raising money to save the Surf and have it declared a nonprofit living museum, with government support. At the main event, Donna Fox pitched in and helped, carrying a large Alhambra water bottle around the dance floor and soliciting donations. "She came back with the whole bottle full of money," says Powers. "You can tell how somebody who was seventeen years old [Ritchie] would definitely have fallen in love with her."

Powers was also "real excited about seeing Don McLean," he recalls. "I'll soon be forty, and the first I knew of Buddy Holly was 'American Pie.' I'm glad I was instrumental in bringing Don McLean to the Surf on the thirty-fifth anniversary of Buddy's death."

Niki Sullivan, now employed in a research division of Sony Corporation, came from his home in Blue Springs, a suburb of Kansas City, Missouri, with his wife, Fran, whom he married in 1965, and their two grown twin sons, Marty and Eryn. While in Clear Lake, the Sullivan twins accepted an offer to open a bar called Sully's. Following the final dance at the Surf, which was attended by twenty-four hundred, Niki returned to Clear Lake almost every weekend in early 1994 to help his sons get Sully's Bar started.

After the Holly memorial dance, the Surf shut its doors, presumably forever. Bruce Christensen resigned as manager and moved away, entering the credit-card business in Nashville. Though Waylon Jennings had said he'd never come back to Clear Lake, his bus and Wayne Newton's bus pulled up at the Surf one day, and Waylon took a final look. In an attempt to save the Surf, Christensen had asked Paul McCartney in 1991 to invest in the ballroom, but MPL Productions had replied that Paul McCartney was not interested in American real estate. Niki wanted to buy the Surf but couldn't raise the funds.

Despite its significance in the history of rock, the ballroom wasn't even on the National Registry of Historic Places. The Surf became another poignant image of small-town America dying; whether in Texas or Iowa, the changes had long since trampled the Mom & Pop establishments that had given birth to Holly and the first-generation rockers. And now the legendary dance halls seemed doomed.

"It is one of those big, glittering ballrooms that once dotted the interior of America like Christmas tree lights, somehow making the world a bigger place to people landlocked in all but dreams," a *New York Times* reporter wrote after a 1968 trip to Clear Lake. Local people waxed nostalgic about their famous landmark. One couple, farmer Laurence Radloff and his wife Evelyn, recalled dancing to the music of Guy Lombardo in the 1930s. Bob Ellsbury, who attended Buddy's concert in 1959 and whose father once managed the Surf, remembered sitting on Louis Armstrong's knee. "The Surf was like having our own major league ballpark," Ellsbury said. "It was a chance to see the stars of the world. It opened up a fantasy world for the whole region." From Glenn Miller to Lawrence Welk, all the greats of the era prior to stadium rock and MTV played one-night stands on the ballroom circuit, sandwiching a gig at the Surf between horrendous bus rides. If the Surf fell to the wrecking ball, it would mark an ignominious end of a musical era in America.

January 1995, Clear Lake—Like the mythical phoenix that rises from its own ashes, the Surf Ballroom was given a reprieve in 1995. The Buddy Holly Tribute Dance and Concert would go on, after all, thanks to the courage of a public-spirited family, the Snyders, and the Clear Lake Chamber of Commerce. The Dean Snyder Construction Company bought the ballroom and undertook an extensive $250,000 renovation. "We've restored it as it was in 1959," said Dale Snyder, one of the three brothers who now run their father's construction firm. A new roof and a new heating system were installed; the old gas turbine boilers were replaced by a water-heating system. The air-conditioning ducts below the Surf were cleaned and painted white, dispelling the ballroom's musty odor. The dance floor was sanded and resealed, and new carpeting was laid down in the lobby. "We now have palm trees and eighty pineapples, just the way it was when Buddy played here," Snyder added. The pine-apples, signifying hospitality, were stenciled on the lobby walls. As if to herald the the Surf's gorgeous new facelift, Weezer, a new rock band, started burning up MTV in January with a scorching video called "Buddy Holly."

By mid-January 1995 the Snyders still had not found anyone to run the Surf, which leases for $8,000 a month. The family appealed to the public, inviting potential donors to "be a part of Surf Ballroom history" by purchasing a "personalized brick paver." All those wishing to have their names engraved on bricks underneath the Surf canopy were asked to send $50 to the Snyders at 806 South Ninth Street, Clear Lake, Iowa 50428. For $150 they'd throw in a brass plaque. PR man Jeremy Powers revealed that his Minneapolis firm was trying to publicize the ballroom's search for a suitable manager. "There are very few rock 'n' roll landmarks left," said Powers. "Besides Graceland and Sun Records, the list is short and getting shorter, every time we lose a Fillmore or a Winterland."

At the last minute the Clear Lake Area Chamber of Commerce stepped in and offered to sponsor the annual Tribute to Buddy Holly, which was held at the Surf Ballroom on February 2–4, 1995. The faithful Maria Elena attended as usual, appearing with DJ Randy Chesterman at the Friday night sock hop. Niki Sullivan came to Clear Lake but spent more time at his sons' bar, Sully's, where, he says in a 1995 interview, "the Regulators from Odessa, Missouri, were playin' good rock 'n' roll, and people in their late fifties were standing on tables rockin'." Sonny Curtis was once again "with the Crickets—Gordon Payne is taking a hiatus," Sonny says in 1995. At the big Saturday night dance, the Fantastic Convertibles, Bobby Vee and the Ricochettes, the Shirelles, and the Crickets rocked the crowd at the Surf till the early morning hours.

Like Buddy Holly's music, the old dance hall seems indestructible. It just keeps on coming back, like a beautiful song.

Acknowledgments

My portrait of Buddy Holly is based for the most part on exclusive interviews with the people who knew him best. The four primary sources I must thank first are Maria Elena Holly, Larry Holley, Sonny Curtis, and Niki Sullivan. I was given the high privilege of interviewing, with no strings or conditions attached, the two people closest to Buddy, his wife Maria Elena and his brother Larry. In my interview with Maria Elena, the more probing and intimate my questions became, the deeper she dipped into the well of memory, even when I asked her to share Buddy's final words to her before he departed on the Winter Dance Party tour. If the second half of this book rings fresh and true as a story of young lovers in Greenwich Village in 1958, I must share the credit with Maria Elena.

Larry Holley was equally willing to explore the past, however painful, even when I asked him to describe his journey to Clear Lake to retrieve Buddy's body after the plane crash. Larry also spoke at length about Buddy's teen years, and if the early chapters have immediacy as a portrait of growing up in West Texas in the 1950s, much of the credit goes to Larry. It was also Larry who helped me understand the conflict Buddy felt between his religion and rock 'n' roll.

I am grateful to my agent, Al Lowman, for giving me the idea for the book and for placing it with the most gifted and sensitive editor any author could hope for: Robert Weil of St. Martin's Press. My book would have been diminished without Bob Weil's help. The efficiency and good humor of his assistant Becky Koh has never wavered. I appreciate the energy and enthusiasm of Andrew Graybill, who found many of the illustrations. With patience and skill, Eric J. Weisberg guided me through the legal vetting of the manuscript. Production editor Mara Lurie held the manuscript together through many changes. Copy editor David Cole offered helpful suggestions. Thomas J. McCormack, chairman and CEO of St. Martin's Press and editorial director of the trade division, delivered the words of encouragement I needed át the outset of this enterprise. Sally Richardson, president and publisher of the trade division, is someone I have admired for

many years, going back to our early careers in New York book publishing. Sally Holloway and Mal Peachey of Virgin Publishing Ltd. of
England have supported this project from the beginning. Don Mc-
Lean, composer of the great song "American Pie," and Elaine Dundy,
author of *The Dud Avocado* and *Elvis and Gladys*, were the first persons outside of my U.S. and British publishing houses to read the
manuscript, and both were generous in their support.

The most gifted of Buddy Holly's musical colleagues, Sonny Curtis,
who predated the Crickets in Buddy's life and has been in and out of the
Crickets over the years, was a wonderful friend and parent to this book.
We spent several days together in Clear Lake, Iowa, in 1993 and spoke
regularly in 1995, just before the book went to press. Sonny's eloquent
song "The Real Buddy Holly Story" is the only work prior to this book
to focus on the duality of Buddy's life, which was both intensely Dionysian
and devoutly Christian.

Niki Sullivan, one of the original Crickets (as well as a third cousin of
Buddy's by marriage), added substantially to our knowledge of Buddy
Holly in the course of several interviews. I'm especially grateful to Niki
for documenting, for the first time, the Crickets' initial discovery of New
York City in 1957 (prior to the famous "black tour") and their trip upstate
to visit Bob Thiele and Teresa Brewer in their home; none of this has
previously been written about. Niki also offered firsthand confirmation of
certain sexual revelations about Buddy, Norman and Vi Petty, and Norma
Jean Berry that first came to light in the *London Daily Mail* in the summer
of 1994.

Immortalized in two of Buddy's greatest songs, "Peggy Sue" and "Peggy
Sue Got Married," Peggy Sue Rackham told me what went wrong in her
marriage to Jerry Allison. Still attractive and beguiling, Peggy Sue fully
lives up to the praise Buddy heaped on her in the two rock classics that
bear her name.

Buddy made a lot of music in West Texas with Larry Welborn, and
I'm thankful to Larry for supplying important facts that no one else could
have done.

The irrepressible Tinker Carlen brought to life Buddy's early years of
wild rebellion. Tinker and I spent a memorable evening at the all-night
Kettle Restaurant in Lubbock, Texas, after Buddy's brother Larry sug-
gested I track him down. I managed to do so with the help of the vivacious
Arlene Burleson, who went to high school with Buddy, and her friend
Jim Fitzgerald.

Although writing a biography is a solitary adventure, the early stages
are intensely interpersonal, and no one could have given me a warmer
welcome to the subject of Buddy Holly than Buddy's niece, Sherry Holley,
whom I met at the Hi-D-Ho restaurant on University Drive in Lubbock.

Sherry is a pretty woman and a gifted singer. Her co-workers at the Hi-D-Ho, Shannon and LeJean Hughes, were also hospitable.

A member of Roy Orbison's original band, Wink Westerners, Charlie Evans, who helped me in 1989 when I was writing *Dark Star: The Roy Orbison Story*, once again came to my aid, picking me up at the Lubbock airport, showing me around the city, and introducing me to local radio personality Jerry Coleman, who knew Buddy and many of the central figures in his life.

Buddy's high school teachers Lois Keeton and Robert E. Knight contributed rare closeups of Buddy at school.

Charlie Johnson put me in touch with his son, Ken Johnson, one of the preachers who officiated at Buddy Holly's funeral. Ken filled in heretofore unpublished details about Buddy's baptism and last rites.

At Tom Lubbock Senior High, I was befriended by Julie Storey, Rickey Woody, and Theresa Martin; and at the South Plains Mall Waldenbooks by Daundria Martinez. Doyle Gammill granted me an interview about Peggy Sue. Standing at Buddy's grave in the Lubbock City Cemetery, I had a moment of warm communion with a Hungarian man named Frank Holly (no relation to Buddy). At the Lubbock Chamber of Commerce, Michael Reeves and Kara Stuller were hospitable and eager to help.

In Clovis, New Mexico, Billy Stull, one of the people closest to Norman Petty for many years, personally showed me through Petty's two studios, on very short notice, and gave me a crucial interview.

Although he is not a primary source, there is one other person who belongs in this group to whom I owe the most: Bill Griggs, founder and president of the now-defunct Buddy Holly Memorial Society. The back issues of Griggs's remarkably scholarly magazines *Reminiscing* and *Rockin' 50s* constitute the main repository of Buddy Holly material. I was able to purchase copies of this incredibly useful collection in Lubbock in 1992. Over the years Griggs and various members of the BHMS interviewed important primary sources, some of them now dead. Herewith my special thanks to interviewers Wayne Jones, Skip Brooks, Bill Malcolm, Bruce Wilcox, Damian Johnstone, Nigel Smith, Larry Corbin, Jack Miller, Lee Jackson, Kevin Terry, Bill Floyd, Jerry MacNeish, Gary McLeod, Hans Goeppinger, Steve Vitek, Dave Skinner, Steve Bonner, Stu Fink, and Margaret NcNie.

Two other Holly fans deserve special mention. Hans Goeppinger of Boone, Iowa, introduced me to Sonny Curtis and arranged our marathon interviews in Minneapolis, Clear Lake, and Mason City. Hans also put me in touch with Jim Weddell, whose interview alters the historical record with regard to when the plane crash that killed Buddy was first discovered. George Blaisdell of Billerica, Massachusetts, generously shared material from his extensive Buddy Holly collection. Just as important were George Blaisdell's many calls to me in Key West, offering friendship and encouragement when they were sorely needed.

In Clear Lake, Iowa, I met Jerry Allison (whom I'd previously spoken to on the phone), Joe B. Mauldin, Frankie Ford, Bobby Vee, Mike Berry, Joan Allison, Chris Hughes, Bruce and Sue Christensen, Don Larson, Neale Winker, Geoffrey T. Williams, Trevor Lailey, Sharon Black, Cathy Gacek, Yvonne Pearsall, Jerome J. Thiele, Marv Jurek, Pat Jurek, Shelley Allison, Brian Mahoney, and Lisa Latham. Subsequently I spoke with countless others from the area, including Karen Lein, Douglas Hines, Elwin L. Musser, Jeremy Powers, Cindy Florer, and Dale Snyder of the Dean Snyder Construction Company.

Others, from all over the U.S. and England, who made kind contributions include Don Bins, Nyal C. Peterson, David Garrard Lowe, Franklin E. Fried, Jim Carr, Bill Munroe, Pat Collins, Jeff Seckler, Lenny Kaye, Brian Mahoney, the late Marion Keisker, the late John R. Lee, Barbara J. Sharp, Melissa Sheahan, Johnny May, Albert Copeland, Tony Szikil, Dick Hankoos, Clive Harvey, Keith Martin, and Maxine Paetro. Special thanks to Waylon Jennings and Pete Curtis for graciously giving me rare photographs.

My revelatory interviews with Sam Phillips, Boots Randolph, and Orbie Lee Harris for my biography of Roy Orbison, as well as the two and a half months I worked with Priscilla Presley on *Elvis and Me* in 1985, gave me rare insights into early rock 'n' roll that have helped me in all that I have written.

This book is also based on written material and on video and audio presentations. At the Mason City Municipal Airport, Jerome J. Thiele, director of aviation, opened the files of the airport commission to me, contributing substantially to my understanding of the events of February 3, 1959. Articles in the *Mason City Globe-Gazette* and the *Clear Lake Mirror-Reporter* were enlightening, especially the expert reportage of Jim Collison, Jeremy Powers, Jeff Tecklenburg, Douglas Hines, and Carol Gales.

Crucial secondary sources included John Goldrosen and John Beecher's ground-breaking biography *Remembering Buddy*; Larry Holley's memoir "The Buddy I Knew!"; William J. Bush's "Buddy Holly: The Legend and the Legacy"; Paul McCartney's *The Real Buddy Holly Story*; Jonathan Cott, Ed Ward, and David McGee of *Rolling Stone*; Douglas Brooker's *Reminiscing*; Alan Clark's publications on Buddy Holly, Ritchie Valens, Eddie Cochran, and the Big Bopper; the radio special "Buddy Holly: The Legend Moves On"; Beverly Mendheim's *Ritchie Valens*; reportage by Sue Frederick, Jim Hoffman, Mark Steuer, Jack Sheridan, William Kerns, and

Larry Lehmer; and interviews by Kurt Loder, Michael Alan Oestreicher, and Pat Kennedy.

Bill Griggs explored the files of the *Lubbock Avalanche-Journal* and turned up many riches. Griggs also contributed generously to the CD section of the discography. Mark Williams at the *Avalanche-Journal* was cordial and informative.

Librarians up and down the East Coast, especially in Florida, Georgia, and Virginia, were eager to help. In Key West, I am grateful to Charles Nundy, Cynthia Lawson, and Marianne Duchardt of the Monroe County Public Library. Jay Brandes of the Troy State University Library in Ft. Walton Beach, Florida, tracked down more than one rare volume for me. I'm grateful to the staffs of the Tifton-Tift County Library in Tifton, Georgia, and the Handley Library Archives in Winchester, Virginia. St. Mary Star of the Sea Catholic Church in Key West helped me interpret the funeral of Ritchie Valens.

As a biographer who often writes of musicians, I am indeed fortunate to have in Key West, where I make my home, a splendid record store. Rogues and Records, operated by the knowledgeable and gracious Dana Moore and Marty Stonely, is a veritable British Museum of the recording industry. The recent addition of Mike McGreevy to the staff assures that Rogues and Records will continue to be one of the friendliest and funkiest spots in town.

The love of one's family is essential during the long and arduous years of writing. My sister Lu Bradbury and brother Bill E. Amburn were generous with their hearts, as always. Joyce Kahlich Amburn and Richard Amburn were especially solicitous, coming to visit me at one point when I was on the road. Bill Manville also tracked me down, driving many miles to bring much-needed fellowship. Cy Egan, to whom this book is dedicated, and his wife, Jean, long ago adopted me as their own, and I am forever in their debt. A veteran newspaperman as well as a stylish writer, Cy devoted many hours to fine-tuning the manuscript and making factual corrections.

Most of this book was written in Key West, where I shared the joys and occasional terrors of daily life with Fred Aanerud, Jerry Doughty, Bill Eccles, Marilyn Johnson, Dennis and Carol Lannon, Alan Keener, Charlie Fallon, Tim Hecht, Pete Peterson, Joanna Jacobson, Rey and Candy Todd, Mike Schuster, Stephanie Hobbs, Annalise and Jane Mannix-Lachner, Wendy Tucker, Dick Epler, Matt Jordan, Dave and Lynn Kaufelt, Michael and Helen Miller, Jimmy Sherman, Pat Doehr, Jon Phillips, Dan and Ellie McConnell, Donnie Callahan, Katie Truax, Frank Cantelmo, and Barbara Ehrenreich.

On research trips, perfect strangers who became fast friends include

Beverly Simpson, Jack Fretwell, and John Greene of Winchester, Virginia; Jerry Barnes of Tifton, Georgia; and Laura Mead of Thomasville, Georgia. In New York, where I saw the delightful British musical *Buddy*, Stanley Bard of the Chelsea Hotel extended a warm welcome and arranged for comfortable quarters, as always.

Shelley Winters continues to enrich my life with love and steadfastness, as do Nell Crisante, Pat Loud, Tyler Hardeman, Jack Larson, Eugenia Trinkle, Kent Henderson, Judy Feiffer, Richard Howard, Florence Rome, Joseph LeSueur, Bill Jamison, Esther Mitgang, Linda Gravenites, Cindy Langford, and Allston and Pepper James.

Several friends died in the years I worked on this book: James Bridges, the brilliant, ever-young director of *Paper Chase*, *China Syndrome*, and *Urban Cowboy*, and lovable Sam Mitnick, with whom I worked in perfect harmony when we were executives at Dell Publishing Company and later at G. P. Putnam's Sons. And I'll miss the laughing voice of the late Joyce Rogers, my dearest friend since college days at Texas Christian University and Columbia University and author of *The Second Best Bed: Shakespeare's Will in a New Light*. Joyce died on Christmas Eve 1994. Her spirit still guides me. I owe the greatest thanks, of course, to the higher power who guides us all, when we're in touch, and even, sometimes, when we're not. Years ago my friend Steve West gave me a crucifix. It has been on the power drive of my computer ever since.

Notes

Full bibliographic details are given in the Bibliography.

Abbreviations

AC: Alan Clark
ACOB: "A Celebration of Buddy Holly: The
  Legend Moves On"
AP: Associated Press
BB: The Big Bopper
BBH: *Big Beat Heat*
BG: Bill Griggs
BH: Buddy Holly
BHMS: Buddy Holly Memorial Society
BHTLL: "Buddy Holly: The Legend and Legacy"
  by William J. Bush, *Guitar Player*
  magazine, June 1982
BM: Beverly Mendheim
BW: Bruce Wilcox
CA: Carroll Anderson
CB: Carl Bunch
CLMR: *Clear Lake Mirror-Reporter*
CW: Charles White
CT: *Chicago Tribune*
DD: Dion DiMucci
DE: Don Everly
DLF: Donna Ludwig Fox
EH: Ella Holley
FM: Fred Milano
G&B: Goldrosen and Beecher
GBOF: *Great Balls of Fire!* by Myra Lewis and
  Murray Silver
GP: *Guitar Player* magazine
HG: Hans Goeppinger
IC: *Iowa Connection*
JA: Jerry Allison
JB: John Beecher
JBM: Joe B. Mauldin
JG: John Goldrosen
JJ: John Jackson
JN: Jack Neal
JP: Jeremy Powers
JT: Jeff Tecklenburg
JW: Jim Weddell
KF: Ken Fuson
KJ: Ken Johnson
KL: Kurt Loder
LAJ: *Lubbock Avalanche-Journal*
LDM: *London Daily Mail*
LH: Larry Holley
LK: Lois Keeton
LL: Larry Lehmer
LOH: L. O. Holley
LR: Little Richard
LW: Larry Welborn

MCGG: *Mason City Globe-Gazette*
MEH: Maria Elena Holly
ML/MS: Myra Lewis and Murray Silver
MS: Mark Steuer
NP: Norman Petty
NS: Niki Sullivan
PM: Paul McCartney
PE: Phil Everly
PN: Philip Norman
PS: Peggy Sue Gerron Allison Rackham
P&T: Jeremy Powers and Jeff Tecklenburg
QOR: *The Life and Times of Little Richard: The
  Quasar of Rock* by Charles White
RK: Robert Knight
RV: Ritchie Valens
VP: Vi Petty
RB: *Remembering Buddy*
RBHS: Paul McCartney's *Real Buddy Holly Story*
RES: Ralph E. Smiley
R50: *Rockin' 50s* magazine
RM: *Reminiscing* magazine
ROA: *Rock of Ages: The Rolling Stone History of
  Rock & Roll* by Ed Ward, Geoffrey Stokes,
  and Ken Tucker
RP: Roger Peterson
SC: Sonny Curtis
TA: Tommy Allsup
TBIK: "The Buddy I Knew!" by Larry Holley
TC: Tinker Carlen
TGBH: "The Guitars of Buddy Holly" by William
  J. Bush, *Guitar Player* magazine, June
  1982
TRSI: *The Rolling Stone Interviews*
TW: *The Wanderer* by Dion DiMucci and David
  Seay
WB: William Bush
WJ: Wayne Jones
WJEN: Waylon Jennings
WJRBH: "Waylon Jennings Remembering Buddy
  Holly" by William J. Bush, *Guitar Player*
  magazine, June 1982

Prologue

3: "Forget about that movie": Author interview
  with LH.
4: "well-built" . . . good looking": Quoted by Lou
  Antonicello in BG, "Duane Eddy and BH," RM,
  p. 11 (undated clipping).

4: then called juvenile delinquency: Author interview with TC. LH says BH took various musical instruments belonging to him, which were kept in the Holley home, to raise money.

4: He got into fights: Author interviews with RK, LW, TC.

4: who carried a chain: Author interviews with LH, TC.

4: far more Rabelaisian: Author interview with TC.

4: fathered an illegitimate offspring: Author interview with NS; PN, "Secret BH: Honeymoon in Acapulco and PS Came Too," LDM, 9/1/94, p. 52.

4: dance in juke joints: Author interview with NS.

4: racially and bisexually: CW, QOR, p. 84 (copyright page lists Richard Wayne Penniman as copyright holder).

4: little-known orgy: Ibid.; author interview with SC.

5: [ingrained Texas prejudices: Author interview with LH (BH "didn't like [a famous rock 'n' roll star, who] had a bigoted attitude, like Buddy used to be").

5: yet crafty as a fox: Author interviews with TC and LH (TC: BH shoplifted and on one occasion took money from a child; LH: BH lifted some musical instruments from the Holley home. JA in G&B, RB, p. 138: although BH wouldn't deliberately have cheated JA and JBM, BH possibly was in arrears to them; there may have been occasions when BH failed to give JA and JBM their share of tour earnings, but JA adds that there were also times when BH paid them amounts in excess of their actual earnings.

5: his manager's wife: Author interview with NS; PN, "Secret BH: Honeymoon," p. 52.

5: "got it on" with: Ibid.

5: He proposed to his: Author interview with MEH.

5: religious fervor temporarily derailed Little: Lazell, Reed, Crampton, Rock Movers & Shakers, p. 301.

5: Scandal damaged Jerry Lee's: ML/MS, GBOF, pp. 1–2, passim.

5: unmercifully hounded Berry: Berry, Autobiography, pp. 203–11.

5: smashup sidetracked Perkins: Stambler, Encyclopedia of Pop, Rock and Soul, p. 515; Stallings, Rock 'n' Roll Confidential, p. 86.

6: the church, the police, the press: JJ, BBH, pp. 200–203, 205–206.

6: harrowing travel conditions: Author interviews with MEH and HG; Ward, Stokes, Tucker, ROA, p. 194; DD, TW, p. 87; TA, RM 15, p. 13; Dodge, Not Fade Away, pp. 160–61.

6: film biography after his: Flippo, "BH Story," quoted in G&B, RB, p. 170.

6: devout fundamentalist Christian: Author interviews with KJ, LH; "What We Believe," Tract #406, Tabernacle Baptist Church: "We are fundamental.... We are premillenial"; Bynum, "Superstar: Jesus Christ Superstar Critically Examined in the Light of the Bible," Tract B-401, Tabernacle Baptist Church.

6: condemned rock as evil: TBIK; Bob Church, BG, RM 27, p. 7.

7: helped shape the new musical: Keith Richards, RBHS; Cott, RS Illustrated History of Rock & Roll, p. 81; Duffy, " '50s," Life, 12/1/92, p. 44.

8: top of the drive-in: illustration, Hi-D-Ho, 6419 University Avenue, Lubbock, Texas; author interviews with Sherry Holley and Shannon Hughes; Jan Fulton qtd. in BG, "Jake Goss: BH's Barber," RM 25, Winter/82, p. 13.

8: "Uncle Buddy used to: Author interview with Sherry Holley.

8: a fire in the belly: EH quoted in RM 43, 7/86, p. 4; EH qtd. in RM 11, 7/79; G&B, RB, p. 23.

8: high spirits: PE told KL that Buddy was so drunk he had to be helped home in "The Everly Brothers," TRSI, p. 146.

Chapter 1

10: "We all sorta spoiled him,": Author interview with LH.

10: he began to cry: TBIK.

10: hard-shell Baptists: "What We Believe," Tract 406: "Five words ... set forth what we believe ... Baptist, Fundamental, Premillennial, Missionary, and Independent ... The Anti-Christ will be manifested here upon the earth and the seven years of tribulation shall begin"; G&B, RB, p. 22.

10: first of them to graduate: "516 Lubbock Graduates to Get Diplomas at Ceremony Today," LAJ, 5/27/55; author interview with LH.

10: as little as $12: Dave Skinner, "A Meeting With Mr. and Ms. Holley on June 12, 1969," RM 43, 7/86, p. 4.

10: from job to job: LAJ, AM edition, 7/10/85.

10: September 7, Labor Day: EH quoted in BG, "Mrs. Holley," RM 4, 9/77, p. 5. It was also Dollar Day in Lubbock, EH added; BH high school English theme quoted in G&B, RB, p. 27.

10: at 1911 Sixth Street: BG, "Tour Schedules, Television Appearances, and Recording Sessions of Buddy Holly," unpublished, 6/29/91, p. 1.

10: dawned cloudy and overcast: References to Lubbock weather throughout: LAJ, 1936–1959.

10: the time Buddy arrived: 3:30 P.M., to be precise: EH quoted in BG, "Mrs. Holley."

10: English and Welsh descent: BG, RM 27, Summer '83, p. 3.

10: one-fourth Cherokee: Ibid.

10: Claremore, Oklahoma: O'Brien, Will Rogers, no publisher or city listed, book found in Tift County Library, Tifton, Georgia, p. 23.

10: of his Cherokee heritage: Rogers, Autobiography of Will Rogers, p. 18.

10: "My ancestors didn't come: O'Brien, Will Rogers, p. 24.

11: 1927, and Patricia in 1929: G&B, RB, p. 13.

11: "too long for such: quoted in ACOB.

11: smiling towheaded: BG, RM 14, 3/80.

11: mother taught him "Have: Buddy Holly: A Rock-'n'-Roll Collection, double LP, MCA 24009; IC.

11: he was five, he won: BH letter to Paul Cohen, 3/2/56, quoted in RM, 3/82, p. 28; reproduced in G&B, RB, p. 36.

11: County Line, a rural: IC.

11: himself on the violin: BH letter to Cohen, 3/2/56.

11: didn't like to study: EH quoted in "Buddy Holly: The Man," IC.

11: Holley children to excel: TBIK.

11: Holley's twin sister: BG, "Buddy in Bronze," RM 17, 12/80, p. 5.

11: "Right after Iwo Jima: BHTLL, p. 76; Travis Holley, ACOB.
11: taught Buddy how to: BHTLL, Ibid.
11: acoustic Epiphone: Ibid.; TGBH, p. 84.
11: "made a clean sound,": Quoted Instant Recall TV program.
12: banjo and mandolin: BHTLL, p. 76.
12: belting "Love Sick Blues,": TBIK.
12: more interested in chasing: Ibid.
12: on sleeping between them: Ibid.
12: "infectious laugh. He just: Author interview with LK.
12: "Because I can see: Ibid.
12: peroxided his hair: Author interview with LH.
12: "King and Queen of: BG, RM 30, Spring 1984, p. 26.
13: Wayne Maines brought his: TBIK.
13: Mahalia Jackson's "Move On: G&B, RB, p. 124.
13: The Baptist gospel singer: Schwerin, Got to Tell It: Mahalia Jackson, Queen of Gospel, passim.
13: precursor of rock: Wexler and Ritz, Rhythm and the Blues, p. 85
13: "a bigoted: Author interview with LH
13: Gatemouth Page's radio: G&B, RB, p. 16.
14: Bluegrass has been: Stambler and Landon, Encyclopedia, p. 477.
14: "big hams . . . push": Quoted in BG, "Mrs. Holley," p. 2.
14: electronics store temporarily: G&B, RB, p. 48.
14: notorious C&W novelty: Malone, Country Music U.S.A., p. 225.
14: PTA open-house: G&B, RB, p. 18.
14: "really impressed,": Quoted in BG, "JA—Part One," RM 23, 6/82, p. 7.
14: Jerry played Fats Domino's: Ibid.; "Allison Recalls How Music Grew," MCGG, 2/1/89.
14: Booker T. Washington: Yanak and Cornelison, Great American History Fact-Finder, pp. 404–405.
14: small black kitten: EH qtd. in BG, "Mrs. Holley," p. 3.
14: "I was ten years: Author interview with LH.
15: "stole, cussed, and chased: Author interview with TC.
15: "choked to death: Ibid.
15: often drove to Mexico: Author interview with Charlie "Slob" Evans.
15: "crotch crickets": Author interview with TC.
15: "I went down and got fucked: Ibid.
15: Buddy's first sexual encounter: Ibid.
16: "grandmother's house,": Ibid.
16: stopped for gas at: Ibid.
16: "wondered if Buddy had: Author interview with LH.
16: "Baptists seem like . . . ": Ibid.
17: never lost his spirituality: Author interviews with LH and PS. PS: "BH was gifted with the white light of Christianity. Music is the food of the soul. Buddy comes from the radiance of the white light of God."
17: underlined his copy of: I found BH's copy of this New Testament book in a box of his memorabilia which BG kindly permitted me to handle and inspect in Lubbock. It was among items the Holley family gave to BG.
17: always kept a copy: BG's Holly memorabilia collection, Ibid.

17: trials, temptations, troubles: Rice and Martin, eds., Soul-Stirring Songs & Hymns, p. 369.
18: "Take it to the Lord: Ibid.
18: "I think I'm going: Author interview with TC.
18: newly discovered pleasures of sex: Ibid.
18: "I'm ashamed of a lot [and subsequent dialogue with TC]: Ibid.
18: baptized by Ben D. Johnson: Author interview with KJ.
18: "I saw the Spirit: Gospel of John, Holy Bible, p. 130.
18: "you are dead to [and subsequent KJ quotations]: Author interview with KJ.
18: Buddy often rose: Ibid.
18: "Just as I am: Elliott and Bradbury, Soul-Stirring Songs & Hymns, p. 282.
19: "He didn't talk a [and subsequent dialogue BH/EH]: BG, "Mrs. Holley," p. 4.

Chapter 2

20: "My son plays the: Quoted in BG, "JN: Story Behind the 'Buddy and Jack' Show on KDAV Radio," RM 44, 9/86, p. 4.
20: "We liked the toe-tapping: Ibid
21: "I played rhythm: "Secret BH: Girl Who Broke Young Buddy's Heart," LDM, 8/31/94, p. 34.
21: temperature regularly hit: LAJ, 9/2/52.
21: In a theme he wrote: Quoted in G&B, RB, p. 27.
21: waving the Westerner banner: "Westerner Alma Mater Song," Westerner, Vol. 31, 1954.
21: "He was still just: Author interview with LK.
22: The winter of Buddy's: LAJ, 2/2/53.
22: girl named Joyce Howard: "Westerner Roundup Day at Lubbock High School," Ibid., p. 1.
22: professional C&W singer: Quoted in G&B, p. 27.
22: him perform during lunch: BG, RM 5, 12/77.
22: wearing tight pants: BG, "LH," RM 14, 3/80, p. 9.
23: "Buddy sidled along the: Author interview with Arlene Burleson.
23: smart-aleck persona: Author interview with SC.
23: who carried a chain: Author interview with LH.
23: "He sat in the fourth: Author interview with LK.
23: he was expelled from: Buddy's theme, G&B, RB, p. 27.
23: destroyed the front: Ibid.
23: electrical engineering as a: EH quoted in BG, "Mrs. Holley," p. 3.
23: last two years of: Ibid.
23: enough of a realist: Ibid.
23: wanted to see Ben Hall: BG, "Ben Hall," RM 22, 3/82, p. 4.
23: Weldon Myrick: Ibid., p. 5.
24: Hi Pockets auditioned them: Hi Pockets Duncan quoted in ACOB; "BH, the Musician," IC.
24: "with a little . . . a star.": Quoted in ACOB.
24: fan mail almost immediately: JN quoted in BG, "An Interview With JN," p. 4.
24: "a beautiful professional job.": TBIK.

24: too small for the: HPD quoted in BG, RM 10, 3/79.
24: "This is Hi Pocket: *Ibid.*
24: His Texas Hot Shots: "Labor Day Dance," LAJ, 9/7/53.
24: recorded the duo on: G&B, RB, p. 178.
25: "The 'Sunday Parties' were: Quoted in BG, "SC," RM 17, 12/80, p. 11.
25: "real hot steel-guitar: *Ibid.*
25: "Sonny started performing: Pete Curtis letter to author, 5/1/95.
25: Adair Music Store: Author interview with SC.
25: "where we'd spend the: *Ibid.*
25: until they fell asleep: BHTLL, p. 78.
25: drank beer and chased: SC song, "The Real Buddy Holly Story."
25: "Sonny Curtis was very helpful: TBIK.
25: he and Bob Montgomery: BG and Larry Byers, " 'Pappy' Dave Stone," RM 34, 1/85, p. 7.
25: radiating sincerity and deference: *Ibid.*, pp. 7–8.
25: "very good,": *Ibid.*, p. 7.
25: their own 2:30 P.M.: *Ibid.*, p. 8.
25: "I had an ulterior motive,": *Ibid.*, p. 7.
26: "They were hits almost: *Ibid.*

Chapter 3

27: *If this guy wears:* Author interview with Orbie Lee Harris.
27: "I would go to: Greg Mitchell, "The History of Rock 'n' Roll," *Crawdaddy*, December 1974.
27: helped Roy with lead: Author interview with Tinker Carlen.
27: "That ol' party boy [and subsequent dialogue]: ACOB.
27: "I feel that I: BG, "18 Interviews (all at once)," RM 20, 9/81, p. 3.
28: "Montgomery remembers him as: "Secret BH: Girl Who Broke," p. 34.
28: dry-cleaning stores in: *Ibid.*, p. 35.
28: more than twenty-six years: BG letter to author, 11/7/94.
28: "Buddy never said a word: Author interview with SC.
28: "I went with a Church: Author interview with LH.
29: "If Buddy had a: Author interview with BG.
29: Brodszky's "I Walk With God": *Commencement Exercises*, Lubbock Senior High School, May 27, 1955, Fair Park Coliseum.
29: Christmas carols: 1955 *Westerner* yearbook.
29: "had hair all over: Author interview with TC.
29: "Echo was not a: Author interview with SC.
29: "I was playing a [and subsequent dialogue]: Author interview with LW.
30: "I'm going to draw: ACOB.
30: remote broadcasts: *Ibid.*
30: at the Lindsey Theater: BG, RM 15, 6/80.
30: "If we played thirty: ACOB.
30: "It's going to be: G&B, RB, p. 20.
30: pronounced it: "School Days," *New Yorker*, 7/8/91, p. 29.
30: "You'll do anything to get: Denisoff, *Waylon*, p. 36.
30: A high-school dropout at fourteen: *Ibid.*, p. 42.
30: "always into some damn: Quoted in *ibid.*, p. 39.
30: burned down a government: *Ibid.*
30: promise as a place kicker: *Ibid.*, p. 42.

30: He'd won first prize: *Ibid.*, p. 40.
30: "He came from a poor: Quoted in *Ibid.*, p. 44.
30: Waylon met Buddy, at seventeen: *Ibid.*, p. 47.
31: "deep brown eyes and: *Ibid.*, p. 83.
31: written when he was fifteen: *Ibid.*, p. 42.
31: "the cowboy Warren Beatty.": Riese, *Nashville Babylon*, p. 56.
31: "honestly crude . . . man, baby' ": Des Barres, *I'm With the Band: Confessions of a Groupie*, p. 166.
31: "Sometimes the same band: *Lost Highway*, p. 208.
31: Buddy frequently lent his: TGBH, p. 86.
31: "Who's got a quarter? [and subsequent dialogue]: Flippo, "*Penthouse* Interview: WJEN," 9/81, pp. 108–112, 142–143; slightly different version, Dan Pietromonaco, "Interview With WJEN," *Billboard's* TWA Airline Service, 1976.
31: appealed equally to hillbillies: Malone, *Country Music U.S.A.*, p. 260.
31: a representative of Columbia: G&B, RB, p. 30.
32: "embarrassing,": · the full quote—"It's kind of embarrassing to listen to those old tapes of me and Buddy, but I wouldn't trade those memories for anything in the world"—occurs in BHTLL, p. 76.
32: "Of course we couldn't: Author interview with LW.
32: "Well, less go back: *Ibid.*
32: "He was ready to: *Ibid.*
32: "Though in appearance Buddy: Author interview with SC.
32: "Scared me half to: PN, "Secret BH: Girl Who," p. 34.
32: "I had to grab: Author interview with RK.
32: "Buddy was cocky, but: *Ibid.*
32: not brawny—nor particularly: Author interview with LH.
33: Buddy took a job: Author interview with RK.
33: "unusually thoughtful, especially: *Ibid.*
33: "Buddy started playing rock: *Ibid.*
33: wore it around her neck: Echo wears Buddy's ring around her neck in photo on p. 9, BG, *R50*, 12/88.
34: if the car was actually Buddy's: BG, "Buddy's New Oldsmobile," RM 35, 3/85, p. 9.
34: Buddy wrecked the car: LH quoted in BH, "Buddy Wrecked the Car!" R50, 4/92.
34: Buddy Holley was not asked: *Commencement Exercises*, Lubbock Senior High School, op. cit.
34: atop the Dunlap Store: Author interview with Robert Knight.
34: "Buddy brought her over: Author interview with LH.

Chapter 4

35: "When Elvis came to: Author interview with LH.
35: "Elvis could get pussy: Author interview with SC.
35: "Without Elvis," . . . "none of: Worth and Tamerius, *Elvis: His Life From A to Z*, p. 89.
35: several times in 1955: *Ibid*, pp. 333–34: 6/3, 10/15, and 10/16/55.
35: group opened for him: Author interview with SC.
35: Hi Pockets once said: ACOB.

35: Winfield Scott Moore III: Worth and Tamerius, *Elvis*, p. 133.
36: Elvis was terribly late: ACOB.
36: "Elvis looked like a: Author interview with SC.
36: Buddy and Elvis intrigued: Bob Montgomery quoted in ACOB.
36: Hi Pockets hobnobbed: Hi Pockets Duncan quoted in *ibid*.
36: "But as far as: *Ibid*.
36: To Bob Montgomery, who: ACOB.
36: "We opened for Elvis: Author interview with SC.
36: "Somebody was wantin' to: Author interview with LW.
37: "Buddy and Elvis got: Author interview with LH.
37: "I wish he had done: TGBH, p. 82.
37: Mrs. Holley loved Buddy's: BH, "Mrs. Holley," p. 4.
37: "I wish I could: Author interview with MEH.
37: "Let me tell you: *Ibid*.
37: Waylon remembers that Buddy: WJRBH, p. 72.
37: "changed Buddy," Waylon later: *Lost Highway*, p. 208.
37: "We got a drummer: Baker, "Roy Orbison, the Life of a Legend," Interview Picture Disk; Ashton, "Last Testament, Blue Angel," BAM, 2/24/89.
37: Buddy said he'd show them; JA quoted in RBHS.
38: Jerry's whole-hearted: *Ibid*.
38: Bob Montgomery and Sonny Curtis were: TGBH, p. 84.
38: "We'd both play: BHTLL, p. 82.
38: he offered to help: BG, "BG Talks to LW," R 45, 11/86, p. 15.
38: driving the '55 Olds: *Ibid*.
38: "Elvis was supposed to: *Ibid*.
38: Known for his bluegrass: Denisoff, *Waylon*, p. 25.
38: King was as good: G&B, RB, p. 30.
38: Buddy was virtually: *Ibid*.
38: "idolized" Elvis, he told: *Ibid*.
39: "Pappy" Dave Stone arranged: BG and Byers, " 'Pappy,' " p. 7.
39: "what it takes.": G&B, RB, p. 32.
39: "Every young songwriter and singer: Tillis, *Stutterin' Boy*, p. 87.
39: "as soon as possible: Quoted in G&B, RB, p. 32.
39: on acetate at KDAV: Quoted in BG and Byers, " 'Pappy,' " p. 7.
40: Paul Cohen, prestigious director: Malone, *Country Music U.S.A.*, p. 95.
40: "I don't care how: WJEN on "The Dick Cavett Show."
40: "asked to have the: Quoted in BG and Byers, " 'Pappy,' " p. 7.
40: "Well, you can bring: ROA, p. 115.
40: When Bob Montgomery realized: G&B, RB, p. 32.
40: "I wasn't able to: Quoted in BG, *Who's Who*.
40: Buddy had attracted Thompson's: G&B, RB, p. 30.
40: from the Lubbock public school: JA in BG, "JA—Part One," RM 23, 6/82, p. 12.
40: for $6 a year: G&B, RB, p. 41.
41: bumped into a blond: Author interview with PS.

41: scribbled her initials: BG, "Buddy's Notebook," RM 5, 12/77, p. 8.
41: boys who were fun-loving: BG in "PS," PS: *Souvenir Program*, 11th Annual BHMS Convention and Rock 'n' Roll Concert, 9/8–10/88, Clovis, New Mexico, p. 2.
41: and had entertaining personalities: *Ibid*.
41: stood in the band room: *Ibid*.
41: "I thought he was: *Ibid*.
41: "Buddy's first crush: *Ibid*., p. 7.
41: "Our relationship: Author interview with PS.
41: They threatened to send: *Ibid*.; BG, *Who's Who*.
41: "It was probably lupus: Author interview with PS.
41: standing beside his car: *Ibid*.
41: "a lot of time: BG, "PS," p. 11.
41: "When the boys didn't: Author interview with PS.
41: Maxine Carrol Lawrence, pregnant: Denisoff, *Waylon*, p. 43; Toepfer, "I'm Not Gonna Put Up With Anything From Anybody," *Photoplay*, 2/74, p. 100.
41: that she wasn't pregnant: Denisoff, *Waylon*, p. 44; Windeler, "Couples," *People*, 9/75, p. 46; Stoop, "WJ: Big Country Singer Hits the Big City," *After Dark*, 4/73, p. 51.
42: Anita Shipley, started dating: *Ibid*., p. 47.
42: They found a shady: Ben Hall in RBHS.
42: Buddy appealed to his: G&B, RB, p. 34.
42: he asked for $1,000: TBIK.
42: "Why don't you just: *Ibid*.
42: "or bust a gut,": *Ibid*.
42: "He blew six hundred: *Ibid*.
42: $249.50: Bacon and Day, *Fender Book*, p. 15.
42: Harrod Music: TGBH, p. 84.
42: on Avenue Q in Lubbock: LH quoted in BG, "1981 BHMS Convention," RM 21, 12/81, p. 23.
42: Buddy made it famous: BHTLL, p. 82.
42: named Clarence Leo Fender: Bacon and Day, *Fender Book*, p. 9.
42: a red sport coat: BHIK.
43: Lansky Brothers: Goldman, *Elvis*, p. 81.
43: "That's how we ended: Author interview with SC.
43: bought a Pro Amp: BHTLL, p. 81.
43: A collection agency was: G&B, RB, p. 34.
43: "Just go on doing: Quoted in Guralnick, *Last Train to Memphis*, p. 237.

Chapter 5

44: hard-drinking C&W recording: Carlisle, *Ragged but Right*, p. 101; Malone, *Country Music U.S.A.*, p. 186; Riese, *Nashville Babylon*, p. 183; Emery and Carter, *Memories*, p. 184.
44: if he were capable: G&B, RB, p. 39.
44: "You don't have the: *Ibid*., p. 43.
44: restraining a volatile and combative: *Ibid*.
45: "chased chicks,": *Ibid*., p. 36.
45: Rosa Parks: Daniel, *Chronicle of the 20th Century*, p. 777.
45: "If the public will: Cited in G&B, RB, p. 38.
45: "Whatever you do, don't: ACOB.
45: showering twenty times a: Author interview with Jerry Coleman.
45: Speedy, a Mexican Chihuahua: Freeman Hoover interview with BH, 11/1/57, Denver, Colorado.

45: "We feel our studio: Quoted in Berry, "NP Recordings Put Clovis on Map," *Clovis News-Journal*, 12/20/59, p. 6.
46: "We have perhaps the: *Ibid.*
46: hit record, "Mood Indigo,": *Ibid.*
46: Nor Va Jak, Petty's: Bernard, "Dual Celebration Tunes in to Cultivation of 'Clovis Sound,' " *Amarillo Globe-News*, 9/4/87, p. 1.
46: Petty was gay: Author interview with NS; PN, "Secret BH: Girl Who," p. 35.
46: Vi bisexual: *Ibid.*; PN, "Secret BH: Honeymoon," p. 52.
46: Berry, was a lesbian: PN: "Secret BH: Honeymoon," p. 52.
46: "If Norman was gay: Author interview with SC.
46: However, Niki Sullivan, another: Author interview with NS.
46: majoring in accounting and: Barnard, "Events Continue Through Weekend," *Amarillo Globe-News*, 9/4/87, p. 1.
46: asked how he could: Bronson, *Billboard Book of No. 1 Hits*, p. 19.
46: "behind a haystack": *Ibid.*
46: where he grew up: Barnard, "Events Continue," *op. cit.*
46: Buddy Holly and Roy Orbison: Bronson, *Billboard Book of No. 1 Hits*, p. 19.
46: first singer-songwriter of: *Ibid.*
47: "Could I get you: Quoted in BG, "Bill Pickering Talks About the Picks!" RM, 21, 12/81, p. 5.
47: "Well, let's see: *Ibid.*
47: "Yes, Buddy told me: *Ibid.*
47: "Can you do anything: ACOB.
47: "Yeah. I'll put you: ACOB.
47: thousand kids poured: BG, RM 10, 3/79.
47: cahoots with the musicians: Author interview with TC.
47: "He was packin' out: Author interview with LH.
47: On May 10 Buddy: BG, "Tour Schedules," p. 2.
47: *The Searchers*: Wayne and Thorleifson, *John Wayne*, p. 116; Gallagher, *John Ford*, p. 332; Magill, *Magill's Survey of Cinema*.
47: Buddy, Sonny, and Jerry: BG, "JA—Part One," RM 23, 6/82, p. 10.
48: compose a song together: *Ibid.*
48: "That'll be the day,": *Ibid.*
48: "Yeah. That sounds like: *Ibid.*
48: they couldn't stop loving: Echo McGuire quoted in G&B, RB, p. 25.
48: made it clear to Echo: *Ibid.*, p. 24.
48: launched on a musical: *Ibid.*, pp. 24–25.
48: Echo's religious convictions: *Ibid.*; author interviews with LH and TC.
48: "didn't have any idea: Quoted in Powers, "Allison Recalls How Music Grew," MCGG, 2/1/89, p. E-3.
48: set on going waterskiing: JA quoted in G&B, RB, p. 41.
48: "a big hassle,": Quoted in *ibid.*
48: bass in twenty minutes: JA quoted in *ibid.*
48: from Lightning Chance: SC quoted in *ibid.*
48: "it was a real serious . . . hard: JA quoted 8/26/78 in BG, "JA," RM 10, p. 8.
48: getting a country song: Owen Bradley quoted in G&B, RB, p. 36; Beecher, liner notes, *BH: Nashville Sessions*, LP/CDL 8038; JA quoted in BG, "JA—Part One," RM 23, 6/82, p. 9.

48: "sing so high, which: JA quoted in BG, "JA," RM 10, p. 8.
49: "the worst song I've: G&B, RB, p. 42.
49: "the biggest no-talent: *Ibid.*, p. 43.
49: "Man, I like 'That'll Be the Day.' ": *Ibid.*, p. 42.
49: and the Three Tunes: Author interview with SC; BH: *The Nashville Sessions*, LP.
49: "I don't remember the: Author interview with JA.
49: Sue Poff, and hanging: Jan Fulton quoted in BG, "Jake Goss: BH's Barber," p. 13.
49: "played on the roof: *Ibid.*
49: previous evening in Amarillo: "LR and Musicians Jailed Following Dispute," LAJ, 8/24/56, quoted in BG, "I Finally Found It!" RM 35, 3/85, p. 6
49: "altogether what we thought: *Ibid.*
49: "change his act somewhat": *Ibid.*
49: Richard was booked on a: *Ibid.*
49: he was carrying $2,669: "LR and Musicians Jailed Following Dispute" quoted in BG, "How's That Again?" R50, 8/92.
50: "disrupted an era, broke: *Mystery Train*, p. 4.
50: "Hey, all right!": JA in RBHS.
50: mixture of five hundred whites: "Rock 'n' Roll Dance Is Shut Down After Disturbance Here," LAJ, 8/25/56.
50: "stopped the blaring beat: *Ibid.*
50: Buddy brought him home: CW, QOR, p. 84.
50: "They got to be: JA in RBHS.
50: "wouldn't let me in,": CW, QOR, p. 84.
50: self-described "glaring homosexual.": Quoted in Timothy White, *Rock Lives*, p. 32; CW, QOR, p. 72, copyright by Richard Wayne Penniman.
50: "If you don't let: LR quoted in CW, QOR, p. 84.
51: "I didn't want to: Quoted in BG, R 35, p. 5.
51: "weren't too happy: p. 84.
51: "That's another fictitious": Author interview with LH.
51: Richard opened Buddy: CW, QOR, p. 84.
51: "We had some great: Quoted in BG, "More on LR," RM 35, p. 7.
51: drawn to heterosexual males: pp. 71–73, 84.
51: "a big penis": Quoted in CW, QOR, p. 71.
51: orgies, often involving his: *Ibid.*
51: "Buddy Holly was a wild boy: *Ibid.*, p. 84.
51: routinely seduced such straight: *Ibid.*, p. 72–73.
51: "some big guy": *Ibid.*, p. 73.
51: invite him to his room: *Ibid.*
51: "Yeah, c'mon. I'd like: *Ibid.*
51: Should the man's equipment: *Ibid.*, p. 71.
51: a wad of money: *Ibid.*
51: bribe the man to fornicate: *Ibid.*
51: "We always had that: Powers, "Allison Recalls How Music Grew."
51: "if you want to live: Quoted in T. White, *Rock Lives*, p. 32.
51: Richard was disowned: *Ibid.*, p. 33.
51: who sold sourmash whiskey: *Ibid.*; Pareles and Romanowski, *RS Encyclopedia of Rock*, p. 332.
51: Richard was gay: T. White, *Rock Lives*, p. 33.
52: "The homosexual should be: Bynum, "Bible and the Homosexual," Tract A-335, Tabernacle Baptist Church.
52: a showdown between them: Author interview with LH.

52: "a lot of the singers: Carlisle, *Ragged But Right*, p. 101.
52: got falling-down drunk: EH quoted in G&B, RB, p. 23.
52: that he was drunk: EH quoted in G&B, RB, p. 23.
52: "Mom, I'm sorry": *Ibid.*
52: "I wasn't really mad: *Ibid.*
53: "We were against: *Ibid.*
53: "on the sly,": *Ibid.*
53: "I couldn't be part: *Ibid.*, p. 24.
53: "it just wasn't what: *Ibid.*, p. 25.
53: "not to care who: *Ibid.*, p. 51.
53: "He run with some: Author interview with LH.
53: and carried a chain: *Ibid.*
53: "Any time anybody: *Ibid.*
53: "Buddy liked everybody, but: *Ibid.*
53: "It's scary if you're out: *Ibid.*
54: "He was about nineteen at the time: *Ibid.*
54: Buddy's friends were complaining: G&B, RB, pp. 22, 24.
54: "Lot of people said: Author interview with LH.
54: Mrs. Holley scolded Buddy: G&B, RB, p. 22.
54: "He was pretty snobbish: Author interview with LH.
54: "Now, Buddy, if you're going to: *Ibid.*
54: "Another thing," Larry continued: *Ibid.*
54: "Thank you," Buddy said: *Ibid.*
54: "I don't know what you said: *Ibid.*
54: "Buddy was just a: *Ibid.*
54: "Lubbock now has its: Fairbairn, "Lubbock Now Has Its Answer to Elvis," LAJ, 10/23/56, pp. 1, 5.
54: at Don Guess's house: BG, "JN; Story Behind," p. 4.
55: thought to be "a ladies lover,": JN quoted in *ibid.*
55: unable to pay his: BG, "SC," RM 17, 12/80, p. 12; G&B, RB, p. 34.
55: Only Don Guess accompanied: G&B, RB, p. 179.
55: C&W star Webb Pierce: *Ibid.*, p. 36.
55: "He needed somebody else: ACOB.
55: Bradley had received his: G&B, RB, p. 36.
55: simply trying to survive: ACOB.
55: to keep Paul Cohen happy: G&B, RB, p. 36.
55: "benefactor" as well as: ACOB.
55: friendly and cooperative: *Ibid.*
56: "passing fad: BG, R50, 10/92, p. 14.
56: "We got the best: *Ibid.*
56: "No, I ain't signing: BG, "JN," p. 5.
56: when it was classified: G&B, RB, p. 43.
56: Decca's marketing gaffe: *Ibid.*
57: Jack had to interrupt: *Ibid.*
57: "He could be quiet: PN: "Secret BH: Girl Who," p. 34.
57: deplored the fact that: Quoted in BG, "Terry Noland," RM 27, p. 7.
57: accepted Buddy's generous donations: Quoted in *ibid.*; author interviews with KJ and TC.
57: "ulcer-prone people are: *Ulcers*, p. 100.
57: "I really didn't get: BG, "LW," RM 45, 11/86, p. 13.
57: American Legion Hall: BG, "Tour Schedules," p. 3.
58: purchase a stand-up: G&B, RB, p. 46.
58: secondhand hearse: Author interview with TC.

58: "Well, I'm not cut: Quoted in BG, "JA—Part One," RM 23, 6/82, p. 12.
58: fondly dismissive about rock: During the 1993 BH Tribute Dance and Concert in Clear Lake, Iowa, Sonny, during his solo performance, said, at one point, "Oh well, it's only rock 'n' roll."
58: Sonny was a better guitarist: G&B, RB, p. 47.
58: "The main thing was: Author interview with SC.
58: tour with Slim Whitman: BG, "SC," p. 12.
58: Philip Morris made him: *Ibid.*
58: didn't exceed a dollar: *Ibid.*
58: to replenish his depleted: *Ibid.*
58: to contribute . . . the best.": *Ibid.*
58: Buddy considered giving up: EH quoted in BG, RM 11, 7/79; G&B, RB, p. 44.
58: "came darn near: Quoted in BG, RM 11.
59: "a hillbilly like Buddy": G&B, RB, p. 46.
59: "a diamond in the rough,": JA quoted in BG, "JA—Part One," RM 23, 6/82, p. 9.
59: he turned Buddy down: G&B, RB, p. 46.
59: hit on Roulette: BG, "JA—Part One," p. 8; G&B, RB, p. 48; BG, "Gary & Ramona Tollet," RM 30, Spring/84, pp. 4–10; BG, RM, 6/82, p. 10.
59: "He went out to: Author interview with NS.

Chapter 6

60: "I'm advising you again: ACOB.
60: sign over a share: BG, "JN," p. 6.
60: "If you can get a hit: Author interview with Billy Stull, who was quoting Vi Petty. The quotation appears in slightly different form in Skip Brooks and Bill Malcolm's interview with NP, published in RM in three parts in 1985.
60: "It's the talent: *Ibid.*
60: temperature hovering around thirty: LAJ, 2/24/57.
60: to leave until after work.: BG, "Gary & Ramona Tollet," p. 6.
60: he frantically put the: BG, "7th BHMS Convention," RM 33, p. 9.
60: After stopping on the: G&B, RB, p. 49.
61: "Norman was a tremendous: Author interview with Billy Stull.
61: Petty was a first-rate: "JA—Part One," p. 9.
61: minimized Petty's role: *Ibid.*, p. 11.
61: "ramrodded" the entire: BG, "Gary & Ramona Tollett," p. 6.
61: They worked until midnight: BG, "Gary & Ramona Tollett," RM 30, p. 6.
62: weren't playing together: JA quoted in BG, "JA—Part One," p. 11.
62: never permitted any girl: TBIK.
62: "I'll give you the: Author interview with Jerry Coleman. Petty himself, in an article by Helen Betty entitled "Creativity in Clovis" in *New Mexico*, 9/60, p. 26, said "a singer is free to pay only the $75 charge per master (plus the union-required fee for extra musicians employed) and sell his own tape." In the same article, Petty claimed that if he became the agent for one of his singers, "about 10 percent of total sales from each record becomes profit for the Norman Petty Agency." In yet another scenario, JA told BG in "JA," RM 10, p. 8, that rather than purchase studio time, they paid NP $15.

62: "Or," he added, "I'll: Author interview with Jerry Coleman.
62: Jerry was the first: G&B, RB, p. 62.
62: But Buddy was adamant: Ibid.
62: "Colonel Parker knows the: Guralnick, Last Train to Memphis, p. 417.
62: Billy Joel: Marsh and Bernard, New Book of Rock Lists, p. 309.
63: scraggly Van Dyke goatee: MacNeish, "Jim Robinson," RM, Fall/83, p. 21.
63: not going to cut it: Ibid.
63: "Well, that poor little: Ibid.
63: Larry Welborn, the bass: LW told BG, "It would bother you a little bit to know that you played on something and weren't getting the money for it, or the recognition."
63: there was no love lost: NP quoted in BG and Bonner, "NP—Part 2," RM 38, 9/85, p. 9.
63: Jerry made Niki feel: In G&B, RB, p. 83., JA says it was "a mutual thing" when Niki said he wanted to leave the Crickets.
63: share Buddy with anyone: In RBHS, JA said it was "weird" after he and BH got married; they couldn't communicate as before; in G&B RB, p. 120, JBM voiced a similar complaint, stating he was "jealous" of BH's wife because she'd divested JA and JBM of BH.
63: "getting cross": Quoted in BG, "JA—Part One," p. 12.
63: used to cut study hall: Ibid., p. 13.
63: Buddy approached Joe B.: Ibid.
63: asked him if he wanted: BG, "Joe Mauldin," RM 16, 9/80, p. 7.
63: Joe B. inquired: BHTLL, p. 90.
63: sixty-two degrees: LAJ, 3/2/57.
64: Elks Club, for $65: BG, "Tour Schedules," p. 3. In NS's memory (BG and Bonner, "NS—Part 1," p. 4), the first gig was at the VFW hall in Carlsbad.
64: "I was very basic: BHTLL, p. 90.
64: They rocked Carlsbad: NS quoted in BG and Bonner, "NS—Part 1," RM 6, 3/78, p. 4; BG, "1981 BHMS Convention," RM 21, 12/81, p. 22.
64: Niki had an educated: Ibid.
64: "It brought the house down": Ibid.
64: Buddy attempted to persuade: JBM interview in RBHS; a slightly different version appears in G&B, RB, p. 54.
64: that kind of bragging: Ibid.
64: to end up a shoe salesman: JBM quoted in BG, "Joe Mauldin," p. 8.
64: Buddy uttered the magic words: JBM interview in RBHS.
64: "fingers to the bone": JBM quoted in G&B, RB, p. 81.
64: but Cohen refused: Ibid., p. 52.
64: including the Scoundrels: BG, "Buddy's Notebook"; BG, "Trivial Trivia," RM 25, Winter/82, p. 25.
65: "Witchcraft," a record: BG, "JA—Part One," p. 13.
65: Finally they consulted an: G&B, RB, p. 53.
65: someone proposed the Grasshoppers: Ibid.
65: Jerry later denied that they: BG, "JA—Part One," p. 13.
65: insect that made noise: Ibid.
65: "make a happy sound: RB, p. 53.
65: collaboration with his mother: EH quoted in Skinner, "A Meeting."

65: for Buddy Knox to cover: G&B, RB, p. 55.
65: Petty offered to take: G&B, RB, p. 55.
65: Petty wanted a cut: BG, "JN," p. 6.
65: "We couldn't lose,": BH interview with Freeman Hoover, 11/2/57.
66: no one in the band: BG and Bonner, "NS—Part 1," p. 4.
66: He called on Columbia: BG, RM, 9/85, p. 8.
66: his office as dog meat: Dannen, Hit Men, p. 62.
66: "The girl has no distinctive: Francis, Who's Sorry Now, p. 59.
66: Though Petty later denied it: Quoted in Brooks and Malcolm, "NP—Part 2, RM 38, 9/85, p. 8: "I did not meet Ahmet Ertegun [of Atlantic] and Jerry Wexler until after we already had two or three hits with Buddy, then they came through New Mexico and wanted to hear some tapes." The historical record is anything but clear on exactly how Petty proceeded to dispose of "That'll Be the Day" in New York. Bob Thiele says in BG, RM 24, 9/82, p. 16, "the master had already been turned down by Jerry Wexler at Atlantic Records, Mitch Miller at Columbia, and Joe Carlton at RCA [when] Murray Deutch stormed into my office." Deutch told G&B, RB, p. 56, that it was he who peddled the demo to the record companies.
66: Atlantic's Jerry Wexler and: Ward, "The Fifties," ROA, p. 154.
66: affiliated with Peer-Southern: Berry, "NP Recordings Put Clovis on Map," p. 6.
66: Deutch wanted a fifty-fifty: Deutch quoted in G&B, RB, p. 56.
66: He rang Bob Thiele: Thiele, liner notes, BH, LP, MCA-25239.
66: Thiele invited Deutch: Ibid.
66: "Please, I don't want any money: BG, "18 Interviews (all at once)," p. 4.
66: "Let's go! It's great!": Thiele, liner notes, BH.
67: "$150 per side and: "Creativity in Clovis," p. 37.
67: "I like to think: Off the Record, p. 61.
67: Petty couldn't believe that: BG, RM, 9/85, p. 8.
67: "right here on this: Ibid., pp. 8–9.
67: "Unfortunately, it wasn't that: Thiele, liner notes, BH.
67: Rachmil and vice president Leonard: G&B, RB, p. 56.
67: "junk": Ibid.
67: Thiele to be insane: BG, R50, 10/92, p. 12.
67: "Fuck it . . . fire me: Off the Record, p. 61.
67: kind of trash-basket label: Thiele, "A Sweet Acquaintance," RM 24, 9/82, p. 16; G&B, RB, p. 56.
67: He struck Deutch as: RBHS.
67: "kind of like going: BH quoted in Shelton, "Southwest's Only Major Recording Studio Operated by Clovis Musician," Amarillo News-Globe, 12/20/59, p. 4-C.
67: Hi Pockets . . . appalled when: ACOB.
67: Neal angrily exclaimed: JN quoted in BG, "JN," p. 6.
68: Buddy shrugged it off: BH quoted by JN, Ibid.
68: invest some of your own: Ibid.
68: shareholder, that he'd finally: JBM quoted in G&B, RB, p. 115.
68: "He sat there for hours: Author interview with Jerry Coleman.
68: "He had a terrible: Ibid.
68: "He liked pizzas real: BG, "Mrs. Holley," p. 3.

68: Steak was another favorite: *Ibid.*
68: okra dipped in a cornmeal: MEH quoted in BG, "Maria Elena," RM 5, 12/77, p. 7.
68: about a scraping process: Author interview with Jerry Coleman.
68: On Coleman's nineteenth birthday: Jerry Coleman quoted in BG, "KLLL radio," RM 7, 6/78, p. 7.
68: Brunswick on March 19, 1957: BG, "Tour Schedules," p. 3.
68: donate a whopping 40 percent: G&B, RB, p. 60.
69: Jerry was lolling on: LH quoted in BG, "1981 BHMS Convention," RM 21, 12/81, p. 23.
69: Petty gave Buddy some: BHTLL, p. 93.
69: Determined to build some: TBIK.
69: to handle a truck: *Ibid.*
69: this was the moment he: *Ibid.*
69: They dashed to a: BG, "Gary and Ramona Tollett," p. 7.
69: they asked Petty if: BG, RM, 9/85, p. 11.
70: Buddy was an inveterate: Author interview with MEH.
70: they were all helping each other: BG, RM, 9/85, p. 11.
70: Petty expected them to keep: Author interview with Billy Stull.
70: "Share and share alike: Author interview with MEH.
70: could be put on salary: G&B, RB, p. 58.
70: his musicians like dogs: *Ibid.*
70: 65–35 percent split: *Ibid.*
70: Ray Ruff, a musician: Jackson, "Ray Ruff," R50, 2/92, p. 19.
71: a male lover who was: Author interview with NS; PN, "BH: The Girl," p. 36.
71: "I can't believe it: Author interview with NS; PN, "Secret BH: Honeymoon," p. 52; PN, "Secret BH: Girl Who," p. 35.
71: "ludicrous. Guys tell each: Author interview with SC.
71: and sit in his car: G&B, RB, p. 64.
71: assuming they'd finally finished: JBM quoted in BHTLL, p. 94.
71: more time on "Words of Love": *Ibid.*
72: "laid, lovingly and well": Amburn, *Pearl: The Obsessions and Passions of Janis Joplin,* p. 165.
72: a favor for Bob: Thiele, "A Sweet Acquaintance."
72: Thiele once told Griggs: *Ibid.*
72: finally convinced Southern Music: NS quoted in BG and Bonner, "NS—Part 2," RM 7, 6/78, p. 3.
72: Someone at the publishing: G&B, RB, p. 65.
72: Diamonds' cover of "Words: Nite, *Rock On,* p. 183; G&B, RB, p. 65.
72: a mere one thousand units: Ward, "Fifties," ROA, p. 154.
73: cosigning the loan papers: TBIK.
73: under the beating it: *Ibid.*
73: hair started turning gray: *Ibid.*
73: *Arthur Godfrey Talent Scouts:* McNeil, *Total Television,* p. 740.
73: twelve percent of CBS's: Metz, *Reflections in a Bloodshot Eye,* cited in McNeil, *Total Television,* p. 56.
73: wracking pain he suffered: McNeil, *Total Television, Ibid.*
73: cost him his reputation: *Ibid.*

73: LaRosa, whom he fired: *Ibid.*
73: Archie Bleyer, whom Godfrey: *Ibid.*
73: uttered a mild expletive: G&B, RB, p. 47.
73: managed somehow to contact: DE quoted in Roger White's *Walk Right Back* cited in BG, RM.
73: He was aware that Don: *Ibid.*
74: "Not Fade Away" for the: PN, *Road Goes On Forever,* p. 37.
74: turned down "Not Fade Away.": *Ibid.;* DE quoted in KL, "Everly Brothers," *TRSI,* p. 145.
74: he was afraid people: DE quoted in Roger White's *Walk Right Back,* cited in BG, RM.
74: "it was nice of: *Ibid.*
74: "Buddy wrote 'Not Fade Away': PN, *Road Goes On Forever,* p. 37.
74: "Ever'body had their: Author interview with LH.
74: "There comes old Turkey Neck": *Ibid.*
74: "Lubbock is a very jealous town": *Ibid.*
74: On May 16, 1957: BG, "Tour Schedules," p. 3.
75: Crickets their usual pay: Author interview with MEH.
75: "Vi only showed me: Author interview with BG, who told me that Robert Linville also "says Norman played the celesta on 'Everyday.' "
75: slapping on his knees: JA quoted in BG, "JA," RM 10, p. 8.
75: "Holly's deepest, wisest, and: *Rolling Stone Illustrated History of Rock 'n' Roll,* Miller, ed., p. 79.
75: Petty went to Nashville: G&B, RB, p. 57.
76: "Only thing I minded about: Author interview with SC.
76: repeatedly playing a catchy: BHTLL, pp. 90–93.
76: "Tell me how,": *Ibid.,* p. 93.
77: Buddy Knox remembers sitting: Quoted in BG, "18 Interviews (all at once)," RM 20, 9/81, p. 4.
77: Holly would play rhythm: Knox quoted in BG, "Buddy Knox," RM 14, 3/80, p. 6.
77: consecutively for twenty minutes: Tom Clay quoted in BG, " 'Guy King,' " RM 15, 6/80, p. 14.
77: he might very well: *Ibid.*
77: such as Buffalo and Cleveland: *Ibid.*
78: 103-degree heat [and subsequent references to 7/57 heat wave]: LAJ, 7/2, 7/8, 7/17, 7/25.
78: after Buddy's niece: BG, "Mrs. Holley," p. 6.
78: "Cindy Lou" had a Latin: NS quoted in BG and Bonner, "NS—Part 2," RM 7, 6/78, p. 3.
78: it was a dud: *Ibid.;* Miller, "NS," RM 30, Spring/84, p. 22.
78: Jaye P. Morgan's "Dawn,": JA quoted in BHTLL, p. 94.
78: "beat the tar out: BG, "Bill Pickering," RM 21, 12/81, p. 6.
78: move his instruments into: NS quoted by Miller, "NS," p. 22.
78: that Jerry should play paradiddles: NS quoted in BG and Bonner, "NS—Part 2," p. 3; PS quoted in BG, "PS," p. 4; JA quoted in BHTLL, p. 94.
78: Jerry asked Buddy if they: NS quoted in BG and Bonner, "NS—Part 2," p. 3; PS quoted in BG, "PS," p. 4.
78: had recently feuded and: Author interview with PS.
78: "Jerry wanted to do: *Ibid.*

78: moved her to Sacramento: BG, *Who's Who*.
78: sustain the steady drumming: PS in "Dick Clark's Golden Greats," a video tape; almost identical version, PS in BG, "PS," p. 4; NS quoted in Miller, "NS," p. 22.
78: "a snare drum with: "JA," R 10, p. 8.
78: instructed Niki to kneel: NS quoted in Miller, "NS," p. 22; NS quoted in BG and Bonner, "NS—Part 2," p. 3.
78: Buddy played all six: NS quoted in BHTLL, p. 94.
78: used nothing but downstrokes: BHTLL, p. 81.
79: jiggered the volume on Jerry's mike: BHTLL, p. 94; JA quoted in BG, "JA—Part One," p. 9.
79: Jerry made a mistake: JA quoted in G&B, RB, p. 76.
79: on the next take: *Ibid.*
79: Only twenty minutes: NS quoted in BG and Bonner, "NS—Part 2," p. 3.
79: "There is something *perfect*: P. 36.
79: Buddy and Jerry cowrote: "NS—Part 2," p. 3.
79: generated the song ideas: P. 64.
79: dropped off the first: "NP," RM 37, 7/85, p. 11.
79: lyrics and a bridge: *Ibid.*
79: they were vulnerable, unsophisticated: NS quoted in G&B, RB, p. 63.
80: Originally entitled "Alla My Love,": BG, *Who's Who*.
80: were deliriously happy: Tilghman quoted in G&B, RB, p. 79.
80: Buddy's cough, which is: BG, "Strange Things in Buddy's Songs," *R50*, 12/88, p. 23.
80: Larry suggested they knock: TBIK; LH quoted in BG, "1981 BHMS Convention," p. 23.
80: someone at Brunswick: *Ibid.*
80: Philadelphia snapped up sixteen thousand: Thiele, liner notes, *BH*
81: a check for $500: LH quoted in BG, "1981 BHMS Convention," p. 23.
81: But surely that was: TBIK.
81: "Performance is better than: Cited in G&B, RB, p. 68.
81: This was proof: Quoted in BG, "Gary & Ramona Tollett," p. 9.
81: a congratulatory wire from: NS quoted in G&B, p. 68.
81: they were too groggy: *Ibid.*
81: "We've got a manager," [and subsequent dialogue]: NP quoted in Brooks and Malcolm, "NP—Part 2," RM 38, 9/85, p. 5.
81: "glorified babysitting job,": *Ibid.*
81: certainly not get married: Author interview with MEH.
81: unsolicited and resented: NP quoted in Brooks and Malcolm, "NP—Part 2," p. 5.
81: Later Petty admitted: *Ibid.*
81: depended on Buddy's father: *Ibid.*, p. 7.
81: surrounded by people who: Author interview with LH, who said, "Buddy was just a wild kid, baby of the family, spoiled."
82: one of the earliest DJs: BG, RM 10, 3/78.

Chapter 7

83: "Around the World": Fox, *Showtime at the Apollo*, p. 206.

83: The Crickets received $1,000: Author interview with SC.
84: mother had been pegging: SC in ACOB.
84: flight from Amarillo to: *Ibid.*
84: from Petty to carry: Marsh and Bernard, *New Book of Rock Lists*, p. 16.
84: stayed at the Edison: *Ibid.*
84: congratulated them on their: NP quoted in G&B, RB, p. 71.
84: in a 1995 interview, Niki: Author interview with NS.
84: "The Crickets had their: SC in ACOB.
84: "kind of a heroes' welcome,": *Ibid.*
84: "We were introduced to: *Ibid.*
85: they went to Philadelphia: *Ibid.*
85: aback when the Cadillacs: JA quoted in BG, "JA—Part One," p. 12.
85: Barlow's group had broken: JA quoted in BG, "Did the Crickets Sue the Crickets?" RM, Summer/84, p. 11.
85: Buddy tried to explain: Freeman Hoover interview, 11/2/57, Denver.
85: one-hit wonders: JBM quoted in RBHS.
85: McPhatter, the headliner, befriended: *Ibid.*
85: "nerves" and lost his: Author interview with NS.
85: Diagnosed with laryngitis: NS quoted in BG and Bonner, "NS—Part 1," p. 3.
85: None of the Crickets professed: NP, Brooks and Malcolm, "NP—Part 2," p. 7.
85: Niki was scared: NS quoted in BG and Bonner, "NS—Part 1," p 3.
85: When Petty joined the tour: G&B, RB, p. 116.
85: "Anyone can sing those songs.": *Ibid.*
85: Niki and Jerry's personalities: NP quoted in Brooks and Malcolm, "NP—Part 2," p. 9; G&B, RB, p. 83.
85: did nothing to alleviate: NS quoted in G&B, RB, p. 83.
85: always side with Jerry: NP quoted in Brooks and Malcolm, "NP—Part 2," p. 9.
85: everyone wanted Niki out.: G&B, RB, p. 83.
85: Gibson electric was stolen: NS quoted in BHTLL, p. 96.
85: the Royal audience was: JA quoted in BG, "JA—Part One," p. 13.
85: heaved a bottle at a black girl: NS quoted in Miller, "NS," p. 23.
86: sixteen-hundred-seat Apollo: Fox, *Showtime*, p. 17.
86: "Uptown, the Apollo was: Holiday with Dufty, *Lady Sings the Blues*, p. 39.
86: could shatter what little: G&B, RB, p. 85.
86: Lone Star lout: *Ibid.*, p. 86.
86: miracle of gentleness: *Ibid.*; BG, "Spotlight on Dick Jacobs," R50, 10/92, p. 13.
86: country bumpkins: G&B, RB, p. 85.
86: the legendary Theresa: Author interview with NS; JBM quoted in PN, "Secret BH: Honeymoon," p. 52. Not everyone agrees that the Crickets stayed at the Theresa. In Floyd, "Crickets' Appearance at the Apollo," RM 28, Fall/83, p. 18, Ted Scott, who performed with Buddy at the Apollo, says that although he stayed at the Theresa, Buddy didn't and was possibly at the Forest.
86: Fidel Castro would choose: Associated Press, "Where Castro Is Staying," 9/30/60.

86: were too innocent, according: JBM, PN, "Secret BH: Honeymoon," p. 52.

87: "I didn't know who: Quoted in KL, "Bo Diddley," TRSI, p. 188.

87: "I don't care if you: Quoted in Fox, *Showtime*, p. 12.

87: four flights down: *Ibid.*

87: then-manager Leonard Reed: *Ibid.*, p. 206.

87: Atlantic's Ahmet Ertegun: *Ibid.*, p. 17.

87: Nor were the Crickets: *Ibid.*, p. 24.

87: producers elected to disregard: Quoted in BG, RM 34, 1/85, p. 1.

87: high up the R&B charts: NP quoted in Brooks and Malcolm, "NP—Part 2," p. 6.

87: began at 10:20 A.M.: Ted Scott quoted in Floyd, "Crickets' Appearance at the Apollo," p. 16.

87: "They were wide awake: Holiday with Dufty, *Lady Sings the Blues*, p. 40.

88: impress the booking agents: Fox, *Showtime*, p. 19.

88: Ed Sullivan, Milton Berle: *Ibid.*, p. 23.

88: better sound *exactly* like: NS quoted in G&B, RB, p. 70.

88: "What's this?": Scott quoted in Floyd, "Crickets' Appearance at the Apollo," p. 17.

88: mentioned in the same breath: *Ibid.*, p. 16.

88: audience from booing them: *Ibid.*, p. 17.

88: a miserable flop: NS quoted in Miller, "NS," RM, Spring/84, p. 23.

88: demoted to the bottom: *Ibid.*

88: dirty, smelly, drafty: Fox, *Showtime*, p. 10.

88: up to the standards: NS quoted in Miller, "NS," p. 23.

88: monitor each other's acts: Fox, *Showtime*, p. 12.

88: authentic bluesy quality: "Crickets' Appearance," p. 16.

89: "Let's open with 'Bo Diddley.': NS quoted in Miller, "NS," p. 23. Slightly different version in G&B, pp. 70–71 and in Fox, *Showtime*, p. 207.

89: were forced to improvise: NS quoted in Miller, "NS," p. 23.

89: the blacks accepted them: *Ibid.*

89: them as a novelty: RBHS.

89: "Hey, another brother out there: Leslie Uggams quoted in Fox, *Showtime*, p. 207.

89: "Oh, that's Buddy Holly!": *Ibid.*

89: "He's *white*, isn't be?": *Ibid.*

89: "He was terrific: *Ibid.*

89: "better than the show: *Ibid.*, p. 10.

89: Hookers masquerading as: *Ibid.*

89: "anything you could want: *Autobiography*, p. 115.

89: "There were drugs back: Quoted in Floyd, "Crickets' Appearance," p. 18.

89: "I loved him dearly,": Quoted in BG, "More on Little Richard," RM 35, 3/85, p. 7.

89: "used to idolize my: CW, p. 84.

89: to lure Buddy and: LR quoted in *ibid.*, p. 73.

89: invited all the Crickets: Author interview with NS; NS quoted in PN, "Secret BH: Honeymoon," p. 52.

89: an orgy was in: Author interview with NS.

89: "carried right on with: NS quoted in PN, "Secret BH: Honeymoon," p. 52.

89: The only whites in: Author interview with NS.

90: "This was definitely not: *Ibid.*

90: Larry Williams was making: *Ibid.*

90: she gave Little Richard oral: *Ibid.*

90: "Everyone else was watching: *Ibid.*

90: he'd been wondering if: LR quoted by NS in PN, "Secret BH: Honeymoon," p. 52.

90: dashingly handsome, mustachioed: Photograph in Nite, *Rock On*, p. 657.

90: "I brought him to: Quoted in CW, QOR, p. 188.

90: Richard purchased some cocaine: *Ibid.*

90: with a gun to collect: *Ibid.*

90: career suffered when: Pareles and Romanowski, eds., *Rolling Stone Encyclopedia of Rock & Roll*, p. 594.

90: for narcotics possession: DeCurtis, Henke, and George-Warren, *Rolling Stone Album Guide*, p. 769.

90: "His red-hot version: *Ibid.*, p. 770.

90: Williams committed suicide: Nite, *Rock On*, p. 656.

90: Richard sang a moving: Stallings, *Rock 'n' Roll Confidential*, p. 90.

90: "I was jacking off,": LR quoted in CW, QOR, p. 84.

90: "sucking my titty.": *Ibid.*

90: Buddy unzipped his pants: *Ibid.*

90: "He was ready: *Ibid.*

90: "She opened up her: *Ibid.*

90: Buddy and the girl had: *Ibid.*

90: "was sucking me,": *Ibid.*

90: they heard Buddy's name: *Ibid.*

90: "he made it, too,": *Ibid.*

90: "He came and he: *Ibid.*

90: "historic occasion.": Clark, *Jack Kerouac*, p. 164; back ad, Kerouac, *On the Road*, Penguin paperback, 1957.

91: "At lilac evening I walked: Kerouac, *On the Road*, p. 180.

91: roof of the Brooklyn Paramount: NS quoted in BG, "NS—Part 1," p. 4.

91: Freed's *Rock 'n' Roll*: BG, "Tour Schedules," p. 5.

91: "Everyone you met was: Quoted in Shaw, "Teen Idols," RS *Illustrated History of Rock & Roll*, Miller, ed., p. 96.

91: Rock was not a: Stallings, *Rock 'n' Roll Confidential*, p. 72.

91: means to wealth and: *Ibid.*

91: easy-listening discount classics: Clark quoted on Merv Griffin television show, cited in *ibid.*

91: "There were no skeletons: Cited in JJ, BBH, p. 170.

91: hot, brightly lit area: McNeil, *Total Television*, pp. 36–37.

92: lip-synched performance: Ward, "The Fifties," ROA, p. 155; Helander, *Rock Who's Who*, p. 90; Stambler, *Encyclopedia*, p. 124.

92: Kenny Rossi: *This Fabulous Century: 1950–1960*, eds., *Time-Life* Books, p. 149.

92: money spread out around them: G&B, RB, p. 138.

92: Joe B. was curious: NP quoted in *Ibid.*, p. 135.

92: arrangement proved unsatisfactory: *Ibid.*, pp. 135–38.

92: expensive baubles: Quoted in *Ibid.*, p. 138.

92: "Norman Petty has put Clovis: "Norman Petty Recordings Put Clovis on Map," *Clovis News-Journal*, December 20, 1959, p. 6.

92: "to break [into] the: *Ibid.*

93: turned into a fistfight: JA quoted in G&B, RB, p. 83.
93: jejune high jinks: Ibid.
93: cut under his left: Author interview with NS.
93: photo showing them celebrating: Ibid., p. 74.
93: feeling very urbane: DE in RBHS.
93: Don says they didn't: DE quoted in PN, Road Goes On Forever, p. 38.
93: Don chided them for: DE in RBHS; DE quoted by JA in BG, "JA—Part Two," p. 8.
93: "They saw what we: Quoted in PN, Road Goes On Forever, p. 38.
93: Phil's Men's Shop: JA quoted in BG, "JA—Part Two," p. 8. Probably mistakenly, BG printed it as "Field's Men's Shop."
93: sleek Ivy League: DE in RBHS.
93: "We got to be: "The Everly Brothers," TRSI, p. 145.
93: they became best friends: PE quoted in McNie, "PE," RM 14, 3/80, p. 14.
94: their circle expanded to: Buddy Knox quoted in AC, "Farewell to Eddie Cochran," Tribute to Eddie Cochran, p. 39; Buddy Knox quoted in BG, "BK," RM 14, 3/80, p. 6; TGBH, p. 84; BG, "Special Tribute to Celebrate the 25th Anniversary of the Crickets," RM 24, 9/82, p. 17.
94: the Young Rockers: Quoted in AC, "Farewell," p. 39.
94: the Village Gate: Knox quoted in BG, "BK," RM 14, 3/80, p. 6.
94: Chuck Berry took them: PE quoted in KL, TRSI, p. 146.
94: "We all got into: DE in RBHS.
94: "There was a real: Ibid.
95: who always trailed along: Knox quoted in AC, "Farewell," p. 39.
95: Don Kirshner's Rock Concert: McNeil, Total Television, p. 209.
95: Eddie Cochran would pull: Knox quoted in AC, "Farewell," p. 39.
95: Cochran rivaled Elvis as: Ibid.
95: "drinking beer and playing: "On the Road With Eddie Cochran: Interview With Dave Shriver," Blue Suede News, Vol. 3, No. 1, Spring/89, p. 8.
95: The "Okie chicks,": Ibid.
95: "Everybody had a good: Author interview with NS.
95: utter a single word: PE quoted in KL, "The Everlys," TRSI, p. 146.
95: "Got her in the back: Ibid.
95: Buddy to improve his physical: Author interview with Jerry Coleman.
95: consulted a dermatologist: Author interview with Jerry Coleman.
95: barber who "kinked" it: Jake Goss in BG, "Jake Goss, Buddy Holly's Barber," RM 25, Winter/82, p. 12.
95: promised him a "quickie.": NS in PN, "Secret BH: Honeymoon," p. 52.
95: Knox's room was trashed: Ray Ruff quoted in Jackson, "Ray Ruff," R50 34, 2/92, p. 19.
95: had been flooded: Ibid.
96: Henry Goldrich: TGBH, p. 84.
96: far too weighty: Ibid.
96: purchasing a Gibson . . . GA series amp: Ibid.
96: a pair of Greyhound: Tommy Tompkins, one of the tour's two bus drivers, quoted in Rossi and Block, "Tommy Tompkins," RM 41, 3/86, p. 5.

96: 3,500-foot-long suspension bridge: 1979 Hammond Almanac, Time eds., p. 242.
96: camping out at the Brooklyn: BG letter to the author, 11/7/94, p. 2.
96: bones under their seats: BG, RM 11, 7/79 (unpaged clipping).
97: Buddy seemed remarkably composed: Bowen quoted in BG, "Jimmy Bowen," RM 20, 9/81, p. 13.
97: "For someone that age: Ibid.
97: "Wasn't that fun?": JA quoted in BG, "JA—Part Two," RM 24, 9/82, p. 8.
97: sew your buttons on: PE quoted in RBHS.
97: shot craps in the back: Cott, RS Illustrated History, p. 81.
97: shrewder or more streetwise: "Tommy Tompkins," p. 5.
97: "in lonely afternoon hotel: p. 126.
97: hitched rides in the: JBM interview, RBHS.
97: tell him his problems: Ibid.
97: "It was a bus loaded: PE interview, Ibid.
98: sleeping with a leggy: Ibid.
98: He was busted during: Author interview with NS.
98: ordered off Tompkins's bus: Tompkins quoted in Rossi and Block, "Tommy Tompkins," p. 6.
98: "a billion volts of energy": G&B, RB, p. 112.
98: kicked a plug out: Ibid.
98: Buddy cursed so loud: NS quoted in G&B, RB, pp. 112–113.
98: Buddy respected Anka's songwriting: NS quoted in BG and Bonner, "NS—Part 2," p. 4.
98: hundreds of ticket-seekers: BG, "Browsing Through Billboard," R50, 2/92, p. 22.
98: "cop plenty of pop": Turner, "Record Reviews," RM 6, 3/78, p. 5.
98: "a newcomer who's broken: Ibid.
98: rushed to a phone: NS quoted in "18 Interviews (all at once)," p. 3.
98: announcing their million-seller: Ibid.
99: whites and blacks on the: NS quoted in BG and Bonner, "NS— Part 2," p. 2.
99: didn't care for the "lifestyle.": NS quoted in Miller, "NS," p. 24.
99: grown up as an only: NS quoted in G&B, RB, p. 82.
99: petty arguments and fisticuffs: Ibid.
99: took out their frustrations: Ibid.
99: The Crickets picked on: Ibid.
99: To Joe B. it was: JBM quoted in G&B, RB, p. 82.
99: who was also dissatisfied: NS and JBM quoted in ibid, p. 83.
99: he wasn't miked on: NS quoted in ibid.
99: his own record deal: JBM quoted in ibid.
99: When he dropped hints: NS and JBM quoted in ibid.
99: The acoustics at Tinker: NS quoted in BG and Bonner, "NS— Part 2," p. 3.
100: "'Blue Days, Black Nights': Amburn, Dark Star, p. 57.
100: "half the writer's share: Author interview with John R. Lee.
100: subsequent efforts at Sun: Author interview with Marion Keisker.
100: "Claudette" to the Everly Brothers: Author interview with Sam Phillips; Roy Orbison quoted

in liner notes, *The Sun Years*, double LP, Sun Record Company.

100: $25,000 in royalties: Author interview with Joe Melson.

100: beautiful girl in "Claudette,": Author interviews with Claudette Frady Orbison's family: Chester and Geraldine Frady, Bill Frady, Paulette Viator, Patty Maddux, Kadon Mahon; author interview with Roy Orbison's son, Wesley Orbison.

100: was dating Little Johnny: Author interviews with Charles Evans and Bobby Blackburn.

100: sexiest of the West: Author interview with Bobby Blackburn.

100: immortal "Pretty Woman" for her: Author interviews with Chester and Geraldine Frady and Wesley Orbison.

100: marked by infidelity: Author interviews with Boots Randolph and Mrs. Anna Dixon.

100: divorce: Author interview with Bobby Blackburn.

100: Brunswick recording artist: Mann, *A-Z of Buddy Holly*, p. 166.

100: became a rockabilly classic: *Ibid.*

100: Rock classics": McGee, "Buddy Holly," *Rolling Stone Album Guide*, DeCurtis et al., eds., p. 324.

100: Buddy's mother deserves part: EH quoted in G&B, RB, p. 93.

101: drum beat from Little Richard's: *Ibid.*

101: her contribution a secret: *Ibid.*

101: Joe B. said he: *Ibid.*, p. 64.

101: Carl Perkins and Buddy: Perkins quoted in BG, "Carl Perkins," RM 19, 6/18, p. 12.

101: "he was *fire*,": *Ibid.*

101: invented his own sound: *Ibid.*

101: "You can't take the: Quoted in Riese, *Nashville Babylon*, p. 12.

101: "You can't even draw: Quoted in Berry, *Autobiography*, p. 135.

101: "There's nobody in Lubbock: Author interview with LH.

101: they were third cousins: Author interview with NS.

101: "There were about thirty-five: *Ibid.*

102: "Norman Petty was actually: Author interview with LH.

102: financial issues were one: NS quoted in Miller, "NS," p. 24.

102: Niki's father tried to: NS quoted in G&B, RB, p. 136.

102: conflicts in the band: NP quoted in Brooks and Malcolm, "NP—Part 2," p. 9.

102: handwriting on the wall: Quoted in BG and Bonner, "NS—Part 1," p. 5.

102: only thing he missed: *Ibid.*

102: "By the time we: p. xi.

102: the infant died on: Dodge, *Everly Brothers: Ladies Love Outlaws*, p. 115.

103: major changes were made: Ward, "Fifties," ROA, pp. 157–58.

103: Cochran's friend Johnny Rowe: Quoted in AC, "Farewell to Eddie Cochran," p. 36.

103: Connie "Guybo" Smith: *Ibid.*, p. 31.

103: Cochran was happiest when: *Ibid.*, p. 27.

103: intimate friends and made: EH quoted in Skinner, "Meeting With Mr. and Mrs. Holley on June 12, 1969," p. 41.

103: Holly and Cochran carried: Mason City (Iowa) Municipal Airport files, office of the director of aviation, Jerome J. Thiele; BG, "Spot-

light on February 3, 1959," R50, 2/89; JT, "Investigator Offers Theory on Fatal Crash," MCGG, 2/1/89; P&T, "Lingering Mysteries of Holly's Fatal Flight," MCGG, 1/29/89; Scott quoted in AC, "Farewell," p. 43.

103: Brenda Lee, who toured: Bufwack and Oermann, *Finding Her Voice*, p. 225.

103: always get a "first count": *Ibid.*, p. 240.

103: finances ended up in a mess: JBM quoted in G&B, RB, p. 64.

103: Buddy was too decent: P. 138.

103: Buddy probably owed them: *Ibid.*

103: .22 in his shaving kit: LH quoted in BG, "LH," RM 14, 3/80, p. 8; BG showed me the shaving kit, which was given to him by the Holley family.

103: a crack shot: Bob Denton quoted in AC, "Farewell," p. 35.

103: "He was . . . into quick-draw: Quoted in Winters, "Old Friends Recall Good Times in Old Neighborhood," *Albert Lea Tribune*, 6/26/94, reprinted in AC, "Eddie Cochran: Legend Continues," p. 52.

103: brandishing his gun: Jack Scott quoted in *ibid.*, p. 43.

103: in front of a bureau: Scott quoted in *ibid.*

103: Jack Scott, a musician: *Ibid.*

104: Ace, who shot himself: Ward, "Fifties," ROA, pp. 98–99.

104: James Dean's fatal: Hyams and Hyams, *James Dean: Little Boy Lost, passim*; Headrick, Jr., *Deanmania, passim*; Devillers, *James Dean, passim*.

104: rabbit hunting: Kaye, "Eddie Cochran," liner notes, double LP, *Eddie Cochran*.

104: "Shrimper, I'm coming home: Quoted in Baenen, "Albert Lee Raises Fuss'n' Holler Over Summertime Singer," *Fairmont* (Minnesota) *Sentinel*, 6/24/91, reprinted in AC, *Eddie Cochran: Legend Continues*, p. 32.

104: Cochran at first struck: AC, "Farewell," pp. 26–27.

104: "Reserved, intense, he can: Quoted in Behle, "Cochran Exhibit Sparks Memories of '50s," *Albert Lea* (Minnesota) *Tribune*, 6/23/94, reprinted in AC, *Eddie Cochran: Legend Continues*, p. 50.

104: Ritchie Valens was still: BM, RV, pp. 27–28.

104: "Little Richard of the: *Ibid.*, p. 27.

105: Ricky had fallen in: Bufwack and Oermann, *Finding Her Voice*, p. 230.

105: their parents objected: *Ibid.*

105: nineteen years her senior: *Ibid.*, p. 231.

105: "Rick Nelson was like: *Ibid.*, p. 230.

105: Ricky would cover many: Selvin, *Rick Nelson*, p. 309.

105: Elvis Presley's girlfriends: Bufwack and Oermann, *Finding Her Voice*, pp. 234–35.

105: "West Coast rockabilly found: *Ibid.*, p. 233.

105: To Sheeley, Cochran was: Sheeley quoted in AC, "Farewell," p. 34.

105: Phil Everly told her: *Ibid.*

105: She became Cochran's girlfriend: *Ibid.*

105: in-crowd included Gene: *Ibid.*, p. 39.

106: gimp-legged, alcoholic Vincent: Stambler, *Encyclopedia*, pp. 720–21.

106: "Irving and Izzie Feld: Author interview with Franklin E. Fried.

106: president of Super Enterprises: Mann, *A–Z of Buddy Holly*, p. 51.

106: "The executives of the company: p. 124.

106: "The way the agency: *Ibid.*

106: They didn't like rock: *Ibid.*
106: Dick Clark Caravan of: *Ibid.*, p. 125.
106: "If you had seven hundred fifty: *Ibid.*, pp. 124–25.
106: "It was almost a guarantee: *Ibid.*, p. 125.
107: "Peggy Sue" for the first: Author interview with PS.
107: "Here comes 'Song.' ": *Ibid.*
107: they were to reconcile: *Ibid.*
107: "Buddy played Cupid,": *Ibid.*
107: "Yes, I'm twirling": *Ibid.*
107: "I love writing and: *Ibid.*
107: call both sides "classics,": *Rolling Stone Album Guide,* DeCurtis et al, eds., p. 324.
107: Rock 'n' roll's port: Brown and Gaines, *Love You Make,* p. 19.
107: sailors—known as "Cunard: PN, *Shout!* p. 50.
107: Liverpool College of Art: Goldman, *Lives of John Lennon,* p. 73.
107: Radio Luxembourg: Brown and Gaines, *Love You Make,* pp. 19–20.
107: "cool": BG, "New . . . Buddy Holly Interview!" RM 16, 9/80, p. 5.
107: "drier.": *Ibid.*
108: He gave it about half a year: *Ibid.*
108: songs that didn't require: *Ibid.*
108: Critical of "That'll: *Ibid*
108: going to butter him up: Freeman Hoover interview, 11/2/57.
108: Freed's manager Jack Hook: NP quoted in G&B, RB, p. 117.
108: could go to hell: *Ibid.*
108: turn them against him: JA quoted in *ibid.*
108: little sign of it: Dale Lowery interview, LP, *Buddy Holly Story,* Vol. II, MA 201185.
109: London's Royal Albert Hall: Smith and Diagram Group, *Rock Day by Day,* p. 54.
109: "In late 1957,": *Shout!* p. 51.

Chapter 8

113: Sullivan filmed the Crucifixion: Quoted in Leonard, *Really Big Show,* p. 40.
113: "Ed's the only man: Quoted in *ibid.*, p. 42.
114: ended up feuding: BG, RM 20, 9/81, p. 12; BG, "Tour Schedules," p. 9; G&B, RB, p. 87.
114: a total farce: NS quoted in ACOB.
114: lose money on the deal: *Ibid.*
114: grim cells: *Ibid.*
114: returned to Studio 50: *Ibid.*
114: all-American football team: *Ibid.*
114: "petrified" them: *Ibid.*
115: "Buddy Holly, Buddy, Buddy: BG, "Ed Sullivan Show," RM 2, 3/77, p. 8.
115: leaped ten points: *BH: Reminiscing,* Brooker, producer, IPBN Public Affairs Presentation, 1979.
115: the most promising: Quoted in BG, "Bits and Pieces," RM 6, 3/78, p. 8.
115: Crickets were not a vocal: Robert Linville quoted in BG, "Clovis's Own Robert Linville," Clovis Music Festival Official Program.
115: the Picks—whose work: *Ibid.*, p. 5.
115: rented a limo: EH quoted in BG, "More Bits and Pieces," RM 19, 6/81, p. 11.
115: He was disappointed: *Ibid.*
115: completely wasted: *Ibid.*
115: all the "Negroes" on: Quoted in RB, p. 75.
116: Larry told Buddy that: BG, "LH," RM 14, 3/80, p. 10.
116: Buddy looked terrible: *Ibid.*, p. 8.
116: have been an ordeal: TBIK.
116: slept for three days: LH quoted in BG, "LH," p. 8.
116: Mrs. Holley once confessed: EH quoted in BG, RM 11, 7/79, p. 8; Skinner, "A Meeting," RM 43, 7/86, p. 4.
116: first royalty check, $192,000: G&B, RB, p. 136.
116: wondered, were their $50,000: *Ibid.*
116: Petty said they'd spent: JBM quoted in *ibid.*, p. 137.
116: offered no records to: NS quoted in *ibid.*, p. 136; JBM quoted in *ibid.*, p. 137.
116: trying to impress the waitress: LH quoted in BG, "LH," p. 8.
116: he'd be washed up: EH quoted in BG, RM 33, 11/84, p. 7.
116: he paid Larry back: LH quoted in BG, "1981 BHMS Convention," p. 23.
116: He promised his parents: Larry Corbin quoted in BG, "KLLL Radio," RM 7, 6/78, p. 8.
116: red-and-white Impala: G&B mentioned the Impala in RB, p. 104; BG revealed that it was red and white in "Bits and Pieces" in an early issue of RM, p. 3 (unpaged, undated clipping, probably the seventies).
116: "I really respect a: BG, "KLLL Radio," p. 8.
117: "I appreciate your carrying: *Ibid.*
117: wanted to bother with: RBHS.
117: symbiosis achieved by Buddy: Quoted in WJRBH.
117: If Niki wants to go: JBM quoted in G&B, RB, p. 83.
117: Niki returned to Clovis: NS quoted in *ibid.*, p. 137.
117: Unbeknownst to the other: *Ibid.*
117: received 10 percent of all: *Ibid.*
117: Petty went back on the deal: *Ibid.*
117: Crickets gave Niki $1,000: *Ibid.*
117: "get along perfect.": Author interview with NS.
117: he blamed Petty for: G&B, RB, p. 83.
117: they wanted Niki out: *Ibid.*
117: remained on the show: BG, "Spotlight on Dick Jacobs," R50, 10/92, p. 14.
118: Petty hadn't miked him: Quoted in G&B, RB, pp. 83–84.
118: swivel-hipped, Elvis-inspired: *Ibid.*
118: Buddy liked his company: *Ibid.*, p. 84.
118: twenty thousand teenagers started forming: BBH, p. 179.
118: grade-B British movie: *Ibid.*
118: "I'm the king: GBOF, p. 140.
118: "*Fats on top,*": *Ibid.*
118: When Buddy got wind: BBH, p. 178; GBOF, p. 140.
118: way to Buddy's heart: GBOF, p. 141.
118: At $5,000 per week: Author interview with SC.
118: "I'll get you more: GBOF, p. 141.
119: Buddy always went for: JBM quoted in G&B, RB, p. 88.
119: the orchestra played Chuck Berry's: GBOF, p. 141.
119: resplendent in a garish tartan: *Ibid.*
119: "Hello, New York, and: *Ibid.*

119: Lubbock newcomer politely but: *Ibid.*
119: Paul Anka sang "I Love: BBH, p. 178.
119: then played a frenzied: GFBOF, p. 141.
119: "supported Buddy's contention: BBH, p. 178.
119: The Everly Brothers appeared: *Ibid.*, GBOF, p. 145; Dodge, *Everly Brothers*, p. 46.
119: Jerry Lee got everyone: BBH, p. 179; GBOF, pp. 142–143; Dodge, *Everly Brothers*, p. 46.
119: left or were on their way: GBOF, p. 143; Dodge, *Everly Brothers*, p. 46.
119: Fats told Freed he'd never: BBH, p. 179.
119: Freed immediately changed the: GBOF, p. 143.
119: breaking the attendance record: Tosches, *Hellfire*, p. 142.
119: ripping their clothing: Dodge, *Everly Brothers*, p. 48.
120: the police laughed and: *Ibid.*, p. 48.
120: center on Eddie Cochran: JBM quoted in AC, "Farewell," p. 39.
120: rooming with the Everlys: Noland quoted in DO, "TN," RM 27, Summer/83, p. 8.
120: head for the Paramount: JBM quoted in AC, "Farewell," p. 39.
120: the pinnacle of Freed's: BBH, p. 179.
120: record manufacturers and distributors: BBH, p. 104.
120: companies were so corrupt: *Ibid.*
120: "had written the song: Berry, *Autobiography*, p. 108.
121: including Terry Noland: Quoted in BG, "TN," p. 7.
121: "a cotton farmer from: RM 16, 9/80, p. 7.
121: Guild F-50: Bush, TGBH, p. 86.
121: "Here, man, you keep: *Ibid.*
121: bring happiness to the: *Ibid.*
122: fame had altered him: JA and JBM quoted in G&B, RB, p. 85.
122: He wouldn't horse around: JA quoted in *ibid.*
122: almost knocked Buddy's glasses: *Ibid.*
122: Buddy ordered everyone: *Ibid.*
122: could indulge in asinine: JA quoted in *ibid.*; JBM quoted in *ibid.*, p. 92.
122: dignity and perquisites of: *Ibid.*, p. 85.
122: "When Buddy went to: Author interview with Jerry Coleman.
122: Dermabrasion . . . chemosurgery: Reardon, M.D., and McMahon, *Plastic Surgery for Men, passim*; Sutton and Lyon, *Cosmetic Surgery, passim.*
122: *Arthur Murray Party*: BG, "Bits and Pieces," RM 15, p. 12.
123: on top of the Paramount: JA quoted in BG, "JA—Part Two," p. 8.
123: Cochran would soon come: Shriver, "On the Road With Eddie Cochran," p. 12; Kaye, liner notes, LP *Eddie Cochran.*
123: Don and Phil would hit: Loder, "The Everlys," pp. 146–47.
123: Little Richard renounced: Smith and the Diagram Group, *Rock Day by Day*, p. 54; Lazell et al, *Rock Movers & Shakers*, p. 301; T. White, *Rock Lives*, pp. 32, 35.
123: Jerry Lee would be: GBOF, pp. 190–200.
123: make a pass at a ninth grader: Presley, *Elvis and Me*, p. 28.
123: give her Dexedrine pills: *Ibid.*, p. 52.
123: disaster and divorce: Ibid., pp. 193–94, 200, 280, 298, 303.

123: Echo McGuire was now: G&B, RB., p. 25.
123: Echo still loved Buddy: Echo McGuire quoted in *ibid.*
123: wife of a rock 'n' roll star: *Ibid.*
124: Jackie Wilson's Producer: BG, "Spotlight on Dick Jacobs," R50 38, 10/92, p. 10.
124: who suggested that Buddy: Dick Jacobs quoted in Jones, "Dick Jacobs," RM 36, 5/85, p. 8.
124: they would often joke: *Ibid.*
124: Rock stars, Petty kept harping: NP quoted in G&B, RB, p. 109.
124: "Naw," Buddy said: Quoted in *ibid.*
125: "Kid'll flip over: BG, RM 19, 6/81, p. 6.
125: $1,200 a night as: BG in Floyd, "Crickets' Appearance at the Apollo," RM 28, Fall/83, p. 18.
125: to sign her breasts: Quoted in Dodge, *The Everlys*, p. 41.
125: "They thought you were: 8/86, cited in Dodge, *The Everlys*, p. 41.
126: "how the guys looked: Cited in *ibid.*
126: "were fighting the current: *Ibid.*
126: "wasn't respectable at all: *Ibid.*
126: "And we all did,": *Ibid.*, p. 42.
126: "cannibalistic and tribalistic.": Cited in Bayles, *Hole in Our Soul*, p. 144.
126: "a barrage of primitive: Quoted in Jahn, *Story of Rock 'n' Roll From Elvis Presley to the Rolling Stones*, pp. 40–41.
126: "means by which the white: Quoted in *Rock 'n' Roll: Early Days*, documentary film aired on PBS, 12/8/86, Paul Montgomery, producer.
126: "Much has been made: "50's," *Rolling Stone*, 576, 4/19/90, p. 48.
126: a target of Communist: McLeod, "Jerry Engler," R50, 10/91, p. 19.
127: political propaganda: Quoted in *ibid.*
127: "Buddy Holly put me: Quoted in PN, *Road Goes on Forever*, p. 38.
127: Buddy was drinking: *Ibid.*
127: "gutless and greedy: *New Book of Rock Lists*, p. 479.
127: He naturally wanted: G&B, RB., p. 98.
127: "He called me from: Author interview with LH.
128: saying he was furious: G&B, RB, p. 115; ACOB.
128: he demanded full royalties: G&B, RB, pp. 115–16.
128: "steaming mad,": *Ibid.*, p. 115.
128: cut "Rave On" in New York: Bob Thiele quoted in *ibid.*, p. 98; NP quoted in Brooks and Malcolm, "NP—Part 2," RM 38, 9/85, p. 9.
128: song about a domestic fight: G&B, RB, p. 97.
128: Petty rejected the first: *Ibid.*
128: Thiele thought better of: Thiele quoted in G&B, RB, p. 98.
128: neither Sullivan nor Petty: BG, "Bill Pickering Talks About the Picks," RM 21, 12/81, p. 8.
128: Sullivan demanded to be told: G&B, RB, p. 87.
128: he didn't know or care: *Ibid.*
129: they must *not* sing: Sullivan quoted in BG, "Tour Schedules," p. 9.
129: banned all rock music: Ward, "Fifties," ROA, p. 171.
129: he was going to walk out: BH quoted in G&B, RB, p. 87.

129: Sullivan resented Buddy's defiance: BG's analysis of the film clip of the show in RM 20, 9/81, p. 12.

129: had an animal act waiting: Leonard, *Really Big Show*, p. 33.

129: he ordered Bo Diddley: *Ibid.*, p.181.

129: Sullivan cheated Bo: Bo Diddley quoted in Loder, "Bo Diddley," TRSI, p. 185.

129: seemed to go wrong: BG, RM 20, 9/81, p. 12; BG, "Tour Schedules," p. 9; kinescope, Canadian TV special, *Roots of Rock 'n' Roll*.

129: like a bush-league: JA quoted in G&B, RB, p. 87.

129: CBS then doubled its offer: *Ibid.*

130: CBS didn't have enough: *Ibid.*

Chapter 9

131: Pan Am Constellation: Johnstone, "Australian Tour," RM 26, Spring/83, p. 8.

131: pick up Jerry Lee: *Ibid.*; GBOF, p. 153.

131: started cracking jokes: GBOF, pp. 155, 157.

131: Buddy, unamused: *Ibid.*

131: "Anchor.": *Ibid.*

131: showed Lewis some lyrics: *Ibid.*, p. 158.

131: scorned them, deciding he: *Ibid.*, p. 156.

131: naked motorcycle ride: Quoted in *Off the Record*, Fink, ed., p. 99.

131: "only for thirty-five": *Ibid.*

131: a cut in his regular: G&B, RB, p. 88.

131: Anka's manager, Bill McCadden: Johnstone, "Australian Tour," *Ibid.*

132: pictures from the plane: NP quoted in BG, "NP," RM 6, 3/78, p. 7.

132: over better than expected: Quoted in BG, R50, 12/88, p. 10.

132: Oahu's Scofield Barracks: BG, RM 43, 7/86, p. 11.

132: Elvis Presley's conquest of Hawaii: Worth and Tamerius, *Elvis: His Life From A–Z*, pp. 8, 245, 278.

132: Ritchie Valens briefly joined: BM, *RV: First Latino Rocker*, p. 98.

132: *guero*: *Ibid.*, p. 23.

132: His repertoire at the: *Ibid.*, p. 28.

132: substituted his own lyrics: *Ibid.*

132: Pan-Am Constellation that had sleepers: JA quoted in BG, "JA—Part Two," p. 5.

132: started a pillow fight: *Ibid.*

133: fire Jerry and hire: G&B, RB, p. 117.

133: she'd married her college classmate: *Ibid.*, p. 25.

133: checked into the Chevron Hotel: Johnstone, "Austalian Tour," p. 10.

133: Buddy was "electric: Quoted in Johnstone, "Australian Tour," p. 10.

133: "overwhelmed" in his initial: *Ibid.*, pp. 10–11.

133: "ill-at-ease . . . inexperienced.": Quoted in *ibid.*, p. 10.

133: Jerry Allison later acknowledged that: *Ibid.*, p. 12.

133: Allison cooled off by hitting: GBOF, p. 158.

133: A non-drinker, Anka: *Ibid.*

133: encouraged Anka to have: *Ibid.*, pp. 158–59.

134: was going to kill him: *Ibid.*, p. 159.

134: Upset and ill, Anka: *Ibid.*

134: Anka scrupulously avoided: *Ibid.*

134: didn't care for Jerry Lee: Johnstone, "Australian Tour," p. 9.

134: "a great fellow [with]: Quoted in *ibid.*

134: "rocked in the aisles: Cited in *ibid.*

134: Pat Barton from radio: Courtesy BG.

134: "I guess he's one: *Ibid.*

134: "quite well." . . . "stayed behind.": *Ibid.*

134: Jerry Lee later told: Quoted in G&B, RB, p. 88.

134: first gentlemen: Taylor, *Rock Generation*, cited in *ibid.*

135: "innate decency" . . . "ascetic": *Ibid.*

135: Jerry Lee insulted the: GBOF, p. 160.

135: so dumb when inebriated: *Ibid.*, p. 159.

135: urinated in an empty: *Ibid.*

135: going to murder: *Ibid.*, p. 160.

135: "pretty horrible.": Quoted in Smith and Johnstone, "Stan Rofe," RM 26, Spring/83, p. 23.

135: "You're hysterical.": *Ibid.*

135: he went back out front: Smith and Johnstone, "Stan Rofe," p. 24.

135: "shook the stadium: Cited in *ibid.*

136: "There's just one problem: Author interview with SC.

136: unassuming and likable: Quoted in Smith and Johnstone, "Stan Rofe," p. 12.

136: "thrilling": Quoted in BG, "Bits and Pieces," RM 5, 12/77 (unpaged).

136: undermined by an untimely: G&B, RB, p. 93.

136: color picture Petty took of Buddy: BG, "Crickets' Stopover in Tropical Hawaii," RM 26, Spring/83, p. 5.

137: blew a valve and stalled: *Ibid.*

137: 40-degree temperature: LAJ, 2/10/58.

137: into buying a Lincoln: Author interview with LH; IC (unpaged); Lehmer, "Holly Almost Drowned in '58 Swimming Mishap," *Des Moines Register* (undated, unpaged clipping).

137: "a skinny guy with a pack: Quoted in BG, "Clovis's Own Robert Linville," 1988 Clovis Music Festival Official Program.

137: overdub their vocals: *Ibid.*, p. 2.

137: only $65 each per: *Ibid.*, p. 3.

137: Tomsco's attitude suddenly changed: Tomsco quoted in BG, "George Tomsco," RB 15, 6/80, p. 4.

137: "spellbound": *Ibid.*

137: inserted some awkward lyrics: BH: *Somthin' Else (Undubbed and Unreleased Version of Some of Buddy's Historical Recordings)*, Coral Records, CR42359, LP: "Take Your Time" (False Start No. 1) and "Take Your Time" (False Start No. 2).

138: Vi an honorary Cricket: BH quoted in Swanson, "BBC Follows BH Trail to Clovis," *Albuquerque Journal*, 6/9/85, C-1.

138: none of the Crickets: BG, "Vi Petty, 9/17/28–3/22/92," R50, 4/92, p. 4.

138: play tunes from sheet: *Ibid.*

138: outspoken and sometimes rude: JA quoted in G&B, RB, p. 99.

138: referred to as "chicks.": *Ibid.*

138: an unlucky fan: *Ibid.*

138: "Hey, forget you,": Quoted in *Ibid.*

138: punched some fans: GBOF, p. 146.

138: got their hands crushed and: *Ibid.*, p. 126.

138: "Animosity toward Jerry Lee's: GBOF, p. 126.

138: groupie wanted to go: McNie, "PE," RM 14, 3/80, p. 14.

138: "If I asked her: Quoted in *ibid.*

149: a Puerto Rican young woman: G&B. RB, p. 105.

149: Provi Garcia: Author interview with BG.

149: "He came in with: Author interview with MEH.

149: tempestuous, passionate woman: *Ibid.*: MEH told me that she and Buddy decided to get married on their first date.

150: "I liked him: *Ibid.*

150: "was not allowed to: *Ibid.*

150: "How are you, Señorita?": MEH quoted in BG, "Maria Elena," RM 5, 12/77, p. 7.

150: Holly tune, "a really: Tobler, "PM 9/13/80," RM 19, 1/81, p. 2.

150: "best-conceived": *Rolling Stone Album Guide,* p. 324.

150: "one of the great rock-'n'-roll songs: *Ibid.*

150: *Cash Box* didn't even: Turner, "Record Review," RM 8, 9/78, p. 9.

150: "The British were certainly: Ward, "Fifties," ROA, pp. 177–78.

151: "Buddy is a very nice: Author interview with MEH.

151: "That still didn't sit: *Ibid.*

151: was born in Puerto Rico: G&B, RB, p. 105.

151: Her father had sent her: *Ibid.*

151: Since 1898, when the United States: Crampsey, *Puerto Rico, passim;* Berbusse, S.J., *U.S. in Puerto Rico: 1898-1900, passim;* Babin, "Special Voice: Cultural Expression," *Puerto Rico,* Carrion, ed., pp. 344–45.

151: overpopulated and undernourished: *Frommer's Comprehensive Travel Guide: Puerto Rico '93–'94;* Delano, *Puerto Rico Mio,* p. 293.

151: escalated from 245,880: Crampsey, *Puerto Rico,* p. 179.

151: "I like *los Estados Unidos:* Thomas, *Down These Mean Streets,* p. 20.

151: *barrio: Ibid.,* p. 103.

151: Maria Elena had held: G&B, RB, p. 105

151: romantically involved with Rita Moreno: Rita Moreno quoted in *Photoplay,* 2/56; *Los Angeles Mirror,* 4/20,61; Harrison Carroll quoted in Kashfi Brando and Stein, *Brando for Breakfast,* pp. 181–82; Manso, *Brando,* pp. 332, 370, 373, 393, 395, 398, 426, 443, 454, 512, 517, 520, 530, 536, 540, 566, 593, 640, 642–44, 790, 907; Holden, *Behind the Oscar,* p. 267.

152: "Buddy's very nice: Author interview with MEH.

152: "That happened: *Ibid.*

152: "José Quintero: *Ibid.*

152: "exactly like Tony: Quoted in *Ibid.*

153: "Though Norman Petty: Brooks and Malcolm, "NP," RM 37, 7/85, p. 8.

153: "Oooh, sure!": Author interview with MEH.

153: "I'll tell you: *Ibid.*

154: "We want to get: Quoted in *ibid.*

154: first consulted with Larry: G&B, RB, p. 106.

154: Maria Elena was four years: *Ibid.,* p. 119.

154: (five, according to: Author interview with PS; PS quoted in BG, "PS," Souvenir Program, BHMS Convention, 9/8-10/88, p. 8.

154: Ella Holley opposed: G&B, RB, p. 106.

154: L.O. would easily be: *Ibid.*

155: they'd initially met in January: 16 cited in Mann, *A–Z of Buddy Holly,* p. 72.

155: "never get beyond the: AC, *BH,* No. 1, p. 46.

155: "whirlwing [sic] thing,": NP quoted in Brooks and Malcolm, "NP," RM 37, 7/85, p. 8.

Chapter 10

156: Escorted by Sonny Curtis: Author interview with SC.

156: combatants for the closing: BBH, p. 194.

156: Berry had seniority: Alan Freed quoted in Tosches, *Hellfire,* p. 146.

156: shows held over seven thousand: Berry, *Autobiography,* p. 112.

156: "Never before had I: *Ibid.*

156: Coke bottleful of gasoline: Tosches, *Hellfire,* p. 146.

157: "Follow *that,* nigger,": *Ibid.*

157: "He wouldn't have known: *Autobiography,* p. 265.

157: duck walk: *Ibid.*

157: jammed together at a music: *Ibid.*

157: His first protégé was: BHTLL, p. 106; Brunswick press release, 1959, quoted in BG, "Lou Giordano," RM 15, 6/80, p. 20; BG, "More About Lou Giordano," RM 36, 5/85, p. 6; Dewitt, "BH: Little Known Facts," *Blue Suede News* 16, p. 13.

157: He came to Buddy's attention: PE quoted in McNie, RM 14, 3/80, p. 14..

157: Joe Villa, who'd: Nite, *Rock On,* p. 541; BG, "Joe Villa Talks About BH and Lou Giordano," RM 22, 3/82, p. 12.

157: two teenage girls their manager: Shannon and Javna, *Behind the Hits,* p. 25.

157: Joe Villa invited Buddy: Villa quoted in BG, "Joe Villa Talks," p. 12.

157: "I can make a record,": *Ibid.*

157: grew fond of him: *Ibid.*

158: her favorite Holly songs: "Maria Elena," RM 5, 12/77, p. 7.

158: "I'm not happy with Norman,": Author interview with MEH.

158: "Norman didn't want to spend: *Ibid.*

158: "wanted to break with: *Ibid.*

158: "not a very kosher: *Ibid.*

158: "Norman . . . knew that I knew: *Ibid.*

158: Norman "to put his name on every: *Ibid.*

159: "Buddy talked to me: *Ibid.*

159: "that Buddy was not going: *Ibid.*

159: "Music is my life,": *Ibid.*

159: "The lineup at the State: BG, RM (unpaged, undated clipping).

159: "every kind of plane: RBHS.

159: Buddy made some . . . sounds: *Ibid.* BG also refers to this interview in RM 43, 7/86, p. 10.

159: a helicopter had crashed: BG, "New Information on TV Appearances by BH and the Crickets," RM 43, 7/86, p. 10.

159: first to urge taking: Quoted in Hoffman, "We Belong Together," *Photoplay,* 5/59, reprinted in AC, RV, p. 35.

159: "We toured together: *Ibid.*

159: "all-around great guy,": BG, "18 Interviews (all at once)," p. 4.

159: gambled large quantities: Quoted in *ibid.*

160: backstage crapshoots: *Ibid.*

160: as much as $3,000: *Ibid.*

160: "way before his: *Ibid.*

160: apparently self-inflicted gunshot: Lazell et al, *Rock Movers and Shakers*, p. 127; BG, "With Our Regrets," RM 27, p 10.

160: Chuck Willis, whose: Monnery and Herman, *Rock 'n' Roll Chronicles 1955–1963*, p. 51.

160: Buddy's favorite guitar: BHTLL, p. 12; BG, "Tour Schedules," p. 12.

160: totaling several pianos: BBH, p. 191.

160: shoving a battered piano: *Ibid*.

160: "smashing $17,000.": 4/14/58, cited in BBH.

160: $150,000: *Ibid*.

160: Irving Feld was surviving, but: BBH, p. 192.

160: fifteen hundred tickets had been: Lehmer, "Holly Almost Drowned in '58 Swimming Mishap," *Des Moines Register* (undated, unpaged clipping from files of Mason City Municipal Airport).

160: Jerry Lee failed to show: *Ibid*.

160: Dickey Doo and the: *Ibid*.

160: hair-pulling broke out: *Ibid*.

160: "a bunch of rednecked: BBH, p. 192.

160: Mayor John B. Hynes at last: *Ibid*.

161: "The dregs of society· p 193.

161: five thousand "hip kids": *Ibid*.

161: Several girls were accosted: Tosches, *Hellfire*, p. 146.

161: The fighting spread: *Ibid*.

161: a riot was about: BBH, pp. 196–97.

161: 60 percent white: Quoted in BBH, p. 193.

161: "Boston always had a lot: Author interview with Cy Egan.

161: grabbing the crotch: Ward, "Fifties," ROA, p. 176.

161: "We don't like your kind: BBH, p. 195.

161: Chuck Berry attempted: *Ibid.*, p. 196.

161: Berry had to run: *Ibid*, p. 196.

161: Montreal at two P.M.: Freed quoted in Ward, "Fifties," ROA, p. 176.

161: Boston Mayor John Hynes again: Tosches, *Hellfire*, p. 146; BBH, p. 201.

161: "rock-'n'-roll paganism.": BBH, p. 201.

161: indicted for inciting: *Ibid*.

161: Senator William D. Fleming: *Ibid*.

161: Their remaining gigs: BG, "Tour Schedules," p. 12.

162: pulling a gun: *Ibid.*: Ward, "Fifties," ROA, p. 177.

162: WINS, outraged by: *Ibid*.

162: The Boston Archdiocese: BBH, p. 202.

162: "corrupting influence on America's: *Ibid.*, p. 203.

162: "There was a time: *Ibid.*, p. 206.

162: Dave Garroway shook: Tosches, *Hellfire*, p. 146.

162: "the Korean postwar youth: *Portable Jack Kerouac*, pp. 559–560.

162: too hot for show business: Ward, "Fifties," ROA, p. 177.

163: "about the most downbeat: *Halliwell's Filmgoer's Companion*, p. 532.

163: "stomach ulcer,": "A Meeting With Mr. and Mrs. Holley on 6/12/69," p. 4.

163: Ariel Cyclone 650cc: BG, "Buddy's Motorcycle," RM 27, Summer/83, p. 16.

163: he'd seen Marlon Brando: JA quoted in G&B, RB, p. 102.

163: he'd owned a Triumph: *Ibid*.

163: beeline for the Harley: BG, "Buddy's Motorcycle," p. 15.

163: with $5,000 in cash: JA quoted in G&B, RB, p. 102.

163: they could never afford: *Ibid*.

164: They took a cab: BG, "Tour Schedules," p. 12.

164: test-ride any bikes: G&B, RB, p. 102.

164: shelled out over $3,000: BG, "Buddy's Motorcycle," p. 16: Jerry's receipt (No. 84005) was for $1,044.63.

164: down the highway to Lubbock: *Ibid.*, p. 15; G&B, RB, p. 102.

164: hail, tornadoes, and rainstorms: "Damaging Storms Again Hit Area," LAJ, 5/13/58.

164: with silver eagle insignias: BG, "Buddy's Motorcycle," p. 15; G&B, RB, p. 104.

164: Crickets tooled around their: RBHS.

164: Jerry's brother James Allison: BG, "Buddy's Motorcycle," p. 17.

164: could use some exercise: *Ibid.*, RBHS.

164: Buddy places an affectionate hand: *Ibid*.

164: "big brother": IPBN Public Affairs Presentation, 1979.

164: "Buyus," later explaining: TV special, 10/58, LP *BH Story*, Side 1, Volume II, Masters, MA 201185/MAMC 9201185, Holland.

164: "Buy us a Coke: Alan Freed in *ibid*.

164: buy us somethin': Buddy Holly in *ibid*.

164: Montgomery, who was still playing: Jack Davis quoted in BG, RM, 1978 (unpaged clipping).

164: playfully reenacting the: BG, "Movies and Slides," RM 9, 12/78.

164: knife fight from *Rebel Without a Cause*: RBHS; BG, RM 9, 12/78 (unpaged clipping).

164: Buzz Gunderson: Hyams and Hyams, *James Dean: Little Boy Lost*, p. 194.

164: James Dean, whose death: Dalton, *James Dean: Mutant King*, p. 281; Headrick, Jr., *Deanmania*, p. 127.

165: Buddy's favorite movie stars: RM 3, 11/84/ p. 10.

165: Jerry seems to be charging: RBHS.

165: Buddy went to his: *Ibid.*; BG, RM 9, 12/78.

165: "It was an English Ariel,": Author interview with LH.

165: oddly unimpressed by the: LH quoted in BG, RM 11, 6/79 (unpaged clipping).

165: "with open arms": Quoted in BG, "LH," p. 9.

165: "I dont think we realized: LH quoted in BG, RM 11.

165: hurried, impatient: "Jake Goss: BH's Barber," RM 25, Winter/82, p. 12.

165: "I usually felt ill at ease: *Ibid*.

165: Jerry Lee Lewis's hometown: Tosches, *Hellfire*, p. 147.

166: "The adolescent confidence: Miller, ed., *Rolling Stone Illustrated History of Rock 'n' Roll*, p. 77.

166: "It's So Greasy: Author interview with TC.

166: "Petty had 'em lined up: BHTLL, p. 98.

166: "flush with money": TBIK.

166: fishing trip to the Brazos: *Ibid*.

166: "I remember that he: Author interview with MEH.

167: He was still growing: Author interview with LH.

167: black shoeshine attendant: Quoted in BG, "Clovis's Own Robert Linville," p. 5.

167: an apartment in Clovis: *Ibid*, p. 4.

167: Orbison continued to record: Amburn, *Dark Star*, p. 55.

167: "Sugartime" originated in Clovis: Jim Caviness, "Charlie Phillips," RM 28, Fall/83, p. 5; author interview with Billy Stull.

167: Buddy Knox, Carolyn Hester: G&B, RB, p. 181.

167: Terry Noland: Buddy Knox quoted in BG, "Buddy Knox," RM 14, 3/80, p. 6.

167: Fred Crawford's [et al.]: I am grateful to BG for playing these rare recordings for me.

167: Shaw's Jewelry Store: Maxine Nation quoted in BG, "Buddy's Wedding Present," R 32, Fall/84, p. 11.

168: to see his old friends the Everly Brothers: Selvin, Ricky Nelson, p. 111.

168: when Jerry Lee pissed: Ibid.

168: Petty, suspicious that Decca: NP quoted in Brooks and Malcolm, "NP," RM 37, 7/85, p. 8.

169: at last freed him: NS makes the point in BG, "NS—Part 2," p. 4, that "Early in the Morning" represented BH's break from the "Crickets' sound."

169: New York Institute of Technology: BG, "Spotlight on Dick Jacobs," R50 38, 10/92, p. 11.

169: the finest recording: BG, "Dick Jacobs," RM 36, 5/85, p. 9.

169: Al Chernet and George: G&B, RB, p. 181.

169: would consider him disloyal: NP quoted in Brooks and Malcolm, "NP," RM 37, p. 8.

169: Jerry graciously said: JA quoted in G&B, RB, p. 101.

169: Petty refused to acknowledge: NP quoted in Brooks and Malcolm, "NP," RM 37, p. 8.

169: lacked vision: Ibid.

169: Buddy purchased a gold chain: BG, "Buddy's Wedding Present," RM 32, Fall/84, p. 11.

169: Petty was aware of: MEH quoted in G&B, RB, p. 118.

169: perfectly well without the Crickets: Ward, "Fifties," ROA, pp. 189–90.

169: "cheap girl": G&B, RB, p. 118.

169: "picked up,": Ibid.

169: went around with numerous: Ibid.

170: The executive denied everything: Ibid.

170: NBC division responsible for: Ward, "Fifties," ROA, p. 183.

170: "Rave On" was singled out: Ibid.

170: "smash the records: Cited in ibid.

170: Everlys could never put it: "Meeting With Mr. and Mrs. Holley on 6/12/69," p. 4.

170: he rued having lost: Quoted in "Everlys," TRSI, p. 145.

170: "I was in a restaurant in Nashville: Amburn, Dark Star, p. 73; Clayson, Only the Lonely, p. 47.

170: Chet Atkins hadn't been: Fricke, "Roy Orbison Remembered," Rolling Stone, 1/26/89, cited in Amburn, Dark Star, pp. 80–81, 240.

171: "Buddy Holly came to visit: Emery and Carter, Memories, pp. 78–79.

171: Fender Precision purchased at: BHTLL, p. 96.

171: Buddy had been drinking: Author interview with Neal Winker, who says Buddy asked one of Winker's friends to buy Buddy a beer in Rhinelander, Wisconsin.

171: "unplanned dip in the river.": "Holly Almost Drowned in '58 Swimming Mishap."

171: logs started turning: JBM quoted in ibid.

171: stayed up all night, drinking: Bob Oestreich, drummer with the Roustabouts, who opened for BH at the Rothschild Pavilion, stated in MS, "Night Before Music Died," Voyageur, Vol. 9, No. 2, Winter/Spring/93, p. 19, that after the dance he met Buddy at a bar and was with him until the early morning hours.

172: he tried to swim across: LL, "Holly Almost."

172: "We knocked and woke him: Author interview with Neale Winker.

172: "Hey, Buddy," he yelled: Ibid.

172: "I'm here to collect my beer,": Ibid.

172: "Buddy made my friend buy him that beer": Ibid.

173: they were suddenly killed: JA quoted in RBHS.

173: Buffalo Springs Lake: Author interview with LH.

173: Owens outboard with a: BG, "Mrs. Holley," p. 3; BG, "BH on Waterskis," R50 36, 6/92, p. 7; Bilas, Waterski, April/92.

173: "bottom of the lake,": "Mrs. Holley," p. 4.

173: "crisp as if they: Ibid.

173: innocent summer of 1958: "LH," p. 9.

173: "salty": Ibid.

173: "Oh, no.": Quoted in RB, p. 106.

173: Ella Holley wasn't the only obstacle: Ibid.

174: Petty was probably correct: JA quoted in G&B, RB, p. 117.

174: "There is a warm side: Author interview with PS.

174: Baptist neighbors felt: G&B, RB, p. 106.

174: "might as well not: Quoted in RB, ibid.

174: "He didn't have a red cent,": Author interview with MEH.

174: hostile and jealous: NP quoted in G&B, RB, p. 118.

174: naive and inexperienced: Ibid.

174: appeared to be undermining: Ibid.

174: "Norman did not want Buddy to get married: Author interview with MEH.

175: "Norman said that Buddy: Ibid.

175: marriage-license affidavit: BG, "PS," Souvenir Program, p. 7.

175: They eloped the following: PS quoted in BG, "PS," p. 8.

175: "what I was doing.": Quoted in G&B, RB, p. 117.

175: "jumping the gun.": Quoted in BG, "PS," p. 8.

175: all going to Acapulco: Ibid.

175: Buddy's father liked Maria: RB, p. 118.

175: a mama's boy, L.O.: Ibid.

175: "come into his own,": Ibid.

175: power she was beginning: Author interview with MEH; Ward, "Fifties," ROA, pp. 189–90; T. White, Rock Lives, p. 45.

175: "mother and father were so: Quoted in "Farewell to BH," 16, reprinted in AC, BH, No. 1, p. 46.

176: "Buddy Charley Halley [sic]: LAJ, 8/16/58.

176: "There wasn't a proper: Author interview with MEH.

176: " 'One karat is enough': Ibid.

176: the temperature hitting 97: LAJ, 8/15/58.

176: "a short—not even: Author interview with MEH.

176: a gold wedding band: Ibid.

176: Jerry played Buddy's record: G&B, RB, p. 107.

176: He tipped pastor Johnson: BG, R50, 8/91, p. 24.

176: not even Maria Elena: Author interview with MEH.

176: "no bank account: *Ibid.*

176: "No. Just Norman: *Ibid.*

176: ample proof: BG, "Second BH Auction," pp. 22, 24. Items from BH's checking account, including the canceled $100 check to Ben Johnson, sold at Sotheby's (lot 621) for $1,650 on 6/23/90.

176: Acapulco, nestled: Video, *Acapulco*, Travelview International; Moldvay and Fabian, *Photographing Mexico City & Acapulco.*

177: they skipped this attraction: Author interview with PS.

177: tension between Peggy Sue and Jerry: *Ibid.*

177: "It was uncomfortable,": *Ibid.*

177: altered after marriage: BG, "PS," p. 8.

177: Buddy was indeed different: *Ibid.*

177: "a happy person: *Ibid.*

177: "I don't think that Buddy: *Ibid.*

177: differences in background and age: Author interview with PS.

177: They all stayed at Las Brisas: Author interview with PS.

177: El Cano, "which was: *Ibid.*

177: They rented a boat: Bilas, *Waterski*, 3/92, cited in BG, "BH on Waterskis," p. 7.

177: Buddy taught her how: *Ibid.*

177: over in Mexico City . . . Hilton: Author interview with PS.

177: "We spent the night: *Ibid.*

177: In the photo, Jerry: BG, "PS," p. 9; G&B, RB, p. 107.

177: Jerry was not as happy: RBHS.

177: "uncomfortable,": *Ibid.*

177: "weird": *Ibid.*

177: abject poverty: Author interview with MEH.

177: move in with Buddy's parents: *Ibid.*

177: even afford to buy groceries: *Ibid.*

177: "My aunt was the one: *Ibid.*

177: "Norman said, 'No: *Ibid.*

178: Buddy's father looked on: G&B, RB, p. 106.

178: the most beneficial thing: Quoted in G&B, RB, p. 118.

178: Ella Holley's apron strings: *Ibid.*

178: "man.": *Ibid.*

178: "She was running Buddy's: Author interview with Jerry Coleman; NP quoted in G&B, RB, p. 121; author interview with MEH, who said JA "felt uncomfortable with the fact that I was making decisions too."

178: "Jerry and Joe B. felt a little: Author interview with MEH.

178: drama beyond his wildest: G&B, RB, p. 117, maintain that Buddy's marriage was the reason for the Crickets' breakup and the rupture of Buddy's relationship with his manager.

Chapter 11

179: Billy Graham: Szatmary, *Rockin' in Time*, p. 54.

179: imposed on unsuspecting teens: Ward, "Fifties," ROA, p. 174.

179: "cheap music": *Ibid.*

179: "largely engineered: Szatmary, *Rockin' in Time*, p. 54.

179: "cretinous goons": Frank Sinatra article in *Western World* cited in Szatmary, *Rockin' in Time*, p. 26.

179: Oscar Hammerstein: *Ibid.*, p. 65.

179: 207 DJs in forty-two: Szatmary, *Rockin' in Time*, p. 66.

179: "Clean up this whole: Quoted in *ibid.*

179: "so bad that it's: BBH, p. 294.

179: "approximately" $100 a month: *Ibid.*, p. 164.

179: Clay admitted that DJs: *Ibid.*, p. 252.

179: "the backbone of American: *Ibid.*, p. 255.

179: "If somebody sent you: *Ibid.*

180: blackballed: *Ibid.*, p. 318.

180: "awash in a sea of alcohol: *Ibid.*, pp. 315, 318, 321–22.

180: Little Richard was studying: Lazell et al., *Rock Movers and Shakers*, p. 301; T. White, *Rock Lives*, p. 34.

180: Elvis . . . was abusing drugs: Presley, *Elvis and Me*, p. 52.

180: Jerry Lee's reputation: Pareles and Romanowski, *Rolling Stone Encyclopedia of Rock 'n' Roll*, p. 327, T. White, *Rock Lives*, p. 49.

180: Chuck Berry would eventually: Berry, *Autobiography*, p. 213.

180: Everly Brothers were close: Dodge, *Everly Brothers*, pp. 51, 64; Loder, "Everlys," RSI, p. 142.

180: "a teenage wasteland,": p. 7.

180: "people kept waiting": Ward, "Fifties," ROA, p. 172.

181: Petty, who refused to: Author interview with MEH.

181: Petty was named sales: NP quoted in Brooks and Malcolm, "NP," RM 37, 7/85, p. 12.

181: "was just sitting around: WJRBH, p. 72.

181: "immensely popular": *Cash Box* cited in G&B, RB, p. 128.

181: high-strung, demanding: Denisoff, *Waylon*, p. 53.

181: $75 a week: Denisoff, *Waylon*, p. 53.

181: "top C&W DJ in: *Cash Box* cited in G&B, RB, p. 128.

181: "began to pitch Waylon: Denisoff, *Waylon*, p. 56.

181: "to see the swingingest: *Ibid.*, p. 55.

181: Supporting his wife and children: *Ibid.*, p. 56.

181: "Maxine stayed at their: *Ibid.*

181: preference for black women: Quoted on p. 56.

181: "I've been with some pretty: Quoted in Riese, *Nashville Babylon*, p. 56.

181: "Buddy liked Waylon: Denisoff, *Waylon*, p. 56.

182: write songs, play them: Quoted in Melhuish and Hall, VHS-PC 105.

182: "local pickers": *Ibid.*

182: "personality DJs": *Cash Box* cited in G&B, RB, p. 128.

182: "Lubbock boys, and we're: *Ibid.*

182: work in the back room: Larry Corbin quoted in BG, "KLLL radio," RM 7, 6/78, p. 7.

182: singing along with it: EH quoted in BG, "Mrs. Holley," p. 4.

182: "looking for the guy": WJRBH, p. 3.

182: pounded on trash: Larry Corbin quoted in BG, "KLLL radio," p. 7.

182: jingles as station IDs: Quoted in video, *Waylon.*

182: Buddy asked if he could: WJEN quoted in BG, "KLLL radio," p. 8.

182: "All I got out: Quoted in Denisoff, *Waylon*, p. 55.

182: "best times of my life,": WJEN quoted in video, *Waylon*.

183: "big old Lincoln": HPD quoted in BG, RM, 3/79.

183: "Let me put it this: *Ibid.*

183: Waylon was his latest: G&B, RB, p. 108.

183: Spur, Texas: *Ibid.*

183: Ray Price's bass: Denisoff, *Waylon*, p.56.

183: "His dad said to Buddy: Quoted in WJRBH, p. 73.

183: "When Waylon Jennings wanted to: Author interview with MEH.

183: "goose bumples.": WJRBH, p. 73.

183: "Buddy knew always that: Author interview with MEH.

183: "he was *smart*, man": WJEN quoted WJRBH, p. 73.

183: go to southern Louisiana: LH quoted in G&B, RB, p. 124.

183: Petty wouldn't provide the: Author interview with MEH.

184: Harry Choates: Horstman, *Sing Your Heart Out, Country Boy*.

184: Waylon was the first: *Waylon*, video.

184: orchid-colored Lincoln: LH quoted in BG, "LH," p. 8.

184: Cadillac: *Ibid.*

184: "pink": *Ibid.*

184: "taupe.": IC.

184: Larry had ended up paying: *Ibid.*

184: drove the Cadillac to Clovis: Jerry Engler quoted in McLeod, "Jerry Engler," R50 32, 10/91, p. 19.

184: "King Curtis helped define: "BH," *Rolling Stone Album Guide*, p. 399.

184: "distinctive, almost: ROA, p. 181.

184: "lickety-split: p. 135.

184: "That'll be five-hundred dollars: Quoted in Denisoff, *Waylon*, p. 57.

184: startlingly different from: LW quoted in G&B, RB, p. 110.

184: increasingly difficult: *Ibid.*

184: "an event,": *Ibid.*

185 Most of Buddy's friends: Denisoff, *Waylon*, p. 57.

185: "just marveling a whole: WJRBH, p. 72.

185: full-time sax man: Wexler and Ritz, *Rhythm and the Blues*, p. 208.

185: stabbed him to death: *Ibid.*, p. 248.

185: "an integral conveyor of: *Ibid.*, p. 127.

185: "loved to eat, shoot: *Ibid.*, p. 248.

185: Buddy had intended to cut: Denisoff, *Waylon*, p. 57.

185: "to see his friends: Quoted in *Waylon*, video.

185: "privileged": Author interview with SC.

185: "Buddy's idea" and added: Quoted in *Waylon*, video.

185: "Jolie blonde,": Horstman, *Sing Your Heart Out, Country Boy*, p. 173.

185: "scared," he remembered the: Denisoff, *Waylon*, pp. 57–58.

185: "I wasn't near ready: *Ibid.*, p. 57.

185: "acquits himself to listenable: Quoted in AC, BH, No. 1, unidentified article dated 5/18/59, p. 47.

186: "interesting, infectious issue: *Ibid.*, 5/30/59.

186: Doug Kershaw: Malone, *Country Music U.S.A.*, p. 312.

186: "an upper, happy all: Quoted in *Waylon*, video.

186: "laughed a lot,": WJRBH, p. 72.

186: "leave while you're ahead: *Ibid.*

186: If a singer retires: *Ibid.*

186: Petty was busily trying: JBM quoted in G&B, RB, p. 120. JBM said that it was in the autumn of 1958 that NP convinced them they'd be robbed of their money if they went to New York.

186: Maria Elena was luring: *Ibid.* JBM said that NP, not MEH, was responsible for breaking up the band by convincing JBM and JA that they must never move to New York.

186: Vi and Norma Jean made: Author interview with MEH; MEH quoted in G&B, RB, p. 119.

186: "hyped" them: *Ibid.*, p. 120.

186: bands ended up broke: *Ibid.*

186: Louis Patsy Giordano: Ralph Giordano, "Lou Giordano!" RM 15, 6/80, p. 1.

187: "B-plus" on both sides: Quoted in AC, "BH," No. 1, article dated 2/7/59, p. 42.

187: The "larks" were Buddy: Ralph Giordano, "Lou Giordano!" p. 1.

187: do "anything: Quoted in "PE," p. 14.

187: "first-rate teen ballad: Cited in Giordano, "Lou Giordano!" p. 2; AC, BH, No. 1, p. 42.

187: Karen Oretti: *Ibid.*, p. 3.

187: "hot hotel": Quoted in TRSI, p. 146.

187: "was having a drink: *Ibid.*

187: inability to navigate: Mendelson, M.D., and Mello, Ph.D., *Diagnosis and Treatment of Alcoholism; Alcoholics Anonymous (The Big Book)*.

187: "strung out," . . . "disaster.": "Everlys," TRSI, p. 147.

187: Everly Brothers were drained: *Ibid.*, pp. 146.

187: Wesley Rose's stranglehold: *Ibid.*

187: exploiting them for money: *Ibid.*, p. 147.

187: "be afraid to take: *Everly Brothers*, p. 40.

187: "rootless, restless, mercurial: "Everlys," TRSI, p. 142.

187: dropping into Manny's: Henry Goldrich quoted in TGBH, p. 84.

188: "every guitar I had: *Ibid.*

188: controlled by her producer: Jones, *Patsy*, pp. 70–71, 119; Nassour, *Patsy Cline*, p. 67.

188: headlining a bill: Robert Linville quoted in BG, "Clovis' Own Robert Linville," p. 3.

188: "had to go to the gym: *Ibid.*

188: The final and most controversial: JBM quoted in G&B, RB, p. 120; JA quoted in *ibid.*

188: "I did not say: Author interview with MEH.

188: "bigshot star": RB, p. 120.

188: his jealousy of Maria: *Ibid.*

188: "brother,": *Ibid.*

189: balked at the prospect: JBM in RBHS; JBM quoted in G&B, RB, p. 120; JA quoted in *ibid.*

189: they hit the bottle: JA quoted in *ibid.*

189: found obnoxious: *Ibid.*

189: "not glamorous: Author interview with MEH.

189: sometimes led to drama: Robert Linville quoted in BG, "Clovis' Own Robert Linville," p. 5.

189: "No, I am from San Juan: *Ibid.*

189: "irritated with Maria Elena": *Ibid.*

189: Jerry complained that the: Quoted in G&B, RB, p. 120.

189: Jerry and Joe B. were drinking: JA quoted in *ibid.*, p. 120.
189: got loaded before noon: *Ibid.*
189: "all the time.": *Ibid.*
189: "shucking it.": *Ibid.*
189: he warned, had better: JA quoted in *ibid.*
189: "tighten up a little bit,": *Ibid.*
189: Maria Elena didn't have: MEH quoted in G&B, RB, p. 134.
190: left him tired and testy: *Ibid.*
190: Bob Linville noticed: Linville quoted in BG, "Clovis' Own Robert Linville," p. 5. *Clovis Music Festival 1988*, p. 5.
190: into the station house: MEH quoted in G&B, RB, p. 134.
190: that he was firing Petty: JBM and JA quoted in G&B, RB, pp. 120–21.
190: "things that he [Petty]: Author interview with MEH.
190: expected Jerry and Joe B. to go along: JBM quoted in G&B, RB, p. 120.
190: Joe B. was against it: *Ibid.*
190: cheated by Yankee record: *Ibid.*
190: share of Prism Records: JA quoted in *ibid.*, p. 121.
190: They did not perform with: G&B, RB, p. 181.
190: "the most inventive music: MS, "BH: Night Before Music Died," p. 22.
191: "perhaps the only instance: MCA's *Complete BH* appears as No. 67 in the Guterman book.
191: "I met them after: Author interview with PS.
191: more effective with violins: NP quoted in Brooks and Malcolm, "NP," RM 37, 7/85, p. 8.
191: "going against them,": *Ibid.*
191: Every time Petty visited: NP quoted in BG, "Spotlight on Dick Jacobs," pp. 11–12.
191: Finally Buddy admitted: NP quoted in Brooks and Malcolm, "NP," RM 37, 7/85, p. 8.
191: "Buddy was growing up,": ROA, p. 189.
191: first major Caucasian rock: Quoted in "Dick Jacobs," RM 36, 5/85, p. 9.
191: New York Philharmonic and: BHTLL, p. 102.
191: One of the songs was dropped: Dick Jacobs quoted in BG, "Dick Jacobs," RM 11, 6/79, p. 3.
191: Don and Phil didn't think it was "right": TRSI, p. 145.
191: Paul Anka had just: Dick Jacobs quoted in BG, "Spotlight on DJ," p. 12.
191: It was impossible, Jacobs: *Ibid.*
192: three hours: Dick Jacobs quoted in RBHS and Jones, "Dick Jacobs," RM 36, p. 9.
192: "fantastic,": Quoted in Jones, "Dick Jacobs," RM 36, p. 9.
192: "pizzicato arrangement for: Quoted in BG, "Spotlight on Dick Jacobs," p. 12.
192: Anka burst into the: BG quoted in "Dick Jacobs," RM 11, 6/79, p. 3.
192: "I wrote this song: Quoted in BG, "On the Air," RM 36, 6/77, p. 8.
192: the atmosphere: Quoted in BG, "PS," p. 3.
192: The musicians included violinists: G&B, RB, *op. cit.*, p. 181.
192: Abraham "Boomie" Richman: Jacobs quoted in Jones, "Dick Jacobs," RM 36, p. 10.
192: "real snobbish: "PS," p. 3.
192: he posed for a photo: BG, "Spotlight on Dick Jacobs," p. 12.
192: "the way he heard it: Quoted in BG, "PS," p. 3.
192: "had not been tried before: *Ibid.*
192: "maturity" the twenty-two-year-old: *Ibid.*
192: "beautifully," she said: *Ibid.*
192: run-through of the: "Spotlight on Dick Jacobs," p. 12.
192: "very apprehensive: "Dick Jacobs," RM 11, 6/79, p. 3.
193: Brenda Lee's: Nassour, *Honky Tonk Angel: Intimate Story of Patsy Cline*, p. 260.
193: Patsy Cline's "True Love": *Ibid.*
193: After the playback of: Jacobs quoted in BG, "Spotlight on Dick Jacobs," p. 12; Jacobs quoted in BG, "Dick Jacobs," RM 11, p. 3.
193: "one hour flat": Quoted in BG, "Spotlight on Dick Jacobs," p. 12.
193: changing nothing: *Ibid.*
193: "flipped out": Quoted in "Dick Jacobs," RM 11, p. 4.
193: a surefire hit: Jacobs in RBHS.
193: deliriously happy: Jacobs quoted in BG, "Dick Jacobs," RM 11, p. 4.
193: Jacobs found that: Jacobs quoted in Jones, "Dick Jacobs," RM 36, p. 9.
193: "leakage": *Ibid.*
193: turned up the "gain": Jacobs quoted in BG, "Spotlight on Dick Jacobs," p. 12.
193: "out cold in the studio: Quoted in "Spotlight on Dick Jacobs," p. 12.
193: Angelic Gospel Singers: G&B, RB, p. 111.
194: "better to the touring": Quoted in RB, p. 134.
194: worried about how the: Jacobs quoted in "Dick Jacobs," RM 11, p. 3.
194: her favorite Buddy Holly performances: Quoted in BG, "ME," p. 7.
194: Peggy Sue announced: Quoted in BG, "PS," p. 3.
194: loved Buddy so blindly: Quoted in BG, "Dick Jacobs," RM 11, p. 3.
194: "best record I've ever: Author interview with LH.
194: She singled out "True: BG, "Mrs. Holley," p. 4.
194: Ray Charles album: Dick Jacobs quoted in Jones, "Dick Jacobs," RM 36, p. 10.
194: "as good a ballad singer: "Spotlight on Dick Jacobs," p. 11.
194: "most un-temperamental artist: *Ibid.*, p. 13.
194: Count Basie sound: Jacobs quoted in Jones, "Dick Jacobs," p. 10; Jacobs quoted in BG, "Dick Jacobs," RM 11, p. 3.
195: Buddy promised to make: G&B, RB, p. 98.
195: objections of Norman Petty: Bob Thiele quoted in *ibid.*
195: Petty would sue, if: CB quoted in BG, "CB," RM 20, 9/81, p. 8.
195: Buddy Holly was finished in show business: JBM quoted in G&B, RB, p. 121. NP's exact words were "we'll starve him to death."
195: "I'm not championing: Author interview with PS.
195: writing a book about: Author interview with BG.
195: "They say husbands and: Author interview with PS.
195: out of her depth: PS quoted in BG, "PS," p. 11.
195: somewhat disconcerting: *Ibid.*
195: When Peggy Sue was asked: *Ibid.*; author interview with PS.

196: "That's where we're gonna: PS quoted in BG, "PS," p. 6.
196: "accept" him: Ibid.
196: Beatles played a doubleheader: Brown and Gaines, Love You Make, p. 104.
196: Mama Leone's, a tourist: Author interview with PS.
196: struck Jerry as painfully: PS quoted in BG, "PS," p. 11.
196: her clothes were as: Ibid.
196: buy some New York clothes: Ibid.
196: "attractive": Ibid. p. 8.
196: "five years older than: Ibid.
196: "Buddy only knew her: Ibid.
196: pocketbook strap, a solid: Author interview with PS.
196: struck a cabinet in: Ibid.
197: the unfamiliar tight skirt: PS quoted in BG, "PS," p. 11.
197: stuck in a subway grate: Ibid.
197: She fell on the: Ibid.
197: he seemed as embarrassed: Ibid.
197: awkward impasse: Ibid.
197: matured faster: Ibid.
197: searching for her identity: Ibid.
197: When Buddy saw her: Ibid.
197: into the theater barefooted: Ibid.
197: protested that she: Ibid.
197: "going to the movie: Ibid.
197: "Buddy was gifted with: Author interview with PS.
197: "There's always a: Ibid.
197: had no children: ibid.
197: opulent house: Author interview with BG.
197: owned the Rapid Rooter: Ibid.
197: their divorce in 1993: Ibid.
197: for her ailing mother: Ibid.
197: sang "It's So Easy.": TV Guide, 10/25/58, reprinted in AC, BH, no. 1, p. 32.
198: blocked the strings: "Robin Luke," RM 5, 12/77, p. 3.
198: 8.4 million: BG, "Browsing Through Billboard," R50, 6/92, p. 23.
198: They lip-synched: BG, "Interviews, Jingles, & Live Performances on Records," RM 26, Spring/83, p. 20.
198: "a lot of dirt": Dick Clark quoted in ibid.
198: "where I can be: JA and JBM in RBHS.
198: "start our own publishing: JA quoted in G&B, RB, p. 121.
198: Buddy was under the impression: Ibid., p. 120; author interview with LH.
198: Buddy was being "headstrong": JBM in RBHS.
198: would rob him if: G&B, RB, p. 120.
198: Jerry and Joe B. went to: Ibid., p. 121.
198: "The boys went to: Author interview with LH.
198: bank account contained $50,000: Denisoff, Waylon, p. 62.
199: knew where he stood: G&B, RB, p. 121.
199: who revealed that they: Author interview with JA; JA quoted in G&B, RB, p. 121.
199: "Buddy ain't ever'thing: Author interview with LH.
199: could make recording stars: JBM quoted in G&B, RB, p. 121.
199: calling themselves the Crickets: Ibid.
199: they fell for Petty's blandishments: Author interview with JA, who said, "Really the reason we

split was because we decided to stay in Texas. We wouldn't have decided to stay there but Norman Petty talked us into staying there and working as the Crickets"; author interview with MEH, who said, "Norman convinced them that they did not need Buddy Holly, that they were the Crickets and that they would make it on their own, and that Buddy was not being fair to them. They believed Norman and felt that that was the way to go."
199: Buddy's money locked in: RB, p. 121.
199: "would produce himself: "NP (Part 3)," p. 6.
199: "We'll starve him to: JBM quoted in RB, p. 121.
199: Buddy called Jerry's house: Ibid.
199: Jerry and Joe B. had not: Ibid.
199: "Where's Jerry and Joe B.?": Author interview with LH.
199: "They went over to: Ibid.
199: who confronted Petty: NP quoted in G&B, RB, p. 121.
199: in front of the Crickets: Author interview with MEH.
199: "We went to Clovis: Ibid.
199: "do better": NP quoted in G&B, RB, p. 121.
199: "not fit": Ibid.
199: started making fun of her: Author interview with MEH.
199: "He got mad and told: Ibid.
199: "in Spanish.": RB, p. 119.
200: "but you don't know: Ibid.
200: Petty demanded an explanation: NP quoted in ibid., p. 121.
200: it wasn't what: Ibid.
200: asked him if he'd definitely: MEH quoted in ibid.
200: Buddy continued to press: Author interview with MEH.
200: Petty dropped his bombshell: MEH quoted in G&B, RB, p. 121.
200: "betrayed," stabbed in the: Ibid., p. 122.
200: "I said, 'Well, Norman: Author interview with MEH.
200: wished the Crickets would: JA quoted in G&B, RB, p. 121.
200: were going to regret: Ibid.
200: welcome to the Crickets': Ibid.
200: "Buddy got real hurt: Author interview with MEH.
200: give up his singing: LOH and EH quoted in G&B, RB, p. 122.
200: "Listen, Buddy,": Author interview with MEH.
200: "real perturbed and real: Ibid.
201: "Of course, everybody knew: Ibid.
201: "Really the reason we: Author interview with JA.
201: "blacks and Mexicans,": MEH quoted in G&B, RB, p. 134.
201: loathed Lubbock's bigoted: Ibid.
201: churchgoing: Ibid.
201: Buddy gave his brother: TGBH.
201: Buddy remained with Snuff: Snuff Garrett quoted in BG, RM 10, 3/78 (unpaged clipping).
201: "the station that other stations: BH quoted in BG, RM 19, Spring/83 (unpaged clipping).
201: to obtain legal counsel: Author interview with MEH.
202: Apartment 4H: Author interview with MEH.

202: No. 11 Fifth Avenue: Author interview with BG, who noted the address when he saw a greeting card that Buddy had sent to Lubbock. However, in my interview with MEH, MEH said their New York address was No. 10 Fifth Avenue.

202: designed by Stanford White: Hahn, *Romantic Rebels*, p. 188.

202: "stood for a fresh: *Ibid.*, pp. 243–244.

Chapter 12

203: Mark Twain was seventy: Kaplan, *Mr. Clemens and Mark Twain*; Harnsberger, *Mark Twain, Family Man*, p. 213.

203: five-hundred-thousand-word autobiography: Twain, *Autobiography of Mark Twain*, 1959 edition, Neider, ed.

203: on the same spot: Author interview with MEH.

203: With Peggy Sue he created: "BH," *Rolling Stone Illustrated History of Rock & Roll*, Miller ed., p. 79.

203: L. O. Holley had suggested: BG, "Our 9th Year," RM 32, Fall/84, p. 1.

203: it sold ten million: BG, "PS," p. 5.

204: "We were paying nine hundred dollars: Author interview with MEH.

204: "a red cent,": *Ibid.*

204: most powerful men in U.S.: Summers, *Goddess*, pp. 272–73.

204: "the boss of bosses: Koch and Rauch, *Mayor*, p. 14.

204: "It was a corner: Author interview with MEH.

204: "the basic stories: *Ibid.*

204: living as a draftsman: MEH quoted in G&B, RB, p. 133.

204: skilled and resourceful: EH in BG, "Mrs. Holley," RM 2, 3/77, p. 3.

204: "late at night or early: Author interview with MEH.

205: Ginsberg and fellow poet: Gooch, *City Poet*, p. 202.

205: Kerouac, who'd just published: Clark, *Jack Kerouac*, pp. 169–70.

205: Joyce Glassman: Glassman, *Minor Characters*, p. 245.

205: "a silent castle for sleeping: Miles, *Ginsberg*, p. 251.

205: "Tom Dooley" had sold: Murrells, *Million Selling Records*, p. 117.

205: "as if they were manufacturing: Quoted in Miles, *Ginsberg*, p. 248.

206: Greenwich Village was settled: Ware, *Greenwich Village*, p. 7.

206: "Buddy loved the jazz: Author interview with MEH.

206: Max Gordon's Vanguard: Gordon, *Life at the Village Vanguard*.

206: "Johnny Johnston had a jazz: Author interview with MEH.

206: walk from club to club: Hentoff, *Jazz Is*; Carr, *Miles Davis*; Feather, *Pleasures of Jazz*.

206: "We were always around: *Ibid.*

206: Gate resounded with the: Author interview with Frank Fried.

206: regulars there: Quoted in BG, "Buddy Knox,"

RM 14, 3/80, p. 6; "Farewell to Eddie Cochran," p. 39.

206: "were probably the only: Quoted in BG, "Buddy Knox," *Ibid.*

206: "The only movie Buddy: Author interview with MEH.

206: "The first pictures that: *Ibid.*

206: from fan Jeff Speirs: Quoted in BG, RM (unpaged, undated clipping).

207: "We were working: Author interview with MEH.

207: flagship recording studio: *Ibid.*

207: "Phil Everly came into town,": *Ibid.*

208: Segovia's albums: MEH quoted in G&B, RB, p. 123.

208: lived in suspense: PE in G&B, RB, p. 110.

208: did nothing to allay: *Ibid.*

208: "Rock 'n' roll is being integrated: Quoted in Ward, "Fifties," ROA, p. 191.

208: "people were always asking: p. 41.

208: one of the few persons: G&B, RB, p. 110.

208: rock 'n' roll had solidly: *Ibid.*

208: experimentation and change. *Ibid.*

208: *Billboard* reported nothing more: Whitburn, *Billboard Book of Top 40 Hits*, pp. 81, 148.

208: He was drinking over: PE quoted in PN, *Road Goes On Forever*, p. 38.

208: "I can remember him: *Ibid.*

208: manufacture a Buddy Holly signature model: TGBH, p. 84.

209: entered into negotiations: *Ibid.*, p. 86.

209: Don cut out the pick: Whitford et al, *Gibson's Fabulous Flat-Top Guitars*, pp. 90–92.

209: "a thinking man,": Quoted in G&B, RB, p. 56.

209: fed up with being: DE quoted in Loder, "Everlys," TRSI, p. 148.

209: slammed his guitar to: *Ibid.*

209: decided to learn Spanish: Author interview with MEH.

209: didn't consider them good enough: MEH quoted in G&B, RB, p. 123.

209: "He wanted so desperately: Author interview with MEH.

210: "I love Mahalia Jackson: *Ibid.*

210: Lana Turner tearjerker, *Imitation*: Schwerin, *Go to Tell It: Mahalia Jackson, Queen of Gospel*.

210: present it to his parents: G&B, RB, p. 124.

210: His favorite part: *Ibid.*

210: "Buddy was a twenty-two-year-old going on: "Chicago Scene," CT, Tempo 2, Section 5, 6/24/88 (unpaged clipping).

210: parents came to New York: BG, "1981 BHMS Convention," RM 21, 12/81, p. 23.

210: "He didn't eat: Author interview with MEH.

211: lessons at a dance studio: MEH quoted in BG, RM 3, 11/84, p. 10.

211: apartment on December 3: G&B, RB, p. 129.

211: ask if the song was any good: MEH quoted in *ibid.*, p. 127.

211: became seriously ill: MEH quoted in G&B, p. 133.

211: As an ulcer sufferer: p. 133.

212: Valentino, died in agony: Shulman, *Valentino*, p. 329.

212: Buddy was ill for the: G&B, RB, p. 133.

212: never again would she: *Ibid.*

212: an almost instant million: Murrells, *Million Selling Records*, p. 446.

212: Buddy Howe and Tim Gale: Denisoff, *Waylon*, p. 58

213: and rejected the offer: *Ibid*, p. 59.

213: "It's sure gettin' to be: Author interview with LH.

213: "Look at this!": *Ibid*.

214: "begged": EH in BG, "18 Interviews (all at once)," p. 3.

214: "It was not really an: Author interview with MEH.

214: "he didn't have any group: Quoted in BG, "18 Interviews (all at once)," p. 3.

214: They were in Clovis: MEH in G&B, RB, p. 140.

214: "had not got any: G&B, RB, p. 145.

214: Sinks tried to ape: I am grateful to George Blaisdell for providing the records of the post-Holly Crickets, including the LP *Crickets: Back in Style*, MCA Records/EMI Records Ltd., liner notes by JB.

214: sign up Larry Welborn: BG, "LW," RM 45, 11/86, p. 15.

214: Terry Noland was also: BH letter to Noland quoted in BG, "Second BH Auction," R50, 8/91, p. 24.

214: had borrowed enough money: TA in G&B, RB, p. 138.

214: $2,500 advance: Denisoff, *Waylon*, p. 62.

214: to shower his family with: TBIK.

214: financially strapped: *Ibid*.

214: a high of forty-nine: LAJ, 12/25/58.

214: CHRISTMAS ARRIVES: *Ibid*.

214: Miss Yvonne Skinner,: *Ibid*.

215: 62 degrees: *Ibid*., 12/28/58.

215: had them completely outfitted: LH in RBHS.

215: the outskirts of town: *Ibid*.

215: always preferred the simpler: Author interview with LH.

215: "play second fiddle: TBIK.

215: "going to hell!": Quoted in BG, "Terry Noland," RM 27, Summer/83, p. 7.

216: "He came in and: Author interview with KJ.

216: "had it made,": Quoted in G&B, RB, p. 132.

216: Morris Fruit and Vegetable Store: *Ibid*.

216: flopped in his hometown: *Ibid*.

216: Buddy Holly homecoming concert: *Ibid*.

216: "up a building higher: "WJEN," RM 25, Winter/82, p. 8.

216: One day Buddy told Waylon: Quoted in WJRBH.

216: "You're the One.": BG, "KLLL radio," pp. 7–8.

216: clapping their hands: WJRBH, p. 74; Larry Corbin quoted in "KLLL radio," p. 8.

216: playing the guitar accompaniment: BG, "More and More About 'More and More,' " RM 43, 7/86, p. 11.

217: offered him a job: Larry Corbin quoted in BG, "KLLL radio," p. 8.

217: as electric-bass: Author interview with MEH; WJRBH, p. 74.

217: Maxine was pregnant: Denisoff, *Waylon*, p. 60.

217: "An artist: *Ibid*, pp. 60–61.

217: a leave of absence: Larry Corbin quoted in BG, "KLLL radio," p. 8.

217: He and Jack Neal, his: BG, "JN," p. 5.

217: "got mad,": RB, p. 140.

217: "I *always* go commercial,": Author interview with MEH.

217: Buddy piloted a Cessna: BG letter to author, 11/7/94, p. 2; LH quoted in RM 42, 5/86, p. 8.

217: Larry was also: Author interview with LH.

217: "behind my back: RB, p. 140.

217: "Buddy's flyin' ": Denisoff, *Waylon*, p. 243.

218: New Year's Eve: TA in BHTLL, p. 106.

218: "get ahold of: CB quoted in BG, "CB," RM 20, 9/81, p. 7.

218: "dyin' to gig": BHTLL, p. 106.

218: March 27, 1909: Millard, *Country Music*, p. 6.

218: innovator of Texas honky-tonk: Malone, pp. 164, 166.

218: prostitutes sat next to him: *Ibid*., p. 167.

218: "I'll Sail My Ship: Millard, *Country Music*, p. 81.

218: "Sweeter Than the Flowers.": Malone, *Country Music U.S.A.*, p. 230.

218: No one in the Odessa: TA quoted in BHTLL, p. 106.

219: for legal reasons: G&B, RB, p. 140.

219: frightening dream: *Ibid*.; Ward, "Fifties," ROA, pp. 193–94.

219: "Anywhere I go: Ward, "Fifties," ROA, p. 194.

219: "Don't worry,": *Ibid*.

219: "and all of a sudden: BHTLL, p. 108.

219: "he intended to make: "WJ," RM 25, Winter/82, p. 10.

219: Waylon quaked at the prospect: WJEN quoted in BHTLL, p. 108; G&B, RB, p. 139.

219: Buddy bought him one: WJEN quoted in WJRBH, p. 72.

219: play it in fourteen days: WJEN says BH gave him 2 weeks in WJRBH, p. 72; in G&B, RB, pp. 139–40, he says it was a week and a half.

219: gave Waylon his albums: G&B, RB, p. 139.

219: "everything he had ever: WJRBH, p. 72.

219: perfectionist: *Ibid*., p. 74.

219: appeal to Tommy Allsup for help: *Ibid*., p. 72.

219: "could sing rock 'n' roll better: *Ibid*., p. 73.

219: "a week or so: Author interview with MEH.

220: "lazy sound,": WJEN quoted in WJRBH, p. 74.

220: borrowed Buddy's Fender: *Ibid*., p. 73.

220: syncopation: *Ibid*., p. 73.

220: "really turned me on,": *Ibid*.

220: The opening guitar lick: *Ibid*., p. 73.

220: *Rolling Stone* rated: Cott, "BH," *Rolling Stone Illustrated History of Rock & Roll*, Miller, ed., p. 81.

220: meticulous detail: *Ibid*., p. 74.

220: "was learning as I went along: WJEN quoted in WJRBH, p. 74.

220: rented hall in New York: BHTLL, p. 106.

220: Waylon sang harmony: WJEN in WJRBH, p. 74.

220: worked on "Gotta Travel On,": *Ibid*.

220: nineteenth-century: Jancik, *One-Hit Wonders*, p. 282.

220: "I'm going to cook: Author interview with MEH.

221: establish a studio band: TA quoted in G&B, RB, p. 126.

221: Buddy invited Noland: "Terry Noland," p. 7.

221: steel guitars and fiddles: TA quoted in G&B, RB, p. 126.

221: $50,000 to 80,000 of Buddy's: G&B, RB, p. 138.

221: "In mid-January: Author interview with BG.

221: "I'm going to Clovis: Denisoff, *Waylon*, p. 62.

221: advance from GAC: BHTLL, p. 106.

221: Allsup, received $250: TA quoted in G&B, RB, p. 136.

221: Waylon received $200: *Waylon*, p. 71.

221: "Buddy was very concerned: Author interview with MEH.

221: Blair House Restaurant: Dick Jacobs quoted in Jones, "Dick Jacobs," p. 9.

222: "very nice": *Ibid.*

222: produced thirteen early Holly: Owen Bradley in ACOB.

222: "went over and talked: *Ibid.*

222: she wanted to go on the tour: Author interview with MEH.

222: driving dangerous if not: Stallings, *Rock 'n' Roll Confidential*, p. 190: "one of the worst winters on record."

222: "I had found out: Author interview with MEH.

222: "The only reason Buddy went: WJEN quoted in Stallings, *Rock 'n' Roll Confidential*, p. 190.

222: "Buddy said, 'I want: Author interview with MEH.

Chapter 13

223: the city was snowbound: TA in BG, "TA," RM 15, 6/80, p. 13.

223: Buddy and his bride: *Ibid.*

223: apprehensive about meeting Ritchie: EH quoted in BM, RV, pp. 108–109.

223: as sixteen-year-old Paul Anka: NS quoted in G&B, RB, p. 112; EH quoted in BM, RV, p. 109.

223: they accompanied "everybody": CB quoted in "CB," RM 20, Spring/81, p. 8.

223: nothing like Buddy had imagined: EH quoted in BM, RV, p. 109; BG, "Bits and Pieces," RM 20, 9/81, p. 5.

223: responded warmly to friendly: BM, RV, p. 22.

223: grown up among gangs: *Ibid.*; Ward, "Fifties," ROA, p. 192.

223: the Silhouettes: Lazell et al, *Rock Movers & Shakers*, p. 524; Clifford, *Harmony Illustrated Encyclopedia of Rock*, p. 180.

223: "Ritchie Valens and I: Author interview with MEH.

224: hadn't yet received his royalties: Stallings, *Rock 'n' Roll Confidential*, p. 191.

224: much-needed guidance: Author interview with MEH; BM, RV, pp. 122–123.

224: "Buddy was talking to Ritchie: Author interview with MEH.

224: "a straight shooter.": "The Dick Cavett Show," televised (or re-run) 9/22/92.

224: beer or shots of: Denisoff, *Waylon*, p. 65.

224: Adrianne Joy Fryon: Gales, " 'Bopper' Died Just as Career Was Climbing," MCGG, E-4, 2/1/88. Gales spells Mrs. Richardson's maiden name "Fryou" but it is spelled Fryon by writer Randall C. Hll in "BB," p. 11, in AC's booklet *BB*.

224: Adrianne was pregnant: Gordon Baxter quoted in Thomas, "Gordon Baxter," RM 19, 6/81, p. 5.

224: "Bee-bop's big and I'm big: Gales, " 'Bopper' Died Just."

224: KTRM "DISC-A-THON,": Hill, "BB," AC, *BB*, No. 3, p. 4.

225: Made of silk: Collier, *Art of Lacemaking*, passim.

225: "little bitty cute: Quoted in Thomas, "Gordon Baxter," p. 5.

225: scheduled to tour Australia: Rogers, "Hidie Hodie Everybody!", reprinted in AC, *BH*, No. 1, p. 47.

225: "I once asked [the Bopper]: Hoffman, "We Belong Together," *Photoplay*, 5/59, p. 35.

225: third most-played song of 1958: Hill, "BB," p. 4.

225: "because there wasn't a mean: Thomas, "Gordon Baxter," p. 5.

225: "I dug Holly's lean: TW, p. 87.

225: He was addicted: *Ibid.*, p. 85.

225: "silent partner in everything: *Ibid.*

225: "hippest, handsomest: *Ibid.*, p. 52.

225: "secret lover,": *Ibid.*, p. 53.

225: "instant courage.": *Ibid.*, p. 51.

225: He joined the Fordham Daggers: *Ibid.*, p. 46.

225: the Baldies: *Ibid.*, p. 48.

225: "converted school bus: *Ibid.*, p. 87.

226: "It snowed on us. BG, "TA," RM 15, 6/80, p. 13.

226: arranged in Chicago: *Ibid.*

226: lowest bidder: Author interview with Hans Goeppinger.

226: "Usually the heater wouldn't work,": BG, "TA," p. 13.

226: "third-class operation,": TW, p. 87.

226: The booker, General Artists Corporation: Ward, "Fifties," ROA, pp. 193–94; Clark, *Big Bopper*, p. 24; MS, "Night Before Music Died," p. 23; J. Dodge, *Not Fade Away*, pp. 160–61.

226: abandoning them to abominable: "Barsalona: Agents," in Spitz, *Making of Superstars*, p. 125; Ward, "Fifties," ROA, pp. 193–94; J. Dodge, *Not Fade Away*, pp. 160–61; Stallings, *Rock 'n' Roll Confidential*, p. 191; G&B, RB, p. 141.

226: engine frequently stalled: TW, p. 87; G&B, RB, p. 141.

226: "dueling guitars: TW, pp. 88–89.

226: "Mama Long," which he'd: BM, RV, p. 24.

226: "played the meanest rhythm: TW, p. 88.

226: luggage racks: *Ibid.*, p. 87.

226: 300 miles long, 118 miles: Hatcher and Walter, *Pictorial History of the Great Lakes*, p. 177.

226: their Milwaukee hotel: Denisoff, *Waylon*, p. 65.

226: took a cab: *Ibid.*

227: Tommy had difficulty: *Ibid.*

227: Would anyone come out: *Ibid.*

227: in twenty-five-below-zero: MS, "Night Before Music Died," p. 23.

227: "There's a very different: p. 104.

227: "I'm going onstage: Author interview with MEH.

227: "a great reception,": BHTLL, p. 108.

227: "Turn that Goddamn: WJEN quoted in *ibid.*

227: "probably the world's: Quoted in Denisoff, *Waylon*, p. 243.

227: "hanging over the bandstand.": "TA," p. 13.

228: decided to go out and: *Ibid.*

228: the city's 1,650 bars: Pierce and Hagstrom, *Book of America*, p. 279.

228: Buddy was homesick: BG, "TA," p. 13.

228: Bunch's feet seemed to be freezing: CB quoted in BG, "CB," p. 8.

228: Buddy and Dion huddled: TW, p. 123.

228: "I got to know Holly: *Ibid.*, p. 88.
228: "bent notes": *Ibid.*, p. 40.
228: local American Motors: Pierce and Hagstrom, p. 279.
228: posed for . . . Szikil: Sterelczyk photo in AC, *Big Bopper*, p. 22.
228: nicknamed "Melvin.": "Tribute to Big Bopper," *Rock 'n' Roll Songs*, 7/59, cited in AC, *BB*, p. 41.
228: Buddy cleared about $500: Denisoff, *Waylon*, p. 71.
228: Tommy gave him a gun: BG, "Spotlight on 2/3/59," p. 9.
228: .22-caliber "Vest Pocket" revolver: "Investigator Offers Theory on Fatal Crash," MCGG, E6, on file at Mason City Municipal Airport, courtesy Jerome J. Thiele, director of aviation, Mason City Airport Commission.
228: serial number 6K5315: BG, "Spotlight on 2/3/59, p. 9.
228: existence of Buddy's gun: "Pistol in Plane Wreck Not Fired," MCGG, 4/10/59, p. 14.
228: Larry Lehmer of the: JP, "1959 Winter Dance Party, Fatal Crash Are Fodder for Aspiring Author," MCGG, 2/9/92.
228: bottom of his toilet kit: BG, "Spotlight on 2/3/59," p. 9.
229: her in "Ooh My Head,": Cott, "BH," *Rolling Stone Illustrated History of Rock 'n' Roll*, p. 80.
229: "I want to do: Author interview with MEH.
229: "jungle food": Tillis, *Stutterin' Boy*, p. 146.
229: she'd used the $65: Hoffman, "We Belong Together," p. 35.
229: Valenzuela died in 1951 from diabetes: "Life and Death of RV," *Modern Screen*, 5/59, reprinted in AC, *RV*, No. 2, p. 38.
229: $140-a-month pension: Hoffman, "We Belong Together," p. 35.
229: She remarried, then: *Ibid.*
229: went to work: *Ibid.*
229: troubles with the law: *Ibid.*
229: "I tell him to be: *Ibid.*
229: few months of rigorous: Sherlock, "We'll Remember Ritchie," *Teen*, 5/59.
230: tape record a greeting: BG, "Trivial Trivia, RM 21, 12/81, p. 28.
230: "all talked on the tapes: WJ, "Fred Milano," RM 8, 9/78, p. 4.
230: "wasn't very religious: *Photoplay*, 5/59, p. 35.
230: Fournier's dance hall [temperature, performance, Sammy's Pizza]: Author interview with Don Larson.
230: Bunch discovered that he'd lost: Denisoff, *Waylon*, p. 65.
230: "Come here," Buddy said: WJRBH, p. 74.
230: Charlie "Papa" Jackson, "Salty Dog Blues": Malone, *Country Music U.S.A.*, pp. 105, 124, 330.
230: "We did country songs: Quoted in G&B, RB, p. 143.
230: "Man, that 'Salty Dog Blues': *Ibid.*
230: photo of Buddy, Waylon: cover photo (Jane Ellefson), RM 27, Summer/83; BG, "New Photos," *Ibid.*, p. 24.
230: "awful": Quoted in RB, p. 144.
230: "every day, maybe twice: Author interview with MEH.

231: propose a reconciliation: G&B, RB, p. 140.
231: "Jerry called me at home: Author interview with MEH.
231: "I think that was: Author interview with LH.
231: "wanted to go to: NP quoted in Brooks and Malcolm, "NP (Part 3)," p. 6.
231: drizzly weather: LL, "How Icy Bus Woe Led to Plane, Rock Immortality," *Des Moines Sunday Register*, "Entertainment Travel," 1-F/4-F, 2/3/89.
231: passing bottles: BM, RV, p. 106.
231: "Silver Satin wine,": Freddie Aguilera quoted in BM, RV, p. 36.
231: which he called "whites,": *Ibid.*
231: a small town situated: Davenport has a population of 10,000, but was smaller in 1959.
231: Buffalo Bill's birthplace: Winckler, *Plains States*.
231: rain turned to sleet: LL, "How Icy Bus Woe."
232: the heater completely conked: CB quoted in BG, "CB," p. 7.
232: Carl Bunch complained: *Ibid.*, p. 8.
232: "Holly and I used: TW, p. 87.
232: designing for George Jones: Denisoff, *Waylon*, pp. 65–66.
232: "I don't know if it: *Ibid.*, p. 66
232: pulling into Mac's Shell Station: LL, "How Icy Bus Woe."
232: "famous" recording: *Ibid.*
232: wanted a blue one: Quoted in BM, RV, p. 104.
232: "If you're going to: Quoted in WJ, "Fred Milano," RM 8, 9/78, p. 4.
233: GAC disapproved of charter: unidentified clipping dated 2/9/59 in AC, BB, p. 24.
233: "I took J.P. up: "Gordon Baxter," RM 19, 6/81, p. 6.
233: buy a radio station: Gales, " 'Bopper' Died Just as Career Was Climbing," MCGG, 2/9/89, E4.
233: "Tommy Allsup wasn't making: Quoted in WJ, "Fred Milano," p. 4.
233: But Ritchie was afraid of: Quoted in BM, RV, p. 104.
233: He'd never been in a small plane: TA in RBHS.
233: "massive rebirth": "CB," p. 8.
233: "to kill, to steal: *Ibid.*
234: "a place to come from: Quoted in Peirce and Hagstrom, *Book of America*, p. 581.
234: stupefying provincialism: Benet, *Benet's Third Edition Reader's Encyclopedia*, p. 566.
234: "icy breath of death: "Ice Palace," *Short Stories of F. Scott Fitzgerald*, p. 67.
234: experimentation with cosmetic surgery: Author interview with Jerry Coleman.
234: "tall, powerful: BG, "Duane Eddy and BH," RM 19, 1986, p. 11.
234: black Levi's suit: BM, RV, p. 66.
234: "Dion had his groupies: *Take Another Little Piece of My Heart*, p. 198.
234: Sue Butterfield: TW, p. 121.
235: "where cars skid: *Duluth*, p. 4.
235: bear smashed through: Bree, *In the Teeth of the Northeaster*, p. 103.
235: "nine months of winter: Hatcher and Walter, *Pictorial History of the Great Lakes*, p. 157.
235: Edmund Fitzgerald: Shanley, "Winds of November," *Cayo*, Vol. 1, No. 7, 1993, pp. 4–5.
235: "white blob,": Bree, *In Teeth of Northeaster*, p.

122; U.S. Department of Transportation, Coast Guard, Marine Casualty Report: S.S. Edmund Fitzgerald: Sinking in Lake Superior on 10 November 1975 With Loss of Life, U.S. Coast Guard Marine Board of Investigation Report and Commandant's Action, Report No. USCG 16732/64216, Washington, D.C., 1977.

235: slammed her onto a reef: Shanley, "Winds of November."

235: "I saw Buddy Holly in Duluth: "Bob Dylan," TRSI, p. 98.

235: known as Bobby Zimmerman: Spitz, Dylan, p. 67.

235: a middle-class Jewish boy: Ibid., pp. 14–15.

235. He wore Hush Puppies: Ibid., p. 70.

235: high-school garage band: Thompson, Positively Main Street, p. 60.

235: Echo Helstrom: Ibid., pp. 68, 82: Spitz, Dylan, p. 57.

235: would one day enshrine: Spitz, Dylan, p. 68, 388: Spitz maintains "Girl of the North Country" was "reportedly" written about Bonnie Beecher, "Bob's old college flame."

235: "Buddy was great.": KL, "Bob Dylan," TRSI, p. 98.

235: "one of the biggest: BG, "Spotlight on 2/3/59," p. 6.

236: "nice little rap,": Bowen quoted in BG, "Jimmy Bowen," RM 20, 9/81, p. 14.

236: "Tell everybody I'm flying,": BG, "Spotlight on 2/3/59," p. 6. In the same article, Frankie Sardo mentions that some of the singers were going to charter a plane.

236: Ritchie called his manager: "Life and Death of RV," Modern Screen, 5/59, reprinted in AC, RV, No. 2, p. 39.

236: Jack's on the Pier: BM, RV, p. 108.

236: "It's thirty-five degrees below: "Life and Death of RV," p. 39.

236: "finish that evening and: BM, RV, p. 108.

236: engine froze and stopped: TA quoted in MS, "Night Before Music Died," p. 18; TA quoted in BG, "TA," p. 13.

236: "The bus finally broke: Quoted in BG, "CB," p. 7.

236: "It was cold: Quoted in RBHS.

236: The piston had gone: BG, "Spotlight on 2/3/59," pp. 6–7, writes that the Iron County Garage was owned by Calvetti's father and uncle; MS, "Night Music Died," p. 18, writes that the wrecker operator who retrieved the bus was Frank Leoni.

237: February 1 was 25 below: Ralph Ansami of Ironwood Daily Globe, told BG, "Spotlight on 2/3/59," p. 7, that the low on 2/1/59 was "officially" minus twenty-five degrees, although out on the highway it was much colder.

237: more like 40 below: Ibid.: The estimate of the temperature on the road was made by Calvetti. Wisconsin's Voyageur magazine also reported minus forty degree F temperature (in MS's "Night Before Music Died," p. 18).

237: trees snap in the wind: Calvetti quoted in BG, "Spotlight on 2/3/59," p. 7.

237: limbs crashing onto the highway: MS, "Night Before Music Died," Voyageur, p. 18.

237: piles up six feet deep: TA quoted in BG, "TA," p. 13.

237: The bus driver was no: Calvetti: quoted in BG, "Spotlight on 2/3/59," p. 7.

237: "feel" bears out there: MS, "Night Before Music Died," p. 18.

237: "newspapers in the aisle: Ibid.

237: hoping to hail down: Calvette quoted in BG, "Spotlight on 2/3/59," p. 7.

237: They stood in the middle: Ibid., p. 6.

237: French explorers, . . . who'd discovered: Bree, In Teeth of Northeaster, p. 20.

237: "We didn't know enough: TW, p. 87.

237: It was an hour: BG, "TA," p. 13.

237: started waving frantically: Calvetti quoted in BG, "Spotlight on 2/3/59," p. 6.

237: "and tried to get: BG, "TA," p. 13.

238: bone cancer: CB quoted in BG, "CB," p. 7.

238: It took two hours: Ibid.

238: alerted the Iron County: Quoted in BG, "TA," p. 13.

238: A posse came out: MS, "Night Before Music Died," p. 18; BG, "TA," p. 13.

238: refused to serve the black: Calvetti quoted in BG, "Spotlight on 2/3/59," p. 7.

238: Unable to walk, Carl: CB quoted in BG, "CB," p. 8.

238: Grand View Hospital: MS, "Night Before Music Died," p. 18; BG, "Spotlight on 2/3/59," p. 6.

238: between Ironwood and Bessemer: When I called the hospital in 1995, the operator explained, "Our mailing address is Ironwood. The hospital is located halfway between Ironwood and Bessemer."

238: frostbite in both feet: G&B, RB, p. 141; "TA," p. 13; BG, "CB," p. 8.

239: Chicago-Northwestern train: BG, "Spotlight on 2/3/59," p. 7. According to Albert Salonen, formerly of Ironwood, train service once linked Hurley to Green Bay and Chicago but was subsequently discontinued. BG bases his conviction that BH took the train on statements from Calvetti, TA, and Salonen.

239: purchase a sleeping bag: BG, "TA," p. 13.

239: case of the flu: WJEN quoted in BG, "18 Interviews (all at once)," p. 3; "TA," p. 13.

239: Ritchie substituted: "Chicago Scene," CT, 6/24/88.

239: One of the Belmonts played: TA quoted in BG, "TA," p. 12.

239: Buddy was the drummer: Ibid., according to MS, "Night Before Music Died," p. 24; BH also enlisted Bob Oestreich, who played drums with the Runabouts from Wausau, Wisconsin, to play in Bunch's absence in Green Bay.

239: "jump out there and: Quoted in RBHS.

239: "held my hand and sang: Quoted in MS, "Night Before Music Died," p. 17.

239: Valens was coming to Lubbock: Cited in BG, "Bits and Pieces," RM 20, 9/81, p. 5; EH quoted in BM, RV, p. 109.

239: supposed to have the following day off: G&B, RB, p. 141.

239: thirty-nine-year-old manager: Oestreicher and Kennedy, "CA," Rave On!, 4/80, p. 10.

240: "if he could get those: BG, "Bob Hale," RM 9, 12/78, p. 7.

240: "the star of that show": WJ, "CA," RM 4, 9/77, p. 4.

240: "just a high-class: Ibid.

240: "really clicking good,": BG, "TA," p. 13.
240: stop using the name: Author interview with BG.
240: same wretched GAC bus: "Death of Singers," CLMR, 2/5/59, p. 1; G&B, RB, p. 141.
240: replacement engine for: BG, "Spotlight on 2/3/59," p. 7.
240: "something happened": TA in ACOB.
240: minus-25-degree: Ibid.
240: to arrive at four P.M.: CA quoted in Oestreicher and Kennedy, "CA," p. 10.
240: they ditched the bus: TA in ACOB.
240: rented school bus: Ibid.
240: "did stay warm: Ibid.
240: "Buddy called from the tour: Author interview with MEH.
240: "Why don't you: "Chicago Scene," CT, 6/24/88.
240: audit of one of Petty's: TA quoted in G&B, RB, p. 138.
240: "infuriated,": Ibid.
241: Ritchie was as fed up: BM, RV, p. 108.
241: "skip out,": Ibid.
241: talking about chartering a: Ibid.
241: concerned that his fatigue: Ibid.
241: another long bus ride: Bob Hale quoted in "Chicago Scene," CT, 6/24/88.
241: at 7:30 or 7:45: Quoted in Oestreicher and Kennedy, "CA," p. 10.
241: the end of the sidewalk: Ibid., p. 12.
241: he'd take their dirty laundry: BG, "TA," p. 13.
241: "didn't want to take a chance: 2/5/59, p. 1.
242: Witke's Restaurant: CA quoted in WJ, "CA," RM 4, 9/77, p. 2.
242: joined by: Fuson, " 'La Bamba' Recalls Day Music Died Here in Iowa," Des Moines Sunday Register, 7/26/87, p. 1–8A.
242: "feel as if that was: Oestreicher and Kennedy, "CA," p. 10.
242: eighteen degrees: G&B, RB, p. 144.
242: "they talked about coming: " 'La Bamba' Recalls Day," p. 1-8A.
242: Anderson agreed to book the stars: Bob Hale in BG, RM 9, 12/78, p. 7.
242: Bob Hale hastened to invite: Ibid.
242: 6,300-square-foot rock-hard: "Enjoy the Convention at the Surf!"—promotional brochure.
242: drifting clouds: Gault, "Iowa's Surf Ballroom Features Drifting Clouds on Ceiling," Dancing USA, 2/84-3/84, p. 16.
242: twenty-two hundred patrons: "Enjoy the Convention at the Surf!"
242: pay telephone inside the lobby: Ibid.
242: the promoters had fulfilled: RB, p. 144.
243: "There's nobody else: Ibid.
243: As Ritchie telephoned: "Enjoy the Convention at the Surf!"
243: Buddy went into Anderson's: CA quoted in WJ, "CA," 9/77, p. 2.
243: "Will you find out: Quoted in Oestreicher and Kennedy, "CA," p. 10.
243: The Bopper joined them: Quoted in WJ, "CA," p. 2.
243: "It was the Big Bopper: Ibid.
243: they wanted to reach the Fargo airport: Ibid.
243: "a good night's rest: Ibid.
243: "How far is the: Quoted in Oestreicher and Kennedy, "CA," p. 10.

243: "encouraged Valens: CA quoted in WJ, "CA," p. 2.
243: Anderson attempted to reach: BG and BW, "RP Story," RM 18, 3/81, p. 6; G&B, RB, p. 142.
243: Jerry Dwyer, the owner: Ibid.
243: Someone at Dwyer's Flying: CA quoted in Oestreicher and Kennedy, "CA," p. 11.
243: $108 for a four-seat: BG, "Spotlight on 2/3/59," p. 7.
243: said they'd call back: Ibid.
243: the past seventeen hours: Van R. O'Brien, Washington, D.C., assistant chief of the Hearing and Reports Division, Civil Aeronautics Board, official investigation into the crash that killed Buddy Holly, quoted in "Study Plane Mishap: Testimony Leaves Cause of Crash 'Up In Clouds,' " MCGG, 2/19/59, p. 13.
243: following day, February 3, off: G&B, RB, p. 142; BG and BW, "RP Story," p. 6.
243: bride of four months: AP, "Pilot's Parents Can't Forget 'Day Music Died,' " MCGG, 2/5/88.
243: until 12:30 A.M., following: G&B, RB, p. 142.
244: Peterson was a Buddy Holly fan: "RP Story," p. 6.
244: "The young man was: Author interview with MEH.
244: "wanted to take these: "Investigator Offers Theory on Fatal Crash," 2/1/89, p. E-5.
244: "in the middle . . . could.": Quoted in AP (dateline: Alta, Ohio), "Pilot's Parents Can't Forget 'Day Music Died,' " MCGG, 2/5/88.
244: not qualified to fly: "Study Plane Mishap," MCGG, 2/19/59, p. 13.
244: His steady date at: BG and BW, "RP Story," p. 6.
244: "very popular" . . . "good Christian,": "RP Story," p. 6.
244: "A thoughtful, considerate: AP, "Pilot's Parents."
244: Art Peterson, Roger's father: BG and BW, "RP Story," p. 6.
244: pilot for Gate City Steel: Ibid.
244: cakes were "superb.": Quoted in ibid.
244: Ross Aviation . . . Graham Flying: Ibid.
245: hardly control . . . and less,": Quoted in official testimony, CAB investigation into crash cited in "Study Plane Mishap," MCGG, 2/19/59, p. 13.
245: to cope with vertigo: Ibid.
245: Peterson had failed his: Ibid.
245: went into a dive: Ibid.
245: "a proper holding procedure.": Ibid.
245: "holder does not meet": BG, "Spotlight on 2/3/59," p. 13; Frederick, "Fourth Star," Griggs, RM 4; "Instant Recall."
245: hired by Jerry Dwyer: BG and BW, "RP Story," p. 6.
245: accounting department of KGLO-TV: CA quoted in WJ, "CA," p. 3; "Four Killed in Clear Lake Plane Crash," MCGG, 2/3/59, p. 1.
245: made him a flying instructor: MCGG, 2/3/59.
245: 711 flying hours: Frederick, "Fourth Star," RM 4, 9/77, p. 4.
245: Jerry Dwyer didn't learn: G&B, RB, p. 144.
245: to help prepare the plane: Ibid.
245: three-and-a-half hour flight: FM quoted in WJ, "FM," p. 4.
245: eighteen degrees with snow flurries: "Crash Hearing Slated," unidentified newspaper clipping

on file at Mason City Municipal Airport.

246: "a gathering Midwest snow: "Singing Star's Body Due Here Today," 2/4/59, unpaged clipping.

Chapter 14

247: It was after eight P.M.: CA quoted in Oestreicher and Kennedy, "CA," p. 10.

247: "Backstage Band Room,": "Enjoy the Convention at the Surf!"

247: "said he was worried: Ibid.

247: 125 to 150 parents: Ibid.

247: gas turbine heaters: Author interview with Sue Christensen.

247: "catch a cold,": FM quoted in WJ, "FM," p. 4.

247: "three or four: Ibid.

247: Buddy leased the plane: WJEN quoted in BG, "18 Interviews (all at once)," p. 3.

247: the Bopper was on the list: CA quoted in WJ, "CA," p. 2; FM quoted in ibid., p. 4.

248: Though Tommy Allsup stated: BG, "TA," p. 13.

248: Milano told Wayne Jones: "FM," p. 4.

248: more people to share the charter fee: TW, p. 89.

248: cost him the equivalent of a month's rent" Ibid.

248: "Holly rounded up Ritchie,": Ibid.

248: Rod Lucier was still hopeful: "Singing Star's Body," LAJ.

248: "filled to the rafters.": Quoted in BG, "Bob Hale," RM 9, 12/78, p. 7.

248: Half a dozen floorwalkers: CA quoted in WJ, "CA," p. 3.

248: "dancing and listening": Quoted in Oestreicher and Kennedy, "CA," p. 10.

248: "I had my jeans: Author interview with Karen Lein.

248: "he can't help it if it's: AC, BH, No. 1, p. 43.

249 "It had the perfect: Ward, "Fifties," ROA, p. 193.

249 "Everybody was out on: Quoted in Hines, "Fans Got Last Glimpse of Holly: Concert-Goers Waved Goodbye at Airport," MCGG, 2/1/89, p. E-7.

249: gold record for "Donna": BM, RV, p. 108.

249: met at an Igniters: Ibid., p. 37.

249: gang dance: Ibid., p. 27. Louis "Skip" Raring, a classmate who lived near Ritchie, explained that "car clubs" such as the all-Anglo Igniters and Drifters and the all-Chicano club Lobos were "essentially . . . just gangs."

249: "Hi, blondie!": Ibid., p. 37.

249: They danced together: Ibid.

249: necked whenever they ran: DLF quoted in ibid., p. 56.

249: her father disapproved of: Freddie Aguilera in ibid., p. 56; DLF quoted in ibid., p. 115.

249: Donna sneaked out to: DLF quoted in ibid., p. 56.

249: too much of a "hassle": Ibid.

249: "You flirt too much,": "Girl Ritchie Left Behind," reprinted in AC, RV, No. 2, p. 45.

249: they split up: BM, RV, p. 56.

249: Ritchie dated Donna's girlfriend: Ibid.

249: wrote the song to get her back: Ibid.; Doug

Macchia, RV's classmate, quoted in Ibid., p. 41.

249: In September 1958: Hoffman, "We Belong Together," p. 34.

249: "Donnie . . . Listen: "Life and Death of RV," Modern Screen, 5/59, p. 38.

249: "Well, he began to: Hoffman, "We Belong Together," p. 34.

249: "We'd broken up about: "They Still Hear RV," Starlife, p. 46.

250: "walking Donna Ludwig to: "Girl Ritchie Left Behind," 16, 7/59, p. 45.

250: "I remember the Bopper,": Author interview with JW.

250: "The Bopper was really: Author interview with Karen Lein.

250: "screaming.": Quoted in Oestreicher and Kennedy, "CA," p. 10.

250: "almost blew the roof: Ibid.

250: fell at 10:30 P.M.: Ibid.

250: "and we came right: Ibid.

250: near as: Ibid.

250: "guy with the glasses: Quoted in BG, "Bob Hale," p. 7.

250: "My name is Mr. Holly: Ibid.

250: and told Hale that Buddy: Ibid.

250: "full of pep: "Death of Singers," p. 1.

250: "Let's confirm that,": Quoted in Oestreicher and Kennedy, "CA," p. 11.

250: plane would be ready: Ibid.

250: "but something happened,": TA quoted in BG, "TA," p. 13.

250: Buddy sang "Gotta Travel On,": IC.

251: "We drank beer . . . booze for you.": Author interview with JW.

251: wipe out tour packagers: BBH, pp. 252, 332; Ward, "Fifties," ROA, p. 245.

251: "It is a measure: Palmer, "Fifties," 4/19/90, p. 48.

251: "fantastic . . . just": Quoted in BG, "Bob Hale," p. 7.

251: "He'd made it this far: TW, p. 89.

251: "I dunno—I was just out: Author interview with JW.

252:"Thank God they never: Quoted in "Bob Hale," p. 7.

252: "There would never again: "Fifties," ROA, p. 245.

252: the final number performed: CA quoted in Oestreicher and Kennedy, "CA," p. 10.

252: ended at 11:55 P.M.: Ibid.

252: $250, thanks to: Quoted in Oestreicher and Kennedy, "CA," p. 11.

252: sixty percent of: Ibid.

252: "I'm down to only: Ibid.

252: "just rolled . . . up: Ibid.

252: Anderson offered Buddy: CA quoted in WJ, "CA," p. 2.

252: suffering from the flu: WJEN quoted in BG, "18 Interviews (all at once)," p. 3; BG, "TA," p. 13.

252: "He was a big man,": Ibid.

252: visit a doctor: RBHS.

252: his new sleeping: BG, "TA," p. 13.

252: if he could take: WJEN quoted in "18 Interviews (all at once)," p. 3.

252: "It's all right with: Quoted in Denisoff, Waylon, p. 66; slightly different version in BG, "18 Interviews (all at once)," p. 3.

252: Waylon was relieved to be: Quoted in ACOB.
252: the fun and the camaraderie: G&B, RB, p. 142.
252: driving Waylon "to drugs,": *Waylon*, video.
252: cold but again hesitated to: WJEN quoted in BM, RV, p. 108.
252: to have his hair cut: Quoted in "We Belong Together," p. 35.
252: remained ambivalent: BM, RV, pp. 25–26.
252: Guardian Angels church: *Ibid.*, p. 104.
253: "What'd you do if you: *Ibid.*
253: a premonition . . . of his career.": "We'll Remember Ritchie," p. 30.
253: "he wished he didn't have: "We Belong Together," p. 35.
253: "was starting to freeze: BG, "TA," p. 13.
253: "I've never been on a: BM, RV, p. 108; TA in RBHS.
253: Tommy shook his head and: TA quoted in "TA," p. 13. RV had asked TA two or three times; in RBHS TA said RV had been bugging him all night for the seat and TA had repeatedly refused.
253: dumped their belongings: TA quoted in BG, "TA", p. 13.
253: Anderson's wife Lucille: WJ, "CA," p. 2.
253: "go back" and make: Quoted in BG, "TA,", p. 13.
253: Ritchie, who was surrounded: *Ibid.*
253: accommodatingly signed their hands: Quoted in BG, "Spotlight on 2/3/59," p. 9.
253: "You going to let me: RBHS.
253: 50-cent piece: BG, "TA," p. 13.
253: "Let's flip a coin,": TA in RBHS.
253: "if you want to: *Ibid.*
253: he wanted to use the Bopper's: G&B, RB, p. 142.
253: "and no more was: BG, "TA," p. 13.
253: coin came up heads: TA in RBHS.
253: "You won the toss": *Ibid.*
253: Tommy asked Buddy to pick: *Ibid.*
254: "Here, take my wallet,": *Ibid.*
254: his nineteenth birthday: Helander, *Rock Who's Who*, p. 129.
254: At 12:05 A.M. Anderson": CA quoted in Oestreicher and Kennedy, "CA," p. 11.
254: frosted windows at the snow: *Ibid.*, author interview with JW.
254: a carload of fans: Author interview with Douglas Hines; Hines, "Fans Got Last Glimpse of Holly," p. E7.
254: driving on the highway dicey: Author interview with JW.
254: "it was spitting a trace: "CA," p. 3.
254: snowing "like mad,": BG, "Bob Hale," p. 7.
254: "We were on our way: Author interview with JW.
254: Mason City, which the stars: Stewart: *Plains States: Smithsonian Guide to Historic America*, p. 332.
254: " 'We had as much: Sheridan, "Death Cuts Short Meteoric Career for Lubbock Youth," 2/4/59.
255: deposited them at Dwyer's: CA quoted in JW, "CA," p. 2.
255: it was 12:15: Quoted in Oestreicher and Kennedy, "CA," p. 11.
255: mood was "jubilant": "BH Tribute: Fans Recall Day Music Died," undated clipping in Mason

City Municipal Airport files; CA quoted in Oestreicher and Kennedy, "CA," p. 11.
255: "charted through the CAA.": *Ibid.*
255: "snow blowing across the: Quoted in WJ, "CA," p. 3; slightly different version in Oestreicher and Kennedy, "CA," p. 11.
255: to see stars: CA quoted in Oestreicher and Kennedy, "CA," p. 11.
255: failed to warn: *Ibid.*; WJ, "CA," p. 3.
255: Buddy asked about the: *Ibid.*
255: from their homes to Fargo: CA quoted in Oestreicher and Kennedy, "CA," p. 11.
255: Rod Lucier was still: "Singing Star's Body," LAJ.
255: parked on the runway: BG, "Spotlight on 2/3/59," p. 13.
255: on runway 17: Jerome J. Thiele, director of aviation, Mason City Airport Commission.
255: single-engine airplane, N3794N: Frederick, "Airplane—N3794N," RM, Spring/83, p. 25. The serial number was D-1019.
255: perfect condition: "Study Plane Mishap," p. 13.
255: pronounced it "fit,": "Investigator Offers Theory," p. E6.
256: "little spiffs": Quoted in WJ, "CA," p. 3.
256: "snow showers": Quoted in JT, "Investigator Offers Theory," p. E6.
256: "That Buddy Holly: Quoted in Hoffman, "We Belong Together, p. 35.
256: "stretch their evening with: Hines, "Fans Got Last Glimpse."
256: "like crazy teenagers.": *Ibid.*
256: pilot was the first: Quoted in Oestreicher and Kennedy, "CA," p. 11.
256: "Holly, why don't you": *Ibid.*
256: he'd forgotten his briefcase: *Ibid.*
256: "picked it up.": *Ibid.*
256: "Who knows how long: *Ibid.*
256: shook hands with Anderson: *Ibid.*
256: two alarming weather advisories: RB, p. 144.
256: failed his latest instrument: BG, "Spotlight on 2/3/59," p. 13.
256: "Holder does not meet: *Ibid.*
256: "beautiful snow": "Fans Got Last Glimpse."
256: "good luck," Anderson later: Quoted in "BH Tribute: Fans Recall Day Music Died," MCGG, 6/1/84, unpaged clipping in files of Mason City Municipal Airport.
256: Dwyer stood in the: 6/24/88; BW and BG, "RP Story," p. 6.
256: waiting for Peterson to call in: BG, "Spotlight on 2/3/59," p. 11.
257: "had taken a nap": "Study Plane Mishap," p. 13.
257: had checked weather: *Ibid.*, p. 2.
257: The wind was from: Collison, "Open Probe of Accident Here," MCGG, 2/5/59.
257: temperature . . . dew point eleven: "Coroner's Investigation."
257: "if there had been: "Study Plane Mishap," p. 13.
257: Billie Rose pulled away: Hines, "Fans Got Last Glimpse."
257: Peterson radioed the tower: RES, "Coroner's Investigation."
257: "incomplete," both the CAB: P&T, "Lingering Mysteries of Holly's Fatal Flight," MCGG, 1/29/89.

257: Peterson told the tower: RES, "Coroner's Investigation."

257: takeoff occurred at "0040-0100": Files of Air Traffic Communication Station, located atop Administration Building, Mason City Municipal Airport.

257: about one A.M.: BG, "Spotlight," on 2/3/59, p. 11.

257: Dwyer, in the tower: CT, 6/24/88.

257: Anderson, on the ground: BW and BG, "RP Story," p. 6.

257: "Ironically," a reporter: 2/4/59.

257: Lucille and Tom: CA quoted in Oestreicher and Kennedy, "CA," p. 11.

257: In the tower, Dwyer waited: CT, 6/24/88.

257: with mounting anxiety: G&B, RB, p. 145.

257: radio silence: RES, "Coroner's Investigation."

257: " 'It looks like it just: CT, 6/24/88.

257: thought it was going up: "Lingering Mysteries."

257: "In any Beechcraft Bonanza: "Spotlight on 2/3/59," p. 14.

257: Peterson had encountered the: BG, "Sheriff Allen," RM 13, 12/79, p. 6.

257: may have lost visual reference: Ibid.

257: nothing was visible but snow: P&T, "Lingering Mysteries."

257: "terrible snowstorm reference.": Ibid.

258: "can either go: "Investigator Offers Theory."

258: Peterson looked at the gauges: P&T, "Lingering Mysteries."

258: His chronic vertigo: Lambert Fechter, flight instrument instructor, in testimony before the CAB, quoted in "Study Plane Mishap."

258: read the gyroscope backward: Ibid.; LH quoted in BG, "Spotlight on 2/3/59," p. 14.

258: crash under full power: P&T, "Lingering Mysteries."

258: "Woke out of a sound: Quoted in BG, "Spotlight," p. 13.

258: "motor was working: Ibid.

258: realized his mistake too late: Duane Mayfield quoted in "Investigator Offers Theory"; author interview with Jerome J. Thiele.

258: frantic prayers: Dodge, Not Fade Away, p. 160.

258: The plane came in level: "Sheriff Allen," p. 6.

258: cruising speed: Terry, "Bob Booe Remembers 2/3/59," RM 29, Winter/84, p. 23.

258: was 172 miles per hour: RM 26, Spring/83, p. 25; BG, "Sheriff Allen," p. 6.

258: landing gear was still retracted: BG, "Spotlight," p. 13.

258: the fuselage split open: "Bob Booe," p. 22.

258: shot from the wreck: Ibid.

258: flying seventeen feet: RES, "Coroner's Investigation," p. 1.

259: the crater it had dug: "Four Killed in Clear Lake Plane Crash," MCGG, 2/3/59, p. 1.

259: left wing snagged the: Ibid.; Bob Booe quoted in Terry, "Bob Booe," p. 22.

259: a furrow fifty feet: I have recreated the path of the plane across the field using a compendium of contemporary accounts, although these sometimes differ in detail. Main sources: Author interview with Elwin L. Musser; MCGG; CLMR; Sheriff Jerry Allen in BG, RM 13; Kevin Terry's "Bob Booe"; Deputy Sheriff Duane Mayfield in JT's "Investigator Offers Theory."

259: crumpling off: Bob Booe quoted in Terry, "Bob Booe," p. 22.

259: then cartwheeled: Ibid.

259: reduced to a ball: Author interview with Elwin L. Musser, who photographed the wreck; Bob Booe quoted in Terry, "Bob Booe," p. 22; RES in "Coroner's Investigation," p. 1 ("The shape of the mass of wreckage approximated a ball").

259: Five hundred seventy feet: RES, "Coroner's Investigation," p. 1.

259: crashed into the fence line: Ibid.; author interview with Elwin L. Musser.

259: "40 feet from the: RES, "Coroner's Investigation," p. 1.

259: skull cracked open from his forehead: RES, "Charles Hardin Holley (born 9/7/36, SSN 450-58-5172): Certificate of Death, 2/4/59," Iowa State Department of Health, Division of Vital Statistics.

259: Half of his brain tissue: RES wrote on Buddy's death certificate, "approximately half the brain tissue was absent."

259: blood gushed from both: Ibid.

259: His face was disfigured: Ibid.

259: his chest was soft: Ibid.

259: His left forearm was: Ibid.

259: "There was a small: Ibid.

259: for ten hours after: G&B, RB, pp. 144–45; "Four Killed in Clear Lake Plane Crash," p. 1; "Death of Singers Here Shocks Nation," CLMR, 2/5/59, p. 1; BG, "Spotlight," p. 11; JT, "Investigator Offers Theory"; RES, "Coroner's Investigation."

259: drifts formed around: RES, "Coroner's Investigation," p. 1.

259: "Some parts of each: Ibid.

259: Scattered all about them: P&T, "Lingering Mysteries"; BG, "Spotlight," p. 8; RES, "Coroner's Report of Investigation (From 205-G), Richard Valenzuela, 2/3/59"; BG, "Sheriff Allen," p. 6.

259: Ritchie had landed: RES, "Coroner's Investigation," p. 1; Certificate of Death, 2/3/59, Richard (unknown) Valenzuela, born 5/13/41, SSN 560-54-7403, Iowa State Department of Health, Division of Vital Statistics.

259: threw him into the adjoining: RES, "Coroner's Investigation," p. 1; Certificate of Death, 2/4/59, Jiles P. Richardson, born 10/24/30, SSN 456-34-6417, Iowa State Department of Health, Division of Vital Statistics.

259: sticking upside down: RES, "Coroner's Investigation," p. 1; Certificate of Death, 2/4/59, Roger A. Peterson, born 5/24/37, SSN 479-48-9009, Iowa State Department of Health, Division of Vital Statistics.

259: one foot jutting: CA quoted in WJ, "CA," p. 3.

259: body was wrapped around: Bob Booe quoted in Terry, "Bob Booe," p. 23; "Four Killed," p. 1; "Death of Singers," p. 1.

259: skin had been flayed: RES, Roger Peterson AUTOPSY: A-8-59, AUTOPSIED: 4/Feb/59, PATHOLOGIC DIAGNOSES . . . PROTOCOL, p. 1.

259: brain stem had been destroyed: Ibid.

260: gross trauma to the brain: Certificates of Death, Ibid.

260: subfreezing weather: RES, "Coroner's Investigation," p. 1; BW and BG, "RP Story," p. 6.

260: 5.4 miles north: Map of crash site, Surf Ball-room, courtesy Bruce Christensen.

260: Airport issued an alert: G&B, RB, p. 145.

260: "early morning fog,": "Four Killed," p. 1.

260: raises questions: G&B, RB, p. 144, re: weather advisories; BG, "Spotlight," p. 12, re: errors in the official CAB report.

260: it didn't have to happen: Author interview with Mason City Municipal Airport Aviation Director Jerome J. Thiele re pilot errors; "Study Plane Mishaps," MCGG, p. 13; P&T, "Lingering Mysteries," MCGG; AP, "Pilot's Parents," MCGG; LH quoted in BG, "LH," p. 9; "For RV: $1½ Million Lawsuit in Local Plane Crash," unidentified newspaper clipping dated 6/26/59, Mason City Municipal Airport files, re: lawsuits; BG, "Spotlight," p. 13, re: lawsuits.

260: The Civil Aeronautics Board eventually: P&T, "Lingering Mysteries."

260: "There's a plane down.": Author interview with JW.

260: seems to corroborate Weddell's testimony: Hines, "Fans Got Last Glimpse of Holly," MCGG, 2/1/89, p. E7, courtesy Jerome J. Thiele, director of aviation, Mason City Airport Commission, Mason City Municipal Airport; author interview with Douglas Hines.

260: "It really blew our: Quoted in Hines, "Fans Got Last Glimpse," p. E7.

260: Dwyer attempted to reach: RB, p. 145.

261: hazy, chilly day: Booe quoted in Terry, "Bob Booe," p. 22.

261: a two-seat Champ: Ibid.

261: twenty-five feet from the ground: Ibid.

261: At 9:35 A.M., eight and a half: Dwyer to CAB, quoted in RB, p. 145.

261: "about 9:00 A.M.,": "Coroner's Investigation," p. 1.

261: around 8:40 A.M. when: "Investigator Offers Theory."

261: "just after I got: Author interview with Elwin L. Musser.

261: Buddy's yellow leather jacket: RES, Certificate of Death.

261: "Jerry said, 'They're in a pasture: Quoted in "Bob Booe," p. 22.

261: A ham radio operator: BG, "Spotlight," p. 11; G&B, RB, p. 146.

261: Lou Giordano telephoned: MEH in BG, "ME," RM 4, 9/77, p. 9.

261: "When I got the: Author interview with MEH.

261: radio on or was watching: BG, "Spotlight," p. 14; MEH quoted in G&B, RB, p. 146.

261: Aunt Provi entered the room: MEH quoted in G&B, RB, p. 146.

261: psychological trauma: Parade, 12/8/91.

262: Ella Holley screamed and collapsed: Author interview with KJ.

262: "Put the radio on,": BG, "Spotlight," p. 14.

262: "an airplane crash in: Author interview with KJ.

262: "Oh, no! It can't: Ibid.

262: "Maybe it was just: Author interview with KJ.

262: "The Lord figured He: Author interview with LH.

262: "God doesn't go around: "CB," p. 8.

262: "Honey, what are you: Ibid.

263: "A cult is a phenomenon: Dalton, James Dean: Mutant King, p. 310.

263: "That was a miserable: Fink, "Don McLean," RM 43, 7/86, p. 8.

263: "Buddy Holly was the first: P. F. Kluge cited in Billboard Book of Number One Hits, p. 305.

263: "American Pie," the biggest record: Whitburn, Billboard Book of Top 40 Hits, p. 474.

263: Governor Morehead School: Milsap with Carter, Almost Like a Song, p. 17.

263: "He sounded so sincere": Ibid., p. 69.

263: overly strict music teacher: Ibid., p. 50.

263: both boys were banned: Ibid.

263: "I mean, I'll never: TRSI, p. 98.

263: "The music of the late: Newsweek, 1974, cited in G&B, RB, p. 161.

264: "We didn't have school: Author interview with JW.

264: "I just lifted the needle: " 'La Bamba' Recalls Day Music Died Here in Iowa," 7/26/87, p. 1.

264: DeAnn Peterson was at: Quoted in WJ, "CA," p. 3.

264: "I was young and: "Pilot's Parents Can't Forget."

264: Eventually she would move: Ibid.

264: Allison out of a deep: BG, "SC," RM 17, 12/80, p. 12.

264: "Hey, man, I've got: Quoted in BG, "JA—Part Two," RM 24, p. 9.

264: from Clovis the previous night: PS quoted in BG, "PS," pp. 9–10.

264: "I thought that there might: Quoted in "JA—Part Two," p. 9.

264: a publicity stunt: JBM on "Instant Recall."

264: " 'No, no, go out: Ibid.

264: It was Jerry who: Brooks and Malcolm, "NP—Part 3," p. 6; BG, "NP," p. 8.

264: "Catastrophic": Quoted in BG, "NP," p. 8.

265: "and the phones never stopped ringing.": BG, "Robert Linville," p. 4.

265: "It depends," said Petty: BG, "Snuff Garrett—2/3/59," RM 29, Winter/84, p. 26.

265: New York Daily News: AC, BB, p. 23.

265: "Did you hear: WJ, "Dick Jacobs," RM 36, 5/85, pp. 9–10.

265: "Crazy, isn't it: Quoted in Hoffman, "We Belong Together," p. 35.

265: "Unchained Melody": Pareles and Romanowski, Rolling Stone Encyclopedia of Rock 'n' Roll, p. 237.

265: "We always fought: unidentified column dated 2/9/59 reproduced in AC, BB, p. 24.

266: "You'd better sit down: "Girl Ritchie Left Behind," 16, 7/59, p. 44.

266: "The macabre fascination: Hines, "Fans Got Last Glimpse," p. E-7.

266: Allen was away in St. Louis: JT, "Investigator Offers Theory," p. E-6.

266: patrol cars carrying reporters: RES, "Coroner's Investigation," p. 1.

266: Life magazine had already requested: BG, RM 32, Fall/84, p. 11.

266: Souvenir hunters wanted to: "Investigator Offers Theory."

266: At 11:15—ten hours: RES, "Coroner's Investigation," p. 1.

266: black Cadillac hearses: Elwin L. Musser photograph.

266: wallet in his pocket: TA in RBHS; RES, "Coroner's Investigation."

266: "As far as I know: "CA," p. 3.

266: listed Tommy Douglas Allsup: RES, "Coroner's Investigation," p. 1; BG, "TA," p. 13.

267: "It was my first: BG, "Spotlight," p. 13.

267: "The wire services were: Author interview with Elwin L. Musser.

267: Mortitians Van Slyker: Ibid.; Musser photo in BG, "Spotlight," p. 12.

267: "gathered Buddy up": WJ, "CA," p. 3.

267: The police were hesitant: RES, "Coroner's Investigation," p. 1.

267: They decided to wait: Ibid.: RES wrote that only three bodies were removed before he left. RP's body could not be removed until permission was granted by the inspector for the CAB and FAA. On p. 2 of Smiley's report he states that field representatives of the CAB did not arrive at the crash site until "the evening of February 3rd. They visited the scene of the crash for preliminary survey before dark that day." In "Death of Singers," a CLMR journalist wrote on 2/5/59, p. 1, that the investigators did not arrive in Clear Lake until "late Tuesday."

267: Guards were posted: JT, "Investigator Offers Theory."

267: field representatives headed by: RES, "Coroner's Investigation," p. 2.

267: From the $193: Coroner's Report of Investigation: Coroner's Transcript of Fees—To County Auditor (Form 205-G), Coroner's Transcript 1784, Investigation of Death of Charles H. Holley, filed 2/18/59, approved 3/2/59, by Elmer Luscomb; Transcript 1783 (JPR); Transcript 1782 (RP); Transcript 1785 (RV).

268: were arterially embalmed: George T. Joyce, M.D., pathologist, "Microscopic Description," p. 4 of RP autopsy.

268: G. W. Wilcox Funeral Home: Coroner's Report of Investigation, Coroner's Transcripts 1784, 1782.

268: the Ward Funeral Home: Ibid., Transcripts 1785, 1783.

268: his tattoo, "R.V.": Certificate of Death.

268: They still weren't sure: CA quoted in WJ, "CA," p. 3.

268: Larry Holley reveals in a 1992: Author interview with LH.

268: Peterson was the only one: "Spotlight," p. 12.

268: various controversies: Author interview with JP, former MCGG reporter; "Pistol in Plane Wreck Not Fired," MCGG, 4/30/59, p. 14; "Revolver Found at Crash Scene," unidentified clipping in Mason City Municipal Airport files; JT, "Investigator Offers Theory"; P&T, "Lingering Mysteries"; BG, "Spotlight," p. 12.

268: four autopsies were done: BG, "Spotlight,"p. 12.

268: " 'missing': Jerry Dwyer quoted in ibid.

268: or covered up,": BG, Ibid.

268: Mercy Hospital in Mason City: Coroner's Report of Investigation, Transcript 1782.

268: the amount of crushing: RP Autopsy, p. 1.

268: "multiple small fragments: Ibid.

268: "$100 autopsy fee: Coroner's Report of Investigation, Transcript 1782.

268: Hundreds of students throughout: Hoffman, "We Belong Together," p. 34.

268: pink stucco house at 13423: Ibid.

268: "We finally got in: BM, RV, p. 111.

268: Concepcion sitting beside: Ibid., pp. 110–111.

269: pride and self-respect: Hoffman, "We Belong Together," p. 34.

269: Concepcion rocked back and forth: DLF quoted in BM, RV, p. 111.

269: clinging to her: "Girl Ritchie Left Behind," 16, p. 45.

269: "I was so proud: Quoted in Hoffman, "We Belong Together," p. 34.

269: at one A.M. Wednesday: "Investigator Offers Theory."

269: "while they were in: Ibid.

269: shipped to California: "Death of Singers."

269: Morales and Bob Keene identified: RV, p. 111.

269: Nobel Chapel Funeral Home: Certificate of Death.

269: black sweater and black skirt: Hoffman, "We Belong Together," p. 34.

269: flag was at half: Ibid.

269: St. John de la Salle: Ibid.

269: Bob Keene said he paid: Keene quoted in BM, RV, p. 111.

269: Requiem Mass was celebrated: AC, RV, No. 2, p. 28.

269: dismal and damp, a thousand: BM, RV, pp. 112–113.

269: Chicano crowd to riot: Ibid., p. 119.

269: Donna Ludwig knocked a photographer's: DLF quoted in ibid., p. 112.

269: Ritchie and Donna had broken up: John Alcaraz, Freddie Aguilera, and DLF quoted in ibid., p. 56.

269: "my silly father: Quoted in ibid., pp. 115–116.

270: wore a black scarf: Photo on p. 26, AC, RV, No. 2.

270: "a good boy: "Life and Death of RV," Modern Screen, p. 39.

270: modest brown casket: 8/60, reprinted in AC, Tribute to Eddie Cochran, p. 20.

270: The officiant, Reverend: AC, RV, No. 2, p. 26.

270: "O gentlest Heart of: Ibid.

270: crew-cut youth from: Sherlock, "We'll Remember Ritchie," Teen, 5/59, reprinted in AC, RV, No. 2, p. 30.

270: "honorary member": "Life and Death of RV," Modern Screen, p. 39.

270: "and cried like a baby: RV, p. 113.

270: No stone would mark: Ibid., p. 122.

270: The stone was engraved: AC, RV, No. 2, p. 26.

271: Broussard Funeral Home in: Certificate of Death.

271: wife arrived from New Orleans: "Death of Singers."

271: blurted over KTRM,: Gordon Baxter in Thomas, "Gordon Baxter," p. 6.

271: "a horrible thing,": Ibid.

271: Bopper's guitar to Dion: 2/60.

271: Presley and Col. Tom Parker: "Texas Concert Will Honor BB," MCGG, 2/1/89.

271: photographer from Life: Hill, "BB," p. 4.

271: "bodily ejected": Ibid.

271: "the other side: Quoted in Thomas, "Gordon Baxter," p. 5.

271: Baxter ran the: Ibid., p. 6.

271: "a spiritual kind of: Ibid.

271: "a sacred offering with: 3/1/59, reprinted in AC, BB, No. 3, p. 25.

271: Roger Peterson had two funerals: "Death of Singers," p. 1; BW and BG, "RP Story," p. 6.

272: "If it wouldn't be for those: "Pilot's Parents Can't Forget."

272: "a delicious lunch: Quoted in BW and BG, "RP Story," p. 6.

272: "The music doesn't bother: "Pilot's Parents Can't Forget."

272: West Texas Aircraft and: BG, "Spotlight," p. 14.

272: "I just wanted to remember: Author interview with LH.

272: "laughing, hollering, and: LH quoted in BG, "LH," p. 9.

272: He took one look: Author interview with LH.

272: They drove out to: Ibid.

272: scraps of metal since shortly: Collison, "Open Probe of Accident Here," MCGG, 2/5/59, unpaged clipping.

272: It was snowing: Sheriff Jerry Allen quoted in BG, "Sheriff Allen," RM 13, 12/79, p. 5.

272: The FAA team, Eugene: photographs in the MCGG, 2/4/59.

272: "faintest idea": "Four Killed in Clear Lake," p. 1.

272: In Dwyer's estimation, the: Ibid.

272: could wind up with only one: Collison, "Open Probe."

272: "We went out in the snow: Author interview with LH.

272: "They had just installed: BG, "LH," p. 9.

273: "misread the instruments": "Lingering Mysteries."

273: "It was a very: Author interview with LH.

273: "These are Buddy's: Quoted in BG, "Spotlight," p. 10.

273: "Just as I was leavin': Author interview with LH.

273: Garrison Keillor: TV newscast, Tifton, Georgia, 8/93.

273: Buddy's pistol would remain: "Pistol in Plane Wreck Not Fired," 4/10/59, p. 14.

273: loaded on a flatbed trailer: CA quoted in WJ, "CA," p. 3.

273: "silverish—a metallic gray: Author interview with NS.

273: had to be grounded: BG, "Spotlight," p. 14.

273: "They had Buddy's music: Author interview with LH.

274: "It was real sad: Author interview with TC.

274: Maria Elena flew from: Author interview with MEH.

274: "killer storm": "Storm Slashes Into East," LAJ, 2/4/59, p. 1.

274: "heavy sheet ice: "Sun Cracks Icy Mantle in Texas," LAJ, 2/3/59, p. 1.

275: "new surge of arctic: "Storm Slashes," p. 1.

275: Waylon Jennings's wife: Ibid.

275: Larry Wilburn and Bobby Burgess: LAJ, 2/4/59, unpaged clipping.

275: "hurried way": Ibid.

275: "buddying up": Freeman Hoover interview, 11/2/57.

275: "only one person: Author interview with TC.

275: Niki to be a pallbearer: NS quoted. in BG, "Buddy's Funeral," RM 8, 9/78, p. 1.

276: a capacity crowd of fifteen hundred: Author interview with KJ.

276: "flew down: Quoted in TRSI, pp. 146–47.

276: had a framed twelve-by-fourteen-inch: Author interview with KJ; "BH Rites Are Held in City," LAJ, 2/7/59.

276: pallbearers included Sonny Curtis: LW quoted in BG, "LW," RM 45, 11/86, p. 16.

276: two of the Roses: Robert Linville in BG, "Clovis's Own Robert Linville," p. 4.

276: Niki Sullivan sat between: NS quoted in BG, "Buddy's Funeral," p. 1.

276: Norman Petty, despite: NP quoted in BG, "NP," RM 32, Fall/84, p. 8.

276: Vi Petty, who just: Author interview with TC.

276: Peggy Sue nervously scanned: PS quoted in BG, "PS," p. 10; BG, R50, 2/89, p. 14.

276: "heavy density of teenagers,": LAJ, 2/8/59; BG, R50, 2/89, p. 14.

276: to sit by herself: PS quoted in BG, "PS," p. 10.

276: "The thing I remember: Ibid.

276: "His bride of less: LAJ, 2/8/59.

276: "I was in Lubbock, but: Author interview with MEH.

277: "There was one pew: Author interview with KJ.

277: "surprised and amazed": NS quoted in BG, R50 11, p. 7.

277: "Ever'body was tryin' to: Author interview with TC.

277: Bill Pickering sang "Beyond: Bill Pickering quoted in BG, "Bill Pickering," RM 21, 12/81, p. 8.

277: "What lies beyond the: Sanville, 40 Gospel Hymn Stories in Horstman, Sing Your Heart Out, Country Boy, p. 39

277: "I don't think the service: NS quoted in BG, "Buddy's Funeral," p. 1.

277: Sunday morning church service: Ibid.

277: "Brother [Ben] Johnson had: Author interview with KJ.

277: "I had never heard: BG, "Bill Pickering," p. 8.

277: long a favorite of Buddy's: G&B, RB, p. 147.

277: passed in front of: NS quoted in BG, "Buddy's Funeral," p. 1.

277: shown no emotion throughout: Ibid.

278: "made it easier: Ibid.

278: Joe B. still thought Buddy: JBM in RBHS.

278: had to go back inside: BG, "Buddy's Funeral," p. 1.

278: Peggy Sue could stand: PS quoted in BG, "PS," p. 10.

278: unable to face the cemetery: Ibid.

278: "sat mostly in silence: "Buddy Holly Rites Are Held in City": LAJ, undated clipping.

278: "There were some tears: NS quoted in BG, "Buddy's Funeral," p. 1.

278: gave them the letter: Terry Noland quoted in BG, "Terry Noland," p. 7.

278: "hating rock 'n' roll: Bob Church, quoted in ibid.

278: "that changed everything: Terry Noland quoted in ibid.

278: "Up to this date: Author interview with MEH.

278: she his eternal bride: MEH told Parade magazine on 12/8/91 that she hadn't changed since the day of BH's death, that although she underwent many changes, it was as if she were walking in her sleep.

278: "to you who for refuge: Author unknown, early American melody, Soul-Stirring Songs & Hymns, Rice and Martin, compilers, p. 154.

278: "They definitely felt that": BG, RM 11, p. 7.
279: Some of them gathered: Author interview with TC.
279: "We all then went: NS quoted in "Buddy's Funeral," p. 1.
279: "Brother Johnson, I want: Author interview with KJ.
279: The original tombstone: BG, "Buddy in Bronze!" RM 17, 12/80, p. 1.
279: an upright guitar: BG, "Reader's Forum," RM 23, 6/82, p. 3.

Chapter 15

283: pilot error: BG, "Spotlight," p. 13; P&T, "Lingering Mysteries"; Mann, A–Z of Buddy Holly, p. 30.
283: rumors of foul play: BG, "Spotlight," pp. 11–13.
283: Delbert Juhl's father: Author interview with BG.
283: finally turned up the gun: "Pistol in Plane Wreck," p. 14.
283: "while clearing small bits: "Revolver Found at Crash Scene," undated and unidentified clipping (probably MCGG) in files of Mason City Municipal Airport, courtesy Jerome J. Thiele; "Pistol in Plane Wreck."
283: pistol were empty: "Revolver Found."
283: rumors spread: BG, "Spotlight," p. 9.
283: "there were no shells: "Revolver Found."
283: "fired all four bullets: Ibid.
283: "only one shot had: BG "Spotlight," p. 9.
283: Stillwagon, was solely interested: BG, "Spotlight," p. 13.
283: report was "pretty sloppy.": Ibid., p. 12.
283: than candy wrappers: Ibid.
283: no drug tests were: RES quoted in ibid., p. 12.
283: after arterial embalming: Ibid.; Dr. George T. Joyce, "RP, Autopsy A-8-59. Autopsied 4 Feb 59," "Microscopic Description—Comment."
283: Blood tests can only: BG, "Spotlight," p. 12.
283: Dwyer denied that the: Quoted in ibid., p. 11.
284: "my pilot was incapacitated: Ibid.
284: "There was more than: Quoted in ibid., p. 12.
284: "I could tell the: Quoted in ibid.
284: was adopted on September 15, 1959: Ibid., p. 13.
284: "we didn't see the report": Ibid.
284: Stillwagon had "overruled": Ibid.
284: "people to move around: Ibid.
284: CAB found that the heaviest: Ibid.
284: the Bopper—was sitting: Ibid.
284: the implication is that Buddy Holly: Ibid.
284: Jerry Dwyer "simply doesn't: Ibid., p. 12.
284: dismissed charges of drug: Ibid.
284: Jeremy Powers, a reporter who: Author interview with JP.
284: plane was sold for scrap: CAB report quoted in BG, "Spotlight," p. 13.
284: "The plane is out here: Lisa Latham and Shelley Allison of Clear Lake, both employees at Mason City Municipal Airport.
285: "It was snowing," . . . "The: Author interview with Jerome J. Thiele.
285: suddenly and mysteriously dropped: BG, "Spotlight," p. 13.
285: Ritchie's mother sued Dwyer: "For Richie [sic]

Valens: $1½ Million Lawsuit in Local Plane Crash," unidentified clipping (probably MCGG) in files of Mason City Municipal Airport, dated 6/26/59, courtesy Jerome J. Thiele.
285: $50,000 from Dwyer's insurance: BG, "Spotlight," p. 13.
285: "The aviation industry was: Author interview with Cy Egan.
285: "His loss was all: Quoted in Denisoff, Waylon, p. 75.
285: The tour manager went into the hotel: WJEN quoted in BG, "18 Interviews (all at once)," p. 3.
285: "Come outside: Ibid.
285: and asked for Buddy Holly's room: TA on "Instant Recall."
285: "Haven't you heard?": Ibid.
286: " 'Boys, they didn't make: "18 Interviews (all at once)," p. 3; G&B, RB, p. 146.
286: "felt guilty," as if: Waylon video.
286: responsible for the accident: Edwards, AP, "Waylon Thinks About Buddy Every Day," MCGG, 6/1/84.
286: "go home,": WJEN quoted in BG, "18 Interviews (all at once)," p. 3.
286: "tough reckoning with himself: with Carter, Reba, p. 257.
286: Tommy found a telephone: TA quoted in BG, "TA," p. 13.
286: "I went crazy: Quoted in Denisoff, Waylon, p. 70.
286: hunched before the TV: TW, p. 89.
286: "There were no survivors": Ibid.
286: "All around me were: Ibid., pp. 89–90.
286: Fred Milano of the Belmonts was sound: FM quoted in "FM," p. 4.
286: "The plane had crashed: Ibid.
286: accompany Buddy's body: Denisoff, Waylon, p. 71.
286: "the people from New York called: CT, 6/24/88.
286: The promoters promised to fly: BM, RV, p. 111.
286: GAC later reneged: G&B, RB, p. 147.
286: Bobby Vee, who lived in: Lazell, Rock Movers & Shakers, p. 527.
286: had been looking forward: Vee, I Remember BH, Liberty LP liner notes, LST-7336.
287: had formed a band: Ibid.
287: Jim Stillman, called the: "Bobby Vee," Clovis Music Festival Official Program, p. 12.
287: christened themselves the Shadows: Vee, I Remember BH.
287: "It was a very bizarre: Larson, "Bobby Vee," RM 15, 6/80, p. 12.
287: audience burst into sobs: Denisoff, Waylon, p. 72.
287: Tommy Allsup seemed a million: Ibid.
287: staring blankly: Ibid.
287: wire service correspondents: AP dispatch, "Show Goes on Despite Death of 3," Independent Journal, 2/4/59 (city not specified, clipping found in files of Mason City Municipal Airport).
287: were properly lit: Vee quoted in Larson, "Bobby Vee," p. 13.
287: Bing Bingstrom: Lazell, Rock Movers & Shakers, p. 527.
287: "were trying to hold back: "FM," p. 4.
287: "screamed, clapped, and whistled: "Show Goes," Independent Journal.

287: "paid tribute to the: *Ibid.*
287: increasing uneasiness as Dion: Williams, "A Star Dies, Another Is Born," *Movieland and TV Time,* 4/61, reprinted in AC, BH, No. 1, p. 54.
287: "and he saw the audience: *Ibid.*
287: Everly Brothers, Little Richard: Vee quoted in Larson, "Bobby Vee," p. 12.
287: Discovered by Bing Bingstrom: Lazell, *Rock Movers & Shakers,* p. 527.
287: "a fair-sized hit": Bobby Vee, *I Remember BH.*
287: Snuff Garrett, who recorded: Lazell, *Rock Movers & Shakers,* p. 527.
288: "Our style was modeled: Bobby Vee, *I Remember BH.*
288: "But then," Tommy later: *Waylon,* p. 72.
288: promoters announced they were: WJEN quoted in G&B, RB, p. 147.
288: "This, after begging us: *Ibid.*
288: canceled one of the: *Ibid.*
288: in Sioux City, Iowa: *Ibid.*; CB quoted in BG, "CB," p. 8.
288: the Shore Acres ballroom: insert in *Playbill,* Shubert Theatre, *Buddy,* 5/91, Vol. 91, No. 5.
288: including Ronnie Smith, who: G&B, RB, p. 147: CB quoted in BG, "CB," p. 7.
288: "I always felt that: BG, "Jimmy Clanton," RM 13, 12/79, p. 11.
288: "eerie,": *Ibid.*
288: Frankie Avalon: Nite, *Rock On,* pp. 19–20.
289: dropped him during the: Stallings, *Rock-'n'-Roll Confidential,* p. 89.
289: substantial interests in music: Pareles and Romanowski, *Rolling Stone Encyclopedia of Rock 'n' Roll,* p. 103.
289: "too hurt, too sad: CB quoted in BG, "CB," p. 8.
289: Ronnie Smith assisted Waylon; Denisoff, *Waylon,* p. 72.
289: tried to play Buddy's: CB quoted in BG, "CB," p. 8.
289: Waylon's applause matched Frankie: Denisoff, *Waylon,* p. 73.
289: "it was a different: Quoted in BG, "Frankie Sardo," R50, 4/92, p. 22.
289: teenager named Doug McLeod: Author interview with HG.
289: "Shock permeated the atmosphere,": Quoted in "Personal Remembrances," IC, 1/31/87, Val Air Ballroom, Des Moines, Iowa, Easter Seal Society of Iowa, Inc.
289: "nervous enough": HG, "Doug McLeod Remembers Last Tour," RM 29, Winter/84, p. 13.
289: betrayed him: G&B, RB, p. 147.
289: bus to Chicago: Denisoff, *Waylon,* p. 73.
289: he'd been drinking vodka: *Ibid.*
289: Tommy Allsup spiked his: *Ibid.,* p. 74.
289: Ronnie had acquired in: *Ibid.,* p. 73.
290: "After the first one: *Ibid.,* p. 74.
290: "We gave it all: TA quoted in *ibid.*
290: Petty immediately sought an: *Ibid.*
290: Maria Elena arranged a: Quoted in BG, "CB," p. 8.
290: "flesh peddlers.": Quoted in Denisoff, *Waylon,* p. 75.
290: "he blamed Norman Petty: *Ibid.*
290: Buddy Holly died intestate: G&B, RB, p. 150.
290: Maria Elena was his sole: *Ibid.*

290: "The only way I got: Author interview with MEH.
290: he promised interviewers: Quoted in "NP (Part 3)," p. 8.
290: Maria Elena Diaz-Hernandez: "Coral Releasing 'New' Holly Tapes," unidentified clipping, dated 9/15/62 in AC, BH, No. 1, p. 52.
290: and had three children: *Parade* magazine, 12/8/91.
290: "When Buddy died: Author interview with LH.
290: "most of the things: Quoted in BG, "Maria Elena," RM 4, 9/77, p. 9.
290: "We got tired of trying: Author interview with LH.
291: Larry's fondest dream: *Ibid.*
291: Ella and L. O. Holley went: CA quoted in Oestreicher and Kennedy, "CA," p. 12.
291: "I want you to: *Ibid.*
291: "The 'death rattle': "Album Sales Keep 'Em Alive," cited in G&B, RB, p. 150.
291: "get masters, get masters: Quoted in BG, "Spotlight on Dick Jacobs," R50 38, 10/92, p. 13.
291: Buddy's priceless apartment tapes: *Ibid.*
291: Jack Hansen assisting: *Ibid.*
292: "reached the Top 30: "No Ballyhoo Is Needed to Sell BH Discs!" reprinted in AC, BH, No. 1, p. 50.
292: "You'll only hurt: Quoted in Kaye, liner notes, *Eddie Cochran,* double LP, UAS-9959; author interview with Lenny Kaye.
293: Allison came to visit him: JBM quoted in AC, "Farewell to Eddie Cochran," p. 39.
293: Sheeley and Vincent were also: Ward, "Fifties," ROA, p. 223.
293: Cochran never regained consciousness: Borie, "Eddie Died in My Arms," *Photoplay,* 8/60, reproduced in AC, *Tribute to Eddie Cochran,* p. 22; Kaye, *Eddie Cochran* LP.
293: "We'll all miss Eddie: "Suddenly There Was No Tomorrow," *Modern Screen,* 8/60, reproduced in AC, *Tribute to Eddie Cochran,* p. 25.
293: into the trucking business: JBM quoted in BG, "Joe Mauldin," RM 15, 6/80, p. 8, JA quoted in BG, "JA—Part Two," p. 10.
293: Jerry became a session drummer: *Ibid.*
293: threatened to withhold them: G&B, RB, p. 150.
293: Buddy's parents took him: *Ibid.*
293: "I have a pair of nailclippers: Quoted in RM 10, 3/79.
293: "terrifically unhappy": Quoted in G&B, RB, p. 150.
293: distrusted New York record: *Ibid.*
294: royalties were to be split: "Coral Releasing 'New' Holly Tapes," p. 52; G&B, RB, p. 150.
294: Jerry felt that if anyone: JA quoted in G&B, p. 152.
294: Jerry was back in the Southwest: *Ibid.*
294: a direct affront to him: JA in G&B, RB, pp. 294–53.
294: convinced that Petty was: *Ibid.*
294: "Sugar Shack" the No. 1: Whitburn, *Billboard Book of Top 40 Hits,* p. 470.
294: "purists" charged that the: Quoted in "NP (Part 2)," p. 9.
294: "slow version": *Rolling Stone Illustrated History of Rock 'n' Roll,* p. 81.

294: "Wishing," an old demo: Lazell et al., *Rock Movers & Shakers*, p. 234.

295: "were done better by: 1/64.

295: Fab Four were simply: George Harrison said in New York on 2/12/64, "In the early days it was Elvis Presley, Carl Perkins, Chuck Berry, Little Richard, and Buddy Holly." Giuliano and Giuliano, *Lost Beatles Interviews*, p. 16.

295: book business in Surrey: BG, "John Tobler Book," RM 16, 9/80, p. 2.

295: "a lot of work": BG, "Mrs. Holley," p. 2.

295: "Musically, the rock 'n' roll: *Man Who Made the Beatles*, p. 67.

295: first forty songs: G&B, RB, p. 159.

295: McCartney revealed in 1987: RBHS.

295: "They play and harmonize: p. 21.

295: Tony Bramwell, who'd once: Norman, *Shout!* p. 53.

295: "Buddy was my very: "Legend of BH," 16, 4/65.

296: "quite unlike anything the: Coleman, *Man Who Made*, p. 110.

296: Buddy's most profound effect: RM 19, 6/81, p. 7.

296: reincarnation of Buddy: *Ibid.*

296: "We're more popular: Cited in Coleman, *Man Who Made*, p. 281.

296: "on the train from Liverpool,": BG, "18 Interviews (all at once)," p. 4.

297: "something . . . like Buddy Holly's: *Shout!* p. 74.

297: Johnny and the Moondogs: *Ibid.*, p. 59.

297: Long John and the: Lazell et al., *Rock Movers & Shakers*, p. 34.

297: "What's happening in Liverpool: Coleman, *Man Who Made*, p. 68.

297: "My Bonnie: *Ibid.*, p. 70.

297: Cavern Club: *Ibid.*, p. 73.

297: 75 shillings each for: *Ibid.*, p. 81.

297: was gay, found the: *Ibid.*, p. 57.

297: to be somewhat ragged: *Ibid.*, p. 73.

297: they rejected the Beatles: *Ibid.*, p. 97.

297: most popular band in: PN, *Shout!* p. 144.

297: They dressed like Buddy: RBHS.

297: EMI had previously: Coleman, *Man Who Made*, p. 108.

297: George Martin recorded them: PN, *Shout!* pp. 158–59.

297: Roy Orbison's high, soaring style: Amburn, *Dark Star*, p. 117.

298: *Sunday Night at the London Palladium*: Coleman, *Man Who Made*, p. 199.

298: Sid Bernstein, an agent: *Ibid.*, p. 200.

298: "The first thing the Beatles: Author interview with David Garrard Lowe.

298: "The way they arranged: Quoted in Schaffner, *British Invasion*, p. 62.

298: " 'Not Fade Away' fully: *Ibid.*

298: "He passed it on: RBHS.

299: "after the American rocker: Schaffner, *British Invasion*, p. 228.

299: had sixteen Holly tracks: BG, "New Albums (Review)," RM 18, 3/81, p. 7.

299: Clapton, rock's future guitar god: Roberty, *Slowhand: Life and Music of Eric Clapton*, pp. 10, 45, 53, 85, 91.

299: Clapton played with the Roosters: Roberty, *Slowhand*, pp. 11–15.

299: Clapton played "Peggy Sue": Schumacher, *Crossroads*, p. 117

299: Clapton covered Buddy's "Well: *Ibid.*

299: No. 6 in England's: "Legend of BH," 16, p. 57.

299: "They said, 'You mean: Quoted in Oestreicher and Kennedy, "CA," p. 12.

299: "Very fine people." . . . some day": *Ibid.* pp. 11–12.

Chapter 16

301: $400,000-a-year bracket: Hendler, *Year by Year in the Rock Era*, p. 150.

301: "an eight-minute chronicle: Ward, "Fifties," ROA, p. 453.

301: dedicated to Buddy: Don McLean quoted in BG, "Don McLean," RM 17, 12/80, p. 6.

301: " 'American Pie' became a tool: Quoted in Fink, "Don McLean," RM 43, 7/86, p. 9.

302: "I can't stand that surfing: Cited in G&B, RB, p. 162.

302: Rock 'n' roll's been going: BG, RM 3, 6/77, p. 5.

302: "like an omen: Quoted in Fink, "Don McLean," p. 9.

302: Kmart employee and sometime: BG, "Editorial," RM 16, 9/80, p. 1.

302: lasted over a decade, . . . Maria Elena and disagreements: BG, "Lubbock's 1986 'BH Festival' Called Off," RM 42, 5/86, p. 10; BG, "Farewell, So Long, Goodbye . . ." RM 28, Fall/83, p. 26; Ernie Conner, Dale Smith, "Letters," R50 31, p. 5; BG, "Editorial," RM 16, 9/80, pp. 1–2.

302: boasted fifty-two hundred members: BG, "International BHMS," 1988 Clovis Music Festival Official Program, p. 16.

302: Netherlands, . . . Canada: BG, "BHMS Members," RM 22, 3/82, p. 23.

303: "I'm not a beautiful: *Linda Ronstadt: It's So Easy*, p. 61.

303: "a bad reputation: *Ibid.*, p. 18.

303: J. D. Souther: *Ibid.*, p. 44.

303: California Governor Jerry Brown: *Ibid.*; Clifford, *Harmony Illustrated Encyclopedia of Rock*, p. 148.

303: "The Eagles backed me: P. 301.

303: Peter Asher: Stambler, *Encyclopedia of Pop, Rock, and Soul*, p. 584.

303: *Simple Dreams*: *Ibid.*, p. 585.

303: her debt to Buddy: BG, "Lubbock Happenings," RM 23, 6/82, p. 4.

303: a mass audience in the seventies: Pareles and Romanowski, *Rolling Stone Encyclopedia of Rock & Roll*, p. 479.

303: "Mother had got behind: Author interview with LH.

304: "Who do you really: Quoted in "PM 9/13/80," RM 19, 6/81, p. 2.

304: "Happy Birthday," . . . Ira Gershwin.: Giuliano, *Blackbird*.

304: $500 million: Brown and Gaines, *Love You Make*, p. 366.

304: richest musician in history: *Ibid.*

304: "a big fan of Buddy's": Quoted in Tobler, "PM 9/31/80," p. 2.

304: On September 7, 1976, the: Tobler, *This Day in Rock*, p. 256.

304: Petty was the guest: Schumacher, *Crossroads*, p. 208.

304: "just great: Quoted in Tobler, "PM 9/31/80," p. 2.

304: "would entertain LW: BG, "LW," RM 45, 11/86, p. 16.

305: Crickets would appear with him: Giuliano, *Blackbird*, p. 312; BG, "JA—Part Two," RM 24, 9/82, p. 12.

305: "I went and seen: Author interview with LH.

305: "I don't hold no grudge: *Ibid.*

305: [McCartney's father-in-law: Tobler, *This Day in Rock*, p. 39; PN, *Shout!* p. 362; Brown and Gaines, *Love You Make*, p. 299.

305: Michael Jackson acquired the: Coleman, *Man Who Made*, p. 306.

305: Brian Epstein's mishandling: *Ibid.*

305: "The Beatles were angry: *Ibid.*

306: John Tobler's *The Buddy Holly Story*: BG, "John Tobler's Book," RM 16, 9/80, p. 2.

Chapter 17

307: voice-over by Paul McCartney: NP quoted. in Brooks and Malcolm, "NP," RM 37, 7/85, p. 9. The interview was conducted on 9/3/83.

307: "very good.": *Ibid.*

307: except Maria Elena: *Ibid.*

307: all wanted more money: G&B, RB, p. 164.

307: "We had favorite-nation: "NP," RM 37, p. 9.

307: went to Florida to see Maria Elena: G&B, RB, p. 164.

307: a Texas businessman: *Parade* magazine, 12/8/91.

307: were named after Buddy: EH and LOH quoted in Skinner, "Meeting With Mr. and Mrs. Holley on 6/12/69," RM 43, 7/86, p. 4.

307: a share of the royalties: G&B, RB, p. 164.

307: title was *The Day the Music Died*: BG, "Movie," RM 2, 3/77, p. 1.

308: buying chicken farms next to: NS quoted in BG and Bonner, "NS (Part 1)," p. 3; JA quoted in BG, "JA—Part Two," p. 11.

308: screenwriter Tom Drake: G&B, RB, p. 165.

308: entitled *Not Fade Away*: *Ibid*; author interview with NS.

308: resistance from Buddy's wife and family: G&B, RB, p. 165.

308: The language was too racy: *Ibid.*

308: Maria Elena didn't care: *Ibid.*

308: Steve Davies playing Buddy: *Ibid.*

309: Gary Busey as Jerry: G&B, RB, p. 165.

308: *Philip Marlowe*: Martin and Porter, *Video Movie Guide 1989*, p. 128.

308: *The Nest*: *Ibid.*, p. 898.

308: Jerry himself took a small: G&B, RB, p. 165.

308: Bob Montgomery also got: *Ibid.*

308: rushes and panicked: *Ibid.*

308: writing off a million dollars: Dewitt, "Little Known Facts," *Blue Suede News* 16, p. 14; G&B, RB, p. 165.

308: warning of legal action: G&B, RB, pp. 165–66.

308: skyscrapers in the background: "Holly Film Was Not Realistic," MCGG, 2/1/89, p. E-8.

308: who chose to shoot: G&B, RB, p. 166.

308: Far more damaging was: JG on IPBN TV film *Reminiscing*.

308: would sue the producers: "Lawrence Holley Sr. Dies," LAJ, 7/10/85.

308: Billy Stull stated: Author interview with Billy Stull; G&B, RB, p. 166.

309: Petty was offered $5,000: Author interview with Billy Stull.

309: "I felt like a nonentity: 9/21/78, cited in G&B, RB, p. 169.

309: Smith knew how to play: *Ibid.*, p. 167.

309: Stroud lacked professional: *Ibid.*

309: credited as the drummer: LP, *Buddy Holly Story*, Epic 35412.

309: "Special thanks": *Ibid.*

309: Gailard Sartain: Fred Travelena quoted in WJ, "Fred Travelena," RM 6, 3/78, p. 7.

309: *Hard Country*: Martin and Porter, *Video*, p. 314.

309: Maria Elena was still under: MEH quoted in BG, "Maria Elena," RM 4, 9/77, p. 9.

309: from 240 pounds to 180: *USA Today* cited in BG, "News Briefs," RM 44, 9/86, p. 2.

309: dyed and cut to resemble: Fred Travelena quoted in WJ, "Fred Travelena," p. 7.

309: Busey, at thirty-three: Mann, *A–Z of Buddy Holly*, p. 25.

309: "It wouldn't be any good: Quoted in "Maria Elena," RM 4, 9/77, p. 9.

310: "if Buddy isn't singing: "Movie," RM 5, 12/7, p. 1.

310: he'd require off-camera assistance: G&B, RB, p. 168.

310: "Gary Busey was a good: Author interview with SC.

310: committed suicide: Mann, *A–Z of Buddy Holly*, p. 25.

310: Dallas, where the movie: BG, "Movie Premiere in Dallas," RM 8, 9/78, p. 2.

310: from Tennessee, and Trini Lopez: *Ibid.*, pp. 1–2.

310: Actor-director Ron Howard: BG, "BH Lives!" RM 7, 6/78, p. 1.

310: "hot and sticky,": *Ibid.*, p. 1.

310: "started seeing Buddy on": "Movie Premiere in Dallas," p. 2.

310: Contradicting his statement: BG, "Movie," RM 5, 12/77, p. 1.

311: that "I loved the movie: Quoted in "Movie Premiere in Dallas," p. 2.

311: Busey had visited Buddy's: Author interview with Don Larson.

311: Svenson later became Larson's: *Ibid.*

311: Busey asked Larson for: *Ibid.*

311: first reunion since January: BG, "Movie Premiere in Dallas," p. 2.

311: "That movie just really: "Holly Film Was Not Realistic," MCGG, 2/1/89, p. 8.

311: "I've got to be: "JA—Part Two," p. 13.

311: Allison had imparted to Busey: G&B, RB, p. 169.

311: Crickets posed with Gary: BG, "Movie Premiere in Dallas," p. 2.

311: captured the moment: *Ibid.*

311: bandleader was Busey's brother: *Ibid.*

311: the whole movie, period,": Quoted in BG, "Joe Mauldin," RM 15, 9/80, p. 8.

311: "J.I. and Buddy didn't: *Ibid.*

311: was glad that someone: *Ibid.*

311: "For some reason," . . . turning.": *Ibid.*

311: "a———": "JA—Part Two," p. 12.

311: "*really* irritated: *Ibid.*

311: The insult had actually: JP, "Holly Film Was," p. E-8.
311: "was all bullshit: Author interview with JA.
312: Buddy's birthplace: JG quoted in BG, "Bits & Pieces," RM 7, 6/78, p. 6; BG, "Movie Premiere in," pp. 2–3.
312: "worthwhile," she told: BG, "Movie Premiere in," p. 3.
312: "It was Buddy and: Ibid.
312: hardly a park or "recreation area,": BG, "Buddy Holly Lives!" p. 1.
312: Busey made a brief: Ibid.
312: "soundtrack album died: A–Z of Buddy Holly, p. 25.
312: "nineteen years after his: This Day in Rock, p. 90.
312: visited with Buddy's parents: BG, "Movie Premiere in," p. 2.
313: gold records to: Ibid., pp. 1–3.
313: platinum record from England: BG, "Bits & Pieces," RM 8, 9/78, p. 3.
313: never expected him to become: Quoted in "Mrs. Holley," RM 2, 3/77, p. 3.
313: an emotional L. O. Holley stood: Quoted in "Ed Cohen & Steve Rash," RM 8, 9/78, p. 8.
313: mother was "proud": Quoted in BG, "Mrs. Holley 7/1/78," RM 11, p. 8.
313: "real pleased": LH quoted in ibid.
313: realistic use of profanity: Ibid.
313: "Cunning tactics by one: Holden, Behind the Oscar, p. 322.
313: Rona Barrett: EH quoted in BG, "Mrs. Holley 7/1/78," p. 8.
314: "That's just about: Ibid.
314: Joe Renzetti took home: Ibid., p. 566.
314: "was hardly the true": PM in RBHS.
314: "she's not talking: PBS-TV Reminiscing.
314: sued for $300,000: "Lawrence Holley Sr. Dies," LAJ, 7/10/85.
314: they'd previously told Griggs: BG, "Mrs. Holley 7/1/78," p. 8.
314: now charged that the: "Lawrence Holley Sr. Dies."
314: innacurately portrayed: Ibid.; G&B, RB, p. 169.
314: settled out of court: Ibid.,
315: "The movie does not: "BH Story," cited in G&B, RB, p. 170.
315: "true-to-life movie": G&B, RB, p. 168.
315: cocaine overdose of its star: "The Other Shoe Drops," The People Column, Miami Herald, 5/10/95, p. 2A.
315: felony cocaine-possession: Ibid.
315: checked himself into California's: Ibid.
315: imprisoned for three years: Ibid.
315: $15,000 to $25,000: Denisoff, Waylon, p. 297.
315: convoy of two Silver: Ibid., p. 295.
315: Buddy Dean: Ibid., p. 82.
315: Jones, a flamboyant barmaid: Ibid., p. 85.
315: Barbara Rood: Ibid., p. 143.
315: Barbara left him: Ibid., p. 168.
315: Jessi Colter: Ibid., p. 169.
315: "wound up in the: "Outlaw Breed," 8/26/74, p. 84.
315: son, Waylon Albright: Denisoff, Waylon, p. 290.
316: drug habit would last: Quoted in VHS, PC105, Hallway Productions, 1990; Riese, Nashville Babylon, pp. 58–59.

316: "$1,500 a day": Riese, Nashville Babylon, p. 59.
316: "$70,000 [in] lawyer fees: Waylon video; Riese, Nashville Babylon, p. 58; Roland, Billboard Book of No. 1 Country Hits, p. 203.
316: trashed four rooms in: Riese, Nashville Babylon, p. 59.
316: soared to sixteen million: Denisoff, Waylon, p. 299.
316: "In times I was down: Ibid., p. 293.
316: who signed autographs for: BG, "Lubbock for 1979!" RM 13, 12/79, p. 4.
316: Tommy Allsup played "True Love Ways": Ibid., p. 2.
316: Niki Sullivan's mother broke down: Ibid., p. 4.
316: bar called Heads Up: CT, 6/24/88, Tempo 2.
316: sculptor Grant Speed was: "BH," City of Lubbock booklet, BH Memorial Foundation, 1979, p. 4.
316: still proudly wore Buddy's Omega: LH quoted in BG, "LH," RM 14, 3/80, p. 9.
316. Waylon watched the statue: BG, "Buddy in Bronze!" RM 17, 12/80, p. 3.
316: gathering of 150: Ibid.
317: Nigel Smith and Adrian: Ibid., pp. 1, 4.
317: "En France, Buddy: Ibid., p. 6.
317: he loved Buddy: Ibid., p. 4.
317: "real fine,": Quoted in ibid., p. 3.
318: needed a gimmick: In "Surf Ballroom: Valens' Last Stage," Des Moines Register, 7/26/87, Darrel Hein, the Surf's owner, said that the Surf only sold out once a year, for the annual BH tribute.
318: KZEV donated a bronze: BG, RM 10, 3/79, p. 1.
319: still clamored in vain: Lazell et al, Rock Movers & Shakers, p. 234.
319: MCA dragged its feet: McGee, "BH," in DeCurtis et al., Rolling Stone Album Guide, p. 324.
319: finally releasing The Complete Buddy Holly: G&B, RB, pp. 191–92.
319: having "one of the: DeCurtis et al, Rolling Stone Album Guide, p. 324.
319: "I only wish Buddy Holly: Gene Sculatti, "Calendar," 5/31/81, Los Angeles Times cited in BG, RM 20, 9/81, p. 6.
319: "Trivial Pursuits" contained no less: BG, "Trivial Pursuit," RM 32, Fall/84, p. 13.
319: Robert Parker's A Catskill Eagle: BG, "News Briefs," RM 38, 9/85, p. 4.
319: as a space alien: Denton, Buddy Holly Is Alive and Well on Ganymede.
319: P. F. Kluge's novel: BG, RM 32, Fall/84, p. 12.
320: "the promoters of the Winter Dance Party: P. 161.
320: The Rocky Horror Picture Show: BG, "New Singles (Review)," RM 18, p.7.
320: "Buddy Holly Handicap,": BG, RM 35, 9/85.
320: starred Debra Winger before: Ibid.
320: couple of newlyweds reported: Cofer, "BH Fans Get Standing Room Only," LAJ, 6/17/93, p. 85.
320: "Buddy—The Singing Piston": Hot Rod magazine, 6/80, p. 122, cited in BG, RM 17, 12/80, p. 16.
320: In Yemen, fans mobbed: BG, RM 20, 9/81, p. 12.
320: Hi Pockets Duncan died: BG, "Who's Who" of West Texas Rock-'n'-Roll Music, unpaged.
320: Snuff Garrett, who'd become: Ibid.

320: Decca's Dick Jacobs: BG, "Spotlight on Dick Jacobs," p. 15; BG, RM 25, p. 11.

320: Bob Thiele was still "alive: letter to author from Bill Munroe, 12/3/93.

320: Norma Jean Berry: BG, NOR-VA-JAK MUSIC DEALT A TRIPLE TRAGEDY, RM 31, p. 11.

320: "Bill" Pickering: BG, "Bill Pickering," RM 35, 3/85, p. 12.

321: Don Guess: Caviness, "Charlie Phillips," RM 28, Fall/83, p. 7; BG, "Who's Who" of West Texas Rock 'n' Roll Music.

321: Country Club bar in Reseda: BG, "Week in Los Angeles," RM 31, Summer/84, p. 10.

321: substituted a new routine: Ibid.

321: "still looking good,": Ibid.

321: recovered from his drug addiction: TW, p. 184.

321: "the language of the: Ibid., p. 185.

321: Fred Milano, one of: Reynolds, "Belmonts in Rhode Island," R50 31, 8/91, p. 7.

321: "not to be interviewed: Author interview with BG.

321: GAC's Irving Feld: Ibid.

321: "has long since retired: A–Z of Buddy Holly, p. 51.

321: Jerry Dwyer declined: BG, "Spotlight," p. 14.

321: "harassment": JT, "Investigator Offers Theory," p. E6.

321: "It must have been tough: Author interview with JP.

322: "bummed around the country: CB quoted in BG "CB, p. 80.

322: so intoxicated he could: Ibid.

322: prison guard: Ibid., p. 9.

322: founding the "Dove Nest: Ibid.

322: Carl appeared on Bakker's: Ibid.

322: inserting religious phrases: Ibid.

322: "The devil knew that: Ibid., p. 8.

322: Sonny Curtis was flying high: BG, "SC Keeps Rollin' Along," RM 20, 9/81, p. 10.

322: Jimmy Bowen: Ibid., p. 14; Nite, Rock On, p. 60.

322: almost dropped Reba: McEntire with Carter, Reba, p. 145.

322: "Ultimately, Bowen didn't agree: Ibid., p. 148.

322: New Traditionalist movement: Ibid., p. 149.

322: most recorded song of 1967: Ibid., p. 73.

322: "Montgomery was polite: Ibid.

322: driving a camper with: BG, RM 30, p. 13.

323: Many of them had to spend: Ibid.

323: of criticizing the Beatles: Author interview with Billy Stull.

323: "In his latter years: Ibid.

323: He lay dying of leukemia: Ibid.; "Petty, 57, Friend, Manager of Buddy Holly, Dies Here," LAJ, 8/16/84, p. A-11; Roberts, "Petty's Musical Genius Influenced Today's Tunes," Clovis News-Journal, 8/19/84.

323: "Norman never spoke of: Author interview with Billy Stull.

324: "Norman was hurt by all: Ibid.

324: "eminence in the recording: "Holly's Album Merits Gold Record for Clovis Man," Amarillo Daily News, 6/1/84, p. 13-A.

324: "Petty still waxes nostalgic: Ibid.

324: "He died unfulfilled,": Author interview with Billy Stull.

324: PETTY, 57, FRIEND: 8/16/84, p. A-11.

324: "It's real sad: BG, "NP, 1927–1984," RM 31, Summer/84, p. 3.

324: "True Love Ways," which was: BG, "NP, 1927–1984," p.3.

324: "Petty took as much: Author interview with BG.

324: suffered a stroke: "Hospitalized Father of Star BH on Critical List," LAJ, 7/8/85.

325: moved to the intensive care: "Holly's Father Still Critical," LAJ, 7/8/85.

325: at eight P.M., he died: "Lawrence Holley Dead at 83," LAJ, 7/9/85.

325: "father of the late: "Services Slated Wednesday for Buddy Holly's Father," LAJ, 7/9/85.

325: The Reverend E. L. Bynum: BG, RM 38, 9/85, p. 3.

325: pallbearers were his barber: "Lawrence Holley Sr. Dies," LAJ, 7/10/85.

325: fall off a bridge: Author interview with LH.

325: one of the ten original: LAJ, 1/24/86.

325: circumstances eerily similar: Bashe, Teenage Idol: Travelin' Man, pp. 276–78; People, 1/20/86; Selvin, Ricky Nelson, pp. 286, 289, 291–92, 294, 296.

325: "I wish Buddy, Elvis, and: Quoted in BG, "News Briefs," RM 42, 5/86, p. 2.

325: rock's "Magnificent Seven": BG, RM 44, 9/86, p. 8.

325: pilot's seventy-one-year-old: "Pilot's Parents Can't Forget."

325: "Mrs. Holly, fifty-five, said: Ibid.

325: "someone can be so: Quoted in Ibid.

326: Peterson's name was included: JP, "Legends of Rock Remembered: Monument Is in Place at Surf," MCGG, 6/7/88.

326: photograph taken during the dedication: CLMR, 6/22/88.

326: "Now that I am: Ibid.

326: she held aloft: Sunday Globe, 6/19/88.

326: Jay P. Richardson, Jr.: JP, "Saturday: Day Music Lives Again," Clear Lake Weekend A.M., 6/16/88.

326: "It's heartwarming to take: Reporter, 6/22/88.

326: film biography of his father: Gales, "Hollywood introduced Son to Bopper," MCGG, 2/1/89.

326: "she tried to put it: Quoted in ibid.

326: Bob Morales: JP, "Saturday: Day Music."

326: actor Esai Morales: BM, RV, p. 138.

326: Marshall Crenshaw: WJ, "Marshall Crenshaw," RM 26, Spring 1983, p. 26.

326: migrant laborer and a farmworker: BM, RV, p. 139.

326: snakeskin was purely fictitious: Ibid.

327: The creative team included: Program, Surf Ballroom, Buddy: BH Story, p. 16; Playbill, Buddy, Shubert Theater, 5/91, Vol. 91, No. 5, p. 63.

327: "an unashamed, rabble-rousing: advertisement for Buddy, Colonial Theatre, Boston, Massachusetts.

327: "big cast . . . big sound: cover, Program, Surf Ballroom, Buddy.

327: party at the Lone Star: Giuliano, Blackbird, p. 312.

327: venerable Shubert Theater: "At This Theatre," Playbill, Buddy, p. 5.

327: "Buddy has them dancin': poster, Shubert Theatre.

327: Hipp's portrayal won him: "Who's Who in the Cast," *Playbill, Buddy*, p. 48.

327: performances in Lubbock: BG, "Buddy—BH Story," R50, 12/91, p. 4.

327: Christopher Eudy: Surf Ballroom program, *Buddy*, p. 7.

327: "The Lubbock audience stood: BG, "Buddy—BH Story," p. 4.

328: Prime Minister John Major: *LDM* cited in BG, "Prime Minister Likes Buddy," R50 35, 4/92, p. 23.

328: take "everything we've got: Author interview with LH.

329: Buddy's Ariel Cyclone: BG, "Buddy's Motorcycle," p. 16.

329: "Mother was losing her mind: Author interview with LH.

329: suffering a heart attack: BG, R50, 12/88, p. 22.

329: "I boxed them up: Author interview with LH.

329: "ardent followers. "Talk of the Town," *New Yorker*, 7/8/91, p. 28.

330: Eddie Murphy arrived at: BG, "Second BH Auction," R50, 8/91, p. 24.

330: Fender Stratocaster fetching $100,000: *Ibid.*, p. 22.

330: "A Lubbock man was: Author interview with BG.

330: "just because it was: "Talk of the Town," p. 28.

330: "sad": *Ibid.*, p. 29.

330: "smooth and engaging: *Ibid.*

330: "brought back in,": BG, "Second BH Auction," p. 24.

330: "a Tiffany flatware: Quoted in "Talk of the Town," p. 28.

330: "I noticed the Hard: Quoted in *ibid.*

330: "flooding the market": *Ibid.*

331: brought in $5,225: BG, RM 31, p. 23.

331: It was still . . . Elvis was the king: various TV newscasts, 6/94; BH prices: BG, "Second BH Auction," pp. 22–24, and BG, RM 31.

331: "Norman had been a: Author interview with BG.

331: "gracious widow who loved: Author interview with Billy Stull.

331: "eccentric cat woman who: Author interview with BG.

331: "They tried to shrink: Author interview with Billy Stull.

332: Panhandle South Plains Fair: Kerns, "Stamp Ceremony to Break Tradition," LAJ, 6/15/93, p. 1B.

332: deal with a T-shirt company: *Ibid.*

332: "dollar value": *Ibid.*

332: "to begin capitalizing: Kerns, "City Gets Windfall From Holly Stamp," LAJ, 6/13/93, pp. 1D–8D.

332: "a small vacant lot, strewn: "Buddy Holly Stamp Excites Hometown," *Fort Worth Star-Telegram*, 6/17/93.

332: "60, divorced, and: 12/8/91.

332: photograph atop page one: James Granger.

332: "He came through the: Kerns, "Holly's Hit List Grows With Hot-Selling Stamp," LAJ, 6/17/93, p. 1.

332: "I hinted. I prayed: Kerns, "Family Appreciates Holly Celebration," LAJ, 6/17/93, p. 85.

332: "astonished" by the city's: Quoted in *ibid.*

332: "given up on the: Quoted in *ibid.*

333: "treating us so well,": Kerns, "Holly Notes," LAJ, 6/17/93, p. 85.

333: "We all know what happened,": "Holly's Hit List," p. 1.

333: handed it to Maria Elena: *Ibid.*

333: Civic Lubbock, Inc., had recently: Kerns, "Family Appreciates," p. B-5.

333: "treasure" and: Kerns, "Holly's Hit List," p. 1.

333: annual summer observance in: LAJ, 6/15/93, p. 1B.

333: 24,571 Holly stamps: Kerns, "Holly's Hit List," p. 1.

333: "to use Buddy's name: Author interview with LH.

334: beneficiaries could not: *Ibid.*

334: name on the toilet paper: *Ibid.*

334: proposed a mammoth Disneyland-type: *Ibid.*

334: percentage of every soft: *Ibid.*

334: "His plan fell through,": Author interview with BG.

334: "multi-event center,": *Ibid.*

334: "The public defeated the: Author interview with Michael Reeves.

Epilogue

335: in its final days: Author interviews with HG and JP.

335: "As president of the: *News Letter: Surf Ballroom*, 5/88, p. 6.

335: "Eddie Cochran Birthday Bash": "Schedule of Events" (program), p. 7.

335: "If you want to vote: Lanpher, "Having a Ball," *St. Paul Pioneer Press*, reprinted in *Music & Dance News*, 2/93, p. 7.

336: "If you were a Cricket: Author interview with BG.

336: "They crisscrossed: Author interview with HG.

337: "It's not advisable: Author interview with Mike Berry.

337: "J.I. [Jerry Ivan]: Author interview with SC.

337: "His alligator mouth: *Ibid.*

337: "Come again?": Author interview with Mike Berry.

337: "He talked the pilot: Author interview with SC.

339: "There was a lot of tension: Author interview with Frankie Ford.

340: she'd never let go: *Parade* magazine, 12/8/91.

340: a healthy catharsis: Author interview with HG.

340: "My favorite: Author interview with JP.

340: Sony Corporation: "Member of BH's Band Recreates Those Days Annually," *Jefferson City (Missouri) News Tribune*, 2/6/94.

340: a bar called Sully's: Author interview with NS.

341: credit-card business in Nashville: Author interview with Sue Christensen.

341: Waylon Jennings had said: Author interview with NS.

341: Paul McCartney was not interested. Author interview with Sue Christensen and HG.

341: Niki wanted to buy: Author interview with NS.

341: "It is one of those: Reprinted in CLMR, 6/16/88.

341: farmer Laurence Radloff and: "America's Mu-

sic Still Waltzes Through the Surf Ballroom," reprinted in CLMR, 6/16/88.
341: "The Surf was like: Quoted in *ibid*.
341: "We've restored it as: Author interview with
Dale Snyder.
342: "We now have palm trees: *Ibid*.
342: $8,000 a month: Author interview with NS.
342: to "be a part: "Be a Part of Surf Ballroom History," advertising mailer, Surf Ltd. c/o Snyder
family.

342: "There are very few: Author interview with JP.
342: appearing with DJ Randy: ticket, "Tribute to
BH," Fri., Feb. 3, 1995.
342: "the Regulators from Odessa: Author interview with NS.
342: "with the Crickets—Gordon: Author interview with SC.
342: the Fantastic Convertibles, Bobby: ticket,
"Tribute to BH," Sat., Feb. 4, 1995.

Bibliography

Books, Newspapers, and Magazines

"A Farewell to Buddy Holly: The Young Bride of a Favorite Young Star Bids Him a Last Goodbye." *16 Magazine*. Undated article collected in *Buddy Holly*. Compiled by Alan Clark. 30th Anniversary Memorial Series, No. 1. West Covina, California: National Rock and Roll Archives, 1989.

Ashton, Martin. "Last Testament, Blue Angel." *BAM*, 24 February 1989.

"At This Theatre." *Playbill: Buddy: The Buddy Holly Story*. Vol. 91, No. 5. New York: Shubert Theater, May 1991.

Babin, Maria Teresa. "Special Voice: The Cultural Expression." In *Puerto Rico*, edited by Arturo Morales Carrion. Nashville: American Association for State and Local History, 1983.

Bashe, Philip. *Teenage Idol: Travelin' Man*. New York: Hyperion, 1992.

Bacon, Tony, and Paul Day. *The Fender Book: A Complete History of Fender Electric Guitars*. San Francisco: GPI Books, 1992

Baenen, Jeff. "Albert Lea Raises Fuss 'n' Holler Over Summertime Singer."

Associated Press. *Fairmont (Minnesota) Sentinel*, 24 June 1991.

Barsalona, Frank. In "Agents." *The Making of Superstars*, by Robert Stephen Spitz. New York: Doubleday, 1978.

Barnard, Karen. "Dula Celebration Tunes in to Cultivation of 'Clovis Sound.'"

Amarillo Globe-News, 4 September 1987.

Bayles, Martha. *Hole in Our Soul: The Loss of Beauty and Meaning in American Popular Music*. New York: The Free Press, 1994.

Bego, Mark. *Linda Ronstadt: It's So Easy*. Austin: Eakin Press, 1990.

Benet, William Rose. *Benet's Third Edition Reader's Encyclopedia*. New York: Harper & Row, 1987.

Berbusse, Edward J. S. J. *The U.S. in Puerto Rico: 1898–1900*. Chapel Hill: University of North Carolina Press, 1966.

Berry, Chuck. *The Autobiography*. New York: Simon and Schuster, 1987.

Bilas, Zenon. *Waterski*, March/April 1992.

Bokris, Victor. *Keith Richards*. New York: Poseidon Press, 1992.

Borie, Marcia. "Eddie Died in My Arms." *Photoplay*, August 1960.

Bree, Marlin. *In the Teeth of the Northeaster*. New York: Clarkson N. Potter, 1988.

"The British Tour of Buddy Holly and the Crickets." Double LP. *Memories of Buddy*. MCA 301735.

Brooks, Skip, and Bill Malcolm. "Norman Petty." *Reminiscing* 37, July 1985.

———. "Norman Petty (Part 2)." *Reminiscing* 38, September 1985.

———. "Norman Petty (Part 3)." *Reminiscing*. Undated clipping.

Broven, John. *Rhythm & Blues in New Orleans*. Gretna, Louisiana: Pelican, 1974.

Brown, Peter, and Steven Gaines. *The Love You Make: An Insider's Story of the Beatles*. New York: New American Library, 1983.

"Buddy Holly Stamp Excites Hometown." *Fort Worth Star-Telegram*, 17 June 1993.

"Buddy Holly Tribute." *Iowa Connection*. Collector's Program. Des Moines, Iowa: The Easter Seal Society of Iowa, Inc., 5 February 1988.

Bufwack, Mary A., and Robert K. Oermann. *Finding Her Voice: The Saga of Women in Country Music*. New York: Crown, 1993.

Bush, William J. "Buddy Holly: The Legend and Legacy." *Guitar Player*, June 1982.

———. "The Guitars of Buddy Holly." *Guitar Player*. June 1982.

———. "Waylon Jennings Remembering Buddy Holly." *Guitar Player*, June 1982.

Bynum, E. L. "Superstar: *Jesus Christ Superstar* Critically Examined in the Light of the Bible." Tract B-401. Lubbock, Texas: Tabernacle Baptist Church.

———. "The Bible and the Homosexual." Tract A-335. Lubbock, Texas: Tabernacle Baptist Church.

Carlisle, Dolly. *Ragged but Right: The Life and Times of George Jones*. Chicago: Contemporary Books, 1984.

Carr, Ian. *Miles Davis*. New York: Morrow, 1982.

Caviness, Jim. "Charlie Phillips." *Reminiscing* 28, Fall 1983.

"Chicago Scene." *Chicago Tribune*, Tempo 2, June 24, 1988.

Clark, Alan. *A Tribute to Eddie Cochran: Never to Be Forgotten*. West Covina, California: National Rock and Roll Archives, 1991.

———. *Buddy Holly*. 30th Anniversary Memorial Series, No. 1. West Covina, California: National Rock and Roll Archives, 1989.

———. *Eddie Cochran: The Legend Continues*. West Covina, California: National Rock and Roll Archives, 1994.

———. *Ritchie Valens*. 30th Anniversary Memorial Series, No. 2. West Covina, California: National Rock and Roll Archives, 1989.

———. *The Big Bopper*. 30th Anniversary Memorial

Series, No. 3. West Covina, California: National Rock 'n' Roll Archives, 1989.

Clark, Tom. *Jack Kerouac: A Biography.* New York: Paragon House, 1984.

Clayson, Alan. *Only the Lonely: The Life and Artistic Legacy of Roy Orbison.* London: Sidgwick & Jackson, 1989.

Clifford, Mike. *The Harmony Illustrated Encyclopedia of Rock.* New York: Harmony, 1988.

Coleman, Ray. *Clapton!* New York: Warner, 1985.

Cofer, Brian. "Buddy Holly Fans Get Standing Room Only." *Lubbock Avalanche-Journal,* 17 June 1993.

Collier, Ann. *The Art of Lacemaking.* London: David and Charles, 1986.

Collison, Jim. "Open Probe of Accident Here." *Mason City Globe-Gazette,* 5 February 1959.

"Commencement Exercises." Program. Fair Park Coliseum, Lubbock, Texas: Tom Lubbock Senior High School, 27 May 1955.

Cott, Jonathan. "Buddy Holly." *The Rolling Stone Illustrated History of Rock & Roll.* Edited by Jim Miller. New York: Random House, 1980.

Crampsey, Robert A. *Puerto Rico.* Harrisburg, Pennsylvania: David & Charles, 1973.

"Creativity in Clovis." *New Mexico,* September 1960.

Dalton, David. *James Dean: The Mutant King.* New York: St. Martin's Press, 1974.

"Damaging Storms Again Hit Area." *Lubbock Avalanche-Journal,* 13 May 1958.

Dannen, Fredric. *Hit Men: Power Brokers and Fast Money Inside the Music Business.* New York: Times Books, 1990.

"Death of Singers Here Shocks Nation." *Clear Lake Mirror-Reporter.* 5 February 1959.

DeCurtis, Anthony, and James Henke, with Holly George-Warren. *The Rolling Stone Album Guide.* New York: Random House, 1992.

Denisoff, R. Serge. *Waylon.* Knoxville: The University of Tennessee Press, 1983.

Des Barres, Pamela. *I'm With the Band: Confessions of a Groupie.* New York: Jove, 1988.

———. *Take Another Little Piece of My Heart.* New York: Berkley, 1993.

Devillers, Marceau. *James Dean.* Singapore: Chartwell. Undated.

Dewitt, Dennis. "Buddy Holly: Little Known Facts." *Blue Suede News* 16.

DiMucci, Dion, with Davin Seay. *The Wanderer: Dion's Story.* New York: Morrow, 1988.

Dodge, Consuelo. *The Everly Brothers: Ladies Love Outlaws.* Starke, Florida: CIN-DAV, Inc., 1991.

Dodge, Jim. *Not Fade Away.* New York: Atlantic Monthly Press, 1987.

Duffy, Bruce. "The '50s." *Life.* 1 December 1992.

Edwards, Joe. "Waylon Thinks About Buddy Every Day." Associated Press. *Mason City Globe-Gazette,* 1 June 1984.

Elliott, Charlotte, and William B. Bradbury. "Just as I Am." *Soul-Stirring Songs & Hymns.* Murfreesboro, Tennessee: Sword of the Lord Publishers, 1972.

Emery, Ralph, and Tom Carter. *Memories: The Autobiography of Ralph Emery.* New York: Pocket Books, 1992.

"Enjoy the Convention at the Surf." Surf Ballroom promotional brochure.

Fairbairn, Mary Lou. "Lubbock Now Has Its Answer to Elvis." *Lubbock Evening Journal,* 23 October 1956.

Feather, Leonard. *Pleasures of Jazz.* New York: Horizon Press, 1976.

"The Fifties." *Rolling Stone.* 19 April 1990.

Fink, Stu. "An Interview With Don McLean." *Reminiscing* 43, July 1986.

Fitzgerald, F. Scott. "The Ice Palace." *The Short Stories of F. Scott Fitzgerald.* New York: Scribner's, 1989.

"516 Lubbock Graduates to Get Diplomas at Ceremony Today." *Lubbock Avalanche-Journal,* 27 May 1955.

Floyd, Bill. "The Crickets' Appearance at the Apollo." *Reminiscing* 28, Fall 1983.

"Four Killed in Clear Lake Plane Crash." *Mason City Globe-Gazette,* 3 February 1959.

Fox, Ted. *Showtime at the Apollo.* New York: Holt, Rinehart and Winston, 1983.

Francis, Connie. *Who's Sorry Now.* New York: St. Martin's Press, 1984.

Frederick, Sue. "The Fourth Star." *Reminiscing* 4, September 1977.

———. "The Airplane—N3794N." *Reminiscing* 26, Spring 1983.

Fricke, David. "Roy Orbison Remembered." *Rolling Stone,* 26 January 1989.

Frommer's Comprehensive Travel Guide: Puerto Rico '93–94. New York: Prentice Hall, 1992.

Fuson, Ken. " 'La Bamba' Recalls the Day the Music Died Here in Iowa." *Des Moines Sunday Register,* 26 July 1987.

Gales, Carol. " 'Bopper' Died Just as Career Was Climbing." *Mason City Globe-Gazette,* 9 February 1989.

———. "Hollywood Introduced Son to Bopper." *Mason City Globe-Gazette,* 1 February 1989.

———. "Texas Concert Will Honor Big Bopper." *Mason City Globe-Gazette,* 1 February 1989.

Gallagher, Ted. *John Ford.* Berkeley: University of California Press, 1986.

Gault, Lon. "Iowa's Surf Ballroom Features Drifting Clouds on Ceiling." *Dancing USA,* 2–3 February 1984.

Giordano, Ralph. "Lou Giordano!" *Reminiscing* 15, June 1980.

"The Girl Ritchie Left Behind." *16,* July 1959. Collected in *Ritchie Valens.* 30th Anniversary Memorial Series, No. 2. Compiled by Alan Clark. West Covina, California: National Rock and Roll Archives, 1989.

Giuliano, Geoffrey. *Blackbird: The Life and Times of Paul McCartney.* New York: Dutton, 1991.

———, and Brenda Giuliano. *The Lost Beatles Interviews.* New York: Dutton, 1994.

Goeppinger, Hans. "Doug McLeod Remembers Last Tour." *Reminiscing* 29, Winter 1984.

Goldman, Albert. *Elvis.* New York: McGraw-Hill, 1981.

———. *The Lives of John Lennon.* New York: Morrow, 1988.

Goldrosen, John, and John Beecher. *Remembering Buddy.* New York: Penguin, 1986.

Gordon, Max. *Life at the Village Vanguard.* New York: St. Martin's Press, 1980.

Griggs, Bill. "A Letter From Buddy." *Reminiscing* 5, December 1977.

———. *A Who's Who of West Texas Rock-'n'-Roll*

Music. Lubbock, Texas: Rockin' 50s Magazine, 1994.

———. "Ben Hall." *Reminiscing* 14, March 1980.

———. "Bill Pickering Talks About the Picks." *Reminiscing* 21, December 1981.

———. "Bits and Pieces." *Reminiscing* 5, December 1977.

———. "Bits and Pieces." *Reminiscing* 6, March 1978.

———. "Bits and Pieces." *Reminiscing* 20, September 1981.

———. "Bob Hale." *Reminiscing* 9, December 1978.

———. "Browsing Through *Billboard.*" *Rockin' 50s.* February 1992.

———. "Browsing Through *Billboard.*" *Rockin' 50s.* June 1992.

———. "Buddy Holly on Waterskis." *Rockin' 50s* 36, June 1992.

———. "Buddy in Bronze." *Reminiscing* 17, December 1980.

———. "Buddy Knox." *Reminiscing* 14, March 1980.

———. "Buddy's Motorcycle." *Reminiscing* 27, Summer 1983.

———. "Buddy's Wedding Present." *Reminiscing* 32, Fall 1984.

———. "Carl Bunch." *Reminiscing* 20, September 1981.

———. "Carl Perkins." *Reminiscing* 19, June 1981.

———. "The Crickets Stopover in Tropical Hawaii." *Reminiscing* 26, Spring 1983.

———. "Dick Jacobs." *Reminiscing* 11, June 1979.

———. "Dick Jacobs." *Reminiscing* 36, May 1985.

———. "Duane Eddy and Buddy Holly." *Reminiscing* 19, 1986.

———. "The Ed Sullivan Show." *Reminiscing* 2, March 1977.

———. "18 Interviews (all at once)." *Reminiscing* 20, September 1981.

———. "Frankie Sardo." *Rockin' 50s*, April 1992.

———. "Gary & Ramona Tollett." *Reminiscing* 30, Spring 1984.

———. "George Tomsco." *Reminiscing* 15, June 1980.

———. "How's That Again?" *Rockin' 50s*, August 1992.

———. "I Finally Found It." *Reminiscing* 35, March 1985.

———. "Interviews, Jingles, & Live Performances on Records." *Reminiscing* 26, Spring 1983.

———. "Jack Neal: The Story Behind the 'Buddy and Jack' Show on KDAV Radio," *Reminiscing* 44, September 1986.

———. "Jake Goss: Buddy Holly's Barber." *Reminiscing* 45, November 1986.

———. "Jerry Allison—Part One." *Reminiscing* 23, June 1982.

———. "Jerry Allison—Part Two." *Reminiscing* 24, September 1982.

———. "Jimmy Bowen." *Reminiscing* 20, September 1981.

———. "Joe Mauldin." *Reminiscing* 16, September 1980.

———. "Joe Villa Talks About Buddy Holly and Lou Giordano." *Reminiscing* 22, March 1982.

———. "KLLL Radio." *Reminiscing* 7, June 1978.

———. "Larry Holley." *Reminiscing* 14, March, 1980.

———. "Larry Welborn." *Reminiscing* 45, November 1986.

———. "Lou Giordano." *Reminiscing* 15, June 1980.

———. "Maria Elena." *Reminiscing* 4, September 1977.

———. "Maria Elena." *Reminiscing* 5, December 1977.

———. "More About Lou Giordano." *Reminiscing* 36, May 1985.

———. "More and More About 'More and More.' " *Reminiscing* 43, July 1986.

———. "More Bits and Pieces." *Reminiscing* 19, June 1981.

———. "More on Little Richard." *Reminiscing* 35.

———. "The Movie Premiere in Dallas." *Reminiscing* 8, September 1978.

———. "Mrs. Holley." *Reminiscing* 2, March 1977.

———. "New . . . Buddy Holly Interview!" *Reminiscing* 19, June 1981.

———. "New Information on TV Appearances by Buddy Holly and the Crickets." *Reminiscing* 43, July 1986.

———. "1981 Buddy Holly Memorial Society Convention." *Reminiscing* 21, December 1981.

———. "Norman Petty." *Reminiscing* 6, March 1978.

———. "On the Air." *Reminiscing* 36, June 1977.

———. "OUR 9th YEAR." *Reminiscing* 32, Fall 1984.

———. " 'Pappy' Dave Stone." *Reminiscing* 34, January 1985.

———. "Peggy Sue." *Buddy Holly Memorial Society Convention Souvenir Program*, September 8–10, 1988.

———. "Robert Linville." *Clovis Music Festival Official Program*, 1988.

———. "The Second Buddy Holly Auction." *Rockin 50s*, August 1991

———. "7th Buddy Holly Memorial Society Convention." *Reminiscing* 33.

———. "Special Tribute to Celebrate the 25th Anniversary of the Crickets." *Reminiscing* 24, September 1982.

———. "Spotlight on Dick Jacobs." *Rockin' 50s*, October 1992.

———. "Spotlight on February 3, 1959." *Rockin' 50s*, February 1989.

———. "Terry Noland." *Reminiscing* 27, Summer 1983.

———. "Tommy Allsup." *Reminiscing* 15, June 1980

———. "Tour Schedules, Television Appearances, and Recording Sessions of Buddy Holly." Unpublished, 29 June 1991.

———. "Trivial Trivia." *Reminiscing* 21, December 1981.

———. "Vi Petty, September 17–March 22, 1992." *Rockin' 50s*, April 1992.

———. "Waylon Jennings." *Reminiscing* 25, Winter 1982.

———. "With Our Regrets." *Reminiscing* 27.

Gooch, Brad. *City Poet: The Life and Times of Frank O'Hara.* New York: Alfred A. Knopf, 1993.

Griggs, Bill, and Steve Bonner. "Niki Sullivan— Part 1." *Reminiscing* 6, March 1978.

———. " Niki Sullivan—Part 2." *Reminiscing* 7, June 1978.

Griggs, Bill, and Bruce Wilcox. "The Roger Peterson Story." Reminiscing 18, March 1981.

Guralnick, Peter. Last Train to Memphis: The Rise of Elvis Presley. Boston: Little, Brown, 1994.

———. Lost Highway. New York: Perennial Library, 1989.

———. Sweet Soul Music: Rhythm and Blues and the Southern Dream of Freedom. New York: Harper & Row, 1986.

Guterman, Jimmy. The Best Rock 'n' Roll Records of All Time. New York: Citadel, 1992.

Hahn, Emily. Romantic Rebels: An Informal History of Bohemianism in America. Boston: Houghton Mifflin, 1967.

Halberstam, David. The Fifties. New York: Villard, 1993.

Halliwell, Leslie. Halliwell's Filmgoer's Companion. New York: Charles Scribner's Sons, 1988.

Harnsberger, Caroline Thomas. Mark Twain, Family Man. New York: Citadel, 1960.

Harvey, Brett. The Fifties: A Women's Oral History. New York: HarperCollins, 1993.

Hatcher, Harlan, and Erich A. Walter. A Pictorial History of the Great Lakes. New York: Bonanza, 1963.

Headrick, Robert Jr. Deanmania. Las Vegas: Pioneer, 1990.

Helander, Brock. The Rock Who's Who. New York: Schirmer, 1982.

Hentoff, Nat. Jazz Is. New York: Random House, 1976.

Hertsgaard, Mark. A Day in the Life: The Music and Artistry of the Beatles. New York: Delacorte, 1995.

Hill, Randall C. "The Big Bopper." Collected in The Big Bopper. Compiled by Alan Clark. West Covina, California: National Rock and Roll Archives, 1989.

Hines, Douglas. "Fans Got Last Glimpse of Holly: Concert-Goers Waved Goodbye at Airport." Mason City Globe-Gazette, 1 February 1989.

Hoffman, Jim. "We Belong Together." Photoplay, May 1959. Collected in Ritchie Valens. 30th Anniversary Memorial Series, No. 2. West Covina, California: National Rock and Roll Archives, 1989.

Holden, Anthony. Behind the Oscar: The Secret History of the Academy Awards. New York: Simon and Schuster, 1993.

Holiday, Billie, with William Dufty. Lady Sings the Blues. London: Penguin, 1956.

Holley, Larry. The Buddy I Knew! Lubbock, Texas: Larry Holley, 1979.

The Holy Bible. Authorized King James Version. New York: Oxford University Press.

"Holly's Album Merits Gold Record for Clovis Man." Amarillo Daily News, 1 June 1984.

"Holly's Father Still Critical." Lubbock Avalanche-Journal, 8 July 1985.

Horstman, Dorothy. Sing Your Heart Out, Country Boy. Nashville: Country Music Foundation, 1957.

"Hospitalized Father of Star Buddy Holly on Critical List." Lubbock Avalanche-Journal, 8 July 1985.

Hyams, Joe, and Jay Hyams. James Dean: Little Boy Lost. New York: Warner Books, 1992.

Jackson, John A. Big Beat Heat: Alan Freed and the Early Years of Rock & Roll. New York: Schirmer, 1991.

Jackson, Lee. "Ray Ruff." Rockin' 50s 34, February 1992.

Jahn, Mike. The Story of Rock 'n' Roll From Elvis Presley to the Rolling Stones. New York: Quadrangle, 1975.

Johnson, Joyce. Minor Characters. Boston: Houghton Mifflin, 1983.

Johnstone, Damian. "The Australian Tour." Reminiscing 26, Spring 1983.

Jancik, Wayne. The Billboard Book of One-Hit Wonders. New York: Billboard, 1990.

Jones, Margaret. Patsy: The Life and Times of Patsy Cline. New York: HarperCollins, 1994.

Jones, Wayne. "Carroll Anderson." Reminiscing 4, September 1977.

———. "Fred Milano." Reminiscing 8, September 1978.

———. "Dick Jacobs." Reminiscing 36, May 1985.

———. "Marshall Crenshaw." Reminiscing 26, Spring 1983.

Kaplan, Justin. Mr. Clemens and Mark Twain. New York: Simon and Schuster, 1966.

Kaye, Lenny. "Eddie Cochran." Liner notes. Double LP, Eddie Cochran. United Artists Records, UAS-9959, Legendary Masters Series.

Kerns, William. "City Gets Windfall From Holly Stamp." Lubbock Avalanche-Journal, 13 June 1993.

———. "Family Appreciates Holly Celebration." Lubbock Avalanche-Journal, 17 June 1993.

———. "Holly's Hit List Grows with Hot-Selling Stamp." Lubbock Avalanche-Journal, 17 June 1993.

———. "Holly Notes." Lubbock Avalanche-Journal, 17 June 1993.

———. "Stamp Ceremony to Break Tradition." Lubbock Avalanche-Journal, 15 June 1993.

Kerouac, Jack. On the Road. New York: Penguin, 1957.

———. The Portable Jack Kerouac, edited by Ann Charters, New York: Viking, 1995.

Kevin, Terry. "Bob Booe Remembers February 3, 1959." Reminiscing 29, Winter 1984.

Koch, Edward I., and William Rauch. Mayor. New York: Simon and Schuster, 1984.

"Labor Day Dance." Lubbock Avalance-Journal, 7 September 1953.

"Lawrence Holley Dead at 83." Lubbock Avalanche-Journal, 9 July 1985.

"Lawrence Holley Sr. Dies." Lubbock Avalanche-Journal, 10 July 1985.

Lazell, Dafydd Reed, and Luke Crampton. Rock Movers & Shakers. New York: Billboard, 1989.

"The Legend of Buddy Holly." 16, April 1965. Collected in Buddy Holly. 30th Anniversary Memorial Series, No. 1. Compiled by Alan Clark. West Covina, California: National Rock and Roll Archives, 1989.

Lehmer, Larry. "Holly Almost Drowned in '58 Swimming Mishap." Des Moines Register (undated clipping).

———. "How Icy Bus Woe Led to Plane, Rock Immortality." Des Moines Sunday Register (undated clipping).

Leonard, John. A Really Big Show: A Visual History of the Ed Sullivan Show, edited by Claudia Falkenburg and Andrew Solt. New York: Sarah Lazin Books, 1992.

Lewis, Myra, with Murray Silver. Great Balls of Fire! New York: St. Martin's Press, 1982.

"The Life and Death of Ritchie Valens." *Modern Screen*, May 1959. Collected in *Ritchie Valens*. 30th Anniversary Memorial Series, No. 2. Compiled by Alan Clark. West Covina, California: National Rock and Roll Archives, 1989.

Linedecker, Clifford L. *Massacre at Waco, Texas*. New York: St. Martin's Paperbacks, 1993.

"Little Richard and Musicians Jailed Following Dispute." *Lubbock Avalanche-Journal*, 24 August 1956.

Loder, Kurt. "Bo Diddley." *The Rolling Stone Interviews*. New York: St. Martin's Press, 1989.

———. "The Everly Brothers." *The Rolling Stone Interviews*. New York: St. Martin's Press, 1989.

Lubbock. Southwestern Bell telephone book. November 1991–1992. St. Louis: Southwestern Bell Yellow Pages, Inc., 1991.

Magill, Frank N. *Magill's Survey of Cinema*. Vol. 4. Englewood Cliffs, New Jersey: Salem Press, 1980.

Malone, Bill C. *Country Music U.S.A.* Austin: University of Texas Press, 1985.

Manso, Peter. *Brando: The Biography*. New York: Hyperion, 1994.

Marcus, Greil. *Mystery Train*. New York: Dutton, 1975.

Marsh, Dave, and James Bernard. *The New Book of Rock Lists*. New York: Simon and Schuster, 1994.

"Member of Buddy Holly's Band Recreates Those Days Annually." *Jefferson City* (Missouri) *News-Tribune*, 6 February 1994.

Mendelson, Jack H., M.D., and Nancy K. Mello, Ph.D. *The Diagnosis and Treatment of Alcoholism*. New York: McGraw-Hill, 1979.

Mendheim, Beverly. *Ritchie Valens: The First Latino Rocker*. Tempe, Arizona: Bilingual Press, 1987.

Miles, Barry. *Ginsberg*. New York: Simon and Schuster, 1989.

Millard, Bob. *Country Music*. New York: HarperCollins, 1993.

Miller, Jack. "Niki Sullivan." *Reminiscing*, Spring 1984.

Mitchell, Greg. "The History of Rock 'n' Roll." *Crawdaddy*, December 1974.

Moldvay, Albert, and Erika Fabian. *Photographing Mexico City & Acapulco*. New York: Amphoto/ American Photographic, 1980.

Monnery, Steve, and Gary Herman. *Rock 'n' Roll Chronicles 1955–1963*. Stamford, Connecticut: Longmeadow Press, 1991.

Murrells, Joseph. *Million Selling Records*. New York: Arco, 1984.

McGee, David. "Buddy Holly." *The Rolling Stone Album Guide*. Anthony DeCurtis and James Henke, with Holly George-Warren, eds. New York: Random House, 1992.

McLeod, Gary. "Jerry Engler." *Rockin' 50s*, October 1991.

McNeil, Alex. *Total Television*. New York: Penguin, 1991.

McNeish, Jerry. "Jim Robinson." *Reminiscing*, Fall 1983.

McNie, Margaret. "Phil Everly." *Reminiscing* 14, March 1980.

Nassour, Ellis. *Patsy Cline*. New York: Leisure Books, 1989.

Nite, Norm N. *Rock On: The Illustrated Encyclopedia of Rock 'n' Roll*. New York: Harper & Row, 1982.

"Norman Petty Recordings Put Clovis on Map." *Clovis News-Journal*, 20 December 1959.

Norman, Philip. *Shout! The Beatles in Their Generation*. New York: Simon and Schuster, 1981.

———. *The Road Goes on Forever*. New York: Simon and Schuster, 1982.

———. "The Secret Buddy Holly: Honeymoon in Acapulco and Peggy Sue Came Too." *London Daily Mail*, 1 September 1994.

———. "The Secret Buddy Holly: The Girl Who Broke Young Buddy's Heart." *London Daily Mail*, 31 August 1994.

O'Brien, P. J. *Will Rogers*. No publisher, city, or copyright date listed.

Oestreicher, Mike, and Pat Kennedy. "Carroll Anderson." *Rave On!* April 1980.

"On the Road With Eddie Cochran: Interview With Dave Shriver." *Blue Suede News*, 3, no. 1 (spring 1989).

Orth, Maureen. "Outlaw Breed." *Newsweek*, 26 August 1974.

Parade, 8 December 1991.

Pareles, Jon, and Patricia Romanowski. *The Rolling Stone Encyclopedia of Rock*. New York: Summit Books, 1983.

Paulk, Suzanne. "Buddy Holly." Memorial pamphlet, 1979.

"Petty, 57, Friend, Manager of Buddy Holly, Dies Here." *Clovis News-Journal*, 19 August 1984.

Pierce, Neal R., and Jerry Hagstrom. *The Book of America*. New York: W. W. Norton, 1983.

"Pilot's Parents Can't Forget 'Day the Music Died Died.'" Associated Press, 5 February 1988.

"Pistol in Plane Wreck Not Fired." *Mason City Globe-Gazette*, 10 April 1959.

"Postal Service Plans Party for Rock 'n' Roll Stamps." Associated Press. *Lubbock Avalanche-Journal*, 15 June 1993.

Powers, Jeremy. "Allison Recalls How Music Grew." *Mason City Globe-Gazette*, 1 February 1989.

———. "Holly Film Was Not Realistic." *Mason City Globe-Gazette*, 1 February 1989.

———. "Legends of Rock Remembered: Monument Is in Place at the Surf." *Mason City Globe-Gazette*, 7 June 1988.

Powers, Jeremy, and Jeff Tecklenburg. "Lingering Mysteries of Holly's Fatal Flight." *Mason City Globe-Gazette*, 19 January 1989.

———. "1959 Winter Dance Party, Fatal Crash Are Fodder for Aspiring Author." *Mason City Globe-Gazette*, 9 February 1992.

———. "Saturday: The Day the Music Lives Again." *Clear Lake Weekend A.M.*, 16 June 1988.

Reardon, James J., M.D., and Judi McMahon. *Plastic Surgery for Men*. New York: Everest House, 1981.

Riese, Randall. *Nashville Babylon*. New York: Congdon & Weed, 1988.

Roberts, Mark. "Petty's Musical Genius Influenced Today's Tunes." *Clovis News-Journal*, 19 August 1984.

"Rock 'n' Roll Dance Is Shut Down After Disturbance Here." *Lubbock Avalanche-Journal*, 25 August 1956.

Roland, Tom. *The Billboard Book of Number One Country Hits*. New York: Billboard, 1991.

Rossi, Nick, and George Block. "Tommy Tompkins." *Reminiscing* 41, March 1986.

Rovin, Jeff. *Country Music Babylon*. New York: St. Martin's Press, 1993.

Schaffner, Nicholas. *The British Invasion: From the*

First Wave to the New Wave. New York: McGraw-Hill, 1983.

"School Days." *New Yorker,* 8 July 1991.

Schulman, Irving. *Valentino.* New York: Trident, 1967.

Schwerin, Jules. *Got to Tell It: Mahalia Jackson, Queen of Gospel.* New York: Oxford University Press, 1992.

Scriven, Joseph, and Charles C. Converse. "What a Friend We Have in Jesus." *Soul-Stirring Songs & Hymns.* Compiled by John R. Rice and Joy Rice Martin. Murfreesboro, Tennessee: Sword of the Lord Publishers, 1972.

Selvin, Joel. *Rick Nelson: Idol for a Generation.* Chicago: Contemporary Books, 1990.

"Services Slated Wednesday for Buddy Holly's Father." *Lubbock Avalanche-Journal,* 9 July 1985.

Shanley, Robin. "The Winds of November." *Cayo* 1, no. 7. (1993).

Shannon, Bob, and John Javna. *Behind the Hits: Inside Stories of Classic Pop and Rock and Roll.* New York: Warner Books, 1986.

Shaw, Greg. "The Teen Idols." *The Rolling Stone Illustrated History of Rock & Roll.* Edited by Jim Miller. New York: Random House, 1980.

Shelton, Gene. "Southwest's Only Major Recording Studio Operated by Clovis Musician." *Amarillo News-Globe,* 20 December 1959.

Sheridan, Jack. "Death Cuts Short Meteoric Career for Lubbock Youth." *Lubbock Avalanche-Journal,* 4 February 1959.

Sherlock, George. "I'll Remember Ritchie." *Teen,* May 1959. Collected in *Ritchie Valens.* 30th Anniversary Memorial Series, No. 2. Compiled by Alan Clark. West Covina, California: National Rock and Roll Archives, 1989.

"Show Goes on Despite Death of 3." Associated Press. *Independent Journal,* 4 February 1959.

Skinner, Dave. "A Meeting With Mr. and Mrs. Holley on June 12, 1969." *Reminiscing* 43, July 1986.

Smith, Joe. *Off the Record: An Oral History of Popular Music.* Edited by Mitchell Fink. New York: Warner Books, 1988.

Smith, Nigel, and Damian Johnstone. "Stan Rofe." *Reminiscing* 26, Spring 1983.

Smith, Steve, and The Diagram Group. *Rock Day by Day.* Enfield, Middlesex: Guinness Books, 1987.

Spitz, Bob. *Dylan.* New York: McGraw-Hill, 1989.

Stallings, Penny. *Rock 'n' Roll Confidential.* Boston: Little, Brown, 1984.

Stambler, Irwin. *The Encyclopedia of Pop, Rock and Soul.* New York: St. Martin's Press, 1989.

———. and Grelun Landon. *The Encyclopedia of Folk, Country, and Western Music.* New York: St. Martin's Press, 1984.

Steuer, Mark. "The Night Before the Music Died." *Voyageur: Northeast Wisconsin's Historical Review* 9, no. 2 (winter/spring 1993).

Stoop, Norma M. "Waylon Jennings: Big Country Singer Hits the Big City." *After Dark,* April 1973.

"Study Plane Mishap: Testimony Leaves Cause of Crash 'Up in Clouds.'" *Mason City Globe-Gazette,* 19 February 1959.

"Suddenly There Was No Tomorrow." *Modern Screen,* August 1960.

Summers, Anthony. *Goddess.* New York: Macmillan, 1985.

"Surf Ballroom: Valens' Last Stage." *Des Moines Register,* 26 July 1987.

Sutton, Cynthia E., and Wanda S. Lyon. *Cosmetic Surgery.* Orlando, Florida: Swan, 1992.

Swanson, D. J. "BBC Follows Buddy Holly to Clovis." *Albuquerque Journal.* 9 June 1985.

Szatmary. *Rockin' in Time.* Englewood Cliffs, New Jersey: Prentice Hall, 1991.

Tecklenburg, Jeff. "Investigator Offers Theory on Fatal Crash." *Mason City Globe-Gazette,* 1 February 1989.

Thomas, Jim. "Gordon Baxter." *Reminiscing* 19, June 1981.

Thomas, Piri. *Down These Mean Streets.* New York: New American Library, 1967.

Time editors. *The 1979 Hammond Almanac.* Maplewood, New Jersey: Hammond Almanac, Inc., 1978.

Time-Life editors. *This Fabulous Century: 1950–1960.* No city listed. *Time-Life* Books, 1988.

Tobler, John. "Paul McCartney 9/13/80." *Reminiscing* 19, January 1981.

Toepfer, Susan. "I'm Not Gonna Put Up With Anything From Anybody." *Photoplay,* February 1974.

———. *This Day in Rock.* New York: Carroll & Graf, 1993.

Tosches, Nick. *Hellfire: The Jerry Lee Lewis Story.* New York: Delacorte, 1982.

TV Movie and Record Stars, February 1960.

Turner, Joan. "Record Reviews." *Reminiscing* 6, March 1978.

———. "Record Review." *Reminiscing* 8, September 1978.

Twain, Mark. *The Autobiography of Mark Twain.* 1959 edition. Edited by Charles Neider. New York: Harper, 1917.

U.S. Department of Transportation, Coast Guard, Marine Casualty Report. *S.S. Edmund Fitzgerald: Sinking in Lake Superior on 10 November 1975 With Loss of Life.* Washington, D.C., 1977.

Vidal, Gore. *Duluth.* New York: Random House, 1983.

Vitek, Steve. "Robin Luke." *Reminiscing* 5, December 1977.

Ward, Ed, Geoffrey Stokes, and Ken Tucker. *Rock of Ages: The Rolling Stone History of Rock 'n' Roll.* New York: Summit Books, 1986.

Ware, Caroline F. *Greenwich Village.* New York: Harper & Row, 1965.

Wayne, Pilar, and Alex Thorleifson. *John Wayne.* New York: McGraw-Hill, 1987.

"Westerner Alma Mater Song." *The Westerner.* Vol. 31. Lubbock, Texas: Tom Lubbock Senior High School, 1954.

Wexler, Jerry, and David Ritz. *Rhythm and the Blues.* New York: Alfred A. Knopf, 1993.

"What We Believe." Tract 406. Lubbock, Texas: Tabernacle Baptist Church.

Whitburn, Joel. *The Billboard Book of Top 40 Hits.* New York: Billboard, 1987.

Whitcomb, Ian. "The Rockers." *The Age of Rock.* Edited by Jonathan Eisen. New York: Random House, 1970.

White, Charles. *The Life and Times of Little Richard: The Quasar of Rock.* New York: Harmony, 1984.

White, Timothy. *Rock Lives.* New York: Henry Holt, 1990.

Whitford, Eldon, David Vinopal, and Dan Erlewine.

Gibson's Fabulous Flat-Top Guitars. San Francisco: GPI, 1994.

"Who's Who in the Cast." Playbill: Buddy: The Buddy Holly Story. Vol. 91, No. 5. New York: Shubert Theater, May 1991.

Williams, Pat. "A Star Dies, Another Is Born." Movieland & TV Time. April 1961. Collected in Buddy Holly. 30th Anniversary Memorial Series, No. 1. Compiled by Alan Clark. West Covina, California: National Rock and Roll Archives, 1989.

Williams, Paul. Rock 'n' Roll: The 100 Best Singles. New York: Carroll & Graf, 1993.

Windeler, Robert. "Couples." People, 29 September 1975.

Winkler, Suzanne. The Plains States: Smithsonian Guide to Historic America. New York: Stewart Tabori & Chang, 1990.

Winters, Georgia. "16 Salutes a Wonderful Boy Whose Tragic Death Ended a Life That Was Just Beginning." 16, August 1960. Collected in A Tribute to Eddie Cochran. Compiled by Alan Clark. West Covina. National Rock and Roll Archives. No date listed.

Winters, Lauri. "Old Friends Recall Good Times in Old Neighborhood." Albert Lea Tribune, 26 June 1994. Collected in Eddie Cochran: The Legend Continues. Compiled by Alan Clark. West Covina, California: National Rock and Roll Archives, 1994.

Worth, Fred L., and Steve D. Tamerius. Elvis: His Life From A to Z. New York: Wing Books, 1990.

Yanak, Ted, and Pam Cornelison. The Great American History Fact-Finder. Boston: Houghton Mifflin, 1993.

Documents

Joyce, George T., M.D. Microscopic Description (section of Roger Peterson autopsy A-8-59).

Smiley, Ralph E., M.D., Acting Coroner. Coroner's investigation. Air crash, Feb. 3, 1959. SW 1/4 Section 18, Lincoln Twp. Cerro Gordo County, Iowa.

———. Roger Peterson, Autopsy: A-8-59, Autopsied 4/Feb/59, Doctor: Smiley.

———. Coroner's Report of Investigation: Coroner's Transcript of Fees—To County Auditor (Form 205-G), Coroner's Transcript 1784, Investigation of Death of Charles H. Holley, filed February 18, 1959, approved March 2, 1959, by Elmer Luscomb.

———. Coroner's Report of Investigation: Coroner's Transcript of Fees—To County Auditor (Form 205-G), Coroner's Transcript 1783, Investigation of Death of Jiles P. Richardson, filed February 19, 1959, approved March 2, 1959, by Elmer Luscomb.

———. Coroner's Report of Investigation: Coroner's Transcript of Fees—To County Auditor (Form 205-G), Coroner's Transcript 1782, Investigation of Death of Roger Peterson, filed February 17, 1959, approved March 2, 1959, by Elmer Luscomb.

———. Coroner's Report of Investigation: Coroner's Transcript of Fees—To County Auditor (Form 205-G), Coroner's Transcript 1785, Investigation of Death of Richard Valenzuela, filed February 19, 1959, approved March 2, 1959, by Elmer Luscomb.

———. Death Certificates: Charles Hardin Holley, Richard (unknown) Valenzuela, Jiles P. Richardson, Roger A. Peterson, Iowa State Department of Health, Division of Vital Statistics.

Radio and Television Interviews With Buddy Holly

Barton, Pat. Newcastle, Australia, 31 January 1958.

Clark, Dick. TV. "American Bandstand." 28 October 1958. LP. The Buddy Holly Story. Vol II. MA 201185.

Hoover, Freeman. Denver, Colorado: 1 November 1957.

Lowery, Dale. Radio Station KTOP, Topeka, Kansas; 5 November 1957. LP. The Buddy Holly Story. Vol II. MA 201185.

Robinson, Red. Georgia Auditorium, Vancouver, British Columbia, Canada, 23 October 1957. Reminiscing 16, September 1980.

Sullivan, Ed. TV appearance, 1 December 1957. LP. The Buddy Holly Story. Vol I. MA 191185.

Related Videos and Radio Shows

Brooker, Douglas. Reminiscing. 1979 Video. IPBN Public Affairs Presentation. Interviews with John Goldrosen, Joe B. Mauldin, Niki Sullivan, Larry Holley.

Clark, Dick. Interview with Peggy Sue Rackham and kinescope of Buddy Holly on 1957 "Arthur Murray Dancy Party."

"Instant Recall." Television program. Includes kinescopes of Buddy Holly's television appearances. Interviews with Maria Elena Holly, Tommy Allsup, Joe B. Mauldin, and Larry Holley.

Montgomery, Paul, producer. Rock 'n' Roll: Early Days. Aired on PBS, December 8, 1986.

McCartney, Paul. The Real Buddy Holly Story. BBC-TV. 1987. Narration by Paul McCartney, who sings "Words of Love." Kinescopes of Buddy Holly on television, abroad, and with Elvis Presley, Johnny Cash, Carl Perkins, Don Guess, Ben Hall, Bill Black, and Scotty Moore in Lubbock. Home movies of Buddy Holly on his motorcycle. Interviews with the Everly Brothers, Keith Richards, Larry and Travis Holley, Murray Deutch, Bob Thiele, Vi Petty, Dick Jacobs, Tommy Allsup, Jerry Allison, and Joe B. Mauldin.

McDaniel, Randy Jack. Radio special, "A Celebration of Buddy Holly: The Legend Moves On." KQ95. 1979–1980. Interviews with Hi-Pockets Duncan, Owen Bradley, Sonny Curtis, Ben Hall, Niki Sullivan, and Larry and Travis Holley.

Waylon: Renegade, Outlaw, Legend (The Authorized Video Biography). VHS-PC 105. Nashville: Hallway Productions Inc. Charlie Dick and Gregory Hall, producers; written by Martin Melhuish and Gregory Hall. Includes an interview with Waylon Jennings about Buddy Holly.

Discography

Singles

Blue Days, Black Nights, Love Me
  Decca D 29854. 45 RPM and 78 RPM. April 16, 1956

Modern Don Juan, You Are My One Desire
  Decca 30166. 45 RPM and 78 RPM. December 24, 1956

That'll Be the Day, I'm Looking for Someone to Love
  Brunswick 55009. 45 RPM and 78 RPM. May 27, 1957

Words of Love, Mailman, Bring Me No More Blues
  Coral 61852. 45 RPM and 78 RPM. June 20, 1957

Rock Around With Ollie Vee, That'll Be the Day
  Decca 30434. 45 RPM and 78 RPM. September 2, 1957

Peggy Sue, Everyday
  Coral 61885. 45 RPM. September 20, 1957

Oh Boy, Not Fade Away
  Brunswick 55035. 45 RPM and 78 RPM. October 27, 1957

Love Me, You Are My One Desire
  Decca 30543. 45 RPM and 78 RPM. January 6, 1958

I'm Gonna Love You Too, Listen to Me
  Coral 61947. 45 RPM and 78 RPM. February 5, 1958

Maybe Baby, Tell Me How
  Brunswick 55053. 45 RPM and 78 RPM. February 12, 1958

Rave On, Take Your Time
  Coral 61985. 45 RPM and 78 RPM. April 20, 1958

Think It Over, Fools Paradise
  Brunswick 55072. 45 RPM and 78 RPM. May 27, 1958

Girl on My Mind, Ting-A-Ling
  Decca 30650. 45 RPM and 78 RPM. June 23, 1958

Early in the Morning, Now We're One
  Coral 62006. 45 RPM and 78 RPM. July 5, 1958

It's So Easy, Lonesome Tears
  Brunswick 55094. 45 RPM and 78 RPM. September 12, 1958

Heartbeat, Well All Right
  Coral 62051. 45 RPM and 78 RPM. November 5, 1958

It Doesn't Matter Anymore, Raining in My Heart
  Coral 62074. 45 RPM. January 5, 1959

Peggy Sue Got Married, Crying, Waiting, Hoping
  Coral 62134. 45 RPM. July 20, 1959

True Love Ways, That Makes It Tough
  Coral 62210. 45 RPM. June 29, 1960

Valley of Tears, You're So Square (Baby I Don't Care)
  Coral 62283. 45 RPM. September 1961. Issued exclusively in Canada

Reminiscing, Wail 'Til the Sun Shines, Nellie
  Coral 62329. 45 RPM. August 20, 1962

Bo Diddley, True Love Ways
  Coral 62352. 45 RPM. April 1, 1963

Brown-Eyed Handsome Man, Wishing
  Coral 62369. 45 RPM. July 29, 1963

Rock Around With Ollie Vee, I'm Gonna Love You Too
  Coral 62390. 45 RPM. June 1, 1964

Maybe Baby, Not Fade Away
  Coral 62407. 45 RPM. April 27, 1964

What To Do, Slippin' and Slidin'
  Coral 62448. 45 RPM. March 15, 1965

Rave On, Early in the Morning
  Coral 62554. 45 RPM. July 22, 1968

Love Is Strange, You're the One
  Coral 62558. 45 RPM. March 17, 1969

That'll Be the Day, I'm Looking for Someone to Love
  Coral 65618. 45 RPM. 1969

That'll Be the Day, I'm Looking for Someone to Love
  MCA 60000. 45 RPM. 1973

Peggy Sue, Everyday
  MCA 60004. 45 RPM. 1973

It Doesn't Matter Anymore, Peggy Sue
  MCA 40905. 45 RPM. May 29, 1978

Memories, A Message From Buddy's Parents
  Prism 100. 45 RPM. May 1980

That Makes It Tough, Norman Petty Talks About the Plane Crash
  Prism 101. 45 RPM. May 1980

You're the One, Everyday Jingle, Peggy Sue Jingle, KSYD Promo
Prism 102. 45 RPM. May 1980

Slippin' and Slidin', Dearest
Prism 103. 45 RPM. September 1981

Albums

Long-Playing 33⅓ RPM (LP's)

The Chirping Crickets
Brunswick BL 54038
November 1957
Not Fade Away, You've Got Love, Maybe Baby, It's Too Late, Tell Me How, That'll Be the Day, I'm Looking for Someone to Love, An Empty Cup, Send Me Some Lovin', Rock Me My Baby (Rereleased in 1962 as *Buddy Holly and the Crickets* CRL 57405/CRL 757405)

Buddy Holly
Coral CRL 57210
March 1958 (later released as MCA 25239)
I'm Gonna Love You Too, Peggy Sue, Look at Me, Listen to Me, Valley of Tears, Ready Teddy, Everyday, Mailman, Bring Me No More Blues, Words of Love, You're So Square, Rave On, Little Baby

That'll Be the Day
Decca DL 8707
April 1958
You Are My One Desire, Blue Days, Black Nights, Modern Don Juan, Rock Around With Ollie Vee, Ting-A-Ling, Girl on My Mind, That'll Be the Day, Love Me, I'm Changin' All Those Changes, Don't Come Back Knockin', Midnight Shift
(Rereleased in 1967 as *The Great Buddy Holly* VL 73811 and later as MCA 20101 [without Ting-A-Ling])

The Buddy Holly Story
Coral CRL 57279/757279
March 1959
Raining in My Heart, Early in the Morning, Peggy Sue, Maybe Baby, Everyday, Rave On, That'll Be the Day, Heartbeat, Think It Over, Oh Boy, It's So Easy, It Doesn't Matter Anymore

The Buddy Holly Story Volume 2
Coral CRL 57326
March 1960
Peggy Sue Got Married, Well All Right, What To Do, That Makes It Tough, Now We're One, Take Your Time, Crying, Waiting, Hoping, True Love Ways, Learning the Game, Little Baby, Moondreams, That's What They Say

Reminiscing
Coral CRL 5 7426/757426
February 1963
Reminiscing, Slippin' and Slidin', Bo Diddley, Wait 'Til the Sun Shines, Nellie, Baby, Won't You Come Out Tonight, Brown-Eyed Handsome Man, Because I Love You, It's Not My Fault, I'm Gonna Set My Foot Down, Changin' All Those Changes, Rock-A-Bye Rock

Showcase
Coral CRL5 7450/757450
May 1964
Shake, Rattle and Roll, Rock Around With Ollie Vee, Honky Tonk, I Guess I Was Just a Fool, Ummm, Oh Yeah (Dearest), You're the One, Blue Suede Shoes, Come Back Baby, Rip It Up, Love's Made a Fool of You, Gone, Girl on My Mind

Holly in the Hills
Coral CRL 57463/757463
January 1965
I Wanna Play House With You, Door to My Heart, Fool's Paradise, I Gambled My Heart, What to Do, Wishing, Down the Line, Soft Place in My Heart, Lonesome Tears, Gotta Get You Near Me Blues, Flower of My Heart, You and I Are Through

The Best of Buddy Holly
Coral CXB-8/7CXB-6
April 1966
Peggy Sue, Blue Suede Shoes, Learning the Game, Brown-Eyed Handsome Man, Everyday, Maybe Baby, Early in the Morning, Ready Teddy, It's Too Late, What to Do, Rave On, True Love Ways, It Doesn't Matter Anymore, Crying, Waiting, Hoping, Moondreams, Rock Around With Ollie Vee, Raining in My Heart, Bo Diddley, That'll Be the Day, I'm Gonna Love You Too, Peggy Sue Got Married, Shake, Rattle and Roll, That Makes It Tough, Wishing

Buddy Holly's Greatest Hits
Coral CRL 757492
March 1967
True Love Ways, Bo Diddley, What to Do, Learning the Game, It Doesn't Matter Anymore, That'll Be the Day, Oh Boy, Early in the Morning, Brown-Eyed Handsome Man, Everyday, Maybe Baby

Giant
Coral CRL 757504
January 1969
Love Is Strange, Good Rockin' Tonight, Blue Monday, Have You Ever Been Lonely, Slippin' and Slidin', You're the One, Dearest, Smokey Joe's Cafe, Ain't Got No Home, Holly Hop

Good Rockin'
Vocalion VL 73923
1971
I Wanna Play House With You, Baby, I Don't Care, Little Baby, Ting-A-Ling, Take Your Time, Down the Line, Now We're One, Words of Love, That's What They Say, You and I Are Through

Buddy Holly: A Rock and Roll Collection
DXSB7-207
August 1972 (later renumbered as MCA2-4009)
Rave On, Tell Me How, Peggy Sue Got Married, Slippin' and Slidin', Oh Boy, Not Fade Away, Bo Diddley, What to Do, Heartbeat, Well All Right, Words of Love, Love's Made a Fool of You, Reminiscing, Lonesome Tears, Listen to Me, Maybe Baby, Down the Line, That'll Be the Day, Peggy Sue, Brown-Eyed Handsome Man, You're So Square, Crying, Waiting, Hoping, Ready Teddy, It Doesn't Matter Anymore

The Nashville Sessions
MCA CDL 3038
Liner notes by John Beecher
Produced by Owen Bradley
You Are My One Desire, Blue Days, Black Nights, Modern Don Juan, Rock Around With Ollie Vee, Ting-A-Ling, Girl on My Mind, That'll Be the Day, Love Me, I'm Changing All Those Changes, Don't Come Back Knockin', Midnight Shift, Rock Around With Ollie Vee

Buddy Holly/Crickets 20 Golden Greats
MCA 3040
May 1978
That'll Be the Day, Peggy Sue, Words of Love, Everyday, Not Fade Away, Oh Boy, Maybe Baby, Listen to Me, Heartbeat, Think It Over, It Doesn't Matter Anymore, It's So Easy, Well All Right, Rave On, Raining in My Heart, True Love Ways, Peggy Sue Got Married, Bo Diddley, Brown-Eyed Handsome Man, Wishing

Memories of Buddy Holly
MCA 301735
1981
Liner notes by Gaatse Zoodsma, founder, Dutch Buddy Holly Music Club
Peggy Sue, Everyday, That'll Be the Day, Heartbeat, Oh Boy, Tell Me How, True Love Ways, Love's Made a Fool of You, Rave On, It's So Easy, I'm Gonna Love You Too, Not Fade Away, Well All Right, Listen to Me, It Doesn't Matter Anymore, Brown-Eyed Handsome Man, Down the Line, I'm Gonna Set My Foot Down, I Guess I Was Just a Fool, Because I Love You, Modern Don Juan, Mailman, Bring Me No More Blues, Last Night, Little Baby, Baby I Don't Care, Valley of Tears Rock Me Baby, You've Got Love, Dearest (Umm Oh Yeah), That's What They Say, Crying, Waiting, Hoping, You're the One

The Complete Buddy Holly
MCA 6-80000
February 1981
Gotta Get You Near Me Blues, Soft Place in My Heart, Door to My Heart, Flower of My Heart, Baby It's Love, Memories, Queen of the Ballroom, I Gambled My Heart, You and I Are Through, Gone, Have You Ever Been Lonely, Down the Line, Brown-Eyed Handsome Man, Bo Diddley, Good Rockin' Tonight, Rip It Up, Blue Monday, Honky Tonk, Blue Suede Shoes, Shake, Rattle and Roll, Ain't Got No Home, Holly Hop, Baby Let's Play House, I'm Gonna Set My Foot Down, Baby Won't You Come Out Tonight, Changin' All Those Changes, Rock-A-Bye Rock, It's Not My Fault, Guess I Was Just a Fool, Love Me, Don't Come Back Knockin', Midnight Shift, Blue Days, Black Nights, Rock Around With Ollie Vee, I'm Changin' All Those Changes, That'll Be the Day, Girl on My Mind, Ting-A-Ling, Because I Love You, Rock Around With Ollie Vee, Modern Don Juan, You Are My One Desire, That'll Be the Day, I'm Lookin' for Someone to Love, Last Night, Maybe Baby, Words of Love, Peggy Sue, Everyday, Mailman, Bring Me No More Blues, Listen to Me, I'm Gonna Love You Too, Not Fade Away, Ready Teddy, Oh Boy, Tell Me How, Maybe Baby, Send Me Some Lovin', Little Baby, Take Your Time, Rave On, You've Got

Love, Valley of Tears, Rock Me My Baby, Baby I Don't Care, It's Too Late, An Empty Cup, Look at Me, Think It Over, Fool's Paradise, Early in the Morning, Now We're One, Lonesome Tears, Heartbeat, It's So Easy, Well All Right, Love's Made a Fool of You, Wishing, Reminiscing, Come Back Baby, That's My Desire, True Love Ways, Moondreams, Raining in My Heart, It Doesn't Matter Anymore, Peggy Sue Got Married, Crying, Waiting, Hoping, Learning the Game, That Makes It Tough, What to Do, That's What They Say, Wait 'Til the Sun Shines, Nellie, Ummm, Oh Yeah (Dearest), Smokey Joe's Cafe, Slippin' and Slidin', Love is Strange, Slippin' and Slidin', Learning the Game, Crying, Waiting, Hoping, What to Do, That Makes It Tough, Peggy Sue Got Married, That's What They Say, Dearest, You're the One, Slippin' and Slidin', Dearest, Love is Strange, Peggy Sue Got Married, That Makes It Tough, Learning the Game, You're the One, Real Wild Child, Oh You Beautiful Doll, Jole Blon, When Sin Stops, Stay Close to Me, Don't Cha Know, Topeka, Kansas, interview, The Ed Sullivan Show (That'll Be the Day, Peggy Sue), Ed Sullivan interview, Alan Freed interview, Dick Clark interview

For the First Time Anywhere
MCA-27059
February 1983
Liner notes by Steve Hoffman
Rock-A-Bye Rock, Maybe Baby (first version), Because I Love You, I'm Gonna Set My Foot Down, Changing All Those Changes, That's My Desire, Baby Won't You Come Out Tonight, It's Not My Fault, Brown-Eyed Handsome Man, Bo Diddley

Legend
MCA MCA2 4184
September 1986
That'll Be the Day, Oh Boy, Not Fade Away, Tell Me How, Maybe Baby, I'm Gonna Love You Too, Words of Love, Rave On, Well All Right, Listen to Me, Everyday, Rock Around With Ollie Vee, It's So Easy, I'm Looking For Someone to Love, Peggy Sue, Think It Over, Heartbeat, Reminiscing, It Doesn't Matter Anymore, True Love Ways

Cassettes

20 Golden Greats (Buddy Holly Lives)
MCA MCAC 1484
1978
That'll Be the Day, Peggy Sue, Bo Diddley, Everyday, Not Fade Away, Oh Boy, Maybe Baby, Listen to Me, Heartbeat, Think It Over, It Doesn't Matter Anymore, It's So Easy, Well All Right, Rave On, Raining in My Heart, True Love Ways, Peggy Sue Got Married, Words of Love, Brown-Eyed Handsome Man, Wishing

Words of Love
MCA MCAC 20260
1985
Rock-A-Bye Rock, Peggy Sue, Well All Right, Words of Love, Reminiscing, Moondreams, Maybe Baby, Tell Me How

The Best of Buddy Holly
MCA HANC 20290
1985
Rock-A-Bye Rock, Peggy Sue, Well All Right, Words of Love, Reminiscing, Moondreams, Maybe Baby, Tell Me How

The "Chirping" Crickets
MCA MCAC 25170
1987
Originally released as Brunswick Records album BL 54038 on November 27, 1957, produced by Norman Petty. Includes liner notes from the original album package and reissue liner notes by Andy McKale.
Oh Boy, Not Fade Away, You've Got Love, Maybe Baby, It's Too Late, Tell Me How, That'll Be the Day, I'm Looking for Someone to Love, An Empty Cup (And a Broken Date), Send Me Some Lovin', Last Night, Rock Me My Baby

Oh Boy
MCA MCAC 20425
1987
Oh Boy, Heartbeat, You Are My One Desire, Listen to Me, Blue Days Black Nights, I'm Gonna Love You Too, That's My Desire, It Doesn't Matter Anymore

Compact Discs

United States

The Real Buddy Holly Story
Live Gold LG 6006
18 tracks including interviews (Red Robinson, Alan Freed, Dick Clark, Dale Lowery, Freeman Hoover), tribute songs, and Holly/Crickets songs overdubbed by the Picks.

Buddy Holly—From the Original Master Tapes
MCA MCAD 5540
20 tracks, digitally remastered: That'll Be the Day, Oh Boy, Not Fade Away, Tell Me How, Maybe Baby, Everyday, Rock Around With Ollie Vee, It's So Easy, I'm Lookin' for Someone to Love, Peggy Sue, I'm Gonna Love You Too, Words of Love, Rave On, Well All Right, Listen to Me, Think It Over, Heartbeat, Reminiscing, It Doesn't Matter Anymore, True Love Ways.

Buddy Holly—Oh Boy
MCA MCAD 20425
10 tracks: Oh Boy, Heartbeat, You Are My One Desire, Listen to Me, Blue Days, Black Nights, I'm Gonna Love You Too, That's My Desire, It Doesn't Matter Anymore, Raining in My Heart, Early in the Morning.

Buddy Holly
MCA MCAD 25239
12 tracks (reissue of 1958 album): I'm Gonna Love You Too, Peggy Sue, Look at Me, Listen to Me, Valley of Tears, Ready Teddy, Everyday, Mailman, Bring Me No More Blues, Words of Love, You're So Square, Rave On, Little Baby.

The Great Buddy Holly
MCA MCAD 31037

10 tracks (Decca-Nashville sessions): You Are My One Desire, Blue Days Black Nights, Modern Don Juan, Rock Around With Ollie Vee, Girl on My Mind, That'll Be the Day, Love Me, I'm Changing All Those Changes, Don't Come Back Knockin', Midnight Shift.

Buddy Holly—For the First Time Anywhere
MCA MCAD 31048
10 tracks (undubbed versions of released songs): Rock-a-Bye Rock, Maybe Baby (Clovis version), Because I Love You, I'm Gonna Set My Foot Down, Changing All Those Changes, That's My Desire, Baby Won't You Come Out Tonight, It's Not My Fault, Brown-Eyed Handsome Man, Bo Diddley.

The Chirping Crickets
MCA MCAD 31182
12 tracks (reissue of 1957 album): Oh Boy, Not Fade Away, You've Got Love, Maybe Baby, It's Too Late, Tell Me How, That'll Be the Day, I'm Looking for Someone to Love, An Empty Cup, Send Me Some Lovin', Last Night, Rock Me My Baby.

Buddy Holly and the Crickets—Vintage Gold
MCA MCAD 37295
4 tracks (3" CD): Peggy Sue, Rave On, Early in the Morning, It Doesn't Matter Anymore.

Buddy Holly—Vintage Gold
MCA MCAD 37314
4 tracks (3" CD): Peggy Sue, Rave On, Early in the Morning, It Doesn't Matter Anymore.

The Buddy Holly Collection
MCA MCAD 2-1-10883
50 tracts (2 CD's—* denotes undubbed version): Down the Line, Soft Place in My Heart, Holly Hop, Blue Days, Black Nights, Love Me, Midnight Shift, Baby Won't You Come Out Tonight*, Changing All Those Changes*, I'm Gonna Set My Foot Down*, Rock Around With Ollie Vee (no sax), Girl on My Mind, Ting-A-Ling, Modern Don Juan, Brown-Eyed Handsome Man*, That'll Be the Day, I'm Looking for Someone to Love, Words of Love, Not Fade Away, Everyday, Tell Me How, Ready Teddy, Listen to Me, Oh Boy, It's Too Late, Peggy Sue, I'm Gonna Love You Too, Look at Me, Little Baby, You've Got Love, Maybe Baby, Rock Me My Baby, You're So Square, Rave On, Fool's Paradise, Take Your Time, Well All Right, Think It Over, Early in the Morning, Heartbeat, It's So Easy, Wishing, Love's Made a Fool of You, Reminiscing, True Love Ways, It Doesn't Matter Anymore, Raining in My Heart, Peggy Sue Got Married (Fireballs dub), Crying Waiting Hoping (Fireballs dub), Learning the Game (Fireballs dub), What to Do (Fireballs dub).

Buddy Holly and the Picks—The Voice of the Crickets
24 tracks (1–21 are the original Buddy Holly and the Crickets cuts subsequently overdubbed by the Picks; 22–23 are by the Pickering Brothers, and 24 is John Pickering's tribute song): True Love Ways, Everyday, Love Me, Don't Come Back Knockin', You're So Square, Reminiscing, Peggy Sue, Well All Right, Midnight Shift, Blue Days, Black Nights, That's What They Say, Rock-a-Bye Rock, Heartbeat, Girl on My Mind, Ting-A-Ling,

I'm Gonna Set My Foot Down, It's Not My Fault, Rock Around With Ollie Vee, You Are My One Desire, Because I Love You, Modern Don Juan, Words, You've Lost That Lovin' Feeling, Buddy Holly Not Fade Away.

England

Buddy Holly—Showcase
Castle CLACD 306
12 tracks: Shake Rattle and Roll, Rock Around With Ollie Vee, Honky Tonk, I Guess I Was Just a Fool, Umm Oh Yeah, You're the One, Blue Suede Shoes, Come Back Baby, Rip It Up, Love's Made a Fool of You, Gone, Girl on My Mind.

Giant—Buddy Holly
Castle CLACD 307
10 tracks: Love Is Strange, Good Rockin' Tonight, Blue Monday, Have You Ever Been Lonely, Slippin' and Slidin', You're the One, Dearest, Smokey Joe's Cafe, Ain't Got No Home, Holly Hop.

Reminiscing—Buddy Holly
Castle CLACD 308
11 tracks: Reminiscing, Slippin' and Slidin' (dubbed slow version), Bo Diddley, Wait Till the Sun Shines Nellie, Baby Won't You Come Out Tonight, Brown-Eyed Handsome Man, Because I Love You, It's Not My Fault, I'm Gonna Set My Foot Down, Changing All Those Changes, Rock-a-Bye Rock.

That'll Be the Day—Buddy Holly
Castle CLACD 309
11 tracks (identical to U.S. 1958 vinyl): You Are My One Desire, Blue Days, Black Nights, Modern Don Juan, Rock Around With Ollie Vee, Ting-A-Ling, Girl on My Mind, That'll Be the Day, Love Me, I'm Changin' All Those Changes, Don't Come Back Knockin', Midnight Shift.

20 Golden Greats
MCA DMC TV 1
20 tracks: That'll Be the Day, Peggy Sue, Words of Love, Everyday, Not Fade Away, Oh Boy, Maybe Baby, Listen to Me, Heartbeat, Think It Over.

From the Original Master Tapes (1st number)
MCA DIDX-203
20 tracks (identical to U.S. MCA MCAD 5540)

Buddy Holly—True Love Ways
MCA DMCA 1302
3 tracks (3" CD): True Love Ways, Raining in My Heart, Words of Love

Buddy Holly—Oh Boy
MCA DMCAT 1368
4 tracks (5" CD): Oh Boy, Well All Right, Mailman, Bring Me No More Blues, Everyday.

For the First Time Anywhere
MCA CMCAD 1712 (also released as MCA CMCAD 31048)
10 tracks (identical to U.S. MCA MCAD 31048).

Buddy Holly—Love Songs
MCA DMCL 1717 (also issued as MCA MCLD 19047)
20 tracks: True Love Ways, Everyday, Listen to Me, You've Got Love, Learning the Game, Send Me Some Lovin', Love Is Strange, That's What They Say, Because I Love You, Raining in My Heart, Heartbeat, Moondreams, Take Your Time, Dearest, Look at Me, You're the One, Wishing, It Doesn't Matter Anymore, What to Do, Words of Love.

Buddy Holly
MCA DMCL 1752
10 tracks (identical to U.S. MCA MCAD 25239).

The Chirping Crickets
MCA DMCL 1753
12 tracks (identical to U.S. MCA MCAD 31182).

Buddy Holly—Golden Greats
MCA DMCM 5003 (also released as MCA MCLD 19046)
16 tracks: Peggy Sue, That'll Be the Day, Listen to Me, Everyday, Oh Boy, Not Fade Away, Raining in My Heart, Brown-Eyed Handsome Man, Maybe Baby, Rave On, Think It Over, It's So Easy, It Doesn't Matter Anymore, True Love Ways, Peggy Sue Got Married, Bo Diddley.

From the Original Master Tapes (2nd number)
MCA DMCMD 7003
20 tracks (identical to U.S. MCA MCAD 5540)

Buddy Holly
Old Gold 6154
3 tracks (5" CD): Peggy Sue, Everyday, Rave On

Buddy Holly and the Crickets
Old Gold 614729
3 tracks (3" CD): That'll Be the Day, Oh Boy, Maybe Baby.

Buddy Holly—Special Limited Edition
Pickwick Box 26
44 tracks (3-CD box set, including Pickwick single CDs 523, 560, and 595. 595 is the same as Pickwick 888).

The Legendary Buddy Holly
Pickwick PWKS 523
14 tracks: Listen to Me, Words of Love, You've Got Love, Learning the Game, Not Fade Away, What to Do, Early in the Morning, Wishing, Love's Made a Fool of You, Love Is Strange, You're So Square, Midnight Shift, Reminiscing, Valley of Tears.

Buddy Holly—Moondreams
Pickwick PWKS 560
16 tracks: Moondreams, Because I Love You, I Guess I Was Just a Fool, Girl on My Mind, I'm Gonna Love You Too, You and I Are Through, Come Back Baby, You're the One, I Gambled My Heart, You Are My One Desire, Door to My Heart, Crying Waiting Hoping, Now We're One, Love Me, Soft Place in My Heart, Have You Ever Been Lonely.

The Best of Buddy Holly
Pickwick PWKS 595
14 tracks: That'll Be the Day, Maybe Baby,
Peggy Sue Got Married, Rave On, True Love
Ways, Bo Diddley, Oh Boy, Peggy Sue,
Everyday, Think It Over, Brown-Eyed
Handsome Man, Heartbeat, Raining in My
Heart, It Doesn't Matter Anymore.

*Words of Love—Buddy Holly and the Crickets—28
Classic Tracks*
Polygram 514487-2
Words of Love, That'll Be the Day, Peggy Sue,
Think It Over, True Love Ways, What to Do,
Crying Waiting Hoping, Well All Right, Love's
Made a Fool of You, Peggy Sue Got Married,
Valley of Tears, Wishing, Raining in My Heart,
Oh Boy, Rave On, Brown-Eyed Handsome
Man, Bo Diddley, It's So Easy, It Doesn't Matter
Anymore, Maybe Baby, Early in the Morning,
Love Is Strange, Listen to Me, I'm Gonna Love
You Too, Learning the Game, You're So
Square, Heartbeat, Everyday.

The Chirping Crickets
Sequel NEMCD 629
12 tracks (identical to U.S. MCAD 31182)

Buddy Holly
Sequel NEMCD 630
12 tracks (identical to U.S. MCAD 25239)

True Love Ways
Telstar TCD 2339
20 tracks: True Love Ways, Everyday,
Heartbeat, Maybe Baby, You've Got Love,
Peggy Sue Got Married, Reminiscing, Love Is
Strange, Learning the Game, Think It Over,
Raining in My Heart, It's So Easy, Words of
Love, Listen to Me, Wishing, Love's Made a
Fool of You, Because I Love You, Fool's
Paradise, Crying Waiting Hoping, It Doesn't
Matter Anymore.

The Rock 'n' Roll Era: Buddy Holly
Time-Life Music RRC-E15
24 tracks: Peggy Sue, Heartbeat, Raining in My
Heart, Everyday, Midnight Shift, Peggy Sue Got
Married, Bo Diddley, Valley of Tears,
Reminiscing, Ready Teddy, That's My Desire,
Brown-Eyed Handsome Man, Rave On, True
Love Ways, You're So Square, You've Got
Love, Lonesome Tears, Listen to Me, Wishing,
Early in the Morning, Love's Made a Fool of
You, Learning the Game, What to Do, It
Doesn't Matter Anymore.

Index